THE GILDED

DANIEL SNOWMAN was born in London. A lecturer at Sussex University in his twenties, he went on to work at the BBC where he was responsible for a wide variety of radio series on cultural and historical topics. A long-time member of the London Philharmonic Choir, and currently a Senior Research Fellow at the Institute of Historical Research (University of London), his books include critical portraits of the Amadeus Quartet and Plácido Domingo and, more recently, *Historians* and a study of the cultural impact of *The Hitler Emigrés*.

THE GILDED STAGE

A Social History of Opera

Daniel Snowman

To Buddy
All good wishes!

[signature]

March 2011

Atlantic Books
LONDON

First published in hardback in Great Britain in 2009 by Atlantic Books,
an imprint of Grove Atlantic Ltd.

This trade paperback edition published in Great Britain in 2010
by Atlantic Books.

1 3 5 7 9 10 8 6 4 2

A CIP catalogue record for this book is available from the British Library.

978 1 84354 467 8
978 1 84354 466 1

Designed by Simon McFadden
Printed in Great Britain by the MPG Books Group

Atlantic Books
An imprint of Atlantic Books Ltd.
Ormond House
26–27 Boswell Street
London
WC1N 3JZ

www.atlantic-books.co.uk

Contents

List of Illustrations

FIRST PICTURE SECTION

1. Carnival in Venice. © Leemage/Lebrecht Music & Arts
2. Ticket for *The Beggar's Opera*. Author's collection
3. Turin's Teatro Regio. AKG-images
4. Wolfgang Amadeus Mozart with Maria Theresa. © Costa Leemage/ Lebrecht Music & Arts
5. Ludwig van Beethoven. © Lebrecht Music & Arts
6. Satirical portrait of Elizabeth Billington. © The Trustees of the British Museum
7. John Philip Kemble, Charles Kemble and Sarah Siddons. Author's collection
8. The *nouvelle riche* at play. Author's collection
9. Weber's *Der Freischütz*. © Lebrecht Music & Arts
10. Riots at the Astor Place Opera House. Library of Congress, Prints & Photographs Division, LC-USZC2-2532
11. Paris Opera House. Library of Congress, Prints & Photographs Division, Photochrom Collection, LC-DIG-ppmsc-05181
12. Wagner's Rhine maidens. © Lebrecht Music & Arts
13. Ricordi's *Tosca* poster. AKG-images/Joseph Martin
14. *Musica e Musicisti*. © Lebrecht Music & Arts

SECOND PICTURE SECTION

1. The Met's Gatti-Casazza and Manhattan's Oscar Hammerstein. © Collection of the New-York Historical Society, USA/The Bridgeman Art Library
2. *Théâtrophone*. Private Collection/The Stapleton Collection/ The Bridgeman Art Library
3. Met stars listening to a live broadcast. The Metropolitan Opera
4. Gramophone advert. Author's collection
5. Costume design for *The Demon*. © Lebrecht Music & Arts
6. *A Night at the Opera*. © Bettmann/Corbis
7. The Paris Opera under the Nazi flag. © Roger Viollet/Topfoto
8. Gala concert at La Scala. © Teatro alla Scala
9. Leontyne Price recording with the Boston Symphony Orchestra. AKG-images

Acknowledgements

While researching and writing this book, I was able to try out some of my emerging ideas through a number of broadcasts, lectures and articles. For BBC Radio 3, I presented a series of six features for which I recorded interviews with a number of experts on opera history in Britain and around the world, and was also able to mine invaluable seams from the sound archives of the BBC and the New York Metropolitan Opera. Some of this material has helped enrich the book and I am grateful to my producer, Kate Bolton, for her help as we prepared these programmes together. My thanks, too, to the editor of *Opera Now*, Ashutosh Khandekar, who kindly invited me to write a series of articles, and nuggets from these, too, have found their way into what follows. I am also grateful to Chatto & Windus for permission to adapt and re-present brief passages derived from material previously published in my book *The Hitler Emigrés*.

Much of the research for *The Gilded Stage* was undertaken in London. As a Senior Research Fellow in the Institute of Historical Research (London University), I had access to all the resources of the IHR and, indeed, the entire University of London library system, while I also worked in the British Library and in the archive collections of the Royal Opera House, Covent Garden, and London's Theatre Museum. My thanks to all concerned. I have learned much, too, from many visits to opera in other parts of Britain and, over the years, to most of the world's great opera centres – where I have often had the pleasure of meeting scholars, archivists and librarians as well as managers, press officers and artists, all of whom have generously helped with my researches and pointed me in useful directions for further study. While working on this book, my operatic peregrinations were also enriched by the opportunity to lead some thirty opera tours for companies such as Martin Randall Ltd, Cox & Kings and others with whom it has always been a privilege and a pleasure to work.

Countless conversations, email exchanges and interviews (some of them recorded) with friends and colleagues in Britain and around the world have proved invaluable, and I am grateful for instruction, help and advice from the following: Julian Anderson, Rosamund Bartlett, Tim Blanning, John Brewer, Stephen A. Brown, Peter Burke, Sir David Cannadine, Margaret Carson, Michael Chance, Peter E. Clark, David Coke, Roger Covell, Julia Creed, Stephen Dee, Gabriele Dotto, Katharine Ellis, Iain Fenlon, Francesca Franchi, Bernard Greenberg, Alison and David Gyger, Ulrike Hessler, Raymond Holden, Eric Homberger, Geoffrey Hosking, Alfred Hubay, Robert D. Hume, James H. Johnson, Paula Kaplan, Thena Kendall, Helene Lindroth, Hugh Macpherson, Dennis Marks, Judith Milhous, Edward Morgan, Gary Murphy, Jiří Nekvasil, Moffatt Oxenbould, Roger Parker, Nicholas Payne, Maurice Pearton, John Pennino, Graham Pont, Sir Curtis Price, Therese Radic, Ivan Ruml, Jan Spacek, Donald Sassoon, Marc Scorca, Elizabeth Silsbury, Somtow Sucharitkul, Gerhard Strassgschwandtner, Jula Szuster, Tanya Tintner, Owen Toller, James Torniainen, Robert Tuggle, Walter Wells, Frank Whitford, Rupert Wilkinson and Hin-Yan Wong. Some of these kindly read through various sections of my text, while Roger Parker (to whom special thanks) was good enough to read and check the entire manuscript. All this expert scrutiny has, I hope, helped save me from too many egregious mistakes.

Remaining errors of fact or judgement remain mine, of course – though I hope few have survived the rigorous production process for which I have to thank Toby Mundy and his colleagues at Atlantic Books. The book was Toby's idea in the first place and I am also grateful to Caroline Knight and Sarah Norman who helped steer the book editorially through various hazards, and to Mark Handsley who transformed the normally mundane job of copy-editing into what became a shared creative process. My thanks, as always, to Dinah Wiener, supportive agent *extraordinaire*. Also, to Janet, whose unquenchable enthusiasms and burgeoning iconographic expertise led me to images, ideas and sources I would never otherwise have encountered. And, finally and alas belatedly, to my parents, whose warm encouragement enabled me as a child to learn and love music and opera in the first place. They would have relished the idea of my undertaking a book which is, at least in part, my grateful homage to their memory.

Introduction

In a letter published in *The Times* (London) on 8 April 1853, a gentleman signing himself 'C.T.' reported that he had been refused admission to the Royal Italian Opera, Covent Garden, 'because the cut of my dress coat was not what it ought to be according to the ideas of the doorkeeper'. With scarcely disguised indignation, he goes on to say:

> I put on my evening suit, with clean linen and everything necessary to have admitted me to any resort of ladies and gentlemen… and according to respectable witnesses at the door (who tendered me their assistance if I would bring forward the case) there could be no objection to it.

After protesting for twenty minutes or so ('and finding all expostulation in vain'), C.T. agreed to leave, retrieved his coat and went round to the box office to ask for the seven shillings he had paid for his ticket. Here, 'the same person who sold it to me refused to refund the money, on the ground that it had been accounted for to the Theatre.' Meanwhile, he noticed several people entering the theatre 'in frock coats and great coats, and others positively dirty'. 'To my certain knowledge,' he says, the attire he wore that evening would have gained him admission 'to any part of any opera house' between London and Naples. 'I returned home,' reports C.T. deeply disgruntled, 'without seeing *Masaniello*.'

That was not the end of the story, for the next day he confronted the manager of the Covent Garden theatre, Frederick Gye, asking for his seven shillings, plus a further five for cab hire. Mr Gye, he reports, 'again referred me to the ticket office, although he could not object to my coat'.

'What redress is there, Sir,' asks our correspondent in a final flourish, 'but the County Court, where I shall, perhaps, obtain my own after loss of time and temper?'

*

Many books about the history of opera concentrate on the traditional trio of composers, works and performers. My shelves – like those of every opera lover – are packed with them (and a quick glance at the Notes will reveal how indebted I am to some of the best). But in addition to being an art form, opera has always been a social, economic and political phenomenon, and elements of each lie between the lines of that indignant letter. The appropriate dress code, the price of a ticket, the behaviour of fellow audience members, the supposed omni-competence of a beleaguered manager, the threat of legal action – all are part of the story. Then there is the work C.T. never got to see. Auber's *Masaniello* (or *La Muette de Portici*) is a stirring piece about a Neapolitan political uprising; when performed in Brussels in 1830 it was said to have aroused local patriotism to such a pitch as to have contributed directly to the achievement of Belgian independence. In *The Gilded Stage*, we explore the broader context in which opera has been created, financed, produced, received and perceived. It is not the operatic stage itself and what goes on within its gilded confines that we concentrate on. Here, our focus is as much on the demand as the supply, not just the production of opera but also its consumption: the many chains of connection linking opera houses and impresarios, monarchs and money makers, art, artists and audiences.

Sometimes, I am tempted to start a campaign to abolish the word opera altogether. After all, it simply means a work. But for many it has become heavily loaded with resonances of grandeur, wealth and 'elitism' (another word I would like to banish). In my campaign I suspect I would have the ghosts of some of the greatest composers on my side. Monteverdi called *Orfeo*, first performed just over 400 years ago, a *Favola in musica*: a fable set to music. So far as I know, nobody at the time used the word opera to describe an art form that, in effect, was an attempt to combine all the arts, as the ancients were believed to have done and as an ambitious production of a movie or musical might aspire to do today: a *Gesamtkunstwerk*, to use the term associated with Wagner. He would be on my side, too.

Opera is certainly the most complex of all the performance arts, the form that attempts to reconcile the greatest number of contributory elements. The longer the chain, the greater the risk of weak links, and opera lore is replete with legendary tales of catastrophes, amusing in retrospect but doubtless appalling when (and if) they actually occurred. Part of the appeal of opera, indeed, is that, as with tightrope walking or motor racing, there is a constant sense in a live performance that something might go wrong. Or spectacularly right. From the start, it was the sheer ambition of opera, the attempt to integrate so many art forms into one transcending arch of aesthetic achievement, that made it so attractive to those who encouraged, commissioned, composed, performed and patronized it. In this sense, opera might be thought of as one of the crowning artistic legacies of the Renaissance.

In *The Gilded Stage*, we follow the story of opera as it spread from the cities of northern Italy through Europe, America and the wider world, becoming a global business in the digital age. The book makes no claim to be a comprehensive history of opera, rather a sequence of 'scenes' from a rich and colourful story. Thus, our historical helicopter lands in a succession of times and places across the operatic map, sojourning for a while in each before taking off again for another. Many of our way stations provide the immediate environment in which some outstanding operatic composers lived and worked. But the helicopter refuels, too, in locations germane to our story not on account of particular composers or works but because of the resonant operatic culture that developed there. Thus, our journey takes us from Renaissance Italy to the Paris of Louis XIV and Frederick the Great's Berlin. Later, we note how the post-Napoleonic settlement, intended to bestow a sense of political stability, came to be undermined by an eruption of cultural nationalism across much of Europe. By the middle of the nineteenth century, attendance at the opera houses of London or Paris might have represented the acme of fashion; but soon the most significant productions were as likely to be staged in Munich or Milan, Bayreuth or Budapest, Prague or St Petersburg.

Nor was opera a European monopoly. The more cultured among the American Founding Fathers encouraged and aped European tastes, while Mozart's librettist and Rossini's first Count Almaviva help take our story to New York and thence to New Orleans and Mexico. We catch glimpses of opera, too, alongside the bravado and bawdiness of the Australian and American frontiers as mining millionaires flaunt their flamboyant and anomalous claim to culture (much as the rubber barons of the High Amazon would later signal their parvenu wealth by erecting an opera house in Manaus). By the late nineteenth century, a typically 'Anglo-Saxon' patron of the New York Metropolitan Opera, that archetypal product of Gilded Age America, might have caught a French work sung by a Czech, Polish and Italian cast led by a German conductor at what came to be affectionately dubbed the 'Faustspielhaus'. Twenty years later, one might have heard Caruso singing Puccini in Havana or Toscanini conducting Wagner in Buenos Aires.

Even Caruso and Toscanini could scarcely have imagined the global reach of opera by the end of the twentieth century. For opera lovers, its worldwide popularity was undoubtedly a cause for celebration. Some, however, felt that the presentation of opera was in danger of becoming too democratized, its jagged edges filed down for mass consumption, exploited and commodified by people primarily concerned to make money out of it. Others sensed opera becoming a museum art appealing to a well-heeled social group contentedly revisiting old masterpieces rather than writing, producing or attending new ones. One reading of operatic history, indeed, might be said to reveal its rise and fall over the course of a 400-year trajectory. Or, perhaps, the gradual democratization of culture as serious music theatre, like artistic endeavour in other fields, struggled to widen the social base of its audiences while at the same time maintaining aesthetic standards. We consider such questions before moving on to one more: where does opera go from here? The book will end with some speculation about possible futures in an era of instant international communications, global finances and interactive digital technology. And we conclude – like *Madama Butterfly* – on an unresolved chord.

*

In writing this book, I have tried to take account of two rather different historiographies. First, there is a large and growing volume of excellent scholarly material on the history of opera, often by people trained as musicologists. Much of it tends to be fairly close-focused, with books and articles concentrating primarily on composers and their works and performers. Second, there is an even larger corpus of material on social history, an approach to the past that was in its infancy when I first encountered it but which has grown and flourished in the decades since. It will be no surprise to toilers in both fields if I say that, until recently, wire fences and closed gates rather than well-trodden pathways often marked the boundary between the two. Of course, the standard traditional biographies of the great operatic composers have routinely mentioned something of their family background and historical environment: Mozart's extraordinary childhood, for example, or Verdi's prominence in *Risorgimento*-era Italy. One could nevertheless read otherwise excellent composer biographies by the fistful and search in vain for anything more than cursory consideration of the wider context of their subjects' lives and work.

Those trained as historians rather than musicologists could be just as territorial. 'That's not my field,' says the Bismarck scholar pressed for a view on Frederick the Great or the Medievalist when asked about the Renaissance. The Americanist will deny expertise on the history of France, the French historian on that of Russia. This is partly a question of intellectual integrity; none of us is omniscient and we all have to defer to experts in 'fields' not our own. Perhaps it also reflects deeper attitudes, however, about the proper nature of historical study. Two or three generations ago, history as taught in the academy tended to concentrate on the great political, diplomatic and constitutional events of the past and the men (for they were mostly men) who effected them. Much of this was to change during the 1960s and 1970s, when, concomitant with the new radicalism of the times, the historiographical barometer swung towards the story of 'ordinary' people whom history had hitherto tended to marginalize or ignore.

Today, social history has been augmented by the emergence of cultural history; here, historians have learned much from anthropology and have brought to the fore such issues as gender, ethnicity and ritual. 'Culture' has thus come to mean many things. What it does not mean to most historians, however, is precisely what it probably signified to their grandparents: painting, architecture, literature and 'classical' music. Just as music history often gives short shrift to the wider context in which composers composed and performers performed, so social or cultural history tends to avoid consideration of the 'high' arts. Perhaps there is a vestigial class bias at work here, as historians intent on elevating the role of 'ordinary' people disdain to consider such 'elite' pastimes as opera – while opera historians prefer to concern themselves with 'great art'.

In recent years, the fences have begun to be breached and the pathways better trodden than before, thanks to the efforts of a number of notable and courageous pioneers. This book is an attempt to build on their work and to pull together into a single volume some of the essential elements of a large story. It is not an encyclopedia, however, and individual readers will doubtless, according to taste and interest, find this or that location, period or personality given too much or too little attention. Sometimes the historical helicopter lands in a particular time or place that demands close and detailed coverage. Elsewhere, relatively flimsy coverage might result from paucity of data. We simply do not know enough about (for example) life at the Mantuan court when Monteverdi's *Orfeo* was first produced, or even with absolute certainty where in the palace it was performed. How widely known would Handel and his music have been in early Hanoverian London, or Mozart and his in Habsburg Vienna or Prague, and what sort of people played in their orchestras and sang in their choruses? Did the Italian immigrant community in late nineteenth-century New York provide a substantial proportion of the audience at the new Metropolitan Opera? Perhaps; but there are no accurate data to substantiate or contradict what must remain a hunch.

So the scope and scale of this book have necessarily been restricted by both editorial considerations and the limitations of available evidence. But if it is necessarily an exercise in historical synthesis, it will not, I trust, read like one of those interminable chronicles that recount 'one damn fact after another'. On the contrary, I have tried to remain aware throughout of the need to keep hold of the big picture, the broad themes that inform the overall narrative. Five themes in particular run through much of the book.

The first is *political*. When a Gonzaga or Wittelsbach duke or a Bourbon monarch promoted opera, the aim was usually to impress someone (a rival ruler, perhaps), while 'popular' opera could often be more subversive. Mozart quit the secure employ of an archbishop to freelance in and around the court of an emperor where he encountered his finest librettist, a Venetian Jew who ended his days in Martin Van Buren's America. Napoleon appeared at the opera to show himself to 'the people' whose cause he was supposedly fighting in foreign lands. In the wake of the French Revolutionary wars, much of central Europe gradually became immersed in a rising tide of cultural nationalism, a theme that many of the producers and consumers of opera embraced and which survived well into the twentieth century – notably and notoriously under the Third Reich. In our own times, public debate about the supposed elitism or popularity of opera has sometimes taken a fiercely political turn.

Alongside politics is *finance*. It is impossible to talk about an art form that aspires to combine all the others – and is therefore liable to be the most expensive – without discussing money and management. Detailed financial information, except for more recent times, is often scanty. Thus, there is only sporadic evidence, and that largely anecdotal, about the wages paid in earlier times to operatic *comprimari* or to the members of choruses or orchestras. We do know something about the sums paid to celebrated soloists and, here and there, the cost of buying a box at the opera for a season or the cost of tickets for individual performances (when these were sold). The foot soldiers are an all-important part of our story, but it is the finances – and debts and deficits – of the field marshals that the historical record tends to preserve. Opera has rarely managed to be self-financing, and if there is one issue that recurs like a rondo theme throughout our story, it is the question of who pays. Or, rather, who picks up the deficit. The story of opera is therefore in part that of a succession of dukes and monarchs, risk-running impresarios, syndicates of bountiful bankers and industrialists, grants from local or central governments, and latterly of various ingenious, more or less tax-exempt schemes to raise money from sponsorship and private donation.

In the course of the book, many different currencies are mentioned, from Venetian ducats via French francs and Italian lire to modern British pounds and US dollars. There is no way these could realistically be converted for comparative purposes into a single currency comprehensible to modern readers. Rather, I have tried to give an idea of monetary values by quoting, alongside (say) a prima donna's fee or the price of a theatre ticket, the typical daily wage of a worker at the time or the cost of a loaf of bread or restaurant meal.

Opera is a *social* phenomenon, too. The shift in the nature of the operatic audience, or at least the broad outlines of that shift, is easily plotted; it parallels other historical changes as power and money moved from the aristocracy, church and higher soldiery to the emergent bourgeoisie and, latterly, to a wider social spectrum. This shift is evident in everything from the physical shape of the opera house itself (for example, the relative absence of boxes and other social distinctions in most modern opera houses), to the way audiences behaved and dressed at the opera and such matters as pricing policy, the style of playbills and programmes, and the food and drink on offer. Equally remarkable is the changing social status of those in the operatic professions – especially, perhaps, among talented women singers to whom opera at times offered a rare opportunity for substantial social and economic improvement.

Alongside these social changes, we also note changes in *technology* that transformed the nature of opera. From earliest times, opera flaunted magical stage effects as Eros flew overhead, Jove or Juno descended from the heavens or the plot's wicked miscreant was dragged, Don Giovanni-style, down into a fiery hell. 'Scenes' and 'machines' were as much remarked as the music or drama. Indeed, the latest scientific wizardry often featured, sometimes in parodic form, in operatic plots (such as the caricature of Dr Mesmer in *Così fan tutte*). We will talk of candle, gas and electric lighting, of gauzes and swimming machines and of the arrival of laser lighting and surtitles. Our story also includes the development of new means of spreading the word (and sounds and sights) of opera beyond the confines of the theatre: music publishing and copyright laws and the successive invention of photography, recording, film, TV, video, and the latest satellite and digital technologies.

Finally, of course, opera is an *art form*, and this book is therefore, to some degree, a cultural history. Here, several great arcs are discernible, each of which parallels broader historical trends. The first concerns the people who actually make opera happen. The singer has always been important, and our story is replete with the supposedly extravagant behaviour, funding and achievements of operatic superstars. But everyone else's relative weight on the scales of significance has shifted radically as our story lurches from what might loosely be labelled as 'patrons' opera' (from the Gonzaga dukes of Mantua to the Austrian Emperor Joseph II), to 'composers' opera' (from Gluck and Mozart to Puccini and Strauss), to 'conductors' opera' (the Mahler/Toscanini era), to 'producers' opera' in more recent times. Who, or what, is the principal attraction when *you* decide to go to the opera?

Then there is the changing nature of the art itself. Broadly speaking, two strands weave their way in and out of our narrative. The first, which we encounter in the courts of late-Renaissance Italy, in Handel, Wagner, Verdi and Benjamin Britten, is what we might dub 'serious' opera, usually through-composed and dealing with heightened emotions, situations and characters. The other, a more 'popular' style of music theatre with catchy tunes and vernacular dialogue, emerges in everything from Venetian *commedia dell'arte*, *The Beggar's Opera* and *The Magic Flute* to Viennese operetta, Gilbert and Sullivan, and beyond. In earlier times, opera goers liked to attend something new, rather like today's cinema audiences. By the early twentieth century, however, it was becoming clear that they preferred to revisit a standard repertoire of acknowledged classics, an emerging 'canon' to which few new works were subsequently added. Running alongside this fundamental change has been the way operatic plots and productions have altered focus over the centuries from high authority and quasi-mythical heroes towards ordinary people and 'victims'. The music of operas, similarly, has tended to shift from stylized aria and recitative towards more integrated music drama, thence perhaps to psychodrama and, in parallel, the popular 'musicals' of recent decades. Ah, but are these 'operas'?

Maybe opera is simply the word we apply to a music drama produced in what we call an opera house; if *Sweeney Todd* is mounted at Covent Garden, it is *ipso facto* an opera.* Some would argue that what distinguishes opera from other forms is that it is aimed to be sung, live, with a properly focused 'operatic' voice capable of projecting without electronic amplification. We all know an operatic voice when we hear it: Bryn Terfel has one, Elton John does not. Perhaps it is safer not to attempt too rigid (or too loose) a definition; opera, like the proverbial elephant, is something most of us recognize when we come across it but would be hard-pressed to describe precisely to someone who had not. So I am not urging a broad, all-embracing new definition of opera; just suggesting we should avoid too narrow a one.

That said, it is hard to avoid the conclusion that opera, at least as widely construed, is an art form which reached its acme during the long nineteenth century, from around the time of Mozart to the death of Puccini. In which case, this book might be said to document the rise, decline and fall (and possible demise) of an elite art form. According to this reading, opera has become at best a museum art, a kind of old-fashioned religion re-enacted inside great temples before a dwindling audience of the devout. Or perhaps we have been chronicling the democratization of opera, the gradual diluting, or 'dumbing down', of a once great art form to the point where any appeal it has beyond the narrow world of the cognoscenti is necessarily derived from the imposition of hype, shock and bogus sex appeal. If, on the other hand, you are of the 'glass half full' disposition, it seems to me that, despite death agonies more protracted than those of Gilda or Tristan, opera is resolutely refusing to die. On the contrary, there are, as I will try to show, potent signs of a revival in this most protean of all art forms.

---

* Stephen Sondheim was quoted (by Norman Lebrecht, *Evening Standard* (London), 14 July 2004) as saying: 'I believe an opera is something that is shown in an opera house in front of an opera audience. The same work in the West End... is a West End show. It's a question of expectation.'

PART I

Down the Road from *Arianna* to *Zauberflöte*
*c.*1600–1800

CHAPTER I

The Birth of Italian Opera

Anna Renzi was Venice's prima donna, one of the leading singers of her day, a 'sweet siren who gently ravishes the souls and pleases the eyes and ears of the listeners', according to one of her admirers, the dramatist and poet Giulio Strozzi. A portrait of Renzi shows an elegantly, expensively dressed young woman. Her richly coiffed hair is bedecked with flowers and jewellery, and her slashed two-tone bodice, tightly gathered in at the waist, is edged with a delicate filigree lace collar and cuffs. In Renzi's hand is a sheet of music, but her eyes are looking out knowingly and confidently at the viewer. A 'woman of few words', says Strozzi, 'but those are appropriate, sensible, and worthy for her beautiful sayings'.

As a young man, the English diarist John Evelyn had visited Venice in June 1645 as part of the Grand Tour he was undertaking. During Ascension week, Evelyn went to hear Renzi in an opera about Hercules in Lydia. He was duly impressed (though he thought 'an eunuch' in the cast 'surpassed her'), and he attempted to describe the attraction of the new art form:

> This night… we went to the Opera, where comedies and other plays are represented in recitative music, by the most excellent musicians, vocal and instrumental, with variety of scenes painted and contrived with no less art of perspective, and machines for flying in the air, and other wonderful notions; taken together, it is one of the most magnificent and expensive diversions the wit of man can invent… The scenes changed thirteen times… This held us by the eyes and ears till two in the morning.

Opera was one of the entertainments presented in Venice as part of Carnival, a winter-time festivity that in theory ran from the day after Christmas until Shrove Tuesday but which in practice came to be extended in both directions. Here were gathered every kind of freethinker: sexual libertarians, disillusioned priests, rich young Grand Tourists like Evelyn, and a stream of louche actors and musicians from all over Italy seeking work, money and audiences in the city most likely to provide them. During Carnival-time, the wearing of masks guaranteed anonymity to their wearers and broke down social (and sexual) barriers. So long as you kept out of trouble with the city authorities, your life was pretty much your own. Evelyn, revisiting Venice in January 1646 'to see the folly and madness of the Carnival', noted 'the women, men and persons of all conditions disguising themselves in antique dresses, with extravagant music and a thousand gambols, traversing the streets from house to house, all places then accessible and free to enter'. Here, 'the comedians have liberty, the operas are open… and the mountebanks have their stages at every corner'. Evelyn records that the 'diversions which chiefly took me up [were] three noble operas, where were excellent voices and music, the most celebrated of which was the famous Anna Rencia [*sic*]', whom he and his companion later invited to supper.

Unlike Florence, Mantua and other northern Italian city-states, Venice was a republic, in many ways an exceptionally liberal, independent-minded one. In 1606, the entire city was, in effect, excommunicated by the papacy for its religious toleration (including towards Protestants). If something was attractive, the Venetian instinct was to flaunt it, perhaps to sell it. The city had long been an essential stopover for wealthy tourists from all over Europe seeking a frisson of danger. In 1594, Thomas Nashe, a contemporary of Shakespeare, published a vivid account in which his characters meet a pimp in Venice who leads them to a brothel, 'Tabitha the Temptresses'. Tabitha apparently maintained a house of such elegance and refinement that, like 'any saint's house', it contained 'Bookes, pictures, beades, crucifixes [and] a haberdashers shop… in every chamber'. Tabitha's whores had not a hair out of place, says Nashe, while on the beds there was 'not a wrinkle' to be found and the pillows were as smooth as a 'groning wives belly'. Nashe's young men had no complaints. 'Us for our money,' he concludes, 'they used like Emperours.' At Carnival time, Venice exploded into a riot of license and danger. Evelyn described the way Venetians would 'fling eggs filled with sweet water, but sometimes not over sweet', while they also had 'a barbarous custom of hunting bulls about the streets & piazzas, which is very dangerous, the passages being generally narrow'. Here, by the waterways of La Serenissima, visitors found an exuberant crossroad between cultures where the legacy of the Renaissance met that of Byzantium, art met commerce, East met West.

For all its flamboyance, Venice was also in decline. The Imperial armies that routed Mantua in 1630 brought plague to Venice a year later, killing a quarter of the city's population of some 150,000 over the next couple of years; fifteen years later, Venice embarked on two decades of recurrent warfare with the expansionist Ottomans, a campaign that drained the exchequer and culminated in humiliating defeat for the Republic in 1669. Deeper, longer-term trends also pointed to inexorable decline as foreign trade gradually diminished and the great trading routes Venice had once dominated were superseded by new roads to the East. Poverty became widespread while the men running the city responded with ever more petty rules and regulations. The Most Serene Republic, it became evident to anyone prepared to peer out beyond the civic mask, was in terminal decay. 'My eyes are very pleased by Venice,' commented the French political philosopher Montesquieu; 'my heart and mind are not.'

Yet, throughout these years, Venice continued to face the world with a broad smile, or at least the fixed semblance of one. Not only during Carnival but throughout the year a sequence of festivals and processions packed the calendar in a triumph of show over substance. Art and artifice acted as an addictive drug, a way of neutralizing traditional moral codes, a permanent diversion from uncomfortable realities. Life imitated art and became something far more comfortable: theatre. Venice was itself the most theatrical of cities, its very fabric providing the greatest spectacle of all: there was theatre on the canals, in the piazzas, in churches, in homes, and people would walk, talk and dress with a vivid sense of theatricality. Above all, this was a city of public theatres, often built by noble families on their vacant city properties, in which travelling troupes of players could usually be sure of a paying audience

In this 1610 engraving from Venice, singers, actors, masquers, jugglers and a snake-charmer perform outside St Mark's. Many smaller piazzas would have witnessed similar scenes, especially during Carnival: a socially mixed crowd enjoying open-air, multi-media entertainment. Cover the piazza and you have the essence of the early opera house.

made up of not just the aristocracy but, potentially at least, of all ranks of society. Performances would typically contain a spoken comedy, interspersed with elements of song and dance and, if the spectators were lucky, some clever stage trickery of the kind that impressed Evelyn. Back in the 1590s, when Thomas Nashe was writing, there were two such public theatres in the vicinity of San Cassiano alone, a short walk west of the Rialto. One of them burned down in 1629 and was promptly rebuilt with brick and renamed the Teatro S. Cassiano. After a further fire and rebuild, it was here at the Cassiano, from 1637, that something like operatic life as we know it today was inaugurated: a form of publicly promoted musico-dramatic entertainment available on a regular or recurrent commercial basis in purpose-built theatres before a paying public.

At the time, the leading musician in Venice and the man in charge of music at St Mark's Cathedral was the seventy-year-old Claudio Monteverdi. Few Venetians would have known that, thirty years before, in the confines of a Renaissance court in Mantua, their *maestro di cappella* had also composed perhaps the earliest genuine masterpiece in operatic history: *Orfeo*.

*

The origins of opera can be dated back a lot earlier still. Throughout history, many societies, often inspired by religio-political motives, have tried to link drama, spectacle, music and movement, and scholars have found fragmentary evidence of some of the words, instruments and stagings used in (for example) Pharaonic Egypt, the amphitheatres of ancient Greece, or the streets and churches and the courtly jousts and banquets of medieval Europe. We have little knowledge of the actual music sung or played in these quasi-ceremonial music dramas, however. In any case, it was probably not until Renaissance times that serious, systematic attempts were made to integrate and to stage all the elements of story and song, words, dance and music. Thus the roots of what we call 'opera' can realistically be traced no further back than the stage jigs and courtly masques of the sixteenth century, the *intermedi* performed between the acts of plays in the Renaissance courts of northern Italy, and that popular semi-improvised Italian theatrical entertainment, the *commedia dell'arte*, which featured much-loved stock characters such as the lovers Harlequin and Columbine, the miserly old Pantalone and the sad but comic Pulcinella.

In the 1570s and 1580s, a number of well-connected Florentine cultural figures used to gather at the home of the military leader and humanist intellectual Count Giovanni de' Bardi, where they would discuss the essentials of music and drama. Among the regular members of the Bardi *Camerata* were the musicians Giulio Caccini and Vincenzo Galilei (father of the astronomer Galileo). Galilei wrote a treatise arguing for a 'dialogue between ancient and modern music': a revival, in effect, of what he believed to have been the

Italian *commedia dell'arte*, with its stock characters and story lines, fed directly into what later became known as opera. Its influence is still evident in Rossini's *Barber of Seville*, Donizetti's *Don Pasquale* and the play-within-a-play in Leoncavallo's *I pagliacci*.

aesthetic ideas of the ancient Greeks and Romans, most notably the complete integration of music and poetry. After Italy had suffered 'great barbarian invasions', lamented Galilei in his *Dialogue*, 'men had been overcome by a heavy lethargy of ignorance… and took as little notice of music as of the western Indies'. Nowadays, he asserted, 'there is not heard the slightest sign of modern music accomplishing what ancient music accomplished'. Neither the novelty nor the excellence of modern music 'has ever had the power of producing any of the virtuous effects that ancient music produced'. Today's musicians, Galilei thundered, 'aim at nothing but the delight of the ear, if it can truly be called delight'. One of Galilei's concerns was about the ways in which texts were set to music. 'The last thing the moderns think of,' he sniffed, 'is the expression of words with the passion that these words require.' And he took particular objection to the fashion for polyphony, in which a number of musical lines run alongside each other, advocating instead the clarity of a single vocal line. This, he thought, was how the music of the ancient world had been able to make so powerful an impact.

Galilei's views were not original to him, and he and his colleagues were swimming with an already powerful tide. Throughout the Renaissance, there had been an attempt, especially but not only in northern Italy, to revive what came to be regarded as the superior culture of the ancient world and to place the individual human being centre stage. Architects, painters and sculptors, poets, historians and philosophers all aspired to build upon the supposedly humanistic principles underlying surviving Greek and Roman models. The Greek Parthenon and Roman Pantheon, the sculptures of Pheidias and Prax-iteles, the works of Aristotle and Virgil – all served as inspiration in the era of Leonardo, Michelangelo, Raphael and Machiavelli. For one cultural form, however, there were no ancient models, and that was music. Philosophers, including Plato, had reflected on the nature and impact of music, and there were plenty of surviving pictures of ancient musicians and music-making and descriptions of musical occasions. But the music itself had vanished. This only served to present a greater challenge to those, such as the Bardi circle, interested in the revival of the ancient arts and learning.

Renaissance art and scholarship received encouragement and funding from some of the wealthiest and most powerful political figures of the day. The munificence of Lorenzo de' Medici ('The Magnificent') helped make Florence a leading cultural centre, while it was the Vatican that commissioned St Peter's and the Sistine Chapel. In Ferrara, the ruling Este family had long been accustomed to putting on elaborate banquets at which musico-dramatic presentations would be performed for the delectation of guests between the many courses. Here, and in Mantua, courtly entertainments would also often feature elegant, classically based pastorals in which the drama would be set to music and include dance sequences. In Florence, the Medici would mark opportunities for political display such as dynastic weddings with not only gentle pastorals but also more impressive (and expensive) forms of stage enter-tainment and, between the acts, a series of extravagant, multimedia *intermedi*. In 1589, the celebrations of a marriage linking the houses of Tuscany and Lorraine culminated with a series of *intermedi* played in the entr'actes of a drama called *La pellegrina*. Devised by Bardi and calling upon the talents of several prominent members of his circle, these included not only spectacular scenic effects but also sequences of richly textured vocal and instrumental music and a ballet. 'Through the depredations of time,' we read in a pamphlet by one who was there, 'we have lost the ability to perform such things with the musical modes of antiquity.' However, although 'presented to the accom-paniment of our modern music', it was evidently to the credit of the composer (Luca Marenzio, who wrote the music to the second and third *intermedi*) that he apparently did 'his utmost… to imitate and re-create the music of antiquity'.

Such *intermedi* – still, theoretically, mini-performances between the acts of a play – could overshadow the play itself. Some complained about this: one did not go to a show for its intermission features. 'The wondrous show – alas! – of the intermedi,' complained 'Comedy' in a line by the sixteenth-century Florentine poet and playwright Antonfrancesco Grazzini. However, if pastorals could be so popular and *intermedi* so potent, some wondered why not extend them. It was thus a natural step to argue, as Vincenzo Galilei did, that music should be played throughout a full-length dramatic performance. Further, Galilei argued that the music should reflect the emotions seen on stage. As in ancient Greece (it was presumed), singers should be given words and music both clearly embodying the feelings they were required to express. To underline the emotions, said Galilei, not only should one melody be played or sung at a time, but the music should follow the natural inflections and rhythms of speech. Galilei composed illustrations of how these principles might work in practice. His compositions have not survived. Some of Caccini's have, however, and are among the earliest embodiments of principles that, with variations, have tended to lie at the very root of what later generations came to call 'opera'.

It would be misleading to suggest that *intermedi* or pastorals simply gave way to the new form. On the contrary, there was at first little substantive distinction between the genres. But it is perhaps not altogether fanciful to date the origins of opera as we have come to understand it to around the year 1600 and, more specifically, the celebrations in Florence in October that year of the marriage of Maria de' Medici to the King of France, Henri IV. The festivities marking the event were highlighted by a performance of a work called *Il rapimento di Cefalo* in which most of the music was by Caccini. Less noticed at the time, perhaps because it took place in the confined space of the Pitti palace, was *Euridice*, with text by Ottavio Rinuccini and music mostly by Jacopo Peri

The Florentine *Intermedi* of 1589 were an early attempt to recreate what was believed to be the ancient world's integration of music, drama and staging. One featured Apollo's descent from the clouds to defeat the dragon Python.

(with some unwelcome additions by Caccini). This is the first opera for which complete music has survived, perhaps the first 'opera' of all. Rinuccini, although not using the term, seems to have implied as much in his dedication to Maria de' Medici, where he wrote (almost as if it were a matter of accepted fact) that 'the ancient Greeks and Romans, in representing their tragedies on stage, sang them throughout' – something, he added, that nobody had done since because modern music was so inferior to that of the ancients.

If the aesthetic origins of opera can be traced to earnest Renaissance theorizing about the Greeks and Romans, the historical context in which it first developed leads us into rather less elevated social and political considerations. Beneath the celebratory surface of the nuptials of 1600, there were severe offstage squabbles between some of the artists. Thus Peri and Caccini competed over which singers the other could use, while the man who directed *Euridice*, the musician, dancer, choreographer and diplomat Emilio de' Cavalieri (another member of the Bardi circle), was excluded from the principal musical offering, the *Rapimento*, and left Florence in disgust for his native Rome. As for the wider political stage, the high hopes some held of this dynastic marriage were to be repeatedly frustrated over the years that followed. Henri IV was assassinated and Maria (now Marie) became the incompetent Regent of France. Ousted by her son, Louis XIII, she realigned herself unsuccessfully with Catholic Spain and by the time she was painted by Rubens in the early 1620s had become something of a frumpy has-been.

Nothing of this was of course visible to the army of notables who attended the spectacular marriage celebrations in 1600. And if the law of unexpected consequences lurked above those Florentine festivities, it was in at least one respect to uncharacteristically benign effect. For before long, the tender new art form, incorporating elements of drama, poetry, music, dancing and acting, took firm root. The creations of Peri, Caccini and the rest involved the painting of scenery, too, and the production of costumes as well as the engineering of ambitious stage machinery, all topped by a style and quality of solo singing never heard before. The results were variable and there was no single word to describe them; each was simply a 'work' (or *opera* in Italian) inspired by the lofty and probably unachievable ambition of integrating all the arts.

One of those present at the wedding festivities in Florence in 1600 was Vincenzo Gonzaga, Duke of nearby Mantua, and he doubtless attended the performance of *Euridice* with his long-term secretary, the poet Alessandro Striggio. A few years later, the Duke's chief musician, Claudio Monteverdi, collaborated with Striggio to produce a far greater work on the same theme.

*

It is February 1607 and we are in the richly panelled room of a Renaissance palace. The room is long and narrow, not particularly large – maybe fifteen metres by eight – and is part of the ground-floor apartment of the widowed sister of the Duke. On this particular occasion, it has been decked up as a temporary theatre, with a curtained dais at one end faced by a pair of comfortable armchairs, a few more basic wooden chairs, and several rows (or raised rings) of seats or benches which are beginning to be filled up by eager, elegantly dressed young men. The room is lit by the naked flames of torches and candles, which give it a warm, wan look, and sufficient light for the more enthusiastic to wave across to each other in lively anticipation of the show they have come to witness. Word has spread that the performance will be rather special, with the actors singing their parts. Suddenly the chit-chat diminishes to silence. The Duke and his entourage enter, take their seats to the accompaniment of a musical fanfare and the show begins.

Was this how things seemed to those who attended the first performance of *Orfeo* in the Gonzaga palace in Mantua? Probably, though there is no documentary evidence enabling us to be sure. Of one thing, however, we can be certain: those present, including the work's creators, Striggio and Monteverdi, as well as the Duke, would have been astounded to be told that, four hundred years later, their *Favola in musica* would have come to be regarded as the first work of consequence in a new artistic genre universally known as 'opera'.

*

While Duke Vincenzo was alive, Mantua regained something of the artistic pre-eminence it had once achieved under his celebrated sixteenth-century predecessor Isabella d'Este. In Isabella's day, many regarded Mantua as the finest city in the world and the ducal palace with its vast sequence of gardens and courtyards the largest building. Mantegna had been retained by the Mantua court, and the architect and theorist Alberti. In 1588, according to the Venetian Ambassador, the city had a population of some 40,000 (of whom one in five were Jews). By the early 1600s, Mantua had suffered a degree of economic and political decline. But it was still one of the largest and wealthiest cities in Italy and the Duke one of the peninsula's most munificent patrons of the arts.

As a young man he had spent much time in neighbouring Ferrara, where his sister was married to the Duke. With their encouragement, the Ferrarese court had become a magnet for Italy's leading artists and poets; it was here that the young Vincenzo befriended the poet Torquato Tasso, who was to spend some of his last years in the Gonzaga court in Mantua. Ferrara was famous, too, for the high quality of its music, especially its virtuoso *concerto delle donne* known to history as the 'Three Ladies of Ferrara'. It was in his sister's court in the early 1580s that Vincenzo developed his aesthetic tastes and his lifelong passion for the performing arts. He was also always a frequent visitor to Florence. Here, the theatre-loving Vincenzo would have seen some of the latest *intermedi*, including perhaps those of 1589 which involved virtually all the major figures associated with the birth of opera.

Vincenzo became Duke of Mantua in 1587, and immediately set about improving the artistic quality of his court. He established a musical ensemble and went on to extend his collection of artworks and the palace that housed them. He brought the Cremona-born Monteverdi to Mantua, and invited the Jewish composer Salomone Rossi to incorporate traditional Hebrew chants into his work as director of instrumental music. Every Friday evening, the Duke held concerts in the palace and he also encouraged, paid for and attended theatrical entertainments. In many ways, Monteverdi was fortunate to be working for such a master. Without the patronage of Vincenzo Gonzaga, and the active encouragement of his son and heir Francesco, Monteverdi would not have been able to undertake an ambitious, through-composed music drama in the new style. It was only through the patronage of Renaissance princes such as Duke Vincenzo that 'opera' came to be established.

Monteverdi had already been working in the Gonzaga court for seventeen years when Prince Francesco proposed he collaborate with Striggio to write *Orfeo*. The 39-year-old composer was by now at the height of his powers, a man of considerable renown whose fame had spread far beyond the confines of Mantua. His books of madrigals had been reprinted many times. But Monteverdi was still a paid hand, a servant like the Duke's head cook or butler and, like them, he had to dance attendance on his princely masters. In Monteverdi's case, that meant producing music for regular concerts and also for a seemingly endless procession of 'special' events and courtly entertainments. Monteverdi found this exhausting: he is overworked, he says in his letters, underpaid and underappreciated. Before 1607 was out, Monteverdi's wife became ill and died and the strain seems to have caused his own health to deteriorate further. Monteverdi went to his home town of Cremona to recuperate (his father was a physician). While there, he was summoned back to Mantua.

Monteverdi could not bear the thought, he wrote at the start of a long letter to the courtier who was, in effect, his line manager. If the Duke insisted on his returning:

> I assure you that unless I take a rest from toiling away at music for the theatre, my life will indeed be a short one...
>
> If fortune favoured me last year by making the Lord Duke invite me to assist with... musical events, it also did me a bad turn... by making me perform an almost impossible task, and furthermore it caused me to suffer from cold, lack of clothing, servitude, and very nearly lack of food... without my being in the slightest degree favoured by His Highness with any public mark of esteem...
>
> If fortune has done me a favour by letting me have so very many opportunities of being commissioned by His Highness, it has also caused me this loss, that the Lord Duke has always spoken to me

This title page for Marinoni's *Fiori Poetici* commemorates the death of Monteverdi in 1643 and is filled with a display of contemporary musical instruments.

about hard work, and never about bringing me the pleasure of something useful…

There is more in this vein. Looking back over his years, Monteverdi concludes that the 'fortune' he had found at the Gonzaga court more often than not felt like 'misfortune' – literally so, since he was often out of pocket. In this, he was not alone. Duke Vincenzo, who as a young man had loved hunting both beasts and men, had squandered a substantial part of the ducal legacy on military campaigns. Yet, despite his depleted treasury, he continued to support a household of some 800 people and – ever more indulgently – his love of the arts. Perhaps it is we, more than Monteverdi, who have cause to be grateful.

We should be grateful, too, to the Duke's two sons, Prince Francesco Gonzaga and his younger brother Ferdinando. Ferdinando was something of an intellectual and an accomplished musician, and it was perhaps to rival his brother's growing reputation that Francesco, heir to the Mantuan throne, commissioned his father's finest artists to devise a work for performance at court during the 1607 Carnival season. If so, the rivalry appears to have been perfectly friendly and fraternal. At one point, as the performance date approached, Francesco wrote to his brother, who was in Florence, asking if he could help arrange the temporary loan ('for a fortnight at most') of a good castrato singer. Ferdinando, it seems, was happy to oblige.

Monteverdi's 'fable set to music' was given just two performances (there was some talk of a third), and then no more until it came to be revived 300 years later in the early twentieth century. At the time of its creation, nobody had any thought of building a repertory or of creating a canon of works that would be performed again and again. Nor were court operas intended to make a profit. They were provided in order to entertain those present: ephemeral extravaganzas, propaganda for the prince who promoted them and produced in order to celebrate a dynastic marriage, a military victory or to impress the rulers of rival duchies or principalities.

*

Orfeo may have arisen out of an existing tradition. Yet even at the time it was recognized as something of a novelty. On the eve of its unveiling, one Mantuan courtier, Carlo Magno, wrote to his brother that the following evening there was going to be a play that promised to be unusual because 'all the performers speak musically'; he would probably be driven to attend 'out of sheer curiosity' – unless (he added) he could not get a seat for lack of space. The performance, it must be remembered, took place in a room in the Gonzaga palace – not what we would recognize as a theatre – before a courtly audience of no more than a few score people. Many or most were members of the Accademia degli Invaghiti. Such academies were, in effect, intellectual clubs of sophisticated, aristocratic culture lovers. The members who attended *Orfeo* would have felt very much at home with its constituent elements. Any educated aristocrat in late-Renaissance Mantua would have been expected to have some musical aptitude. As the author and diplomat Baldassare Castiglione had written in his book *The Courtier* eighty years before, any man worthy of the name 'Courtier' should, besides 'understanding and being able to read music', also be capable of playing various instruments. Such a man would also have learned to dance, so that the members of the audience assembled in the Mantua palace in February 1607 would have been well equipped to appreciate the skills of Monteverdi's and Striggio's performers. They would also have known the Greek myths (the story of Orpheus and Eurydice being one of the most popular) and been familiar with such basics of classical theatre as the interpolation of dance sequences between scenes, the Chorus commenting on the drama, the Aristotelian unities of time, place and action, and the solemn, cathartic conclusion. They would have understood the power of myth as allegory and been interested to see how librettist and composer had attempted to integrate their respective contributions into the evening's entertainment. Renaissance art had long taken its themes from religious and mythical subject-matter and most early composers of opera, like other artists, believed themselves to be telling moral tales via the aesthetic principles of the ancient world. Thus, while Monteverdi and Striggio were doubtless keen when writing *Orfeo* to demonstrate how the Mantuan court could outstrip a work based on the same story produced a few years earlier for the Medici in Florence, they were typical of their time in drawing upon the mythologized history of the ancient world for their theme. Monteverdi, indeed, went on to create operatic treatments of the Ariadne and Ulysses sagas and crown his career with the cautionary *L'incoronazione di Poppea* (*The Coronation of Poppea*).

For the most part, therefore, he and Striggio would have had a knowledgeable and discriminating audience. Anyone invited to attend a high-profile entertainment put on by the Medici or the Gonzagas would have expected to see a costly multimedia entertainment created and performed by the finest artists and designed to appeal to both the intellect and the senses. The story might be an affecting rendition of a familiar ancient myth, perhaps with a pastoral theme, whose performers would have been expected to be able to act, sing and dance. As for scenery and stage effects, these would be the most spectacular that the latest technology and a deep ducal purse could obtain: clouds and sunbeams that carried gods across the heavens, winds and waves that evoked turbulent lakes and oceans, the smoke and fire of hell. To the assembled members of the Accademia degli Invaghiti, then, *Orfeo* would have been an eagerly anticipated piece of musical theatre of a kind not infrequently produced in the courtly palaces of northern Italy at the time.

One of the major detective mysteries of recent musicological research concerns the identity of the room in the Mantua palace in which *Orfeo* was performed. The regular Friday evening concerts evidently took place in the Sala degli Specchi, the Hall of Mirrors (but which room was this? The one visitors see today is a grand salon in eighteenth-century decor). *Orfeo* does not seem to have been performed there but in 'a room in the apartments which the Most Serene Lady of Ferrara [that is, Duke Vincenzo's sister, the widow of the Duke of Ferrara] had the use of' – maybe on the ground floor beneath what is now the Sala Pisanello. To date, the room has still not been definitively identified.

Orfeo was evidently a great success. Or at least Duke Vincenzo considered it so, according to his son Francesco, who wrote to his brother that their father had ordered it to be given again a week later, this time with women in the audience. In 1609, *Orfeo* was published (with a different ending, causing much perplexity to subsequent scholars). Publication was not an indication that there was a lucrative potential market for Monteverdi's masterpiece. Rather, it was undertaken for the greater glory of the Gonzagas: an opportunity to furnish a lavish souvenir of a grand and costly event, a glossy

Monteverdi's *Orfeo* was first performed in a room in a palace in 1607. Two years later it was published, but its next full performance was nearly three centuries later.

programme to remind people what spectacular entertainments the Mantuan court was capable of providing. Publication – like the commissioning of the work in the first place – was as much a political as an aesthetic statement.

To this day, the great palace in Mantua and the nearby Palazzo Te overwhelm the visitor with superb paintings, sculptures and tapestries, including an entire room frescoed by Mantegna, while to music lovers, of course, this was the home of the father of opera. But the Gonzagas could be hard taskmasters and, after the death of Duke Vincenzo, Monteverdi at last quit their employ for Venice to take charge of music at St Mark's. In 1628, the Gonzagas tried to solve their recurrent financial problems by selling many of their treasures to England's new king, that avid collector of art Charles I. Shortly thereafter, Mantua, like much of the Po Valley, was drawn into the wider European catastrophe of the Thirty Years War and in 1630 the city and its treasure houses were sacked. By that time, Monteverdi was safely in Venice.

*

Venice's Teatro Cassiano belonged to the Tron family and it was they who reconstructed the theatre after the fire and agreed to lease it to a pair of visiting musicians from Rome. Francesco Manelli and Benedetto Ferrari arrived in Venice in 1636 and were given employment by Monteverdi in the choir at St Mark's. Monteverdi was entrusted not only with the composition and performance of liturgical music in Venice's principal church but also with maintaining the quality of music-making in the city as a whole. In Manelli and Ferrari, he had engaged a pair of highly entrepreneurial artists. Within a year of their arrival, they had obtained permission to open the rebuilt S. Cassiano as a public opera house.

Their first production, *L'Andromeda*, for which Manelli wrote the music and Ferrari the text, proved popular and they came back the following year with another opera. Soon several other Venetian theatres had been adapted, sometimes by the aristocratic families that had built them such as the Vendramin or the Grimani, to become opera houses. Hitherto, opera had been a predominantly courtly entertainment created to mark a specific occasion. In Venice, for the first time, operas began to be composed and performed in order to entertain a paying public in buildings designed for the purpose. The works themselves, as before, were new (it would be a long time before the idea took hold of a 'canon' of established operas), but for the first time the venues and the dates of performances came to be decided according to commercial rather than political criteria.

The new trend was unmistakable and brought Monteverdi back to an art form that he had earlier done so much to develop. He revived *Arianna* to inaugurate opera at the Teatro S. Moisè in Carnival 1639/40, and later that season produced *Il ritorno d'Ulisse in patria* (*The Return of Ulysses*) at the Teatro S. Cassiano. Monteverdi's great culminating achievement, *L'incoronazione di Poppea,* was produced for the Carnival season at another of the 'new' Venetian opera houses, the Teatro SS. Giovanni e Paolo, which was owned by the Grimani family.

*

Any historian (or opera lover) looking back at the cultural world of late-Renaissance Florence, Mantua or Venice might be forgiven for experiencing a frisson of excitement at what was, in effect, the birth of a great art form that has given pleasure from that day to this. Something similar, moreover, was also beginning to emerge in a region whose rulers, paradoxically as it might seem, traditionally placed the strictest constraints upon what was permissible on the theatrical stage: papal Rome. As home of the papacy, the Eternal City had long attracted men of money and power. It had also given work to some of the greatest artists. Bramante and Bernini, Michelangelo and Raphael worked here for the church, as did Palestrina. No religion, moreover, laid greater emphasis than the Roman Catholic church on theatricality, with its colourful costumes, crooks and mitres, crosses and incense, communal incantations, dramatic readings, paintings, processions and the awe-inspiring buildings in which much of this was housed. And at its centre: music, the art that, above all perhaps, provided a route to the Almighty as the ethereal voices of the renowned papal chapel choir soared high above the stave to heaven.

The Catholic authorities in Rome had long been aware of the value of secular theatrical performance outside the church itself and some had positively encouraged and promoted it; the Jesuits put on public performances of plays in Rome throughout the seventeenth century. There were limits to what the ecclesiastical authorities would sanction, however. Any music or drama had to be appropriately uplifting in content and style, and, as in the church itself, women were normally barred from performing. But if God was omnipotent, the ecclesiastical authorities were not. Thus, they exercised little control over the rich and varied theatrical fare regularly promoted in the magnificent homes of Rome's secular aristocracy who – unlike their counterparts in Florence or Mantua – were not constrained by the dominant presence of a single, central secular political authority. Rome was, in fact, the scene of a great deal of musical and theatrical activity, and of their combination in the new fashion, when, in 1623, the Jesuit-trained Cardinal Maffeo Barberini was elected Pope Urban VIII. He was to reign for twenty-one years until his death in 1644.

The Barberini family were well known as generous patrons of the arts, and the new Pope soon showed how none of this had to stop just because he had ascended the throne of St Peter. In an extreme example of papal 'nepotism', Urban went on to make his brother and two of his nephews cardinals and a third the Prefect of Rome. The family accumulated great wealth and power, some of which they placed in carefully chosen artistic projects which they rightly assessed would redound to their credit. One of the Pope's new nephew-cardinals, for example, went on to build the great Barberini palace in the via delle Quattro Fontane and to found the Barberini Library, later acquired by the Vatican. And the Barberini encouraged the growth of opera in Rome, sometimes pastoral, sometimes epic, always spectacular. Only men and boys (and castrati) were permitted to perform, and subject-matter had to be appropriately uplifting. Thus, as early as 1632 the enormous theatre in the Barberini palace presented a work based on the life of Saint Alexis (*Il Sant'Alessio*) for which sets were designed by Bernini and the libretto was written by Giulio Rospigliosi, a young priest serving Urban VIII who would himself later become Pope. Performances in the Barberini palace must have been breathtaking to hear and to behold: huge, costumed concerts before grandiose baroque scenery, all enlivened by the latest magical stage effects before audiences said to have been up to three thousand or more. For *Sant' Alessio*, reported one who was present, there were four main scenes, the first

Productions of opera in the Teatro Barberini in papal Rome could be truly grandiose,
whether they dealt with the epic or (as here in *La Vita Humana*, 1656) the pastoral.

representing 'the city of Rome with its palaces', the second Hell 'from which
emerged a quantity of devils', the third the saint's tomb or mausoleum, and
the fourth 'a glory of Paradise where one saw St Alexis with a quantity of
angels'. It was one of the finest spectacles ever produced in Rome, he reported,
going on to note that the entire hall 'was draped in red, blue, and yellow satin
with a canopy above of the same material'.

Where Urban and his family led, others followed, so that Rome became,
if fitfully, an important centre of activity during the pivotal early years of
operatic history (an importance it was to recapture briefly during the sojourn
there in the 1660s and 1670s of that eccentric but influential émigrée, ex-
Queen Christina of Sweden). Rome was also to play an important, if negative,
role a little later in our narrative as a wholesale migration of talented performers (especially women and castrati) helped nourish the growth of opera
elsewhere.

＊

It would be disingenuous to suggest that the history of opera 'began' in
Mantua in 1607 or in Venice or Rome a few decades later. But Monteverdi's
court opera *Orfeo* can reasonably be seen as the earliest major example of
what came to be dubbed *opera seria*, and it was in the public theatres of mid-

century Venice that many of the rules of the opera 'business' were first tried and tested. And it was the figure of Monteverdi, above all, who bridged these two nascent operatic worlds. One of the musicians Monteverdi engaged at St Mark's was a boy soprano from Crema. As Francesco Cavalli grew up, his musical talents were recognized and nurtured by Monteverdi and in his twenties he was organist at the church of SS. Giovanni e Paolo, later moving to St Mark's itself. He also married a wealthy widow, thus guaranteeing a degree of financial independence. Cavalli wrote a string of operas for S. Cassiano with the librettist Giovanni Faustini, producing altogether some thirty operas for the Venetian theatre. He took over the Cassiano from the Manelli–Ferrari company for a while (the theatre was later run by Faustini's brother Marco), and he also continued to collaborate with his mentor, Monteverdi. Most of Cavalli's own operas have long been forgotten (though the Early Music revival of the past thirty-odd years has familiarized opera lovers with *La Calisto*). But as a man of both musical and entrepreneurial talent, Cavalli holds a crucial place in operatic history as the art form gained rapid popularity not only in Venice but all over Italy and beyond. So do the Faustini brothers – especially perhaps Marco Faustini, possibly the first important impresario in operatic history.

CHAPTER 2

The Opera Business, Italian Style

An operatic impresario such as Marco Faustini was what we would now call a manager, the person who would lease a theatre from its owners, run it for a season and hope to make a net profit. If you hold the magnifying glass closer, what you tend to see is a man forever juggling and struggling as his attention is demanded by a succession of casting decisions, rebellious instrumentalists, recalcitrant carpenters and scene-shifters, temperamental *prime donne* and, always, the problem of how to balance artistic and financial considerations, maximize audiences and, somehow, pay his artists. In the Venice of Marco Faustini, the finances of promoting opera were precarious in the extreme. Sometimes external forces would intervene: in the mid-1640s when Venice embarked on war with the Ottomans, Venetian opera theatres closed down for a couple of seasons (though there seem to have been some opera performances outside Carnival-time). More often, problems arose from a musical score that was not ready on time, a malfunctioning stage set, a show that did not prove popular at the box office or – most frequently, perhaps – an artist who went sick (or claimed to be). In February 1654, towards the end of the 1653/4 season, the singer Anna Felicita Chiusi received a stern letter from the two impresarios in charge of the Teatro S. Apollinare, where she was supposed to be appearing. Chiusi, it seems, had asked to be paid the rest of her wages. The management were unmoved:

> If you do not come to perform for the rest of the Carnival as you are required, for whatever reason and under whatever pretext, we are informing you that you are responsible for all damages and expenses that in any way come to us as a result of your failings.

Chiusi wrote a spirited response saying she had been 'gravely ill' and had informed the management of this, adding that 'if you do not pay me what I am owed immediately, I will pursue those avenues of justice available to me'. She was not the first opera singer, and far from the last, to try and extract money from management by threatening court action.

Anna Renzi was one of a number of celebrated Venetian *prime donne* to come from Rome, where, as we have seen, there was a vigorous musical culture but one that, officially at least, excluded women from any but the most devout form of stage performance. The journey from Rome to Venice in the seventeenth century was hazardous and expensive (and took nearly a fortnight), and the hiring impresario would have had to pay the travel and accommodation costs of any 'foreign' singers he engaged, and, perhaps, those of the singer's spouse and servant. A prestigious singer such as Renzi might, however, be put up free of charge in one of the palaces of the local theatre-loving nobility, a form of subsidy that lifted a major financial burden from the shoulders of the impresario.

A surviving contract for the 1643/4 opera season gives some indication of Renzi's celebrity and power. It also hints at the growing impact of opera. In the contract, the impresario Girolamo Lappoli offers Renzi a fee of 500 silver Venetian scudi, payable in four instalments. This was the equivalent of 750 ducats, vastly more than the 100-ducat annual salary of a top soloist at St Mark's Cathedral. St Mark's was a powerful magnet for any music-loving visitor to Venice, especially while Monteverdi (who died in 1643) remained its music director; but opera, only recently introduced, was rapidly becoming popular.

In her contract of December 1643, Renzi was required to attend rehearsals, but only those that took place in the theatre 'or in the house where the Signora Anna is residing'. Furthermore, she was provided with a box in the theatre which she could use throughout the season. If 'Signora Anna' is taken ill and unable to complete her agreed run of performances ('che Dio non voglia' – 'God forbid' – says the contract), Renzi will be paid half the agreed fee; if the season is pulled off for any other reason, the impresario who runs the theatre is obliged to give Renzi her entire fee.

A sizeable proportion of every impresario's budget went into paying star singers, especially the leading ladies, the great *virtuose*; it was they above all whom audiences flocked to see, and their income and bargaining power rose accordingly. During the 1658/9 opera season in Venice, singers' fees accounted for 42 per cent of all production costs. Between 1658 and 1668, the composer's fee received by Cavalli, high by the standards of the day, remained constant; meanwhile, the singer Giulia Masotti earned four times as much as the composer in 1666 and nearly six times as much three years later. Another prima donna, who had earned 350 ducats in 1658, considered 600 ducats too little in 1665.

The presence of a top singer could go a long way towards guaranteeing a successful season, but poor singing could bring about its wreck and leave the management with a sizeable end-of-season bill. In which case, someone – the impresario, the box-holders, the nobleman who owned the theatre or a named 'guarantor' – had to pick up the pieces. Marco Faustini, like many an operatic manager from his day to ours, could find himself besieged by employees demanding to be paid and having to resort to ever more ingenious delaying tactics. Sometimes, a prima donna would be allowed to keep her costume in lieu of money. When Chiusi was in dispute with the Apollinare management about her fee, she tried to cling on to her gold brocade dress as collateral before being ordered by the courts to return it.

Some well-known soloists were from Venice itself, or the Veneto area, often permanent or temporary transfers from the church, a career move that continued well into the eighteenth century. Others came from all over Italy, attracted by Venice's vigorous and potentially lucrative theatrical culture. An impresario like Faustini would have developed an intelligence network throughout the peninsula and beyond. One of his correspondents, having attended a performance in Verona to hear a singer in whom Faustini was interested, wrote that she 'displeased me so greatly that she became insupportable'. Another writes from Rome of a particular singer that she is 'a most singular *virtuosa*, but her voice is very small and for your theatre she does not seem to me to be suitable'.

If the star singers, especially the women, were highly paid, everything else in this most complex and costly of art forms was of necessity cheesepared. Less important singers, often recruited from St Mark's for the season and keen to augment their meagre ecclesiastical salaries, would typically earn less than a tenth of the fee given to the prima donna. Numbers of participants were kept low. Thus Cavalli's Venetian operas were written for an appreciably smaller instrumental ensemble than Monteverdi would have had

An elaborate stage set designed by Giacomo Torelli for Venice's Teatro Novissimo in 1643. Visitors to the opera often commented on the visual excitements on offer more than on the musical and dramatic ones.

in mind when writing for his Mantuan masters half a century earlier. During
the 1651/2 season at Venice's S. Aponal theatre, Cavalli played the keyboard
in an opera orchestra consisting of as few as half a dozen players. Sets and
stagings could be expensive and elaborate, while the thirteen scene changes
noted by Evelyn were not exceptional. 'Every scene in the drama,' wrote the
theatrical memoirist Cristoforo Ivanovich in 1681, 'is expected to entail a
change of scenery, and the invention of the machines must be extravagant.
These are the reasons why expenses grow heavier every year.' A shrewd
impresario could offset costs by reusing sets, props and costumes in other
productions. Furthermore, a popular show might be repeated as many as
twenty or more times during the season; it had to be if the impresario was to
have any chance of amortizing his costs. When Marco Faustini took over the
Cassiano theatre for the 1657/8 season, he presented a new opera that played
twenty-five times to an aggregate audience estimated at over 7000. There are
modern parallels here: not with the way most modern opera houses do their
business but with the production of a Broadway or West End musical, when
a new work is mounted to great fanfare, repeated for as long as it continues
to attract audience revenue – and is then closed. As with the modern musical,
Venetian opera provided as many flops as hits.

Nowadays, we tend to revere the memory of the composers of operas but
tend to forget the names of the people who wrote the text, the *libretto* (or 'little book'). The reverse was often the case in earlier times. In Venice, the
musical composer was normally a contracted professional while the librettist
was often a member of the professional or political classes, perhaps a young
nobleman, who wrote plays as a spare-time occupation. Giacomo Badoaro
rose to become one of the most influential figures on Venice's governing body,
the Council of Ten. In the preface he wrote to his text for Monteverdi's Venice
opera, *Il ritorno d'Ulisse*, Badoaro wrote that 'the world knows that my pen
fights to defeat boredom, and not to earn glory'. Nicolò Minato, at the time
a busy lawyer, wrote in the foreword to one of his opera texts that 'I have
robbed myself of some hours of sleep to give you this drama', adding: 'I swear
to you that the sun has never seen me with pen in hand.' Francesco Melosio
claimed in a preface in 1642 that 'I write out of mere whim [*per mero capric-
cio*]', a phrase also used by Giacinto Andrea Cicognini, in his preface to
Cavalli's *Giasone* (1649), who added that his whim 'has no other aim than
to give pleasure'. Paradoxically, the very fact that the librettist – unlike the
composer – was not usually a professional could render him all the more
important and enable him to pull the political, artistic and sometimes the
financial strings. It was his text that the composer was contracted to set to
music, he who established from the outset what scenery, costumes, dances and
the like would be required, he who arranged for his 'little book' to be published and marketed. In the candle-lit auditoria of Venice, it was the libretto
as much as the transient show on stage that many seem to have relished and

some still retain signs of wax drippings. People collected their libretti much as enthusiastic opera goers today make a collection of their programmes; one Venetian doctor had over seventy of them in his library.

The composer was simply one of a number of paid artisans whose skills contributed to the overall production of opera. Most were (like Cavalli) composer-performers who also sang, played the keyboard, taught music, all the time moving in and out of both the liturgical and theatrical worlds, and, among other things, set libretti to music when contracted to do so. The more successful found salaried jobs: several overlapping ones if they were lucky. The prolific Venetian opera composer Pietro Andrea Ziani worked as organist at a convent, published both sacred and secular music, and also sang for a while in the chapel at St Mark's before obtaining a senior court post in Vienna. A composer like Ziani or Cavalli might have been recognized as especially talented, and he would typically have been paid a sum for his score and further money for helping perform it. But the printed libretti of Venetian operas often did not even mention the name of the man who had written the music. Understandably, perhaps, since the actual music performed on any given night might have included work by other hands. Thus the band might play an interlude illustrating a war scene or divine anger written by someone else popular at the time. Or perhaps a new singer found a particular number lying awkwardly on the voice and the original composer was unavailable. In this case, the impresario might commonly commission a more manageable aria from someone else. Nobody took offence at this. In 1665, the opera composer Antonio Cesti, one of whose works was due to be produced by Marco Faustini, wrote to the impresario suggesting whom the impresario might like to approach, 'should it be necessary to delete, add, change, or do anything else with the music'. By the later years of the seventeenth century, any well-known prima donna – the person the audience had come to see – would be likely to interpolate into her performance one of her favourite arias from another work in order to show off her vocal prowess to best advantage. As opera became popular not only in Venice but all over Italy, singers would carry these 'suitcase arias' from one engagement to the next and, if they sang them well, nobody objected. This practice continued until well into the nineteenth century (and into our own times in, for example, the party scene in Johann Strauss's *Die Fledermaus* or the lesson scene in some productions of Rossini's *Barber of Seville*).

Theatres in Venice were small and audience numbers low by modern standards. This was partly a function of the way they were financed. Venetian opera houses did not contain the copious grand circles and dress circles of today, but were ringed with boxes; the Cassiano contained three tiers of boxes and the SS. Giovanni e Paolo four, with in each theatre a total of over 150 boxes in all. For those people who could afford one, a box at the opera provided a social centre, a home-away-from-home which they could rent for the season and in which they could hold court and entertain their friends night after night if they wished. One of the first things an impresario would do, therefore, on taking over management of an opera theatre, would be to solicit sizeable sums from the local plutocracy in return for permanent or seasonal ownership of a box. In 1653, when the Teatro S. Luca was being rebuilt after a fire, its manager increased the annual box fee from 20 to 25 ducats and asked the box-holders for two years' rental in advance (when he tried to raise the fee eight years later to 30 ducats, he met with resistance and had to climb down). The social importance attached to owning a box at the opera is illustrated by a letter from 1672 sent to the Doge by John Dodington, the official British Resident in Venice, in which he asks the 'Most Serene Prince' to obtain opera boxes for him in two of Venice's leading theatres. 'I do not ask for them for my own satisfaction or taste,' says Dodington, with what we might regard as astonishing frankness:

> seeing, as I declare, that I do not love music. As regards poetry, I do not esteem it, and I do not understand the theatre. The only reason I ask for this favour is so that I may keep up appearances: my most recent predecessor had boxes, and all the other residents currently at this court have them.

In many ways, the archetypal opera house as we know it – the horseshoe-shaped auditorium ringed with boxes – has its origins in Venice. Its original inspiration may have been the amphitheatre of ancient times, but in its more modern reincarnation opera house design derives from the piazzas in which street theatre would have taken place. Imagine a small, more or less enclosed Venetian piazza with a performing troupe in the middle. Watching it is a crowd of passers-by while, above, a second more privileged audience looks down, semi-visible, from the privacy of the surrounding balconies. Cover the piazza with a domed roof and you have the rudiments of an opera house.

A further respect in which Venice was midwife to the birth of public opera is that individual members of the public could buy tickets, or *bollettini*, for a particular night's performance on a 'first come, first served' basis. It would be disingenuous, however, to suggest that opera became a form of mass entertainment. Even a large Venetian theatre could not normally accommodate an audience of more than a few hundred and figures suggest that, except perhaps on the opening night of a new work or the last night of the Carnival season, theatres were far from full. Cavalli's *La Calisto* was first shown during the 1651/2 season at the S. Aponal, a theatre with a capacity of about 400; it ran for only eleven performances with audiences on two of the nights barely reaching more than fifty. Furthermore, members of Venice's working classes would have been most unlikely to attend the opera, if only because the price of even the cheapest ticket was often the equivalent of more than a day's wages, while wealthy box-holders would often sit in on the same opera night after night. At a generous estimate, therefore, aggregate attendance might have reached no more than about seven or eight thousand over the course of a successful season, representing a small and utterly unrepresentative proportion of the city's overall population, which in 1655 was estimated as 158,000 and swelled during Carnival-time.

So one must not exaggerate the popular significance of publicly performed opera. Audiences would still have been predominantly drawn from the nobility and wealthier citizenry and the art form remained, as it always has been, something of an acquired (and expensive) taste. The question remains as to why, when this art form began to reach out to a new, wider audience, it succeeded in doing so first of all in Venice. Several partial explanations suggest themselves.

In some ways, commercial opera was a direct by-product of the Venetian Carnival. Artistically, Venice with its long-established tradition of popular theatre provided a fertile seed-bed for the budding new form, while much traditional theatrical fare (including aspects of *commedia dell'arte*) translated easily into early opera. There were social reasons, too, why opera began to take root in seventeenth- and early eighteenth-century Venice. By now, as the grand triumphs of earlier Venetian history faded into distant memory and a new, more commercially minded nobility came to replace the old, the formal social hierarchies of earlier times became loosened. At the opera house (as on the piazza or the gondola), masks were designed to disguise personal status and individuality, offering opportunities to contravene social norms with a degree of guaranteed impunity unthinkable in ducal Florence or papal Rome. One of the attractions of the Venetian theatre, in other words, was that, during Carnival at least, it provided a forum for licensed licentiousness in a public environment in which, paradoxically, privacy could be preserved.

In Venice, theatregoers could buy tickets from a box office much as their successors do today.

Economically, opera benefited from the fact that members of the Venetian nobility obtained pride and prestige from building and owning a public theatre (in sharp contrast, again, to the practice in Mantua or Florence). The Grimani family, for example, relished the chance to open their theatres to a wider public: the Teatro SS. Giovanni e Paolo was built by Giovanni and Paolo Grimani specifically for public performance of opera, and the family went on to own no fewer than four Venetian opera houses. In addition to the goodwill this produced, the noble family owning an opera theatre also stood a fair chance of earning a tidy sum from rentals. In 1661, Andrea Vendramin earned some 5000 ducats from property and leases, one thousand of which came from the lease of his family's theatre, the S. Luca. Sometimes an opera season incurred a net loss; Cavalli's early attempt at theatre management came to a painful end in 1644 when he had to hand back the Cassiano, still owned by the Tron family, with substantial unpaid debts. But if a deficit had to be underwritten from time to time by noble owners and patrician box-holders, it seems they were not necessarily averse to having to subsidize further their own entertainment. As a French commentator reported in 1683, the nobility of Venice patronized the great opera theatres more for their *divertissement particulier* than for any financial profit that might accrue, since income from opera 'did not normally furnish half the expense'. This pattern – of wealthy economic magnates pouring money into an essentially non-profitmaking enterprise – provides yet another example of how the early history of opera in Venice set the course for much that was to follow.

All this helped nurture the emergence of commercial opera. It was also both effect and cause of the continued erosion of the once almost unassailable authority of the church. Indeed, during much of the seventeenth and eighteenth centuries, throughout Italy as a whole, there was a tussle for musical supremacy between these two institutions, church and theatre, as singers, instrumentalists and composers found their allegiance swinging from the one to the other. Cavalli (like his mentor Monteverdi) began his career as a church musician, a *maestro di cappella*, yet he moved increasingly into the composition of opera, the form for which he was most celebrated in his lifetime and remembered today. The conflict between the spiritual and commercial is spectacularly illustrated in the lives and careers of some of the castrati.

*

It was in order to sing 'like angels' that castrated boys were brought into Italian church choirs. In Rome, the papal choir had long aspired to music that evoked heaven and as women and girls were banned from church performance the most obviously angelic voices were those of prepubescent children. But boys' voices broke. Hence the gradual acceptance, and later the full-scale promotion, of the adult castrato singer, a practice that began at the turn of the sixteenth and seventeenth centuries (precisely around the time the first operas were being composed), reached its peak in the eighteenth century and finally died out in the nineteenth. We have no way of knowing quite what the voices of the great eighteenth-century castrati sounded like or appreciating the impact they had upon their listeners.* The immense fame and fees of singers like Senesino and Farinelli suggest a phenomenon comparable to that of such celebrities of a later age as Caruso or Pavarotti.

The Catholic church did not officially condone the practice of castration, nor was it the first institution in history to accept it. However, some early Christians had had themselves castrated in order, as they thought, to ensure a life of chastity and abstinence, an ideal that retained a powerful hold among many believers in seventeenth-century Italy. By that time, castration was generally illegal unless carried out with the express agreement of the boy concerned. But a number of recorded instances suggest the decision was reached consensually between the boy and his father and, in some instances, a singing teacher; all would have known of the career opportunities castration could make possible. Sometimes the initiative seems to have come from the boy himself. In 1613, a young orphan in Rome was reported as having wanted to have himself castrated so that he could serve the Duke of Mantua; later, two boys worried about losing their vocal prowess if their voices broke petitioned the Duke of Modena for financial help in getting themselves castrated. The celebrated singer Luigi Marchesi was said to have been castrated on his own insistence and against his parents' wishes. Often the operation was performed when the child was no more than about eight or nine, so the suspicion must remain that it was usually the parents of a talented young son with a good voice who made the decision in the hope of using the lad's vocal abilities as a possible route out of poverty.

Castration may or may not have led eventually to a successful career as a singer. The more immediate benefit for a boy from a poor family was that, with luck, he might be taken under the wing of a kindly tutor, or a church institution, and receive board and lodging and a rudimentary education – with music and singing as a principal subject of study – that would probably not otherwise have been available. In Naples, there were four highly regarded charitable institutions expressly set up by the church to care for the poor and orphaned and to bring them up as devout Christians. Here, young castrated boys from poor families were sent and trained in what was regarded as the 'conservation' of the great traditions of the church and its music. These *conservatori* provided early homes for many of the great operatic castrati, all of them trained initially to perform music for the greater glory of God.

---

* The well-known recordings by Alessandro Moreschi, the 'last castrato', made in the early twentieth century, provide an intriguing relic more interesting for the fact that they exist at all than for the artistic quality they reveal. Moreschi was evidently a man of moderate vocal talent, well past his prime by the time these recordings were made.

Daily life in the conservatoires, as in any religious institution at the time, was highly disciplined. Typically, a boy would be required to get up before daybreak, sing the praise of the Lord while getting dressed and washed, then attend chapel. During the day, the boys would wear the distinctive cassock and surplice of their particular conservatoire and be expected to behave at all times in a dignified fashion. Meals were taken communally but in silence, followed by a half-hour of 'recreation'. There is some evidence that the young castrati (or 'eunuchs') tended to be treated with greater care than the other boys, for these frail children, their mutilated bodies acquiring a pathetic semblance of adult maturity, were angels in the making. At one of the Naples conservatoires, the Santa Maria di Loreto, it was noted in 1699 that 'due to the dampness of the place the voices of the eunuch students are somewhat lacking in strength' and they were subsequently provided with thicker winter underwear. At another, the Sant'Onofrio, the young castrati were sometimes served richer food than the other students, while the steward at the Poveri di Gesù Cristo noted that he had bought seventeen rolls of provolone 'for the eunuchs'. The English music historian Charles Burney described a visit to the Sant'Onofrio in 1770. By then, the tradition of training castrati at the great Neapolitan conservatoires was past its heyday. However, what Burney found confirmed the impression of many who had preceded him. He noted that boys ate, slept and practised in the same overcrowded rooms and was evidently taken aback by the cacophony that resulted. Out of thirty or forty boys who were practising, he wrote, scarcely two were playing the same piece. There was one haven of quiet. There were, says Burney, sixteen castrati in the college, 'and these lye by themselves in a warmer apartment upstairs than the other boys for fear of colds, which might endanger or injure the voice'.

It has been estimated that there were probably never more than a few hundred castrati singers at any one time, and that numbers probably started declining from around 1750. Yet the practice of castrating young boys for a life of church music was to have an immense effect upon the world of opera. This was not its intention, but it was a major consequence. Throughout the later seventeenth century and much of the eighteenth, opera composers and audiences in Italy and beyond relished the exquisite, unearthly sound of the castrated male singer. No church chorister ever received anything like as much public adulation or financial recompense as a celebrated opera singer; in London, in the 1730s, Senesino and Farinelli could command fees of up to £1500 per season.

The fascination with castrati went beyond the merely aesthetic, however, as popular speculation became widespread about their supposed sexual capacities. Many castrati were believed to have had intimate relationships with women. Caffarelli boasted of them, Siface was assassinated by the brother of his beloved, while the young soprano Caterina Gabrielli was said to have been transformed into a great beauty by her love affair with yet another castrato, Guadagni. How

Castrati Senesino and Berenstadt are portrayed as hugely overgrown pre-pubic boys flanking the Italian prima donna Cuzzoni.

far these relationships were fully sexual, only the participants would have known. If they were, one attraction might well have been the knowledge that there was no danger of pregnancy: 'faithless woman,' said the castrato Tenducci to his erring wife when she became pregnant, 'you can see that this child is not mine since I cannot give to anyone what I do not possess myself.'

Interest in the castrati fed into a wider fascination at the time with the ambivalent wonders of nature and of science, with the real and the apparent, with masks and masquerades, sexual titillation and ambiguity, and an apparently insatiable appetite for 'curiosities' and the freakish. In Vienna, when Mozart went to live there, crowds would visit the Schönbrunn Palace gardens, where the chief attraction was an elephant. A few years earlier, in 1767, the crew of HMS *Dolphin* had returned to England after circumnavigating the globe and were widely reported to have encountered a tribe of nine-foot-tall 'Patagonian giants'. Some of the castrati, too, were portrayed as absurdly and grotesquely overgrown: large-scale little boys with the powerful chest cavities of the mature singer yet with residues of pre-pubescent puppy fat and no facial hair. Most of them, wrote the French jurist Charles de Brosses after a visit to Italy in 1739:

> grow big, and as fat as capons, their hips, rump, arms, throat and neck as round and chubby as a woman's. When you meet them at a gathering, it is astonishing, when they speak, to hear a little child's voice

emerging from such a colossus. Some are very pretty: with fair ladies
they are smug and conceited and, if rumour is to be believed, much
in demand for their talents, which are limitless.

They were popularly reputed to be selfish, temperamental and unreliable,
not unlike the 'diva' of more recent times. There was doubtless some truth
to this image, but it was also something of a caricature. When Burney
encountered the elderly Farinelli in Bologna in 1770, he found a tall, thin,
courtly gentleman clearly modest about past glories. They met initially in the
library of the great musician and teacher Padre Martini; 'what he is doing
will last,' said Farinelli, adding that his own achievements were 'past and
already forgotten'. Later, over dinner in the singer's elegantly furnished home,
Farinelli waved aside Burney's desire to write about his life and career but
was very helpful in furnishing Burney with detailed information about
Domenico Scarlatti. Later, in Naples, Burney met another of the great castrati, Caffarelli, by then a very youthful-looking 63-year-old (and still
singing). Caffarelli, notorious in earlier years for his overweening arrogance,
was 'very polite and entered into conversation with great ease and cheerful-
ness', asking courteously after various English acquaintances.

Many castrati with successful careers in the opera theatre nevertheless
retained their links to the church, doubtless out of a mix of genuine piety
and as a kind of pension plan. Caffarelli, for all his international *réclame*,
remained on the books of the Naples royal chapel for most of his life.
Guadagni, having been dismissed from his church choir because of his
unauthorized theatre engagements, made great efforts to be reinstated,
finally being readmitted eighteen years later. Antonio Maria Giuliani, a relatively minor figure who lived in Modena, sang in (and later directed) the
cathedral choir for many years; but he also took occasional jobs on the
opera stages of Venice and elsewhere and worked as *répétiteur* in the Modena
opera house.

As opera spread across Italy and beyond, however, the musical attractions and opportunities of the church showed signs of decline. In Venice,
something close to forty members of the St Mark's choir also appeared in the
city's opera theatres between 1660 and 1725. In Rome in 1728/9, the papal
chapel found itself recruiting three castrati all of whom had spent the previous few years on the opera stage. A document from Rome in the middle of
the eighteenth century complains of the multiplicity of theatres here and elsewhere in Italy who offer castrati 'excessive salaries' so that 'these singers no
longer set much store by the Papal Chapel'. Lesser chapels around the peninsula found it even harder to recruit the singers they needed. During the 1740s
and 1750s, that in Loreto had to grant repeated leave to its singers (including
seven castrati) to enable them to take up operatic engagements, while by 1779
the chapel of S. Maria Maggiore in Bergamo could only hope to recruit a

young castrato to its choir if it agreed to release the singer for the entire Carnival period with full pay.

The decline in the authority of the Catholic church may have coincided with the rise in the popularity of opera and, in particular, of the castrato singer, but its causes went much deeper. The Counter-Reformation, launched in Italy in the sixteenth century to oppose the spread of Protestantism in Europe, had largely run its course, while Enlightenment rationalism was making increasing inroads into the traditional faith. By the later decades of the eighteenth century, the church began to experience some difficulty finding high-quality recruits not only for its choirs but also for the priesthood itself. Yet, in some degree, Rome was the architect of its own decline: the ecclesiastical ban on women appearing on the theatrical stage or in the pontifical chapel had helped lead directly to the emergence and celebrity of the castrato. Opera's gain was thus the church's loss. By the later eighteenth century, if Burney is to be believed, 'all the *musici* in the churches... are made up of the refuse of the opera houses, and it is a very rare thing to meet with a tolerable voice' in any church in Italy.

*

If Venice saw the beginnings of commercial opera and Rome was responsible for the earliest forays by castrati into opera, the most important centre of music-making in Italy for much of the eighteenth century was Naples. Naples was by far the largest city in Italy – bigger than any other European city except London and Paris – and richly cosmopolitan. Greek, Roman and Byzantine rule had each left their mark; since medieval times Naples (and therefore much of southern Italy) had fallen under the hegemony of a succession of rulers, culminating with the great Spanish Habsburg Emperor Charles V. The Spanish continued to govern under a series of viceroys until the early eighteenth century, when they were replaced by the Austrians. Austrian rule was never secure, and in 1734 a Bourbon prince, the son of a Spanish king and an Italian duchess, ousted the Austrians in their turn and re-established Bourbon hegemony throughout southern Italy as King Charles III. One of the first projects he initiated was the building of a huge opera house as an adjunct to the royal palace. Inaugurated on the monarch's name day in 1737, the great theatre was named the Teatro San Carlo, a vast edifice whose richly embellished royal box, at the apex of the horseshoe, had the capacity of four ordinary boxes and was three storeys in height. In this impressively regal house, audiences of over 2000 would attend 'serious operas' (*opere serie*) that, in the allegorical form of Greek gods or Roman Emperors, would tend to mirror the power structure of the people observing them.

The city was not new to opera in 1737. As in Florence, there had been experiments linking drama and music in Naples as early as the sixteenth century. And it was in the smaller theatres of Naples that traditional *commedia dell'arte* had led to what became known as *opera buffa* in which the stock characters would sing and speak their drama in language, and rudimentary stage settings, that were identifiably local. Publicly performed opera was first produced in Naples in 1650, only a few years after its introduction in Venice. New operas were normally showcased each season in the Viceroy's private theatre and then transferred to the adjacent public theatre, the S. Bartolomeo. It was to supervise the new season in the S. Bartolomeo that the 24-year-old Alessandro Scarlatti, born in Palermo and educated in Rome, was summoned by the Viceroy in 1684.

Scarlatti stayed for most of the rest of his life writing numerous operas himself as well as adapting Venetian works for the Neapolitan stage. It was in considerable part through his example and leadership that the city came to vie with Venice as Italy's foremost centre of opera. For the rest of the eighteenth century, Naples remained an irresistible magnet to every musician of ambition or prominence, especially those who were to make their names composing *opere serie*. When the Saxon-born George Frideric Handel was a young man, he spent three years honing his lyrical gifts in Italy, composing a dramatic cantata when in Naples in 1708 (*Aci, Galatea e Polifemo*) which included a bass aria requiring the singer to leap operatically from a top A to low D, a range of two and a half octaves. A little later, another leading young German composer, Johann Adolf Hasse, lived in Naples for a few years, soaking up all he could learn from Scarlatti. In later life, after Hasse had settled in Dresden, he met de Brosses, who asked him what he thought of French music. 'The famous composer, known as *il Sassone* [the Saxon], nearly choked with anger,' reported de Brosses, and he quoted Hasse as adding: 'God keep me from ever seeing or hearing any music other than Italian, because no other language can sing, and there can be music only in Italian.' For good measure, Hasse was particularly rude about French music, considering the French language full of hard, unsingable sounds 'detestable in music'.

It was to Naples, too, that the Rome-born Pietro Metastasio, the century's most influential librettist of *opera seria*, initially came to work before later moving to Vienna, while in May 1770 Mozart, then aged fourteen, was brought to Naples by his father for a month. Mozart *père* wrote home that, despite unseasonably cold weather, Wolfgang was keen to get a tan. Wolfgang, meanwhile, wrote to his sister that the Naples opera house was beautiful, but he had noticed that the King 'has had a rough Neapolitan upbringing and in the opera he always stands on a stool so as to look a little taller than the Queen'.

From the moment it opened, the Teatro San Carlo quickly established itself as a major tourist attraction to all with an interest in music. '[T]he royal theatre in Naples,' gushed de Brosses in 1739, shortly after its inauguration, 'is of a prodigious size, with seven ranks of loges served by corridors and a deep, spacious stage fit for large-scale constructions in perspective.' He described King Charles III and his wife as just about the ugliest royal couple ever to rule Naples. But they were, it seems, much loved and their opera house was a stupendous success.

*

De Brosses admitted to some shame when he saw the number of opera houses in Italy; in the whole of France, he confessed (not quite accurately), 'there is no real auditorium except the one in the Tuileries which is hardly ever used'. Lord Stanhope, on a visit to Milan in 1733, noted that opera 'is the chief entertainment of all the strangers here', partly no doubt because, unlike other forms of theatrical entertainment, the fact of its being performed in a foreign language was regarded as of negligible importance. Letters and memoirs by upper-class gentlemen visiting Italy on the Grand Tour frequently mention visits to the opera. The French author and cleric the Abbé Coyer attended a performance at the San Carlo which was 'interspersed with marches, battles and triumphs, all carried out on a grand scale' – and all the more impressive because the King's own horses were used. Another visitor to the Naples opera observed with breathless admiration that 'the men fight as though at war… These are not wretched men picked up on street corners, as happens in Paris and London, but real soldiers trained in military skill.' The fare on offer in Turin was equally impressive. When an English Grand Tourist, Edward Thomas, visited the Teatro Regio in 1750 a few years after it opened, he thought its performances the finest in Europe, going into raptures on account of both 'the music and the machinery'. It was the sheer grandeur of the place, and of its productions, that most impressed. 'You might see cities taken by storm and elephants on the stage,' he wrote, 'with their castles and as it were whole armies drawn up.' Sometimes there might be 'above 40 dancers together with a chorus of above 200 persons in gorgeous apparel'. Thomas Brand, a 'bearleader' (that is, someone who accompanied a rich young aristocrat and helped manage his tour), reported in 1783 that the Turin house was 'immense': 'In the ballets, in triumphal entries and other great shows, there are sometimes 70 horse manoeuvring upon the stage at a time, real horse of the Piedmontese cavalry: and there is room in the house for 3,200 seated spectators.'

Size, however, wasn't everything. Many reported on the sheer quality of operatic entertainment in Italy. As early as 1709, Lord Charles Somerset went to Bologna, where he visited the opera and thought the performance 'extraordinarily delicate and fine'. He noted that locals esteemed it merely 'of the middle rank', from which he deduced that 'the excellent music of this country excel[s] any that we can pretend to'. It would, he concluded, be 'the highest vanity for us in England to compare the best of any of our new operas to that which was counted but indifferent among the Italians'.

Other visitors reported that Italian singers had a tendency to shout. Burney put this down in part to the sheer size of some of the theatres, which were

Pescheurs de Corail. Monsieur frere unique du Roy. Monsieur le Duc d'york. le Duc D'anuille. le Comte de Guiche. le petit Comte de S. aignan fils. le Marquis de Mirepoix. M.rs Sainte et de la Chesnaye; les S.rs Bruneau. S.re Frè Langlois et Raynal.

Early opera was often enlivened by exotic, imaginative or outrageous costume designs, such as this one for a coral fisher for Cavalli's *The Marriage of Thetis and Peleus*.

so big, he said, that 'in order to be heard thro' space and noise [the singers] seem in a perpetual bawl'. There were other criticisms, too. One dissatisfied visitor to Naples saw 'a miserable thing they called an *opera buffa*', while a tourist in Florence noted sourly that the management was in the hands of people 'whose only interest is to get money'.

Many foreign visitors were particularly illuminating about the behaviour of audiences. When David Garrick visited the Turin opera in the 1760s, he was taken aback not only by the general noisiness of the crowd but by the way the players would move out of character to exchange words with members of the audience. Samuel Sharp wrote in 1767 that 'it is so much the fashion at Naples, and, indeed, through all Italy, to consider the Opera as a place of rendezvous and visiting, that they do not seem in the least to attend to the musick, but laugh and talk through the whole performance, without any restraint.' A few years later, Burney found the 'inattention, noise and indecorum' of the Italian operatic audience 'quite barbarous and intolerable' – another reason, he thought, why singers sometimes had to 'bawl' to be heard. Burney contrasted this, perhaps a little unrealistically, with what he described as the 'silence which reigns in London and Paris', which he approved of as 'an encouragement to the actor as well as a comfort to the hearer'. Visiting the opera in Florence in 1788, Charles Abbot enjoyed the splendid 'scenery and dresses' but noted that 'the company paid very little attention to the performance except at particular airs'. The buzz of conversation, he added, 'actually prevented us very often from hearing the singers, though we were seated within three rows of the stage'.

To some extent the behaviour of Italian opera audiences, so often berated by educated foreign visitors, arose from the fact that opera had been made commercially available in Italy earlier than elsewhere. As a result, even in a court theatre like the San Carlo, it was common practice for people to stroll in after the performance had begun, to chat audibly, wave to friends across the auditorium and to eat, drink, smoke and perhaps play cards or chess. Chess, noted de Brosses, 'is perfect for filling the emptiness of… long recitatives, and music for breaking one's excessive concentration on chess'. 'The hour of the theatre,' wrote the British visitor William Beckford, with all its 'mobbing and disturbance… is the happiest part of the day, to every Italian, of whatever station; and the least affluent will sacrifice some portion of his daily bread, rather than not enjoy it.'

Few attended to the opera in a reverent frame of mind in order to appreciate what we might consider 'great art'. Rather, the opera was a little like a modern jazz club: somewhere sophisticated to go to with friends, while away a long evening and, in passing, enjoy the highlights of whatever entertainment was on offer. It was not actually *bon ton* to listen to the opera, said de Brosses, except to the 'interesting places'. As at a jazz club, or a palm court orchestra in an old-fashioned café, one might applaud an individual musician for a particularly virtuoso showpiece. Indeed, one might (as at a pop concert) get caught up in the excitement and sing along, or at least hum along, with the principals or, as at a spectacular musical today, gasp and maybe applaud at exciting musical or dramatic moments. However, for the most part, opera (opined the Abbé Coyer) 'is for conversation, or for visiting box to box'. People do not listen to most of the music, he said, but they do go into ecstasies 'for arias'. Not, be it noted, for old favourites, as in today's opera houses. 'No one wishes to see an opera, a ballet, a stage set, or an actor that was seen the previous year,' wrote de Brosses, a view endorsed by an anonymous visitor to Turin in 1782 who noted that 'the music is never attended to by the people of the country unless [it is] a new opera and the first representation perhaps – or a favourite air by a favourite singer'. When the celebrated castrato Senesino returned to Naples, reported de Brosses, 'people cried: "What's this? We have seen this actor before; his singing will be old-fashioned."' On the other hand, a new work might attract many of the same people night after night, the theatre serving them as a kind of club. As de Brosses noted dryly, the fondness Italians had for going to the opera was 'more remarkable for the constancy of their attendance than for the attention they bestow upon it'.

Typically, the audience would be stratified. This did not need to be legislated; ticket prices would generally see to it that attendees knew their place. On the 'parterre', or ground level, were rows of benches on which people – all men in some theatres – would sit: assorted intellectuals, priests, military officers and other middle-rank functionaries, plus perhaps the composer and librettist of the piece and their friends. A painting of the newly opened Teatro Regio in Turin shows the bewigged occupants of the front few rows of parterre benches. Some are watching the performance (in one case through a telescope), others are chatting to their neighbours, looking around or passing the time reading quietly. A young girl is selling oranges, someone else drinks, while an armed guard ensures that order is preserved. De Brosses compared the parterre benches in an Italian opera house to those in a church: 'one sits on them'. There the similarity ended, for:

> the din of cabals in favour of the actors, of applause while a faction's favourite is singing (sometimes even before he begins), of echoes responding from the very highest loges, of poems dropped or shouted in praise of the singer is unceasing; an ear-splitting noise so unpleasant, so indecorous, that the first rank of loges is made uninhabitable by it.

It could be even noisier behind the parterre benches. Here, having to stand, would be a gaggle of jostling servants, the people who had to convey their noble masters to and from the theatre and, in general, be prepared to satisfy their every whim. In Venice, this was where the *gondolieri* would congregate. The upper reaches of the house would take the form of a series of horseshoe levels, the higher semi-circles tending to be frequented by people preferring not to be seen, such as young blades with their mistresses. As for the first-level boxes immediately above the parterre, plus those a tier or two higher in the biggest houses, these provided the domain of the rich and powerful.

Although the social levels were carefully stratified, they were not exclusively so and there was considerable interchange between them. A young man from the parterre might pay an obligatory social call to a *grande dame* in a first-level box before joining his girl in the obscurity of the higher reaches of the house. In Venice, the racier aristocrats in the boxes, doubtless masked, would sometimes spit on the common people below and see if they could score a direct hit; this practice, it seems, was met not with surly resentment but with high-spirited repartee and 'pulling very funny faces'. Gladstone noticed this spitting as late as the 1830s (when his wife left Naples because of the stink).

*

In winter time, when it was costly to keep draughty homes warm, the Italian opera theatre provided all possible creature comforts for those wealthy enough to afford it. In some of the grander opera houses the seasonal rent for a box could cost five times the annual income of an average citizen. The French travel writer Jérôme de Lalande commented that the boxes were so comfortable that their owners might spend 'one quarter of their lives there'. This was where one saw friends, entertained, did business, passed much of one's leisure time and caught up with all the gossip. Every lady's box, wrote William Beckford, 'is the scene of tea, cards, cavaliers, servants, lap-dogs, abbés, scandal and assignations; attention to the action of the piece, to the scenes, or even to the actors, male, or female, is but a secondary affair.'

Across the candle-lit auditorium, people would survey the audience through opera glasses or lorgnettes, wave to acquaintances and take note of who was wearing what or squiring whom. Every now and then the King or Viceroy or maybe a victorious general might turn up, in which case one would turn towards the VIP box, smile, applaud and hope to be seen doing so. For a little more privacy, or obscurity, it was always possible to withdraw to the back of the box, behind the curtain, to indulge in a discrete tête-à-tête. Even indiscretions had their etiquette. During the 1748/9 season in Parma, the 23-year-old Casanova proposed taking his lady friend Henriette to the opera every night. When Henriette asked coyly whether that was not excessive, Casanova explained that they would get themselves talked about if they were *not* to be seen at the opera. Indeed, they would probably have to leave town. Very well, said Henriette, but take a private box as little exposed as possible. Casanova did his best to comply, taking a box up in the second tier, but warning Henriette that, as the theatre was small, 'a pretty woman could not fail to be noticed'. Henriette, having perused the 'list of foreigners then in Parma' and satisfied herself that none were known to her, agreed to run the risk and attend, but did so that first night 'without rouge and without a candle' – and resolutely used her opera glasses to look at the stage all evening and nowhere else. 'No one seemed to be curious about us,' reports Casanova, 'so we went home well satisfied, in the bosom of peace and love.'

*

As the eighteenth century progressed, ecclesiastical establishments in Rome, Naples and elsewhere faced increasing difficulties. Venice, meanwhile, continued its dizzy decline as a European power while consolidating its reputation as a flamboyant leader in the arts. Here, Tiepolo painted his spectacular canvases, Goldoni and Gozzi brought subtlety and intrigue to theatrical comedy while the idea of publicly performed opera, pioneered in Venice, spread across Italy and, indeed, north of the Alps into Central Europe. What had begun as an elegant *divertissement* for the nobility, and continued to provide a forum for the display of power and wealth, was also by now firmly established as a popular form of commercial entertainment, its clientele in some places reaching far down the social scale. Every city had its opera house. Many had several. Most of the great Italian houses best

known to history date from the eighteenth century: the Argentina in Rome
(1732), the San Carlo in Naples (1737), Turin's Teatro Regio (1740), the
Teatro Comunale in Bologna (1763), Milan's La Scala (1778) and the Fenice
in Venice (1792).

The French Revolution, which broke out in 1789, would transform everything it touched, including the history of opera. Five years after the opening
of La Fenice, Venice was occupied by French troops and the great Venetian
Republic brought to a precipitate and ignominious end. In Rome, castration
was outlawed and the Pope banished. As for the great city of Naples, it
remained the capital of a kingdom; it was just that the King was Napoleon's
brother-in-law and one of his generals.

CHAPTER 3

Opera Crosses the Alps – and the Channel

Italian opera spread across Europe like wildfire. But the cliché needs qualifying. The Thirty Years War (1618–48) had brought operatic development to a virtual halt, almost killing it in the bud in Central Europe where music theatre was to remain deeply Italian-influenced for a further century and a half. By the time the war came to an end, swathes of Central Europe had become little more than a wasteland. The power of Spain had receded, that of Austria and Sweden been severely curtailed. Did any countries benefit from the Thirty Years War? England, perhaps, whose own civil wars kept her out of those raging on the Continent. A few German princes whose political independence was strengthened by the Peace of Westphalia of 1648. Much of the Italian peninsula, which, despite the Habsburg presence in the north and in Naples, remained largely unscathed by battle. And France.

Here, as elsewhere, Italian operatic influences were powerful – at least as long as the Italian-born Cardinal Mazarin was France's First Minister. Mazarin assiduously moulded the tastes of the young Louis XIV, bringing a succession of Italian composers and performers to Paris for the education of his royal charge. Cavalli's works were performed at court (later Cavalli himself came to Paris at Mazarin's request for a protracted but unproductive stay). And it was under Mazarin's tutelage that Louis befriended a young Italian immigrant, Giovanni Battista Lulli, later naturalized (and known to history) as Jean-Baptiste Lully. Lully shared his king's love of music and dance; when Louis married, it was Lully who wrote special dances for the occasion, interspersed into an opera by Cavalli.

Everything the French King Louis XIV did was theatre, from his ceremonial rising in the morning to his retiring at night: a succession of ritualized performances each played out before a carefully chosen audience. If you were one of the privileged few invited to participate or observe, you felt duly honoured – though you were also put on your mettle as you could be as easily dismissed from the royal presence as invited. It may have been an honour to be summoned into His Majesty's bedchamber or to watch the Sun King sup; but etiquette demanded a deep bow before the royal bed, whether or not the monarch himself was in attendance, and you had to be sure to remove your hat before the dining table set for the King. Louis himself, an accomplished dancer and aesthete in his youth, played the starring role to perfection, 'as dignified and majestic in his dressing gown as when dressed in robes of state or on horseback at the head of his troops,' wrote the astute royal watcher Saint-Simon. At no court was etiquette more formal, ritual more detailed, than that of Versailles, where the *Roi Soleil* maintained his headquarters from 1682. If life imitated theatre, theatre had come by then to imitate life as a succession of spectacular multimedia shows made Louis XIV and his court, in opera as in so much else, the centre and envy of Europe.

*

In 1672 Louis issued a proclamation: 'being well acquainted with the intelligence and great knowledge acquired by our dear and beloved Jean-Baptiste Lully in the field of music,' pronounced the King, he instructed Lully to establish 'a Royal Academy of Music in our good city of Paris, which shall be composed of a number and quality of persons which he shall deem suitable... in order that they may perform before us, whenever it shall please us, musical pieces.' It was understood that the core of the Academy's activities was to produce opera and, significantly, the King insisted that it be 'equal and similar to' those of Italy. Lully, evidently a man of great energy and imagination, used his conspicuous elevation to make himself in effect the supreme controller of music throughout the kingdom. He also had a bitter streak and was ruthlessly territorial and pugnacious, regularly caught up in the vindictive personal quarrels and rivalries that inevitably arose within the confines of a closed and competitive court. When local entrepreneurs in provincial France applied for the right to perform operas or concerts, Lully generally controlled the decision, often enriching himself in the process. For all that, Lully seems to have had an uncanny ability to mastermind the kind of grand, somewhat fawning multimedia performance that chimed perfectly with the requirements of the increasingly assertive reign of the *Roi Soleil*. With Molière, Lully produced a succession of what became known as *comédies ballets*. Other works were billed as *ballets lyriques*, *tragédies lyriques* or *tragédies en musique*. All were essentially regal festivities, highly stylized theatrical rituals performed before the King and court in Paris and later at Versailles. This was the King's opera, performed within the palace confines by the Académie (which everyone called the Opéra) under the control of its royally appointed director. As for the works on show, these, in the *bon mot* of the music historian Richard Taruskin, 'were the courtiest court operas that ever were'. Only those invited by the monarch could attend, and the audience was seated according to strict hierarchy. Louis XIV became famous for the lavish generosity with which he entertained the French nobility. This was politically shrewd. Nobody could refuse an invitation to visit Versailles and attend the magnificent *divertisse-*

Jean-Baptiste Lully's *Fêtes de l'Amour et de Bacchus* performed at Versailles. All the arts (and court artists) were brought together under Louis XIV in a conscious attempt to harness culture to the greater glory of the regime.

ments performed there. And once safely ensconced, not even the most powerful and ambitious could make political mischief while the captive of the King. Opera at Versailles – both the work of art and the occasion – was essentially political.

So it was with all the arts and sciences. All were organized, for the greater glory of the regime, under a string of official 'Académies'. Central control could of course be stifling; no ambitious artist, writer or musician could hope to flourish except within these official structures and much that was produced under the regime was otiose. However, to anyone with talent who was prepared to accept the rules, the opportunities on offer were considerable. Indeed, Louis and his chief minister, Colbert, were at pains to attract the finest creative minds they could. While Colbert (unlike Mazarin) evinced no strong personal interest in culture and the arts, he was resolute in his insistence that Versailles should become home to the best France had to offer. Thus, at various times during Louis's long reign, not only Molière and Lully were in attendance but the playwrights Corneille and Racine. Boileau wrote his histories at Versailles, Bossuet his sermons and Saint-Simon his vivid memoir of life at court. The maxims of La Rochefoucauld were penned under the aegis of the *Roi Soleil*, as were the fables of La Fontaine and the fairy tales and folktales of Charles Perrault, the creator of Cinderella and Little Red Riding Hood, whose day job was as adviser to Colbert. The King's chamber music was supervised (and his daughters taught the harpsichord) by Lalande, while he had himself painted by Lebrun and Rigaud, his palace designed by

Le Vau and his gardens laid out by Le Nôtre. No other regime in Europe, at the time or later, could compare in cultural magnificence and munificence with that of Louis XIV. And none used its artistic splendour more single-mindedly for political purposes. To Louis, culture was an important weapon in his overall project: to achieve military, diplomatic and therefore political hegemony across Europe.

Looking back, we rightly regard with admiration the artistic achievements of the court of Louis XIV, not least the multimedia musical extravaganzas masterminded by Lully. It is worth remembering, though, that the cost of Versailles and of the theatrical events promoted there was in the last analysis born by millions of people who were granted no access to them. It was the same in most of the courts of Europe, large and small, for a century and more thereafter. Taruskin reminds us that opera, like most surviving art music, was 'the product and the expression of an elite culture'. So far, so uncontroversial, says Taruskin. But he invites his readers to consider another form of words: that early opera was the product and expression of 'a tyrannical class' and was 'only made possible by the despotic exploitation of other classes'. Opera not only contributed to the impoverishment of the lower classes; it sometimes killed them. When court opera first began to seep over the borders of Italy northwards, one duke sold his subjects as mercenaries in the Thirty Years War – slave-soldiers, essentially – in order to finance his operatic habit. Much of the art encouraged by Louis XIV and his imitators and successors involved great expenditure by the rich and powerful, partly as a way of displaying their authority over any disposed to question it. Thus, when opera is nowadays labelled 'elitist' by its enemies, they are not entirely wrong: for it was in some degree created by a small ruling elite for its own entertainment on the backs of its impoverished subjects.

*

Versailles became the most exclusive venue for the performance of opera in France. But there was also opera at Fontainebleau, where the court adjourned for a few weeks each autumn, while performances of more intimate works were mounted in the Tuileries palace. There was opera just across from the Tuileries, too, in the Palais Royal, home of the Orléans branch of the ruling Bourbon family. The Palais Royal – unlike Versailles, Fontainebleau or the Tuileries – contained a purpose-built theatre open to the public. It was Lully who had proposed the Palais Royal as a venue for opera, haughtily commandeering the place from Molière's acting company, and it was here that Lully's elaborate productions would transfer after they had been premiered at court. While he was alive, Lully maintained a virtual monopoly, sanctioned by the King, over what opera would be produced, by whom and where. After his death in 1687, things relaxed a little. The number of new productions and performances at the Palais Royal increased and by the early eighteenth century the Opéra regularly presented three or four performances per week, virtually around the year. Starting time was supposedly 5.15pm; in practice, it was often a little later (that is, once all the singers had arrived). This may have been the Palais Royal, home of the Duc d'Orléans, but, as had happened earlier in Italy, opera had effectively made the transition from court opera to public opera.

The Palais Royal could hold an audience of over 1200 people, more than half of whom (all men) would have been standing downstairs in the large parterre, perhaps behind a few rows of benches in the orchestra facing the stage. The theatre would have been hot and stuffy, especially in the over-crowded parterre, which, as in the larger Italian theatres of the time, was on occasion packed with hundreds of assorted city rowdies, drunken servants, frustrated soldiers on leave and impecunious aesthetes keen to follow the show. There were frequent scuffles and occasional fights. As in many Italian theatres, too, armed guards would patrol the Palais Royal during performances.

Higher up, there were rows of boxes which the wealthy aristocrats of Paris were invited to rent, perhaps for two or three years at a time. At the very top of the house was the *paradis* – 'the gods' we would call it – where seats (on hard benches) were cheap and young people could enjoy a night out without too much supervision from their elders. The most prestigious seats in the house were the boxes on the first level, some of the larger containing as many as a dozen well-upholstered seats. To the wealthy occupants of these boxes, in Paris as in most of the great opera houses of Europe, it was bad form to arrive at the theatre on time. Rather, you digested a late lunch, took your time at your *toilette* and turned up at your leisure during the course of the evening once the show was under way. As late as the mid-nineteenth century, Flaubert makes fun of Dr Bovary for thinking you have to arrive at the opera before it begins. A ticket to the opera was like an invitation to a dinner party; if one were so naïve as to turn up at the time on the card, one would be regarded as having arrived too early.

Once in your box in the Palais Royal, you looked out over a rectangular-shaped theatre. The boxes faced across at each other rather than towards the stage and the principal show was other people. After all, auditorium and stage alike were candle-lit throughout the evening, with little variation of lighting level to differentiate the performance from the intervals except the slow and careful raising and lowering of the chandeliers in the auditorium and onstage with a series of ropes and pulleys, and perhaps the partial covering of the (candle) footlights.

We, looking back, tend to find candles pretty or quaint and relish their romantic presence on elegant dining tables. Some sense of what a candle-lit opera house might have been like can be obtained at Drottningholm, the eighteenth-century court theatre outside Stockholm. Here, the authorities strive after historical authenticity, though constrained by modern health and safety regulations, and the Drottningholm auditorium is illuminated (and the retail outlet enriched) by wonderfully flickering imitation candles which are in fact powered by electricity. If we could be transported back into the seventeenth and eighteenth centuries, however, we would probably be shocked by the impact of candle lighting in the theatre, for it provided a permanent smoky haze which often impeded a clear view of the stage and of others in the auditorium, smelled bad, and could cause coughing and soreness to the eyes.* Things could be worse still for the performers, who had to speak, sing, act and dance under such trying circumstances. Candle lighting was dim (it has been estimated that the total illumination provided by some eighty-eight candles in the auditorium of London's Drury Lane theatre would have been about the equivalent of a modern 75-watt electric bulb). Not surprisingly, perhaps, the better-off members of opera audiences brought their own candles with which to light themselves to and from their seats, read their libretti and see their neighbours. During the course of a long performance, dripping candles had to be trimmed, dying ones snuffed and new ones lit – onstage and off. Candles were a constant fire hazard. Throughout the centuries, until the introduction of electric lighting in the late nineteenth century and even beyond, the history of theatres is in part the melancholy story of a sequence of horrific and often fatal conflagrations. The Palais Royal succumbed to fire in 1763 and was replaced by an enlarged auditorium in 1770 which itself burned down eleven years later, after which the Opéra moved to a new purpose-built opera theatre – the first in Paris – near the Porte Saint-Martin.

*

For all the rambunctiousness of audience behaviour at performances at the Opéra, this was, nonetheless, the 'court' opera, the linear descendant of Lully's Académie Royale de Musique, a theatre – or succession of theatres – which Louis XV and (less commonly) Louis XVI would attend. Here, the *tragédie lyrique* reigned supreme. Meanwhile, a lighter, more authentically popular form of entertainment also emerged in Paris during the eighteenth century. This was what came to be known as *opéra comique*.

Opéra comique had a number of theatrical ancestors. For centuries, the great Paris fairs held in Saint-Germain and Saint-Laurent had included, as part of their appeal, staged popular entertainments, complete with song, speech and dance, somewhat in the style of the *buffo* shows popularized by troupes of touring Italian players trained in *commedia dell'arte*. What gradually emerged was not quite 'opera', perhaps, nor necessarily 'comic' in the

---

* Burney, visiting the opera in Milan in 1770, walked out because 'the lights at the opera house… affect my eyes in a very painful manner'. Marie Antoinette faced a similar problem; after attending the Opéra in 1784, she wrote to complain about all the smoke in the auditorium at Porte Saint-Martin, though there wasn't anything much the management could do about it.

Popular theatrical performances (often an early version of what was to develop into *opéra comique*) would aim to catch the passing crowds at French fairs such as that of Saint-Laurent* or Saint-Germain.

modern sense, but a style of *comédie* whose principal feature was its alternation of song and spoken dialogue: broadly speaking, a French equivalent of Italian *opera buffa* or German-language *Singspiel*. As such, it aimed to reach a far wider cross-section of society than its more aristocratic counterpart. By the late seventeenth century and early eighteenth, the evident popularity of the theatrical entertainments put on at the Paris fairs was coming to be considered something of a nuisance if not an actual threat by those in charge of bona fide opera at the Palais Royal and by their colleagues at the Comédie Française. True, Louis XIV had expelled Italian players from France for what was deemed the licentiousness of their performances. But to many, that only made the legacy of what they had introduced the more alluring.

The stage was set – for once the cliché seems appropriate – for a century of rivalry between competing companies, each of them offering versions of music drama and jostling with each other for audiences and for the theatres in which to perform. It would be misleading, however, to suggest that these theatrical rivalries and manoeuvrings represented a scene of chronic disruption and subversion. On the contrary, all the companies yearned for stability: not only institutionally, but artistically too. Take the 'lower' end of the market. By mid-century, there was little to differentiate the shows mounted by the Opéra-Comique and those of the Comédie-Italienne. The former (once regarded askance by a suspicious establishment) now had its own Paris theatre,

* Where the Gare de l'Est stands today.

while the latter, despite its Italian provenance, had achieved respectability by performing in French. In 1762, the two companies were merged. Gradually, both the shared art form and the audiences became more refined, so that it would have been hard for an objective observer to have detected, in any *opéra comique* or its reception, any seriously subversive social or political message. The composer André-Modeste Grétry, who bridged the worlds of opera and *opéra comique*, became celebrated among the bluest of blood – not only in Paris but across Europe – for works like *Richard Coeur-de-Lion*, with its heroic invocation of the virtues of kingship.

Operatically at least, Paris was thus in many ways a singularly unrevolutionary city during the decades leading up to the Revolution. A glance at the repertoire of the Opéra reveals much that was traditional. Thus, Paris remained the home of the *tragédie lyrique*, that highly wrought combination of words, music and dance in the classical manner once associated with Lully and by now with Rameau. These aristocratic diversions continued to be mounted at the Palais Royal until the Porte Saint-Martin was opened just a few years before the Revolution. What disputes there were tended to be cerebral, aesthetic and philosophical: not the sort of thing any monarch or government need worry about. It was at the Opéra that battle was joined in 1752 in the *Querelle des Bouffons*, an intellectual sparring match between the defenders of the high seriousness of French opera and those advocating the more expressive style of Italians such as Pergolesi. Much ink was spilt in this celebrated 'quarrel', but no blood. A quarter-century later, the operatic cognoscenti launched upon another dispute, this time between the respective merits of the latest works of Gluck and those of his (alleged) rival Piccinni. These 'wars' were fought with passion in the intellectual presses of the time, as fashions and preferences very gradually shifted. It was not really until the 1770s and 1780s that Italian – or at least Italianate – opera began to triumph as composers such as Salieri and the young Cherubini introduced new works to Paris. By now, too, the operatic reforms of Gluck came to be acknowledged as having outmoded Rameau and the more traditional forms of *tragédie lyrique* with the result that much of the core baroque repertoire (revived with great success in our own times) became eclipsed.

Was it revolutionary for Italian opera to become accepted in the French capital, or for a new, more expressive kind of opera to replace the Enlightenment formalities of *tragédie lyrique*? Perhaps. These were certainly powerful portents for what was to flower in Paris a few decades later and render it the operatic capital of the world. But for the time being, in Paris as in much of Europe, audiences for opera (*real* opera as opposed to the *comique* variety) remained by and large aristocratic by blood and conservative in their tastes, preferring to attend new settings of often familiar texts. Despite whatever new depths of musical and dramatic imagination a composer such as Gluck breathed into the operas he created, the results remained firmly in the tradition of *opera seria*, in which characters were invested with courtly dignity and moral seriousness. If audiences came away from performances at the Opéra with a message, it would not have been one of revolution; rather, the paramount importance of traditional values of morality, social stability and political hierarchy. Just as audiences across Europe would have done as they emerged from Grétry's *chef d'oeuvre*, their ears ringing with its celebrated romance, 'O Richard, ô mon Roi!'

*

If opera in eighteenth-century France became a peculiarly French affair, nowhere was it more cosmopolitan than in London. Indeed, it was a measure of the cosmopolitanism of the English capital that one of its most highly bruited forms of entertainment was Italian opera written by a *Kapellmeister* from Saxony.

One of the things people nowadays tell visitors to Halle, a small town now just a couple of hours' drive from Berlin, is that in the years since German reunification many of its brightest youngsters have left to seek fame or (at least fortune) elsewhere. It is a story prefigured by Halle's most celebrated citizen, Georg Friedrich (or George Frideric) Handel, who was born there in 1685 but died nearly seventy-five years later in his elegant home in London. Handel was baptized in the Liebfrauenkirche, the late-Gothic church that dominates the Halle marketplace. The baptismal font is still there, as is the Reichel organ on which the adolescent Handel would play a few years later. A short walk, and you are at the austere Calvinist cathedral where, at seventeen, he became church organist.

Halle could not hold Handel, his prodigious talent demanding a larger stage. In Hamburg, he played in the opera orchestra and composed several works which were performed there. He travelled to nearby Lübeck (like his exact contemporary Bach a couple of years later) to meet the organist and composer Buxtehude. Buxtehude seems to have offered Handel a post as church organist which he turned down, supposedly because a condition of taking the job was marriage to Buxtehude's unappetizing daughter. In any case, Handel's interests were rapidly turning from the liturgical to the dramatic. It was opera that interested him, and that meant going to Italy. For four years, Handel absorbed the musical culture of Florence, Venice, Rome and Naples, befriending not only influential composers such as Corelli and the Scarlattis, but also the aristocratic and ecclesiastical magnates who supported them. He returned to Germany in 1710, armed with recommendations to several of the most brilliant courts, notably that of the Elector of Hanover, who took the gifted young man into his service. A year later, Handel requested and obtained permission to visit that great commercial hub of the musical world and of much else besides – London.

*

London was by far the biggest city in Europe: a vast, sprawling, bustling metropolis of half a million or more, a commercial and industrial capital whose port and river provided a gateway to and from the wider world. Here, financial speculation and peculation dwelt cheek by jowl, alongside every gradation of wealth and poverty, industry and idleness, puritanism and licentiousness, coffee house and whorehouse. There was a sense of freedom in London unmatched on much of the Continent, where monarchs and churches had traditionally kept strict control over forms of cultural expression. In England, by contrast, the monarchy had undergone a series of formidable trials, each of which had further weakened its powers and ambitions. Some monarchs – Charles II, for example, or William III's co-regnant Queen Mary – enjoyed patronizing the arts and theatre but were in no position to control them. It is true that, after the Revolution of 1688–9 which overthrew the Catholic King James II, the avowedly Catholic John Dryden had to relinquish his Poet Laureateship. But Dryden was not imprisoned or hanged, and he turned his talents to writing texts for the 'semi-operas' composed by his friend Henry Purcell. Music and the arts thrived during these years. Or, rather, the arts like everything else responded to the invigorating and sometimes chilly market economy, allied to a system of aristocratic patronage, that emerged in the decades following the Restoration of the monarchy in 1660. Looking back, we celebrate the theatrical imagination of Congreve and Wycherley, the satirical pen of Defoe and Swift, the portraiture of Kneller and Lely, the buildings of Wren and Hawksmoor and the music of Purcell. But there were as many snakes as ladders awaiting the unwary.

London in the time of Purcell and Handel was a huge commercial city containing extremes of wealth and poverty – and a rich and varied cultural life largely unregulated by political authority.

Take, for example, the ill-fated venture into theatre management by that formidably talented soldier, playwright, architect and landscape gardener John Vanbrugh. Vanbrugh had a vision: he would design, build and run a new theatre – the Queen's Theatre in the Haymarket – and make it the first in Britain to be devoted to the public performance of all-sung opera; not opera alone, but a mixed season including semi-opera and stage plays, the latter presumably making sufficient profit (he must have calculated) to finance the former. It was probably a madcap idea from the outset. For a start, there was precious little operatic repertoire to choose from; audiences would not be attracted by the reappearance of old works, nobody in England was writing good new ones and the market for imported Italian opera was yet to be tested. For a while, Vanbrugh's company of singers and actors struggled along, watching helplessly while his rival, Christopher Rich at Drury Lane, mounted successful productions of Italian-style operas in English translation. At one point, Vanbrugh developed the idea of trying to combine all of London's drama and music theatre under his leadership, a move perfectly calculated to arouse the most virulent objections from Rich, the current theatrical supremo. Eventually, after much complex politicking, Vanbrugh achieved what perhaps he had aimed for from the start: an official pronouncement by the Lord Chamberlain of a division of labour, starting in 1708, whereby Rich would take control of London's two licensed acting companies while Vanbrugh was presented with an opera monopoly at his new theatre on the Haymarket. Both parties were delighted. Rich, an aggressive man who clearly enjoyed power and money, had regained a monopoly he had lost back in 1695. As for Vanbrugh, he quaffed gleefully from a chalice that he ought to have realized was poisoned.

There was nothing new about having music on the English theatrical stage. It had been there at least since medieval times. Shakespeare wrote songs into his plays, while Nell Gwyn was as renowned for her singing as for her acting and her other accomplishments. During the Restoration era, opera – or drama-with-music – had been produced and financed by London's two officially licensed theatres in Dorset Garden and Drury Lane: a shrewd promoter could mount a popular comedy fairly inexpensively and, with the profits, put on a few performances of a multimedia extravaganza such as *King Arthur* or *The Fairy Queen*. For a few years following Purcell's premature death in 1695, the vogue continued for semi-spoken, semi-sung English-language entertainments, Christopher Rich promoting a number of productions at Dorset Garden and Drury Lane, but ran out of steam by about the turn of the century. Meanwhile, sharp-eyed promoters were not slow to note the growing popularity in the great courts of the Continent of all-sung Italian opera. But could fully-fledged opera be promoted in England, where there was no Gonzaga duke or Bourbon monarch prepared to pay for it? If one were to put on nothing but operas, without subsidy, bankruptcy would surely soon loom.

Vanbrugh discovered this harsh but self-evident truth within weeks of embarking upon the final chapter of his ill-judged venture in January 1708. After twenty-three performances of opera at the Queen's Theatre, Vanbrugh found he had spent over £4000 and taken in less than £3000. As the books began to slide rapidly into the red, he applied to the Queen for a subsidy of £1000 to help finance his losses and was turned down. Perhaps the importation of famous foreign singers would enable him to bring in an audience while raising ticket prices; Vanbrugh had already been paying his singers more than his actors, but he soon discovered that the cost of Italian superstars would have been prohibitive. By May, Vanbrugh had transferred management of the Queen's Theatre to Owen Swiney (or McSwiny), and had gone off to busy himself with the construction of Blenheim.

A year later, Swiney unexpectedly inherited all of Christopher Rich's actors, who, rebelling against Rich's harsh management style, defected en bloc to the Haymarket with the blessing of the Lord Chamberlain. Once again, spoken and sung drama were under the same roof. Genuine harmony was not fully restored, however, until Swiney agreed to pay the actors the same high salaries he was already paying his singers. Meanwhile, the presence in the company of a number of expensive Italian singers, notably the castrato Nicolini, helped raise artistic quality and audience size, but set the company down the ludicrous path of multilingual performances while helping plunge it further into debt.

For several years, a succession of similar shenanigans beset the London scene as one hapless theatrical manager after another wriggled awkwardly between the conflicting demands of popular entertainment and high finance. In 1710, Swiney quit the Haymarket for the Drury Lane theatre, ceding control to William Collier, an ambitious MP. Collier handed day-to-day management of the Haymarket to a young man called Aaron Hill. Hill was ousted less than a year later – but not before he had mounted *Rinaldo*, an opera for which Hill himself had drafted a text (based on Tasso) and for which the musical score was provided by the 25-year-old Handel, currently resident in London. Handel is said to have written the score of *Rinaldo* in a fortnight, not as remarkable as it sounds for the work contains some fifteen numbers previously composed for other occasions.

*

When Handel arrived in England in 1710, the nation had for some years been undergoing a period of sustained factional ferment. Whig opinion, still haunted by memories of the Catholic King James II, ousted in the 'Glorious Revolution' of 1688, had adamantly supported war against Louis XIV, originally masterminded by the impeccably Protestant King William III and later effectively prosecuted by their hero Marlborough. To the true Whig, a degree of religious liberty and tolerance for dissent was even more important than strict adherence to the ancient principles of hereditary monarchy. It was in this spirit that the Act of Settlement of 1701 decreed that if William III and his sister-in-law Anne were both to die without issue, the crown would bypass the Catholic Stuarts and go to the nearest Protestant branch of the royal family, the Hanoverians. William, a childless widower, died in 1702 and was succeeded by Anne. Five years later, her kingdom was expanded under an Act of Union that brought together the crowns of England and Scotland. By the time of Handel's first visit to London, it was becoming increasingly clear that Queen Anne was unlikely to provide the new united kingdom with a live male heir and that the Act of Settlement might have to be invoked upon her death. In 1714, the Queen died, the Act came into effect and, controversially, Handel's former employer the Elector of Hanover was pronounced king of a united Britain. A year later, the Stuarts, with considerable support in Scotland and from many English Tories as well as from Catholic sympathizers on the Continent, made a determined but ultimately doomed effort to recapture the crown they believed rightfully theirs.

There is no evidence of Handel's political views, except in the sense that, like the good, practical businessman he was, he managed – despite a sometimes brusque personality – to avoid biting the various hands that fed him. He doubtless knew that Vanbrugh and most of his Kit-Kat Club friends who had originally helped finance and sustain the Queen's Theatre in 1705 were Whiggishly inclined. But by the time Handel was domiciled in London, the volatile and unstable political atmosphere must have given him pause as he composed Italianate operas to texts packed with battle scenes and legendary leaders, aware that any parallels with the present, however nuanced, would immediately be picked up by members of his politically sensitized audiences. As a German Protestant who had spent time in Rome, furthermore, he must also have been deeply aware of the ambivalence of the market for whom he was writing towards all things Italian. On the one hand, Italy was the home of high culture. Nothing was more attractive to a wealthy, educated Englishman at this period than the legacy of ancient Rome and the Renaissance. Lord Burlington, Handel's earliest important patron in England, had his London mansion renovated in the Palladian style and another neoclassical pile erected in Chiswick to house the artworks he had brought back from his Italian travels. An opera such as *Rinaldo*, deriving from Tasso, fed directly into this Italophilia. On the other hand, as we shall see, anything essentially Italian – and particularly Italian opera – could also arouse ferocious prejudices, especially among those (the vast majority) who did not go to it. One way and another, it must be said that the English soil on which Handel first planted his solidly Saxon feet and Italianate training must have been something of a financial, political and cultural minefield.

*

Handel was hugely admired, but not uncritically, or by everyone. Joseph Goupy's engraving, satirising Handel's big appetite, was entitled '*The Charming Brute*'.

Or perhaps a desert, at least operatically. As Handel's first biographer, Mainwaring, acknowledges, 'I am afraid there was little [music] to boast of, which we could call our own. At this time Operas were a sort of new acquaintance.' The appearance of *Rinaldo* on the London stage, therefore, was something of a milestone in operatic history. But perhaps that is to look at the past through the distorting prism of what we know came later. When it was first produced, on 24 February 1711, the day after Handel's twenty-sixth birthday, *Rinaldo* was a huge success. The presence of Nicolini in the title role, and a series of spectacular stage effects masterminded by Hill, certainly added to its initial acclaim and it was given fifteen performances between February and June, taken to Dublin the following year and revived in subsequent London seasons as Handel's fame grew. Initial box office receipts were moderate, however, scarcely enough to pay the basic expenses of all involved. Handel himself received only £186 7s. 11d. of an agreed payment of £430, while the copyist took away the score after every performance until Collier was able to pay him. The situation had not been helped by the fact that Joseph Addison made great fun of the extravagance of *Rinaldo* and of Italian opera in general in the pages of his new magazine, *The Spectator*. Addison reported how he encountered a man in the street carrying a cage full of birds evidently destined for the opera production. He imagined the birds making an entrance 'in very wrong and improper Scenes, so as to be seen flying in a Lady's Bed-Chamber, or perching upon a King's Throne' – and, naughtily, the 'inconveniences' the birds might drop upon the heads of those in the audience.

Later in the same report, Addison told his readers, reassuringly, that:

> the Opera Rinaldo is filled with Thunder and Lightning, Illumina-tions, and Fireworks; which the Audience may look upon without catching Cold, and indeed without much Danger of being burnt; for there are several Engines filled with Water, and ready to play at a Minute's Warning, in case such Accident should happen.

However, Addison expressed the hope that the owner of the theatre, a good friend of his, had been wise enough 'to *insure* his House before he would let this Opera be acted in it'. Meanwhile, Addison's co-editor, Richard Steele, noted that Italian opera was not the only show in town. Steele preferred *Whittington and His Cat*, not least because it contained no eunuchs and was performed 'in our own Language'.

In June 1711, Handel returned to Germany, increasingly confident of his artistic powers and reputation and determined to come back to London (which he did towards the end of the following year). Meanwhile, the theatri-cal scene he left behind him continued to lurch from crisis to crisis. Swiney, having run into severe financial and personnel problems at Drury Lane, returned to the Haymarket theatre once more, but in January 1713 fled to the Continent to escape bankruptcy proceedings, leaving 'ye Singers unpaid and ye Scenes and Habits also unpaid for'. Opera struggled on intermittently at the Haymarket, managed (if that is the right word) by the Swiss-born Johann Jakob Heidegger. The political and financial uncertainties generated by the death of Queen Anne in 1714 and the subsequent Jacobite rebellion did opera no favours, and the whole enterprise finally juddered to a complete halt after a short season in 1716/17. Thereafter, no Italian opera was produced in London until 1720. The wonder was that its demise had not occurred earlier. By now, an objective observer of the London scene at the time might have been forgiven for believing that England's faltering attempts to promote Italian opera – any kind of opera, indeed – were terminally doomed.

*

In the event, far from doomed, it was about to undergo a spectacular revival, launching London on a trajectory that, after many further fits and restarts, would eventually lead to its becoming one of the operatic capitals of the world. Several things saved Italian opera in London, all of them highly improbable. The first was the accession to the British throne of George I. The Act of Settlement and Act of Union must have seemed pretty arcane fare to the Elector of Hanover in his palace in central Germany, and at first he was said to have been unenthusiastic about acceding to their bizarre proposals. However, his advisers reassured him that they added to his credibility at home and, in any case, the likelihood of his taking the British crown seemed fairly remote (Queen Anne was repeatedly pregnant). So that when Queen Anne did indeed die without live issue, her crown was inherited by a somewhat per-plexed German Protestant who scarcely spoke or understood English. He did, however, have a reasonable understanding of Italian and loved Italian opera, attended it frequently and contributed financially to its revival.

It did not hurt that the foremost composer in London was the King's former *Kapellmeister*. Handel had obtained the Elector's permission to revisit England in late 1712 having undertaken to return to Hanover in due course. If there was some embarrassment a year and a half later when the two men met in London (as Mainwaring reported), it did not last long. By now, Handel was receiving an annual pension of £200, granted by Queen Anne shortly before her death, and living in Burlington House in Piccadilly, where he would have encountered many of the principal patrons and play-ers in London's vigorous musical and artistic worlds. Inevitably, given the parlous state of the Haymarket theatre (now renamed the King's), Handel gave little attention to the composition of opera during the first few years of George's accession.

All that was to change in 1719 with the creation of the Royal Academy of Music. This was a joint stock company, established by royal charter and financed by subscription (and a modest royal grant), which was set up in order to place opera production at the King's Theatre on a secure footing. The idea was that the subscribers, who all came from the nobility and landed gentry, would inject a healthy mix of artistic and economic acumen into their management of the Academy, their investment leading – they hoped and presumed – to a healthy return. Opera in London, in marked contrast to else-where, continued to be run as a capitalistic enterprise in private hands.

As so often before and since, the history of the Academy reveals a group of highly experienced and competent figures blinded by their love of opera into acting with financial recklessness in the untenable belief that the pro-duction of opera could make them a profit. It did not. Nor, to be fair, did much else at this moment, the run-up to the South Sea Bubble (which burst towards the end of 1720). Despite the presence among the directors of such people as Vanbrugh and Heidegger, whose earlier experiences must surely have given them heed, the Academy proved to be yet another financial catas-trophe, going bankrupt by 1728.

During its brief life, however, the Academy – fuelled by the attentions of an opera-loving monarch and a composer of genius – provided a framework for some of the most magnificent works and performances of Italian opera seen until that time. One of the first things the Academy did was to send Handel off to the Continent on a talent-hunting expedition (he was especially asked to secure the services of the great castrato Senesino, who made his London debut in 1720). On his return, Handel composed *Radamisto*, which was premiered to great acclaim in the King's Theatre in April 1720. Present, in a public display of their recent (if uneasy) reconciliation, were both the King and the Prince of Wales. For the next few years, until the demise of the Academy, much of Handel's time was devoted to opera at the King's Theatre, which continued throughout this period to be managed by Heidegger. A French visitor wrote a letter that included a detailed description of what he saw and heard. The company, he acknowledged, had 'sent for the best voices [and] the most skilled instrumentalists in Italy' to which they had added 'the best from Germany'. The orchestra was 'very loud' (it included twenty-four violins), though the chorus consisted of only four voices. The auditorium was 'small and in very poor taste' and there were 'candles everywhere'. Among 'people of quality', he was surprised to note, 'there are few who are keen on music'. Which was a pity because, as he had to admit, the overtures to Handel's operas were 'very fine' and there were 'arias with string accompaniment and wonderfully rich harmony which leave nothing to be desired'.

Handel was at the acme of his powers. So, as it happened, were some of the most famous Italian opera singers of the age, many of whom he engaged for the Academy and for whom he went on to compose what became some of their most famous roles. Handel was, of course, an employee of the Academy, not one of its directors, and did not always have his own way and was probably not best pleased when, for example, the Academy commissioned works from a rival composer of Italian opera, Bononcini. But Handel had grown in confidence and authority, well able by now to deal with a vocal superstar like the dumpy but divine-voiced Francesca Cuzzoni. Cuzzoni made her London debut in 1723 in Handel's new opera, *Ottone*. Mainwaring describes a rehearsal at which Cuzzoni refused to sing her first aria ('Falsa immagine'). Handel, unabashed, addressed the Italian prima donna in his gruffly German-inflected French, saying, 'Oh! Madame (said he) je sçais bien que Vous êtes une veritable Diablesse: mais je Vous ferai sçavoir, moi, que je suis Beelzebub le Chéf des Diables.' With this, Mainwaring says, Handel 'took her up by the waist, and, if she made any more words, swore that he would fling her out of the window'.

Opera in the eighteenth century was one of the very few professions in which talented women could climb out of the traditional social roles assigned to them and ascend the social and economic ladders. Not to the very top, perhaps. A singer was still an entertainer, indulged by the aristocracy but

In London in the 1720s, fierce rivalry broke out among the opera-going public between adherents of the Italian sopranos Faustina Bordoni and Francesca Cuzzoni. Here, both ladies are portrayed as rivals for the attention of a third superstar, the castrato Senesino, the 'Demi-Man', whom they are welcoming to England.

never their social equal. Financially, however, a celebrated prima donna like Cuzzoni could demand considerably higher earnings than Handel, a mere composer.* Nor was she alone. By 1726, the Academy was running into severe difficulties and the King's Theatre was (yet again) in crisis and, knowing that audiences were always looking for the latest novelty, they engaged at considerable expense another celebrated Italian prima donna, Faustina Bordoni (who later married the composer Hasse). The theatre hoped the presence of Senesino, Cuzzoni and Faustina would save it and Handel boldly created roles for all three in his opera *Alessandro*. Casting Faustina and Cuzzoni in the same opera was always going to be risky: Handel carefully gave each the same number of arias to sing, both had to be 'in love' with Senesino and the ladies even had to sing a duet. *Alessandro* was a stupendous success. Then Senesino went sick and, in his absence, the rivalry between the two ladies – or at least their partisans – increased. When Handel's next opera, *Admeto*, opened in January 1727, the audience was absurdly partisan; if admirers of Cuzzoni applauded, those of Faustina hissed and booed, and vice versa. In June, at a performance of Bononcini's *Astianatte*, things reached a

---

* Cuzzoni's salary in London in the 1720s seems to have been at least £1500 at a time when most principal singers (better paid than actors) were earning around £200–£300 per annum, and when a pound would secure a pair of decent seats at the opera and for a penny you could buy a pot of beer. Cuzzoni's wealth did not last. She died in obscurity and extreme poverty in Bologna in 1778 aged eighty-two, supporting herself in her last years, it was said, by making buttons.

crisis. At first, reported the *British Journal*, the contention was 'only carried on by Hissing on one Side, and Clapping on the other; but proceeded at length to Catcalls, and other great Indecencies: And notwithstanding the Princess Caroline was present, no Regards were of Force to restrain the Rudeness of the Opponents.' The contentiousness was said to have spread to the principals themselves, who, it was reported, pulled 'each other's coiffs... It is certainly an apparent Shame that two such well bred Ladies should call Bitch and Whore, should scold and fight like any Billingsgates.'

*

A few days later, it was reported from Osnabrück that King George I had died – shortly after signing an Act giving Handel naturalization. For a while, the rivalry between Bordoni and Cuzzoni was forgotten in the solemnities accompanying the funeral of one monarch and the accession of another. Indeed, to most people, other than those who attended it, opera was of little account. A theatre such as the King's could hold comfortably no more than seven or eight hundred (900-odd at a push), and Drury Lane somewhat fewer. Then, as now, far more people did not go to opera than did and, as today, the absentees had strong opinions about an art form they did not care to sample. Opera, people sniffed, was foreign: it displayed overblown, effete emotions, was performed in a language ordinary British people did not understand and was sung by Italians (which meant Catholics), among them those ludicrous but tragic half-humans, the castrati. Staging was widely deemed to be absurdly extravagant, spectacle taking precedence over drama as altos (male and female) pretended to be real men. In sum, Italian opera tended to undermine the fighting spirit, the patriotism and, indeed, all the good solid virtues of the Englishman: all very easy to ridicule if (like Addison and Steele) you were so disposed. William Hogarth, advocate of the Roast Beef of Old England, had fun portraying the mindless rich going to operas while a wheelbarrow man sells waste paper made up of the works of Shakespeare, Dryden and Ben Jonson. In *The Enraged Musician*, Hogarth showed a bewigged aesthete (doubtless an effeminate Italian from the opera orchestra) with his hands over his ears as ordinary Englishmen and women sing, blow pipes and bang drums in the streets below.

And Hogarth portrayed *The Beggar's Opera*. *The Beggar's Opera* was premiered in 1728, the very year of the Academy's demise, at the Lincoln's Inn Fields theatre, which was under the management of John Rich (son of the late Christopher). To a text by John Gay, *The Beggar's Opera* stood in stark contrast not only to Italian opera but also to previous English-language opera, which had usually tended to present the elevated sentiments of ancient gods and monarchs and the like. Here, instead, was a clever arrangement of well-known ballad tunes set to new words, stitched together to create a popular entertainment that anyone could enjoy. Gay parodied Whig politics,

In Hogarth's *The Enraged Musician*, the vulgar boisterousness of a rowdy, cosmopolitan London crowd causes distress to a hyper-sensitive violinist who is prevented from getting on with his practice. But just above the parrot in the upper left-hand corner, a poster hints at more popular musical fare: *The Beggar's Opera*.

Italian opera and much else besides while featuring the thrills and spills of the lowest of London's lowlife. The show even included a spat between two loud-mouthed women and everyone would have recognized in Lucy and Polly, the two inamoratas of the highwayman hero Macheath, the counterparts of Bordoni and Cuzzoni. In Hogarth's famous print, both of the women – watched by an onstage audience of aristocrats – beg for their lover, who is centre stage, to be released from his irons.

The Beggar's Opera was an immediate hit,* running for a record sixty-two performances in its first season. Every theatrical manager in Britain sought to produce it, or at least the latest ballad opera. It would not be true to say that *The Beggar's Opera* put an end to Italian opera in London. For all its popularity, it had no significant successor (Gay's own sequel was suppressed), and after a while the vogue for new ballad operas petered out somewhat. Nor did it end Handel's career as an operatic composer: major works – *Orlando*,

---

* Not with everyone. The French visitor who had admired Handel's operas at the King's Theatre also attended *The Beggar's Opera* and found it 'a kind of comic opera... all ballads with worthless music', adding, 'I would bore you if I told you about the country dances at the end.'

Ariodante, *Alcina* and *Serse* among them – were still to come. But it certainly flowed into a continuing stream of resentment towards the form. 'Leave us, as we ought to be/Leave the Britons Rough and Free!' said a lampoon addressed to Cuzzoni back in 1725, while Swift in 1728 wrote of the 'Un-natural Taste for Italian musik among us, which is wholly unsuited to our northern Climate, and the Genius of our People, whereby we are overrun with Italian Effeminacy, and Italian Nonsense.'

For the time being, Handel continued as the reigning presence controlling Italian opera in England. Indeed, Heidegger put him in total command of opera at the King's after the collapse of the Royal Academy of Music, and the composer promptly went off again to Italy to trawl for singers, returning with a netful of new stars. By now, Handel was revered by many, but resented by some. He had what we might now regard as a high-handed management style, falling out with, among others, his castrato star Senesino, whom he sacked. He seems to have aroused a degree of antipathy, too, among some of the mightiest in the land. Handel was by now living in Brook Street in Mayfair, an up-and-coming district frequented by the upper gentry: a mere artist who, not content with the patronage of the nobility, was beginning to act as though he were one of them. Even Prince Frederick, the new Prince of Wales, seems to have taken against Handel, perhaps resenting the composer's closeness to *his* father, now King George II. At any rate, a group of wealthy and noble Londoners led by the Prince clubbed together to found what amounted to a rival opera company, dubbed the 'Nobility', which opened in 1733. At first, the Nobility, with the Neapolitan Nicola Porpora in tow as 'house' composer, appeared to ride high, especially after they also secured the services of Farinelli, the greatest castrato of the age, for their second season. The two companies fought head to head, both determined to showcase the most magnificent performers and performances money could buy, the Nobility managing to oust Handel from the King's Theatre, where, predictably, Farinelli proved a sensational success.

However, for all the publicity generated by the rival companies, it soon became clear that they were competing for a limited and possibly shrinking market. After a while, even the novelty of Farinelli's presence began to wear off. Audiences fell away, as did revenue, and the Nobility faced the prospect of bankruptcy. People began to gossip about Farinelli – yet another grotesque Italian, said the envious – who was sponging up stupendous sums from a financially ailing company. As one song of the time put it:

> And there the *English* Actor goes,
> With many a hungry Belly,
> While heaps of Gold are forc'd, Got wot,
> on Signior *Farinelli*

In one of his engravings (no. 2 of the *Rake's Progress* series), Hogarth portrays a musician at the harpsichord behind whom is a scroll describing the gifts which 'Signor Farinelli the Italian Singer Condescended to accept of ye English Nobility & Gentry for one Nights performance of the Opera Artaxerxes'. These include 'a Gold Snuff box Chac'd with the Story of Orpheus charming ye Brutes'. Brutes? Hogarth evidently did not think much of the audiences Farinelli sang to either (not altogether surprising, perhaps, considering that it was after *Artaxerxes* that a lady is said to have cried out ecstatically, 'One God, one Farinelli!').

Opera was expensive and its stars astronomically paid – there was no getting away from that. Though, as one contemporary satirist pointed out, you didn't *have* to attend:

> But why this Rout about a lousy Shilling?
> Keep out, and sh—t, cries T— if you're not willing.
> In England now can Musick be too dear,
> The Fiddles of all Italy transplanted here?
> They strive to charm not Souls that grudge their Chink:
> And Musick ne'er was fram'd for Men who think:
> Or would so many thoughtless Boobies run
> To squeaking Op'ra's till they're half undone?
> Or Ladies worship Farri as a God?
> Who, say some Criticks, rather is Rod,
> Or Scourge to lash the Follies of the Age,
> And drive all Sense and Virtue from the Stage.

So opera was an Italian import patronized by the rich and mindless, Farinelli no God but a wooden actor, and the whole exercise a 'Scourge to lash the Follies of the Age'. The satire is aimed at the Nobility. But it applied just as pointedly to Handel's company (which was offered a temporary home in the newly built theatre at Covent Garden, where the proprietor was John Rich). After the inevitable demise of the Nobility, Heidegger brought Handel back to the King's, where the composer no doubt obtained some wry satisfaction from having seen off the opposition. But these were difficult years for Handel (in 1737, he suffered an uncharacteristic bout of bad health). Paradoxically, the very presence of two competing Italian opera companies in London, with consequently inadequate audiences at both, may itself have helped contribute to the decline in popularity of the art form. It has been calculated that there were probably no more than about 1200 families in London at the time with the social and financial clout to take out a subscription to an opera season; many of them would have been understandably reluctant to continue doing so as the rival companies stretched resources and divided audiences. In any event, by the later 1730s, Handel found himself

The image of the informal statue of Handel by Roubiliac, commissioned for London's Vauxhall Gardens, was widely reproduced.

turning away from Italian opera and increasingly towards English-language oratorio.

This shift of emphasis proved to be a smart career move. Once Handel had doffed the dubious mantle of Italian opera and enveloped his broad shoulders in the more respectable cloth of Protestantism and Englishness, his fame began to reach an ever-wider audience. His airs were performed in London's latest attraction: the Pleasure Gardens in Vauxhall, opened by the entrepreneur Jonathan Tyers in 1732. Tyers wanted Vauxhall to appeal to a far wider social spectrum than that which patronized the opera (rather as *The Beggar's Opera* had done). Where Handel's melodies had been played at the King's Theatre to audiences in the hundreds, at Vauxhall they would be enjoyed by the thousands. Here, visitors of all sorts would come and spend a summer evening eating, drinking, wandering, flirting and enjoying the musical entertainment on offer. Tyers was one of Handel's greatest admirers. He also knew how useful Handel could be to him. In 1738, he commissioned a little-known French sculptor, Louis-François Roubiliac, to create a statue of Handel to adorn 'the Grove', a central location in the park. When it was revealed, Roubiliac's work was a sensation, showing the composer relaxed, wigless and with his legs crossed. For all its informality, there was no doubting the message. As Handel plucked at a lyre, a little angel or *putto* at his feet, this was a statement of both the immediate accessibility and of the eternal appeal of his music. But it was an anglicized Handel rather than the German composer of Italian operas who was lionized at Vauxhall, most famously when in April 1749 his 'Fireworks Music' was given a public rehearsal at Vauxhall, prior to its official premiere, before an estimated crowd of 12,000 who had fought and shoved and tied up much of London's traffic in order to attend.

The Roubiliac statue was the first public monument in Britain to be erected to a living artist – one who, moreover, was palpably capable of linking high art with commercial appeal. In the years to come, as one Handel oratorio after another equated the triumphs of ancient Israel with the virtues of contemporary Britain, this German-born exponent of Italian opera came to be embraced by an ever-wider public as the pre-eminent voice of all that was best about his adopted homeland.

By the 1740s, while Handel was achieving new triumphs with *Messiah* and *Judas Maccabaeus*, a series of struggling and faltering managements at the King's continued to produce whatever Italian operas they could get hold of, recurrently losing money and alienating audiences. Handel died in 1759, and in his final years he could have been forgiven for reflecting that London's operatic world had by now completely bypassed the Italian-inspired art form to which he had made so powerful a contribution in his youth. Indeed, much of the opera on display in London by this time must have been, as Dr Johnson put it, an 'exotick and irrational entertainment'.

CHAPTER 4

Cultural Confluence in Mozart's Vienna

The Swedish Queen Lovisa Ulrika, like many eighteenth-century monarchs, loved French drama and opera and had it performed in her court theatre, the Slottsteater in the royal palace complex in Drottningholm, the 'Queen's Island' a little west of Stockholm. In August 1762, on Lovisa Ulrika's name day, the whole court was assembled for a performance when the troupe's leading tragedienne rushed into the auditorium shouting 'Fire!' – in French. The royal family and aristocracy, it is said, were saved while the Swedish-speaking servants and *hoi polloi* were at first nonplussed and several were killed. Four years later, Queen Lovisa Ulrika inaugurated a new theatre, the one we know to this day. Lovisa Ulrika was the sister of King Frederick II ('the Great') of Prussia. He, too was a cultural francophile, preferring to speak and write in French, not German (which he despised); Frederick called his exquisite home in Potsdam 'Sans Souci' and invited Voltaire to come on an indefinite visit as a valued guest. 'Our language and literature,' wrote Voltaire, who heard not a word of German spoken in the court of Frederick the Great, 'have made more conquests than Charlemagne ever did.'

The French 'Sun King' cast a long shadow. During his reign and for long thereafter, rulers everywhere tried with varying success to ape the grandeur of Louis XIV, building a string of grand palaces – each with its statutory court opera theatre – across Europe. Yet his legacy was regarded with profound ambivalence.

On the one hand, no young aristocrat's education was deemed complete without a thorough grounding in French language and literature. In Russia, with its open frontiers to the West, Peter the Great and his successors encouraged the best and the brightest to enter the Russian diplomatic academy, where they would be taught the cultural skills and tastes of their French counterparts. Peter introduced Western-style entertainments at court, too, a practice continued on a larger and grander scale by the female emperors who succeeded him, particularly the Empress Elizabeth in the 1740s and 1750s and Catherine the Great from 1762. French dancers and ballet masters (and Italian singers and instrumentalists) packed the Tsarist court throughout the century. It was much the same elsewhere. In Vienna, the Habsburg Empress Maria Theresa married a French-speaking former Duke of Lorraine, and their daughter Marie Antoinette went on to marry the French Dauphin. In Munich, when the Bavarian Elector wanted a new court theatre alongside his palace, he entrusted the job to François Cuvilliés, a dwarf and former court jester whom he had earlier sent to Paris to study architecture.

There was also antagonism, however, towards much that France was seen to represent. Despite Frederick the Great's love of French culture, for example, the music-loving monarch was determined that opera, as both art and entertainment, should acquire a new mien. Shortly after taking power in 1740, he ordered the construction of an opera house: not as in France as an adjunct to the royal palace but separate, free-standing, a great neoclassical temple to art. To this day, over a quarter-millennium after its original construction, Frederick's opera house, now the Berlin Staatsoper, has pride of place in the heart of town on Unter den Linden. He also had a stage built within the royal palace and both there and in the new opera house many operas were produced during his reign, often under the detailed supervision of the King himself. At first, the audience was generally restricted to those with official invitations: that is, the court and senior army officers. But, gradually, members of the wider public were able to buy tickets and attend (always provided, of course, they were appropriately attired). Frederick frankly needed the revenue this would provide. He was fighting a series of almost non-stop wars between 1740 and 1763 and, like other rulers across Europe at the time, he found he had to let the public into his opera house simply to keep it financially afloat.

Much of Frederick the Great's reign was devoted to war, but one of the first acts of the music-loving monarch was to order the construction of a free-standing opera house – still there over 250 years later as the Berlin Staatsoper.

As for the works performed, Frederick did not encourage the peculiarly French style of *tragédie lyrique*, with its mix of highly stylized musical and balletic set-pieces. His tastes, rather, had been formed as crown prince when he had enjoyed the new, Italian-style operas of Hasse. It was to Italy that he sent his court composer, Graun, on a quest to gather up the finest composers, singers, dancers, librettists and instrumentalists. 'A German singer?' the King was said to have expostulated; 'I should as soon expect to receive pleasure from the neighing of my horse!' The music at Frederick's court may have been by German composers (notably Graun himself); but the texts, and most of the leading performers, were Italian. Much the same was true at the lighter end of the repertoire. Despite the gradual emergence at this time of the popular style of German opera known as *Singspiel*, a form of quasi-pantomimic speech-and-music entertainment with German-language dialogue, it was rather to Italian *opera buffa* that Frederick turned. For some fifteen years or more, his capital was one of the operatic capitals of the world. This heyday of opera in Berlin was only brought to an end by Frederick's other great obsession: military expansion. The opera house closed down during the Seven Years War (1756–63), and by the time it reopened Graun was dead. The King's preoccupations were increasingly military and, without his advocacy, interest in Italian opera among the Berlin nobility waned, its place in their affections being increasingly taken by *Singspiel*. Ironically, the various operatic currents that had flowed through Frederick's Berlin finally came together in its great rival for pre-eminence in the German-speaking world, Vienna.

*

The first of these was French. In Vienna, as in Frederick's Berlin, the writers and thinkers who came to be most esteemed were not those who wrote in German but people such as Montesquieu and Rousseau, while French was the language of the elite (Maria Theresa's husband never learned to speak German properly). And as Prussia's military wrath raged against France in the 1750s, Maria Theresa's canny Francophile Chancellor, Prince Kaunitz, engineered an end to the traditional enmity between Austria and France by creating a series of Franco-Austrian alliances. He was also instrumental in establishing in Vienna a French theatre company. As in Berlin, culture was deemed to speak with a French accent. But here, French opera was welcomed too.

The man in charge of music in Vienna in the 1750s was Count Giacomo Durazzo, a highly cultured and Francophile Italian diplomat who was encouraged to promote French opera and ballet at the Burgtheater, adjacent to the royal palace. The personnel involved in these productions reveal another cultural stream; among the principal singers Durazzo brought to Vienna were Caterina Gabrielli* and the castrato Gaetano Guadagni (later Gluck's first Orfeo), while the ballet master was Gasparo Angiolini. Metastasio, the most prolific and successful operatic librettist of the eighteenth century, was living

Vienna's Kärntnertortheater, home of popular *Singspiel* in Mozart's day. The 'Carinthian Gate Theatre' stood by the city walls, near the site of today's Sacher Hotel.

and working in Vienna throughout these years, as was (from 1761) his great nemesis and another Kaunitz protégé, Ranieri Calzabigi. In Vienna, as in Berlin, it was acknowledged that the *fons et origo* of opera, that most ambitious of art forms, lay south of the Alps. The very word 'opera' was Italian, as indeed was the entire language of music. Durazzo seems to have seen it as his task to graft what he understood as Italian opera onto existing French styles.

Vienna's ruling elite might have admired French culture and Italian music and music makers. But it was a German-speaking city, and Durazzo's remit included the popular theatre at the Carinthian Gate, the Kärntnertortheater (that stood roughly on the site of today's Sacher Hotel), where he staged *Singspiel*. In 1776, the Emperor Joseph II, keen to promote 'national' (that is, German) culture, set up a German-language Nationaltheater in Vienna. This involved dismissing the existing Burgtheater company, thereby lowering the quality and quantity of French drama and Italian opera on offer in

* Among Gabrielli's claims to fame is the riposte she is said to have uttered to Catherine the Great when the Russian Empress invited her to sing at court. Gabrielli explained that her fee would be 5000 ducats. The Tsarina exclaimed that none of her field marshals received such a sum, to which La Gabrielli is said to have replied: 'Very well, then, Your Majesty must invite her field marshals to sing!' The court of Catherine the Great employed a number of distinguished Italian musicians, among them such operatic composers as Galuppi, Cimarosa and Paisiello.

Vienna (the experiment did not last long, and would be forgotten had it not given the world Mozart's *Die Entführung aus dem Serail*). Today, we hear little of the French *tragédies lyriques* or *opéras comiques* of mid-eighteenth-century Vienna, or of its Italian *opera seria* or German *Singspiel*. Yet it is from these three variegated and disparate roots that some of the mightiest operatic forests were to grow.

*

In 1765, a couple of years after the end of the Seven Years War, Maria Theresa's husband, the Emperor Francis Stephen, died. On his death, she announced that she would take a subordinate role as Dowager Empress, while day-to-day running of the empire would be undertaken by her son, the Archduke Joseph. For fifteen years, this memorable duo reigned in tandem until Maria Theresa's own death in 1780, when her son became in name as well as in fact the Emperor Joseph II.

By the 1760s, audiences to opera, even in some of the most exclusive court theatres, were likely to include a wider section of the population than would ever have had access to Versailles. Tim Blanning has argued persuasively that there was already emerging what we would recognize as a 'public' for opera, and that this – and no longer just the whim of kings and princes – came increasingly to influence the nature and quality of what was performed. In part, this was a result of sheer economics: opera was the most expensive of the arts and had of necessity to produce revenue in the form of ticket sales, especially at a time when national exchequers were being drained by war. But it was also a consequence of a broader change whereby any social, political or cultural idea or artefact gradually came to need at least a degree of public acceptance or acquiescence if it were to acquire the stamp of legitimacy. And that applied to opera. Opera that could not draw a 'public' was not likely to be performed.

As the social profile and status of opera audiences began to shift in the later eighteenth century, so too did that of composers. Earlier musicians such as Bach, Telemann or Vivaldi had mostly been salaried artisans, composing and performing as required and answerable to their aristocratic, ecclesiastical or civic paymasters. They might move from job to job, that is from one court, church, theatre or municipal authority to another. Most probably did so with the eventual aim of finding the best post in which to 'settle down'. Like today's top professors (or master chefs), a famous composer-performer might get the occasional call to work temporarily elsewhere; but, for most, home was where the main salary or pension was paid and accommodation and food provided. Without these, a composer's income, in an age without adequate copyright or royalty laws, could be precarious in the extreme. As for mere performers, they had long carried a somewhat louche reputation and lay further still down the ladder of social status. Casanova in his twenties took a job playing the violin in one of the theatres in his native Venice. 'My profession was not a noble one, but I did not care,' wrote Casanova later, adding that he soon acquired all the habits of his 'lowly comrades' and going on to describe with relish the drunkenness, debauchery and cruel pranks which (he virtually implies) came with the job.

A serious composer would normally have occupied a rather higher plane than a mere pit musician and would have commanded greater respect. But composers remained resolutely excluded from the top social circles for whom they worked. Bach's letters (like some of Monteverdi's) are full of resentment for what he regarded as the inadequate financial and social rewards he received. The authorities in Leipzig (wrote Bach in 1732) are 'odd and little interested in music, so that I must live in almost continual vexation, envy, and persecution'; a year later, he described his situation as one in which he was 'constantly exposed to undeserved affronts'. Haydn, by contrast, worked as *Kapellmeister* to the Esterházy court throughout much of his long career and wore the Esterházy livery like any other house employee: a highly respected and well-rewarded member of a noble household which, like a medieval castle, was a complete but self-enclosed society providing for every human need.

*

Mozart, a generation after Haydn, was a young man in a hurry. A *Wunderkind* shown off by his ambitious and entrepreneurial father Leopold to the courts of Europe, he learned as a boy to relish his talents and the attention they stimulated. When Leopold brought him to play at the Habsburg court in Vienna, the six-year-old was roundly applauded and presented with not only an honorarium but also a magnificent court outfit that had belonged to the Archduke Max. Everyone seems to have enjoyed the visit, not least the Emperor Francis Stephen, who challenged the boy to play a simple piece of music with the keys of his instrument covered. Wolfgang not only did so but cheekily asked the distinguished court composer Wagenseil to turn the pages for him. When at the end he threw himself onto the lap of the Empress Maria Theresa, she scooped him up and gave him an affectionate kiss. There is even a story that, when the boy slipped on the polished floors of Vienna's Schönbrunn Palace, he was helped up by the Princess Marie Antoinette, whom he thanked profusely, adding that when he was grown up he would marry her. If he had done so, not only his own history but that of France and the wider world would have been somewhat different.

It would of course have been unthinkable for someone like the son of a jobbing musician from Salzburg to marry a Habsburg princess. When, a decade later, another of Marie Antoinette's many brothers, the Archduke Ferdinand, was thinking of taking Mozart into his service, the Empress wrote to him saying that Ferdinand could employ the young Mozart if he wished; she wouldn't stand in his way. But she warned him not to burden himself with 'useless people' and to avoid 'giving titles to people of that sort' who, she said, 'go about the world like beggars'.

Mozart did not know about this exchange, and of course was not employed by the Archduke. But he did take employment a few years later, like his father Leopold, with the new Archbishop of Salzburg, Count Hieronymus von Colloredo. Wolfgang considered himself more talented than most of his social superiors and chafed under the yoke of a man he regarded as an unsympathetic employer. In early 1781, soon after the death of Maria Theresa and the accession of Joseph II as Emperor, Archbishop Colloredo moved temporarily to Vienna, instructing much of his official household (including Mozart, who was in Munich at the time) to join him. They installed themselves in the Deutsch Ordenshaus, the House of the Teutonic Order, in Singerstrasse, behind St Stephen's Cathedral. Mozart's letters back home to his father burst with indignation about the way he is treated. Why, he even has to have his meals at the servants' table, below the Archbishop's valets (but at least above the cooks) – he, Mozart, who as a boy had been feted by kings and emperors! Every time Mozart made a request, he was thwarted by Colloredo's chief steward, Count Arco, whose duties seem to have included putting the pushy young musician firmly in his place – in particular, when he repeatedly requested permission to stay in Vienna when the

It is easy to see Leopold Mozart as a harsh, judgmental father who pushed his son into musical precocity. However, Wolfgang seems to have enjoyed his youthful travels, absorbing all the musical styles to which he was exposed.

party was due to return to Salzburg. Mozart was eventually dismissed with a
kick on the backside. Very well. He would stay in Vienna. 'Salzburg is no
longer the place for me,' he reflected to his father – unless, of course, he
should have the opportunity of returning Count Arco's kick! So Mozart
remained in the capital and, brimming with confidence, embarked upon an
arduous and somewhat novel kind of career: that of the 'free artist' who
would live off whatever commissions and performances he could muster.

Mozart's attitude to his archiepiscopal employer was not unique. Even
Haydn began to express irritation as his increasingly international reputation
seemed to redound not to his credit but to that of his aristocratic superiors.
'I didn't know if I was a *Kapell*-Master or a *Kapell*-Servant,' he said in a letter of 1790; when he wanted to travel (which he did, to England, to enormous
acclaim), he was only enabled to do so after the death of his long-standing
princely employer, Prince Nikolaus Esterházy. Many musicians nursed a sense
of grievance at the constant reminders of their low-to-middling position in
the social order during the eighteenth century, particularly those associated
with opera. By the 1780s, Mozart may have had occasional privileged access
to the Emperor, Joseph II, a ruler with a passionate and informed interest in
music and the theatre. When Mozart and his wife were invited to court occasions, they dressed up to the nines, whatever their precarious finances, and
hired carriages for the occasion. But most of the Viennese aristocracy probably regarded the Mozarts' natural habitat as lying closer to those amiable
but socially unpresentable theatrical folk they worked with. People such as
his most important librettist, Lorenzo Da Ponte.

*

Da Ponte was born to a Jewish family in the Veneto. He converted to Catholicism as a teenager and was evidently sufficiently devout to enter the priesthood
a few years later. But he soon succumbed to more worldly Venetian pleasures
and spent much of his adult life embarking upon, and escaping from, a
sequence of financial and sexual scandals. Forced to leave Venice, Da Ponte
lived briefly in Dresden and in 1781, armed with a letter of recommendation
to the court composer Salieri, he settled in Vienna. At the time, the Emperor
Joseph II was still trying to encourage German-language theatre and opera.
He abandoned this a couple of years later, reinstated Italian opera and
appointed Da Ponte poet to the imperial theatre, a post he held until 1790,
when the Emperor died. Da Ponte's racy and entertaining *Memoirs*, written
many years after the events recounted, may be packed with self-serving fabrications, or exaggerations, but the Vienna sections are full of anecdotes
about how cleverly he managed to get round recalcitrant court functionaries
and, mere scribbler that he was, get the ear of the Emperor. It was Da Ponte
who (by his own account at least) persuaded Joseph to permit performance
of a new opera he and Mozart were working on based on Beaumarchais's

recent play *The Marriage of Figaro*, which the Emperor had banned as being of dubious taste and politically subversive.

According to Michael Kelly, the Irish tenor who sang in the first performance of *Figaro*, this was one of three operas being written around the same time (the others were by Salieri and Righini) 'and each composer claimed the right of producing his opera for the first'. The contest raised much discord, it seems, 'and parties were formed'. Kelly describes the personalities of the competing composers: Salieri, the *maestro di cappella* to the imperial court, was 'a clever, shrewd man, possessed of what Bacon called, crooked wisdom', while Righini 'was working like a mole in the dark to get precedence'. As for Mozart, he was the most relaxed and affable of companions, says Kelly; he loved punch and was an excellent billiard player. On matters of music, however, Mozart could be uncompromising. At Sunday concerts, which Kelly used to attend, Mozart was 'always ready to oblige; but so very particular, when he played, that if the slightest noise were made, he instantly left off'. Deeply aware of his own superior musical abilities, Mozart was 'as touchy as gunpowder' at the idea of *Figaro* competing for precedence with works by Salieri and Righini, and he 'swore he would put the score of his opera into the fire if it was not produced first'.

The mighty contest was put at an end, Kelly records happily, by an order of the Emperor that *Le nozze di Figaro* 'be instantly put into rehearsal'. But Mozart's (and Da Ponte's) travails were not yet over. Count Rosenberg, the man in charge of court spectacles, had been told the work included a scene containing a dance sequence. Did the *signor poeta* not know, he asked Da Ponte, that the Emperor had forbidden dancing in his theatre? The *signor poeta* did not. Whereupon the pompous Count tore out the offending scene and placed the pages carefully on the fire.

Da Ponte hurried to Mozart, who was desperate. 'It was a task for me to calm him,' Da Ponte recalled. 'But at length I begged him to allow me just two days' time, and to leave everything to me.' The opera was due to be performed at the Burgtheater and Da Ponte tells us he managed to invite the Emperor to attend the dress rehearsal, where at first everything went well and was greeted with applause. Then came the 'pantomimic scene between the Count and Susanna' during which the orchestra plays and the dance occurs. The orchestra remained silent and there was no dance; instead, the Count and Susanna simply gesticulated and the whole thing looked like a dumb show. 'What's all this?' the Emperor exclaimed, and called for Da Ponte for an explanation. Da Ponte showed him the libretto, in which he had restored the dance scene. The Emperor, nonplussed, asked the obsequious Rosenberg why the ballet was cut and received the weak answer that no dancers were available.

'But can't they be procured at some other theatre?' asked the Emperor, and was told that they could.

The captivating 20-year-old Nancy Storace: the English-born soprano was Mozart's choice as Susanna in the 1786 premiere of his *Le nozze di Figaro*.

'Very well, let Da Ponte have as many as he needs.'

In less than half an hour, Da Ponte tells us, twenty-four dancers had appeared and the offending scene was rehearsed and reinstated.

All of which pleased Da Ponte (and doubtless Mozart) mightily, though the *signor poeta* explains how his clever little manoeuvre also served to make Count Rosenberg hate him all the more and seek future opportunities for revenge.

*

Figaro was a moderate success in Vienna, the imperial capital. But it was a *succès fou* in Prague. 'Here they talk about nothing but *Figaro*. Nothing is played, sung or whistled but *Figaro*. No opera is drawing like *Figaro*. Nothing, nothing but *Figaro*.' Mozart's letter of 15 January 1787 to his pupil, friend and fellow Mason Gottfried von Jacquin is one of his most frequently quoted and it nicely conveys the breathless excitement of his first protracted visit to Prague. So popular was *Figaro* that its composer was commissioned to write a new work which would have its premiere here. However, the quotation from Mozart's letter, if taken out of context, can be deeply misleading and raises the question as to who exactly would have been doing the talking, playing, singing and whistling.

In Mozart's time, Prague was the capital of Bohemia, a province of the empire in which a large Czech population was ruled by German-speakers who took their cue from Vienna. If some ambitious Czechs felt constrained to learn German, the compliment was scarcely reciprocated. The German language was used as a tool of policy by the Habsburgs, Joseph II following his experiment with a 'National Theatre' with the introduction of German (rather than Latin) as the official language for governmental communication. In the German-speaking world, the Emperor's encouragement of the vernacular language for use in the arts and in governmental communications was viewed as progressive, but in the outposts of the empire, such as Bohemia, it was widely regarded as a further signal of the hegemony of Vienna. As yet, there was no especial tension between those who spoke German and those who used Czech; that would come later. But in Prague, as elsewhere, language indicated a clear sociopolitical divide: the wealthier, more educated citizens spoke and wrote German, though they might resort to Czech when addressing their butlers, dressmakers or coachmen.

Mozart, though not an aristocrat, was a celebrated 'German' from Vienna who was known to the Emperor. So he tended to mix with the upper strata of Prague society, particularly its more liberal-minded, artistically inclined aristocracy. After an exhausting three-day coach journey across wintry Moravia and Bohemia, he and his wife stayed with the enlightened, music-loving 'Old' Count Thun, the dedicatee of Mozart's 'Linz' Symphony, whose palace in Prague's fashionable 'Lesser Town' had long been noted for its musical performances. Soon after his arrival (Mozart reports), after a late lunch complete with musical entertainment, he was driven off by another music-loving aristocrat (Count Canal) to a ball at the home of a third (Baron Breitfeld, or Bretfeld). Here, as he reported in his letter to von Jacquin, all the most beautiful women in Prague were reputed to gather ('*you* ought to have been there my friend!'). Mozart himself neither danced nor flirted with any of them, 'the former, because I was too tired, and the latter owing to my natural bashfulness'. However, he obtained a lot of pleasure just looking on as people 'flew about in sheer delight' to various popular arrangements from his latest hit, *Figaro*. It was at the Breitfeld ball, not in the taverns or streets of Prague, that Mozart noted that everyone talked about 'nothing but *Figaro*'.

Which is not to say that Mozart went unnoticed by the rest of Prague. His presence was reported in the local press (his name appearing in the *Prager Oberpostamtszeitung* as 'Mozard' which, to German-language readers, would have sounded correct). And there are a host of stories, none easy to authenticate, of Mozart's popularity with ordinary Czechs, among them the washerwomen on Kampa (a small peninsula beneath Prague's Charles Bridge) who supposedly sang melodies from *Figaro* as they went about their work. Niemetschek, Mozart's first biographer, reports that 'a piano version of *Figaro* was made by one of our best masters, Herr Kucharz; it was arranged for wind parts, as a quintet and for German dances; in short, Figaro's tunes echoed through the streets and parks; even the harpist on the alehouse bench had to play "Non più andrai" if he wanted to attract any attention at all.'

Mozart's first visit to Prague lasted about a month and the composer was evidently at his happiest. Not only *Figaro* but also his new Symphony in D (ever afterwards known as the 'Prague') received excellent performances and brought their composer the kind of unbridled acclaim he had never quite achieved in supposedly more sophisticated Vienna. And by the time Mozart embarked upon the journey home, he had in his pocket an invitation to return: a commission from the impresario Pasquale Bondini to write a new opera especially for his theatre.

What we call the Estates Theatre was the creation of an enlightened, art-loving Bohemian aristocrat, the *Oberstburggraf* Count Franz Anton Nostitz: his gift to the people of Prague. A neoclassical structure, its pediment still bears the motto *Patriae et Musis* ('To the Homeland and the Muses'). The *Patria*, of course, was Germany; as Joseph II himself pointed out, the new Nostitz Theatre would provide a contribution to the German 'national' spirit he was so keen to foster. The birth of the new theatre was not without controversy. It was built on a vacant square alongside Prague's venerable Charles University and some complained that it would blot out the natural light from the lecture rooms. This, replied defenders of the scheme, would be more than compensated for by the enlightenment emanating from the theatre. Building commenced in 1781 and the theatre opened two years later with a performance of a play by Schiller. Count Nostitz soon put the daily administration of his theatre into the hands of Bondini, but he retained an interest in the theatre until his death in 1798, after which it was taken over by the Bohemian Estates. In later years, the area around the Estates Theatre – like that adjacent to London's Covent Garden – became well-known as the city's principal fruit market.

So when Mozart came to Prague in January 1787, his *Figaro* was performed in the newest, largest and most prestigious theatre in town. The money Bondini offered Mozart for the new commission was not princely. But the composer's finances were by now in a parlous state and, in Vienna at least, opportunities to earn were limited. Nobody is quite sure who first thought of an opera on the Don Juan legend. Da Ponte of course attributed the idea to himself. If so, he did not make things easy for his composer colleague. Da Ponte tells us he spent the summer of 1787 working on no fewer than three libretti: one for Martín y Soler (to which he decided to devote his mornings), one for Salieri (afternoons) and in the evenings he would write for Mozart. Da Ponte can hardly be accused of laziness. In his memoirs he said he put in twelve-hour days at his desk. But his methods were unorthodox to say the least. Parts of his *Don Giovanni* are more or less directly 'inspired by' the text written a couple of years earlier for another opera on the same theme composed by Gazzaniga. Then there were Da Ponte's ways of gaining and retaining inspiration:

> A beautiful girl of sixteen – I should have preferred to love her only as a daughter, but alas..! – was living in the house with her mother, who took care of the family, and came to my room at the sound of the bell. To tell the truth the bell rang rather frequently, especially at moments when I felt my inspiration waning... At first I permitted such visits very often; later I had to make them less frequent, in order not to lose too much time in amorous nonsense, of which she was the perfect mistress. The first day, between the Tokay, the snuff, the coffee, the bell, and my young muse, I wrote the first two scenes of *Don Giovanni*...

– as well as substantial scenes for both the other composers.

When Mozart and his wife returned to Prague in the autumn, the score of *Don Giovanni* was still incomplete. The Mozarts were given lodgings in a house in the Kohlenmarkt called the 'Drei Goldenen Löwen' ('Three Golden Lions') which is still visible from the upstairs salon in the Estates Theatre, while Da Ponte also came to Prague for a few days and stayed in an adjacent building. The two men were said to have been able to communicate with each other window to window.

On the first night, according to one report, the coaches began arriving at the theatre as early as half-past five, with finely dressed ladies looking for the entrance in 'a sea of mud'. After Mozart's triumphant visit to Prague earlier in the year, it was only to be expected that a loyal following would be present at the premiere of his next opera, one written especially for them. If the aristocracy were there in force, so were their retainers. As the city's *eleganti* negotiated their way through the mud, the upper parts of the house were apparently already full. Dangerously so, it seems, for the galleries 'had an almost frightening aspect'. Up there:

> people were shoulder to shoulder, and the last row of the audience, who were holding on to the iron rails between the pillars, seemed about to fall on to the rows below. Over the hum of the excited crowd, you could barely make out the voices of the servants, who were going round offering 'beer and sausages' to the insatiably hungry gallery spectators, while down below the cry rang out 'lemonade, almond milk'.

The audience at the 1787 premiere of *Don Giovanni* enjoyed lemonade and almond milk, beer and sausages – and a richly inventive *dramma giocoso* which included a seductive serenade. The new opera was a huge success, and Mozart left the theatre with the applause still ringing in his ears. No wonder he loved his 'Praguers'.

This audience may not have made up a complete microcosm of Prague society. But it seems to have included representatives of not only the wealthier, almond milk-drinking local aristocracy but also of the larger, Czech-speaking, beer-drinking artisan and servant class. Few would have understood every nuance in Da Ponte's Italian libretto (it was another twenty years before Prague would hear *Don Giovanni* in German translation and 1825 before a Czech version became available). Most would, however, have appreciated the rich musical inventiveness with which Mozart had invested this *dramma giocoso*, and the singing of an outstanding cast (among them Bondini's wife, who sang the part of Zerlina). The evening was a resounding success, and it was with the thunderous applause of his first-night audience still ringing in his ears that Mozart is supposed to have said happily: 'My Praguers understand me.'

*

In Vienna, things were different. When *Don Giovanni* was performed before the Emperor, he told Da Ponte that, while he thought it excellent, 'it is no tasty morsel for the teeth of my Viennese.' When Da Ponte reported this to Mozart, the composer came up with a spirited response: 'Just let them have time to chew on it.'

Perhaps Joseph II had other things on his mind. That same year, the Habsburg empire found itself at war with the Ottomans to the east, and the Emperor decided that he personally would supervise military operations. In general, the city to which Mozart returned after the Prague premiere of *Don Giovanni* frankly had little money or attention for musicians. The Turkish wars demanded the entire attention of the Emperor, straining and draining the imperial budget, and in order to help pay for increasing military expenditure many among the Viennese nobility had to reduce their social and artistic commitments. When Mozart tried to organize a series of benefit concerts in 1790, he received virtually no subscriptions. The world in which Mozart had launched his freelance career so optimistically was collapsing around him. Before long, the French Revolution, which had broken out in 1789, would not only bring down the French aristocracy but threaten to impose its doctrine of social equality throughout the known world.

In 1790, Joseph II died, to be succeeded by his brother Leopold. With the Turkish wars in abeyance (temporarily as it proved), Leopold was scheduled to visit Prague to be crowned King of Bohemia, and Mozart was invited to write an opera to celebrate the event. The job had originally been offered to Salieri who had turned it down on the grounds that he had so much other work to complete. Mozart might legitimately have said the same: at the time he was frantically busy working on two other very different kinds of commission, *The Magic Flute* and a Requiem Mass. But he desperately needed the money, and he had already made a number of attempts, so far to no avail, to attract the attention of the new Emperor. Perhaps he was foolish to agree to undertake the new coronation opera. On the other hand, it was a prestigious commission and Mozart had known nothing but triumph in Prague.

La clemenza di Tito is a traditional *opera seria* based on a much-used Metastasio libretto telling of the great generosity of spirit of the Roman Emperor Titus. Just the thing to celebrate the coronation of a new ruler, one might think, and the work contains some inspired arias and ensembles. Once again, Mozart seems to have completed the score dangerously close to deadline (during the three-day coach journey, according to some reports), with his pupil and friend Süssmayr helping out with the recitatives. This time, however, Mozart was writing not to entertain the people of Prague but as a formal homage to the imperial party, and his efforts met with far less success. It is said that his older rival, Salieri, who was much in evidence during the Prague celebrations, did his nefarious best to outshine Mozart (and, somewhat improbably, that the new Empress dismissed *Clemenza* as 'una porcheria tedesca').

Mozart was understandably demoralized and fell ill. Even before leaving Prague for the journey back to Vienna, he turned his attention to *The Magic*

Flute, which was due to be performed a mere three weeks later before what would undoubtedly be a far more *gemütlich* audience. And then there was that Requiem to complete; at least this might help restore his seriously depleted finances…

*

For all his talent and celebrity, Mozart remained 'merely' a musician, Da Ponte 'merely' a poet. Only a tiny handful of their colleagues (such as the librettist Metastasio and the court composer Salieri) were able to attain serious money and social esteem. As for those who performed their works, a handful of singers, actors or dancers became rich and famous or had private means. Most, however, were like the 'travelling players' whom Hamlet instructed, troupes of 'wandering minstrels', usually led by an actor-manager, who were called upon and then discarded with equal insouciance by the cities in which they installed themselves.

The most famous player-manager of Mozart's day, certainly to us, was Emanuel Schikaneder, the man who commissioned and produced – and appeared in – Mozart's *Die Zauberflöte* in 1791. Schikaneder was a German-born playwright, singer, composer and theatrical entrepreneur and director who first got to know the Mozarts during an early stint in Salzburg. During many years on the road, Schikaneder honed his versatile theatrical skills and built up a reputation as a highly polished performer, not least in serious drama (in 1777 he appeared as Hamlet at the Munich court theatre with such success that he had to repeat the final scene as an encore). In 1784, Joseph II saw him in Pressburg (now Bratislava) and later had him invited to perform in Vienna. In 1789, Schikaneder moved into the Theater auf der Wieden, where he specialized in *Singspiel* with magical stage effects for which he would commission musical settings of what were often his own texts and cast them from his own company. Schikaneder was a successful and popular player-manager for much of his career, though that did not immunize him from the precariousness of the theatrical life (in his case bankruptcy and mental breakdown followed by an early death). We can get a glimpse of this life by entering the Theater auf der Wieden, or Wiedner theatre, the venue in which the *Magic Flute* was premiered.

This was not just a theatre; it was part of a village, or community. Schikaneder's biographer describes the complex as a 'monstrous' series of houses and apartments linked to each other around half a dozen courtyards, a maze-like complex containing craft shops, a church, a mill, wells, places to eat and drink and, just off one of the courtyards, a theatre capable of accommodating an audience of up to a thousand. It was in many ways what we would today call a housing estate. The complex, which was finally pulled down in the twentieth century, was popularly known as the Freyhaus (or Freihaus) and was situated a short walk south from the Kärntnertor, one of the

The playwright-actor-manager Emanuel Schikaneder as the bird-man Papageno in the original 1791 production of *Die Zauberflöte*.

main entries into the walled city of Vienna itself. Why 'free house'? A century before, the Starhemberg family had received the land from the crown with all taxation waived in perpetuity, so later generations could charge tenants somewhat less than the going rate. In this people-packed enclave of amiable chaos, Schikaneder's theatrical troupe (his 'children') lived, worked, played, ate, drank – and performed for a large and appreciative public.

The Freyhaus theatre kept decor simple and ticket prices low. There were boxes, but the great majority of the audience sat on benches on the ground floor (or in a balcony, which Schikaneder added). If you wanted to get a good seat, it was best to get there early. One habitué described how he would arrive in mid-afternoon and sit for three hours 'bathed in heat and sweat and impregnated by the garlicky fumes of the smoked meats being consumed' before the performance began. As likely as not, the theatrical fare on offer

The playbill for *Die Zauberflöte* 'by Emanuel Schikaneder'.

would be the latest *Singspiel* written, directed and performed by Schikaneder himself. His was the name at the top of the bill, and one would have had to search hard, and perhaps in vain, to find that of whoever had added the music. As with today's audiences flocking to see a ballet or film, it was rarely the person who wrote the score who provided the principal attraction. Thus, it was Schikaneder's *Zauberflöte* that people wanted to see at the Wiedner theatre on 26 September 1791. Two months later, Mozart's body lay in an unmarked grave, his Requiem still incomplete.

*

It is easy, and perhaps comforting, to look back at the Vienna of Joseph II as a golden age of music and opera. Above all, of course, because it happened to be the time and place of Mozart's flowering, but also because of the benign influence of the Emperor himself. Joseph ruled over one of the most extensive empires in history, his sprawling realms packed with what we would call ethnic and cultural tensions while at the same time abutting powerful neighbours with whom he was sometimes at war. Yet the man at the centre of this empire somehow found the time and the intellectual energy to maintain an active interest in music and theatre. Indeed, it seems there was little he loved and cared about more. As a young Habsburg prince, Joseph had been trained by the finest musicians in Vienna, among them Wagenseil, and later, in addition to running his empire, seems to have acted like a hands-on Intendant of his court theatre. He particularly loved and encouraged opera (it is no coincidence that both Haydn and Mozart concentrated on operatic composition during Joseph's ten years at the helm). We find the Emperor suggesting and rejecting topics for operatic treatment, reading and commenting on proposed libretti and perusing musical scores with quasi-professional expertise. Early in Mozart's sojourn in Vienna, the Emperor presided over a piano duel between Mozart and the composer and pianist Muzio Clementi: 'Allons, fire away,' said Joseph when it was Mozart's turn (having privately made a bet that Mozart would win). In 1786, as entertainment to mark a visit by the Governor-General of the Austrian Netherlands, Joseph arranged that Mozart and Salieri both produce a short, light-hearted operetta, about opera itself, to be presented in succession at either end of the Orangery at the Schönbrunn Palace. Mozart wrote a piece about a beleaguered impresario while Salieri's, entitled *Prima la musica e poi le parole*, touched on a long-standing operatic dispute: which is prior, the music or the words?

Da Ponte, too, benefited from Joseph's benign interest. It was through the Emperor's direct intervention that Da Ponte got to write his first libretto for Martín y Soler, a collaboration that later found fruit in the highly successful *Una cosa rara* (which Mozart quotes in the second act of *Don Giovanni*). Where the court led, many followed. Haydn, Mozart and Beethoven all received generous aristocratic patronage; the Baron Gottfried von Swieten bestowed his enlightened largesse upon all three. Any music lover is in debt to Joseph II for the practical encouragement he was able to give in the Age of Mozart.

Yet the reasons why late eighteenth-century Vienna has earned a favoured place in musical and operatic history extend beyond the benign influence of an enlightened Emperor and the coincidental presence of a sequence of musical masters. During these years, Vienna was expanding rapidly and (as the story of the Freyhaus has suggested) a great deal of activity was spilling out of the old city walls into the new suburbs. Voluntary associations sprouted up all over Vienna – reading groups, choral societies, the Masonic lodges of which Mozart and some of his friends were members – while a small music publishing firm such as Artaria began to find a new, lucrative market. In some respects, oddly enough, Joseph II's Austria was perhaps less receptive to musical culture than in his mother's day. 'It was formerly a strong custom,' wrote a Viennese writer looking back in the 1790s, 'that our great princely houses maintained their own house orchestras, at which they cultivated the leading spirits of music.' This 'worthy custom has been lost,' he lamented, 'to the detriment of music'. To some historians, the musical fame of Joseph II's Vienna is in part attributable, paradoxically, to this very decline. One of the reasons the imperial court and its theatre played so important a part in the musical history of these years, in other words, was that many of the lesser courts, needing to economize, found themselves no longer able to do so. As aristocratic power and influence eroded, the importance of the imperial court and the example it set correspondingly rose. And if the Emperor happened to set high store on music and opera, this message was not lost on an increasingly insecure nobility. It is a seductive argument. However, real economic decline and the accompanying erosion of aristocratic power and influence did not really set in until some years after the death of Joseph II and of Mozart.

Another possible explanation links the contemporary fame of Mozart and (more so, perhaps) the young Beethoven to the emergence at the time of a new bourgeoisie. Certainly, the reputation of these celebrated musicians spread far beyond the aristocratic circles that primarily sponsored and patronized them. But here, too, some reservations are in order. Of subscribers to a Mozart concert series in 1784, half came from the 'high' nobility, 42 per cent from the lesser nobility and wealthier townspeople – and a mere 8 per cent from the 'bourgeoisie'. All this represented a tiny proportion of the population as a whole. The Viennese nobility in Mozart's time numbered perhaps 3 per cent of the city's total population (of 230,000) and the middle class of *Beamten und Bürger* (civil servants and wealthier citizens) probably no more than a further 4 per cent. Yet these two groups constituted something like 90 per cent of the audience at Vienna's Burgtheater, where Mozart's *Entführung*, *Figaro* and *Così* all had their premieres. It would be another two generations at least before Vienna would see the emergence of a substantial professional and mercantile music-loving middle class of the kind already establishing itself in London.

One should be wary of romanticizing the Vienna of Joseph II's day and regarding it as a haven of cultural civility honouring its artists. A handful may have received encouragement at the highest levels. But many another suffered neglect and hardship. Mozart's Vienna was in this respect not unlike the Hollywood of the 1930s or 1940s: an irresistible magnet for aspiring talent which embraced and celebrated a tiny fraction of those who threw themselves upon its mercies but discarded the great majority without ceremony. Nor did fame necessarily translate into money or social status. Mozart himself, notwithstanding the annual pension the Emperor bestowed upon him from 1787, faced recurrent financial difficulties during his last years; his pension was about the equivalent of the annual subscription for a box at the Burgtheater. It may be true that the leaders of Viennese taste were gradually edging towards the romantic idea of the musical 'genius'. But if that meant pouring extravagant praise upon the few, most artists, like today's would-be pop singers (or most wannabe film stars), slipped through a net containing notoriously large holes.

So Mozart was lucky. He went to seek his fame and fortune in a city that, for a variety of complex historical reasons, gave promise of both – at least, to the few. And it was in the Vienna of Joseph II that Mozart composed some of the immortal works of opera that have been revered across the world ever since, not to mention a succession of other works of genius. In that respect, certainly, the Vienna of the 1780s was indeed a golden age.

However, if the ladders reached high, the pitfalls were equally abundant, even for the fortunate ones the system had embraced. Mozart earned good money but seems to have managed it poorly. He and his wife Constanze were expected to attend court functions from time to time, and that meant maintaining an elaborate wardrobe, while the couple owned far more furniture than could fit comfortably into any of the many apartments in Vienna they moved into, even the biggest in the Domgasse. When Mozart heard that Salieri would grace a performance of *Die Zauberflöte* with his presence, the composer hired an expensive carriage to take him to and from the show. In addition, Constanze was often pregnant and in need of a succession of expensive cures. One way and another, Mozart got badly into debt in his final years; over a four-year period, he sent a score of increasingly desperate letters to his fellow Mason, the textile manufacturer Johann Michael Puchberg, begging for loans.* Some have suggested that Mozart's financial problems may have been exacerbated by illegal gambling in which he incurred debts of honour that could not be written down but that had to be paid at once.

Mozart's international fame was growing during his last years, but in Vienna itself his popularity and therefore his earning power were beginning to fade. He was no longer a novelty. In 1787, on the death of Gluck, Mozart finally received an official imperial appointment but on a considerably smaller salary than Gluck had received (800 florins per annum in contrast to Gluck's 2000). When *Don Giovanni* was first played in Vienna after its triumphant premiere in Prague, it was nothing like as ecstatically received. All this must be seen against a background of growing economic malaise, exacerbated by the ferocious demands of the Turkish wars. As concert subscriptions dried up and aristocratic establishments reduced or dismissed their house orchestras, the pool of unemployed and therefore economically insecure musicians

---

* It has been estimated that during those years Mozart earned something over 9000 gulden – far more than the 1000 or so gulden per annum that a normal middle-class family would have expected to live off in Vienna at the time – while Puchberg appears to have loaned him a further 1500.

seeking work became ever larger. In addition, in an era before the introduction of adequate copyright laws, when Mozart's compositions were performed outside his immediate circle he would normally receive no compensation.

When Mozart decided in his mid-twenties to quit his employment with the Archbishop of Salzburg and to settle in Vienna, therefore, he was embarking upon a highly precarious route. For he was stepping outside a time-honoured form of employment, secure but constricting, and – like the medieval knight throwing off the livery of his lord – entering the new, economically insecure world of the independent artist, an untested domain that we, with chilling accuracy, refer to as that of the freelance. 'There is no monarch in the world whom I should be more glad to serve than the Emperor [Joseph II],' Mozart wrote to his father from Vienna in 1782; 'but I refuse to beg for any post.' This was a bold statement, implying a more elevated view of the proper status of the artist than was held by most of the people he encountered during his years in the imperial capital. As late as 1798, half a dozen years after the death of Mozart and nearly a decade after the outbreak of the French Revolution, the following ad appeared in a Vienna newspaper:

> Wanted: A musician… who plays the piano and can sing well too, and is able to give lessons in both. This musician must also perform the duties of a *valet-de-chambre*.

Nothing more eloquently places the musician into his social stratum. The romanticization of the artist was still some way off in the future.

PART II

Revolution and Romanticism
c.1800–1860

CHAPTER 5

Napoleon and Beethoven

At times, Beethoven was something of a romantic liberal. 'Love liberty above all things,' the young man wrote in a friend's album a few years after the outbreak of the French Revolution. And he added: 'Never deny the truth, even at the foot of a throne!' A decade later, when Napoleon had himself crowned Emperor, Beethoven denounced his former hero furiously as being no more than an ordinary mortal who would probably go on to crush the rights of man underfoot and become a tyrant. Beethoven had planned to dedicate his new symphony to Bonaparte, but the angry composer famously defaced the title page and instead the work became known to posterity as the 'Heroic', or 'Eroica'.

Beethoven also knew that if he wanted butter on his bread it could best be provided by the educated elite, and that still meant the hereditary aristocracy. Once Beethoven had established himself in Vienna in the early 1790s, he soon found himself feted by the titled nobility who invited him to compose and perform chamber works in the elegance of their private palaces before elite audiences of at most a few score. 'I do not write for the masses,' expostulated the irritable composer in 1806 at the director of the theatre where his opera *Fidelio* was first performed. 'I write for the cultured!' Beethoven was not arguing about art; he was haggling about money. The management of the Theater an der Wien had agreed to share the takings with the composer, but his opera had not succeeded in attracting a sell-out audience. Beethoven had been begged to adapt the music in various ways to give the opera wider appeal, but he had refused. 'The cultured alone will not fill our theatre,' explained the director as calmly as he could. 'To make a profit we need the masses and since you have refused to make any concessions to them in your music you yourself are to blame for the low returns.' Then came the clincher: 'If we had paid Mozart the same share of the profits on his operas, he would have become a rich man.' At this, Beethoven demanded back his score and stormed out.

*

When Mozart quit the employ of Archbishop Colloredo and settled in
Vienna to work as a freelance, he was, as in so much else, ahead of his time.
There had been independent artists in the past (Handel, once he had had settled in London, lived mostly off a pension from the crown plus his earnings
from a series of separate commissions). But Mozart's move from Salzburg to
Vienna may be taken as emblematic of an historical shift. His early mentor,
'Papa' Haydn, had been content to spend almost all his long working life in
the employ of the Esterházy princes. Mozart's successors, such as Beethoven,
faced a new and more precarious existence as traditional social and economic
relationships came to be questioned and familiar hierarchies gave way, under
pressure from the French Revolution and Napoleonic wars, to a new world
of greater social mobility – downwards as well as upwards. Within a few
years of Mozart's death, much of the apparently immutably hierarchical
social and economic system he had seen as a boy had been overthrown. In
Paris, the little Austrian princess to whom he had played in the Schönbrunn
Palace had gone on to become the Queen of France and later been beheaded.
Soon, from Madrid to the gates of Moscow, the air reverberated with cries
for liberty and the earth with the thud of armies and their cannonry. Rulers
were ousted and their palaces and titles assumed by victorious foreign generals. Old wealth gave way to new or to none, food supplies were looted or cut,
and countless villages and villagers – and hundreds of thousands of soldiers
– were trampled into the mud.

Yet Napoleon might be said to have created as much as he destroyed.
Inspired by a vision of a modern, united Europe of rationally governed
nation states, he introduced political constitutions in territories he con-
quered, signed a Concordat with the papacy and abolished feudalism and
other antiquated social and economic systems. It was Napoleon's proud
boast that he would reward merit wherever he found it; in every soldier's
knapsack, it was said, lay a marshal's baton. He reformed the obsolete and
corrupt French judicial system, too, ordering a codification of the laws along
rational, Roman lines. The *Code Napoléon*, subsequently adopted in many
of the territories that French forces occupied, still provides the basis of the
legal system in parts of Europe as well as across the Atlantic in Louisiana.
And, as we will see, Napoleon had cultural ambitions too.

Artistic responses to the French Revolution and the wars that followed
were occasionally immediate and direct, covering the gamut from the official
and celebratory (great open-air musical *fêtes*, or Jacques-Louis David's
grandiose portraits of Napoleon) to the appalled (Goya's *Disasters of War*).
However, as events unfolded on a vast and almost apocalyptic scale, most
artists were as bewildered by them as everyone else and few felt driven to try
and transfer the enormity of what was going on around them into serious
aesthetic form. Thus the producers and consumers of opera in Napoleon's
own time did not expect to see theatrical portrayals of Robespierre, Marie

On 13 November 1805, Napoleon's troops occupied Vienna. Later in the month, the premiere of Beethoven's *Fidelio* was given before a depleted and largely indifferent audience, the most conspicuous members of which were French officers.

Antoinette, the Paris crowds or the *Armée de la République*. If the impact of external events on the operatic world was indirect, it was nevertheless profound as many creative artists felt impelled to inject an element of moral elevation into the works they produced: tales which (like the cowboy movies of a later age) portrayed dark derring-do finally defeated by the superior forces of virtue. By far the most famous and lasting opera to have been created during the period of the Revolutionary wars was written not in Paris but in a city occupied by French troops and, at the time of its premiere, by the Emperor himself: Vienna.

Fidelio is about an unswervingly devoted wife who, against all odds, manages to rescue her unjustly imprisoned husband. Many ideas came together in *Fidelio*. Originally named by Beethoven *Leonore* after its principal character, the opera celebrates the heroic ideal of married love (its subtitle) – something of an obsession with the agonizingly moralistic Beethoven whose extravagant romanticization of womanhood prevented him from finding real love in his own life and led him to ruin that of his poor sister-in-law.

If Beethoven's personal preoccupations inform some of the most elevated passages in the eventual score, the roots of *Fidelio* found earlier and deeper nourishment in French soil. By the time Beethoven settled in Vienna in 1792, Mozart was dead, as were the Emperor Joseph II and his brother and successor Leopold. All eyes were turned to France, where the *ancien régime* was being systematically destroyed. The liberated Bastille may have turned out to be largely devoid of political prisoners; but its symbolic downfall and the mass euphoria that followed unleashed a frenzy of popular rhetoric and action that left much of Europe agog and incredulous. For many imaginative youngsters of Beethoven's generation, the French banners proclaiming 'Liberty, Equality, Fraternity' provided an inspirational slogan. Even for those living under a relatively benign regime such as that of Britain, young artists like Wordsworth, Coleridge, Blake or Burns could hardly fail to find enticing some of the ideals newly ascendant across the Channel. Yet, as each new Revolutionary tide consumed the waves that had heralded it, doubts grew. Not only the aristocrats and crowned heads of Europe, but reflective conservatives such as Edmund Burke, warned of the dangerous consequences to the wider world of Revolution run wild.

The French Revolution was a *real* revolution; its progenitors wanted to undo the whole of previous history and start again with *L'An Un* – 'Year One'. The entire old order was under threat: at first in France, and potentially everywhere. In Austria, the traditional aristocracy on whom Mozart had depended so heavily was severely shaken by the cataclysmic events across Europe in the last years of the eighteenth century and the first decade of the nineteenth. Many of the princes who had patronized and paid the young Beethoven when his star first burst upon the scene ran scared as war with France and the accompanying inflation placed further strain upon their already depleted social and financial status.

For all this, the Vienna in which Beethoven composed *Fidelio* remained a proud, traditional, imperial city, in which a battered but time-honoured social hierarchy remained largely intact, in honour if not in wealth. The Austrian aristocracy continued to praise and pay their star composer and performer as they had done when he first arrived. Back in the 1790s, the Prince and Princess Lichnowsky had invited the young man to live in their palace as a guest, while as late as the winter of 1808–9, after Beethoven had broken with the Lichnowskys in the most ungracious manner and was considering leaving Vienna for good, we find Prince Lobkowitz, Prince Kinsky and Beethoven's erstwhile pupil the Archduke Rudolph clubbing together to offer him a pension for life if only he would stay in the capital. Even in adversity, Beethoven was shrewd at marketing himself and his talents, biting one hand, perhaps, but going on to lick another.

The generosity and forbearance of such people might strike us as extraordinarily indulgent towards someone who could be spectacularly sullen and ungrateful. Of course, they stood to benefit too; such was the celebrity of Beethoven that his benefactors gained reflected glory. Beethoven knew this and made good use of it. It was for the princes and the archdukes that Beethoven played and composed, they whose money and approbation he craved.

The symbiotic link between Beethoven and his aristocratic backers may help to explain why, for one whose output had already been so prolific, he came relatively late to opera. He had heard opera as a young man at the court of the Elector in Bonn and played viola in the opera orchestra. But Beethoven's primary skill was at the keyboard and it was as a piano virtuoso that he was feted throughout his first decade in Vienna. Opera and symphonic composition required a larger, more public (and more costly) ambience for their performance; these were not Beethoven's primary concern, nor that of his noble patrons. The vogue for Italian opera continued in Vienna, it is true, while the Schikaneder company continued to commission and perform German *Singspiel* in the Theater auf der Wieden. Such entertainments must, however, have seemed increasingly irrelevant, in Vienna as in many another anxious European capital, once the French began to carry the banner of Revolution abroad and found, in Napoleon, a genius capable of inspiring and leading them in this ambitious quest.

*

Napoleon was well aware that France had provided an artistic and intellectual benchmark for every court in eighteenth-century Europe, a paramountcy he was determined to revive, especially once he became emperor. 'No opera,' he pronounced in 1810, 'may be staged without my authorization.' Earlier, he had issued a series of decrees that reduced the number of theatres in the capital while attempting to raise the standards of those that remained. Napoleon was not especially knowledgeable about music ('What is this piece *Don Giovanni* that they want to do at the Opéra?' he is said to have asked in 1805), but he seems to have been genuinely fond of Italian opera, a predilection that may have derived in part from his Corsican roots. Whatever his personal tastes, Napoleon understood the value music and opera could provide for his regime. Whenever he was back in Paris and there was an event he wished to mark, he would make a point of visiting the Opéra. It was here that he celebrated his military victories, formally presented his second wife Marie-Louise, and celebrated the birth of his son. During his reign, Napoleon attended the opera more often than any other nineteenth-century French head of state.

Part of the reason was that Napoleon, the legatee of an egalitarian revolution that vowed to overthrow all that preceded it, was careful to create, or re-create, symbols of continuity with a hierarchical past. The Revolution may have abolished the *ancien régime* and dispossessed its aristocracy. But Napoleon assiduously set about creating a new aristocracy, bestowing over 3000 titles of nobility by the end of his reign, mostly to people who had never held titles before, while the very language and regalia of the Napoleonic Empire were calculated to evoke that of Ancient Rome. The monarchy is dead; long live the empire.

In such a climate, opera provided a perfect opportunity for appropriate display, a culturally approved venue in which the Emperor could make highly publicized appearances before a large but controlled crowd of admiring spectators. Back in 1800, when word had spread of an alleged assassination attempt, it was to the opera that Napoleon hastened in order to show *le tout Paris* that their First Consul was alive and well. The opera represented hierarchy, power, continuity, stability, affluence. Napoleon knew this; so did everyone else. When he attended the opera, often arriving in mid-evening and in mid-act, the audience – and even the artists – would applaud. The cheering and clapping were evidently spontaneous enough. But the plaudits were doubtless reinforced by a semi-circle of boxes right across the theatrical horseshoe containing top governmental officials, among them highly visible representatives of the army and police.

The audience would have been markedly different from that of the Old Regime, not only in its composition but also in its behaviour. The social and economic power of the hereditary aristocracy, if not eliminated, was by now largely replaced by that of the new, post-Revolutionary meritocracy, the senior civil servants, bankers, merchants and members of the liberal professions who stood to benefit under Napoleon and the subsequent Restoration of the monarchy. These were the people who, alongside a few beached whales from an earlier era, paid for boxes at the opera – not, significantly, on an annual or lifelong basis as their aristocratic predecessors had tended to do, but more often for a particular performance. This meant that, unlike in the past when the same powerful and wealthy elite would congregate night after night, the precise composition of audiences began to vary considerably from one week to the next so that the house would contain people new to each other and, often, to the entire experience of attending the opera. One consequence was that a certain distance, or formality, began to creep into the ways audience members regarded one another, their behaviour becoming somewhat more reserved. They might interrupt a performance to cheer the Emperor; but only after checking that everyone else was doing the same thing.

Another characteristic of the new audience noted by long-term visitors was its increased attentiveness to what was actually being acted and sung on stage, if only out of good manners. A publication from 1802 advised readers that it was impolite to talk, yawn or blow one's nose loudly while music was being played, while an etiquette book of 1819 noted how audience members would call out to others to be quiet and not to interrupt the show. From our twenty-first-century perspective, we may look back and (a little patronizingly) admire these new opera goers for their greater concentration on the performance. But any increase in theatrical decorum was probably also symptomatic of a new audience slightly abashed by its greater access to the plush playgrounds of the former elites it had displaced. Such audiences were not likely to prove politically combustible.

For all these reasons, Napoleon was keen for music and opera to flourish in France, especially after his reorganization of the theatres. Opera under the empire was, indeed, remarkably well financed and patronized when one takes into account the draining effect of almost constant war. Paris played host to some of the best-known composers of the period: not just Frenchmen but also many Italians who had flocked to the capital in the hope of catching the Emperor's eye, or ear. Napoleon was particularly partial to the singing of the castrato Crescentini, whose rendition of Zingarelli's Romeo is said to have reduced him to tears; his admiration went so far as to award Crescentini the Lombardy Cross of the Crown of Iron, normally presented for valour on the battlefield. One of Napoleon's favourite composers was the ageing Paisiello, whom he commissioned to write a mass for his coronation as Emperor in 1804, while Spontini's masterpiece, *La vestale*, received its premiere (on the recommendation of the Empress Josephine, it was said) in Paris in 1807.

*

Of all the Italian musicians in Paris, the most important (not in his particular case a Napoleonic favourite), a man who was to dominate much of French musical life as composer and pedagogue for half a century, was Luigi Cherubini. Cherubini was one of the very few contemporary composers whom Beethoven came to regard with the greatest respect. He made a major impact in Vienna in 1802 when Schikaneder, whose company had just moved to the Theater an der Wien, decided to put on his opera *Lodoïska*. It was a triumph – virtually Schikaneder's first since *Die Zauberflöte* more than a decade earlier. In due course, Cherubini was commissioned to write a new opera especially for Vienna. His collaborator was to be the poet (and secretary of the court theatres) Joseph von Sonnleithner, the man best known to history as the librettist of Beethoven's *Leonore*.

By now the environment in which Beethoven lived and worked had shifted. The strings which had earlier bound the young man so closely to his aristocratic Viennese patrons continued to loosen, musical performance moving more and more into publicly accessible theatres and concert halls. Here, members of the nobility might find themselves mingling with the untitled representatives of the new bourgeoisie. Culturally, meanwhile, Vienna came increasingly under the spell of France, the dominant new European power. French opera enjoyed a new vogue, and the star to follow was Cherubini. Shortly after the production of *Lodoïska*, Schikaneder approached Beethoven with the text of an opera he might write, an idea the composer took up for a while with sporadic enthusiasm. But while Schikaneder returned to *Singspiel* and pantomime performances, Beethoven's imagination was ignited by a French text on which (he wrote in early 1804) he had already begun to work.

The text was a play entitled *Léonore, ou L'amour conjugal*. It was written in 1794 at the height of the French Revolution and supposedly based on

The first proprietor of the Theater an der Wien (which opened in 1801) was Emanuel Schikaneder who put on Mozart's *Die Zauberflöte* to packed audiences. In 1805, to a markedly cooler reception, Beethoven's *Fidelio* had its premiere in this theatre.

a real-life episode in Touraine. In Beethoven's opera, Leonore, the steadfast wife of a political prisoner, disguises herself as a young man, goes to work for the jailer and manages to rescue her husband, Florestan, just before he is to be put to death by the wicked prison governor. The play had already been used as the basis of an opera several times before Beethoven came to it, and was one of many stories, especially popular in the years following the storming of the Bastille, about unjust imprisonment and heroic rescue. Such themes were popular well before the French Revolution (earlier 'rescue' operas include Mozart's *Entführung* of 1782 and Grétry's *Richard Coeur-de-Lion* a couple of years later). But the immense symbolic impact of the taking of the Bastille etched itself into the creative imagination and a number of operas were written in the 1790s and the early new century that emphasized not just the literal rescue from prison but, more broadly, the moral confrontation between tyranny and freedom and the capacity of the properly inspired individual to right self-evident wrongs. These are the themes Beethoven was at pains to highlight as he completed his work in the first half of 1805.

While Beethoven was completing *Leonore* (or *Fidelio*, as the theatre entitled the piece) and awaiting its first performance, the *Grande Armeé* of Napoleon was massing against the Austro-Russian alliance arrayed against him. By the autumn, Napoleon set his sights on Vienna, which duly came under military threat for the first time since the Ottoman siege of 1683.

On 13 November 1805 (three weeks after Trafalgar), French forces occupied Vienna – followed by the Emperor, who installed himself in the Schönbrunn, the very palace in which the infant Mozart had performed to the Empress Maria Theresa nearly half a century before. As the forces of Napoleon were approaching Vienna, many of Beethoven's most loyal backers fled, their great houses subsequently occupied by French generals; others stayed, hoping to retrieve what little status and dignity they could under trying circumstances. The approach of the French was a catastrophe for Prince Lobkowitz, for example, a man whose friendship and finance had seen Beethoven through countless crises and to whom Beethoven dedicated the 'Eroica' Symphony after his disillusionment with Napoleon. Lobkowitz left Vienna shortly before the French arrived, his magnificent palace soon commandeered by General Hulin.

Thus, it was under the dark cloud of French occupation – and only a fortnight before Napoleon's crushing victory over the Austrians and their allies at the decisive battle of Austerlitz – that Beethoven's opera had its premiere. *Fidelio* was presented in the Theater an der Wien on 20 November 1805 before a depleted and largely indifferent audience, the most conspicuous members of which were French officers.

The opera received little more than muted praise. Part of this can be attributed to the political climate in the city; few in Vienna, Austrian or French, would have had much stomach for theatrical entertainment. And the piece was undoubtedly difficult to absorb. The rehearsal period, in the composer's presence, had been quite fraught at times. Beethoven had written a difficult, florid aria for the 'baddie', the prison governor. The bass Sebastian Mayer, singing the part, found passages of the aria difficult and sensed he was not being helped by a recalcitrant orchestra. Mayer was married to Josepha Weber, a sister of Mozart's widow Constanze (and Mozart's first Queen of the Night in *Zauberflöte*). At rehearsal, Mayer struggled with his aria, snorted with rage and finally hurled at Beethoven the words: 'My brother-in-law would never have written such damned nonsense!'

After its tepid reception, Beethoven withdrew the piece but consented to spend an evening at Prince Lichnowsky's palace with a small group of friends in order to go through the opera to see how it might be improved. Years later, one of those present, the young tenor Josef August Röckel who was about to take over the role of Florestan, the prisoner who is rescued, wrote a vivid description of what took place that night. Beethoven was not a man to take criticism easily. 'Not a single note,' the composer shouted when he was implored to make cuts and adjustments. Evidently about to storm out, he was only persuaded to sit down again when the Princess Lichnowsky 'put her hands, folded as if in prayer, on the precious score, looked up with indescribable mildness at the furious genius and, lo – his rage melted under her look, and he sat down again, resigned'.

The evening dragged on until after midnight, Beethoven still adamant that nothing in the score would be altered. Again, it was the Princess who saved the situation. She looked at Beethoven with a 'beseeching look' and asked: 'Must your great work remain unappreciated and disparaged?' 'It is sufficiently rewarded by your approval, gracious Princess,' Beethoven responded and made to go. Suddenly, reports Röckel:

> it was if a stronger, more commanding spirit had possessed this delicate lady; almost kneeling and putting her arms round him, she spoke passionately: 'Beethoven! No – your greatest work, and you yourself, must not fail like this! God will not have it so, who has placed the sounds of purest beauty in your soul – the spirit of your mother will not have it so, who at this moment begs and admonishes you through me – Beethoven, it must be! Give in! Do it in memory of your mother! Do it for me, for your only, your truest friend!'
>
> The great man with the Olympian head stood long before the angelic admirer of his muse; then, as his hand brushed back a lock of hair from his face, it was as if a beautiful dream had entered his soul, and he cried, his eyes turned heavenward full of emotion, 'I will do it – do it all; for you – for my mother!' And at the same time he respectfully raised up the Princess towards him and gave his hand to the Prince, as if in a pledge. And we all stood around them deeply moved, for we all even then felt the significance of this great moment.

At last, the hosts and their guests could relax and enter the dining room. Beethoven, still brooding, ate little. Röckel, sitting opposite him, wolfed down the food that was placed in front of him, a fact that Beethoven commented on in his surly way. 'I was so hungry,' Röckel replied nervously, 'that I paid no attention to what I ate.' Beethoven responded with a weak joke, saying that that must be why Röckel played the starving prisoner so naturalistically earlier in the evening. You must always be sure to starve yourself before a performance, he added, and success will be guaranteed. As Röckel pointed out tactfully in his account, 'everyone laughed and seemed to enjoy the fact that Beethoven was joking again more than the joke itself.'

Thanks to the combined efforts of the Prince and Princess and their guests, Beethoven was eventually prevailed upon to make various amendments and the partly revised version was given (with Röckel as Florestan) the following spring. This time, the reception was better, but not sufficiently so to guarantee more than a couple of performances or much revenue for the composer (it was at this time that Beethoven stormed that he did not write for the masses). Beethoven demanded his score back and it is one of the minor miracles of musical history that, nearly a decade later, this obstinate

Beethoven was shrewdly aware of the importance of his wealthy aristocratic backers. His *Pathétique* Sonata of 1799 was dedicated to Prince Lichnowsky.

man was prevailed upon to dig it out and make further revisions to produce the *Fidelio* the world has come to love.

During the intervening years, Beethoven made no attempt to write other operas. It was a form to which he was probably not temperamentally suited. In any case, once Austria had become fully involved in the war against France (Napoleon reoccupied Vienna in 1809), Vienna would hardly have provided the ideal environment for the production of anything so complex and costly, even for a composer of more equable mien. Everyone had to come to terms with the fact of the continuing wars, and Beethoven, his deafness obviously incurable and worsening, found his inner demons increasingly difficult to control. Money was always a problem. 'I wish that I were above having to wrangle and bargain with publishers,' he had once said, 'and could find one who would decide once and for all to pay me an annual salary, in return for which he would have the right to publish everything I compose, and I shouldn't be slothful in composing.'

It was not until the cumulative campaigns against the French in Spain and Russia, and the mammoth 'Battle of the Nations' in Leipzig in 1813, that it seemed the apparently invincible Napoleon could after all be defeated. Beethoven, ever the grumpy revolutionary who nonetheless knew where power and money lay, accepted a commission to mark the British success in the Peninsular Campaign incorporating variations on the British national anthem, 'God Save the King'. The result, *Wellington's Victory*, popularly known as the 'Battle' Symphony, is easily despised as an inferior *pièce d'occasion* written on autopilot in order to obtain for its composer a little short-term fame and money. But the first performance in December 1813 was ecstatically received and it was given repeat performances (in the Redoutensaal in the Imperial palace) shortly afterwards. As Allied troops entered Paris and the final defeat of the French loomed, Beethoven found his reputation soaring atop a tidal wave of optimistic triumphalism.

Buoyed by his success, Beethoven allowed himself to be persuaded to look once again at his prison opera. He made a number of changes and adaptations, significantly adding a final scene in which the faithful Leonore and her liberated husband, emerging from the dungeon into bright daylight, are lauded by an honest and honourable Minister of State and cheered by the welcoming crowds for their courageous defiance of political tyranny. The overall effect of Beethoven's changes was to broaden its focus. Where the original version was a tale of personal courage and tenacity, *Fidelio*, as produced in Vienna in May 1814 in the wake of Napoleon's arrival on Elba became a universal celebration of freedom and the downfall of tyranny.

That autumn, the leaders of the victorious powers re-gathered in Vienna for the Congress at which they would plan the shape of post-war Europe. Before they got down to serious business, they were given a night at the theatre. Nothing but the best would do for the assembled emperors, monarchs, princes and prime ministers. They were taken to a performance of *Fidelio*. A century and a half later, another gathering of pan-European peacemakers would adopt a melody by the curmudgeonly composer of *Fidelio* as their official anthem.

CHAPTER 6

After Napoleon: Opera as Politics, Art and Business

> Standing once more in the theatre, I found again that sense of awe and ecstasy. If you search to the farthest frontiers of Europe, you will find nothing to rival it… This mighty edifice, rebuilt in the space of three hundred days, is nothing less than a *coup d'état*: it binds the people in fealty and homage to their sovereign far more effectively than any *Constitution*… From prince to waiter, all Naples is drunk with joy.

Stendhal, the French novelist and opera lover, was typically exuberant in his enthusiasm for the San Carlo opera house in Naples, rebuilt in time for King Ferdinand's birthday in January 1817. The auditorium, wrote Stendhal, was 'a symphony in silver and gold, while the boxes are blue as the deep sky'. The rapid rebuild was undoubtedly a cause of widespread celebration. When the old theatre burned down, Neapolitan memories of the recent French occupation were still fresh and some proclaimed noisily (on no evidence) that the conflagration must have been the work of Jacobins. The Bourbon monarchy, reinstated as part of the post-Napoleonic settlement, gave promise of stability and Ferdinand himself was an attractive king. 'I can conceive of nothing more majestic,' rhapsodized Stendhal, 'than the sumptuous royal box, which is set over the central doorway, borne aloft by two huge golden palm-trees, each of natural size.'

The Neapolitan Bourbons were not the only beneficiaries of the final defeat of France. Throughout much of Europe, traditional monarchies and empires were reinforced or reinstated by the Congress of Vienna, dangerous traces of political freedom repealed and already powerful states further strengthened. Bonapartism had been an unmitigated disaster and nothing like it must ever be permitted again, agreed the victors as they resolutely tried to reimpose the past upon an uncertain future. Yet to many who felt they had enjoyed a taste of *liberté*, the Vienna settlement provoked resentment and anger. Stendhal may have been right in reporting the popularity of the restored monarch when the opera house reopened. Yet within three years the King of Naples was having to face down a revolt whose principal demand was the installation of a constitution – a pattern repeated with variations in a dozen or more European capitals over the next thirty years.

If it was difficult and dangerous to express overtly subversive political views, some sought covert ways of doing so. Suppose, for example, one were to dress up the message in the mantle of art and place it not in the present but in the past? When the chorus in Verdi's early opera *Nabucco* sang elegiacally of their *patria perduta*, their lost homeland, they were garbed not as nineteenth-century patriots but biblical Hebrews, while it was the medieval Scots in his *Macbeth* who mourned their *patria oppressa*. Whether or not such operatic set-pieces were always intended to be (or always received as) coded political messages is a question to which we will return. What is striking is how many operas of the post-Napoleonic decades were placed in the historical past. Not, be it noted, the very recent past, nor that of classical myth and antiquity. More often a colourful, imaginative re-creation of medieval chivalry and Renaissance derring-do: love and treason in Roman Gaul, the bravery of William Tell or the Neapolitan revolutionary Masaniello, the heroism and destructiveness of the Crusades, the Massacre of St Bartholomew's Day and the emotional turmoil besetting England's Ann Boleyn and Elizabeth I. 'Historicism' was not a monopoly of opera (or of political dissent): witness the huge popularity of the historically based fiction of Walter Scott and Victor Hugo, while architects embraced classical and 'neo-Gothic'

An accurate portrayal of the past was not a primary concern of the Romantic Age. Windsor Castle takes on a neo-Gothic look in this scene from Donizetti's 1830 Tudor-era opera *Anna Bolena*, designed for Milan's Teatro Carcano by Alessandro Sanquirico.

styles, poets and painters rediscovered Arthurian chivalry and the theatre saw a growing vogue for 'historical' sets and costumes. It was a romanticized past people sought, not a real one. Nobody went to Wagner's *Rienzi* or Bellini's *I puritani* in the expectation of seeing an historically accurate portrayal of medieval Rome or the English Civil Wars. The attraction, rather, was the heightened emotions suggested by the exotic setting as librettists and composers placed their princes and priests, their saints and sinners, their warriors and their feisty womenfolk in extreme situations demanding extreme responses.

This newly unbridled emotional expressiveness came to be reflected not only in the stories of popular operas in post-Napoleonic Europe but also in their musical treatment. The drums and the wind and brass bands that had accompanied Napoleon's armies also criss-crossed Europe via its operatic stages and continued to do so long after his defeat and demise. Berlioz and Verdi, for example, recruited the military band as a means of turning up the emotional heat in their music; the offstage *banda*, indeed, became something of a cliché of many early Verdi scores, while Berlioz's massive 'Hungarian March' became one of his most famous compositions. Gradually, the operatic orchestra became larger and more sonorous: trombones became standard features, while the percussion department would often make all sorts of sounds unimaginable to Haydn or Mozart. Anything that could add dramatic effect became acceptable: Verdi used a wordless male chorus in *Rigoletto* to suggest the ominous wind preceding a storm, while the unconstrained life of a gypsy encampment in his *Il trovatore* was evoked by the rhythmic beating of an anvil. Choruses became larger as composers elevated the 'people' into a principal player in their dramas, a tendency particularly marked in Paris – partly no doubt in homage to the memory of the Revolution but also because the Opéra provided composers with large professional resources on which to call. The chorus at the Opéra had fifty-nine singers in 1831, rising to eighty-two by 1836 (the year Meyerbeer's massive *Les Huguenots* had its premiere). However, the looming presence on stage of the 'people' was not confined to French *grand opéra* and there are plenty of communal carousings, prayers, dirges, oath-swearings, celebrations, processions and uprisings, too, in operas by Rossini, Weber, Wagner, Bellini and Verdi (including Verdi's Hebrew slaves in *Nabucco* and Bellini's warlike Gauls in *Norma*).

Furthermore, large-scale emotions demanded appropriately striking productions. Stage design took on new life as imaginative artists such as Alessandro Sanquirico in Milan and Pierre-Luc-Charles Ciceri in Paris strove to re-create visually the spirit and scale of the romantic dramas their designs would showcase. Sets would typically reveal a richly embellished foreground featuring the evocative architecture of an earlier age, opening out onto a distant landscape bordered perhaps by a moving diorama instead of a static backcloth. Stage designers were further aided by the replacement of candle light by gas.

This produced a steadier, brighter form of lighting and offered the opportunity of far greater contrasts of light and shade on stage (and, once pilot lights were introduced, the ability to extinguish or relight any particular batten). Gas was scarcely less dangerous than candles and there seems to have been no reduction in the number of theatre fires. But these hazards were, perhaps, compensated by the opportunities gas provided for the creation of not only vivid scenery but also romantic costumes and spectacular stage effects. One of the appeals of Auber's *La Muette de Portici*, first produced in Paris in 1828, was the fact that, at the culmination of the opera, its (silent) heroine Fenella leaps into the smoking abyss of an erupting Mount Vesuvius.

With larger shows, bigger theatres and heavier orchestration, moreover, came a vogue for bigger voices. In particular, the 'dramatic' tenor voice as we would recognize it became increasingly prominent, especially in the kind of heroic, romantic parts that in earlier times might have been written for castrati. Adolphe Nourrit was one of the great singer-actors of his day and a sequence of powerful tenor roles was composed for him by Rossini, Auber, Halévy and Meyerbeer. Meanwhile, audiences accustomed to the falsetto tones and head voice of earlier times thrilled to the sound of tenors such as Donzelli and Duprez who were capable of delivering high notes with a new kind of baritonal muscularity.*

With the heightened emotions on stage, some of the artists who embodied them came to be regarded as being as important as the art. 'When Madame Pasta sings,' gushed Stendhal, words were inadequate to describe the 'visions of celestial beauty which spread before us in dazzling glory' or the 'ineffable mysteries' and 'vistas unknown, unfathomable, deep-hidden in the recesses of the human heart' which her art revealed. Outstanding singers had long attracted an ardent following, especially those (such as Farinelli) capable of scaling the highest peaks of pitch and passion. What was new was the way this romantic reverence also came to be applied to other kinds of musician, notably composers, and indeed – especially in the German-speaking world – to music itself.

The great transitional figure was Beethoven, the archetypal Romantic genius: the deaf musician, the wounded giant, Prometheus struggling to loosen his chains, a wild, brooding, unhappy man brimming over with almost uncontrollable emotions which he struggled to mould into artistic form by dint of almost superhuman willpower. Like other aspects of romanticism, the idea of the artist as god-like genius had roots deep in the eighteenth century. But it flowered in the early decades of the nineteenth, and the young Beethoven himself was not averse to playing a part in his own gradual adoption into the new pantheon. At his funeral in 1827, the narration written by the poet Grillparzer famously evoked not God but Art. Beethoven (like Christ) had been wounded by the thorns of life, said Grillparzer. Where had he sought

---

* Rossini, however, remarked that Duprez's chest-tone high C in *Guillaume Tell* sounded like 'the squawk of a capon whose throat is being cut'.

A huge crowd assembled at Beethoven's funeral in 1827 at which Art – not God – took pride of place in the eulogy penned by the poet and dramatist Franz Grillparzer.

refuge? '[I]n thine arms, O thou glorious sister and peer of the Good and the True, thou balm of wounded hearts, heaven-born Art!'

In due course, music came to be elevated to a status akin to that of religion and the great musician to that of a god or high priest. When Liszt played the piano (or Paganini the violin), audiences swooned and true believers craved and collected relics of such occasions. Liszt, wrote George Eliot in *Daniel Deronda*, was 'understood to be adored by ladies of all European countries with the exception of Lapland'. Balanced critics, such as Friedrich Wieck (father of Schumann's wife Clara) wrote that Liszt 'excites terror and astonishment' and that his 'passion knows no bounds', while an English admirer, Henry Reeves, after seeing Liszt perform in Paris in 1835, wrote: 'I saw Liszt's countenance assume that agony of expression, mingled with radiant smiles of joy, which I never saw in any other human face except in the paintings of Our Saviour.' In *Daniel Deronda*, Eliot created her own neo-Lisztian figure in the shape of the magnetic and arrogant Jewish musician Herr Klesmer (the Hebrew for 'melody'). Klesmer, she said in a burst of almost Germanic abstraction, was one whom nature had made generously and had then 'added music as a dominant power… finding expression for itself not only in the highest finish of execution, but in that fervour of creative work and theoretic belief which pierces the whole future of a life with the light of congruous, devoted purpose'. The romantic apotheosis of the supremely gifted musician recurred throughout the century and probably reached its acme with Wagner, who aimed to redeem Mankind by his art and to have it performed in what amounted to a temple built for the purpose.

For all his overarching aspiration, however, Wagner saw his work as lying in direct succession to that of such quintessentially romantic German figures as Beethoven and Carl Maria von Weber, both of whom he revered. In the immediate aftermath of the Napoleonic wars, one of the most popular and influential German operas was Weber's *Der Freischütz*, first performed in Berlin in 1821. It is set in the wake of another protracted conflict (the Thirty Years War) and the curtain goes up on a crowd of happy, ordinary folk relishing the long-awaited return of a kind of normality, a celebration of what audiences immediately recognized as the traditions, values, songs and dances – and 'spirit' – of the German people. By the 1820s, the old universalism proclaimed by the *Grande Armée* of the French Revolution retained little appeal anywhere in Europe. Much better to cultivate your own garden, that of your own people, your own folk, your own nation.

*

The roots of cultural nationalism lie deep in eighteenth-century history. Mozart thought of himself as culturally 'German' and his Emperor, Joseph II, tried to establish a 'German' national theatre. Neither envisaged a German state. The political nationalism that became so widespread in the nineteenth century was a separate phenomenon. But in post-Napoleonic Europe, a shaky sense of political pride was often reinforced by ballast provided by the arts and culture. In Russia, for example, which had so nearly succumbed to French invasion, the final defeat of Napoleon signalled a profound sense of relief, of regaining one's homeland, of patriotic pride as Russians gradually started to look back once more to time-honoured national traditions, Russian church music, Russian folktales. Pushkin hymned Russian heroes and the Russian soul in his poetry while the composer Glinka created operas based on Russian history (*A Life for the Tsar*) and Russian folklore (*Ruslan and Ludmilla*). Meanwhile, the ethnographer and folklorist Afanasiev began the laborious job of noting down the tales he heard on his travels in the hope of publishing them – much as the Brothers Grimm had done in Germany. In Vienna, the capital of the most multicultural of European empires, Chancellor Metternich was more concerned with maintaining political control over the far-flung Habsburg lands than whether Italians, Croats, Czechs, Hungarians or Poles were dancing their traditional dances or speaking or singing in their local languages. From the perspective of Vienna, Austrian Italy doubtless looked like some kind of political unity, at least on the map. But on the ground, regional and local differences abounded. If a young Parmigiano like Verdi had wanted to visit his future librettist, the Venetian Francesco Piave, he would have needed a passport and would have had to cross a series of customs barriers, while an ordinary peasant from Parma or Lombardy would have found the dialect of someone from the Veneto (let alone a Neapolitan) almost incomprehensible.

Language became an increasingly resonant issue as Italian intellectuals and aesthetes, seeking the outlines of a genuinely national identity, argued about which regional dialect was the most 'correct' form to speak and write, the consensus being that it was Tuscan, the language of Italy's greatest poet, Dante. In 1827, the Milanese writer Alessandro Manzoni published his novel *I promessi sposi* (*The Betrothed*), a wonderful and wittily told yarn, set in the seventeenth century on the borders of the Duchy of Milan and the Venetian Republic, about a young couple, Renzo and Lucia, who become separated, go through every imaginable trial and hardship, and are brought together again in the final pages. The novel has many fine qualities, but one of its principal claims to historical importance is that its author laboriously rewrote the work in the Tuscan idiom, its final publication in 1840 providing one of the landmarks in the quest for a sense of *italianità* that marked so many of the cultural strivings of the middle decades of the century.

While Manzoni was wrestling with the fate of Renzo and Lucia, the Czech language, too, was receiving renewed attention and becoming a newly powerful vehicle of literary and intellectual discourse. The first history of the Czech people was written (initially in German, then published in Czech) by the Moravian historian František Palacký, while the funeral in 1847 of Josef Jungmann, the compiler of the first Czech dictionary, provided the opportunity for a huge public demonstration of grief. In Prague's Estates Theatre, where Czech-language drama could only be performed on Sundays and holidays, people flocked to hear the latest works of the playwright J. K. Tyl. Tyl's comedy *Fidlovačka*, set to music by the Czech composer František Škroup, was premiered at the Estates Theatre in 1834; it was in this opera that the patriotic air 'Where is My Homeland?' first appeared, later to be adopted as the Czech national anthem.

Music became a particularly potent embodiment of aspirant national culture. In Hungary, the young composer and conductor Ferenc Erkel was engaged in 1838 by the newly formed Hungarian National Theatre and went on to compose a succession of operas celebrating the legendary heroes of Magyar history, notably *Hunyadi László*, first performed in 1844. The Polish composer Stanisław Moniuszko infused his opera *Halka* with the rhythms of traditional Polish dances while, in exile from a homeland divided among the surrounding empires and therefore politically nonexistent, the poet Adam Mickiewicz and the pianist and composer Frederic Chopin kept alive the suppressed cultural aspirations of the Polish people. As the operas of Verdi, with their rousing choruses, began to appear in Milan, Venice, Florence, Bologna, Rome and Naples, they came to provide one of the few shared experiences that could be enjoyed by Italians across the entire peninsula – a vital link between Italy being merely (in Metternich's dismissive phrase) a 'geographical expression' and its eventual unity and statehood.

None of which is to suggest that such artists and intellectuals were necessarily political revolutionaries. Verdi's opera *Nabucco* about the Hebrew slaves was dedicated (as was his next work) to a Habsburg duchess, while Palacký was bitterly criticized by more radical Czech patriots for his refusal to advocate the dismantlement of the Habsburg empire. As for young patriots such as Hugo, Wagner or Glinka, they could hardly be described as narrow nationalists. Yet all – like Manzoni, Škroup and Erkel – created works that strove to embody the cultural aspirations of their respective 'nations'. It was in memory of Manzoni ('our saint') that Verdi later composed his *Requiem*.

It may seem strange to modern eyes to couple liberalism and nationalism. Nowadays, 'liberal' thinking usually embraces a considerable degree of *inter*nationalism, of transcending national boundaries, while passionate 'nationalists' are more inclined to advocate walls of exclusion – of goods, services and unwanted people. But to Verdi or Palacký and many another like them, nationalism did not have to be destructive or exclusionary. Their aspiration, rather, was for a form of government in which reasonable Italians (that is, moderate-minded constitutionalists) governed Italians, reasonable Czechs governed Czechs and so forth, rather than distant Austrians. By the later 1840s, Verdi was preoccupied with his operatic commissions and probably did not have a carefully formulated political position other than a generalized belief in the ultimate goal of a constitutionally governed united Italy; Palacký, while keen to throw off the yoke of German culture, advocated nothing more politically radical than a kind of multinational federation.

Then, in 1848, revolution sprouted across much of the Continent. Everywhere, it seemed, republicans, nationalists and liberals rose up against unrepresentative and often repressive regimes. The by now atrophied regime of Louis Philippe was overthrown in Paris as was that of Metternich in Vienna. In Frankfurt, a collection of idealistic, would-be parliamentarians met to lay the foundations of a liberal, united Germany while an independent republic was declared in Hungary. South of the Alps, Austrian rule came under fierce pressure under the inspiration of the republican leader Giuseppe Mazzini. Venice broke loose and was declared once more to be a free, independent republic. Most dramatically of all, the citizenry of Milan managed against all odds to oust their Austrian masters during the course of five delirious days (the *Cinque Giornate*) in March. Verdi, who had been working in Paris, came rushing back to Milan to exult in the news, writing to his librettist, Piave (who was now a 'Citizen of the Venetian Republic'):

> The hour of liberation is here; be sure of that. The people want it: and when the people want it, there is no absolute power that can resist...
> Yes, yes, a few years more, perhaps a few months, and Italy will be free, united, and republican...

Piave had been corresponding with Verdi about music, but for the moment the ecstatic composer would have none of it:

> What has got into you? Do you think that I want to bother myself now with notes, with sounds? There cannot be any music welcome to Italian ears in 1848 except the music of cannon!

By the end of the year, Verdi had completed an overtly nationalistic new opera, *La battaglia di Legnano*, that was produced in republican Rome (the Pope having fled) and which opens with a chorus proclaiming 'Viva Italia!'

Alas, for the visionaries of 1848, few of their dreams were to last as the old regimes returned and reinforced their rule. The following year, the Pope was reinstated in the Vatican while the Austrians reasserted themselves in Milan and eventually Venice. In Dresden, the authorities crushed a revolution which had demanded a liberal constitution and whose vociferous supporters had included Richard Wagner and his friend the architect Gottfried Semper, both of whom were forced to flee. Wagner, with the active help of Liszt, went initially to Weimar and thence, with false papers, via Paris, to Switzerland. To Verdi as he resumed work as a composer, and to Wagner as he settled down in Zurich (where he wrote more prose than music), the year of revolutions had provided an excess of both expectation and disappointment. Better not to harbour unrealistic hopes for the future. To those who had witnessed and participated in the uprisings and been uplifted by them, the 1848 revolutions were not so much a portent for the future as the product and culmination of previous decades of uneasy discontent.

*

During the 1848–9 revolutions, the Pope was forced into exile and Rome declared a Republic. Verdi's contribution to this brief political triumph was an opera about a twelfth-century Italian victory against the Holy Roman Empire, *La battaglia di Legnano*.

It is tempting to see opera during these decades as having been a form of sur-
rogate political opposition, a camouflage for incendiary political sentiments,
its composers, librettists, audiences and impresarios seeking to share coded
political messages. Any Italian listening to the patriotic choruses Verdi planted
into one opera after another in the 1840s could hardly fail to have been
stirred. 'You have the world; leave Italy to me!' sings the defending Roman
general, as he tries to keep at bay the invading Huns in Verdi's 1846 opera
Attila.

Nor was it just in Italy that opera donned the livery of political aspiration.
Auber's *La Muette de Portici* was an emotionally supercharged spectacular set
in Naples at the time of the 1647 revolution led by the local fisherman
Masaniello against the Spanish Viceroy. It was an overwhelming success when
produced in Paris in 1828. A couple of years later, while a flurry of real revolutions swept through parts of Europe, *La Muette* was due to be produced at
the Théâtre de la Monnaie in Brussels, a city that, while still part of the
Netherlands, was at the time much exercised with talk of insurrection.
Popular mythology has it that a performance of *La Muette* in August 1830
triggered a spontaneous revolt that led to Belgian independence. Recent
research has modified the picture somewhat. But the emotions aroused by
the opera undoubtedly provided a powerful tributary that flowed directly into
what proved to be an irreversible current.

At times of political repression,
opera sometimes provided a
rare opportunity for opposition.
In Brussels in 1830, the emotions
aroused by an opera about a
seventeenth-century revolution
overflowed into the irreversible
current that led to Belgian
independence.

The idea that opera functioned as a coded form of political subversion would seem to be reinforced by the censorship it often had to confront, especially in Italy. Verdi, for example, recurrently ran into difficulties with the censors. And it is true that he (far more than Rossini or Bellini, for example) had an active interest in politics and was fired by the idea of a liberal, united Italy as a young man. However, it is important to separate fact from mythology. Verdi's encounters with the censors were much more strenuous after 1848 than before, and during those earlier years it was more often the religious than the political content of his operas that caused offence. Thus his early work *I Lombardi*, a celebration of *italianità* set in Crusading times, included a scene in which the chorus cries out 'Guerra! Guerra!' in response to a feverish proclamation from our hero that 'The Holy Land will be ours!' But what exercised the Cardinal Archbishop of Milan was a scene in which a converted heathen becomes baptized, and it was only after an 'Ave Maria' became a 'Salve Maria' that the work was allowed to be shown. Furthermore, the nature of the censorship Verdi encountered varied from one part of Italy to another. Everywhere (as continued to be the case in Britain until 1968), a new theatrical work had to be passed by the censor before it could be performed, but religious censorship was particularly stringent in papal Rome and political censorship in Naples (where the opera house was part of the royal palace), while in these years the representatives of the Habsburgs in the north were relatively lenient.

What is surprising is not that Verdi as a young man had so many brushes with the censor but that they were not more bruising, that what might seem the most incendiary aspects of his early works – the blatantly nationalistic sentiments in one opera after another – were not what primarily caught the critical censorial eye. It is simply anachronistic to ascribe to Verdi or his librettists or audiences in the early and mid-1840s the fervent political ambitions that crystallized later. Some Italians yearned for a united Italy, others urged a kind of Lombard League of the north, some wanted a constitutional monarchy and others a republic. Such dreams did not bother the authorities overmuch so long as they were poetically and allegorically expressed. We know that revolutions broke out in 1848–9 and that just over a decade later Italy's various 'foreign' regimes were ousted and the peninsula united. But nobody knew this beforehand. It was not then but much later that 'Va, pensiero' became widely adopted as a quasi-national anthem and that Verdi himself became revered as the embodiment of Italy's national aspirations. Back in what he later called his 'years in the galley', he was adopting and adapting the heightened rhetoric that was the standard theatrical language of the day, placing his operas in exotic times and locations and lacing them with politically elevated sentiments designed to send audiences home happy.

Moreover, if the authorities were somewhat more lenient than we might have expected in applying political censorship, it was in their interests too that audiences should enjoy a night out at the theatre. During the decades following the Napoleonic wars, a host of new opera houses sprang up across Italy and old ones (such as the exquisite Teatro del Giglio in Lucca) were lovingly renovated. No town could be held in any regard, declared the percipient Englishman Keppel Craven after touring southern Italy, unless it could afford a theatre season. Everywhere, from the great regional capitals of the north down to even some of the most provincial townships, civic pride was manifested in its theatre as local councils aped the manners of their former aristocratic masters. By the time Verdi was setting out on his career in the early 1840s, the opera house was almost as ubiquitous in parts of Italy as the cinema a century later, and fulfilling many of the same functions. Rather as people across America would later troop to see *Gone with the Wind*, their predecessors up and down the peninsula from Bergamo to Bari – certainly, the better-heeled among them – would have been keen to catch the latest opera. Opera was often the only popular diversion available to many people in a country where, unlike in Germany, France or Britain, there were as yet few museums, libraries, choral societies or clubs (let alone chamber ensembles or symphony orchestras). Here, as at the royal and ducal courts of earlier times, the local citizenry could relish lavish entertainments that reflected back to them their own sense of social and economic advancement. And what did they see on stage? Noisy choruses advocating war and patriotism, to be sure; but also earnest advocacy of such archetypally bourgeois virtues as honour, loyalty, duty.

Those who produced new operas knew their market, and prudent self-censorship usually ensured that a new work contained little the authorities need worry about (though the military and police would normally be present throughout, just in case). No impresario, after all, went into the business of opera with the intention of having his house closed down. Capitalism, not subversion, was the spur. Nor did the political authorities like to shut down a theatre, a step that was far more likely to exacerbate political rumblings than eliminate them. An open, well-attended theatre was a venue in which all the local opinion formers would congregate and where they could be kept under constant observation. Even in the immediate wake of the revolutions of 1848–9, one of the first things many of the restored regimes in Italy did was to reopen their opera theatres for business, preferably with shows that would prove popular. Once Milan was securely back under Austrian control, the authorities chose to put on Verdi at La Scala, just as they did in Naples where revolt had been brutally suppressed right outside the San Carlo theatre itself. It was not the political allegiances of a composer that weighed most heavily with the restored rulers of post-revolutionary Italy but his ability to fill the opera house. Here was the pre-eminent place for the ruler to display himself, fully in charge and happily smiling and waving to his subjects. So long as nothing on stage was blasphemous or directly threatening to social order, the censors could afford a longish leash. And if opera audiences purred with satisfaction at the end of the evening (and loyally applauded the monarch or minister if he chose to attend), everybody went away happy and those in government could be confident they had little to worry about.

*

Opera was not only an art form but also a business. For many who entered it in post-Napoleonic Europe, it proved a particularly demanding one as new market forces increasingly replaced the old-fashioned patronage systems that had once provided a regular livelihood for people like Haydn or Leopold Mozart. A few composers might hold salaried posts, though these were now more likely to be at music academies or opera houses than with bishops or princes. A handful of the most outstanding (and well-connected) musicians, as we have seen, became celebrated almost to the point of reverence: the 'geniuses' or quasi-gods whose inner fire enabled them to express in artistic form the passions felt by ordinary mortals. For most, however, a lucrative commission one month would hold no guarantee of another the next, while many had to supplement an irregular and inadequate income with bouts of teaching. For the budding composer, there was as yet only the most rudimentary career structure, no efficiently organized music industry of a kind we would recognize with its internationally enforceable contracts, effective copyright legislation and royalties and the rest. In such a world, many composers doubtless starved in the proverbial garret and remain unknown to history, but many among even the most talented found they had to struggle for recognition and income. For years, Berlioz, Schumann and Wagner were better known and paid for their journalism than for their musical compositions, while Beethoven, Schubert, Bellini, Donizetti, Weber and Verdi all suffered periods of severe financial, physical and even mental strain.

In much of Europe, certainly in Italy, music had long been regarded as a craft, often handed down from father to son rather like carpentry or coalmining. Just as the cobbler or farrier had traditionally taught his sons to make and mend shoes, the one for people and the other for horses, so the church organist or choirmaster would impart his skills – that is, his means of earning a living – to his. Not only to his own sons, perhaps, but also to others who would join him as apprentices. By the nineteenth century, formal craft apprenticeships were largely a thing of the past as youngsters attended schools and acquired the rudiments of a more general education. But a form of apprenticeship, or pupillage, survived. Donizetti, for example, who was born in poverty in Bergamo in 1797, greatly benefited by being attached early in life to a benign teacher. Simon Mayr, the local *maestro di cappella* and a successful operatic composer, opened a small music school financed by a local charity. Primarily intended to train choirboys, the school offered free musical education and one of its first pupils was the nine-year-old Donizetti. From the start, Mayr recognized the boy's talents, took a detailed personal interest in his development and later helped him to obtain his first commissions.

By the time Donizetti was embarking upon his career, several things were beginning to work in favour of the composers of operas in Italy. With the proliferation of new and renovated theatres came the opportunity for more performances, and with performances came money. Most of this, initially at least, went not to the composer but to the man who had commissioned the opera, the impresario. Like Marco Faustini 200 years before, the nineteenth-century Italian impresario was a middleman, a kind of operatic fixer. Typically, he would lease the theatre from its owner (usually for a single season at a time), put together repertoire and casts, and promote his shows as aggressively as he could in the hope of paying off his debts and making some surplus cash for himself.

One of the most successful was Domenico Barbaja, the impresario who enticed Rossini, Bellini and Donizetti to work at the San Carlo opera house in Naples. Today, much of the vast royal palace to which the San Carlo is attached is a museum, and the Bourbon monarchy and the 'Kingdom of the Two Sicilies' over which it reigned have long since gone, swept away by Italian unification, while Barbaja's palazzo on nearby via Toledo houses medical offices and rental apartments. Yet the opera house remains very much the theatre Barbaja would have known when he ran it on behalf of the King of Naples, its portico still topped with the legend 'REAL (that is, Royal) TEATRO DI S. CARLO'. Barbaja was a new kind of entrepreneur (he is the man who introduced to the already rich Italian diet the idea of mixing whipped cream with coffee or chocolate). A poorly educated Milanese, Barbaja knew little about art but a great deal about earning money, making his initial pile managing the gambling tables in the foyer of La Scala. He had an enviable capacity for drawing on the talents of others, 'sniffing the odour of true merit', in the words of a contemporary, 'like a fox that, even from afar, raising its muzzle in the air, catches the scent of a pullet'. Barbaja's operatic empire gradually expanded and came to include major theatres in Milan and Vienna. An amiable man, whose word (said the composer Pacini) was as good as a written contract, Barbaja assiduously developed the careers of those he employed, bringing Rossini to Vienna, where the composer of *Il barbiere di Siviglia* sought out the ageing and apoplectic Beethoven.

A shrewd impresario might make good money, especially if he stayed on the right side of the (noble or civic) owners of the theatre who were his ultimate employers. But the empire he ran could be beset with innumerable little local difficulties. Thus, we find Barbaja desperately trying to persuade the singer Adolphe Nourrit to stay in Naples in 1838 (he offered him *William Tell*) since otherwise the San Carlo season would be left with no star tenor. Then there was the problem of finding a decent chorus and orchestra. Opera work was seasonal and most singers and instrumentalists were in effect migrant labour. One can imagine the backstage gossip during a short, demoralizing season in small-town Salerno or Senigallia to the effect that, according to Arturo's friend Carlo, who heard it from his wife's cousin Andrea, you could earn twice as much in Odessa or Buenos Aires. And even if the impresario's chorus or orchestra were safely intact, what was he to do when a deadline was approaching and a promised libretto or score had still not materialized? In 1832, the impresario Alessandro Lanari signed up Bellini to compose a work for performance the following spring at the Fenice in Venice. The text would be by Bellini's frequent collaborator and one of the best and busiest librettists in Italy, Felice Romani. The trouble was that Romani was too busy; he had four or five other libretti to complete and was constantly behind schedule. Bellini, becoming desperate, eventually took his problems to Lanari who, lest he have a big hole in his schedule, finally resorted to the police to demand the presence of the dilatory librettist in Venice to complete his work.

Verdi's big break a decade later came about after he helped the impresario running La Scala out of a somewhat similar quandary. As Verdi recalled it many years later, he had run into Bartolomeo Merelli by chance in the streets of Milan. Merelli greeted the young man, took his arm and led him

Verdi's 1842 opera about Nebuchadnezzar was his first major success. Its chorus of Hebrew slaves in Babylon, crying out for their lost homeland, is often said to have fuelled the demand for Italian independence from Austrian hegemony. But was the opera really considered that subversive at the time?

to his office. La Scala it seems was due to present a new opera but the composer to whom the job had been assigned had refused to cooperate, claiming he did not like the libretto. But it's a wonderful libretto, Merelli exclaimed, pressing it into Verdi's hands and inviting him to set it to music. Verdi was in no mood to comply. Now in his late twenties, he had made a faltering start as a composer and over a short period had endured the multiple tragedy of losing both of his two children and then his wife. Merelli was persistent, Verdi recalled, so the composer reluctantly took the wretched libretto home (feeling sick all over) and flung it down on the table, where it fell open at the lines 'Va, pensiero, sull'ali dorate'. Verdi was transfixed. He couldn't sleep. Before long, he tells us, the music of *Nabucco* was racing through his head: the opera that first made him famous. Verdi undoubtedly dramatized in retrospect the story of how he emerged from what had seemed like terminal despondency to become the most feted young composer in Italy. But it is another reminder of the perennial hazards facing the operatic impresario in an age when, every season, his audiences were baying – and paying – for something new.*

In a good season, a shrewd operatic impresario like Barbaja, Lanari or Merelli could make money. So, up to a point, could the author of a successful text. Few librettists achieved the kind of fame enjoyed by the more prominent among their predecessors from the eighteenth century, when an opera such as *Didone abbandonata* was routinely regarded as by Metastasio rather than by one of the forty-odd composers who set his text to music (and *Die Zauberflöte* was advertised as being by Emanuel Schikaneder). By the 1830s, it was Bellini's *Norma* or Donizetti's *L'elisir d'amore* that people went to hear, even though both works benefited from a text by Felice Romani; in Paris, similarly, it was Meyerbeer's (rather than Eugène Scribe's) *Robert le Diable* or *Les Huguenots* that drew the crowds. Many librettists are scarcely known to history, and some (such as Solera and Piave, important early collaborators with Verdi) ended their lives in poverty. But the most talented and prolific, such as Scribe and Romani, were in constant demand and able to make a tidy fortune. Romani wrote some ninety texts, which were set by thirty-four composers, while Scribe's productivity was higher still, both men becoming better known and better recompensed than many of the lesser composers who set their words to music. Audience members could buy the libretto to an opera and, if they wished, follow the text as the plot unfolded

---

* The title of Verdi's opera acquired unexpected prominence after a meeting in Vienna in 2002 between representatives of Austrian, Hungarian, Romanian, Bulgarian and Turkish gas and oil companies. Their aim was to develop a gas pipeline from the Caspian Sea through to Central Europe that would avoid going through Russia. A consortium was set up, after which the delegates went off to the Vienna State Opera, where they enjoyed a performance of *Nabucco*. Later, over dinner, the question arose: what should the new pipeline be called? Flushed with the success of their mission (and some excellent Austrian wines), they unanimously agreed to christen their creation 'Nabucco'.

or take it home and look over it later. Scribe amassed an enormous fortune from his plays and opera libretti; as early as the 1820s, he was living in an elegant country estate and, with some 2–3 million francs to his name, was probably the richest playwright in Europe.

Money was also beginning to flow into the coffers of music publishers, such as Ricordi, founded in Milan in 1808, initially as a printing works. Giovanni Ricordi was a Milanese violinist (he worked for a while in a little marionette theatre) and music copyist. After an apprenticeship in Leipzig, at the time and long afterwards a leading centre of music publishing, where he learned about the latest printing techniques, Ricordi returned to Milan and set up shop. The first piece of music he published was for guitar, figuring, doubtless correctly, that there was a guitar in every home and someone keen to play it. In 1825, Ricordi took what proved to be an all-important step when he bought the musical archives of La Scala, Milan, where he had worked as a prompter, thus coming into possession of a large number of original scores. Since most opera performances at the time were of new works, the Scala management was probably not too worried about the removal of vast quantities of music that was simply lying around unperformed. Existing operas were revived periodically (for example, if a composer or librettist did not deliver a new commission in time), and Ricordi figured he could make some money by renting out the parts. In the longer term, the Scala archive provided the basis of what was to become one of the most important of all operatic publishing houses as the idea developed later in the century of a 'repertoire' or 'canon' of masterworks to be replayed year after year. Even during the company's heyday, it preferred to rent out rather than sell operatic parts, thus keeping some control over performances, while it made substantial sums by selling vocal or instrumental reductions of operatic favourites. During the 1850s (the period of Verdi's *Rigoletto*, *Il trovatore* and *La traviata*), the Ricordi catalogue typically included twenty or more transcriptions of all or parts of popular operas arranged for piano solo or duet (original keys or 'easy level'), flute solo or duet, flute and piano, solo violin, violin and piano, string quartet, accordion, and a variety of wind instruments (for example, clarinet, trumpet, bassoon, horn) with piano accompaniment – not to mention piano medleys and 'fantasies' of varying degrees of difficulty.

Even more than the impresario, librettist or publisher, it was the celebrity singers who stood to make big money out of opera. It was they whom audiences came to hear, they who commanded vast fees – the women, perhaps, even more than the men. People like Giuditta Pasta, Maria Malibran and Giulia Grisi were the pop stars of their day, earning far more than the composers whose music they sang. In a society in which women were generally restricted to traditional domestic roles, opera was one of the few fields in which a woman of talent could rise up the social scale and achieve great wealth and status. In 1829, when a cheap restaurant meal could be obtained

Casa Ricordi, founded in Milan in 1808, had become the most important Italian publisher of opera by the time of this 1850 print, the composers on their books including Verdi and, later, Puccini. The Ricordi offices adjacent to La Scala are now the home of the Scala Museum.

for a franc or thereabouts, Malibran was reported as earning over 90,000. This was exceptional (and complained about in the press), but a top operatic soprano such as Pasta could earn up to 1000 francs for a performance, with an annual income of some 30,000. The German soprano Henriette Sontag married a Sardinian diplomat and, after some complicated manoeuvring, was herself made a countess, while by mid-century Malibran's sister, Pauline Viardot, was hosting one of the most prestigious salons in Paris. Not everyone, of course, rose to such starry heights, and the workload could be ferocious. A soprano engaged in Naples claimed she had to sing twenty-six operas in a single year, including a full-length Donizetti work that she had to learn in six days. Giuseppina Strepponi, Verdi's future wife, once sang the title role in *Norma* six times in a week (while pregnant), and Pasta, the first Norma and one of the most celebrated of sopranos, sang herself out well before final retirement from the stage. In her prime, however, a singer of Pasta's stature would have wielded considerable power in the opera house. When Verdi was starting out, it was normal for the prima donna to have a lot of influence over the repertory she would sing, what costumes she would wear, which of her arias should be cut and which extraneous ones (her 'suitcase arias') added. Moreover, composers were usually quite prepared to adapt their music to the demands of their star performers, for they knew that their marketability would be enhanced if a famous singer took a shine to a particular work and went on to perform it elsewhere. 'Maestro Rossini' (said the composer's contract for *The Barber of Seville*):

> commits himself to deliver the score by the middle of January [1816] and to adapt it to the voices of the singers; he further commits himself to make all those changes that may be deemed necessary both to the success of the music and to the convenience of the singers...

Ten years later, when Pasta agreed to appear at London's King's Theatre, her contract guaranteed her not only a large fee but also the right to choose which roles to sing and which costumes to wear. It also included a clause asserting that Madame Pasta alone:

> will choose the actors, the distribution of the roles, the absolute direction of all that which regards the rehearsals, and all else for the *mise en scène* of the said operas.

No-one, it continued imperiously:

> will have the right to intervene in the rehearsals nor interfere with anything concerning the performance of those operas.

The composer remained very much at the beck and call of other more powerful players. For writing an opera, he would typically be offered a one-off fee, subject to negotiation, paid once the opera had opened. Donizetti was forever chasing new commissions, sometimes finding himself obliged to compose three or four operas in a year and, in his later years, dashing frenetically from one European city to another to supervise rehearsals of his latest work. Bellini, by contrast, learned how to bargain for the highest sum he thought he could get away with so as to have as long as possible for composition.

Normally, a composer's contract also required him to be present at the first three performances, directing from the keyboard, and that would bring in a bit more money. Thereafter, nothing. Many operatic composers lived in penury. Even the score a composer had written was not his property but that of the commissioning impresario, and in the early part of the century it was he – not the composer – who could, if he so chose, offer subsidiary rights to a publisher (or copyist) to print and sell some of the more popular arias or duets. More often than not, he would not bother. And since there was still no enforceable copyright on musical scores, the most popular were frequently pirated so as to avoid rental fees. That is to say, a vocal score would be re-orchestrated by a local musical hack and the resulting performance passed off as a Donizetti or Bellini 'original', not unlike today's fake Gucci bags and Rolex watches. It was a kind of flattery, in a way, but desperately hurtful to its victims. 'I beg you to announce in all the newspapers that [you are] the sole proprietor of *Anna* [*Bolena*] and *Elisir*,' wrote an anxious Donizetti to Ricordi in 1833, 'and that any other copy is false.'

When Donizetti was in his declining years and Verdi starting out, the composer still came well down the financial ladder. No wonder Verdi complained later that the low status and hard work of his early years was comparable to having to row in a Roman galley. Yet already things were changing. As early as 1843, the 29-year-old Verdi was negotiating with the opera management in Venice over his contract for a new opera. Verdi insists that he should have a say over which artists will perform his new work, that there should be 'all the rehearsals necessary for a good performance' and that he should have the right to adjust the final scoring of the opera 'until the rehearsal before the dress rehearsal'. As for the fee, Verdi proposes it be delivered in three equal instalments: on his arrival in Venice, at the first orchestral rehearsal and the final sum after the dress rehearsal.

It may not have been true that 'every Italian' knew and whistled the popular arias of the day. Even the largest opera houses could accommodate only a tiny fraction of their local populations. Those who never attended the theatre might nevertheless still get to know some of the tunes. The military band, legacy of the Napoleonic wars, turned up not only in the orchestral brass and timpani that Rossini and Verdi wrote into their operatic scores, but in the piazza or city park where, as people sipped their coffee or wine, the local band would entertain them with the latest operatic oompahs (courtesy of Casa Ricordi, unless it was playing from pirated scores). Or, if it was not the brass band, perhaps the barrel organ or an aspiring young singer. A company like Ricordi was able to take advantage of the invention of lithography which, by saving wear and tear on engraved plates, facilitated far larger editions and thus enabled operatic vocal scores and band or piano reductions to be marketed around the world. A corresponding growth of the press brought information about opera, and even pictures of its composers, to the notice of an ever-wider, increasingly literate readership. All of which, alongside the development of the railway and improved road networks, helped stimulate the establishment of new opera houses and opera companies throughout Europe as well as in the Americas and elsewhere. So that already by the mid-1840s (unlike the 1780s, when, *pace* Mozart, not everyone in Prague could have been singing *Figaro*), operatic hits such as Rossini's *William Tell* galop would have been widely performed throughout Europe and beyond. As operatic music and those who wrote it became better known, it was only a matter of time before the composer would climb his way up the economic cliff face.

The story is told of three popular composers who met for a drink at a *café chantant* in Paris in the mid-1840s. As they sat and chatted, they found themselves entertained by someone who, in order to attract customers, was singing some songs by these very men. When they stood up to leave, the threesome announced that they refused to pay for their drinks unless they were also compensated for the commercial use of their compositions. I do not know whether Verdi knew of this incident. But he was already acting as though he did.

CHAPTER 7

Opera Reaches New York –
and the Wider Frontier

By the time of Mozart's death, his librettist Lorenzo Da Ponte, a man forever on the run, had quit Vienna, making his way across Northern Europe – including, briefly, revolutionary Paris – and thence to London, where he found employment at the King's Theatre, Haymarket. After a succession of scandals and bankruptcies, Da Ponte fled to New York in 1805, later moving to Sunbury (Pennsylvania) and Philadelphia, working at first as a grocer and general merchant and then teaching Italian and dealing in Italian books. In 1819, Da Ponte returned to New York, where he devoted himself to the dissemination of Italian culture in his adopted city, publishing his memoirs and, in his latter years, becoming the first professor of Italian at Columbia College. Courtly, toothless, with a gentle Voltairean smile, Da Ponte seems to have found a degree of tranquillity in New York in his old age, celebrated as the librettist of the by-now legendary Mozart and a man capable of discoursing (in a slight but elegant foreign accent) with equal facility about the literary works of Virgil, Dante or Tasso, or the finest European music and drama of his own times.

Perhaps 'tranquillity' is not quite the right word. For this was a man whose personal and imaginative restlessness lasted into extreme old age. How was it that there was no Italian opera in so self-consciously cultured a city as Philadelphia? Da Ponte toyed with the idea of bringing it there himself. There was none even in New York, the most cosmopolitan city in America. Like a dog with a juicy bone, Da Ponte continued to chew away at what to him was both problem and opportunity. Then, in his mid-seventies, Da Ponte tasted red meat: a troupe, led by Manuel García and his 'incomparable daughter' Maria, was coming from London to America, 'and in fact to New York, to establish the Italian opera there – *desiteratum* of my greatest zeal'.

*

There had been opera of a sort in America even before Independence, but it had had a chequered history. Theatre of any kind was fiercely condemned by the Pilgrim Fathers. Life in Puritan New England, they preached, was tough and the daily fight for food, shelter and survival rendered virtually any form of entertainment superfluous, not a part of the European cultural heritage they were keen to transplant to their City on a Hill. There is 'much discourse of beginning Stage-Plays in New England', sniffed the Puritan cleric Increase Mather in 1687, adding darkly that 'last year Promiscuous Dancing was openly practised.' Mather concluded that 'the Natural Effects of Stage-Plays have been very pernicious… Persons who have been corrupted by Stage-Plays,' opined the Puritan preacher, 'are seldom, and with much difficulty Reclaimed.' The Quaker leader William Penn, too, was scathing about the dangers of theatre. 'How many plays,' he asked, 'did Jesus Christ and his apostles recreate themselves at? What poets, romances, comedies, and the like did the saints make use to pass their time withal?' In the words of the poet Michael Wigglesworth, author of *The Day of Doom* (1662):

> The wicked are brought to the Bar
> Like guilty Malefactors,
> That often times of bloody Crimes
> And Treasons have been Actors

To such men, music may have been permissible, but only if reserved for liturgical purposes. Psalmody, not operatic arias, lay at the heart of the Anglo-American musical tradition.

Further south, in the colonies of Virginia and South Carolina, life was at first equally precarious, but a somewhat more tolerant attitude developed. By 1718, while any kind of sustained theatrical or non-liturgical musical culture was still anathema in much of New England, the thriving city of Williamsburg, Virginia, boasted its own purpose-built theatre, and over the years that followed a scattering of theatres and of travelling theatrical troupes appeared up and (mostly) down the Atlantic seaboard. Productions often included music and were commonly called 'operas'. As early as 1735, in Charleston, South Carolina, a theatrical entertainment was produced by the English actor and playwright Colley Cibber, with musical interpolations and a pantomime as an afterpiece. Gay's *Beggar's Opera*, produced in New York in 1750, rapidly became popular and led to a succession of American 'ballad operas' that strung together a sequence of popular airs with updated words linked by rudimentary dialogue and a simple, feelgood plot. Light and comic operas by popular English composers were soon performed in the American colonies; a Philadelphia newspaper reviewed Arne's *Love in a Village* in 1767, half a dozen years after its London premiere. There was still plenty of resistance, especially in New England. In the very year that New Yorkers first revelled in *The Beggar's Opera*, the Massachusetts legislature enacted a law prohibiting all theatrical production.

By the outbreak of the Revolution, certainly, a few cultured enthusiasts knew – and some played and sang – the latest compositions of the current

European masters. One of the striking exhibits at Thomas Jefferson's home in Monticello, Virginia, is a fiddle on which the great statesman and polymath might have played the latest airs. Benjamin Franklin, an enthusiastic music lover, played the harp and guitar, invented the glass harmonica and went on to devise a theory of melodic and harmonic consonance. But to even the most cosmopolitan-minded Virginians or (especially) New Englanders, the hymns of Isaac Watts, Charles Wesley or William Billings – the rough, disabled tanner and collector of *The New England Psalm Singer* – would probably have been more familiar than the latest airs of Gluck or Haydn. Billings regarded the singing of psalms as a way of getting people to meet, get together, share a spiritual quest. As the Revolutionary troops went into battle against King George's Redcoats, his four-part hymn 'Chester' became something of a rallying cry, just as psalms had been for Cromwell's Ironsides over a century earlier.

War was no time for trivial entertainment and, not surprisingly, there is little record of operatic or even of much theatrical performance in the American colonies from the mid-1770s through the early 1790s. Yet in Boston, the occupying British defiantly disregarded the theatre ban, performing *The Beggar's Opera* and *Love in a Village* and even turning the Bostonians' hallowed town meeting house, Faneuil Hall, into a temporary playhouse. Among the British generals, General Burgoyne was an accomplished playwright while General Clinton took his violin with him on military campaigns. George Washington, though personally no aesthete, thought that theatrical entertainment could help maintain military morale, arranging for his officers to give a performance when their fortunes were at their lowest ebb at Valley Forge.

There was musical theatre, too, in New Orleans, an emerging European outpost on the Gulf coast that was heir to strong Spanish and French influences and was sold by Napoleon in 1803, with the rest of France's vast Louisiana territories, to the newly sovereign United States of America. The sale did not, however, mean that Yankee culture would predominate. On the contrary, New Orleans and its little theatre on the rue Saint-Pierre became something of a beacon of French *outre-mer* culture. Here, *opéra comique* thrived: between 1806 and 1810, there were over 350 performances of 76 different works by 32 composers. Occasionally, Italian or German works were staged, but usually in French translation. Performances were amateur but evidently popular. The theatre on rue Saint-Pierre was replaced by a larger one, the number of works and performances increased further, and even African slaves were permitted to attend (although separated from the rest of the audience). During the first third of the nineteenth century, it was in New Orleans, not the great cities in the north-east, that European opera – especially French opera – was most likely to be heard. When there was opera in Philadelphia, Boston or New York, it was most likely a touring company from New Orleans that was on show.

Which is not to imply that the northern cities lacked musical theatre. Here, however, the predominant cultural influence was English. *The Beggar's Opera* and its many pale successors continued to be popular, while in the principal cities there was 'serious' opera, too. Philadelphia, for example, prided itself on the quality of its musical and cultural offerings. But the opera on offer in Philadelphia's Chestnut Street theatre was most likely to be by Arne, Dibdin, Linley or Shield, or perhaps by Philadelphia's own Francis Hopkinson (except if a visiting New Orleans company brought Grétry, Méhul or Boieldieu). As for Italian opera in Italian, Lorenzo Da Ponte was astonished to find it almost totally lacking. Until the arrival of the Garcías in 1825, that is.

*

Manuel García has many claims to operatic fame, not least as father of two of the nineteenth century's most celebrated singers, Maria Malibran and Pauline Viardot, and of one of its most famous voice teachers (and inventor of the laryngoscope), Manuel García Jnr. Born in Seville in 1775, García senior gained early renown as a versatile singer and composer, many of his light operettas being performed across the Iberian peninsula and beyond. In his early thirties, García left Spain, honed his vocal skills and toured France and Italy, specializing in the Italian repertoire. In Rome in 1816, he sang the tenor role (Almaviva) in the premiere of Rossini's *Barber of Seville*. In 1824, we find García in London, where he published a book of singing exercises and opened an academy of singing. And it was in London that he negotiated with a prominent visiting New York businessman, Dominick Lynch, to undertake a trip to America. The following year, García and his troupe embarked for the New World.

Back in 1802, García had sung the role of the Count in the Madrid première of *Le nozze di Figaro* and was later to become a celebrated exponent of the title role in another Da Ponte opera, *Don Giovanni*. This bespoke versatility of the highest order: Rossini's Almaviva is a high, often florid tenor role, the Count in *Figaro* a baritone and the bass-baritone role of Don Giovanni rather lower still. Vocal categories may have been less fixed in those days, with transpositions and 'upper' or 'lower' options common and pitch something like a semitone lower than now. Nevertheless, García's vocal abilities, allied to his proven accomplishments as a composer, were unusual and impressive. Then there was García's wife, also an accomplished singer, Manuel Jnr, a budding baritone – and the 'incomparable' Maria, then seventeen yet already widely known for her vocal and dramatic prowess. Pauline, too, was in tow, though a small child at the time. García *père* was a cruel and even brutal parent and his long-suffering children doubtless bore lifelong emotional scars as a result. But, by whatever means, he had certainly generated a nest of exceptional talent.

One of the operatic roles sung in New York by Manuel García was Rossini's Otello. The English actor Edmund Kean, playing Shakespeare's Othello in the same theatre on alternate nights, attended García's performance and enthusiastically congratulated him afterwards.

The Garcías' American visit was a calculated gamble. In many ways, the signs were propitious. By now, the internecine, often interfamilial acrimony associated with the American Revolution was receding into history while earlier political factionalism was correspondingly submerged into what became known as the 'Era of Good Feelings'. As for the sectional tensions that were later to spark civil war, these were effectively swept out of view, at least for the time being, by the Missouri Compromise of 1820, a political fudge that permitted the new and expanding nation to admit one slave state and one free state, thus preserving the balance in the US Senate. Internationally, the new nation exuded a new sense of confidence, its president (Monroe) asserting in 1823 that the USA would regard any attempt by a European power to extend its influence anywhere in the Western hemisphere as a threat to America's own peace and safety. This was splendid rhetoric. But for many years to come it meant very little in practice. Overall, and for all the bluster, Europe and North America were experiencing an unaccustomed period of peace, prosperity and mutual trade.

New York became particularly prosperous. Situated on the Atlantic seaboard but served by the Hudson River, it was by now a major trading centre boasting a large hinterland market (which was soon expanded still further by the opening of the Erie Canal). Moreover, the city was attracting a new wave of European immigrants, stimulated by stories of New World prosperity and the introduction of a regular transatlantic packet in 1818 that guaranteed to run 'full or not full'. Many of the most entrepreneurial settled in the city of debarkation, trailing memories of the culture they had left behind.

So García had some reason to believe that fertile soil awaited the operatic seed he wished to import. The enterprise, he knew, would not be easy. The perilous Atlantic crossing, undertaken in October 1825, was expensive and hazardous and entailed well over a month under sail. On board the *New York* with the Garcías was the socialist idealist Robert Owen, en route to set up a utopian colony in New Harmony, Indiana. Owen's son kept a diary which has survived. He describes what he refers to as 'our Italian party' singing what he supposes to be 'Italian catches, glees and humorous songs, in the highest spirits, apparently extemporizing with the most perfect ease and harmony. Amongst other amusements they imitated the Scotch bagpipes to perfection.' The initial jollity soon evaporated, however, as a fortnight of fierce gales forced passengers to take to their bunks and 'occasioned many ludicrous scenes during dinner and at other times'.

Immediately on arriving in New York in early November, García got down to the job of recruiting an orchestra and chorus from whatever talent he could find; standards were inevitably likely to be patchy (his orchestra consisted of only twenty-five players), while García himself was fifty and past his vocal best. Above all, there was no guarantee that New Yorkers would be interested in what the visitors had to offer; the path to operatic glory, then and since, was strewn with the detritus of defunct peripatetic theatrical troupes that had been bankrupted by strenuous and ill-advised tours. Professor Da Ponte might have been delighted that the Garcías were bringing Italian-language opera to America. But would anyone bother to show up at New York's Park Theatre down near the Battery (a house with a capacity of some 2000 spectators) to see music theatre in a language scarcely any of them understood, with admission prices a good 25 per cent higher than usual? Opera was an expensive, foreign-bred form of elite entertainment, still carrying something of the aristocratic patina of its courtly origins. How would it go down in the commercial capital of the most self-consciously egalitarian nation on earth?

García decided to play safe and present as his main attraction Rossini's *Barbiere di Siviglia*. Da Ponte did all he could to help promote the García performances, hoping Italian opera would finally take root. He tells how he overheard one of his students discussing the García visit somewhat irreverently. 'Finding his notions erroneous,' writes Da Ponte, 'I remarked in jest: "Silence, King Solomon! You know nothing of music yet!"' Some time later, Da Ponte took the young man and some of his other students to a performance of *Il Barbiere* and, he reports, 'that admirable music caught them up,

New York's Park Theatre, where in 1825 Manuel García brought high-quality Italian opera to North America. Today the area is known for the park that houses City Hall, just off lower Broadway, but tucked away behind Park Row is 'Theater Alley', providing a clue to what once stood there.

along with the rest of the audience, into a sort of ecstatic spell'. The errant student, it seems, was converted.

So were a sizeable number of New Yorkers. Although the season was not widely advertised ahead of time, it was well reported, as much for its novelty value as for its artistic proficiency. After the first night, the *New York Evening Post* of 30 November 1825, wrote as follows:

> *The Opera.* – Last evening was presented at our Park Theatre, and for the first time to an American audience, this elegant and charming sister of the Drama. The house was open at half past 7, and before 8 o'clock the hour of commencing, it was quietly and entirely filled…

One senses a touch of relief: New Yorkers had not disgraced themselves by refraining from attending an event so elevated, so 'European'. During the previous few days, people had been asking in the columns of the press what was the appropriate attire for attendance at Italian opera, the proper time to arrive and the correct etiquette during the performance. According to the English actress Clara Fisher Maeder, the audiences would take their cue from that leading social lion and operamane Dominick Lynch, who sat in a prominent seat or box every opera night, and applaud whenever he did. The members of the opera audience were clearly keen to impress their visiting artists and (doubtless) the attendant press, and did not want to make fools of themselves. They need not have worried. 'An assemblage of ladies so fashionable, so numerous & so elegantly dressed, was probably never witnessed in our theatre,' wrote the reporter from the *Post*. And not only fashionable ladies. In the expensive boxes were some of New York's most prosperous merchants, plus a scattering of prominent intellectuals: the novelist James Fenimore Cooper was there, and so was Napoleon's brother, Joseph Bonaparte, the exiled former King of Spain, while the slightly less elevated strata of the European immigrant community poured into the dollar-a-seat pit and the 25-cent gallery. When trying to assess the art form itself, the man from the *Post* found himself almost lost for words:

> In what language shall we speak of an entertainment so novel in this country, but which has so long ranked as the most elegant and refined among the amusements of the higher classes of the old world? ... Until it is seen, it will never be believed that a play can be conducted in *recitative* or singing and yet appear nearly as natural as the ordinary drama. We were last night surprised, delighted, enchanted; and such were the feelings of all who witnessed the performance. The repeated plaudits with which the theatre rung were unequivocal unaffected bursts of rapture.

The writer goes on to comment on the performance, noting that the style of acting 'differs widely from any to which we have been accustomed'. Among the male performers, in particular, he was struck by 'the variety, novelty and passion of their expressive, characteristic and unceasing gesticulation'. The ladies, by contrast, acted with 'remarkable chasteness and propriety, never violating good taste nor exceeding the strictest bounds of female decorum'. Special note is made of the contribution of 'the daughter, Signorina García', who 'seems to us a being of new creation... equally surprising us by the melody and tones of her voice and by the propriety and grace of her acting'.

The García tour got off to a rousing start and went on to play to good houses. García had been right to begin with a run of Rossini's sparkling *Barbiere*. More Rossini operas followed (*Otello*,* *Cenerentola*, *Tancredi* and *Il turco in Italia*), plus some of García's own compositions. As the year turned, however, and the New York winter took hold, houses were not always as full or enthusiastic as they had been at the outset, performances probably became somewhat routine and a succession of coughs and colds inevitably felled some of the artists. García resorted to yet more Rossini. At which point, Da Ponte suggested that, admirable as Rossini was, García might do well to vary further what was on offer – for example, by putting on 'my *Don Giovanni* set to music by the immortal Mozart'. As recounted by Da Ponte, García responded

---

* Edmund Kean was in New York performing Shakespeare's *Othello* in the same theatre on alternate nights; he attended García's opening performances of the Rossini adaptation and enthusiastically congratulated him afterwards.

enthusiastically: 'If we have enough actors to give *Don Giovanni*, let us give it soon,' he said. 'It's the best opera in the world!' Da Ponte's understandable delight was tempered by the fact that the company did not include a singer capable of singing the role of Don Ottavio. So Da Ponte himself undertook to find one and, from his own pocket and with the help of friends and students, found the necessary funds. And so, on 23 May 1826, *Don Giovanni* had its North American premiere, to Da Ponte's original Italian text, in the presence of its elderly librettist. The performance itself was packed with accidents and inadequacies, but García as the Don and Maria as Donna Elvira covered themselves with glory and, by popular request, the opera was given another nine times.

The Garcías stayed in New York for a total of nine months and gave seventy-nine performances of nine different operas. Da Ponte seems to have been as thrilled by the whole visit as García himself must have been, writing in his memoirs what 'great an interest I took in the continuance and success' of the enterprise. Until now, Italian opera had stubbornly failed to take root in North America. The García tour seemed to have changed all that, as the correspondent of the *New York Evening Post* recognized at the time:

> We consider the question whether the American taste will bear the Italian Opera is now settled. We predict that it will never hereafter dispense with it. Nothing could have been more judicious and liberal, if they wished that it should obtain a permanent establishment among us, than the course the managers have pursued. They have brought out at once a large number of first rate performers, and we may boast that we begin with as good a *troupe* as London, Paris or Naples can furnish...

Henceforth, America would have Italian opera: New World commerce and democracy had extended the hand of welcome to Old World high culture. But notwithstanding the *Post*'s breathless boast, it would be some time before regular performances comparable to those in London, Paris or Naples would routinely be available in the USA. It was one thing for wealthy New Yorkers to part with a few dollars in order to attend a prestigious passing show; after García had come and gone, these same people doubtless paid similar amounts to attend the French opera seasons brought by troupes from New Orleans. It would have been quite another thing for these embodiments of the profit motive to put big money into something so predictably *un*profitable as a permanent Italian opera company or a dedicated opera house. García thus left New York as lacking in Italian opera as he had found it. He came, he was seen, he was applauded and paid – and he left.

García followed his New York season by taking all his money and most of his troupe (minus Maria) to Mexico. Here, he was taken to task for performing in Italian and was obliged to translate his Rossini offerings into Spanish. He was later caught up in the anti-Spanish sentiment that accompanied the Continent-wide movement towards national independence and robbed of all his New World earnings. Eventually returning to Europe impoverished, García continued to perform with what was left of his voice, picked up his career as a composer and spent his last years highly admired both as a teacher of singing and as the father of one (and, it gradually became apparent, two) of the great singers of the age.

As for Da Ponte, he continued to harbour hopes of building on what García had pioneered. He was irritated by the fact that New Yorkers paid to hear what he regarded as inferior French operas performed by inferior visiting musicians from New Orleans. So, by now in his early eighties, Da Ponte poured his still considerable energies into promoting and helping to finance another Italian troupe, led by Giacomo Montresor, which performed Italian opera in New York in 1832 and went on to appear in Philadelphia. Old age had evidently not diminished Da Ponte's lifelong predilection for restless and sometimes misjudged enthusiasms, and at eighty-three we find him helping coordinate efforts to raise the funding for an 'Italian Opera House' to be erected on New York's Church and Leonard Streets. This theatre, the first ever built in the USA exclusively for use as an opera house, opened in November 1833 to great fanfares of optimism, and showcased some of the Montresor singers and a repertoire largely consisting of Rossini. Alas, the enterprise lasted only two seasons, each of which ended with a substantial deficit, while Da Ponte's involvement with the Montresor enterprise and the opera house lost him both money and friendships.

Americans were discovering the hard way what Europeans had long known: that opera – the fully-fledged, properly rehearsed performance of an art form that combines all the others – can never make a commercial profit. In this new American world of free enterprise and market-led economics, there were no bountiful monarchs or dukes keen to use opera as a way of impressing their rivals, no wealthy aristocrats happy to rent expensive opera boxes as a display of social extravagance. Indeed, it was precisely to eliminate such Old World anomalies that the new nation had been wrested from its former European masters in the first place. And there was another thing. Perhaps opera – particularly Italian opera – with its larger-than-life characters (both on and off the stage) expressing extravagant, overheated emotions was simply inappropriate for a down-to-earth nation that was busy setting up townships, establishing territories and struggling to make a living from the earth and the riches that lay beneath. As Americans elected Andrew Jackson to the presidency and looked optimistically yet apprehensively towards the limitless lands to their west, little attention or money was concentrated on the cultural legacy of Europe. Was Da Ponte's great mission a failure? Would the seed of Italian opera never flourish outside Europe? He may have reflected so as he lay dying in his ninetieth year. If so, he was to be proved spectacularly wrong.

*

> There is no corner in the world where – if they have a theatre and two instruments – Italian opera is not sung. When you go to the Indies and the middle of Africa, you will hear *Il trovatore*.

Verdi was writing from London to his lifelong friend Count Opprandino Arrivabene in 1861 and doubtless exaggerating a little. But only a little. By now, Italian opera, or at least excerpts from Italian operas, could be heard on every continent. There was opera in Havana, Buenos Aires and Montevideo, in Adelaide, Melbourne and Sydney, in New Orleans, New York and San Francisco, Cape Town, Cairo and Bombay.

Most of the places where opera took root were outposts of European culture where it provided a reminder of home to Italian or Spanish émigrés, British colonial administrators, German and Scandinavian pastors and missionaries, and a host of assorted merchants, farmers, gold and silver speculators, and other panhandlers and adventurers. Not all were opera lovers, of course. But most, like travellers and migrants everywhere, tried to garb themselves in at least the outer garments of their former life. If they could not carry their childhood home on their back, they could bring out evocative elements of it as they settled and became more affluent in their new environment. Mid-nineteenth-century Melbourne or Buenos Aires were hardly London or Milan, while the burgeoning gold-enriched towns of San Francisco or Ballarat were better suited to the bar and the brothel than to grand opera. But the presence of 'opera' on many of these remote frontiers of European civilization remained a potent symbol of success. Just as people shipped out crinolines and top hats, dinner sets and a piano, they would also import opera and, if finances were available, build an opera house: a reminder, perhaps, of the gentility they had left behind. Often enough it was a false reminder: theatres that rarely or never mounted performances of operas were still called opera houses. The remnants of nineteenth-century 'opera houses' are to this day scattered across the old mining states of Colorado, Nevada and California, while the 'Opera House' district of Bombay was long synonymous with the city's vice trade. Yet everywhere, 'opera' was widely regarded as an indication of wealth, social achievement, status.

In Australia, European art music arrived soon after settlement. Regimental brass bands entertained British officers with the latest hit tunes while more sober fare was available in church on Sundays. Meanwhile, at balls and soirées, colonial administrators and their wives, eager for news from 'home', enjoyed the latest airs by English composers such as Henry Bishop. If the fare on offer was not as sophisticated as that available in Europe, audiences in

Verdi was scarcely exaggerating when he said you could hear his operas in Africa. The Cairo opera house, which had staged the world premiere of *Aida* in 1871, held a charity ball a dozen years later at which much fun was clearly had by all. Note, inter alia, the 'Scotch' reel among the fezzes and the undignified donkey ride home afterwards!

Sydney and Melbourne could nevertheless hear occasional (mostly English-language) performances by touring companies of excerpts, or edited-down versions, of such popular operas as Weber's *Der Freischütz* or Mozart's *Die Zauberflöte*, or the works of English composers like Wallace or Balfe, much as their counterparts were doing in Boston, Philadelphia or New York.

By the 1840s, there was opera (of a sort) in most of the main towns in Australia. Adelaide was founded in 1836 by Nonconformist free settlers and German pastors. The denizens of this 'City of Churches', proud of their high cultural standards, brought out with them a library of worthy books and within four years had built the Queen's Theatre, which, along with other theatres that sprang up in the infant city, came in due course to host various operatic touring companies.* George Coppin, a local actor-manager, produced 'grand opera' in Adelaide in the late 1840s before relocating to the goldfields of Victoria in 1851 and for many years working out of Melbourne. Coppin toured his artists around the country, as for a while did the Grand Italian Opera Company of Eugenio and Giovanna Bianchi (Italians who had settled in San Francisco). By all odds the most important company in Australia was that controlled by the Irish-American entrepreneur William Lyster. Basing his company in Melbourne, Lyster organized a regular series of tours throughout the 1860s and 1870s, bringing over a company of predominantly Italian and other European (and American) soloists, picking up a scratch orchestra in Melbourne, and later taking his troupe around the coast to cities further afield, recruiting small local choruses as he went. One of Lyster's tenors was Pietro Cecchi, who later became teacher to the young Melba. Lyster's epic tours would last a year or more, with the company remaining in residence at one of the larger towns for a couple of months at a time.

It was the discovery of gold that fuelled the growth of opera in Australia. Melbourne, capital of the gold-rich state of Victoria, experienced a business and building boom in the 1850s and began to shoot ahead of Sydney as the leading city in Australia (in its own eyes at least). For some forty years, until everything was brought to a standstill by the Depression of the 1890s, Melbourne remained the rich, proud capital of a wealthy state in which financial speculation was more likely to succeed than fail. Job opportunities were plentiful, land values rose rapidly and new industries were established on easy credit as networks of roads and railways began to link the principal centres across the state and Cobb & Co introduced Australia's earliest significant bus company. For a canny building contractor like Nellie Melba's father, the Scottish-born David Mitchell, Melbourne and its surrounding districts offered rich rewards as people poured in from across Australia, as well as from Britain and the USA and elsewhere, seeking a new, affluent life. There were houses to build, churches, schools, civic amenities.

* The Queen's (its yellow-fronted classical-revival façade now restored) was to double as the local law courts for a while and was even used as a horse bazaar and later a car park.

After the discovery of gold in California, and here in the Australian state of Victoria, a host of variably talented entertainers – among them a number of operatic vocalists – crossed continents in pursuit of a quick profit.

And theatres. Like arrows to a target, every kind of artist and entertainer, too, sped to Ballarat, Bendigo, Geelong and above all to Melbourne. The operatic soprano Anna Bishop (the second wife of Henry Bishop) and her harpist lover Nicholas Bochsa turned up, as did her rival Catherine Hayes, the 'Swan of Erin'. So, indeed, did that notorious actress, dancer and mistress of monarchs, Lola Montez. It was in Melbourne that not only Coppin and (later on) Lyster but every would-be promoter of the arts made his base.

✻

Gold fuelled opera in America too. In 1847, the old Mexican province of Alta California was ceded into American hands; the USA now stretched from coast to coast, and people across the Union rejoiced in the 'manifest destiny' evidenced by their spectacular new acquisition. In 1849, gold was discovered and a year later California celebrated its formal entry into the Union as the thirty-first state. These were heady days. From all over the continent, men set out for California to seek the latest version of the American dream: life, liberty and the pursuit of happiness, all boosted by a large pot of gold. There were hazards of course; every 'forty-niner' knew that. On the golden frontier, basic amenities were poor, food and water of variable quality, disease widespread, medicines in short supply. In this rudimentary, mostly male frontier society, tempers, like fortunes, rose and fell with alarming rapidity; crime was rampant and policing indifferent. The tacky mining camps and wooden townships were susceptible to fire whenever the winds rose; substantial portions of San Francisco, in effect if not *de jure* the capital city of the new territory-become-state, were burned down half a dozen times in eighteen months. Yet for all this, huge numbers of people continued to turn up in the hope that they would be among the lucky ones and strike gold. Or, if they were unlucky in the goldfields, would enjoy a future blessed by perpetual sunshine and an abundance of good land. California offered a vision of frontier life at its elemental best.

Theatres sprang up like hydra heads. In San Francisco, there were something like a dozen of them. They were lit by candles or whale oil (gas didn't arrive until 1854); most burned down in the fire of May 1851 and were promptly rebuilt. Here, as in Victoria after the discovery of gold in Australia, people craved entertainment – of almost any kind. In 1850, the pianist Henri Herz presented a series of concerts (with a local flautist and baritone) that included selections from popular classics, including opera. With the influx of Chinese labour to work the mines came the importation of oriental theatre, including Chinese opera, which seems to have attracted and baffled in equal measure the large non-Chinese audiences who attended. In addition, San Francisco offered a wide choice of more obviously popular vaudeville shows at which variably talented dancers, instrumentalists and operatic vocalists might alternate with acrobats, tightrope walkers, fire eaters and the occasional performing animal. This was cheap fare for the most part, the raucous (mostly male) audiences talking, drinking, smoking, chewing, heckling and spitting their nonchalant way through the performance. A notice in 1851 'respectfully advised gentlemen that if they must eject tobacco juice…, they be particular to eject it on their own boots and pantaloons instead of the boots and pantaloons of others'. But the theatre was marginally more ennobling, perhaps, than the relentless gambling, cockfighting, drunkenness, prostitution, gunslinging and rampant robbery in and around the streets outside.

The performers at some of these theatres knew they stood to earn a quick buck out here or, if they were really lucky, a bucket of gold nuggets. Anna Bishop, with Bochsa in tow, after an arduous journey down from New York, across Nicaragua and then up the Californian coast, recouped at her very first San Francisco concert in 1854 all their expenses to date. Catherine Hayes, too, swanned around California singing songs and arias to hordes of sentimental Irishmen and retired on the proceeds. Some of the most successful operatic performers consisted of small family groups from Europe (as the Garcías had been): a husband and wife team, with maybe a brother and sister-in-law and assorted youngsters – the standard migrant family group lighting out for the putative wealth and good life of a new world. Many were Italians (such as the Pellegrinis, who brought Italian opera to San Francisco as early as 1851, or a little later the Bianchis, who were to settle there), their presence perhaps having been stimulated not only by gold but also, in some cases, by the failed revolutions of 1848 back home. Some headed from San Francisco up to Sacramento or else, in the wake of the Comstock Lode, to Eureka or Piper's Opera House in Virginia City in Nevada; others to Australia after the gold strikes in Bendigo and Ballarat.

If the rewards dangling before these performers were enticing, the potential hazards were commensurate. For migrants from Europe, travel to the American West before the establishment of the transcontinental railroad in 1869 was normally either by sailing ship round Cape Horn or else across the Panama isthmus (unless you were hardy enough to risk crossing the Rockies by wagon). One way or another, this was bound to be a lengthy, perilous and uncomfortable journey. The Cape Horn route was often prolonged further (and possibly rendered more lucrative) by stopovers in such cities as Rio, Montevideo and Buenos Aires and then, on the way up the West Coast of Latin America, in Valparaiso, Lima and perhaps in Mexico before finally docking in San Francisco Bay. When Henri Herz performed in San Francisco, he was nearing the end of a tour covering all the majors centres in North, South and Central America. The voyage to Australia could take even longer and until the opening of the Suez Canal in 1869 included no operatic stopovers except possibly Lisbon and Cape Town. Hotels for the intrepid traveller could be insalubrious and dangerous, rooms (and even beds) often shared with strangers, food and water risky to ingest. One opera singer, arriving in San Francisco in the wake of the gold rush, described how 'we made a tent of our bedsheets and camped on Telegraph Hill. Then we erected a knock-down house and added a lean-to kitchen which also serves as a dining room.'

Things soon improved. By the latter decades of the century, every aspiring middle-class family had a piano (the 'altar' of the bourgeois home), and young ladies were encouraged to learn to play the latest operatic airs from the piano reductions that European publishers like Ricordi distributed in cheap editions right around the world. By now, improved forms of transport had rendered international and even intercontinental travel a good deal more reliable, comfortable and (relatively) inexpensive. A network of railroads gradually came to link up the main cities of the USA and, a little later, those of Australia (the two sides of the Andes were not linked by rail until 1910), while the steamship came to replace sailing vessels, halving the time required for a transatlantic crossing. New commercial shipping and railway companies sprang up and adopted strict timetables to which, by and large, they managed to adhere. Meanwhile, hotel standards were raised by improvements in hygiene, and would-be travellers found their forward planning further facilitated by the invention of the telegraph.

If new technologies helped solve problems, they also created some novel ones. John Henry ('Colonel') Mapleson, the flamboyant British operatic entrepreneur, led a number of European opera troupes to America in the

Once America's coasts became linked by railroad, opera spread more rapidly to San Francisco and elsewhere in the West.

1870s and 1880s and his memoirs are packed with stories of anxious Atlantic crossings, missed connections, derailments and the like. Pressing the new American railroad system to its limits, Mapleson would take some 150 or more singers, dancers, instrumentalists and technicians clear across America and back with performances almost every evening, often hundreds of miles apart. Typically, a weary company would be herded into its special train in the early hours. One night, en route to Chicago:

> the engineer saw that he was unable to get to that city in time for our engagement the same evening. He therefore telegraphed back to Pittsburg [*sic*], and the railroad officials there telegraphed on to Fort Wayne to have two extra locomotives ready for us. Our train was then cut into three parts, and sent whizzing along to Chicago at a lively rate... By leaving at two o'clock in the morning we arrived at four the same afternoon at our next destination, in ample time to perform that evening.

In 1886, Mapleson found himself in San Francisco halfway through an American tour with a large company and no funds. There was no alternative but to bivouac in the open. 'Frisco,' he reflected, lay 'at the end of the American world; it is the toe of the stocking beyond which there is no further advance'; it was full of people who had scraped together the resources to get there but never found the funds to leave. So he was not altogether surprised when a deputation from his Italian chorus announced that their members were considering defecting from the company and seeking local employment. Some said they would get by selling bananas or ice cream; 'others proposed to start restaurants, or to blacken their faces and form themselves into companies of Italian niggers.' Mapleson played for time. Fortunately, these 'light-hearted and light-pursed children of sunny Italy' seemed content for the next forty-eight hours to enjoy the macaroni they cooked in the open air, washed down by cheap Californian wine, and passing the time 'by card-playing, cigarette smoking, and the exercise of other international vices'. Again, Mapleson tells us he was able to pull the proverbial rabbit out of the hat and save his beleaguered company. But he is also honest enough to catalogue a plethora of sicknesses that plagued his exhausted company during the course of this most strenuous of tours.

It would be hard to overstate the strains and hazards of life on the road for these peripatetic operatic performers. When Anna Bishop and Bochsa left California for Australia in late 1856, the voyage took nine weeks and nearly killed Bochsa (he died shortly after arrival in Sydney). Even the superstars, with their fabulous money and their personal cars and cabins, were not immune. As late as 1901, when Nellie Melba undertook a trans-Pacific voyage, from Vancouver to Brisbane, her ship broke down no fewer than four times 'and lay heaving on the burning waters for hours, and sometimes a whole night at a time'. This was Melba's first visit to Australia since she had achieved celebrity in Europe and America, and she went on to undertake an exhaustive concert tour of her home country, going on to New Zealand. In later years, she returned with fully fledged opera. 'Oh, those hotels of the Australian Bush!' Dame Nellie was later to gush, referring to the 'backblocks' of her homeland as 'perhaps the most remote outposts of the white race in any part of the world' where 'the only means of communication is on horseback for the young… and by buggy for the old'. As she toured hot and dusty small-town Australia, Melba recalled grandly, she would sleep 'on the local bed reserved for celebrities' and, next morning, 'lie back and listen, for already the carts and trucks and bullock-waggons [*sic*] have started to roll in from the outlying districts – all expectant for the great event, my humble concert.' Deeply touching; but hardly what she was accustomed to in London, Paris or New York.

*

To our eyes and ears, the operatic entertainment on offer in mid-century Melbourne, Sydney or San Francisco would often have seemed a curious hybrid,

When Nellie Melba, 'Australia's Gifted Daughter', arrived in Lilydale, Victoria, in 1902, she was welcomed like royalty.

the 'original' work severely edited, cut and simplified for popular consumption, but with the addition of new dialogue and additional songs and dance routines. In San Francisco in 1851, the Pellegrinis offered Bellini's *La sonnambula*; what they in fact presented was something like a multilingual highlights concert, with little or no scenery or chorus, to the accompaniment of a handful of instruments. Reviews suggest their shows were presented with a male chorus of perhaps half a dozen, no women's chorus and an orchestra of at most a dozen or fifteen players (many of them German immigrants). Not infrequently, operas would be cut to little more than half their original length so that the theatrical billboard might offer an operatic double-bill, or, more commonly, an opera preceded or followed by an equally 'edited' play or ballet. Acting seems to have been rudimentary: hand on heart to signify love and/or sincerity, hand on brow to indicate emotional pain and hands out wide to milk applause at the end of an aria. Costumes and sets, too, tended to be multipurpose standard issue: a painted mountain panorama might be unrolled for *Sonnambula* one night and *William Tell* the next, a castle or night sky made to serve for both *Lucia* and *Freischütz*, while Lucia's costume might be disguised with a coloured ribbon or two and adjusted to fit the company's Gilda.

Nevertheless, where there was 'opera', there was usually an audience. People dressed up for the opera, sometimes extravagantly so. Indeed, it sometimes seemed that the roughest communities aspired to produce the most smartly attired audiences, as if the newly rich in these tough, remote New World frontier communities were striving to convince each other that the values of the Old World had not been jettisoned and that European culture and civility had been maintained.

Putting on the finery was one thing; knowing how to behave when you attended the theatre was another. People dusted down their best hats for the opera, sometimes wearing them throughout the performance (perhaps in part to keep their hair free of candle drippings from the chandeliers above). In the prospectus for an opera season in Sydney in 1834, patrons had to be reminded that 'neither Bonnets nor Hats will be allowed to be worn in any of the boxes' while, in the upper tiers, it was 'particularly requested that all gentlemen will be seated during the performance'. Then there was the problem of how to react to the show itself. We have already encountered New Yorkers in the 1820s, uncertain when they should applaud and taking their cue from a well-known socialite sitting in a prominent box and applauding whenever he did. By mid-century, especially in the American West, audiences were less inhibited: a successfully executed aria might be rewarded by gentlemen twirling their hats on their sticks and a burst of yelling, stamping and whistling, while a bad performance would elicit hisses and catcalls. European visitors were wont to remark how Americans would interrupt the music with their applause (or catcalls), to a degree unheard of in London, Paris or Vienna. The transatlantic contrast was nicely expressed by Mark Twain after attending the opera in Hanover, Mannheim and Munich. 'In Germany,' he wrote in 1880, 'they always hear one thing at an opera which has never yet been heard

The frontier opera house in Leadville, Colorado, erected in 1879 by the mining magnate Horace Tabor. Tabor's Opera House still stands and has recently undergone renovation. Its founder's fortunes (and misfortunes), especially Tabor's love for 'Baby Doe', became the subject of an opera by the American composer Douglas Moore, made famous by Beverly Sills.

in America, perhaps, – I mean the closing strain of a fine solo or duet. We always smash into it with an earthquake of applause.' Germans go to opera because they like it 'with their whole hearts', concluded Twain. Most Americans go 'in order to learn to like it' or 'to be able to talk knowingly about it' – the latter humming along with the music 'so that their neighbors may perceive that they have been to operas before'.

Not everyone in the new towns of America or Australia attended the opera. Some, indeed, flatly refused to go. Opera – unlike oratorio – was a branch of theatre which, with its sets and costumes and its portrayal of depraved human emotions, was a notorious sink of sin and iniquity. Worse, opera was a foreign, Italian, Catholic branch of theatre: all the more to be despised, if tacitly, by hard-working respectable Protestants. David Mitchell was not amused when his daughter Nellie, after a stint in a remote spot in Queensland with an incompatible husband and a young child, decided she wanted to return South and take singing lessons with an Italian tenor. But in his tight-lipped way Mitchell was a kindly man. He knew his headstrong daughter was set on trying her luck in opera and that that meant going to Europe. In 1886, he was appointed to represent the state of Victoria at the Indian and Colonial Exhibition in London. 'I am going to take you too, lassie,' he announced one day; 'we sail in six weeks.' Melba recalled later that this was perhaps the greatest thrill of her life. More, her father agreed to give her an allowance for an initial period. If the 'lassie' had the talent she said she did, she'd find her own way; if not, she'd always be welcomed back home.

Nellie Melba's first trip back to Australia was nearly sixteen years later. How different, she reflected, was her homecoming from her departure:

> Then, I had been an unknown girl, setting out on a lonely and arduous adventure; now they had put red carpets down for me, they sent their mayors and their corporations, their officials, their leaders of art and literature and society to meet me, they pelted me with flowers.

After disembarking in Brisbane, she undertook a long, slow train journey across huge expanses of drought-afflicted southern and eastern Australia as spring moved into summer. When she finally arrived, there were more tumultuous crowds to contend with. But it was her father, by then elderly and ill, whom Nellie yearned to see above all when she got back.

CHAPTER 8

L'Opéra

Every visitor to Paris knows the Opéra. It is one of the largest buildings in a city of magnificent edifices, a landmark surrounded by splendid cafés, hotels and restaurants. The Opéra is a Métro stop, a district of Paris, a meeting place of the *grands boulevards* and of those countless tourists, shoppers, students and business men and women who prance or slouch along them. And it is still an opera house, probably the biggest, most opulent in the world, *the* Opéra de Paris. This, many reflect as they visit its plush gilt-and-marble interiors or gawp at its imposing façade, was the home of opera when Paris ruled the operatic world, an impression doubtless reinforced by the spectacular image of the building presented in the Andrew Lloyd Webber version of Gaston Leroux's *Phantom of the Opera*. How could a building with (many believe) over two thousand rooms and an underground lake have been anything less? It would be more accurate to say that Charles Garnier's Opéra, like Edwin Lutyens's New Delhi, was inaugurated just in time to celebrate a chapter of history that was already more or less closed.

*

In the first half of the nineteenth century, Paris was the centre of the operatic world. The post-Napoleonic Restoration brought back the Bourbon monarchy and much that the *ancien régime* had represented. Yet much, too, had been changed irrevocably by the Revolution and its aftermath. Paris was a large, cosmopolitan city, a teeming metropolis in which *le peuple* knew they could never again be disregarded (and periodically rose up to remind those in government of the fact). Many among the wealthier and more educated classes may have been relieved by the reappearance of 'business as usual'. But they also seem to have been at ease with their cultural cosmopolitanism, celebrating foreigners in their midst such as Rossini, Bellini and Verdi, Jews like the composer Fromental Halévy – and even Jewish foreigners, most famously Meyerbeer, Offenbach and the poet Heinrich Heine. It was to Paris that the greatest singers came to find their loudest acclaim and highest fees, here that the grandest productions were mounted and famous composers wrote their

In the exclusive environment of the Paris salon, people would gather to enjoy a night of food, drink, elegant sociability, the card tables, and entertainment provided by the latest musical stars. This is where many people would first have become familiar with the operatic 'hits' of Donizetti or Verdi.

most ambitious works. Chopin and George Sand went to the opera in Paris. So did Delacroix and Balzac and Stendhal. Rossini and Donizetti composed their last masterpieces for Paris, both of them living in the French capital for a period of their lives. Berlioz loved and hated the opera in Paris; so, in their own ways, did Wagner and Verdi, both of them periodic visitors. No composer could be said to have ascended to the peak of the operatic world until his work had been well received in Paris.

It was in the exclusive environment of the salon, just as much as in the theatre, that many among the Parisian elite became most familiar with the latest 'hits' by Donizetti or Verdi. In earlier times, the salon has been largely the preserve of the traditional French aristocracy or, latterly, the Napoleonic social elite. In Restoration Paris, the city grew apace and a new moneyed bourgeoisie began to aspire to the lifestyle and leisure pursuits appropriate to wealth and status. This required as grand a house or apartment as one could afford in which to display elegant furnishings, expensive clothes and efficient staff and to hold elegant parties. By now, the guitar, once a frequent accessory in educated households, was coming to be replaced by that emerging icon of bourgeois respectability, the piano. What better than to hold a musical soirée at which the latest virtuoso pianist would play variations on themes from Rossini or accompany a pretty soprano in airs by Bellini with coloratura embellishments? At the salon of the Countess Merlin or a little later chez the Princess Belgiojoso or the Countess Marie d'Agoult, the Parisian glitterati would gather to enjoy a night of food, drink, sophisticated sociability, card tables at which large sums could be insouciantly won or lost – and musical entertainment provided by artists such as Sontag, Grisi, Chopin, Paganini or Liszt.

For the guests who attended them, the salons were a much valued form of social cement in a world seemingly in constant flux. And for those who made the music, they provided a high-profile, low-anxiety showcase in which to appear before the nation's high and mighty. The salons were especially valuable, perhaps, to younger performers to whom they offered an important stepping stone towards a career in the opera house or on the concert platform. Any debutant who did well on the salon circuit stood to gain a tidy fee and a collection of influential friends on whose admiration any savvy musician could then capitalize. Friedrich von Flotow (the composer of *Martha*) described the procedure: the thing to do, once you had begun to get some recognition in the salons, was to announce a concert, send a clutch of top-price tickets to all the hostesses you knew and, with luck, they and their friends would all turn up to hear you. Musicians, however talented, were not regarded as the social equals of those for whom they performed. After one salon, Marie d'Agoult, the mistress of Liszt, described Sontag (the future Countess Rossi) as 'intoxicated by the presence of aristocracy and good breeding' and trying to play the great lady herself without success. Yet a social catch like Rossini could expect a substantial fee simply for agreeing to appear as guest of honour at a fashionable salon. When Rossini returned to Paris in his mid-fifties for what proved to be the last ten years of his life, he and his (second) wife held a regular *samedi soir* in their Paris apartment in the rue de la Chaussée d'Antin or in their house in Passy on the edge of the Bois de Boulogne. Here, a long line of distinguished guests would queue up for the privilege of an audience with their celebrated host (a process Verdi found distasteful) and enjoy outstanding performances by the top musicians of the day as well as rising young stars such as Adelina Patti. 'What a spectacle!' wrote the music publisher Giulio Ricordi of a Rossini soirée as he struggled to recall the names of 'all the Marquises, the Baronesses, the ministers and ambassadors who were paying court to the celebrated Maestro'. It was in such salons, in an era before radio and recordings, that the great and the good of Paris could familiarize themselves with the operatic highlights of the day, the music that everyone felt they ought to know.

Where did they go if they wanted fully staged, costumed, rehearsed performances of opera, complete with chorus, ballet and orchestra? The story is complicated: over these years, there were a dozen or more opera houses in Paris, most of which burned down at one time or another. It is easier, perhaps, to remember that (in consequence of the rationalization of the theatres of Paris under Napoleon in 1806–7) there were essentially three main operatic companies, or institutions, each of which moved from time to time and place to place.

*

First, there was the Opéra, the direct descendant of Louis XIV's (and Lully's) Académie Royale de Musique. In the time of the first Napoleon, this was based at the Théâtre National on the Square Louvois, just across from the old Bibliothèque Nationale (alongside the rue de Richelieu). Here, the operas of Méhul and Le Sueur (Berlioz's teacher) shared the stage with those of Gluck, Mozart, Paisiello and Spontini. This was the theatre to which Napoleon hastened in December 1800 in order to show he had survived an assassination attempt. Twenty years later, another assassination attempt, this time a successful one against the Duc de Berry, caused the theatre to be closed down. The hapless duke stood to inherit the French throne and was murdered as he left the Opéra in February 1820 by a deranged workman set on eliminating the entire Bourbon family. The assassin failed in his attempt to end the Bourbon line (the Duke's widow was carrying his child). But, by an exquisite unfolding of the law of unexpected consequences, he did succeed in closing down the opera house. After the murder of the Duc de Berry on the steps of the Opéra, it was unthinkable (and risky) for King Louis XVIII or anyone loyal to the Bourbon monarchy to spend an evening's entertainment at such a site.

Eighteen months later, a new theatre was completed in the nearby rue le Peletier, and it was in the Salle Peletier that the Opéra saw its glory days. This was the home of *grand opéra*. What audiences wanted at the Peletier – and what shrewd opera managers provided – were big five-act spectaculars (complete with a statutory ballet scene), through-composed and sung in French by a large cast and chorus, preferably culminating with noisy and colourful fires, floods, earthquakes and general mayhem. Year after year, decade after decade, a succession of sumptuous productions were staged here, often to Scribe texts and with music by Auber, Halévy or Meyerbeer. Rossini's last great masterpiece, *Guillaume Tell*, was written for the Opéra. So were Donizetti's *La Favorite* and Verdi's *Les Vêpres siciliennes* (both of them Scribe operas), as well as *Don Carlos* and Wagner's 'Paris' version of *Tannhäuser*.

People talked of the Peletier as a temporary home of opera, a stopgap before they built the big one everybody envisaged. However (like the original New York Metropolitan), it lasted a lot longer than many expected or wanted and, despite living under an almost permanent sentence of being superseded, fulfilled its primary function to most people's satisfaction for over half a century. It was the destruction of the Salle Peletier by fire in 1873 that provided the eventual incentive to complete the Opéra Garnier.

They sang in French, too, at the Opéra-Comique. Like the Opéra, the Comique had been formally recognized in the Napoleonic reforms of 1806–7 and was equally constricted as to the kinds of piece it could produce. Until the legal noose was loosened in the 1860s, it could only put on works in which spoken dialogue separated the musical numbers. Premieres at the Opéra-Comique included *Le Postillon de Longjumeau* (famous for a bravura aria at the top of the tenor register) by Adolphe Adam, the composer of *Giselle*, Auber's hugely popular *Fra Diavolo* about a lovable outlaw (complete with chorus of dead nuns) and a work whose sprightly overture features in concert programmes to this day, Hérold's *Zampa*. It was at the Comique that the composer Halévy gave encouragement to a young German Jewish cellist in the orchestra, Jacques Offenbach, whose ambition was to compose light operas of his own. Ticket prices at the Opéra-Comique, like its theatrical ambition, were lower than at the Opéra, as were the social pretensions of its audiences. But the Comique was an opera house, not a showcase for pantomime or vaudeville like the Porte-Saint-Martin or the Funambules. It was at the Opéra-Comique that Armand Duval first set eyes on the wealthy and elegant Marguerite Gautier, the Lady of the Camelias in the Dumas novel. Over the years, a series of financial disasters and fires rendered the Opéra-Comique particularly peripatetic before it finally settled into the Salle Favart, where it remains to this day (though the present building is the third on the site).

Earlier, the Favart had been home for a while to the equally nomadic Théâtre-Italien. Buffeted by periodic fire, chronic mismanagement and recurrent bankruptcy, the 'Italiens' (or the 'Bouffes' as it was also known) somehow survived, often on the back of governmental largesse. It was here that the real opera lovers – the *dilettanti* like Stendhal – could get to hear Italian opera sung in Italian by the leading Italian singers of the day. In the early 1820s, the works of Rossini were perennial favourites.* In 1823, Rossini himself visited Paris on his way to London, was massively feted, and was back the following year with a lucrative contract in his pocket from the French government whereby he agreed to reside in Paris for at least a year (he stayed for five), composing new operas and directing revivals of his earlier ones. Paris had successfully bagged the biggest operatic celebrity in the world, the man Stendhal hailed in a famous literary flourish as the successor to Napoleon. Rossini's official empire, however, extended no further than the directorship of the Italiens and even this little domain stretched the amiable composer's limited administrative skills. Within a couple of years, he was relieved of his managerial responsibilities and given a generous government pension in the hope that new operas would sprout from his fertile pen.

It was in the Salle Favart during the 1830s that the Italiens probably achieved the acme of its fame, witnessing premieres of new works by Bellini and Donizetti interpreted by the greatest performers in what is widely

---

* In 1822, 119 of 154 evenings at the Italiens were devoted to works by Rossini; in 1825, 121 out of 174.

regarded as a golden age of singing. This was no showcase temple of the arts, no grand, golden Garnier. The Favart stood, as it does today, facing a tiny square tucked away between a series of narrow side streets untouched by the grandiose reconfigurations of Haussmann. Here, in this unpretentious space, Malibran sang, and Grisi, Pasta, Rubini, Tamburini and Lablache. The building in which they sang has, however, long gone. In January 1838, it caught fire and one of the directors (a close colleague of Rossini) was killed after jumping from an upper window. The Italiens had a further lease of life, moving a few years later into the Salle Ventadour. The company was finally wound up in the 1870s after the completion of the Garnier. Today, the old Ventadour is occupied by the Banque de France.

*

As their names implied, the Opéra, Opéra-Comique and Théâtre-Italien supposedly fulfilled different functions, reflecting a tidy, Napoleonic division of labour. Each had its official contract, its *cahier des charges*, defining and limiting what it was and was not allowed to produce so that, in theory at least, there was a strict consonance between institution and artistic genre. Thus, opera with spoken dialogue could only be produced at the Opéra-Comique, French *grand opéra* (and *petit opéra*: through-composed but without ballet) at the Opéra and Italian-language works at the Italiens. The two principal opera companies, the Opéra and Italiens, performed on different days of the week. The aim was to minimize competition between the two and create maximum collegiality. The administrative links between them became manifest when, during (and after) Rossini's directorship, the Italiens was placed directly under the ultimate control of the Académie Royale de Musique (that is, the Opéra) – no bad thing since it guaranteed the beleaguered company some funding from the government purse. In practice, there was a degree of overlap, rivalry and back-biting between the two companies almost from the start. During the early 1820s, while the Italiens showcased one highly acclaimed Rossini production after another, the Opéra experienced a continuing slide in subscriptions to boxes, which its management tried in vain to halt with warmed-up favourites by Gluck and Grétry. Success bred success, and as top artists signed up to the Italiens, standards at the Opéra fell further.

The Opéra fought back. The Revolution of July 1830 finally put paid to the old Bourbon monarchy, installing in its stead the Orleanist branch under Louis Philippe. The 'July Monarchy' was widely heralded as signalling the ascendancy of bourgeois values, a new situation well illustrated at the Opéra by the man appointed to run it, Louis Véron. Véron became director in 1831 and was offered an entirely new kind of contract: for the first time in the history of the Opéra, this venerable royal institution was to be run as a kind of private–public partnership. That is to say, it would remain under the ultimate supervision of the government and receive a substantial (but diminishing)

The backstage *foyer de la danse*, where men were permitted to mix with the dancers before – and after – the performance.

annual subvention. Within these constraints Véron was permitted to raise and spend money as he wished, taking for himself any net prófit. It was an attractive formula for someone who, like a number of other successful opera impresarios, was probably more of a money-maker than an aesthete. As a young man, Véron had made his pile marketing a chemical paste as a cold cure, rather as Barbaja had made money from his coffee formula and management of the gambling concession at La Scala. Véron was also an experienced journalist and a gifted publicist who went on to become a leading newspaper owner. During his tenure at the Opéra, Véron refurbished the Salle Peletier, split up some of the larger boxes and in general tried to increase the number of seats, adjust ticket prices and strengthen the theatre's subscription system. One of his innovations was to give specific numbers to seats and tickets.* Under Véron, the auditorium was redecorated, becoming less spectacular than before but more user-friendly. Only men were allowed to sit in the orchestra stalls and the shrewd Véron insisted they retain their right of access to the Green Room (the *foyer de la danse*) where the ballerinas limbered up before the show, a privilege probably also valued by some of his impecunious *danseuses*. Curtain-up, which old-timers remembered being at 5pm and had been changed to 7pm in 1803, now became later still to accommodate people coming to the opera from work or across town.

* Previously (and not only in France), it was common for those with seats in the orchestra stalls to send a servant to the theatre early in order to secure the best seats. Berlioz (*Memoirs*, p. 80) describes how as a young man he and his friends would arrive early at the Opéra for this purpose.

Véron resigned after four years; after yet another reduction in the government subvention, he realized that, for all his entrepreneurial flair, it would be easier to make money elsewhere. Did his reforms help widen the social base of the Opéra audience? Véron certainly liked to claim so; he wrote later that his aim had been to make the Opéra the 'Versailles' of the bourgeoisie. Analysis of subscriptions and other kinds of audience data during these years suggests, however, that at both the Opéra and the Italiens those attending the opera continued to be disproportionately the titled and the wealthy. In 1833/4, nearly one third of all subscribers to the Opéra had titles of nobility. A further 20 per cent of subscriptions went to representatives of the world of high finance: those wealthy, upper-middle-class merchants, bankers and speculators who inhabit the novels of Balzac. As for the *petite bourgeoisie*, a seat at either of the main opera companies was probably beyond the financial means (or taste) of the threadbare schoolteacher or *curé*, and out of the question for members of the rapidly growing working class that even now was swelling the population of Paris to a million and more. A well-paid blacksmith in Paris working in the coach-building industry during the 1830s and 1840s might have received an annual salary of around 1500 francs, a baker not much more than a thousand and a shoemaker as little as 800 francs at a time when basic outlay on food and drink for an average family of four could be as high as 500 francs. And then there was the rent to pay. For most such people, tickets to the Opéra, which were priced between 2.50 and 7.50 francs (a little higher at the Italiens, lower at the Opéra-Comique), would have seemed an unnecessarily extravagant expense. The implications become clear if one multiplies these figures by thirty: few among today's working classes, on a family income of £30,000 or even £40,000 (or euros or dollars), with around £15,000 going on basic living expenses, would make a habit of spending £225, or even £75, on an opera ticket. This was the world of Rodolphe and Mimì, of Murger's *Scènes de la vie de Bohème*. A Christmas Eve splurge at the Café Momus was one thing. But the opera? No. A night at the Opéra-Comique, possibly (where you could snog in the gods for as little as a franc a seat). More likely, a Parisian worker or *petit bourgeois* (or student, poet, painter or seamstress) with a little saved up for entertainment would make for one of the town's cheap pantomime or vaudeville shows, for which entry could be obtained for 50 centimes or less.

There is a further reason, too, why it is surely false history to suggest that the new bourgeoisie replaced 'the aristocracy' as the bulk of the opera audience. The management – even that self-styled bourgeois Louis Véron and certainly the government functionaries to whom he was answerable – did not *want* the opera audience to be too downmarket. The aim of Véron's pricing policy (in the words of the secretary to the government body to whom he was responsible) was to 'attract more people to the house, without lowering the Opéra to an inferior level'. One had to be careful, said his report, not to 'risk attracting to the Opéra inferior classes whom one might hold in high esteem but with whom good company does not like making contact'. And 'good company' meant those with wealth and 'breeding'. The aristocracy may have been weakened by the French Revolution, but it was far from eliminated and its numbers had been augmented by the new nobility created by Napoleon. Despite the supposedly bourgeois credentials of the July Monarchy, a man with a title continued to command respect and there is little doubt that the aristocracy, old and new, continued to be a commanding presence at the opera in Paris throughout the second quarter of the nineteenth century and beyond.

It is probably disingenuous, therefore, to suggest that Véron simply replaced the old aristocracy with the new bourgeoisie as the mainstay of his audiences. What is more likely is that there was a partial merging of the two. Younger members of the titled nobility entered not only the church or army as their predecessors had done but the new commercial professions, mixing on increasingly easy terms of social equality with the emerging financial and mercantile elite. The Opéra hardly attracted a mass following. By mid-century, however, its audience base had undoubtedly widened.

*

As the composition of the opera audience altered, so did the way it behaved. We have seen how in the eighteenth century the opera was often regarded by its aristocratic patrons as a social diversion, a kind of club where the privileged and wealthy might turn up several evenings a week during the season, take in part of the show and meanwhile chat, play cards, eat, drink and do business. Elsewhere in the theatre, servants and others would stand at the back of the 'orchestra' or sit on uncomfortable benches upstairs and enjoy themselves as best they could. Everywhere, people would come and go and there would be a certain amount of noise and bustle, interspersed with periodic applause, laughter and an occasional 'shush!' when a particularly exciting or moving passage was in progress. And the whole thing might stop in mid-performance for a special round of applause if the ruler should happen to turn up.

In the Orleanist France of the 1830s and 1840s, as new forms of wealth and status merged with old and the audience catchment area for opera became enlarged, *habitués* began to notice unfamiliar faces in the house. These newcomers were unlikely to turn up at the opera every night. They had other things to do with their time and money and probably had work to go to the following morning. To such people, the idea of a night at the opera could arouse qualms. Some of these were aesthetic: 'Will I enjoy the show, or understand its finer points?' Then there were the social qualms. How exactly did one buy tickets (should it be done by sending a servant, what is a reasonable amount to pay, did a ticket guarantee a seat, was there a reservation fee)? What was the correct dress code? When were you supposed to applaud?

A box at the Paris Opera
in 1834. But whom is he
really looking at?

Should you eat beforehand or afterwards? What time could you expect to get
home? In Véron's reconstructed Salle Peletier, with some of the old lavish
boxes reduced in size and grandeur, you and your spouse might turn up and
find yourself sharing a four-person box with another couple you had never
met before. Should you talk to them? Share an interval drink? Perhaps. But
your comportment would inevitably be more stiff and guarded than in earlier
times. With *embourgeoisement* came a new *politesse*. One result was that
people seem to have attended more closely to what was on stage.

   At the same time, their expectations probably shifted about the kind of
productions they chose to attend. For many, no doubt, a night at the opera
remained little more than a pleasant diversion, as it has continued to be to
multitudes of their successors today. Others, perhaps picking up something of
the reverence for the arts that was coming to be adopted in the German-
speaking world, went to the other extreme, regarding music as almost tantamount to religion and attending the opera with the solemn mien adopted by the
devout when in church. Berlioz portrays himself as one such when a young
man, describing his almost obsessive attentiveness when visiting the Opéra: if
a neighbour talked once the overture had begun, Berlioz made sure he was
silenced with the sarcastic observation 'Damn these musicians, they're prevent-
ing me from hearing what this fellow is saying.' For most, the opera in Paris
was perhaps less than religion but more than mere *divertissement* as productions became ever more ambitious and audiences quieter and more attentive.

The processes fed off each other. Opera houses became bigger and more comfortable as they attempted to set their net to catch a larger, more diverse public. For those who attended, even if they sat in the less expensive seats and the house was hot and leg-room cramped, it was no great trial to sit through several hours of high-octane theatricality if the performance looked and sounded good. Furthermore, the show was likely to resonate with some of their own preoccupations. Not directly, of course; most operas at this time, as we have seen, were set in ostensibly remote times and places and it was another half-century or more before the arts dealt overtly with the triumphs and tragedies of daily life. But it is not difficult to spot the popular appeal as librettists, composers and designers created a succession of 'grand operas' portraying huge (often menacing) crowd scenes, brave individuals struggling (usually in vain) against superhuman forces, and heartfelt appeals by the fragile and vulnerable for the protection of God, nation and honour. As top singers were aggressively marketed by entrepreneurial operatic managers and every production advertised as surpassing even the stupendous heights achieved by the last, audience expectations were correspondingly raised. And an expectant audience anticipating a sensational show with famous singers in the leading roles tends to get to the theatre in good time and watch in silence once the curtain rises.

*

Opera in Paris was big news. The comings and goings of Rossini, Grisi or Rubini were regularly reported and widely discussed, the leading performers achieving a level of celebrity and financial recompense not unlike that of today's sporting superstars. It is worth remembering, however, that the number of people attending opera did not compare with the numbers attending modern rock concerts or football matches; nor were the private lives of opera singers as widely known or discussed. The great majority of people, even in a great operatic centre such as Paris, probably had little or no interest in opera or the time, energy or money to attend it. And if you did not actually go to performances (or read the expensive specialist press), you could have no more than a limited impression of what they were like. You might be familiar with some of the more famous operatic tunes from the outpourings of a local band or barrel organ or a music-box. But this would give little idea of the spectacular multimedia theatricalities produced by Véron and his team at the Opéra, the sheer bravura of a Malibran or Pasta or the sparkling wit conjured up by a score by Auber.

A further qualification should be made, too. We are talking primarily about the French capital, not the entire country. There was opera elsewhere than in Paris. Thus, Nourrit quit the Opéra in 1837 and embarked on an ambitious tour (interrupted by illness) with appearances scheduled not only in such cities as Brussels and Antwerp but also in Lille, Marseille, Lyon,

Toulouse and Bordeaux. The historian Jean Mongrédien makes a valiant attempt to describe the nature of opera in provincial France, especially Lyon, in the early nineteenth century. But the overall impression then and later in the century is of chronically poor singing and playing and slipshod production. In *Madame Bovary*, Dr Bovary and his erring wife go to a performance of *Lucia* in Rouen. Emma spends the whole time identifying with the lovelorn Lucia and imagining running off with the tenor, Lagardy. Flaubert uses opera, as many nineteenth-century authors were to do, as a resonant backdrop for erotic fantasy. But part of his irony is that, as he makes clear, the performance itself scarcely warranted it; Lagardy, for all his 'sound and fury', evidently 'came nowhere' alongside the likes of Tamburini or Rubini.

No. For high-quality opera in France one had to go to Paris until well into the twentieth century. The reasons are not hard to find. France (like Britain) had been a more or less united country for many centuries, its political, economic and cultural life dominated by what went on in its capital city. Very different were Italy and Germany, each of them long a collection of separate, independent states with no single polity or geographical region dominant. Thus, where Rome, Naples, Florence, Venice, Milan and Turin (or Hamburg, Berlin, Frankfurt and Munich) might vie for operatic pre-eminence, there was no such competition in France. Paris was overwhelmingly dominant: the seat of government, the headquarters of the church and the army, the site of the nation's leading university, the magnet attracting France's leading businesses, publishers, artists and intellectuals. And Paris, far and away more than anywhere else, had opera. Paris was the opera capital of France and, perhaps, of the world. If a young Frenchman such as Rastignac, the figure at the centre of Balzac's *Père Goriot*, yearned for social success, it was at the opera in Paris that he had to be seen. The Opéra-Comique had the frothiest fare and was the cheapest to get into; early in the novel, we see Rastignac adjusting his cravat and posing to impress the women in the first galleries of the Opéra-Comique. But he rapidly sets his sights higher. He endures a hazardous 'first day on the battlefield of Parisian civilization', and soon learns that 'People with a box at the Italiens have heaven's own luck!'

The women made for the opera in much the same spirit, or so Balzac tells us. One of Old Goriot's obnoxious, uncaring daughters 'owns a side-box at the Opéra and... laughs very loudly to attract attention', while Mme de Beauséant attends both the Opéra and the Italiens with lover and husband in attendance, the latter tactfully leaving the box once they are installed. Foedora, the heartless fashion victim in *La Peau de chagrin* (*The Wild Ass's Skin*), ignores the music and instead puts herself on show, spending the entire evening peering through her opera glasses from box to box. The opera is where the expression of extravagant emotions is permissible, not only on stage but off as well, a place of great art, yet faintly disreputable: an irresistible combination. 'Upon my word,' says the handsome Charles (in *Eugénie Grandet*) to his pretty

In Rossini's heyday, the Théâtre Italien was where the world's top singers used to perform to audiences that included such opera lovers as Chopin, Balzac and Delacroix. For a while, the company was based in a theatre just off the Boulevard des Italiens on the site of today's Opéra Comique.

cousin, 'if you were in a box at the Opéra, and dressed in full fig, my aunt would be quite right to think of deadly sin, for all the men would be envious and all the women jealous.'

Not all the attendees at the opera were would-be social lions, lubricious viscountesses or nouveau riche financiers. Some were primarily there because they loved opera. Stendhal identifies (and doubtless caricatures) two categories. The first are the pedants whose 'perceptions of notes, modes and keys are sharpened to an incredible degree of accuracy' but whose souls are indifferent to even a hint of passion. The pedants are impeccably dressed, he says, and can reel off in a slightly nauseating manner 'the entire history of musicology, interwoven with a vast rigmarole containing every detail of the vocal characteristics of every *prima donna* who has appeared on the Italian stage for the last twenty years, every date of every first appearance, of every *premiere*'. But there was a second cluster of operatic obsessives: the *dilettanti* (of whom Stendhal himself seems to have been an early exemplar). Etymologically, the word suggests people who 'delighted' in opera and found it 'delectable' while, today, we tend to use the term to imply a certain lack of seriousness. Either way, it gives little idea of the emotional intensity described by Stendhal. If the 'pedant' displayed nothing but cold cerebration, the *dilettante* was the archetypal romantic: slightly untidy in appearance and listening to the music in a trance-like ecstasy of rapture, mouth agape, features drained of vitality, only his eyes revealing something of the fiery recesses of his soul. And then, at the end of a power-fully delivered operatic set-piece, pouring out his pent-up feelings in an uncontrollable orgasm of enthusiasm.

Nor were the *dilettanti* the only ones to raise the roof with their bravos. This was the heyday of the 'claque', a group of people paid ahead of time, usu-ally by a principal singer, in return for guaranteed applause. Nowadays, the claque has a bad name. I do not know any singer who admits to having paid a claque in recent times or any opera manager who admits to running a theatre in which the system is still permitted to operate. For a singer to pay for applause smells to our nostrils as unsavoury as a sleazy industrialist paying for a politi-cal honour. Yet such negotiations have a long and not entirely dishonourable history. During Véron's time at the Opéra, the system was formalized and above board, the leader of the claque Auguste Levasseur being hired by the management for a sum which he could then augment in various ways. For each performance, Levasseur would be allocated a batch of tickets which he would then distribute to his *claqueurs*; some received their tickets free of charge while others paid Levasseur a reduced price. Levasseur would work out in consulta-tion with the management precisely where applause was required, and he would also, of course, call upon the principal artists for their kind considera-tion. Woe betide the foolish singer who did not pay! Careers could be made and destroyed by the claque. Venal? Perhaps. But every opera management or star singer was and is grateful for enthusiastic and vociferous applause, and Levasseur was sufficient of a connoisseur not to back losing horses. What was the difference, after all, between paying for a claque and paying for press pub-licity? Loud, ecstatic applause, like glowing press coverage, was good for business, made everyone happy and helped spread the word, bringing people in to later performances. We still do the one, but frown on the other.

*

As the regime of Louis Philippe lost its initial flair, the large-scale, romantic escapism of grand opera seems to have acquired strengthened appeal for many. If so, the message was not entirely lost on the government. In July 1836, for a state memorial for those who had died six years earlier in the rev-olution that had brought it to power, the regime put on at the Hôtel des Invalides one of the largest, most ambitious musical works ever composed: Berlioz's gigantic *Messe des morts*, complete with four widely separated brass bands for the 'Tuba Mirum'. Four years later, the Invalides was the set-ting for even greater romantic outpourings when, to tumultuous acclaim, the government re-interred the remains of Napoleon, brought back from St Helena. The regime hoped to benefit from the manoeuvre. But the event only served to make Parisians yearn all the more for the lost glory of yesteryear. In February 1848, Paris sneezed and not only the French provinces but much of Europe caught a cold. The recurrent French malady that proved so infec-

tious was revolution. The great, glowering crowds so beloved by opera audiences in the 1840s strode off the stage and into the streets, threatening law
and order everywhere. Or that is how it might have looked if you happened
to occupy a threatened throne. Alternatively, you might have seen the revolutions (like the operas) as featuring brave but downtrodden souls struggling
for freedom against well-nigh insuperable odds. Offenbach, by now in the
early stages of his career as virtuoso cellist and embryonic composer, fled
with his young family to his childhood home in Cologne – only to run
straight into revolution there, too.

In France, there was at first something almost farcical about the revolution of 1848 as bloated old Louis Philippe, once the great hope of the rising
bourgeoisie, was forced off the throne with the crowds baying outside his
window. 'Sire, the troops are lining up with the Reds, you must abdicate at
once,' he was advised by his anxious son, the Duke de Montpensier. Laboriously, the King, who was lunching with the family, turned to write out an
abdication statement while Montpensier tugged at his sleeve to hurry. Louis
Philippe finished the statement and handed it over, muttering plaintively: 'It
takes time to abdicate.' Eventually, he took his bag with one arm and his wife
with the other and swept out, saying, 'I abdicate, I abdicate.' France was a
republic once again; but not for long.

*

Prince Louis Napoleon, nephew of the great Bonaparte, had nothing special
to commend him except his name. But ever since his youth, spent largely in
exile, he had proved adept at exploiting his principal asset. As a young man,
he had spent much time in England, first visiting in 1831, and he soon discovered that, even here, his name opened doors which he straightway entered
for purposes of both social advance and political intrigue. Prince Louis's
transparent ambition verged on the reckless and the French government, even
as it ceremoniously repatriated and reburied the remains of the 'Great'
Napoleon, found it prudent to place his irritating nephew under house arrest
in a gloomy fortress some distance from Paris. In 1846, Louis escaped,
thereby enhancing his reputation as a romantic adventurer. Once again, he
fetched up in England and it was from here that he watched the overthrow of
the French monarchy in February 1848 and the ineffective republican government that succeeded it. By the end of 1848, he had made a triumphant return
to his homeland and was installed as president of France. Four years later, as
the result of a bloody *coup d'état* but to the ecstasy of many in France who
had yearned for a return of *la Gloire*, he, like his uncle before him, became
Emperor.

The Emperor Napoleon III never forgot his ties to England and was
assiduous in courting, and attempting to emulate, the popular monarchy
across the Channel. Just as London had held a Great Exhibition in 1851,

Paris mounted a World Exhibition in 1855 whose principal contribution to
the gaiety of nations (this was at the height of the Crimean War) was the
Bouffes Parisiens, a tiny theatre adjacent to the fair site at which audiences
were entertained nightly by the latest clever concoctions by Offenbach. From
the Emperor's point of view the highlight of the Exhibition was the appearance of Queen Victoria and Prince Albert, a nice piece of diplomatic
reciprocity four months after a state visit he had made to London.

Napoleon III and his Spanish wife the Empress Eugénie had been much
feted in Windsor and Buckingham Palace during their trip to London. The
highlight of their visit was a command performance of *Fidelio* at the Royal
Italian Opera, Covent Garden, followed by a ballet, to which they were
accompanied by the Queen and Prince Consort. They set off from Buckingham Palace at around 9.30pm. Just before leaving, noted Queen Victoria in
her diary, 'the Emperor upset his cup of coffee over his cocked hat, which
caused great amusement.' It was evidently a jolly evening all round. On the
way to the opera house, crowds cheered the two royal couples, waving flags
embossed with the initials 'N.E.' and 'V.A.', which, Napoleon helpfully
pointed out to the Queen, spelled out the name of the river on which St
Petersburg was built. The royals arrived at about 10pm, between the two acts
of the opera. They entered the auditorium to immense cheers and then the
two national anthems were played. Throughout the rest of the performance,
the Queen and Emperor were seen to be chatting genially to each other,
Victoria apparently reminding him how they had first met in 1848 at a public breakfast at a villa in Fulham for the benefit of baths and washhouses in
the East End of London. When *Fidelio* came to an end, the curtain went up
to reveal the entire opera company, a guards' band and a hundred members
of the public who had paid for the privilege. The two national anthems were
again performed – this time sung by all on stage – after which the royals
waved goodbye (presumably not waiting for the ballet) and departed for a
late supper back at the palace.

Half a dozen years later, Napoleon III initiated the project that would
culminate in the great opera house in Paris. Attempting to reproduce true
Bonapartist *Gloire*, the Emperor provided extravagant funding for culture
and the arts. Indeed, he went on to sanction the removal of an entire district
to make room for Charles Garnier's vast new opera house while Haussmann master-minded the city centre's complete renovation through the
creation of its *grands boulevards*. All were part of a master plan whereby the
Emperor, priding himself on having inherited the global perspectives of his
uncle, strove to make France once again a major international power, forging
close links with his royal counterparts in London and intervening as Italy and
Germany engineered their tortuous routes towards unity.

A series of ill-advised adventures led to war with Bismarck's Prussia and
everything came tumbling down in 1870–71 as France suffered the ignominy

When the Emperor Napoleon III and the Empress Eugénie visited London in April 1855 as the guests of Queen Victoria and Prince Albert, their hosts took the French couple to the opera – a courtesy reciprocated (above) in Paris a few months later.

of military defeat. While Paris was under siege, the shell of Garnier's incomplete mammoth opera house was used to shelter military supplies. Napoleon III never got to see the finished building or the grandiose imperial entrance Garnier had included in his plans, for the Second Empire was overthrown, the imperial couple fleeing to that perennial home of political émigrés, Britain. Meanwhile, their former subjects had the humiliating experience of witnessing the victors celebrate their triumph in that French holy of holies, the palace of Versailles, with the declaration of a new, united German Empire. After the horrors of war, siege and the brief but bloody reign of the Commune, few Parisians had any stomach for grand opera, let alone the time or money. Ironically, Napoleon III's opera house was finally completed, with some misgivings, by the austere republican regime that succeeded him. The old theatre in the rue Peletier succumbed to fire in 1873, and it was in response to this that work was speeded up on the Garnier, which opened in 1875. Debussy later described Garnier's opera house as a cross between a railway station and a Turkish bath.

CHAPTER 9

Fires of London

Well into the early hours of Wednesday, 5 March 1856, London's Covent Garden theatre rang to the sound of revelries as hundreds of men and women in fancy costumes, their mood fuelled by alcohol and sexual promise, danced across the floor of the great auditorium to the music of a giant band. This overnight *Bal Masqué* was the culminating event of a two-day 'Carnival benefit' that, according to the correspondent of the *London Journal*, had by then deteriorated into something of a drunken orgy. The women were:

> disgustingly attired, and the majority, by their language and gestures, betrayed the station and localities from which they had emerged to flaunt their scarcely disguised figures in the glare of a satanic revelry.

As for the 'males' (there were, says our reporter, no true 'men' present'), they:

> consisted of thieves, gamblers, roués, and numbers whom we strongly suspect paid for their night's debauchery out of the tills or cash boxes of their employers... Their occupation was tobacco smoking, deep drinking, and uttering the most depraved language in the metropolis.

To this puritanical eye, the scene at Covent Garden must have been something akin to Sodom and Gomorrah. And like them, it was doomed to destruction. The theatre was brightly lit that night by gas jets in an array of chandeliers close to the ceiling, immediately above which were the carpenter's shop and storage space. A pile of rubbish on the storeroom floor seems to have started smouldering during the evening. Miraculously, it was only at 5am, as the remaining 200 people or so were singing the National Anthem and preparing to disperse, that the fire took hold. There was a precipitous rush for the exits, during which (*The Times* reported the next day)

'Hissing, groaning,
yelling, howling, bray-
ing, barking, and hoot-
ing': Covent Garden's
'O.P.' Riots of 1809,
as seen by Isaac Robert
Cruikshank.

KILLING no MURDER. *as Performing at the Grand National Theatre*

several women 'were trampled on, and some were carried out fainting, but
none were seriously injured'. There was something hideous, the *Times*
report continued, 'in this sudden change from mad revelry to ghastly fear' as
wreaths of smoke, 'with here and there a lambent flame, began to curl from
under the proscenium into the body of the theatre'. At 5.30am, by which
time everybody seems to have managed to evacuate the building, the roof collapsed. Later that day, as word spread across London, condolences poured in
from all directions. '[I]mmense numbers of people were attracted to the scene
of the conflagration,' said *The Times*, distinguished visitors including the
Queen and Prince Albert, from which (the paper averred) 'some idea may be
formed of the deep and general interest which this calamitous event has
awakened among all classes of the inhabitants of the metropolis'.

The destruction of the Covent Garden theatre may have been a calamity,
but it was far from unique. It has been estimated that there were some 1100
major auditorium fires during the nineteenth century. Leading opera houses
were destroyed or severely damaged by fire in virtually all the world's great
opera centres, among them not only London but Barcelona, Berlin, Dresden,
Moscow, Munich, Naples, New York, Paris, Prague, St Petersburg and Venice.
The average life of a nineteenth-century theatre or public assembly room has
been estimated at around eighteen years.

Nor was the 1856 fire the first to have struck Covent Garden. The original theatre, the creation of John Rich, dated from 1732 and burned down
in 1808. Its replacement a year later proved formidably expensive – as did
famous foreign stars such as the soprano Angelica Catalani – so the management felt obliged to convert what had previously been a popular gallery
into revenue-producing private boxes and to raise ticket prices across the
house. A concerted campaign to reinstate 'Old Prices' greeted the company
when the new theatre opened, on 18 September 1809:

every sound from the stage being drowned in a continued hissing, groaning, yelling, howling, braying, barking, and hooting noise; accompanied by exclamations of Old Prices! No Rise! No Catalani! No Private Boxes! No Seven-shilling-Pieces! and many others of a like import.

A graphic account has come down to us of what came to be dubbed the 'O.P. Dance', a nightly ritual in which the audience called out the two letters 'O.P.' as loud as they could, every participant 'accompanying the pronunciation of each with a beat or a blow on the floor or seat beneath him with his feet, a stick, or a bludgeon'. The result 'was one of the most whimsically tantalizing banters, or torments, that could be conceived'. After some two months of this, the management had to compromise. On 16 December, pit prices were reduced from four shillings to three shillings and sixpence, and some of the private boxes opened up to the public. '[O]n the cessation of hostilities,' recounts one historian, 'an *OP Medal* was struck to commemorate the victory.' Not surprisingly, 'owing to loss occasioned by the fire and the O.P. Row, and by the great expenses attending a concern of such magnitude, the establishment was heavily burthened with debts.'

Operatic managements always are. One thing that marks out opera from most other businesses is that its production costs have regularly run ahead of income. No farm, factory or finance house that routinely incurred large deficits would long survive. When sales of gentlemen's wigs, ladies' stays or shellac gramophone records went out of fashion, manufacturers stopped producing them. Yet the cost of producing opera has almost always exceeded the revenue provided by ticket sales. One way of getting round this was by putting on a 'mixed bill', only part of which consisted of opera. Indeed, the 1809 Covent Garden theatre, like its predecessor, was not primarily a stage for opera at all. For that, audiences normally had to attend the King's in Haymarket (renamed Her Majesty's on Queen Victoria's accession in 1837) or periodically Drury Lane theatre, at either of which a typical evening's entertainment in the 1820s and 1830s might include not only an opera – in whole or part – but also a scene from a ballet, a few solo items from a celebrity singer and perhaps an act from a popular play. Theatre managers resorted to other strategies, too, in their efforts to make ends meet and, if lucky, produce a profit. In the mid-1830s, the manager of Drury Lane, Alfred Bunn, was also the lessee of the Covent Garden theatre for a couple of seasons. A hard-driving man forever in search of a profit to reap and a cost to cut, Bunn would sometimes require his artists to appear in both his theatres on the same night, so audiences had to wait while performers in the one finished their roles and ran across to the other. Around 9.30pm, passers-by might see Bunn's entire *corps de ballet*, or actors 'half attired, with enamelled faces and loaded with the paraphernalia of their art', as they scurried past. At Christmas time, 'when this state of alternation was at its height, the female figure dancers pattered from one house to another six times during the evening, and underwent the operation of dressing and undressing no less than eight.'

Not until 1847 did the theatre alongside London's Covent Garden fruit and vegetable market become primarily associated with the performance of opera, and it did so as a result of its victory over a rival house. The previous year, Benjamin Lumley, owner and manager of Her Majesty's, having renovated and redecorated his Haymarket theatre at a cost of £10,000, lost the services of his music director, the Italian-born Michael Costa. Costa's departure from Her Majesty's was widely reported and his correspondence with Lumley published. Standards dropped, morale in the house was low and in due course most of Lumley's leading singers deserted. Lumley effectively staked the future of Her Majesty's on the 'Swedish Nightingale', Jenny Lind. Lind delayed her arrival, capriciously as it appeared to many (and almost insupportably as it must have seemed to Lumley), and negotiated to the end about her contract.

The problems at Her Majesty's created corresponding opportunities elsewhere. In 1846, two Italians acquired the lease at Covent Garden with the intention of turning it into an opera house, the 'Royal Italian Opera'. The interior was radically restructured, the three tiers of boxes raised to six, galleries added above, and the whole house made capable of seating a capacity audience of some 2250. Work was done at great speed, with teams of men (over a thousand in total) working in relays around the clock in order to get the building ready for reopening on 6 April 1847. The two Italians went bankrupt and fled to the Continent, as did their successor, Edward Thomas Delafield, who by 1849 managed to lose over £60,000, a colossal sum in those days, in just two seasons. Perhaps Delafield's most important legacy was that he had appointed Frederick Gye (1810–78) as what we would now call his artistic director. A year after Delafield's departure, Gye (who pronounced his name with a soft 'G') acquired rights to the Covent Garden lease. Gye, that is to say, was contracted to pay an annual rental to the 'Proprietors', the ultimate owners of the lease granted by the Duke of Bedford on whose land the theatre stood. Gye was to remain at London's Royal Italian Opera – the Covent Garden theatre and the company it housed – for nearly thirty years.

*

Mid-Victorian London vied with Paris as the operatic capital of the world. Britain had never been the *Land ohne Musik* of caricature, and London could boast top performers and performances, initially in the Haymarket and Drury Lane theatres and (increasingly) at the Royal Italian Opera. The most celebrated performers of the day, such as the singers Mario and Grisi, commuted between Paris and London. Weber composed *Oberon* in London

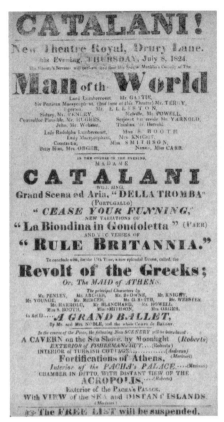

When is an 'opera house' not an opera house? Two playbills from the 1820s.

(where he died) and Mendelssohn accompanied Queen Victoria at the piano and played duets with Prince Albert. Verdi disliked the British climate and promptly developed a throat infection when he first visited in 1847; he found the servants 'rougher than rocks' and the food loaded with too much spice and pepper. But if gastronomical taste in London was uneven and, Weber complained, its restaurants unconscionably dear, the city's aesthetic taste was arguably the most sophisticated in Europe. The main attraction of London for Verdi (as it had been for Weber and was to be for Wagner) was the money and prestige it offered; Verdi confided to a friend that in London he could make four times as much for a new opera as in Naples or Milan. In mid-century London, the gala opening of an opera season would vie with the 'Great Stink' or the rebuilding of Parliament as front-page news. London may not have initiated or premiered many of the latest operatic hits; but it provided them with a superb showcase – especially at Gye's Royal Italian Opera, Covent Garden.

Frederick Gye was the son of a highly innovative entrepreneur who had made an early fortune in the wine and tea businesses. In 1821, Gye Snr bought what had once been London's most popular leisure and entertainment venue,

Vauxhall Gardens, but his stewardship coincided with Vauxhall's decline. All this was closely observed by his son, who had acted as his father's assistant and taken over management of Vauxhall, and their relationship gradually soured. If young Frederick Gye inherited anything from his father it was an acute awareness of the challenges and potential pitfalls of theatrical management. During the mid-1840s we find him running 'promenade' concerts at Covent Garden led by the flamboyant French composer-conductor Louis Jullien, and in 1847–8 an unsuccessful season of English-language opera at Drury Lane, also led by Jullien. Thereafter, most of Gye's energies went into the running of his 'R.I.O.' at Covent Garden.

Gye's first priority was to establish that his theatre, and not Her Majesty's, was regarded by audiences and artists as London's principal opera house. The defection of many of Lumley's singers and of Costa to Covent Garden proved a huge boon for Gye. But Lumley fought back ferociously.

Whenever operatic managements have gone head to head as rivals, as Gye and Lumley did at their respective theatres, two things have tended to result. First, potential audiences have been spoiled for choice, at least for a while. Back in the 1730s, opera-loving Londoners were offered the latest Handel opera in one theatre and Farinelli in another; in the 1880s, New Yorkers would be able to choose between the fare on offer at the Academy of Music and the new Metropolitan Opera while, twenty years later, the Met would confront new competition in the form of Oscar Hammerstein's Manhattan Opera. The second outcome is usually that the jam becomes spread too thin. Operatic talent, audiences and money are rarely so abundant as to sustain two competing companies, and one or both generally run into difficulties. And so it was in London after 1847. For a while, Lumley and Gye made various attempts to acquire control of each other's theatres. They also squabbled over artists, notably the soprano Johanna Wagner (a niece of the composer), whom Gye snatched from under Lumley's nose – only to be prohibited from letting her appear by a last-minute court injunction from Lumley, to whom she was contracted. Lumley ran into further financial difficulties and by 1853 was forced to announce that his forthcoming opera season would be cancelled and his theatre closed. Several people, including Gye, made a bid for Her Majesty's over the next couple of years or so, but to no avail. The Covent Garden theatre was now, effectively, *the* home of Italian opera in London: in the words of London's premier music critic, Henry Chorley, the 'old house' was 'fairly beaten out of the field by the new one'.

Throughout his time at the top, Gye kept detailed diaries. These have survived and are packed with revealing details about the mid-Victorian operatic world. The entries frequently touch on the politics of the time, take us in and out of banks and law courts and illustrate the importance Gye attached to retaining contacts in government and at the court of Queen Victoria. We read of Gye's meetings with the great, the good and the titled, and we accompany him to and from continental Europe, learning much en route about travel conditions, food, drink, hotel rooms and his methods of keeping *au fait* with what was going on back home. The diaries teem with the names and activities of every major figure in the operatic world of the time, including some of opera's most celebrated singing stars such as Mario, Grisi and Patti. Above all, perhaps, they illustrate the absolute centrality of finance to the successful promotion of opera. All this can be seen in microcosm during the critical period immediately before and after the Covent Garden fire of 1856.

*

The story of the fire can be traced back to an apparently insignificant diary entry the previous autumn, on 27 September 1855. 'I received a letter from Anderson,' writes Gye, 'about taking the R.I.O. for the pantomime season.' An entertainer named John Henry Anderson, known professionally as 'The Wizard of the North', wanted to rent the Royal Italian Opera over the Christmas period. Gye agreed to meet Anderson. The bargaining proceeded over the next few days and Anderson 'agreed to take R.I.O. after Xmas & to give me £2000 for ten weeks' (though as late as 21 October, writes Gye, Anderson still 'quibbled at the money – £1000 – I requested in advance').

This talk of wizards and pantomimes may sound bizarre to modern ears. There was no round-the-year opera or opera company in mid-Victorian London (or anywhere else for that matter). Gye's Covent Garden opera season would normally last no more than about four months, from mid-April until mid-August, a period of operatic force-feeding during which the theatre would typically stage three or four performances of some fifteen or more works with overlapping casts. Artists, including famous foreign soloists, were contracted for the season and required to sing a total of (say) fifteen performances in five different operas. For much of the rest of the year, Gye would often travel abroad (frequently with his son and eventual successor Ernest) seeking talent for his next season, having meanwhile organized other ways of making money from his theatre. Hence the presence at London's Royal Italian Opera over the 1855–6 Christmas period of the redoubtable 'Wizard of the North'. On 1 January 1856, Gye noted: 'Went to see Anderson's conjuring & the pantomime at the R.I.O. for the first time – the whole very dull & the pantomime poor.' Maybe. But the Wizard was conjuring up good money for his proprietor.

On 9 February, Gye departed for the Continent on one of his talent-scouting expeditions. 'Left London Bridge Station at 8.30pm,' we read in the diaries, catching up with Gye as he checks into his Paris hotel the following day. 'We were at the Bristol about ten this morning in a very good apt – no 9 – 2nd floor looking on to the Place Vendôme.' Then it's straight down to work.

> Called on Mario… who said Lumley had been trying to induce
> Calzado, a Spaniard and the present manager of the Italian Opera
> here, to open Her Majesty's Theatre next season – that he had offered
> him £20,000 do it… but what this sum was for, whether for repairs,
> salaries, rent or for all or any I could not make out – nor could Mario.

With Gye it's always business first, then art. That evening, Gye went to the
opera to see Mario in Verdi's recent hit, *Il trovatore*. The soprano, he noted,
had 'a very agreeable sweet voice not <u>very</u> powerful'. She was 'tolerably good
looking [but] certainly not worth 45000 francs for 4 months which she asks'.

A few days later, Gye received a letter from Madrid from the baritone
Giorgio Ronconi 'in which he seems totally to forget that he is <u>engaged</u> for
the coming season & asks £1200 for 3 months (instead of 4) and says he cannot come until May 1 when in April I want him most – what a rascal!' So on
17 February, Gye set off from Paris to Madrid: an easy air hop these days,
but in 1856 the journey took Gye through Bordeaux, Bayonne, to San
Sebastian thence to Vittoria and Burgos. On the 20th he writes in some exas-
peration: 'This is the morning we <u>were</u> to have arr'd in Madrid but <u>are</u> little
more than <u>half</u>way!' And on the 21st: 'After a most tedious journey we
arrived at Madrid at 6 o'clock this evening having been 85 hours on the
road!' Where he stays is condemned as 'a most wretched dirty hole'. The
hotel, it seems, had 'some miserable rooms over a 10th rate restaurant – food
and beds in fact everything filthy and bad!'

That night, Ronconi was to sing in Rossini's *La Cenerentola* so, 'after a
wash and some dinner (!)', Gye set straight off for Madrid's 'Theatro Real
[*sic*]' noting that the Queen of Spain was present. After the show, Gye went
round to see Ronconi and they agreed to meet the next day when the singer
bargained with the beleaguered manager. 'He tried to get me to give him
£400 per month instead of £300,' reports Gye plaintively. Eventually, Gye
managed to obtain Ronconi's cooperation by enlisting the singer in a revealing little conspiracy. 'I begged him to let me be able to say to his brother
artists that he had kept to his signed arrangement and promised him that if
I had a moderately good season I would make him a present of £200 above
his salary.' Not as much as the singer had hoped for, but enough to buy his
services.

The next day, Gye received a telegraph from Anderson saying he would
like to give a *Bal Masqué* at Covent Garden. Gye knew all about masked balls;
he had held them at Covent Garden himself as recently as December with
Jullien at the head of a vast orchestra of 110 players. On that occasion,
reported *The Times* approvingly (18 December 1855), the theatre had been
'decorated and "fitted up"… with equal good taste and splendour' and there
was 'more bustle and animation and less vulgarity on the part of the motley
throng than we remember at these entertainments for some years'. At around

1.30am, 'the crowd began to thicken; the dancers assumed an extra liveliness (and) the lookers-on became considerably more jovial and obstreperous (while guarding, be it understood, a praiseworthy decorum).' The fact that the occasion had not contravened the boundaries of acceptable taste and behaviour was attributed to Gye, 'whose experience in these matters is proverbial'. But the prospect of a *Bal Masqué* at Covent Garden, while he was abroad and held under the aegis of the Wizard of the North, was not something Gye was keen to countenance. 'I telegraphed,' he says, '& refused this.' Anderson was not prepared to take no for an answer, announced the event, and asked again, more pressingly. It was only after a series of refusals from Gye and a final appeal from Anderson (who thought he would face ruin if the event were cancelled) that Gye, with the greatest reluctance, acceded and the *Bal Masqué* went ahead a couple of weeks later. With catastrophic consequences.

Back in Paris on 3 March, Gye continued to prepare for his forthcoming opera season. Two days later, on the 5th, Gye records that he was up at 7.30am having slept poorly. He seems to have dozed off again when, 'at ¼ past 8', he received a telegraph 'dated London 5 o'clock saying how Covent Garden Theatre is on fire and the house cannot be saved… I was horror struck.' There follows a confusing (and perhaps confused) entry to the effect that he could not obtain a copy of Bradshaw to find out the times of sailings to Britain ('but knew the Boulogne boat crossed at 8 this morning'). Somehow, Gye made his way back to London and, the next day, 'drove to Bow St & beheld the ruins & fearful wreck of the poor theatre & all my vast collection of property – and all my hopes of the most promising season I had ever looked forward to crushed…'

❉

Over the next few weeks, Gye had to face in heightened form every aspect of the opera business – artistic, social, political and above all financial. Essentially, he had two problems to solve. The more urgent was to find a way of mounting the ambitious opera season he had been due to open at Covent Garden in about five weeks' time. Contracts had been signed and repertoire chosen but Gye desperately needed to find a suitable venue. He also needed to give some thought to his longer-term problem: that of finding a permanent home for his opera seasons.

Even more immediate, however, was the distasteful task of assessing his losses. The day after the fire, Gye spent much of his time at the site of his ruined theatre, particularly mourning the loss of his 'splendid collection' of music, 'now so complete as to require little further outlay', all of which had been destroyed. So had the theatre's sets, costumes and props, not to mention a number of priceless art objects including four Hogarths that had hung in Gye's room. Overall, Gye reckoned his losses must have amounted to 'at the

In the early hours of 5 March 1856, at the conclusion of a *Bal Masqué* at Covent Garden, there was a 'sudden change from mad revelry to ghastly fear' as fire swept through the theatre.

very least £30,000' while the insurance was for only £8000. 'Anderson's conjuring things,' Gye notes dryly, 'were packed up [and] were got out.' Anderson had also managed to retrieve his props and profits, while a few other objects, including Costa's piano, were saved.

The building itself, in which Gye as lessee had invested much of his own money, was a total loss. It was also grossly under-insured, according to a report in *The Times* the following day, because:

> subsequent to its re-erection, after being burnt down in 1808, no in-surance-office would issue a policy upon it. To reassure the public against the alarm then created the architect took pains to erect a tank on the roof of the theatre, calculated to hold 18 tons of water which... could be thrown upon any part of the building at a moment's notice.

Four firemen were permanently on duty to check the system. But the system did not work the night it was most needed because, explained *The Times*, 'instead of visiting every part of the theatre, as was their duty, the fire-men on this occasion confined themselves to the more genial atmosphere of the stage.' Buried in the *Times* report of the fire is a paragraph noting that this was not the first theatre to burn down on Anderson's watch and that his own City of Glasgow Theatre, opened in 1844, had suffered the same fate. For a while Anderson seems to have been regarded as part-villain and part-laughing-stock. *Punch* published a cruel piece of doggerel that included the lines:

> Of the Wizard of the North,
>   Sing the Tuesday night's renown,
> When he let the gas burst forth,
>   And burnt the playhouse down.

Gye, by contrast, was showered with sympathy and goodwill. But he was widely regarded as having been ruined financially. A succession of his immediate predecessors at the Royal Italian Opera had all gone bankrupt, as had countless ambitious operatic impresarios elsewhere. It was hard to imagine that Gye could escape a similar fate.

The only person in London to be pleased by Gye's woes was Lumley. If Lumley's problems at Her Majesty's Theatre a few years earlier had created new opportunities for Covent Garden, the seesaw was now spectacularly reversed. Lumley had been in Paris when Gye was there, but later wrote that on 4 March (the day before the fire) an 'uncontrollable impulse seemed to urge me to return to London'. Lumley arrived on the morning of the 5th and was 'startled by the announcement' that Covent Garden had just burned down.

He was more than startled. Lumley, whose own theatre was still closed, was positively thrilled by the news. Indeed, his *Reminiscences* read at this point like a vengeance aria sung by an ecstatic Verdi baritone. 'The destruction of the rival establishment,' writes Lumley, 'had changed, as if by the wave of a magic wand, the whole aspect of my affairs.' Relieved from the 'fatal rivalry' between the two houses, he says, Her Majesty's Theatre might once again 'look forward to a career of prosperity' and 'could sail forth upon a new venture'. By this one event, gushes Lumley, 'difficulties appeared to have shrunk into nothing. What in men's eyes had been mountains now appeared molehills.' He sees himself aided by what he describes as a 'friendly hand' as all the patrons and supporters of his theatre urge 'that every possible step should be taken for the immediate opening of the establishment'. Once again, says Lumley exuberantly, 'I… saw the sceptre of management brought within my reach.' He mentions that Gye (whom Lumley does not deign to name) made approaches to Her Majesty's Theatre, 'But he found me too strong in the field already.' On 19 March, a fortnight after the Covent Garden fire and directly occasioned by it, 'the momentous decision was taken that the theatre should open for the season of 1856!'

Meanwhile, Gye had been racing around London like a Fury as he sought a site for his company. The most urgent problem was that his opera season

In Venice, Carnival (between Christmas and Lent) saw an annual explosion of official and unofficial theatre as the city attracted sexual libertarians, disillusioned priests, rich Grand Tourists, and a stream of actors, dancers and musicians from all over Italy seeking work, money and audiences.

'Serious' opera could surely not be about highwaymen and beggars, but it was the *Beggar's Opera* – not Handel – that became London's hottest ticket from 1728.

In Turin's new Teatro Regio, people scan the rest of the audience from six layers of boxes, while in the 'pit' men sit on benches, turn round to chat, are served food and drink and are kept in order by the presence of an armed guard.

It was not every little boy that
dared jump onto the Empress's
lap. Mozart with Maria Theresa
at Schönbrunn Palace, as imagined
a century later.

Even as a young man, Beethoven had a
reputation for being unkempt, irritable
and a prodigiously gifted musician.

The English soprano Elizabeth Billington was the archetypal prima donna of her day. In this satirical portrait of 1802, she is portrayed as enormously fat, opening her mouth as anxious theatre directors administer large doses of money in order to restore her to full vocal health.

The actor-manager John Philip Kemble was in charge of the Covent Garden theatre when it burned down in 1808. In this Gillray print, he, his brother Charles and their sister Sarah Siddons solicit funds for rebuilding from the generous Duke of Northumberland. In the background, theatrical colleagues dance in the smoking ruins.

London Published by W. S. Fores 50 Piccadilly Augt 9th 1817

May I die if there is'nt Sir George!! — charming man!! as I live he's looking this way — O! the dear fellow!! Vide the Opera box.

The *nouvelle riche* at play, as portrayed by George Cruikshank in 1817. 'Sir George' is obviously of far greater interest to this lady than whatever is on stage.

Weber's *Der Freischütz*, first performed in Berlin in 1821, is a celebration of a nation at peace and a romantic evocation of wider, mysterious forces. The original stage sets for the Wolf's Glen scene, where magic bullets are cast to the accompaniment of ominously supernatural sounds and visions, resembled this painting by the romantic artist Caspar David Friedrich.

GREAT RIOT AT THE ASTOR PLACE OPERA HOUSE, NEW YORK.

The opera house in New York's Astor Place was closed down in the wake of an 1849 riot that left many dead and the building itself pock-marked by bullets.

A 'cross between a railway station and a Turkish bath'? That was certainly not the view of those who were fortunate enough to attend the inauguration of Charles Garnier's magnificent Paris Opera House in 1875.

At the first Bayreuth Festival, in 1876, Wagner's Rhine maidens, supported by crude swimming machines, included the young Lilli Lehmann (centre), later one of the great figures in operatic history, and her younger sister Marie.

By the early 1900s, the music publisher Ricordi was already 'branding' its products – rather as top Hollywood studios were to do a generation later.

was due to begin just over a month later; its opening would almost certainly have to be delayed. But Gye also had to consider the longer-term question of whether to try and rebuild his theatre and, if so, exactly where. Reading his diary, it seems there was scarcely a grandee he did not approach, an important office un-entered, a door in the musical, political or financial world un-knocked on, a powerful hand unshaken as Gye sought a way out of his impasse.

On 7 March, two days after the fire, Sir Charles Barry, the architect of the Houses of Parliament, 'called to express his sorrow'. Gye asked him if he thought the government might find a piece of ground for a new opera theatre. Barry guessed they might and told Gye he thought such a proposal would have the support of Queen Victoria and Prince Albert. One possible site, suggested Barry, might be Trafalgar Square alongside the National Gallery. Gye asked Barry whether he would agree to be the architect. Barry courteously declined but said he would be happy to offer advice.

Day after day, Gye anxiously rides his two horses. One idea after another is pursued for a while; most are abandoned as impracticable. Gye visits Her Majesty's in the Haymarket with the idea of leasing it, perhaps for the long term, and gets his experienced master carpenter Henry Sloman to measure the theatre. Even with considerable renovation, Sloman finds it would hold a far smaller audience than Gye had been led to believe.

Gye begins to consider the possibility of erecting a new theatre on the site of the old. He visits the office of the owner, the Duke of Bedford, whose agent tells him that 'the Duke would not rebuild the theatre himself but had no

Despite the best efforts of the firemen, Covent Garden could not be saved. On his return from Paris, Frederick Gye beheld 'the ruins & fearful wreck of the poor theatre'.

reason to suppose he would object to grant a new long lease for it to be rebuilt.' A glimmer of good news at last. Then Colonel Phipps at Buckingham Palace tells Gye that, while Queen Victoria might agree to patronize the building of a new theatre, 'she could not lend her name if it were a joint stock company.'

Turning again to his more urgent problem, Gye realized that this year's opera season would have to start later than planned. At no point did he seem to contemplate cancelling it entirely: not only had all his artists been contracted, but Gye did not want to risk losing the loyal audiences he had built up over recent years. It occurred to him that a series of large-scale concerts might help provide work for the singers and entertainment for his audiences while producing much-needed revenue. With this in mind, Gye went to see Fergusson, the new manager of the Crystal Palace, now in Sydenham, to propose a series of concerts, including a benefit night that the Queen might attend.

Meanwhile, Gye was still frantically searching for a theatre to house his opera season. In the event, salvation lay just down the road from his burned-out theatre. The Lyceum lay at the southern end of Bow Street, and Gye called on its manager to discuss possible terms. After much bargaining, the two men reached broad agreement. Gye said he would give a definite answer at the end of the following week, once he had been able to ensure he had all his artists on board. That, in turn, meant asking them, at very short notice, to accept a salary cut for what would have to be a curtailed opera season, and to augment their earnings by agreeing to do concerts at the Crystal Palace. Gye spelled all this out to his conductor, Michael Costa. Costa, we read in the diaries, 'did not like the Crystal Palace – said he would consider and let me know'.

That same day, Friday 14 March, Gye received a letter with the good news that the Crystal Palace directors approved of his idea of holding concerts there and asking for a detailed proposal the next day. This he was not in a position to do. Nonetheless, duly summoned, Gye 'Drove gig to Crystal Palace' on the Saturday and explained that 'I must see the artistes who were on their way from Petersburg, that I could not insure [*sic*] Costa's services and that the day must be <u>Wednesday</u> not Saturday' – to all of which the directors made no objection, asking Gye to provide them with an estimate for twelve concerts.

For every step of every ladder Gye ascended, there seemed to be an accompanying snake waiting to swallow him. None was more lethal than his old adversary Lumley, by now on the verge of announcing his own opera season at Her Majesty's. Lumley had his theatre but as yet an inadequate roster of artists, while Gye had contracted his singers but had no theatre. So Lumley sent an emissary to ask whether Gye would be prepared to sell his artists to him and, if so, for how much. Gye's diaries seethe with indignation: 'I told him that

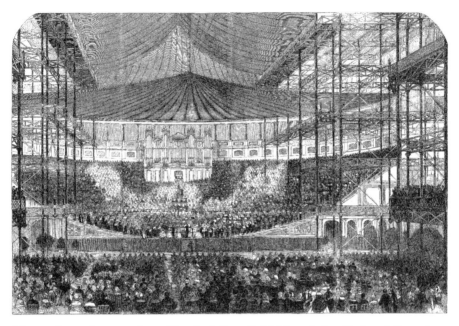

After serving as the centrepiece of London's Great Exhibition of 1851, Sir Joseph Paxton's 'Crystal Palace' was moved to Sydenham in south-east London where it became a venue for giant concerts (and – if the management were lucky – giant audiences). The Crystal Palace burned down in 1936.

without asking what sum [Lumley] proposed to give me I must decline on the ground that… my artistes are not under his management.' For good measure, he reminded his interlocutor that 'in 1852 Lumley had made me a similar proposal offering me £5000 a year & I refused on the same grounds.' In which case, Gye was asked, would he like to reconsider making use of Her Majesty's Theatre? No, he would not, responded Gye, bringing the painful conversation to a close with the information that he was 'just at the point of settling with another theatre, indeed that I was almost committed now'.

Almost committed, but not quite. Everything, for Gye, was in a state of flux. Yet decisions had to be made, some of them urgently. Gye writes about a further meeting with Costa, who, to Gye's evident dismay, 'said he had considered about conducting the concerts at the Crystal Palace & could not do it'. Gye pleads with the conductor, saying that if Costa pulls out, 'the singers would do so too & it was the only means by which I could hold the troupe together as the Lyceum was so small it could not [produce] enough money to pay all expenses.' Costa replied by pointing out that 'the C. Palace Co had made him many offers themselves all of which he had refused.' Clearly, this meeting required all the persuasive powers at Gye's disposal. Eventually, doubtless to Gye's great relief, Costa 'consented to conduct <u>two</u> concerts [on the condition] that it were announced that it was to assist me – & he said he did it as a personal favour to me'.

At last, it began to look as if the pieces in Gye's two complex jigsaw puzzles might slot into place. From the Duke of Bedford's agent, Gye heard that the Duke would be prepared to grant him a new lease of eighty-five years on the site of the Covent Garden theatre at a rent of £1200 a year. Perhaps a new theatre on the site of the old might be feasible. Meanwhile, he signed an amended agreement with the Lyceum to take over the theatre in a month's time, subject to his securing all his leading singers. Many of these were scattered across the Continent, blissfully unaware of the revised terms Gye was now having to offer them: a 3½-month rather than a four-month season for a fee reduced by 25 per cent, with the opportunity of making up the leeway by giving concerts at Crystal Palace. Gye set out immediately for Paris and made at once for his most important artists.

'Called on Grisi,' he writes, '& explained to her my intentions about the Lyceum [and] that I wished all the artistes to make the reduction of a ¼ on their salaries.' He then told her about the concerts he was planning to give at the Crystal Palace, something she and Mario had not previously been contracted to do. 'I had to ask them to do both things,' reports Gye, doubtless relieved when Grisi 'said at once she would do anything in her power'. With Mario and Grisi on board, the rest would surely follow. Overall, Gye's Paris trip was successful, but it was not without its anxieties. 'Lumley arr in Paris last night,' writes Gye on 24 March, '& I hear is really concerning himself with a view to open his theatre.' Gye, all the more anxious to get his season signed and sealed, waits 'anxiously all day' for a confirmatory telegraph from the Lyceum.

Then it's back to London, where Gye's life becomes a frantic kaleidoscope of meetings and messages. On 3 April, he goes to Crystal Palace to sign his contract with the manager – who is away ill. Then to the Lyceum, where the proposed opera season is due to open in less than a fortnight. Gye finds the theatre 'in a peacefully dirty state, not a bit of furniture or thing of any kind to use'.

Meanwhile, it seems the Crystal Palace directors have come up with various objections that need to be sorted out before they can empower Fergusson to sign his copy of the contract. Gye agrees to meet them.

He calls on the Bedford office to discuss the new lease on the Covent Garden site and is pleased to hear that, if he takes it, he would not be obliged to pay the ground rent of £1200 for the first year.

On Saturday, 5 April, Gye goes to meet the Crystal Palace directors again. There is much discussion about ticket pricing, and the directors talk of not admitting season ticket holders, which Gye says would be 'a very great mistake'. Sir Joseph Paxton, the architect of the Crystal Palace, is present and he and Gye chat after the meeting about how best to illuminate the proposed concerts.

On 7 April, Colonel Phipps lets Gye know that the Queen would like a larger box at the Lyceum than she had previously been given at that theatre.

On the 8th, reports Gye, 'Col. Phipps said the Queen had decided on having 3 boxes thrown into one instead of the stage box she has usually occupied at the Lyceum Theatre.'

Then comes a letter from Paris that arouses in Gye the deepest anxieties, not to mention an uncharacteristic touch of paranoia. It is from the tenor Enrico Tamberlik:

> saying he could not accept my new propositions!!! I was thunderstruck: for his brother had written or telegraphed that he would no doubt do as other artists. I can't help thinking that Costa must have heard something of this for today he came & said he was sure I could not open on Tuesday & that he thought I was deceiving him when I said so – I assured him I intended – & yet he did not seem satisfied – moreover he was to have called the chorus today & he has not & I have sent him their engagements to correct & get printed & signed but he has not.

For once, Gye exhibits what look like signs of panic. However, he was not a man to be deflected from his chosen course of action. With Lumley breathing down his neck, he had no time to lose. The competition between the two was intense and, once more, Gye was determined not to cede victory to his rival. On 9 April 1856, barely a month after the Covent Garden fire, two adjacent announcements appeared in the classified ads in *The Times*. The first read:

> HER MAJESTY'S THEATRE – It is respectfully announced that Her Majesty's Theatre will RE-OPEN early in May. Engagements of great interest have been effected both in Opera and Ballet, and the best exertions used to make the arrangements worthy of the occasion. The prospectus will shortly be issued.

Immediately below was another, far more specific:

> ROYAL ITALIAN OPERA – Mr Gye begs most respectfully to announce that he will, during the present season, give the OPERA at the ROYAL LYCEUM THEATRE.

Gye's advertisement goes on to name his singers: first the women, starting with Grisi, then the men, starting with Mario and including Signor Tamberlik 'for a few nights only, previous to his departure for Rio Janeiro [*sic*]'. Costa is announced as music director and Gye lists the ladies who will provide the 'Divertissements' and a repertoire of seventeen operas (including 'Verdi's new opera, *La traviata*'). 'The subscription will be for forty nights,'

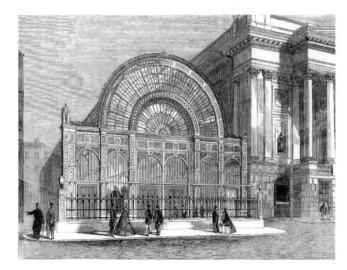

The 'Royal Italian Opera', the third theatre on the Covent Garden site, was designed by Edward Barry (son of Sir Charles Barry, the architect of the Houses of Parliament). It opened in 1858, and the adjacent Floral Hall a couple of years later.

concludes Gye's ad, 'commencing Tuesday next, April 15, on which occasion will be performed Verdi's new grand opera IL TROVATORE'.

In the event, Gye, with no theatre to his name, opened as announced with a season at the Lyceum, his artists rallying round in his time of need. The opening night was 'so successful', opined *The Times*, 'as to augur well for the prospects of the Royal Italian Opera in its present asylum; and Mr Gye, the manager, may be congratulated on having thus far weathered the tempest that threatened to annihilate him.'

Three weeks later, Her Majesty's reopened for the first time in four years with what proved an equally successful season. London's 'opera wars' looked set to resume. They soon fizzled out. In 1858, a new 'Royal Italian Opera' arose on the site of the old Covent Garden Theatre designed by Sir Charles Barry's son, Edward Barry. By the time of the opening, on 15 May, Gye was consigned to his bed by nervous exhaustion. But the theatre opened triumphantly with a gala performance of Meyerbeer's *Les Huguenots* that began late and went on so long that at 12.30am, with an act still to go, the stage manager announced to a weary audience that it might be wiser to call it a day and for everyone to go home. Gye soon recovered from his sickness and remained in charge at Covent Garden for another two decades, surviving a further succession of artistic, legal and financial hazards until his death as a result of a shooting accident.

As for Lumley, he was eased out of his interests in Her Majesty's and in 1858, a few months after the opening of Gye's new Covent Garden theatre, retired altogether from the business. Nine years later, Lumley's old theatre, Her Majesty's, succumbed to fire.

PART III

Opera Resurgens
c.1860–1900

Culture and Politics in Central and Eastern Europe

'The beloved Czech nation will not die!' – the stirring vision of the future, uttered by the mythical Princess Libuše at the climax of Smetana's opera avowedly celebrating the ancient roots of the Czech people. There is still a frisson of excitement in the auditorium of Prague's National Theatre whenever Smetana's heroine projects these words out towards the audience. It was with *Libuše* that the theatre was inaugurated on 11 June 1881. Then, in August, it burned down thanks to a negligent tinsmith working on the roof. A nationwide outpouring of dismay was followed by an equally widespread readiness throughout the Czech lands to contribute to the rebuilding. On 18 November 1883, the National Theatre reopened, complete with the latest electric lighting and decorated with richly elaborate artwork representing the stylized and heroized history of the Czechs. Once again the work performed was *Libuše*.

Cultural nationalism was not new to the Czech people or to Prague. Like other cities, Prague had witnessed a failed revolution in 1848, thereafter reverting to what it had been in Mozart's day: a Bohemian outpost of Habsburg rule, controlled by German-speaking representatives of a government based in Vienna. When the young Bedřich Smetana first came to Prague in 1843, he spoke and wrote German, like any educated Bohemian, calling the city's great river, for example, by its German name, the 'Moldau'. Any incipient aspirations to Czech nationhood were monitored, censored and suppressed. Instead, Czech nationalism, like that in Italy or Hungary, increasingly adopted cultural forms. A fundraising campaign was begun in 1850 (and permitted by the authorities) with the aim of financing a Czech-language theatre in Prague. Before long, a 'Provisional' Czech theatre began to arise on the banks of the river which Smetana, earnestly struggling to improve his sketchy Czech, soon learned to call the 'Vltava'. Prague in mid-century was modernizing and expanding. In the process, it became inexorably an increasingly 'Czech' city as Czechs poured into the city in their thousands and Austrian hegemony perceptibly diminished. In 1866, when Habsburg armies succumbed to the superior forces of Bismarck, Prague suffered the humiliation of occupation

The symbol of emerging Czech nationalism: Prague's National Theatre ('Národní Divadlo')
built in the 1880s on the banks of the Vltava.

by Prussian troops. And when, a year later, a degree of political autonomy
was granted to Hungary, this redoubled the parallel aspirations of the
Czechs. In May 1868, when the foundation stone was laid of a proposed
Czech National Theatre (to replace, or incorporate, the earlier 'Provisional'
theatre), crowds estimated in excess of 60,000 descended on Prague to witness
the ceremony and accompanying celebrations: a quasi-political demonstration
of unanticipated magnitude. Many communities from throughout the Czech-
speaking lands and beyond contributed their own 'foundation stones',
including one from the Czech community in Chicago.*

A measure of the impact of Prague's new National Theatre can be
gleaned from the fact that the city's German community promptly built an
opera house of its own in another part of town: the richly embellished Neues
Deutsches Theater (now the 'State' Theatre), opened in 1888. The rivalry
between the two communities continued, as symbolized by the way their
respective opera houses each tried to outdo the other. However, as the proportion of Czechs in the population of Prague continued to grow, so did their
cultural and political confidence. In the early twentieth century, the Great
War finally brought the Habsburg Empire to an end, the peace treaty that followed it establishing a new nation called Czechoslovakia: the first time the
Czechs had had a self-governing state of their own since 1620. To mark the
event, in November 1918, the great Czech soprano Emmy Destinn sang the

* Some of these stones are displayed in the lower depths of the National Theatre (alongside
an exhibition illustrating the history of the theatre).

title role of *Libuše*. Later in the century, further performances of *Libuše* were mounted to mark the end of the Nazi occupation in 1945, the renovation of Prague's National Theatre in 1983 and, in January 1990, the collapse of Communism.

Opera, in Prague as elsewhere, clearly became a conspicuous embodiment of the national aspirations that swept through much of Europe during the nineteenth century, many composers – like Smetana – setting to music the great myths of their respective national histories. Nor was it just a question of subject-matter; listen to the dances in Smetana's *Bartered Bride* or the great choruses from Mussorgsky's *Boris Godunov* and you hear a composer trying to invoke in music what he imagines to be the 'national character' of his people (rather as Verdi had done earlier). Cultural nationalism was catching. However, it did not necessarily threaten or weaken the jurisdictions that incubated it. The Austrian Habsburgs may have seen their authority waning as Italians, Czechs and Hungarians grew in confidence and assertiveness. Further east, the Russian bear simply tightened its grip on its dissident minorities while vouchsafing a degree of aid and comfort to those who celebrated their national culture.

*

There is no better evocation in literature of the absurdity of opera than Natasha Rostov's visit to the opera in *War and Peace*. The overture is already playing when the Rostovs arrive in their box. In the auditorium there is a buzz of conversation until the curtain rises and a hush descends. To Natasha, her pretty young head full of romantic anxieties, it is the performance in the permanently lighted auditorium that primarily attracts her attention. She notes the 'pomaded heads in the stalls' and 'half-naked women in the boxes'. As for the opera itself, she watches it spasmodically and finds it grotesquely mannered. In the opening scene there is a fat girl sitting on a bench to the back of which a piece of green cardboard is glued. Later, a man with stout legs in silk tights goes up to her, sings and waves his arms about. In the second act there is a cemetery scene with a round hole in the backdrop to represent the moon. In one scene, a bare-legged man leaps very high in the air, making quick movements with his feet, for which he was apparently paid a prodigious sum. The evening is not wasted, however, for the handsome Anatole appears at the end and squeezes Natasha's arm as he helps her into her carriage.

By the time Tolstoy was writing *War and Peace* in the 1860s, he and other intellectuals were increasingly turning away from purely Western influences, seeking inspiration instead in traditional Russian and Slavic sources. The disaster of Russia's defeat by France and Britain in the Crimean War led to much agonized debate about the nation's supposed shortcomings. Discontent was widespread. Semi-secret political societies sprang up advocating a crude form of communism, anarchism or nihilism. Fearing revolution, and perhaps in response to genuinely liberal instincts, Tsar Alexander II instituted a series of reforms, among them the emancipation of the serfs and the introduction of new judicial and penal codes. It was with his encouragement that the Mariinsky theatre was built in St Petersburg in 1860. Soon afterwards, music academies were founded in St Petersburg and Moscow, the former led by Anton Rubinstein. In 1862, St Petersburg saw the world premiere of an opera by Verdi, no less: *La forza del destino*.

Much of this represented genuine enlightenment. But many were still smouldering during these years over the Crimean debacle, resentful at how the supposedly Christian West had 'betrayed' Russia by fighting alongside Ottoman Turkey. The West was revealed as perfidious, its much-vaunted cultural supremacy a cover for economic imperialism. Such attitudes seem to have spilled over into the reception of *Forza*. The opera house was one of the few public spaces in Tsarist Russia in which radical-minded intellectuals could legally assemble, and a demonstration by a group of Russian nationalists intended to disrupt the Verdi premiere was apparently only thwarted by the overwhelming applause for Verdi personally. Critics pointed out the dramatic weaknesses of the piece, while many people were said to have resented the fact that Verdi received a fee far higher than would ever be paid to a Russian composer.

During these years, the cry went up once more to move away from false Western influences, to turn instead to true Slavic values and drink at the pure well of Mother Russia. To some, this suggested an almost mystical surrender into the bosom of the church, to others a systematic study of Russian and Oriental (that is, central Asian) folklore and ethnography. The influential critic Vladimir Stasov became one of the foremost advocates of a 'national' culture, arguing for a more characteristically Russian style of music than anything on offer at the new conservatoires. Under his leadership and that of the composer Balakirev, a group of largely amateur young musicians, deliberately eschewing the academy with its heavy emphasis on the German classics, taught themselves and each other about Russian music and its traditions. In addition to Balakirev, the group came to include Cui (a military engineer), Borodin (a chemist), Rimsky-Korsakov (a naval officer) and an ex-guardsman, civil servant and serial drinker, Modest Mussorgsky. It was Stasov who first dubbed them 'the mighty handful'.

Balakirev and his friends sought inspiration far from Moscow and St Petersburg, turning to the giant hinterland of remote, provincial Russia: the icons and tolling bells of the small-town monastery, the songs of bargees on the Volga, the wooden huts and houses of the steppe-lands, the folktales and dance rhythms of the Caucasus, the mighty warriors and shamanistic magic of the 'Orient' – the world evoked in parts of Borodin's *Prince Igor*, Rimsky-Korsakov's *The Golden Cockerel* and *Scheherazade* and Stravinsky's *Firebird*.

In this 1871 caricature of Russia's 'Mighty Handful', Cui can be seen on the lower left with Balakirev standing above him wielding a baton. The central figure in national costume blowing a horn and beating a drum is Stasov. Rimsky-Korsakov is portrayed as a crab while the arrogant rooster leading the parade is Mussorgsky.

Many operas, certainly, were placed in historical Moscow: for example, Mussorgsky's *Boris Godunov* and *Khovanshchina*. But these, too, evoked a potently mythologized Russia, a Muscovy of the mind with its Old Believers and Holy Fools, a world in which the native wisdom of the 'people' (or of 'Nanny') proves wiser than the decisions of kings and generals. Thus, the artistic inspiration of the 'national' school of composers sailed freely across an imaginative map of time and space.

The resulting works were nevertheless firmly anchored where they were produced: in St Petersburg and Moscow. There was opera elsewhere, not least in some of the major centres of non-Russian populations such as Odessa, Kiev, Tbilisi (where the great bass Fyodor Shalyapin grew up) and the Baltic capitals. However, these cities were essentially local outposts of tsarism, their theatrical offerings and audiences necessarily mirrors of the tastes and styles of St Petersburg. None was a centre of emergent national culture. The Italians and Czechs might have developed national operatic styles in conscious opposition to Vienna; but as long as the Tsars were firmly in place there was little likelihood of a distinctively 'Latvian', 'Georgian' or 'Ukrainian' operatic culture emerging. Alexander II's administrative and judicial reforms were sparingly applied outside the Russian homeland while non-Russian languages were proscribed in print and any signs of Polish, Lithuanian or Ukrainian nationalism repressed. 'Liberalism', it seemed, was strictly limited and for Russians only.

Alexander II was assassinated in 1881. His son and successor, Alexander III, pressed ahead with a ruthless policy of Russification, though one by-product of his government's rationalizing zeal was the repeal of an 1803 decree that had made Russia's theatres a crown monopoly, the new government thereby permitting the establishment of private theatres. One of the most notable was run by the railway millionaire and art lover Savva Mamontov. Mamontov was an influential patron of the arts in late nineteenth-century Russia, a kind of latter-day Renaissance prince. As a young man, he had developed a fine operatic bass voice; in his maturity, Mamontov ran his railway business at a profit and ploughed much of his money and time into the arts. His estate at Abramtsevo, north-east of Moscow, became a magnet for a group of young painters, sculptors, architects, ceramicists and folklorists whom Mamontov encouraged to recapture traditional Russian subjects and skills. One of the ideas to emerge from the Abramtsevo artists' colony was the establishment in 1885 of the Mamontov Private Opera in Moscow. Mamontov himself was actively involved in every aspect of the company's work as it mounted magnificent productions of new Rimsky operas and introduced Shalyapin to Moscow audiences. This bold enterprise did not last long. In 1900, in response to questionable but wounding accusations of business misdealings, Mamontov faced trial and his Private Opera company collapsed, its memory cherished later by those who savoured its influence on Diaghilev, the Ballets Russes, Chagall, Benois and Stravinsky.

Until the Revolution of 1917, the history of opera in Russia was virtually tantamount to that of its two great western cities. In St Petersburg and Moscow, a tiny, highly privileged minority of the population went to see a small repertoire of approved works, by French or Italian composers or acceptable Russian 'nationalists', performed in a handful of theatres. Some probably attended to what was on stage scarcely more than Tolstoy's Natasha had done. Others would have been excited by the big voices, swirling costumes, catchy rhythms and vivid stagecraft as opera came to be increasingly decked in national colours. To a highly centralized tsarist state pursuing an aggressively 'Russian' policy, opera was an acceptable diversion. There was political *sub*version a-plenty for the authorities to worry about. But none of it came from what was presented by Mamontov or composed by Mussorgsky or Rimsky or their friends. In any case, little of what these men produced was known outside an enclave of metropolitan initiates. Few people outside the circle, indeed, had ever heard of them.

*

Everybody had heard of Richard Wagner. He was living in Switzerland at the time of the Franco-Prussian War and rejoiced in the creation of a united

German Empire. Like Hans Sachs in *Die Meistersinger*, Wagner was devoted to Germany and German art, a cultural patriot to his sensitive fingertips. But like the gods, giants and dwarfs in the *Ring*, Wagner was also perpetually plagued by the need for gold. Not from avarice, of course; Wagner was far too high-minded for that. But to finance his ever-grander artistic schemes.

Wagner had the misfortune to grow up in a world in which traditional forms of regal and aristocratic patronage were much diminished while the professional ladders on which future composers would ascend were not yet securely in place. If Verdi suffered from what he would later dub his years in the galley, Wagner's early years read almost like a travel agent's catalogue. Born in Leipzig in 1813, he fetched up for variable periods in Dresden, Würzburg, Königsberg, Riga, London and Paris before returning to Dresden. During much of this time, Wagner was recurrently in debt, surviving by a combination of good luck (he and his wife Minna escaped from Riga, pursued by creditors, in cloak-and-dagger fashion), hard work, inherent talent and unquenchable self-confidence. His most trying time was probably the demoralizing two and a half years he and Minna spent in that operatic cosmopolis, Paris. Wagner, now in his late twenties, was desperate for the opportunity to perform his emerging *oeuvre* but, despite initial goodwill and helpful contacts from Meyerbeer and others, he was largely ignored and had to eke out a precarious living by making arrangements of other people's music and writing often splenetic articles about what else was on offer. At one point, Wagner was threatened with imprisonment for debt before eventually obtaining a regular, salaried post at the Dresden court opera, where his early operas were produced to considerable acclaim. Wagner's Dresden triumphs ended in May 1849 with a hasty retreat after his revolutionary involvements; when he fled Dresden he was, yet again, deeply in debt. For thirteen years, Wagner lived in exile from his native Saxony, mostly in Zurich where he devoted himself largely to prose works and early drafts of what were to become his mature masterpieces. Later, we find him in Venice, then Paris again, moving in 1862 to Vienna (having by now shed Minna). Despite an extensive international concert tour which Wagner hoped would recoup his debts, he again found himself threatened with arrest for debt. In March 1864, he fled Vienna for Stuttgart, where he stayed with friends. Wagner was deeply demoralized and desperate for funds. He felt – and said quite openly – that the world owed him a living, he who gave the world so much beauty. Clearly he was in despair. Then, in early May, an emissary appeared with a letter from the King of Bavaria.

Wagner had never lacked admirers keen to help, and he was especially adept at courting – and often abusing – the most generous among them. Meyerbeer, so kind to the young man in Paris, received little but scorn from the mature Wagner, while he rewarded his Zurich benefactor Otto Wesendonck by falling in love with his wife, Mathilde. Liszt, who had helped Wagner

King Ludwig II of Bavaria decorated his palaces with Wagnerian motifs, and is here portrayed as King Lohengrin, complete with an entourage of swans and watched over by a Wagnerian man-in-the-moon. The 'Mad' King is easy to make fun of; but without his munificence Wagner could probably not have completed the *Ring* or created the Bayreuth Festival.

escape from Dresden and was later to become his father-in-law, was regarded by Wagner as something of a nuisance in later life. Then there was that eccentric reincarnation of an earlier, almost obsolete era of royal patronage and Wagner's most devoted admirer of all, King Ludwig II of Bavaria.

Ludwig came to the throne as a youth of eighteen on the death of his father in March 1864 and one of his earliest acts as king was to invite his idol to court in Munich, pay off Wagner's debts and give him a regular stipend. Ludwig was a beautiful, callow, homosexual youth much given to romantic maunderings. In addition to his generosity to Wagner, he is best remembered as the builder of extravagant fairy-tale palaces such as Neuschwanstein and the never completed Herrenchiemsee, which was intended to outdo Versailles. An unsuccessful effort to get the unworldly monarch to marry ended in tragi-comedy and his short life ended in 1886 (three years after Wagner's death) face downwards in Lake Starnberg.

Munich had long been one of Europe's great operatic centres, proud of a tradition going back to 1653, the longest continuous record outside Italy. For a century and a half, opera in Munich was the private prerogative of the Wittelsbach court, Bavaria's ruling family, who entertained their guests from the 1750s onwards in their exquisite Residenz theatre designed by Cuvilliés. It was here that the young Mozart had one of his earliest triumphs with an *opera seria*, *Idomeneo*. The city expanded, and its new theatre was opened in 1811: a great Corinthian-columned Greek temple, nowadays the home of the Bavarian State Opera. The new Nationaltheater contained (as it does today) 2100 seats – which at the time represented something like 4 per cent of Munich's entire population of around 54,000; an equivalent theatre in modern London or New York would be required to seat some 400,000 patrons. Munich's National Theatre, like so many, burned down a few years later, but was rebuilt with money raised from a beer tax (this was Bavaria after all) and reopened in 1825, topped by the double pediment that still makes it distinctive. This was the house, and the opera-loving city, to which Wagner was invited by the new King of Bavaria in 1864.

Ludwig was ecstatic at having Wagner in personal tow. 'I am nothing, HE everything,' wrote the besotted youth in his diary, and referred to Wagner as 'godlike' and 'the Unique and Incomparable One'. One project Ludwig and Wagner discussed in Munich was the idea of a festival entirely devoted to opera, complete with a theatre overlooking the River Isar for which designs were drawn up by Gottfried Semper. It did not happen, but the seeds were sown. Wagner soon managed to make himself unpopular around the court and in the city generally. People said he thought of himself as joint ruler of Bavaria and began referring to him as 'Lolus Montez'.* Jealousy was perhaps inevitable towards anyone so close to the monarch (and the civil purse), especially someone as preternaturally arrogant as Wagner, while the composer's reputation was not helped by the fact that he had started an affair with Cosima, the wife of Ludwig's court music director Hans von Bülow (and daughter of Liszt and Marie d'Agoult). By the end of 1865, the moonstruck monarch had no alternative but to dismiss Wagner, who, followed by Cosima, went to live in Switzerland overlooking Lake Lucerne. From afar, Wagner continued to court the King, shrewdly keeping him up to date with his work. While not officially reinstated, Wagner was frequently invited back to Munich and it was here, in the great National Theatre just outside the royal residence, that the world first heard *Tristan*, *Meistersinger* and the first two episodes of the *Ring*.

When Germany was united in 1871 under an emperor, the King of Bavaria was permitted to retain his title and perquisites. This enabled Ludwig to continue his periodic subventions of Wagner and his work. Without the attention and money he was able to bestow, Wagner would very likely never have completed the *Ring* and would certainly not have been able to fund and build the Bayreuth Festival Theatre in which the full cycle was first performed.

Wagner was not the first or last artist to behave obsequiously towards a wealthy patron, and too much has probably been made of how Wagner used and abused his monarch's goodwill. Ludwig was generous, and people around him resented this. However, the sums were not large. It has been calculated that, over the nearly twenty years of their relationship, Wagner

*Lola Montez was the mistress of the King's grandfather, Ludwig I of Bavaria.

received an aggregate amounting to less than the King spent on the bed-chamber at Herrenchiemsee, or about a third of the amount spent on the bridal carriage for the royal wedding that never took place. Furthermore, the King often turned Wagner down. After Wagner had left Munich and begun to think of planning his festival and theatre elsewhere, Ludwig insisted, against the composer's urgent requests, that premieres of the first *Ring* operas take place (in what Wagner regarded as inferior productions) at his court theatre. Later, as Wagner's dream of a festival in Bayreuth ran into funding problems and was repeatedly postponed, he kept begging Ludwig to offer a guarantee which the King's ministers advised against.

One has some sympathy for Wagner; here was a man of stupendous talent driven by a powerful artistic vision that he was determined to see materialize. Yet it is hard to warm to his constant irritation whenever the world refused to give him what he wanted, or to his rank dissimulation – one biographer calls it lying – as he repeatedly tried to squeeze money out of his agonized monarch. In February 1874, Wagner had a meeting with represen-tatives of the royal household. They told him that the King could not agree to an unqualified guarantee to underwrite Wagner's soaring costs but would lend him a substantial sum on the understanding that the stage decorations etc. would be collateral until the debt was repaid. Reasonable enough, one might think. But Wagner returned home in an ill-humour, Cosima noted, and there are recurrent entries in her diary during these years showing how vexed Wagner was at the way the King had let him down.

*

Wagner, and the Bayreuth Festival he finally inaugurated in 1876, might be seen to represent the acme of nineteenth-century romanticism, not only in the nature of the works performed but in the very way in which high art and the artist were regarded. The composer did not call his creations 'operas', preferring the term *Gesamtkunstwerk*: work that integrated all the arts. Thus, Wagner not only wrote his own texts and scores, but strove to direct productions of his work too, always with the eventual aim of erecting a new theatre built specially for the purpose. Wagner's inspiration – like that of the earliest creators of opera – was the theatre of classical Greece. Just as the *Ring* was conceived as a tetralogy analogous to the *Oresteia* by Aeschylus, the sense of occasion shared by those present and the space in which the work should be performed were also to have parallels in ancient Athens. The Festival Theatre itself he planned to be a simple, largely unadorned wooden structure, its auditorium (roofed in Bayreuth if not in Athens) fan-shaped, with no aisles, so as to create excellent sightlines from every seat. Lights would be lowered throughout and great trouble taken to create a near-perfect acoustic. The orchestra was to be covered by a curved hood so that audiences would not be distracted by the sight of conductor or instrumentalists and

Ever since the first Bayreuth Festival in 1876, true Wagner lovers have tended to regard the Master's theatre atop the 'Green Hill' with almost religious awe, a kind of musico-dramatic Mecca.

orchestral sound would meld and not overpower that of the singers. Elsewhere, people may have gone to the opera to show off their finery or mix with the mighty; at his Bayreuth Festspielhaus Wagner expected them to come for the sole purpose of concentrating on high art. This was a holy site for a single purpose, almost more temple than theatre. Wagner's original idea was that singers would give their services free for the privilege of serving his art and that audiences, like congregations, would not be asked for anything so squalid as payment for admission. This particular aspect of Wagner's mission proved impracticable given the stupendous pre-Festival bills he ran up (not to mention the penury of many of his singers), and the whole project would have foundered and left Wagner in permanent debt had it not been for a further generous loan from the increasingly cash-strapped but still besotted King of Bavaria.

Against all odds, the Bayreuth Festival did take place in August 1876. Liszt was there, of course. And Nietzsche (still an admirer, though not for long) and some of the best among the younger generation of composers, including Grieg, Saint-Saëns and Tchaikovsky. The Kaiser, Wilhelm I, blessed the Festival with his presence and was welcomed by Wagner to his new temple. How did you bring it off, he asked Wagner affably (though, on leaving, the Kaiser stumbled awkwardly down a doorstep and according to Cosima it took all Wagner's strength to hold him and save him from possible death).

The Festival was not an unmitigated success. The little Franconian town was not prepared for the size of the invasion and some visitors had difficulty finding accommodation while many had difficulty finding food. Tchaikovsky wrote of 'restless people, wandering through the town… seeking to satisfy the pangs of hunger'. After one performance, he noted what he called the 'battle' for a place at the theatre restaurant – a battle most people inevitably lost, only to find that every seat at every inn in town was also taken. He saw one woman, the wife of a prominent Russian, 'who had not eaten one meal during the whole of her sojourn in Bayreuth'. Coffee, reported Tchaikovsky, was her sole succour.

It was easy to make fun of the logistical inadequacies; also, of some of the less felicitous technical paraphernalia of the stagings such as the primitive 'swimming machines' in which the Rhine maidens (among them the young Lilli Lehmann) had to cavort. Or the fact that the newly installed stage lighting periodically malfunctioned. But musically, the performances must have been magnificent and the fact was that, against almost insuperable odds, Wagner had succeeded in his mammoth ambition. He had created what, by any standards, most agreed was one of the greatest single artistic achievements of any single human being and raised the money to build a theatre and mount a festival so that it could be performed in near-ideal conditions.

*

If the first representation of the *Ring* at Bayreuth was a high point in the history of nineteenth-century romanticism, how far was Wagner also representative of German nationalism? From his home alongside Lake Lucerne he followed the Franco-Prussian war in detail. At first, he had some sympathy for the French prime minister, Emile Ollivier (a brother-in-law of Cosima Wagner); Ollivier, he commented, was 'a good and intelligent person' but shared 'his country's insolence' and this had robbed Ollivier of his senses and forced him into war. Wagner was exhilarated as Germany became united, admired Bismarck, wrote poems extolling the German troops and spoke of the new Kaiser as possessing 'qualities which the Universal Spirit needs in order to achieve great things'. Wagner and Cosima (notwithstanding her Hungarian father and French mother) were German patriots. Thus, Wagner upbraided his doctor for daring to question the German right to take Alsace and Lorraine. The idea of all Germans pulling together was particularly appealing; how uplifting it must be, wrote Cosima in her diary, 'for Bavaria, Saxony, and Württemberg to be fighting now as a German army!' To celebrate the Prussian victory, Wagner wrote a sententious piece of patriotic nonsense (which he called 'A Capitulation') in which he cruelly ridiculed the recent suffering of the French.

There were limits to Wagner's German patriotism, however. For a start, it was primarily cultural. He was devoted to German art and culture, a passion that led him to investigate the history and mythology of the German past, its literature and its music and to try to draw them together. But Wagner's tastes and interests went far wider. In addition to his love of things German, he was an avid reader of Aeschylus and Sophocles, Gibbon, Scott and Byron, loved the lyrical cantilena of Bellini and was a frequent visitor to Italy (where he died). He read Renan's *Life of Jesus* and the *Bhagavad-Gita* and, like Verdi, he revered Shakespeare.

Nor did Wagner's pride in German culture spill over into uncritical political nationalism. When asked to write a special march to mark the coronation of the Kaiser, he did so with the greatest reluctance and turned out a bombastic piece in which he took little pride, and within a very short time was becoming highly critical of the new nation. In 1873, he was prepared to acknowledge to a lunch guest that the German armies had displayed impressive strength. But he went on: '[We] are anxiously waiting to see whether this strength can extend to other fields', adding 'I am not to be counted among the ranks of present-day patriots.' Wagner considered himself 'nailed on the cross of the German ideal', something of which the new Germany fell far short in his view. 'We might at a pinch have a German Reich,' he said in 1874, 'but we have no German nation.' Inevitably, perhaps, the unification of Germany, like that of Italy (and perhaps like the German reunification of more recent times), proved to be something of a disappointment to some who had invested such high hopes in it.

The year of the first Bayreuth Festival, 1876, was also the year in which the United States celebrated the centenary of its independence. Wagner, desperate for funds, composed a march for the Philadelphia Centennial Exposition, a highly lucrative commission that helped his Festival pot to keep simmering, if not to boil. Later that year, after the Bayreuth Festival had come and gone, Wagner was forced to contemplate a pile of unpaid bills, including loans he was due to repay to the exchequer of the Bavarian King. Irascible, weary and often ill, Wagner went to London in spring 1877 to conduct a series of concerts at the recently opened Royal Albert Hall which, however, failed to make a profit.

Ten days after his return, we find Wagner talking about moving to the United States, earning proper money and never returning to Germany. Once planted in his mind, the idea grew. He would start a centre of musical education in America, he said. Perhaps in Minnesota. By 1880, he was adamant. America was 'the only place on the whole map which he can gaze upon with any pleasure', reported Cosima. Sick, miserable and increasingly misanthropic, Wagner was by now regarding his fellow Germans with increasing scorn, seemingly incredulous that they did not love (and finance) him more generously. In May, even as he began to struggle with what was to become his final masterpiece, *Parsifal*, Wagner was wondering bitterly what his art had to do with 'these cruel and indifferent people'. He 'wants to leave the Reich and take out American citizenship', noted Cosima. And on 1 September 1880 she quotes Wagner as saying: 'I have made up my mind to go to America.'

*

By the end of his life, Wagner was widely regarded as an iron-willed genius who, like his adored Beethoven, had single-handedly sculpted the very essence of human experience into artistic form. In Wagner's hands, art transcended mere artifice, aiming, rather, at the redemption of humanity. 'Wagnerism' became almost a disease to some, a faith to many. Many worshipped at the shrine. Others detested him and his work (Tolstoy made ruthless fun of the *Ring*, pronouncing it a model of 'counterfeit art'; but then, as we have seen, Tolstoy was prone to make fun of opera in general). Few who knew of Wagner and his works remained indifferent. For most reasonably educated, middle-class people across the world, it was almost impossible *not* to know about him. In Naples, Wagner took a tram into the city and was offended by an encounter with a German headmaster who recognized him (most celebrities would have been delighted). And as the piano became a *sine qua non* of every genteel drawing room, eager young amateurs everywhere propped up in front of them the latest popular medleys of Wagneriana.

Wagner was the most Protean of artists. Was he a passionate Christian or a blasphemous heretic, a saint or a sybarite? There was plenty of evidence in Wagner's life and music for almost any view. A revolutionary (and friend of the anarchist Bakunin) who had had to flee for his life from Dresden, Wagner courted kings and Kaisers; a transcendental symbolist whose *Ring* (thought Bernard Shaw) was a searing critique of rampant capitalism; a high-minded idealist who was not above writing a showy piece of nonsense if the money was good. Fifty years after the Master's death, his indisputable artistic genius allied to his assertive Germanness and crude anti-Semitism enabled Hitler to expropriate Wagner as a supposed precursor of Nazism; to this day his music is avoided in Israel.

In Britain, Shaw was an early convert, while among the most evocative *fin-de-siècle* illustrations of Wagner's sado-erotic imagination are the drawings of Beardsley. To the poet Yeats and the composer Rutland Boughton, on the other hand, it was the transcendental, mystical quality that appealed, as it did to the Russian composer and pianist Skryabin. In Italy, a rising generation of musicians and artists took their cue not from Verdi but from Wagner; some of Puccini's early scores are steeped in 'Wagnerismo', as are the writings of that epitome of Italian romantic nationalism D'Annunzio. In France, Baudelaire and Berlioz paid early court, followed by Gounod, Saint-Saëns, Chabrier, and writers such as Mallarmé and Romain Rolland. The young Renoir made a pilgrimage to Palermo for the honour of painting the Master, Proust wrote of his alter-ego Marcel spending a reflective afternoon playing through excerpts from *Tristan* and Fauré composed his popular

Tristan invites Isolde to drink the magic potion in this illustration by Aubrey Beardsley: Wagner as portrayed through the filter of *art nouveau*.

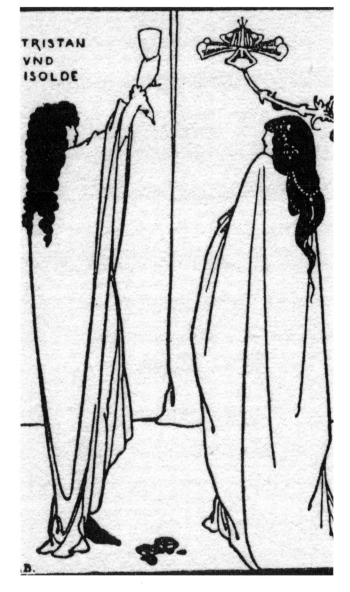

tribute, 'Souvenir de Bayreuth'. The Austrian composer Bruckner regarded Wagner with a degree of awe verging on idolatry. And in America, where the Master dreamed in vain of emigrating, the Wagner virus took particularly powerful hold.

CHAPTER 11

New York's Gilded Age

The Metropolitan Opera, New York, began as an Italian house, then became a German one. That is to say, it produced everything in Italian in its first year; then, during the rest of its first decade, it mounted a lot of Wagner and was led by German conductors. Its early roots and subsequent flowering lay in soil nourished by decades of immigration, especially from Germany and Italy. Giuseppe Giacosa, the Italian dramatist (and librettist to Puccini), visited America in 1898 and later described the bustle and squalor of the Italian settlements he had found in New York and Chicago:

> People live there out of doors, in view of the inclement climate, a sign of how much worse must be the inside of their homes... Ragged, thin men wander about from one shop to another or gather around the entrance of a saloon from which they are served the bitter dregs of the beer bottles retailed in healthy places to healthy people... the women carry on in full view all the pitiful tasks of their domestic life. They suckle their children, sew, clean the faded greens which are the only substance of their soup, wash their clothes in greasy buckets, untangle and arrange their hair...

In every window were portraits of Garibaldi and the King of Italy and the Italian tricolour. These flags, observed Giacosa, aroused 'both a sense of tenderness and a sense of shame' among people caught between nostalgia for a forsaken homeland and unfulfilled dreams of a better life in a new world.

Immigration to America was nothing new, of course, but by then the sheer number of arrivals was unparalleled. With the advent of steam shipping, trans-oceanic travel was faster and more efficient than ever before. When Manuel García and his family had brought Italian opera to New York in 1825, the voyage had taken several weeks under sail; by steam, the transatlantic crossing could be done in about ten days. It was also a lot cheaper, especially once shipping companies began fitting out their steamers for passengers rather than freight. By the early new century, the annual number

Italian immigrants crossing the Atlantic to the New World.

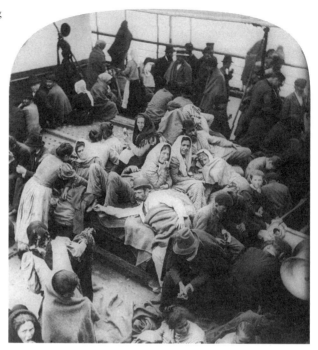

of immigrants to America was often close to a million; in 1907, the figure reached 1,285,000. Altogether, well over 15 million arrived during these years, helping to double the overall population of the USA from a little over 50 million to something close to 100 million in scarcely more than a generation.

Also new was the geographical distribution from which the bulk of this migration came. In the 1870s and 1880s, a series of droughts and poor harvests, industrial recession and political uncertainty in Northern Europe, exacerbated by a sequence of wars, led many from Germany and Scandinavia to follow the traditional path to America, where the economy was said to be booming and good jobs and cheap land were available. Others began to arrive from China and Japan, settling initially on the West Coast and going on to help build factories, roads and railroads. Increasingly, the bulk of 'new' immigrants came from Eastern and Southern Europe: the large Jewish populations of modern New York, Chicago and Los Angeles mostly date from this period. Above all, there were Italians, especially from the *Mezzogiorno*, young men (and some women) who had picked themselves up from the parched fields of Calabria and Puglia or the disease-infested slums of Palermo or Naples and somehow found the wherewithal to journey from the Old World to the New. In 1880, Italian arrivals in the USA totalled about 12,000; by the eve of the First World War the annual figure had climbed to 300,000.

All migrant groups bring something of their background with them: their language, styles of dress, cuisine, customs and beliefs. Thus, parts of the Midwest were dotted with German and Scandinavian émigré communities with their Lutheran churches and beer-houses. In her novel *The Song of the Lark*, Willa Cather writes of a young Swedish-American girl, Thea Kronborg, who is raised in a tiny township in the newly admitted state of Colorado. The Kronborgs are a devout, God-fearing family, and the only form of self-expression available to Thea is when she is permitted to play the organ, and later to sing, in her father's church.

Very different were the 'China Towns' and 'Little Italys' that sprang up in America's burgeoning cities. New York, the most cosmopolitan of them all, already boasted a rather superior 'German town', east of Central Park, where professors, bankers and musicians talked high culture and consumed *haute cuisine*. Meanwhile, the city's Lower East Side, where the new passenger steamers delivered their human cargo, was fast becoming a replica of Naples with its street singers, pasta houses and its laundry lines strung between the tenement blocks.

For all its poverty and squalor, New York's Little Italy provided a social springboard for many. As the city underwent a building spree, Italians supplied a substantial part of the labour force, bringing skills as masons and stucco workers. They began to enter the lower rungs of the service industries, too, working as barbers, fruit dealers, waiters or chefs. Some found their way as entertainers, perhaps in the boxing ring or baseball diamond – or signing up as members of a theatre chorus. If you had a voice, it might provide a conduit out of the slums and into the mainstream of the American dream. To many Italian Americans, an ideal role model was provided by Enrico Caruso:

New York's Little Italy: a replica of Naples.

once a product of the Neapolitan slums and now an internationally celebrated opera singer.

America was changing. In a famous lecture delivered in 1893, the historian Frederick Jackson Turner said that the Frontier was closed. All the land
between the Atlantic and Pacific had now been claimed, most of it occupied.
In consequence, a new American identity was emerging. It was no longer
the movement westwards that defined the nature of Americans. Rather, it
was the Old World cultures from which they had come. The covered wagon,
the cowboy, the homestead, the house on the prairie: these rapidly became
the subject of myth. What was new was emerging not in the prairies and
the mountains, but in the heart of the big cities. Thea Kronborg knew this
instinctively and (like her creator) took the train east. By the end of the century,
America was urban, urbane and (as we would nowadays say) multicultural.

It was also wealthy. Within a decade or so after the end of the Civil War,
from the later 1870s, the market-based business economy of the north was
booming. Big money begat even bigger money: Harriman and Vanderbilt
accumulated immense fortunes from railroads, Rockefeller from oil, Andrew
Carnegie with his steel company and J. P. Morgan from a vast financial
empire with tentacles reaching into every sector of industry. For these apostles of new wealth and others like them, this was truly a 'Gilded Age' in
which unprecedented riches seemed to be available to anyone with the talent
and energy to pursue it. Personal income was not taxed, while the concentration of economic power into a small number of hands was as yet scarcely
limited by trades unions or anti-trust laws. Meanwhile, the nation's old, antebellum ascendancy, from their grand fastnesses in Boston and New York,
looked with disdain and some alarm upon America's economic *parvenus*.
You might buy your carpets from them, opined one hostess, but that was no
reason to invite them to walk on them. Did the nouveaux riches of Gilded Age
America have no qualms about their vulgar acquisitiveness?

They did, and one of the ways to overcome them was to buy culture.
That meant European culture. 'We'll read *Faust* together... by the Italian
lakes,' muses Edith Wharton's scion of new American money (whom she
even names 'Newland' Archer) as he contemplates his lady love at the opera
in the opening chapter of *The Age of Innocence*. Willa Cather picks up the
same theme. 'I'd like to go to Germany to study, some day,' says Thea, the
aspirant young singer in *The Song of the Lark*, as she echoes the words of
her teacher, the mysterious and omniscient Professor Wunsch (Professor
Wish); 'it's the only place you can really learn.' A tense, self-obsessed young
woman ill at ease in small-town Colorado, Thea uses her voice as a passport
to escape her stifling background and to travel initially to Chicago and thence
to Europe, returning to become a leading soloist at the Metropolitan Opera.
Thea makes few close relationships, but she eventually marries Fred, of
whom Cather reports that 'When he was in Chicago or St Louis, he went to

ball games, prize-fights, and horse-races. When he was in Germany, he went to concerts and to the opera.' Fred is something of a bon viveur and gastronome. When he was in Germany, 'he scarcely knew where the soup ended and the symphony began.'

Germany meant culture – above all, music: the pre-eminent cultural form that, not dependent upon verbal or pictorial representation, travelled most easily. Theodore Thomas, America's best-known conductor, set up a series of special concerts for young people and for 'Working Men' and led a series of orchestras in New York, Cincinnati (whose Festival he founded and directed) and Chicago, all of them full of German-born players. Music was good for you, it seemed. 'But Mr Bergmann,' someone told the conductor of the New York Philharmonic, 'the people don't like Wagner.' 'Den dey must hear him till dey do!' Bergmann is said to have replied. They soon learned. One day, a train carrying an orchestra conducted by the indefatigable Thomas had to change engines in a cattle town in Colorado. As the musicians stretched their legs on the platform, a collection of local cowboys congregated and demanded a concert there and then or they would not let the train proceed. Eventually, Thomas himself pulled out his violin and lulled them, Orpheus-like, into acquiescence and a Wagnerian soprano in his party sang to them – after which (said a local newspaper) 'there was loud cheering and hurrahing, and as the train pulled out the enthusiastic cowboys fired a hundred guns into the air.' Meanwhile, back in urban America, middle-class families, like their European counterparts, were buying their first pianos, their daughters learning to play *Für Elise* and Schubert's *Marche Militaire*. And perhaps an air by Rossini and the 'Wedding March' from Wagner's *Lohengrin*.

*

Opera was not new to America when the Metropolitan opened its doors in 1883. Earlier in the century, Da Ponte may have failed in his efforts to establish Italian opera on a permanent basis in his new homeland, but a regular flow of European singers had continued to cross the Atlantic in the hope of filling their coffers with American gold. Opera, and opera singers, carried a patina of excitement, of Old World glamour, and there were plenty of New World entrepreneurs prepared to stake a fortune on this exotic European art. P. T. Barnum, best known for revealing Tom Thumb to the world and America's most successful showman, conceived the fantastical idea of bringing the prim, moralistic Jenny Lind, the 'Swedish Nightingale', to America on an extensive tour that would enable her to dispense high culture to the thirsting multitudes while incidentally making both him and her multimillionaires in the process. When Lind arrived in New York in September 1850, even Barnum was taken aback to see a crowd of some 30,000 people at the dockside to greet her. For nine months, Lind criss-crossed America for Barnum,

America's great showman, Phineas T. Barnum, drums up support for his latest sensation, the 'Swedish Nightingale', Jenny Lind.

singing up and down the East Coast and travelling as far afield as New Orleans in the South and as far west as St Louis and Madison, Wisconsin. Lind gave nearly a hundred concerts, and stayed on for a further year under her own management. Everywhere Lind went she was greeted with the kind of hysterical crowds that popular singers like Sinatra or the Beatles were to experience a century later, her hotel mobbed, and tickets to her concerts exchanging hands at grossly inflated prices. Gloves and bonnets were named after her, music was dedicated to her and her image was everywhere.

Back in the more sophisticated East, there was opera of a kind in most of the major cities. In New York, the Irish-born William Niblo put on public entertainments in 'Niblo's Garden' on lower Broadway, a kind of Vauxhall Gardens with open-air music and ice cream in summertime and an enclosed theatre for more serious operatic offerings. Then there was Castle Clinton, built in 1811 as a fort off the Battery on the southern tip of Manhattan island. Later joined to mainland Manhattan by landfill, 'Castle Garden' as it became known functioned from the 1820s as a place of public entertainment, was roofed over in the 1840s, and was a concert hall and theatre until 1855, when it was requisitioned as an immigration reception centre (the predecessor to Ellis Island). It was at Castle Garden that Jenny Lind made her American debut to an audience of more than 6000 people, each of whom had paid at least $3 for a seat.

There was full-scale opera, too, mostly mounted in theatres in lower Manhattan, domain of New York's wealthiest. The Montresor company, promoted by Da Ponte in 1832, performed not (as the Garcías had done) in the somewhat dingy Park Theatre but in an elegant conversion of a portico-ed, be-columned classical revival mansion that had once been Aaron Burr's estate in Richmond Hill. Here, New York's *eleganti* could sit in dazzling comfort listening to the finest Europe had to offer. But there were not enough of them to make the opera pay, and Richmond Hill soon followed the Park into decline. Da Ponte's opera house, opened in 1833, proved no more successful; nor did the Italian opera promoted by Ferdinand Palmo in the mid-1840s that performed in a converted property on Chambers Street. Touring opera companies still visited occasionally, with varying success. A company from Havana, which appeared at both Niblo's and Castle Garden in 1847, also made forays to Boston and Philadelphia and returned in 1850 and 1851.

In 1847, New York saw the opening of a new opera house, between Broadway and Fourth Avenue, where Astor Place and 8th Street converge. The Astor Place Opera House was yet another Parthenon-derived temple of the arts, and it was strategically placed at the top of Lafayette Place, an elite development where the Astor family and several others among New York's aristocracy of wealth had their mansions. Yet Astor Place, too, was to fail. In spring 1849, as revolution continued to smoulder across Europe, Nativist supporters of the American actor Edwin Forrest, furious that his English rival Macready was starring at Astor Place, marched on the theatre. The national guard had to be called in. By the time the mob was quelled, the opera house was pock-marked with bullet holes and in the street outside over twenty people were dead. With them, in effect, serious theatre and opera in Astor Place also died.

New York's rich and fashionable could not do without their opera, however, and the tragedy of Astor Place was quickly exorcized with the inauguration in 1854 of a new opera house, a little further uptown, in the fashionable neighbourhood of 14th Street and Irving Place, near Union Square. The sheer scale of the New York Academy of Music bespoke the optimism and ambition of its creators. They were going to put on all the best and latest operas sung by the finest singers Europe had to offer: it was here, in 1859, that the sixteen-year-old Adelina Patti, already a celebrated singing *Wunderkind*, made her full operatic debut in the title role of *Lucia di Lammermoor*, no less. The Academy was also the home of the city's new orchestra, the New York Philharmonic, founded in 1842. All the *bon ton* of New York attended the opera at the Academy. Walt Whitman was a regular member of the Academy audience, and the opera left a deep impression:

Across the stage with pallor on her face, yet lurid passion,
Stalks Norma brandishing the dagger in her hand

wrote Whitman in his poem 'Proud Music of the Storm'.

> I see poor crazed Lucia's eyes' unnatural gleam,
> Her hair down her back falls loose and dishevel'd.
> I see where Ernani walking the bridal garden,
> Amid the scent of night-roses, radiant, holding his bride by the hand,
> Hears the infernal call, the death-pledge of the horn.

And he went on to invoke equally vivid memories of operas by Rossini, Meyerbeer, Gounod and Mozart as well as one of his favourite singers:

> The teeming lady comes,
> The lustrous orb, Venus contralto, the blooming mother,
> Sister of loftiest gods, Alboni's self I hear…

The Academy of Music, like smaller opera theatres elsewhere in the country, soon ran into familiar problems. The way such houses normally worked was similar to that pioneered earlier in Europe. That is to say, the theatres would be owned, entirely or in large part, by their stockholders, principally the box-holders. The box-holders would not normally expect to contribute to annual running costs; their chief contribution lay in their having bought the boxes, usually in perpetuity, as a way of helping finance the building in the first place. They would appoint a board of management and lease the theatre out to an impresario. There was no resident company. Rather, the impresario's job, in consultation with his board, was to buy in the finest entertainment their money could afford, and to recoup the costs by filling the house. Touring opera troupes were booked and great stars such as Patti or Christine Nilsson sang at the Academy from time to time. Opera was expensive, and European divas especially so, and it soon became evident that grand opera could not pay for itself. Impresarios were replaced, new ones appointed. Concerts of symphonic music and popular classics were held at the Academy, and the building was leased out for a plethora of social and charitable events, prestigious tea parties, balls and the like. But the hard fact was that the New York Academy of Music, principally erected as an opera house, was home of an art form that routinely incurred financial loss. Inevitably (and of course most would have anticipated this), the Academy box-holders were called upon to help fund the deficit themselves.

There was big money in New York; that was not the problem. Earlier in the century, John Jacob Astor had assumed the proprietorship of the Park Theatre, while the richly upholstered boxes at Richmond Hill for the Montresor season had been owned by some of New York's finest. In the 1870s, the stockholders of the Academy of Music appointed a new board presided over by the fabulously wealthy August Belmont, and Belmont doubtless understood

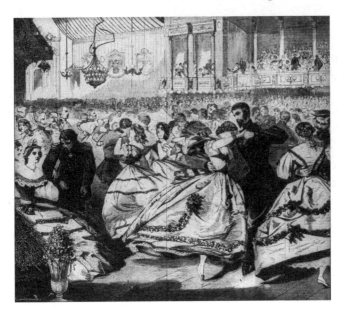

The New York Academy of Music was home not only to opera but also to a plethora of prestigious charitable and social events, such as this 'Russian ball' in November 1863 to mark the visit of a Russian warship.

what was expected of him. He was of German-Jewish origin (the name was a translation of Schönberg), knew and cared about opera, and frequently and generously underwrote the recurrent deficits at the Academy. Opera retained its cachet; the Academy was one of the places in New York at which the old aristocracy of wealth most liked to parade in all its finery. If you were a Roosevelt or a Schermerhorn, you had a box at the Academy and liked to be seen using it. Or, perhaps, letting it occasionally to someone of almost equivalent social prestige. But the hard fact was that, outside the ranks of a few rich people keen to buy themselves some social standing and European culture, plus a few cognoscenti like Whitman, grand opera in foreign languages had limited appeal – even in New York, by far the most cosmopolitan city in America. From the day the Academy of Music opened in the 1850s, the boxes were packed with the great and the good; but, on opera nights at least, there were recurrent rows of unfilled seats. It would be another forty years before New York contained enough European immigrants with sufficient disposable time and income to help provide opera with a guaranteed audience.

There was another problem, too. Opera was widely regarded as the most 'elite' of all the arts, originating as the entertainment of dukes and princes, involving European artists singing in Italian or German and portraying emblematic characters expressing extravagant emotions in dramatically implausible situations. The very origins of the USA lay in the deliberate overthrow of old-fashioned, hierarchical European values ('all men are created equal,' the Declaration of Independence had proclaimed). If the snooty denizens of Lafayette Place chose to go to the opera, it had little appeal to their neighbours in the Bowery, if only because it was so expensive. Furthermore, the Academy was next door to Tammany Hall, headquarters of the

Irish-dominated Democratic Party machine; opera was hardly likely to prove a natural habitat for the party apparatchiks who reported to hard-bitten politicos like 'Boss' Tweed. What could be more foreign – in all senses of the word – to the self-consciously democratic spirit of the New World than opera? Opera was not by Americans, many asked, so why should they want to go to it? As for the nation's aristocracy of wealth, supposedly apostles of free enterprise and laissez-faire economics, how could they squander their riches on an art form that could not pay for itself and that few wanted? If they poured money into opera and opera houses, wasn't that a betrayal of the very values that had made them so spectacularly successful right here in America? In all ways, therefore – socially, economically and politically as well as artistically – opera was widely regarded as exclusive in a society proud of its inclusiveness. Opera, in a word, was unpatriotic.

In the difficult years after the Civil War, a dispassionate observer in America might have been forgiven for anticipating that the precarious, flickering little flame of opera would sooner or later sputter and be extinguished. Fabulous European divas might continue to undertake lucrative concert tours; for this, as for other kinds of circus and freak shows, undoubtedly there was a market. But properly rehearsed, high-quality music drama with sets and costumes and a well-drilled orchestra and chorus? What had this to do with the new frontiers of imagination being stimulated by the challenges of post-war Reconstruction, the conquest of the Western Plains and pell-mell industrialization?

But opera in America did not die. On the contrary, its flames were soon fanned into vigorous life by the inauguration of what was to become America's greatest opera house, the New York Metropolitan.

*

The Met was the product of greed. As Gilded Age America poured new wealth into the pockets of steel and railroad magnates, bankers, finance wizards and shyster politicians, they too wanted boxes at the opera. None covet the trappings of traditional status so keenly as the newly rich. And if the riches are very new indeed, and perhaps a little insecurely held, the covetousness knows few bounds. Thus, the scions of new wealth craved membership of New York's most elite clubs: the Union, the Knickerbocker and that bastion of the super elite, the Patriarchs. They wanted to own mansions on Fifth Avenue and in Newport, Rhode Island, to dine at Delmonico's and to dress their wives in the latest Worth gowns from Paris. And they wanted their boxes at the opera. Belmont, whose remit was to keep the Academy of Music afloat, could doubtless have made good use of any money that came the Academy's way, old or new; he himself was a kind of bridge figure between the two. But the antebellum Yankee aristocracy who owned the boxes at the Academy had no intention of sharing their privileges with the city's nouveaux riches, however bountiful that *richesse* might be. And even if they had been prepared to do so, they could not; there were simply not enough boxes to go round. The Academy of Music contained thirty boxes.* And it seems that when Mrs Vanderbilt applied for one, there was none available.

The Vanderbilts were among the wealthiest of America's wealthiest. When the railroad king, Commodore Cornelius Vanderbilt, died in 1877, he bequeathed to his son William Henry a sum of close to a hundred million dollars (which 'Billy' Vanderbilt went on to double). What could be more natural than that, with this colossal fortune at their disposal, Billy's wife Alva should wish to display her finery in a box at the opera? If you have more money than anyone else ('I am the richest man in the world,' Billy would boast genially), you are not used to being gainsaid. Alva Vanderbilt certainly was not. So when she was refused a box at the Academy, her husband took up the cause. Maybe things were more complicated than that. What is certain is that, in April 1880, George Warren, the Vanderbilt lawyer, made forceful representations to Belmont and his fellow Academy stockholders. It was not just Mrs Vanderbilt's grievance that had to be put right; there were others among New York's newly wealthy, too, who wished to grace the opera with their presence.

The Academy was placed in a quandary. Those among their stockholders who were lucky enough to own a box rarely chose to relinquish so visible a symbol of social status. There were not enough to go round as it was. Then there was the unstated but universally acknowledged fact that the wealthy old New York families who adorned the Academy's boxes did not particularly wish to be tainted by the proximity of new money. 'Conservatives cherished it for being small and inconvenient,' wrote Edith Wharton of the Academy in the opening pages of *The Age of Innocence*, 'thus keeping out the "new people" whom New York was beginning to dread and yet be drawn to.'

In response to Warren, the Academy announced that, with a certain amount of reconstruction, they could cobble together a further twenty-six boxes; that was the absolute maximum the building could accommodate. It was not enough. Within a week, Warren announced that the clients he represented, many of them disgruntled Academy stockholders, had decided to put together the money to found a new opera house of their own. Here, Alva Vanderbilt would get her box.

So would a lot of other people. Ownership of a box meant ownership of part of the theatre; that is, you had helped pay for the theatre in the first place. And if you owned part of the theatre it was only right and proper that you should be able to display yourself as such whenever you chose to appear and (of course) at no further cost. So when the new 'Metropolitan Opera' emerged – further uptown once more, between 39th and 40th Streets on Broadway, just below what became Times Square – one of the features everyone would remark upon would be its boxes. There were to be 122 of them spread over

* According to Kolodin; only eighteen according to Mayer.

four tiers, and they would seat something like a quarter of the entire 3500-strong audience. Here, opulently arrayed for all to see, was the new wealth – and by implication the new power elite – of New York and therefore of America.

The night the Met opened was one of the most brilliant New York society had seen. What made it especially remarkable was the fact that, for the first time in the city's history, two important opera houses were functioning in New York on the same night. For, *miraculo miraculi*, that beached whale of the old Yankee elite, the Academy of Music, was thriving once more. And for that, it had to thank its current manager, that eccentric Englishman 'Colonel' Mapleson.

Born in London in 1830, Mapleson learned the piano and violin, worked for a while as an operatic tenor then went into musical management, at various times organizing seasons of opera at all of London's principal lyric theatres: Drury Lane, the Lyceum, Her Majesty's and (in brief and uneasy partnership with Gye) Covent Garden. A man of irrepressible energy and entrepreneurial spirit, Mapleson went to America, where he honed further his genius for putting together operatic troupes, raising the finances and getting the show on the road. Mapleson's spectacular successes just about outweighed what he himself acknowledged as his equally dramatic failures.

Opening night at the New York Met featured a celebrated Swedish soprano starring in a French opera based on a German story sung in Italian before an English-speaking audience.

Money for Mapleson, as for most promoters of opera before and since, was always a problem. Patti, it seems, regularly held Mapleson to ransom, but was such a phenomenally gifted singer, and such a crowd-puller, that he acceded to her every request, bejewelled private railroad coach, $5000 fee (per appearance!) and the rest. Mapleson's memoirs, written in the late 1880s, are often unreliable, but they provide a richly humane entrée into the problems and practicalities of a forgotten era that might ring bells of sympathy among some of today's operatic impresarios. At one point, Mapleson prints a contract between Patti and himself. Madame Patti, it states, 'shall be free to attend Rehearsals, but shall not be required or bound to attend any', while it was she, not the management, who would choose the costumes she was to wear. In these respects at least, Patti's demands were no more excessive than those of most other leading operatic ladies of the time.

Mapleson is wickedly amusing about the rivalry between Patti and the almost equally celebrated soprano Etelka Gerster, who, Patti thought, had the 'evil eye'. Patti was heard to mumble 'Gerster' whenever anything went wrong and Mapleson describes his Herculean efforts to keep the two ladies apart when on the same tour. On one occasion, the press reported with great excitement that, after a sensational Patti concert, the Governor of Missouri had given the great prima donna a kiss. Gerster, asked by a journalist what she thought of the incident, replied that she did not understand the fuss, adding: 'there is nothing wrong in a man kissing a woman old enough to be his mother.'

In 1881, Mapleson led the New York Academy ensemble on a mammoth tour. The highlight was the first Cincinnati Opera Festival ('undoubtedly the most daring musical enterprise ever attempted in America or any other country'). They took the train from St Louis, their previous venue, at 1am, arriving in Cincinnati around 3pm the following day, spent the rest of the afternoon hunting up hotels and boarding-houses and went on to a stage rehearsal for *Lohengrin*. The company, which included an orchestra of 150 and a galaxy of star singers with worldwide reputations, remained in Cincinnati for a week, performing no fewer than eight different operas to audiences of up to 8000. From Cincinnati, they went on to Detroit, Syracuse and Albany before returning to New York, where, appropriately downsized, they resumed normal work at the Academy.

The following year, Mapleson returned to Cincinnati, to even greater acclaim, this time with Patti as star attraction, and he managed to persuade Patti to appear back at his home house, the New York Academy of Music, during the forthcoming season, notwithstanding the presence of Gerster on the Academy's books. Mapleson had a particular reason for this. The new Metropolitan Opera House was approaching completion and the Met's board and general manager, Henry Abbey, were haemorrhaging money in their attempts to obtain the services of the world's most famous singers. Mapleson, determined to try and beat Abbey at his own game, managed to secure both

Patti and Gerster. Not for the first or last time in operatic history, a kind of arms race built up as two rival companies competed for ultimate primacy. The city's opera lovers found themselves spoilt for choice. On 22 October 1883, the Academy gave *La sonnambula* with Gerster. That night, New York's Metropolitan Opera opened its doors for the first time. On show was *Faust* with Christine Nilsson.

*

The rivalry between the two opera houses, the old and the new, had been exciting the New York press and public for weeks, like the gossip and speculation preceding a prize fight. As the 'Metropolitan' gradually took shape behind its encasement of scaffolding, large crowds ambled up Broadway to stand and stare. The architect, Josiah Cleaveland Cady, had never designed a theatre before, and the most interesting thing about the building, at least from the outside, was what it was not. Unlike virtually all the great opera houses of Europe – unlike Richmond Hill, Astor Place or the Academy, indeed – this was emphatically *not* an Athenian temple of the arts. There was no Greek pediment or portico to hallow the entry place, no Greek or Latin inscription, no Corinthian columns. Rather, a pair of seven-storey apartment buildings (or were they offices?) faced with yellow brick. Mapleson, indeed, dubbed it sourly the 'new yellow brewery on Broadway'. One could, if aesthetically inclined, see in the curved arches of the windows a hint of the then fashionable neo-Renaissance style. Overall, however, this building spoke not of art but of money. How would this latest and grandest of American opera theatres measure up? As opening night approached, the *New York World* informed its readers that 'the social world waits with eager expectancy the result of the musical contest on Monday night, which will... certainly continue, if not increase, the jealousies and rivalries engendered between prominent families.'

On the day itself, reported the *World*, a crowd of some 10,000 pressed onto the sidewalks and tried to catch a glimpse of the opening-night celebrities, just as their successors would do half a century later at Hollywood premieres. The performance was advertised as commencing at '8 precisely' (too early, complained New York's wealthiest, not wishing to wolf down their dinner). At 8pm, there was still 'a jam of carriages' while 'a double stream of full-dressed ladies and gentlemen was pouring into the house'. At 8.23, when the conductor finally lifted his baton to begin, 'people were still pouring in from every side'. Never mind. The new opera house, 'with its brilliant assemblage presented a dazzling sight. No such audience had probably ever been seen in America... Diamonds flashed all the way round from one pole of the great horseshoe... to the other, and costumes of the richest material shone in every hue.'

What everyone wanted to know was whom the diamonds belonged to. In other words, who among New York's elite attended the Metropolitan Opera that night – and who remained loyal to the Academy? This, too, was amply

The New York Metropolitan Opera, on 39th Street and Broadway, was one of the great jewels of Gilded Age America.

reported. The *World* listed the occupants of the boxes at the Met opening night and what the ladies were wearing. Thus, Mrs Wilson in Box 9 'was attired in white satin covered with crystal embroidery. The corsage was low and sleeveless and her ornaments were diamonds and pearls.' A few boxes along, Mrs Turnure 'wore ruby velvet en train' while her daughter 'wore pink satin and brocade made en train… with square neck and trimmed with lace and pearls'. And what about Mrs Vanderbilt, resplendent in Box 35, as she relished her moment of triumph? Her costume, a 'trained dress of pale blue brocaded satin had the front covered with point lace flounces. The neck was cut square and her ornaments were diamonds.'

All who entered the auditorium that night were initially astounded at its opulence. Here was no apartment block or office building, but a vast horseshoe-shaped theatre on traditional European lines richly bedecked with silks and satins. Perhaps it was too big. Sightlines from many seats were poor and a singer lacking a large voice was tempted to shout. Parts of the house were stiflingly hot, while the corridors were distinctly draughty. Backstage facilities were rudimentary and scene-changes took an age. As for the opening performance itself, this was treated by the critics, if not the ecstatic audience, with reservations. Nilsson, in particular, was not quite the singer she had been a decade or more earlier. That did not prevent her from being presented, after the 'Jewel Song', with 'a huge casket containing a solid gold wreath and two massive gold pins of elaborate and costly workmanship'. After tumultuous applause, Nilsson held the crimson velvet casket down so that the audience could see its contents, then placed it on a chair and duly encored the aria, addressing herself this time to her new gift. Encores were de rigueur on such occasions. Indeed, it was a mark of the failure of the Mephistopheles that his entrance aria was not encored: 'a devil who cannot secure an encore for the "Song of the Golden Calf" must be accounted a very poor devil indeed,' wrote one critic.

All in all, however, the evening was accounted a great success. William H. Vanderbilt, it was reported, 'developed an unusual degree of sociability during the evening' as he went from box to box (three of them his own) and 'was apparently in excellent spirits'. The house was packed, the audience enthusiastic, the performance as good as anything Europe had to offer, and Vanderbilt and his friends thrilled at the visibility and status offered by their new gathering place. Henry Abbey, who was not only the Met's general manager but also lessee of the theatre, had good reason to smile as the final curtain calls finally ended around 12.30am and he could lock up his theatre for the

Christine Nilsson as 'Margherita' in the Italian-language version of Gounod's *Faust* with which the Metropolitan Opera House opened. So popular was *Faust* in the Met's early years, along with the works of Wagner, that some dubbed the theatre the 'Faustspielhaus'.

night. His patrons were tired but happy. And of course New York's wealthiest would not have had to get up particularly early the following morning.

Meanwhile down at the Academy, Mapleson also had a packed audience. He spent much of the evening in the stockholders' room and he, too, it was reported, was 'wreathed in smiles and bustled to and fro, now presiding over a freshly opened bottle of champagne and drinking the health of the Academy with one of the stockholders, again rushing over to speak to some reporter who had entered in quest of information'. Every now and then, he would take time off to listen to part of the opera: '"By Jove! you can't beat that, you know," said the Colonel, as Gerster's voice in one aria in particular died away, to be succeeded by thunders of applause.' It is not clear whether it was the aria or the applause that had most excited Mapleson. Either way, he knew he had a big success on his hands. He was even able to announce that Gerster had received a friendly letter from a most unexpected source: Patti, her great rival 'encouraging [Gerster] to do her best and keep enthusiasm up until she arrives when, she says, "We'll go in and conquer everything"'.

The usual Academy box-holders were much in evidence, led by Mr and Mrs August Belmont. 'I would not go in the other house,' one box-holder was quoted as saying, 'even to rehearsal', while another agreed, saying that if you so much as put your foot in it 'you are numbered with the other crowd'. An intrepid few (and their names were also reported) managed to make an appearance at both houses in the course of the evening. One box at the Academy remained empty; Mrs Caroline Astor, that supreme bellwether of New York society, evidently uncertain which way it would be prudent to jump, had apparently not yet 'returned from the country'.

*

Both houses were presenting 'Italian' opera. Mostly, that meant opera by Italians, but not always. Rather, it meant opera *in* Italian. Thus, on the opening night at the Met, as the somewhat matronly Nilsson playing Gounod's Marguerite skittishly plucked the petals from off her daisy, she sang 'm'ama!' and not 'il m'aime', just as she had done a decade earlier at the Academy where, in Edith Wharton's delicious phrase, 'an unalterable and unquestioned law of the musical world required that the German text of French operas sung by Swedish artists should be translated into Italian for the clearer understanding of English-speaking audiences.' Faust's great aria 'Salut! demeure, chaste et pure' was rendered 'Salve! dimora casta e pura'. *Carmen* was sung in Italian, and *Martha* and Wagner's *Lohengrin*. Italian was the *lingua franca* of the operatic world; with its pure and open vowels, it was also a wonderful language in which to sing. It is true that in France much opera was performed in French, in Germany in German, in England English. But the top international stars all sang in Italian. Thus, if an American impresario wanted to book a Swede like Lind or Nilsson, a Hungarian like Gerster, Poles such as

Sembrich or the De Reszke brothers, a Frenchman like Plançon or Maurel, or such English-speakers as Patti or Nordica, he was more likely to succeed if financial inducements were backed up by an invitation to sing in Italian.

So New York's two opera houses, Abbey's Metropolitan and Mapleson's Academy, went head to head, each offering a glamorous, star-studded Italian autumn season aimed at attracting the very acme of New York society. By December, both companies were on the road undertaking extensive winter tours. For a year, New Yorkers (not to mention the opera-loving populations of cities as far afield as Boston, Philadelphia, Detroit, Chicago, Indianapolis, St Louis, Minneapolis, Pittsburgh, Cleveland, Cincinnati, Montreal, Washington, Baltimore and Buffalo) found themselves treated to a surfeit of Italian opera. Sometimes, repertoires would overlap. So, on rare occasions, would the two companies: in January 1884, the Mapleson and Abbey troupes found themselves staying in the same Chicago hotel, with all the *prime donne* – among them the Academy's Patti and Gerster and the Met's Nilsson and Sembrich – staying along the same corridor!

Abbey and Mapleson were in a fight to the finish. At first, it looked as though Mapleson would beat his rival. Before the first season was completed, it became clear that the finances at the Metropolitan were not adding up. This was hardly a surprise to those involved. Once the money for the new opera house itself was in place, Abbey would have had to engage a large chorus and orchestra, costume and scenery designers and an army of backstage staff. And the Met's stockholders had encouraged him and his assistant Maurice Grau to spend whatever was necessary to engage the finest singers the world had to offer: in effect, to indulge in a bidding war with Mapleson. It may not have been true (as Lilli Lehmann reported later) that every costume, shoe and stocking at the Met was provided by Worth of Paris. But while Mapleson's Academy could recycle sets and costumes from earlier shows, every production at the Metropolitan (nineteen of them in that opening season) was brand new. The lavish Met sets and costumes on display certainly received plaudits. Never in the annals of American opera, gushed one critic, 'have such magnificent scenery and dresses been displayed' and he went on to compare the difference between 'the truly regal and scenic appointments of the new Opera House' and 'the drab and nasty daubs which disgrace the Academy' with that between one of New York's 'aristocratic' neighbourhoods and one of its worst slum districts.

All this cost money and much of Abbey's expenditure had to be financed from ticket sales. The Met's box-holders, occupying a sizeable proportion of the house, hardly expected to shell out more for the privilege of sitting in seats for which they had already paid. So ordinary ticket prices at the Met were necessarily higher than those at the Academy. Once the initial excitement of the new house had died down, furthermore, audience levels dropped off somewhat, while touring, with its travel and hotel costs, was always a finan-

Adelina Patti was one of the most gifted singers of the nineteenth century but also one of the most demanding. The impresario Colonel Mapleson acceded to her every request, including a $5000 fee (per appearance!) and a bejewelled private railroad coach.

cial risk. By the time Abbey and Grau brought their company back to New York for their spring 1884 season, cash was haemorrhaging. Abbey felt obliged to inform his stockholders that he would be unable to continue as general manager for a further year unless they were prepared to write off his losses. They were not. Within a year of its opening, the Metropolitan Opera nearly closed.

The stockholders knew from the outset that opera, lavishly staged and sung in a large house, could never pay its way. Their president, James A. Roosevelt (a fourth cousin of Franklin D. Roosevelt), had said as much to a newspaper reporter in March 1882 before the Met had opened. Indeed, it almost seemed a matter of pride to some that good opera *couldn't* pay for itself. 'Do they suppose that when we build an Opera-house we want to make a shop of it?' asked a 'Young Society Man' in a satirical column published in the *World* a couple of days after the Met opening. 'Thank heaven, we *spend* our money at the Opera; we don't make it there.' Opera, opines one of the

Met matrons he encounters, 'is the only place left where we can sanctify our lives by losing money. Let us keep it pure and undefiled!'

A waspish caricature, no doubt. But a WASP-ish one, too, for it was from New York's white, Anglo-Saxon Protestant community that the Met's money was principally derived and they were no longer representative of the city as a whole. Perhaps the Met stockholders had expected the city's burgeoning Italian community to pack the house, nostalgic for *Lucia* and *Sonnambula*. There were certainly plenty of Italians in the orchestra, including the two leaders, 'Signors Ciofi and Giovi'.* But few people were prepared to spend something like a full day's wage for the privilege of sitting in the further reaches of this vast house and struggling to get home just a few hours before they were due back at work.

Watching all this from his redoubt on 14th Street, Mapleson was understandably triumphant. He had, it seemed, seen off the opposition, though, on hearing of Abbey's problems, the Colonel graciously acknowledged 'some regret at hearing of the downfall of this not very clever showman'.

However, any reports of the demise of the Metropolitan were premature. For, at this point, an unlikely saviour presented himself to the stockholders, like the swans and doves and silver-armoured knights of opera. Except that Leopold Damrosch was an earnest, somewhat professorial German, deeply committed to serious music and not at all to quixotic gestures. Damrosch also had an impressive record as a musical entrepreneur. As a young man, he had worked with Liszt in Weimar and directed the Breslau orchestra before coming to New York in 1871. Here he set up and conducted not only the New York Oratorio Society but also, in due course, his own orchestra, the germ of what soon became the New York Symphony, whose president in 1884 was Hilborn Roosevelt, nephew of the Met's James Roosevelt. As Damrosch's son Walter later recounted events, Hilborn Roosevelt mentioned to his Uncle James that a temporary solution to the Met's dilemma might be to invite Damrosch to lease the house for a season of German opera 'as Italian opera was evidently on the wane and Wagner, especially, on the ascendant'. In due course, Damrosch was offered a salary of $10,000 (a sum it would have taken Patti two nights to earn!) for which he would become manager of the opera for a year, promote a season of German-language opera and himself conduct the bulk of the performances. Damrosch (his son reports) was delighted at this opportunity to fulfil 'the dream of his life, the introduction of the Wagner music-dramas to America, and to sweep away forever the artificial and shallow operas of the old Italian school with which Mapleson... and others had until then principally fed our public'. In May 1884, Damrosch sailed for

---

* Of the 73 members of the Met orchestra during its first (1883/4) season (excluding the 20-person 'military band'), 45 by my count have Italian names and a further 16 German-sounding names. The Met corps de ballet consisted entirely of Italian names; but one wonders how many of those were fabricated.

Europe, returning to New York in August with all his contracts made, and immediately plunged into work. Somehow, he managed to run his new company, train his orchestra and singers and conduct the performances. By January 1885, business was so successful that Damrosch agreed to a reduction in his salary (to $8000) in return for a share of profits, and he began to plan a second season. By now, Damrosch was deep into rehearsal for *Die Walküre*, which opened on 30 January 1885 and which he went on to conduct five times in eight days. Desperately overworked, Damrosch took ill and on 15 February he died.

What Leopold Damrosch had begun, Walter Damrosch continued, aided by the inspirational conductor Anton Seidl. Seidl had lived and worked with Wagner in Bayreuth, and in New York he set new standards. For fully seven seasons, the Met was a German house. Not only Wagner was sung in German, but French works such as *Faust*, *Guillaume Tell* and *La Juive*. So successful was the Met in its new German guise, indeed, that the normally ebullient Mapleson found it impossible to continue at the Academy, quitting after a disastrous 1886 season with one final shaft aimed at the Met: 'I cannot fight Wall Street.' The Academy itself soldiered on, housing a succession of touring companies, and was eventually demolished in 1929. Today, a discreet plaque in the entry foyer of the ConEdison building on Irving Place between 14th and 15th Streets notes that this was once the site of 'New York's leading concert hall and opera house'. One could be forgiven for not noticing it.

German opera was a commercial success where Italian opera had failed. Was it true (as Walter Damrosch claimed) that Italian opera was 'on the wane'? Not at all. Italian opera was precisely what the Met stockholders most wanted, not long Wagnerian operas with no superstars or memorable arias. They got their wish eventually. But for the time being their house had to be German to survive. The reasons were partly demographic, partly cultural. By the 1880s, the German population of New York – people, that is, with origins in the German-speaking lands of Central Europe – numbered something in excess of a quarter of a million, with similarly large numbers settled in many of America's other major cities. The Germans were not necessarily the largest national or ethnic group in the American cities in which they dwelt, but they were often among the most prominent and socially coherent. Relatively well-heeled and well-educated, they actively promoted their cultural legacy, bringing German culinary and sartorial styles to America, attending lectures and supporting German-language publications. And they would turn out for concerts. Music was Germany's most powerful and portable export, the cultural inheritance that all acknowledged as *nonpareil*. It was to Germany that every aspiring young American musician (like Cather's Thea Kronborg or Marcia Davenport's Lena Geyer*) felt it necessary to make a pilgrimage.

There was a further reason, too, why German opera was so successful at the Metropolitan, and that was financial. The simple fact was that Wagner, for all his complexities, was cheaper to stage than Bellini or Donizetti. Costumes and sets for Wagner were more or less copies of those used in Bayreuth and could be made cheaply in Europe. In addition, Wagner operas did not require the Met to compete for expensive superstar singers (especially once Mapleson quit the Academy). Even a celebrated artist like Amalie Materna, Bayreuth's Brünnhilde, earned a fraction of the inflated fees that had been demanded by the likes of Nilsson and Patti. Singers such as Materna, Max Alvary, Emil Fischer or Lilli Lehmann, all highly talented performers, were accustomed to working as members of ensemble companies in Germany, where *Walküre* or *Tristan* was not an opportunity for lucrative solo pyrotechnics but a *Gesamtkunstwerk*, a serious gathering together of all the arts to which each had a contribution to make. In this spirit, Damrosch offered good contracts but not extravagant ones, and was able to reduce the cost of top price seats.

So when the New York Metropolitan put on seasons of German-language opera, it was appealing to a ready-made audience. The box-holders might have been disconcerted by Wagner (when is the correct time to be seen arriving? which scene contains the best bits? when should you have your supper?), but the vast upper reaches of the house were filled on most nights, not only with a large and enthusiastic audience but also with the sounds of big Wagnerian voices that carried to the furthest reaches of the building. Wagner sold on the road, too. During the 1888/9 season, Seidl presented the entire *Ring* for the first time in Philadelphia, Boston, Milwaukee, Chicago and St Louis, with Lilli Lehmann as Sieglinde and Brünnhilde.

After a while, as the Wagnerian novelty began to wear off, more Italian and French operas (sung in German) crept back into the Met repertoire. In 1891, the stockholders decided to offer the lease to Abbey and Grau once more. Then, in 1892, the theatre burned down. Had the fire occurred in 1893, a year of severe economic recession, who knows whether its stockholders would have rebuilt it? As it was, many lost heart (as well as money) and withdrew when the property was sold to the newly formed Metropolitan Opera and Real Estate Company. This company was essentially an oligarchy of thirty-five people of immense wealth and power; they rebuilt the Met and – literally – owned it. When the theatre re-emerged, people noted that its decor and sightlines were (in some parts of the house) improved. The *New York Times* reported that the theatre now contained electric elevators and that there were 10,000 electric lights in the house, half of them for use on the stage. Seating capacity had been increased by several hundred and room

---

* In Davenport's novel, Lena's Italian coach says she 'ought to go to Germany and begin there as an unknown in an opera house like Stuttgart or Frankfurt; with her genius she would soon be noticed all over the country and quickly become recognized in Europe. Which, they both knew well, was the prerequisite for real stature at the Metropolitan' (*Of Lena Geyer*, p. 59).

found for as many as 1500 people to stand. To find this space, the number of boxes had been correspondingly reduced. A 'democratic' innovation? To some degree, yes. By now, sections of New York's Italian community were climbing up the ladder of employment and wealth, and an enlarged opera house with swathes of relatively inexpensive seats proved an attraction. In its report of the Met reopening, the *New York Times* noted the presence of the 'immense number of foreign folk of education and breeding'. The cosmopolitan character of the city, it acknowledged (with some reluctance, one senses), 'is no longer sustained by peanut vendors, sellers of bananas, dealers in cheap flowers, pastry cooks, and waiters alone'. No. The 'life of the town at present is varied by Italians, by Germans, by Frenchmen, by Spaniards, and even by Greeks of the highest class'. Last night, concluded the *Times*, all these 'made the triumph of Italian opera a melodious Babel at the Metropolitan'.

In other ways, the Phoenix-like re-emergence of the Metropolitan represented a reassertion of the most anti-democratic instincts in New York. Thus, the decrease in the number of boxes in the auditorium made the visible occupation of a box even more desirable than before. The new owners of the house allocated to themselves the sumptuous boxes in what came to be known as the Diamond Horseshoe and they came to be regarded as occupying the very summit of New York society at a time when social status was something of an obsession to both those who had it and those who did not. Owners would let or lease their boxes on certain days of the week so that different people occupied the boxes on different nights. Thus, William Vanderbilt and his family and guests might occupy Box 6 on Mondays (the socially all-important evening) and Wednesdays, letting it to another party on Fridays and matinees. The important thing was not occupation, but ownership. As Kolodin remarked:

> If you 'owned' you were 'in'; if you merely 'rented', you were more than out – you were socially nonexistent. Needless to say, those who 'rented' swallowed their unhappiness with this caste system, but extended it a bit farther by looking down on those who neither owned nor rented, but merely bought tickets.

Kolodin makes this 'caste system' sound very silly, which from our later perspective it was. However, as he adds, those who took it seriously took it very seriously indeed. And that included not only the wealthy oligarchs and their million-dollar wives nonchalantly flaunting their wealth in their Monday night opera boxes but a wider, deferential society that was evidently thrilled to see them there. After opening night, the fawning *New York Times* went into raptures, regaling its readers with reports about the:

> pearly human fleshtones that lurked in rich measures of arms and shoulders and bosoms; the exquisite convolutions of silken hair –

'All that Society Can Boast in Beauty, Elegance and Culture': enjoying Wagner's *Die Meistersinger* from the comfort of a box at the New York Metropolitan Opera.

here shining like ebony, there gleaming like gold; the faces set as flowers are set upon their stalks, now bent upon the stage in silent, immobile ecstasy, now suddenly revealed in conflicting flashes when the curtain sank, as if loth to shut out the glorious blaze of form and color on the stage; the incessant quiver, like the play of Summer lightning reduced to globuled sparks, of diamonds here, diamonds there, diamonds everywhere – all these flashing, gleaming, flickering, blazing, dancing…

It's obvious where the man from the *Times* had his eyes fixed all evening!

Shrewd observers were quick to recognize not only the heaving bosoms and glistening diamonds but the precise identities of the families who occupied the boxes – especially those in the Diamond Horseshoe – and also the complex ways in which those families, like all aristocratic elites, were interconnected. Some of the relationships were commercial. In the centre of the horseshoe, for all to see, was Box 35, now the domain of the banking magnate John Pierpont Morgan, while friends or business associates of his owned Boxes 5, 8, 9, 10, 12, 16, 18, 21, 26, 27 and 33. Then there was the Vanderbilt clan, whose friends, extended family and sundry business associates owned Boxes 1, 3, 13, 17, 22, 23, 24 and 25. There was a small contingent, too, of hangovers from the old Academy, men (and their ladies) who had swallowed their pride and come over, as they inevitably must, from the defunct fortress of old money to the gleaming palace of the new. Foremost among these was J. J. Astor, whose wife, Caroline, was the uncrowned arbiter of New York society. With Mrs Astor ensconced in her box at the Met, the prestige of the opera house was complete.

Thus, the New York Metropolitan Opera, having nearly collapsed during its inaugural season, had defeated its rival, the Academy of Music, gone on to draw in new audiences and was now re-emerging as one of the central *loci* of power and status in America. In the words of one historian of the period, 'the Metropolitan Opera House, perhaps more than any other civic institution, embodied the values of the city's late nineteenth-century aristocracy.'

The Metropolitan Opera, rebuilt and to some extent refashioned, reopened on 27 November 1893 to an audience that the *Times* headline reported as 'Representing All that Society Can Boast in Beauty, Elegance, and Culture'. Once again, with *Faust*. But this time in French. The new Met was now launched on a career that would soon make it, against the odds and despite rather than because of its earlier history, the greatest international opera house in the world.

CHAPTER 12

Prima la donna

Much of our story is about men, among them great composers, leonine con-ductors and ambitious managers. But from the outset, the prima donna has assumed a powerful place in the operatic narrative, both on and off the stage. From Anna Renzi and Francesca Cuzzoni via Pasta and Patti to Callas, Suther-land and Caballé, some of the greatest plaudits (and pay cheques) have been reserved for the top female singers.

The nineteenth century, above all perhaps, was the era of the diva, the prima donna. Previously, the most famous and highly paid singers, espe-cially but not only in Italy, had often been the great castrati while by the early twentieth century the mantle was falling on the shoulders of the heroic tenor. Between the era of Farinelli and that of Caruso, however, many of the most celebrated were women: Malibran, Pasta, Grisi, Lind, Patti and the rest. Their talents were enormous, their incomes prodigious, but a close reading of their lives reveals how very hard they, and their male counterparts, worked to achieve their supremacy (often from a very early age). This should come as no surprise: genius, said Edison, is one per cent inspiration and 99 per cent perspiration. But in the theatrical world, par-ticularly that of opera, a few percentage points should also be reserved for other factors.

For a start, having the right parents helped. Many operatic composers or performers came from musical families: the Bachs, Couperins, Scarlattis, Boccherinis and Puccinis all provided at least one composer of genius, while Bellini's father and grandfather were (like Puccini's) church organists and composers and Richard Strauss's father a leading horn player. Singing, too, often ran in the family. Manuel García not only had a distinguished career himself but was also the father of one of the nineteenth century's leading singing teachers and of two of its most famous *prime donne*, Malibran and Viardot. The Grisi sisters were highly regarded singers in the first half of the nineteenth century as were the De Reszke brothers in the 1890s. Gabrielli, Sontag, Lilli Lehmann, Patti, Tetrazzini and Ponselle also had sisters who sang, and Lehmann's parents were both singers too.

A number of famous sopranos seem to have been encouraged in the early part of their careers by the presence of a powerful parent-cum-chaperon, usually a mother keen to impress the world with her daughter's talents. The American soprano Geraldine Farrar, a contemporary of Caruso, wrote a memoir in which she penned alternate chapters in her own persona and as though written by her mother. Life with mother for an aspiring prima donna could be a little stifling. 'My brain,' wrote Clara Louise Kellogg, a slightly earlier compatriot of Farrar, 'would have developed much more rapidly if I had been allowed – no, if I had been *obliged* to be more self-reliant.' One can only learn from one's own mistakes, said Kellogg, adding that 'By protecting me, my mother really robbed me of much precious experience.' In the 1920s, the mother of the noted soprano Claudia Muzio was forever in attendance, but it seems the two women scarcely spoke. Yet if Kellogg's testimony to mother love was tinged with reservations and Muzio's with near enmity, another American prima donna, the great Wagnerian soprano Lillian Nordica, was unstinting in her gratitude, recording that her omnipresent mother:

> shielded me from everything unpleasant that might distract me from my work. Her devotion to me and to my career meant the sacrifice of home ties, and the very giving of her life that we might enjoy the privilege of study and travel together.

A good teacher could make all the difference between success and failure, and here too, a sense of lineage developed. The pupils of Manuel García Jnr included not only Jenny Lind but also Mathilde Marchesi, who was responsible for training an entire generation of famous *bel canto* sopranos, including Melba. One of Marchesi's pupils, Estelle Liebling, taught Galli-Curci and later Beverly Sills. Lilli Lehmann in retirement taught a number of outstanding young singers of the next generation, among them Geraldine Farrar and Olive Fremstad. In Marcia Davenport's novel about Fremstad's alter ego, Lena Geyer, we read that Lehmann insisted 'Lena' learn every role in French and Italian as well as German. 'You never know when you can rise by stepping into a cast where nobody thought of putting you,' says Davenport's Lehmann, 'and you must be capable of everything. I am.' Farrar recorded that Lehmann 'was a hard taskmaster and demanded the ultimate', but that she 'found in me an energy equal to her own'.

Sometimes, the teacher–singer relationship could be distinctly ambivalent. Blanche Marchesi, the daughter of the great Mathilde and herself a successful singer, noted with sadness how the immaculate but icy soprano Emma Eames showed little gratitude to her venerable teacher once she was successfully launched on her career. Melba revered Madame Marchesi but, like Mary Garden later, found her intimidating. Garden described Marchesi

Mathilde Marchesi could be an intimidating presence, but she was a formidable singing teacher, her pupils including a succession of outstanding sopranos, among them Nellie Melba.

as 'an old, curt, haughty woman who came forward like an empress and just deigned to bow to you'. Marchesi announced imperiously to Garden that she would make her into a coloratura soprano; this was of no interest to Garden, who endured Marchesi for three weeks before determining to quit. Many years later, Renée Fleming, while idolizing Elisabeth Schwarzkopf and learning much from her, found her classes the kind of circumstance that would 'reduce almost anyone to a quivering bowl of Jell-O'. Worse still was the experience of the young Marilyn Horne. In the 1950s, Horne went to work with the great German soprano Lotte Lehmann (no relation to Lilli), who was by then living and teaching in Santa Barbara, California. As Horne recalled it, she had hardly opened her mouth before Lehmann laid into her with such venom that Horne could almost feel the physical sting of her words. 'Your Cherman vas a disgrrrace,' Lehmann began, adding (somewhat ironically, thought the trembling Horne), 'You haf no rrright to zink a lenkvich zo poorly.' And all that before she got on to the musical side of things.

It has become something of a commonplace to bemoan the way some singers are tempted to undertake too much when still young, thus risking ruining their voices and shortening their careers. However, the historical record suggests that there is nothing new about the seductions and dangers of undertaking strenuous work from an early age – or about older wiseacres shaking their heads disapprovingly. 'What pupil is allowed to study for three years in these days, when everybody is impatient to get money and fame?' wrote an exasperated Mathilde Marchesi in the 1890s. The voice, added

Madame, was 'the most tender, the most fragile, of all instruments', one that needed careful nurturing. Nor was Marchesi entirely wrong. The demands of the operatic profession have always been exacting, and in the nineteenth century were sometimes dauntingly so. Yet Schröder-Devrient, Malibran, Catalani, Sontag, Lind and Patti were all highly regarded operatic stars well before they were out of their teens; Schröder-Devrient, the soprano whose Leonore (in *Fidelio*) so inspired Wagner, first performed this demanding role at the age of seventeen. Nor did an early start necessarily presage an early conclusion. Patti made her celebrated recordings in her sixties while the doughty Ernestine Schumann-Heink, who first sang Azucena aged seventeen, bade farewell to the New York Met with Wagner's Erda when seventy.

Such singers were also more likely to cross between what we tend to think of as more or less hard and fast vocal categories. Malibran, for example, excelled as Rossini's Cenerentola and in Bellini's light and airy *La sonnambula*, as well as being an exponent of the more muscular heroine of *Fidelio*. Later, the most celebrated *fin-de-siècle* singer of Carmen, a role usually regarded as written for a mezzo soprano or even contralto, was Emma Calvé, a Marchesi-trained soprano, while Lilli Lehmann became not only the greatest Isolde of her age but also a consummate singer of Mozart and of Schubert lieder.

Was each of these women a 'prima donna' or 'diva'? In popular parlance, such terms have come to connote a person whose temperament and behaviour are imperious, capricious and self-serving. Callas has entered popular mythology as much for walking out of a performance attended by the President of Italy or spitting in the face of a warrant-server as for the quality of her singing. She was not the first to attract the wrong kind of attention. In 1833, when Schröder-Devrient was in Dresden supposedly learning a role in a new opera, a witness wrote to Spontini (who was general music director in Berlin) describing how the lady had 'had the rudeness, in a moment of impatience, to throw her part at the feet of the composer and stamp on it'. Later, when rehearsing another opera in her home, it seems Schröder-Devrient was constantly distracted by books, pictures and 'importuning' visitors. The letter concludes that if the diva ever got to know about this letter 'she would kill me for certain. I therefore implore you to make sure this does not happen.'

If the great prima donnas of history were not always 'difficult', many seem to have been fiercely independent-minded women. They had to be, especially in times when a 'good' marriage was often the only socially acceptable way a woman could ensure her long-term economic well-being. Until well into the nineteenth century, and the twentieth in some places, a woman was not permitted to own property, while most forms of money-making work beyond the age of thirty (servant, shopkeeper) were almost by definition public admissions of marital failure. A woman might become a nun (like several of the sisters of Francesco Rasi, the first Orfeo, or, three centuries later,

Prima donna in tigress mode. Callas had come offstage after a performance of *Butterfly* in Chicago in November 1955 when a US Marshal, doing no less than his duty, approached to present her with a court summons on behalf of an aggrieved former manager. The photo of what happened next was reprinted around the world.

Puccini's sister Iginia). Or a singer – or courtesan: two professions widely associated in the public mind (both being seen as giving sensual pleasure in exchange for money). Anna Renzi, who flourished in the 1640s, was casually written down by an opera goer of the time as a 'courtesan'; more than two centuries later, the English social commentator Henry Mayhew made the same more or less automatic link.

Many of history's celebrated songstresses tried to combine marriage and career, with variable results. Some seem to have been happy in their marriages, especially those whose husbands were able to provide a sense of security and stability not always available in the theatrical world. Occasionally, two people in the 'business' seem to have achieved a successful partnership. The marriage between Handel's star soprano Faustina Bordoni and the composer Johann Adolf Hasse lasted half a century until Faustina's death aged eighty. Giuditta Pasta and her husband played generous hosts at their villa on Lake Como to a procession of admiring friends, among them Bellini, Donizetti and Prosper Mérimée. Pasta's husband had been an operatic tenor but (like Marta Domingo, a budding young soprano) had had the sense to relinquish his career in favour of that of a spouse self-evidently more talented. In more recent times, it was Joan Sutherland's husband, the conductor Richard

Bonynge, who first recognized and developed Sutherland's virtuoso vocalism and later conducted many of her performances.

However, for many an operatic prima donna, long-term domestic partnership proved a chimera, the ferocious demands of the profession all too often militating against an easy or relaxed domestic life. Nobody would complain when a wife (or husband) brought home a large pay cheque. But few people, male or female, would have found it easy to cohabit happily with a partner whose job demanded excessive hours of work, often until midnight and beyond, interspersed with frequent sojourns far from home. From the 'Three Ladies' of sixteenth-century Ferrara (one of whom was murdered by her jealous courtier husband) to the brief marriages of Maria García to Eugène Malibran in the nineteenth century and of Callas to Giovanni Battista Meneghini in the twentieth, countless women singers have sought security in the arms of unsuitable partners. Melba soon grew out of the restrictions of her early marriage to an Australian farmer, though not before she had born him a son. Muzio's marriage was a catastrophe. So were all three of Nordica's. Tetrazzini was reduced to suing her third husband for financial extortion.

For some of history's most celebrated *prime donne*, the social and public acclaim they achieved seems to have been in inverse proportion to their long-term domestic stability and happiness. On the one hand, operatic superstardom could enable an outstanding singer to climb up the greasy pole of social success. We have seen how the top salons of nineteenth-century Paris vied to attract the leading singers of the day; by the early twentieth, Melba was the toast of every aristocratic home in London. But Melba was still a

By 1900, Nellie Melba had become a very *grande dame* indeed.

performer, never quite on equal terms with her hosts, a fact painfully attested by the frequent name-dropping in her memoir, and she had to keep her affair with the Duc d'Orléans within strict bounds of discretion. As we have seen, there was nothing new about such relationships. Aristocrats had often had affairs with singers, actresses, dancers and the like; on both sides, this almost went with the territory, a form of more or less transient mutual benefit. However, the external conventions had to be maintained. Melba may have been made Dame Commander of the British Empire, but a mere opera singer, however distinguished, could scarcely marry the Pretender to the French throne. Such a union would have caused an insuperable social embarrassment to him and probably the end of her career as a performer. In some ways, the successful actress or prima donna was treated rather as a celebrated black jazz musician might have been in inter-war America: admired by the upper reaches of society while excluded from total acceptance.

Yet, for all the formal constraints traditionally separating patrons and performers, the world of opera did offer singers a prospect of social and economic improvement. For an outstanding female singer, indeed, it provided perhaps the most spectacular route of all to any who wished to fly out of the traditional gilded cage of domesticated womanhood. Celebrated actresses had long attracted extravagant attention and admiration. Yet few women except a handful of modern movie goddesses have rivalled the kind of income commanded by the operatic 'prima donna'. The Met pay books are revealing. In 1900–1901, the conductor Walter Damrosch received a weekly salary of $400. A chorus member earned $15 per performance and, at the top end of the scale, Melba $1850. For forty-nine performances plus a Sunday concert over a 5½-month season, Melba earned the astronomical sum of $92,500. During the same period, Judels, the office boy, earned $377.50. By the early 1900s, Caruso was getting $2000 per performance at the Met and Melba, at Oscar Hammerstein's rival Manhattan Opera, $3000.

During the course of the twentieth century, things evened out somewhat. A career structure developed enabling talented young singers to progress through the conservatoire system and a series of clearly signposted nursery slopes towards the well-plotted summits of the operatic professions, while trades unions and health and safety legislation helped protect the weaker members from penury. The fees commanded by Callas or Sutherland, while substantial, were not remotely comparable to the prodigious amounts earned by their top-dollar predecessors. As for the twenty-first-century prima donna, she turns up to rehearsal with everyone else, probably wearing jeans and a T-shirt, perhaps doing the shopping on the way home afterwards.

Opera has always been an exacting business for its performers, offering large rewards to the few while at times barely more than subsistence to the many. In a profession as intensely competitive as international sport, the chances of rising to the top were always remote. Hence perhaps the fierce battles, real or

A cease-fire during *The Siege of Corinth*? Beverly Sills and Marilyn Horne.

imagined, between rival divas (or their partisans) with which operatic lore
is replete: Faustina vs Cuzzoni, Patti vs Gerster, Melba vs Tetrazzini (and,
later, Toti dal Monte), Jeritza vs Lotte Lehmann, Callas vs Tebaldi. And lest
I give the impression that such rivalries are more mythical than real, consider
these passages from the autobiographies of, respectively, Marilyn Horne and
Beverly Sills describing what happened when the two young American singers
appeared together at La Scala, Milan, in 1969.

The opera was Rossini's *Siege of Corinth* and it was Sills's Scala debut.
On opening night Horne was in her dressing room being made up as the
young warrior Neocle: 'standard army issue, complete with sword and
shield'. Her dresser let slip that a gentleman was at that very moment with
Sills going over the pictures and publicity releases to be forwarded to the
American press and that they were pulling out all the photos that had Horne
in them. Off marched Horne in feisty mode. Though 'appropriately garbed
in armour', she recalled, 'I had fortunately forgotten my sword.' She entered
Sills's room and announced to the flummoxed publicity man: 'if the *New
York Times* runs a picture and I'm *not* in it, I'll find you when I get back to
the States and smack you right in the face, you son-of-a-bitch!' The courtly
gent was utterly taken aback, 'not to mention a certain strawberry blonde

who stood by innocently fluttering her eyelids'. And to think, Horne added, 'that I had been the one who had suggested Beverly in the first place... I felt I had extended my hand in friendship and Beverly had bitten it.'

And Sills's version? She and Horne had never met before their Milan engagement, and Horne's first words, apparently, were: 'We might as well get it out into the open – I prefer Sutherland to you.' As for the dressing room confrontation, Sills's publicist, she recalled, 'tried explaining that he was working for me, not for the *Times*' and had no control over which pictures the US press would or would not use. Horne 'bellowed a bit more and then stormed out'. Later, during the Scala run, Sills was featured on the cover of *Newsweek*. And she flatly denied that it was Horne who had first suggested her to the Scala.

Both ladies went on to have sensational careers, two of the great singers of the twentieth century. But the history of opera is littered with the bones of talented women who fell by the wayside, sometimes given a helpful shove by a rival. Overall, however, rather as 'good' news tends not to get reported, spats between fiery divas have probably been far less common than normal, collegiate friendships. Horne and Sutherland not only sang magnificently together but also became close friends. Fleming recounts the many support-ive friendships she had with other singers (including Horne), especially valued at moments when her own career faltered. If the image of the prima donna is of a fierce harridan tearing out the hair of her rival, let us recall the particularly high stakes for which they compete. Back in the days of Pasta or Patti, the prizes must have seemed particularly seductive at a time when many women were caught in a life pattern of recurrent pregnancy and childbirth and the attendant demands of homekeeping. Or else threadbare spinster-hood. For those with the talent and willpower, the operatic profession held out the possibility of genuine liberation from gilded cage to gilded stage and beyond.

✳

When our children were small, my wife and I discussed introducing them to opera and ballet. Something soft and easy to begin with, like *Swan Lake* or *The Magic Flute* (in English) perhaps. Then I recalled my first introduction to opera. I was eight and my father took me to a performance of *Rigoletto*, a rip-roaring work about sex and murder, two topics I did not yet know much about. However, I was perfectly capable of recognizing big, bold pas-sions as they came pouring across the footlights. That night, I laughed with the lascivious Duke, loved with the vulnerable Gilda and wept at the end with her bitter, bereaved father. A generation later, we took the kids to *Carmen*.

In many well-loved operas, the principal woman is killed off at the end in a kind of expiation of sexual guilt (Lucia, Norma, Gilda, Marguerite, Car-men, Manon, Salome). Some transgressive women (Senta, Isolde, Aida, Tosca) choose to join their lovers in death or oblivion. In a number of works (such as *La traviata*, *Les Contes d'Hoffmann*, *La Bohème*), it is not just the death of the heroine but her sickness that evidently heightens the excitement, while several of the most seductive operatic figures to late nineteenth- and early twentieth-century audiences embodied the further frisson of ethnic 'other-ness', among them Aida, Dalila, Sélika in Meyerbeer's *L'Africaine*, Leïla from Bizet's *Pearl Fishers*, the gypsy girl Carmen, Lakmé, Thaïs, Butterfly and Salome.

The theme of the attractive yet vulnerable and transgressive woman who contravenes social norms and then suffers for her 'sins' recurs again and again in the literature of the later nineteenth century: Emma Bovary, Anna Karenin and Zola's Nana are only three of the more famous examples. They – like Verdi's Violetta, Gounod's Marguerite or Puccini's Mimì – did what respectable ladies were not supposed to do, thus providing a focus for both male and female sexual fantasy while also, in the women's subsequent suf-fering and death, enabling a cathartic sense of moral rectitude to prevail as the frail, pale sinner reaches her deeply romanticized end. Male fantasies in particular seem to be encapsulated in many of the most popular operas of the time (all of them written by men): the sado-erotic desire to become the lover of an alluring younger woman for a while, and then to encounter some form of crisis through which to engineer her eventual disappearance from the scene. Such patterns of behaviour were hardly unknown at the time, and a number of operas (including *Traviata* and *Bohème*) were based on literary texts of thinly disguised autobiography. Where better to link life and art than in the privileged environs of the theatre, where such fantasies could safely be stimulated through the heightened emotions of art – and, perhaps, sublimated in the show after the show?

Opera and the opera theatre as sexual stimulant? Think of their twentieth-century successors, film and cinema, of the young couple canoodling in the back row, the press gossip about the supposed sexual activities of movie celebrities or the widespread publicity afforded any film that allegedly comes close to portraying 'real sex' or a morbid portrayal of death on screen. Sex and murder were, and remain, dangerous topics, proscribed except within very specific limits. When a man like Don Giovanni or Verdi's Duke of Mantua feels free to seduce any attractive woman he encounters, he is portrayed as doing more than ruining the lives of his victims; he is defying and perhaps disrupting the entire social order at whose apex he nominally stands. Today, Don Giovanni or the Duke would probably land up in jail for rape, kidnap or child abuse. When these operas were created, and in many places well into the twentieth century, the only publicly acceptable form of sexual relation-ship was consensual intercourse between a man and a woman in marriage. The killing of another human being, similarly, was officially sanctioned only at times of war or, under carefully defined conditions, in self-defence. Of course, theory and practice did not always chime, and to many, from the puritanical cleric to the free-thinking playwright or composer, it was the aberrant rather than the conventional that tended to arouse the greater interest.

The opera stage was one of few public locations where normally repressed feelings could be extravagantly and legitimately displayed. The overheated passions featured in so many operas were usually conventionally heterosexual. Yet a conspicuous segment of the audience for opera has probably always included homosexual men. Whitman, as we have seen, adored opera; so did Proust (especially if he could listen to it in the immaculate privacy of his own bedroom).* Then there were the opera-loving 'fops' and 'dandies' in the first half of the nineteenth century who, while 'not remarkable for talent' according to one observer, were 'considered to lead the fashion in dress'. They were, it seems:

> forward in coats and cravats, were well up in shirt collars, could have passed a most creditable examination in that most exact science – the art of making a tie for a neck-cloth, were advanced in pantaloons, erudite in cambric shirt fronts and fancy waistcoats, and familiar with the best models of gloves, silk stockings, boots and pumps.

At Her Majesty's Theatre in London's Haymarket, these peacocks would assemble in what came to be dubbed 'Fops' Alley', a wide aisle running from the back of the stalls area through to the orchestra. A wit in the satirical magazine *Punch* tried to imagine the sentiments of one of its occupants:

> Fops' Alley, how enchanted,
>   I take my stand in thee;
> And think what eyes are planted,
>   From every side, on me!

By the 1840s, the term 'Fop' was becoming 'extinct', wrote Benjamin Lumley, by then in charge of Her Majesty's, while the 'Dandy' was 'all but antiquated' (and the 'Swell' had not yet risen to his 'recent supremacy'). Lumley, presumably needing to install extra stalls seating as he went into competition with Gye at Covent Garden from 1847, brought Fops' Alley to an end. But he thought a description might be of interest to 'younger opera-goers, among the male sex especially':

> It was the practice of the day for all the more 'exquisite' and fashionable of the male operatic patrons to quit their boxes or their scanty stalls during various portions of the performance, and to fill the vacant spaces in the centre and sides of the pit, where they could laugh,

*For Proust and *théâtrophone*, see p. 282.

lounge, chatter, eye the boxes from convenient vantage points, and like-
wise criticise and applaud in common. The 'meetings and greetings'
that took place… were looked upon as an essential portion of the
evening's entertainment. All that was aristocratic, distinguished,
fashionable, or (still more) would-be fashionable, met, swarmed,
greeted, babbled in an ever-seething, ever-varying crowd.

The 'Fops', 'Dandies' and 'Exquisites', like the *dilettanti* Stendhal described,
were not necessarily homosexual. But their predilection for outlandish
apparel, not to mention their fiercely expressed operatic expertise, marked
them out as among the ancestors of a later generation's obsessive and posses-
sive 'opera queens', drawn to the emotionally heightened experience offered
by the opera house with its velvet and gilded decor, the flamboyant emotions
and extravagant stagings of the works themselves and their (sometimes literally) larger-than-life performers. No assertively gay male, listening to the
music of a conventional pair of operatic lovers, would presumably identify
directly with either Alfredo or Violetta, Carmen or José, Rodolfo or Mimì.
Yet something about the hothouse heterosexuality of opera has evidently provided a powerful magnet for many homosexual men.

A Dandy fainting or — An Exquisite in Fits. Scene a Private Box Opera

To the truly sensitive soul, the emotions aroused by opera can be insupportably intense.
In this 1818 etching by Cruikshank of a group of 'Exquisites' in an opera box, a dandy lies
back fainting in a chair supported by three others. 'I must draw the curtain or his screams
will alarm the House', exclaims the man on the left, while another comments: 'That last Air
of Signeur Nonballenas has thrown him in such raptures we must call a Doctor immediately!'

A number of possible hypotheses have been advanced. The sexual passions portrayed on stage, it has been suggested, are sometimes so extravagant as to verge on parody. They are not the real affections of ordinary people but theatrically overheated passions that go far beyond anything normally regarded as acceptable and they often end with painful or violent death. Homosexual love, too, has historically been regarded as transgressive by society, so the gay man develops a kind of subversive identification with the impossibly over-heated emotions and 'camp' decor of opera, the 'unreal' love ending in tragedy portrayed on stage. Opera, says Wayne Koestenbaum in *The Queen's Throat*, a book tinged with eloquent sadness, 'has always suited those who have failed at love'.

Furthermore, many operas from earliest times have featured cross-dressing and other forms of disguise, either as part of the plot or as part of the casting. Throughout the first two centuries of operatic history, many of the most celebrated performers were castrated men, while all three of the operas Mozart composed to texts by Da Ponte involve characters dressing up as other people. The tradition continued through the nineteenth century and into the twentieth. Thus, Beethoven's Leonore (in *Fidelio*) and Verdi's Leonora (*Forza*) are required to disguise themselves as men, as is Gilda in the last act of *Rigoletto*. Disguise (though not cross-gender dressing) is recurrent throughout the *Ring* as Alberich becomes a toad, a giant becomes a dragon and Siegfried dons headgear that enables him to disappear altogether. In one of the most popular operas of the early twentieth century, Strauss's *Rosenkavalier*, the curtain goes up on the immediate aftermath of love-making between a countess and her young man, both of them played by women singers, while the central figure in Britten's *Curlew River* is a 'Madwoman', set for a tenor. Meanwhile, the revival of baroque and classical repertoire brought to the fore, in the absence of genuine castrati, that quintessentially androgynous voice, the countertenor. The opera house thus continued to maintain its reputation as a showcase of extravagant disguise and gender ambivalence.

The magnetic appeal of opera for the assertively gay man, the 'opera queen', has often been focused on star singers, especially sopranos. There is a further analogy here with the film fan, passionate not so much about roles but the people portraying them. The word 'fan' is of course an abbreviation for 'fanatic' – a word that easily springs to mind whenever partisans of Callas and Tebaldi, for example, or Gheorghiu or Netrebko would square off about the merits of their preferred diva. Koestenbaum tells how, when Jenny Lind threw her shawl from a balcony, fans were said to have ripped it up and fought for the pieces, while a Melba fan in Russia broke the diva's autographing pencil with his teeth so other friends could retain a 'relic'. Anyone who has been backstage after a highly charged performance by a powerful singer will have encountered the crowd of excited fans whose state of emotional arousal resembles that of the anxious lover desperate for a gesture of intimacy.

The singer, having portrayed a romantic lead all evening, comes to be idolized as one backstage. Prominent among the scrum of admirers are likely to be gay men.

Singing is an elemental, physical activity, far more expressive of self than any other form of music-making. The voice is the person. It is through our mouths, more than with anything else in our bodies, that we express our emotions: our love and hate, fear, fury, anxiety, tenderness. It is with our mouths that we curse those we hate, kiss those we love; the mouth is a visible orifice of sexual action and attraction and the sounds that emanate from it are loaded with coded meanings. On the opera stage, these meanings become overt, exaggerated even, as the strutting characters sing rather than speak their lines. Emotions are poured out at high volume; they have to be to reach the limits of a large unamplified theatre. And, at pivotal moments, at high pitch: when emotions are stretched close to breaking point people tend to scream, to yell, to 'raise' their voices. The highest voice on the operatic stage is that of the soprano, a voice type often required to portray a role combining high sexual charge with raw feeling and requiring of the singer the capacity to cry out high-octane emotions at high pitch and high volume. Anybody capable of responding to opera will have experienced the frisson of excitement as a great dramatic soprano pours out her heart in, say, Violetta's 'Amami, Alfredo'. But the erotic (or desperate) outpourings of a tragic female heroine, expressing high passion, seem to have held a special place among gay opera lovers, the role becoming subordinate to its interpreter. It was Grisi's or Malibran's or Callas's Norma (or whatever) that became the emotional focus. Terrence McNally's 1985 play, *The Lisbon 'Traviata'*, focuses in part on the gay obsession with Callas and the minutiae of her recorded performances.

Callas, in her own life, experienced extremes of both passion and desperation; her untimely death, indeed, might be seen as having resulted in part from her inability to come to terms with these. In her art, she came to be seen, like a number of other gay icons, as having striven to lift her act; a vulnerable female victimized by an oppressive society who, during her cruelly foreshortened career (or life), managed to transcend her victimhood and convey in her art an impressive toughness and resilience. Something of the same could be seen in the life and art of Edith Piaf, for example, or Judy Garland (both of whom died young), or in the *faux* manliness of Bette Davis or Joan Crawford or big-voiced or big-bodied singing stars such as Ethel Merman, Montserrat Caballé or Jessye Norman, all of whom attracted a substantial gay following. It was evidently not just flute-like coloratura virtuosity that excited but the powerful projection of the resilient woman: women who seemed possessed of a kind of masculine resolution, who could soar the vocal heights of female sensuality, women whose art may have been erotically charged but were capable of expressing themselves with the forcefulness of men. Women, if you like, who 'fought back'. Here, perhaps, in the operatic atmosphere of licensed gender confusion, is a further clue to the magnetic appeal of opera, and particularly of certain female singers, for gay men.

On the face of it, there might not seem to be much in common between today's opera queen and the uptight, top-hatted opera goer of yesteryear. But if styles and attitudes have changed, those two perpetual preoccupations, sex and suffering, desire and death, have remained central. In the nineteenth century, the dreaded disease was 'consumption'; that is, tuberculosis. Theatre audiences seeing a sexually active young woman 'consumed' by this wasting sickness might well have understood it to be a polite euphemism for syphilis (a taboo subject that remained unmentioned even in a celebrated play in which it provided the central theme: Ibsen's *Ghosts*). Today, people are less fearful of either TB or syphilis; there are cures for both. Nowadays, the rampant disease that consumes its victims is AIDS. When the *Bohème* story was updated to become the Broadway musical *Rent*, it was not from 'consumption' that the Mimì figure was made to die but from AIDS, while a moving scene in the 1993 film *Philadelphia* features the Tom Hanks character, a gay lawyer fired because he is HIV positive, listening to a Callas recording and trying to explain to his uncomprehending attorney the emotional depths it touches. Every opera house and audience has been depleted by the cruel depredations of AIDS. The subtext of *La traviata*, wrote Wayne Koestenbaum in *The Queen's Throat*, was that pleasure would kill Violetta just as AIDS killed gays. Early death became, understandably enough, something of a gay preoccupation. A long list of celebrated divas died premature or tragic deaths, among them Malibran, Sontag (of cholera, on a tour of Mexico), Nordica (after a shipwreck off Java), Cavalieri (killed in a Second World War bombing raid) and Grace Moore (air crash), and in more recent times Kathleen Ferrier, Lucia Popp and Lorraine Hunt Lieberson.

To Koestenbaum (and, he suggested, to gays more generally), love of opera was an elegiac experience, an exercise in nostalgia for a lost world, a Proustian quest for souvenirs from a dead, unrecapturable past. He writes of the pleasure of listening, alone, to great recordings of opera sung by artists of the past; one senses the almost onanistic ecstasy he seems to have obtained from the experience. Opera as necrophilia. The invention of recording, according to Koestenbaum, helped 'kill' opera by encouraging people to listen to pre-existing rather than new repertoire. Recording, he pointed out, dated from the same period as the category 'homosexual'. Perhaps, for a gay community depleted by AIDS, the catharsis of romanticized love and death performed on record by a great prima donna, herself long since dead, acted as a balm, if only momentary, for those who had survived.

CHAPTER 13

The Lion Tamers: The Ascendancy of the Conductor

As the Viennese watched their new opera house emerging in the 1860s, they were characteristically acerbic and outspoken in their criticisms, much to the dismay of its two principal architects; both were dead (one from suicide, the other, deeply demoralized, from a stroke two months later) when the building opened in 1869. When Mozart and Beethoven had lived in Vienna, the city was still encircled by its protective walls, but these were demolished in the middle of the nineteenth century and replaced by a great horseshoe-shaped highway, the 'Ring', a glittering necklace around which were erected a succession of self-consciously 'historicist' pearls: a neoclassical Parliament, a pseudo-medieval City Hall, a neo-Renaissance University, a Gothic, slightly Disneyesque Votivkirche. And, at the apex of the horseshoe, Vienna's great Court Opera House. This was the first to go up: a heavy neo-Renaissance-style edifice that replaced the old Kärntnertortheater.

It was still the Hofoper – the 'Court Opera' – in 1897 when Gustav Mahler took over as director. In the intensely Catholic city of Vienna, some found it surprising that the Habsburg court should agree to the appointment of a Jew to the post. Mahler was born and raised on the borders of Bohemia and Moravia, his parents typical of the increasingly assimilated Jewish bourgeoisie emerging in the eastern reaches of the Habsburg empire. The Mahlers lived in the bustling little market town of Iglau; here, a local military garrison maintained a band that the boy often heard when it marched down the road or performed in the town square. Mahler's father began life as a carter, going on to run a successful tavern and distillery. Ever keen to improve himself, he was a voracious reader, and the family acquired a small library and a piano which Gustav soon learned to play. A precocious and talented young musician, he was educated at the Vienna music academy and went on to take a number of conducting jobs at small theatres, moving on to junior posts in Prague and Leipzig, thence to the artistic directorships of the Budapest and Hamburg operas and, after what most understood to be a conversion of convenience to Catholicism, to the Court Opera in Vienna.

The Vienna Court Opera (today's State Opera) which opened in 1869.

By now, Vienna was in many ways an extremely modern city, with its efficient tram system, electric street lighting and sophisticated cafes and restaurants. Culturally, it was a somewhat febrile mix of high art, heedless hedonism and almost pathological anxiety. This was the city in which Klimt and his colleagues noisily seceded from the salon art of their predecessors and celebrated the gaudily sexual, while the guilty erotic secrets of the subconscious were uncovered by Freud and dramatized by Schnitzler and Wedekind. Schnitzler highlighted what many regarded as the deep-seated hypocrisy of *fin-de-siècle* Austro-Hungarian society, at once publicly polite and privately licentious, a false glitter brilliantly evoked, too, in the operettas of Lehár and Kálmán and ruthlessly satirized by Karl Kraus – like Freud and Schnitzler (and Mahler) a product of non-sectarian, assimilated Viennese Jewry. The darker, neurasthenic sides of life were further explored by Richard Gerstl and Egon Schiele in their canvasses and in the overripe, darkly perfumed, post-Wagnerian musical romanticism of Zemlinsky and his young pupil Schoenberg.

New styles became evident, too, in architecture and design as leading figures recoiled from the fancy-dress historicism of the buildings around the Ring. Otto Wagner helped develop the style of art known as *Jugendstil*, with its characteristic use of quasi-symbolic squares, curves and rectangles, while the American-influenced Adolf Loos eschewed decor altogether. This was a culture determined to express the previously inexpressible, to portray the hitherto unportrayable, a world in which artists and intellectuals consciously pushed back boundaries, investigated the unknown, and celebrated, caricatured or excoriated the self-indulgent foibles of fallible humanity. It was a culture of self-conscious decadence, cultivated hothouse emotions, sometimes almost pathological. Wedekind's Lulu opens the Pandora's box of her overheated sexuality conscious that it will lead to many violent deaths, including her own. Gerstl committed suicide; so did that most searching of mathematicians Ludwig Boltzmann. It was also, at least in its higher reaches, a small, self-regarding, somewhat incestuous world. Gerstl's death followed his affair with Schoenberg's wife, who was the sister of Zemlinsky. Mahler lived in an apartment block designed by Otto Wagner, and the violinist leader of his orchestra, the Vienna Philharmonic, was his brother-in-law, Arnold Rosé. Mahler's young wife Alma, a former Zemlinsky pupil (and intimate), had an early flirtation with Klimt and, during her marriage to Mahler, a serious affair with the architect Walter Gropius (whom she later married); she also had a relationship with the painter Kokoschka who, after their affair was over, attended the opera with a full-size Alma look-alike doll. Mahler himself famously sought out Freud for an afternoon of intensive if instant psychotherapy. Sex and death, love and hatred, creation and destruction, generation and degeneration: these themes were ubiquitous as the crumbling façade of Habsburg Vienna, still nominally ruled by the aged Emperor Franz Joseph, hurtled towards collapse.

Such was the cultural world into which the brilliant, earnestly intense 37-year-old Mahler stepped, with his awkward, irregular gait, in 1897. Initially appointed as *Kapellmeister*, Mahler was promoted to director of the Court Opera before the year was out. Constitutionally, Mahler was a servant of the crown, all his decisions requiring rubber stamping from on high. And his appointment coincided with a shift to the right by the Viennese electorate which had installed a city government dominated by the Christian Socials under the stridently anti-Semitic *Burgomeister* Karl Lueger. In the event, the court stood loyally by Mahler, and the Emperor himself was heard to say that he would never let decisions be dictated by anti-Semites.

If Mahler managed to avoid direct political confrontation, at least at first, his reign at the Hofoper was never devoid of controversy. A more compliant director might have kept his head down and quietly got on with conducting

Gustav Mahler, director of the Court Opera, at his desk. Mahler would not abide sloppiness, and was said to have been like a lion tamer in the way he sometimes disciplined his musicians.

nice, traditional productions. But Mahler was a stubborn perfectionist, a man to brook no compromise whether in politics, love or art; even his conversion to Catholicism, he claimed (while never denying his Jewish origins), was undertaken for ideological reasons. Tradition, he emphasized, amounted to *Schlamperei*, sloppiness, laziness. Mahler would have none of it. He wanted artists who were prepared to rehearse and singers who could act. Those he thought not up to the job he sacked, and to those he engaged he could be a harsh task master. For a decade, this brilliant, troubled man made the Vienna opera his fiefdom, controlling every aspect of repertoire, casting and production to an extent few practising musicians can ever have done before.

Mahler was no arrogant power maniac. On the contrary, he was a man of few airs and graces. He was evidently quite content to travel to and from work by tram in Vienna and later, when a highly paid celebrity conductor in New York, on the subway. He seems scarcely to have been aware of the bruised egos his brusqueness could cause. It was simply that he was fanatically devoted to his art. Nobody at the Hofoper worked harder than its director. Mahler was in the house day and night, sitting in on rehearsals, frequently conducting performances himself, and somehow finding the imaginative energy each summer to pour out the great song cycles and mammoth symphonies for which he is best known today. To Mahler, music was far more than art; it was a gateway to a heightened spiritual consciousness.

Word soon spread in the little hothouse of Viennese cultural life that something of a revolution was occurring at the Hofoper under its fanatical director. Any night of the week, a new generation of outstanding young singers, coached by musical assistants of the calibre of Franz Schalk and Bruno Walter, could be heard in superb performances of opera. Scores were normally played uncut. Moreover, Mahler introduced a great deal of contemporary work from all across Europe: Tchaikovsky was played at the Hofoper, and new works by Puccini, Saint-Saëns, Richard Strauss and Pfitzner, while Mahler also presented outstanding new productions of Mozart and Wagner which he himself conducted. Many experienced musicians, not to mention the more discriminating critics, openly regarded Mahler as the greatest conductor they had ever encountered.

To Mahler, all aspects of operatic production, not just the music, had to make artistic sense. During his tenure, he engaged as director of scenic and costume design one of the major products of the Vienna Secession, Alfred Roller. Roller, building on the theories of the Swiss scenic designer Adolphe Appia and with Mahler's enthusiastic support, dispensed with old-fashioned clutter, featuring instead electrically lit stage pictures characterized by a primal clarity which focused audience attention on the core atmosphere of the piece being performed. Nor did Mahler limit himself to artistic matters. He insisted that latecomers be excluded from the auditorium until the interval, and he tried (in vain) to banish the claque.

It used to be said (it still is occasionally) that the man in charge of the Vienna opera was the second most important person in town – second, that is, to the man running the country. Mahler and his doings were constantly in the press; people who could not name a politician knew and relished the latest chitchat about Mahler and his star singers: where they lived, the clothes they wore, their favourite foods and, discreetly of course, their love lives. People pointed out Mahler in the street and followed him as he clip-clopped his earnest way, perhaps in deep conversation with a colleague, to and from the opera house. In these early days of photography, he was snapped in the street (as Verdi had been). And ordinary people wanted to see Mahler doing what he was famous for: conducting opera. By now, Vienna's tram system brought the First District and its opera house within manageable and inexpensive reach of all parts of town. Furthermore, the Hofoper offered plenty of cheap seats in its upper reaches, while anyone prepared to stand all evening could gain admission for an even lower sum.

Mahler was widely admired; revered even. But not everyone loved him. Up close, he could be difficult to work with. A 'musical tyrant' was the verdict of the formidable singer Ernestine Schumann-Heink, describing how Mahler would bang away repeatedly about a single note until she got it right. Another soprano (with whom he later had an affair) wrote of the brusque way Mahler dismissed the rehearsal pianist when she first came to audition for him, and then went on to reduce her to tears. One Mahler watcher reported that he treated his musicians the way a lion tamer treated his animals. The tenor Leo Slezak, a member of Mahler's Vienna company, described what happened when he requested leave to make a guest appearance elsewhere:

With my heart thumping, I would step into the room.
    'Herr Director, I should like to sing in Graz on two evenings so I

am requesting four days' leave.'

    'What, are you crazy? You've only just been away!'

Slezak pointed out politely that it was in fact many weeks since he was last away. Mahler decided to check. On his desk was a panel with some twenty-five or thirty buttons, each of which would summon a member of staff. Mahler lunged at it, hitting some dozen buttons with the flat of his hand. Doors popped open on all sides. 'No, not you. Out!' yelled Mahler as one after another of his unwanted colleagues retreated again in some trepidation.

    Many years after Mahler's death, his wife Alma was asked how he had been regarded by the musicians who played for him. She answered succinctly: 'He was feared.'

✳

Never before in operatic history had the conductor so completely ruled the roost – or tamed the lions. The very idea of a professional conductor had only emerged a few decades earlier. Until the nineteenth century, orchestral forces were generally small and could be held together by an alert first violinist, or a centrally placed *maestro di cembalo* – often the composer of the piece (a role Donizetti and Rossini were still expected to perform on the first three nights of a new opera). As composers began to write for larger forces, the job of coordinating an operatic performance became increasingly complex. More was required than that the harpsichordist occasionally wave his head or the leading violinist his bow. In France, in a tradition dating back to the seventeenth century, the main musical beat might be marked with a

Nobody (not even Liszt in this cartoon of 1869) could keep an orchestra of Wagnerian proportions together with just a nod from the harpsichord.

stick or baton striking the floor or perhaps a music stand (Lully died as a result of a gangrenous infection after striking himself accidentally in the foot in this way). Later music lovers such as Rousseau took exception to the noise caused. By the early decades of the nineteenth century, performances at the Paris Opéra began to be coordinated by a *chef d'orchestre* who would wield a thick, short baton a little like those passed by athletes in relay races. Elsewhere, a conductor might beat time with a scroll of paper like those in the hands of Roman statues. The composer Ludwig Spohr was (or claimed to have been) the first to conduct with what we would recognize as a baton and the idea evidently caught on during the 1820s and 1830s. This did not necessarily mean the noise had stopped; Berlioz, visiting the San Carlo opera house in Naples, complained about the conductor's bow (or baton?) being tapped audibly on the music desk, but was told that otherwise the players would not have been able to keep time together.

Increasingly, as opera audiences demanded ever more lavish staging and larger choruses, far more came to be expected of the conductor than that he merely indicate the tempo from an instrument; there was no way a work like Wagner's *Tannhäuser* (1845) or Meyerbeer's *Le Prophète* (1849) could be satisfactorily directed from the first violin. So the fiddle was abandoned as the maestro came to concentrate all his attention on what the forces arrayed before him were playing and singing. Proper rehearsal time was required and this, too, tended to increase the prominence of the conductor in the musical hierarchy. A division of labour developed whereby singers might be rehearsed by a preliminary *maestro concertatore*, the overall performance being brought together at a later stage by the man who would conduct the actual performances, the *direttore d'orchestra* (a situation familiar to opera choruses today). With increasing musical coordination came enhanced ambition: as conductors began to rehearse detailed matters of intonation, tempo, balance and overall interpretation, composers reciprocated by building ever-greater complexity into their scores. Thus was born the profession of conductor, the most famous among them gradually assuming something of the mystique that formerly surrounded instrumental virtuosi such as Liszt or Paganini.

At first, most conductors were primarily composers. Operatic productions were generally of new or recently written works, and it was common for the composer to be actively involved in early rehearsals. Often, as we have seen, it was the singers who called the shots, they who would tell the maestro how they planned to perform, they who would request (read 'demand') changes from the generally accommodating composer. Gradually, however, composers began to assert their primacy; *they* were the ones who would decide how their pieces should be performed.* Berlioz, constantly railing at

* In 1847, an increasingly confident Verdi notoriously put his *Macbeth* soloists through their gruelling paces day after day, hour after hour, right up to the time the opera's world premiere was about to commence.

During the nineteenth century, as orchestras became larger and music more complex, the independent profession of 'conductor' emerged with – eventually – that universally recognised sign of authority, the baton. In the 1820s, Weber used a scroll to control his orchestra.

Verdi, conducting in the 1870s, resorted to something more solid.

the putative inadequacies of conductors, did his best to promote his own works (and earn some decent money) by taking them on tour and conducting them himself; unusual among composers in that he lacked instrumental expertise, Berlioz also wrote one of the first treatises on the nature of conducting. In Germany, Mendelssohn proved an inspirational conductor at the Leipzig Gewandhaus; like Wagner a little later, he was an outstanding exponent not only of his own works but also of compositions by revered predecessors. After watching Wagner conduct, the Kaiser is said to have remarked that he could now see what a good general could do with an army. Mahler is best known to posterity for his compositions, while Furtwängler and Klemperer would like to have been; to them, the process of musical interpretation was essentially subordinate to that of creation.

In a sense, Furtwängler and Klemperer were too late. That is not to say that a latter-day composer would not be called upon to conduct or vice versa; Leonard Bernstein and Pierre Boulez prove the contrary. But already in Mahler's time, the roles of composer and conductor were tending to diverge as both became more demanding. Furthermore, public taste was tending increasingly towards an existing 'canon' of works and this, too, contributed to the rise of the specialist conductor. Audiences became less interested in the latest creation by a little-known composer. What they craved was new interpretations of sanctified classics: Bülow's Beethoven, perhaps, or Mahler's *Don Giovanni* or *Walküre*.

*

In contrast to the German- and English-speaking worlds (and Paris), Italy was something of a musical backwater. It may sound perverse to say this of a nation that produced Rossini, Donizetti, Bellini and Verdi, not to mention singers, theatres and audiences in abundance to celebrate their works. But if Italian opera and its exponents were enthusiastically received across the world, the wider musical world did not much visit Italy. The great symphonies and chamber works of Haydn, Mozart, Beethoven and Schumann made only slow and laborious inroads south of the Alps, tending to be regarded as too long, too 'intellectual' and too difficult to play. The first performance in Italy of Beethoven's Third ('Eroica') Symphony took place in Genoa nearly half a century after its composition. In Lucca, Puccini's birthplace and home of a well-regarded opera house, the first performance of a full-length symphony was probably that of Haydn's 'Farewell' as late as 1881.

Even operatically, Italy was something of a desert. Musically and dramatically, standards were often poor. Italy's music academies were chronically underfunded and the level of the new nation's orchestral playing often rudimentary. Opera choruses tended to be assembled on a seasonal basis, like fruit pickers, from local working people – cobblers, cooks and the like, few of whom could read music, keen to earn a few extra lire. Not infrequently, this operatic equivalent of Falstaff's ragged army would suffer a bout of collective drunkenness or hold management to ransom by demanding an instant wage increase under threat of strike.

Italian unification, so widely celebrated when it happened, had rapidly soured. Many of the kingdoms, duchies and principalities swept away by the *Risorgimento* had been in the habit of subsidizing their own opera houses. As the new all-Italian government gradually found its feet and assumed responsibility for the entire peninsula, it inevitably looked some-what askance at such recurrent debts. No government, probably, could have fulfilled the miracles expected of it, and a series of bad harvests and stock-market failures in the 1870s led to widespread economic and social distress. Emigration from Italy accelerated, especially from the impoverished South, while industrialization stubbornly refused to take off and Mafia corruption increased. A succession of beleaguered administrations, desperate to retrench, tightened further their subventions to opera houses, passing responsibility for these to the various municipalities. Some opera houses closed down while many were forced to reduce their seasons. This produced armies of demoralized instrumentalists, choral singers and soloists all looking for non-existent jobs and, of course, led to further emigration to the Americas and elsewhere.

Then there was the Verdi problem. After all the excitement of unification had died down, Verdi frequently pronounced himself a farmer rather than a composer as the intervals between his compositions widened. Meanwhile, new operas by other Italian composers did not remotely measure up. Verdi himself felt increasingly estranged from the prominent younger generation of musicians and artists then emerging, the *Scapigliatura* (the 'dishevelled' or 'bohemians'), a loose, self-consciously avant-garde brotherhood that included the poet and composer Arrigo Boito, the musician Franco Faccio and the poets Emilio Praga and Ferdinando Fontana. Verdi was such a giant that, other than emulate or imitate him (out of the question), they had little option but to try to bypass him. Publicly distancing themselves from the way the altar of Italian art had been 'befouled like the walls of a brothel' (a comment deeply offensive to Verdi), they turned to foreign influences, at first French and later German, especially Wagnerian. Little was produced that lasted, wounds were healed, and both Boito and Faccio went on to notable collabo-rations with the aged maestro. But one by-product of *scapigliato* exuberance was a growing Italian openness to ultramontane cultural influences in, for example, the works of Puccini and Busoni. 'Here is the tomb of the greatest composer of the century!' wrote the young Arturo Toscanini on a postcard to a friend in 1899; the card was sent from Bayreuth and showed the grave of Wagner.

*

Toscanini, born in Parma in 1867, seven years after Mahler, was to become the most famous of all Italian conductors, the iron disciplinarian of genius, the *maestro di maestri*. But he was not the first. As early as the 1840s, Angelo Mariani had caught the eye (or rather the ear) of Verdi and later became his conductor of choice until the two fell out in the 1870s. Mariani was an important predecessor of Toscanini and Mahler, a single-minded, somewhat austere disciplinarian determined, like them, to maintain a degree of artistic control over all aspects of operatic production. It was Mariani who conducted that first Italian performance of the 'Eroica' Symphony and, in 1871, the first Wagner opera ever to be performed in Italy (*Lohengrin*, at the Teatro Comunale, Bologna). Mariani's younger contemporary, Faccio, having found scant success as an operatic composer, also became an outstanding conductor. It was to Faccio's baton at La Scala that Verdi entrusted the first Italian performance of *Aida* and, in 1887, the world premiere of *Otello*. In the cello section at the *Otello* opening was the nineteen-year-old Toscanini.

Toscanini had already achieved considerable acclaim the previous summer. On tour with an itinerant Italian company in Rio de Janeiro, he had rescued the opening night by taking over a performance of *Aida* after the conductor had proved incompetent and his deputy fallen foul of the audience. So able was Toscanini, and so grateful the company management, that he was asked to abandon his cello and conduct the rest of the tour – eleven operas, all of which he conducted from memory. During his twenties, Toscanini took a variety of conducting posts, notably at the Teatro Regio in Turin, where he introduced Wagner and led the world premiere of *La Bohème*. In 1898, a year after Mahler had become director of the Vienna Hofoper, Toscanini was appointed artistic director of La Scala, Milan, in harness with a new general manager named Giulio Gatti-Casazza.

Milan's great opera house dated back to 1778 and lay on the site of a former church, the Santa Maria della Scala. At first, the theatre was something of a cultural outpost of the Habsburg empire, its opening production a work by the Italian-born Viennese court composer Salieri. The building was largely financed by subscriptions from the wealthy nobility who owned its six layers of boxes, while operating income was boosted by the gambling concession which turned the Scala foyers into a virtual casino (run for a while – at great profit to himself – by Domenico Barbaja). After the defeat of Napoleon, Habsburg authority was re-established in much of northern Italy, a subsidy introduced for the financing of La Scala, and the gambling abolished.

Milan soon emerged as one of the principal opera centres in Italy – *the* centre by mid-century when, with a population of around 200,000, the city had some ten theatres that put on opera, the three principal ones (La Scala, the Canobbiana and the Carcano) capable of seating altogether over 7000 people. On and off throughout much of the mid-nineteenth century, La Scala was run by Bartolomeo Merelli, the impresario we encountered encouraging the young Verdi to help him out of a crisis by writing *Nabucco*. Merelli, openly pro-Austrian, went to live in Vienna after the 1848 revolutions, returning to run La Scala again in the early 1860s. By this time, the traditional, somewhat ad hoc impresarial system was beginning to change, at least in the major cities. Theatre owners, now having to look to the government of united Italy for financial help, realized that longer-term planning was becoming essential if opera seasons were to have any chance of proving artistically and financially successful. Meanwhile, the role of the conductor, too, was evolving; by the time Toscanini was appointed to La Scala, he was not alone in regarding the job as extending far beyond the mere rehearsal and conducting of performances.

The appointment of Gatti-Casazza and Toscanini was thus a statement that, henceforth, La Scala would be run on new lines. True, Milan was a more prosperous city than most and La Scala the nation's most prominent opera house. But, even here, budgets were tight and audiences often small and unenthusiastic. In 1897, the national government in Rome decided to cut its losses, handing over management of La Scala to the city of Milan, which soon afterwards turned off the financial tap. A little later, the theatre closed down. Enter Gatti and Toscanini.

*

'The theatre is intended to be full, not empty. That's something you must always remember': the wise words of the 85-year-old Verdi to the 29-year-old Gatti-Casazza as Gatti prepared to take up his post running La Scala. Verdi spoke slowly, emphasizing each syllable, as he told Gatti to read most attentively the box office reports. These, 'whether you like it or not', said the wily old maestro, 'are the only documents which measure success or failure... If the public comes the object is attained.' Easy to say (especially if you are Verdi); hard to achieve.

Gatti came to La Scala from Ferrara where he had been chairman of the board of directors of the city's Teatro Comunale. His father had fought for Garibaldi in 1860 in Sicily, where a friend and colleague was the father of Arturo Toscanini. Later an officer in the Italian army and eventually a member of the Italian parliament, Gatti Snr was a cultured man who took on a number of public roles, among them the head of the direction at the opera in Ferrara, a role in which his 24-year-old son succeeded him in 1893. By then, Giulio had qualified as a naval engineer and done a maths degree and a year's military service. But what he loved was opera. When he became chairman of the Ferrara board, his principal job was to keep an eye on the impresarios the board appointed to do the day-to-day running of the theatre and to make sure that the municipality and the box-holders, who subsidized the local theatre, got value for money. Gatti felt he had to be both Don Quixote and Sancho Panza, the idealist and the realist: he had to have the wild, creative ideas and also the down-to-earth capacity to execute them responsibly. One day in February 1898, one of Gatti's sopranos, claiming gypsy ancestry, took his hand to tell his fortune and informed him then and there that he was soon to change jobs. 'I see that in the lines of your hand in an indisputable manner,' she exclaimed. Four months later, Gatti received a letter from a prominent Milan journalist who had been campaigning for the reopening of La Scala suggesting he might like to consider becoming its boss. The music director, he was told, would be Arturo Toscanini. Gatti took the letter to his parents for advice. 'My dear young fellow', said his father, 'easy things are made for fools and simpletons. It is the accomplishing of difficult things that marks the strong man.' As his mother commented, it seemed the fortune-teller had been right.

Gatti was appointed not as an old-fashioned impresario but as a salaried general manager on a five-year contract. His first order of business was to supervise the reopening of Italy's most famous theatre. But first he had to get into La Scala: not easy, as his entry was blocked on his first day by a gruff, scowling character who demanded to know who this young interloper was. Once he had got his legs under the table, Gatti immersed himself in urgent matters of finance and management. He was responsible to a board headed by the opera-loving Duke Guido Visconti and Arrigo Boito. Boito, it transpired, had been behind the appointment of Toscanini. Funding for the theatre was guaranteed by a combination of box-holder revenue and the creation of a new society of shareholders which established an initial operating fund. Overall, the auguries could hardly have been better as the new duo got down to work.

Gatti-Casazza (with his 'children' in this cartoon by Caruso) spent a decade at La Scala before going on to run the New York Metropolitan Opera.

In swept Toscanini: not so much a new broom as a hurricane. Toscanini demanded and obtained total artistic control. He would choose the operas to be performed and appoint the singers and the members of the orchestra and chorus, while only he could prescribe how much rehearsal time each production required. Toscanini insisted on taking control of the visual and scenographic side of things, too, reserving the right to decide upon design and designers. Like Mahler in Vienna, Toscanini concerned himself with the latest theatrical lighting and insisted the house be dark during performances and that ladies in the orchestra stalls remove their hats. He dispensed with the old Scala curtain that rose from the ground revealing performers' feet and knees before their faces, and had it replaced with one that opened horizontally. Nothing escaped Toscanini's notice. There was a tradition (not only at La Scala but in many opera houses during the nineteenth century) of presenting a ballet with, or within, every opera performance. This provided a kind of excessive sweet course that was fine if you were an aristocratic night bird with an eye for the ballerinas but which prolonged the evening inordinately if you had work to go to in the morning. The practice was curtailed. Toscanini did not win all his battles; he tried, and only partially succeeded, to end the practice of giving 'encores' when a singer was particularly warmly applauded after an aria. Toscanini – like Mahler – was determined to train audiences to attend the theatre in a frame of mind to concentrate on a work of expertly integrated musico-dramatic art. It was with Wagner that this pre-eminent Italian conductor chose to inaugurate his reign at this greatest of Italian opera houses: *I maestri cantori di Norimberga*.

Toscanini had much in common with Mahler. Short of stature yet oozing charisma, these two Napoleons of the opera house experienced and aroused the strongest passions, not least in their relationships with the opposite sex. Both had intense affairs with singers with whom they worked, though neither, it has to be said, seems to have allowed amorous emotions to dictate artistic policy. On the contrary, both were fanatical in their quest for artistic integrity. Toscanini would rehearse vast, complex scores from memory, dumbfounding members of the orchestra by identifying and correcting even the minutest errors in their instrumental parts. His players, perhaps awed by the domineering figure in front of them, would regale friends with stories of Toscanini's legendary temper, the way he broke a baton in fury or walked out of a rehearsal (or even a production) of which he disapproved. Mahler's players, similarly, would get a cheap gasp from stories out of school about their conductor's faulty baton technique ('Could you hold it a little higher please, maestro?') or the casual cruelty with which he would pick on an individual instrumentalist to criticize in mid-rehearsal. However, while the players were in the presence, they were mesmerized. So were audiences when Mahler or Toscanini was in charge.

There were important differences between the two. Constitutionally, Toscanini was blessed with greater vitality; despite his restlessness and chronic

insomnia, he was to continue working well into his eighties while Mahler
died at fifty. Mahler – like his protégé Bruno Walter, but unlike Toscanini –
was widely admired for his conducting of Mozart, while Toscanini was a
great champion of Puccini. Above all, Mahler was the last of the great com-
poser-conductors, the acme and culmination of a great historic trend.
Toscanini, by contrast, was perhaps the first truly outstanding exemplar of
a profession that is still very much with us, that of the conductor *per se*. With
these two figures, the ascendancy of the maestro reached a peak.

    Fate brought the two men together, but not in Vienna or Milan. At La
Scala, Toscanini's wholesale reforms and fiery manner soon landed him in
difficulties which even the kindly Duke Visconti or the equable and diplomatic Gatti could not always resolve. Everybody recognized Toscanini's
artistic genius, of course; when Verdi died in Milan in 1901, it was naturally
Toscanini who led the music when gigantic crowds came out to say farewell
to their beloved maestro. But trouble was brewing at La Scala from as early
as Toscanini's second production, *Norma*, when he decided at the final
rehearsal that standards were simply not high enough and demanded the
production be promptly cancelled. Toscanini's refusal to allow encores produced howls of protest from the galleries, while traditional patrons objected
equally vociferously when the ballet was removed from opera nights. More
ominously, friction began to develop between Toscanini and Giulio Ricordi,
head of the publishing firm (and the man who had coaxed Verdi back from
retirement to write *Otello*). For many years, Casa Ricordi had controlled not
only the scores it possessed, which included most of those of Verdi, but performance rights too; they would only rent out full operatic scores if
productions were guaranteed to conform to the standards they demanded.
Fundamentally, the gentlemanly publisher and the fierce young conductor
had the same goal in mind. But it was perhaps inevitable that Toscanini, a
man evidently incapable of diplomatic niceties (and deeply committed to
Wagner), would gradually arouse the resentment of Giulio Ricordi – a
breakdown in relations that could have serious consequences for a major
opera house.

    In November 1902, Visconti died and his son took over as chairman of the
Scala board. The young Duke lacked his father's sympathetic understanding
of Toscanini's artistic perfectionism and it was not long before the conductor relinquished his Scala baton to pursue a freelance career. Gatti had him
back at La Scala in 1906 (when Toscanini insisted on the construction of a
proper orchestral pit, an innovation Giulio Ricordi derided as another example of Toscanini's relentless Wagnerism). Then, in 1907, it was announced that
both Gatti and Toscanini would be leaving at the end of the season and sailing to New York. Gatti had been appointed general manager of the Metropolitan Opera. As for Toscanini, he had agreed to share the job of principal
conductor with a colleague, hardly characteristic of the dictatorial maestro

everyone in Milan had learned to love and hate. But the conductorial colleague in New York was to be Gustav Mahler.

*

The man who invited Gatti-Casazza and Toscanini to the Met was Otto Kahn. The Metropolitan, hitherto run as a business supposedly devoted to making money for its shareholders, had recently been reconstituted as a not-for-profit organization with Kahn, a shrewd and wealthy investment banker, as head of its production company. It is easy, through the rosy glass of history, to romanticize the house Gatti and Toscanini came to, with its glittering Diamond Horseshoe listening night after night to Caruso, Melba, Farrar and the rest. But the backstage reality that greeted Gatti was sombre. The stage itself struck him as too short and too narrow and completely lacking in modern equipment of any kind. Rehearsal and storage space were hopelessly inadequate, sets and costumes often having to be left out overnight in all weathers. Soon after he arrived, Gatti poured out his woes to Kahn, who was well aware of the problems. Don't worry, said Kahn sympathetically, promising Gatti that a new opera house answering all his needs would be built 'within two or three years'; in the event it took fifty-eight.

Gatti encountered other problems too. One of them had arisen from the sheer popularity opera had achieved by now in New York. Oscar Hammerstein (like August Belmont and Otto Kahn) was a German-Jewish immigrant who had made his pile in America and loved to spend it on opera. After a series of shaky theatrical ventures, Hammerstein re-sorted his finances and concentrated on what he believed to be his big chance. Taking advantage of the perceived woes of the Metropolitan, he determined to take on the arrogant Met and beat it at its own game. Hammerstein's Manhattan Opera, based in a no-frills purpose-built theatre just a few blocks away, opened in December 1906, aiming to attract a new audience of ordinary music-loving New Yorkers who would be able to hear great stars singing good, popular works for a moderate ticket price. Stars cost money, of course, which Hammerstein

A dinner held in honour of Gatti-Casazza and Toscanini at the Hotel St Regis, New York on 22 November 1908.

aimed to recoup through box subscriptions and expensive seats in the orchestra stalls, thus enabling all the upper parts of the house to undercut the Met.

If Hammerstein's bold venture failed, it was not for want of trying. Nellie Melba, the most celestial of the stars he attracted, gives a (doubtless richly embellished) idea of how persuasive Hammerstein could be. Melba was staying in Paris when she received a visit from 'a determined man of Jewish persuasion, shortish, thin and dark, with piercing black eyes'. At the time, Melba was trying to reduce her workload and, in particular, avoid New York for a season or two. Hammerstein explained to Melba that he was building the biggest and finest opera house in the world, 'And I can't do it without you.' Melba explained she had no intention of going to New York the following year:

> OH: I shall give you fifteen hundred dollars a night.
> NM: Please don't discuss terms, Mr Hammerstein, because I assure you that is useless.
> OH: Oh, you'll come all right (pause). What do you say to two thousand?
> NM: If you offer me twenty thousand I shall still say the same thing.
> OH: It'll be the biggest thing you have done yet. Oscar Hammerstein says so.
> NM: And Nellie Melba says "No". I have no intention of going. Good morning, Mr Hammerstein.

Melba goes on to say that had anyone else been so importunate she would have been very angry. But there was something in Hammerstein's 'naïve determination' that appealed to her. Every few days, Hammerstein called on Melba, wrote notes or telephoned. He even turned up one day when Melba was in the bath and battered at the door:

> OH: Are you coming to America?
> NM: (between splashes) No!
> OH: I'll give you two thousand five hundred a night.
> NM: Not for ten times the money.
> OH: And you can sing as many nights as you like.
> NM: Go away!

Most people quailed before the imperious Melba. But not Hammerstein. He burst in one day while the prima donna was reading *Le Figaro* over a leisurely breakfast:

> OH: It's all settled. You're to have three thousand dollars a night.
> NM: But I've told you a hundred times…

OH (interrupting): Never mind about that. Three thousand dollars a
night, and you open in *Traviata*.

– at which Hammerstein drew from his pocket a large bundle of thou-
sand-franc notes, scattered them all over the carpet and left 'like a whirlwind'.
Melba picked the notes up and took them to the bank, explaining that the
money was not hers and must be kept safely until Mr Hammerstein called
for them. He did not. Instead he turned up one last time, breezily saying
that, despite Melba's lofty protestations, she'd come.

She did. And she loved it, particularly 'the exhilaration of battles, rivalries, difficulties galore'. For perhaps the only time in her life, the feisty prima
donna had met her match. But then, as she herself said: 'I love a good fight.'
She also liked money. And the success that comes with power. 'I am Melba,'
she said to herself. 'I shall sing where and when I like, and I shall sing in my
own way.' The applause at the end of her opening-night *Traviata* reminded
her of what Cecil Rhodes had described to her as the supreme sensation in
life: power. Melba was by far the biggest star in Hammerstein heaven; when
she was billed to sing, the house sold out.

In its first season (1906/7), the Manhattan Opera made a profit and
clearly constituted a major threat to the Metropolitan. Hammerstein was
heartened. New subscriptions rolled in, as did new audiences. Hammerstein
claimed the first season had brought $750,000 to the box office. If this sounds
an improbable figure, it is worth remembering that the population of greater
New York nearly doubled between 1890 and 1910, from 2.5 million to 4.75
million. The Italian community in New York at the time of the Manhattan
Opera was some half a million strong. Buoyed by his success, Hammerstein
engaged not only Melba but further outstanding singers, too, such as Mary
Garden and Luisa Tetrazzini. He also decided to build a second house, this
time in Philadelphia. The Met became seriously alarmed. The engagement
of Gatti and Toscanini was part of the Met's counter-offensive.

The immediate result was that in 1908/9, opera-loving New Yorkers were
once again treated to an *embarras de richesse*: two opera companies vying
with one another, each determined to produce the more magnificent performances. Gatti began his first Met season with a flourish even Hammerstein
could not rival. On Saturday, 14 November, a couple of nights before the New
York opening, the Met company inaugurated the newly built Brooklyn Academy of Music with Farrar and Caruso in *Faust*. On the Monday, Toscanini
opened the Met season proper with Caruso in *Aida* and the next night saw
Bohème in Philadelphia – again starring Caruso. *Walküre* followed on the
Wednesday night, *Butterfly* with Farrar and Caruso (and Toscanini) on
Thursday and on the Friday night a *Traviata* in which the tenor fell ill and was
replaced by Caruso. And the Saturday matinee? *Tosca* – with Caruso. Gatti's
star tenor had sung six different operas in three theatres in eight days.

The American soprano and film star Geraldine Farrar had everything: beauty, brains and a fine voice. A national celebrity, she was pursued by hordes of young (and not so young) 'Gerryflappers'.

New York audiences relished the flamboyant rivalry between the Met and the Manhattan, not only because of the array of talent on display but also because of such welcome amenities as the Met's introduction of elevators (both front of house and backstage), and the city's new subway system with its hub at Times Square virtually alongside the Met and a short walk from the Manhattan. As in the 1880s, when the new Met went head to head with New York's Academy of Music, each of the combatants sustained injuries. Hammerstein's (like Mapleson's before him) were the more serious as he over-reached himself. Many of the top singers in New York had followed Caruso's example and stayed with the Met, while the Philadelphia enterprise proved too costly for Hammerstein to sustain. Negotiations between Hammerstein and the Met resulted in the Met buying the Philadelphia theatre and Hammerstein himself barred from producing opera in any major US city. For the second time in its 25-year existence, the New York Metropolitan Opera had beaten off a serious rival.

*

In New York, as in Milan, Toscanini made waves, some of them tidal. At his very first rehearsal with the Met orchestra, he made a little speech, then launched straight into *Götterdämmerung*, conducting as always without a score. Although Toscanini and Mahler said respectful things about (and doubtless to) each other, the presence of these two redoubtable *maestri* in the same house could hardly fail to lead to difficulties. Once ensconced, Toscanini insisted on conducting *Tristan*, hitherto very much Mahler territory, and it was not long before Mahler left for the less contentious (and highly lucrative) pleasures of the concert hall. Meanwhile, Toscanini made it absolutely clear to

Giulio Gatti-Casazza with Arturo Toscanini and Geraldine Farrar. Did Gatti know of their affair?

his singers who was boss. Caruso and Farrar were the darlings of Met audiences. Yet Toscanini had no hesitation in upbraiding the tenor at rehearsal for not singing full voice. And when Farrar objected to a tempo Toscanini adopted, saying that, as she was the star, he should follow her, he is said to have replied dismissively: 'Mademoiselle, the stars are all in the heavens. You are but a plain artist, and you must obey my direction.' Perhaps this little fracas arose from the tensions that were to lead Toscanini and Farrar into what became a deep and agonizing personal relationship.

Toscanini stayed at the New York Metropolitan until 1915. According to his biographer, Farrar had given him an ultimatum: she would end the affair unless he left his wife and family for her, something that Toscanini, a Roman Catholic and doubtless desperately torn, simply could not get himself to do. He later said he left because he found the quality of work at the Met mere routine, acceptable perhaps to the 'artisan' but not to any true artist. However, there was a third reason, too, for Toscanini's departure. A patriotic Italian, he was keen to do whatever he could for his nation, and by 1915, much of Europe, including Italy, was at war.

PART IV

Opera in War and Peace
*c.*1900–1950

CHAPTER 14

Opera Goes West

In autumn 1897, an Italian company touring Mexico came up across the border for a few dates. In the as yet tiny settlement of Los Angeles they decided to include a novelty by one of the rising young stars among Italy's younger generation of composers. Their calculated risk evidently paid off, for the *Los Angeles Times* noted on 15 October 1897: '*La Bohème*, Puccini's operatic romance of the land of poverty and good fellowship, was the vehicle in which the great singers of the… company gave voice to their talents last night, and it was a performance to remember.'

By the turn of the century, opera was beginning to find a wider public in North America, not only in New York and other great cosmopolitan centres such as Boston and Philadelphia, but out west, too. In San Francisco, a German immigrant named Joseph Kreling had opened the Tivoli theatre in 1879, initially for operetta and other light fare, but by the 1890s had found a large and loyal audience for opera. It has been estimated that during the first decade of the twentieth century some 2225 performances of opera were presented in San Francisco. It was here in 1905 that Tetrazzini had her first major North American success. A year later, Caruso was tumbled out of his hotel bed by the notorious earthquake the night after singing *Carmen* on tour with the Metropolitan Opera.

There was opera in Chicago, too. Over half a century earlier, Chicago and San Francisco had had a kind of operatic baptism within a few months of each other. In 1850, a version of Bellini's *La sonnambula* was given in Chicago by members of the tiny 'Manvers–Brienti Italian Opera Company' (three singers and a piano), while the Pellegrini troupe performed excerpts from the same work in San Francisco in early 1851. In those days, Chicago was a rapidly growing trading centre and San Francisco the hub of the gold rush; in neither was opera much of a priority. Both cities, however, were soon transformed by the railroad: Chicago, already linked by water via the Erie Canal to New York, became the main hub linking East Coast America to its vast western hinterland, while the completion of the coast-to-coast railroad network confirmed San Francisco as the most important city in the western half of the continent. In the later nineteenth century, attempts were made in both cities to establish permanent venues for operatic production, a lofty aspiration finally achieved in the twentieth.

*

Chicago, still scarcely more than a frontier post in the 1830s, had a 3000-seat opera house by 1865, courtesy of a Yankee-born whisky millionaire and philanthropist, Uranus Crosby, who was intent on bringing high culture to the people in his adopted town. Crosby's theatre was flanked by commercial outlets which were intended to help finance the opera. In his opening season (fractionally delayed because of the assassination of President Lincoln), Crosby presented around a hundred performances of nearly forty different operas in what was basically a railroad and meat-packing town, though audiences probably included a liberal representation of the reasonably comfortable Scandinavian and German migrants who had recently settled in and around Chicago. Like many wealthy operatic patrons before and since, Crosby soon found his finances ricocheting unpredictably, and a raffle to save the theatre, while successful in its outcome, smelled rigged and nearly landed Crosby in jail. In 1871, six years after it was opened, Crosby's Opera House burned down in the fire that consumed much of the city.

For a decade and more, Chicago had other priorities than the building of an opera house. Moreover, recurrent recession and labour disputes, culminating in a bomb thrown at the police at a labour rally in the Haymarket in

Crosby's Opera House, a magnificent 3000-seater, was opened in 1865 at the end of the Civil War when Chicago had a population of scarcely more than a quarter of a million.

1886, led many Chicagoans to look with suspicion upon 'aliens' (especially Germans and Italians) and at 'foreign' entertainments. However, some among Chicago's more enlightened elite felt that the city's social tensions might be alleviated by the presence of high culture. In 1885, the property millionaire and philanthropist Ferdinand Peck had bankrolled an opera festival in Chicago's Interstate Industrial and Exposition Building in Grant Park. The building, more suited to political conventions than grand opera, was adapted by the German-born architect Dankmar Adler and the young Louis Sullivan, and the festival – which featured Mapleson at his most extravagant – proved a huge popular success. Altogether, Mapleson's company presented thirteen different operas in a fortnight to an aggregate audience estimated by the local press at some 190,000, including houses of eleven or twelve thousand on Patti nights. When they presented *Aida*, reported Mapleson, Patti could hardly get from her dressing room to the stage, 'the wings and flies being crowded with some 2,000 persons... Together with these were some 500 supernumeraries with blackened faces, in oriental garb, chasing round to try to find their places, others with banners arranging their dresses.' Amidst all this chaos, Patti was only able to leave her dressing room with the aid of the local police, 'but was surrounded immediately by crowds of ladies with pens and ink and paper, requesting autographs just as she was going on to sing her *scena*'.

At the end of the festival, Mapleson was honoured with the freedom of the City of Chicago, while Peck announced his belief that the 'continuation of this annual festival, with magnificent music, at prices within the reach of all, would have a tendency to diminish crime and Socialism in our city by educating the masses to higher things'. Peck's rather touching idealism led him to envisage a permanent auditorium that, in sharp contrast to the Metropolitan Opera, with its flashy boxes, lately inaugurated in New York, would be able to house 'conventions of all kind,... mass-meetings, reunions of army organizations, and, of course, great musical occasions in the nature of festivals, operatic and otherwise'. Chicago, in other words, should have what New York had: but bigger, better – and for everyone.

Chicago's 4200-seat Auditorium was the city's answer to the New York Met. Once again, Peck obtained the architectural services of Adler and (for the interior design – complete with electric lighting) Sullivan. Working as a junior apprentice on the project was Frank Lloyd Wright. As with Crosby's, the Auditorium complex was built to accommodate commercial outlets: not just a few stores this time, but a vast hotel. It was inaugurated in 1889, but opera had not stopped in the interim. While the Auditorium was in the planning stage, not only Mapleson but also the New York Metropolitan had come to Chicago on several highly publicized visits; indeed, the rivalry between the two was partly fought out in Chicago with local opera goers the principal beneficiaries. What the city really needed, they began to think, was

Chicago's Auditorium which opened in 1889. The Auditorium's first tenant was the Chicago
Conservatory of Music and Dramatic Art and it is now part of Roosevelt University.

their own permanent company: it was this, plus a resident orchestra, that the
Auditorium was designed to accommodate.

Chicago's population, perhaps a third of a million at the time of the fire,
grew something like fivefold over the next thirty years, outstripping every
other city in the country bar New York. At a time before most American cities
had paved roads, Chicago led the way with the electric trolley car while also
becoming a major railroad hub. Meanwhile, the thrusting new city was setting the nation's architectural standards with a string of spectacular new
buildings downtown and along the lakefront. By the early new century,
Chicagoans could spend a relaxed summer evening out in nearby Ravinia
Park, enjoy a concert of light classical music or perhaps a truncated opera performance, and catch a convenient train back into town afterwards.

The Chicago Orchestra was founded in 1891 with Theodore Thomas as
its conductor. But it was another twenty years before Chicago had its own
opera company – or, rather, found a multimillionaire couple prepared to spon-
sor one. Harold F. McCormick was boss of the International Harvester
Company and his wife the daughter of John D. Rockefeller. They provided a
potent brew: money from agriculture and from oil, Mid-West interests allied

to East Coast urbanity, the very epitome it must have seemed to many of all their city aspired to as it sprang to life again in the decades following the fire. McCormick's Chicago Grand Opera Company* was a by-product of the territorial feud between two New York-based outfits: the Metropolitan and Manhattan opera companies, both of which dreamed of expanding their activities westwards. The Met continued to visit Chicago, bringing especially starry casts (and Toscanini) during the years it was under threat from Oscar Hammerstein. And it was Hammerstein's evident desire to take control of opera in Chicago as well as New York that led Otto Kahn of the Met to contact Chicago's movers and shakers and form the committee, under McCormick, that set up the Chicago Grand in 1910.

It was not long before the neonate began to assert its independence of both parents. In this, it was greatly aided by the emergence of its own superstar, Chicago's answer to the Met's Geraldine Farrar. Mary Garden was born in Aberdeen but made her name in Paris. A tough and spirited personality offstage, Garden touched audiences with the intensity of both her singing and her acting. She excelled in the works of Massenet and was Debussy's first Mélisande. Brought to America by Hammerstein, Garden caused a sensation as Salome, Strauss's erotically charged princess, as she lasciviously kissed the decapitated head of John the Baptist. If Hammerstein's overstretched ambition helped kickstart the new Chicago company, his collapse apparently enabled Chicago to acquire many of his productions, complete with sets, props and costumes, as well as many of his artists. The inaugural performance by the new Chicago company on 3 November 1910 was led by Hammerstein's leading conductor, Cleofonte Campanini. Two days later, Mary Garden appeared in *Pelléas*. For a decade, Garden entranced Chicago audiences with her portrayals of the delicate, the vulnerable and the sensual. In January 1921, the feisty Scot was made director of the company (or, as she is said to have preferred, its *directa*). A better singer than manager, Garden engaged a stable of extravagantly expensive European artists and spent too much on productions (notably the world premiere of Prokofiev's *Love of Three Oranges*) and the company had to be bailed out one last time by McCormick. By now, he and his wife had separated, a world war had come and gone, Campanini was dead and Chicago was rapidly becoming more noted for its bootlegging and its gangsterism than for its opera.‡ After barely a year at the top, Garden returned to her day job. Or, rather, her night job.

*The names given to Chicago's successive 'permanent' opera companies are bewildering and include the Chicago Grand Opera Company, the Chicago Opera Association, Chicago Civic Opera, the Chicago City Opera Company, the Chicago Opera Company and, from the mid-1950s, Lyric Opera of Chicago.
‡ Opera and gangsterism were not perhaps entirely unrelated, especially among Chicago's large Italian population. It was reported that after one prominent bootlegger was gunned down, he was found to have four opera tickets in his pocket.

The Scottish-born soprano
Mary Garden, who excelled
in roles such as Mélisande,
Thaïs and Salome and
became a major star
– and briefly director –
of the Chicago Opera.

Enter yet another beneficent millionaire. Samuel Insull, head of the
Edison Company, was not only the man on whom Chicago (and its opera)
depended for its electricity. He had also been, since his childhood in London,
a passionate lover of opera. And what does a super-wealthy operatic Croesus
do? He builds his company a new opera house, especially if he lives in a city
which has become a byword for architectural excellence. Insull's Civic Opera
House is the theatre Chicago's opera goers know today. As you enter, you do
not see a gilded Italianate horseshoe so much as a highly practical rectangu-
lar seating area, from front to back one of the deepest most opera goers are
likely to encounter. Mary Garden described it as a 'long black hole' and
thought it looked more like a convention hall than an opera house. However,
audience members could see and hear from wherever they were seated, and
singers, if at first inclined to bawl, soon discovered that the acoustic rendered
them audible in the furthest reaches of the house. Furthermore, the theatre
was designed to incorporate all the latest facilities the older Auditorium

conspicuously lacked, including substantial wing and overhead space to accommodate elaborate stagings. Insull, no less than his predecessors, hoped that commercial earnings would help finance the opera. Aware that inadequate revenue had been produced by Crosby's shops or the Auditorium's hotel, he encased his theatre in a forty-two-storey office block. The Civic Opera House opened, with *Aida*, on 4 November 1929. A few days earlier, the New York stock market had crashed.

Insull's dream, that rentals from the copious office space embracing his Civic Opera House would help finance the opera, was transformed into a nightmare by the Depression. Opera in Chicago lurched from 'mediocrity to disaster' according to its historian, Robert T. Marsh. Unlike the New York Met, which attempted to help amortize costs by giving many repeat performances of each production, Chicago, fearful that audiences were dropping off, reduced its number of performances thus increasing the cost of each. In the 1930/31 season, the Met put on 225 performances of 45 works while Chicago mounted a mere 90 (of 33 productions), dropping to 83 (of 27 productions) the following year, nothing in 1932/3 and, for the rest of the decade, limped along with at most 30- or 40-odd performances per season.

The advent of war helped boost the city's economy; but opera in Chicago, lacking its own stable of singers and long dependent upon the importation of top artists from elsewhere, continued to decline. The best nights, whether at the Civic or in Ravinia, were those distinguished by the presence of visiting stars from the Met. There would have been no opera in Chicago at all during the 1943/4 season had the Met not filled the gap by adding the city to its tour schedule for the first time since 1910. All this hardly added up to the kind of resident company that McCormick, Campanini, Garden and Insull had once envisaged. Overall, concludes Marsh, the first fifteen seasons in the new Civic Opera House were 'the least distinguished in the history of Chicago opera'.

The operatic desert continued after the war, watered by visits from New York. The Met continued to include Chicago on its tour until 1947 and sporadically thereafter, while the thrusting young New York City Center Opera (later New York City Opera) visited each season from 1948 to 1953. These seasons proved there was an audience for opera in Chicago and that, by now, a well-managed resident company could probably find the requisite financial backing. The inauguration of what became Chicago Lyric Opera in 1954 may have looked to some like yet another fancy reorganization of an enterprise that had failed many times before. But not to the youthful troika who founded it: the conductor Nicola Rescigno, a businessman in insurance and real estate named Lawrence Kelly, and Carol Fox, a determined young woman who loved singing and was determined to run something. Soon after the company was launched, Rescigno and Kelly quit. But Fox went on to run Chicago Lyric Opera for over a quarter

Chicago's Civic Opera House, embedded in a high-rise office block, was Samuel Insull's gift to his adopted city. Some thought it resembled a giant armchair and dubbed it 'Insull's Throne'.

of a century. One of the more successful women to direct an opera company, she was succeeded by another, Ardis Krainik, in 1981. Today, the auditorium of Chicago's Civic Opera House is officially known as the Ardis Krainik Theatre.

✻

In San Francisco, a resident opera company was established in 1923 and its opera house inaugurated nine years later at the height of the Depression. Here, the most important name was not that of a millionaire entrepreneur but of an Italian musician: Gaetano Merola. Merola was born in Naples in

1881, the son of a violinist. Educated at the Naples conservatoire, Merola migrated to New York at the end of the century and worked at the Met and for Hammerstein before moving West in 1921. He took a job as a voice teacher and became something of a 'catch' with San Francisco's cultural elite as well as among the city's North Beach Italian community. One day, Merola attended a Stanford University football match down the peninsula in Palo Alto. It is not recorded whether or not he enjoyed the game. What we do know is that he was very impressed by the acoustics of the immense bowl which enabled him to hear every note from the marching band. In summer 1922, Merola took over the stadium for the presentation of grand opera. And he meant grand. Merola borrowed whatever he could from his Italian friends and from local banks, arranged for a stage to be built at one end of the field, formed an orchestra and choir and engaged Giovanni Martinelli, one of the world's top tenors, to star in performances of *Pagliacci*, *Faust* and *Carmen* which Merola himself conducted. 'One was delighted,' wrote the society editor of the *San Francisco Chronicle*, 'to observe how all classes, including the Italian fruit vender [sic] or one's favourite cafeteria cashier, to the leaders of the smart world, were all to be seen at the opera.'

The week-long experiment was a great success in every way except (inevitably, perhaps) economically. It took more than a financial deficit to discourage Merola. He bearded every Bay Area business he could, spoke at fund-raising lunches and dinners and persuaded the city of San Francisco to let him repeat his operatic experiment in autumn 1923, this time in the covered environment of the Civic Auditorium. As Merola and his colleagues began to scent the real possibility of creating long-term resident opera in San Francisco, they came up with what at the time was a novel method of raising funds. In addition to their appeals to the local mogulry, they also invited ordinary citizens, in return for a relatively small sum ($50), to become founder members of the company. The scheme not only brought much-needed cash to the coffers of the infant company; it was also much touted and praised by the Bay Area press as a splendid example of Californian democracy at work. Above all, they praised their volcanic Neapolitan, who bubbled over with all-consuming enthusiasm but was also blessed with the practical abilities of a skilled administrator. If costumes were lacking in the early years, singers were invited to bring their own, while period-style props and furnishings would be begged and borrowed from some of the society hostesses Merola was careful to cultivate.

The Civic Auditorium – a big, unwieldy space with a poor acoustic – was never intended to be more than a temporary home for what Merola was determined to mould into a permanent company. It was better, he said, to have an opera company without an opera house than the other way round. But he wanted both. By 1928, work began on an adjacent pair of civic buildings, across from San Francisco's City Hall (and designed by the same architect),

Most American opera houses have been erected by private finance. In San Francisco, the War Memorial Opera House was built at the behest of the city fathers and opened in 1932, at the height of the Depression.

as a memorial to American Veterans who had died in the Great War. One of the buildings would contain a concert hall, the other an opera house, the first in America to be municipally owned. Despite the onset of Depression, the War Memorial complex went ahead; indeed, the city fathers took some comfort in noting that building costs proved lower than originally anticipated. On 15 October 1932, San Francisco's War Memorial Opera House opened, with Merola conducting a gala performance of *Tosca*. Here, thirteen years later, the Charter of the United Nations was signed.

Until his death in 1953, Merola devoted himself to what he regarded as his life's work. Recalling his own young days (and perhaps with a weather eye on his company's precarious finances), Merola frequently placed relatively untried singers in his casts, giving them the incomparable opportunity of performing over the years alongside such operatic giants as Martinelli, Gigli, Pinza and De Luca. And he took his troupe up and down the coast, from Seattle and Portland in the north to San Diego and – most frequently – Los Angeles in the south.

*

The company that gave *La Bohème* in Los Angeles in 1897 was not a totally isolated visitor to Southern California. A decade earlier, Patti had sung at

'Opera wars', November 1908. The rivalry between the Metropolitan and the Manhattan Opera companies was widely reported. Here, the Met's Gatti-Casazza and Manhattan's Hammerstein grab every singer they can get their hands on.

The *Théâtrophone* was directly linked to the stage of the theatre or opera house (just the thing for someone like Proust, who loved music but hated going out unless he had to).

Opera on the airwaves: Met stars in costume (including Rosa Ponselle, centre) listening to their colleagues during a live broadcast.

The Gramophone Company marketed itself as eclipsing the more limited pleasures of the concert hall or opera house. With the invention of recording, it proclaimed, you could 'choose your own programme, hear the world's most famous artists and play as many encores as you please'.

Anton Rubinstein's 1871 opera *The Demon* was revived in Moscow soon after the 1917 Revolution. This design for the Demon's costume was created for the Opera of Workers' Deputies in Moscow in 1919 by Aristarkh Lentulov, the avant-garde Russian artist whose work influenced Malevich and Kandinsky.

Operatic life is easily parodied, but rarely with as much gusto as in the 1935 Marx Brothers classic, *A Night at the Opera*. Here, in a bravura scene of choreographic chaos, Groucho manages to enjoy himself as everyone pours into his tiny stateroom – and brother Harpo relaxes above the fray.

During the years of occupation, Paris had visits from a string of top German opera companies, including one in 1941 from the Berlin Staatsoper, led by Karajan, which Winifred Wagner was invited to accompany.

La Scala, Milan, was bomb-damaged during the war. The theatre reopened on 11 May 1946 with a gala concert conducted by the seventy-nine-year-old Toscanini. The emotion of the occasion was intensified by the fact that it marked the maestro's first appearance in Italy since he had fled from Fascism.

The great days of opera recording. *Top*: the American soprano Leontyne Price, *c.* 1960, during a recording with the Boston Symphony Orchestra. The conductor is Erich Leinsdorf. *Bottom*: recording Benjamin Britten's *The Burning Fiery Furnace* (1967). In the control booth are Britten (centre) with Peter Pears (nearest camera) and producer John Culshaw. Culshaw also produced the Decca *Ring* cycle conducted by Georg Solti.

By the twenty-first century, opera audiences could enjoy the formal elegance of Glyndebourne or join the crowds in New York's Times Square and watch big-screen relays 'live' from the Met.

Das Rheingold, Thai-style. Wagner's *Ring* was developed for Bangkok Opera by its founder-director, Somtow Sucharitkul.

The Bregenz Festival features a huge open-air stadium from which thousands of spectators can watch massively amplified, spectacularly designed opera performances produced on a stage that floats like a giant liner on the edge of the lake. This is the design for David Pountney's 1999 production of Verdi's *A Masked Ball*.

Mott's Hall on Main Street, the same year that Mrs Thurber's National Grand Opera Company of New Jersey had appeared at the new Hazard's Pavilion. When the Metropolitan Opera first visited Los Angeles in 1900, Melba sang *Bohème* (and the Mad Scene from *Lucia*) on opening night, and the *Los Angeles Times* reported that large numbers converged from all over the region upon Hazard's (at Olive and Fifth Street, later the location of LA's Philharmonic Auditorium). A contingent from Pasadena, said the *Times*, 'swept up before the very door in a special trolley car all blazing with lights and gorgeousness', while fifty people came from as far away as San Diego. The annual visits from the Met ended abruptly after the company was caught, and many of its instruments, sets and costumes destroyed, by the San Francisco earthquake and fire of 1906. But by 1910, when Los Angeles had a population of over 300,000, the Census reported that it contained a higher proportion of working musicians than any other town with a population of 10,000 or more. Los Angeles continued to attract a steady stream of musicians and 1919 saw the creation of a new orchestra. For years, the LA Philharmonic struggled from crisis to crisis, playing in a variety of halls around Los Angeles and Orange County in an effort to build up funds and audiences. The orchestra survived, its most highly publicized and attended concerts being those in the Hollywood Bowl, a glorious natural setting capable of accommodating audiences of 20,000 or more. Sometimes, the Bowl played host to operatic performances: there was a spectacular *Carmen* in 1936 and a *Walküre* in 1938 in which, according to one account:

> the classic 'Ride of the Valkyries' was breathtaking, as live snow-white horses, twice the usual number in most productions of the opera, with twice the usual number of Valkyries astride them, galloped down a distant hill on to the Bowl stage… [and] thunder and lightning and smoke boomed and crackled and billowed from the mountain-top set, accompanied by the delighted and excited shrieks of the audience.

There was indoor opera in Los Angeles, too. In the 1920s, a kind of 'San Francisco South' was set up in LA, under Merola's leadership, but it was killed off by the Depression, as was a plan to build a Grand Opera House (on Olive Hill). From 1937 until 1965, the San Francisco company itself came to Los Angeles, where it played a regular season at the Shrine Auditorium, a 6000-seater better suited to basketball, while in 1948 the Met included Los Angeles in its tour once again.

By now, many felt the city was ripe to form its own resident opera company. A magnet for outstanding artistic talent, Los Angeles attracted many of Europe's most gifted musical migrants. Klemperer had conducted the LA Philharmonic in the 1930s, and, after the war, Schoenberg and Stravinsky both lived in Los Angeles. So did the composers Korngold, Eisler, Gershwin,

Krenek and Foss. Performers such as Heifetz, Szigeti, Piatigorsky, Horowitz and Iturbi made their homes in Los Angeles, while conductors including Walter, Stokowski and Ormandy were frequent guests. André Previn learned his craft in Los Angeles, as did Leonard Slatkin, and the movie industry continued to draw wave upon wave of singers, dancers, instrumentalists, musical arrangers, actors, directors, stage designers, prop and costume makers. By the 1950s, Southern California was teeming with musicians and music lovers and was the home of a first-rate orchestra and the Roger Wagner Chorale, while its universities offered some of the finest musical education in the country.

There was even a Los Angeles opera company, a tiny, somewhat frail infant founded in 1952 by an Italian musician named Francesco Pace. Each year, Pace assembled an ad hoc company and produced a two-week season which reached respectable artistic heights and attracted enthusiastic audiences. Yet Pace's company struggled to remain solvent. Many found this puzzling, among them Bernard Greenberg, a young Los Angeles lawyer, who in a 1959 report aimed at Pace's potential donors noted that Los Angeles was 'the largest metropolitan area in the world without a resident opera company'. It had a population 'on wheels with more leisure time, higher income and better climate' than anywhere comparable. When companies such as the Bolshoi Ballet or the San Francisco Opera visited Los Angeles, wrote Greenberg, they could always be sure of large audiences. Looking at the wider picture, he noted that 'more and more opera [was] being performed throughout the United States', while 'American artists now star in many of the European opera companies instead of the reverse'. Greenberg's hope was that Los Angeles might eventually have a permanent, resident company with its own opera theatre. As we shall see, this double dream was eventually to become a reality twenty-five years later.

CHAPTER 15

Spreading the Message

In his biography of his father, Enrico Caruso Jnr quotes a 1913 exchange between the tenor and a friend who had asked him how much he earned from his recordings:

> 'Guess,' replied Papa.
> '$10,000,' the friend said tentatively.
> 'Right,' he answered. 'Only I make that monthly, you know.'

It would not be true to say that Caruso 'made' the phonograph or that early recordings brought opera to a truly 'mass' audience. But recording was one of a number of new technologies, all pioneered around the turn of the century, which helped to spread the word (or sound) more widely than ever before.

By the early 1900s, many wealthier people were becoming familiar with the camera and telephone and were able to receive the latest mass-produced daily newspapers. There were picture palaces, too, where audiences could relish the latest moving pictures, while just as exciting was that much-discussed product of Mr Henry Ford's inventiveness and entrepreneurship, the automobile. Within a few years, people were beginning to listen to gramophone recordings, and were reading with near incredulity about the Wright brothers' experiments with manned flight. They might have read about another scientist, too, the Italian émigré physicist Guglielmo Marconi, who arrived in London in 1896 with a bundle of devices promising the prospect of the 'wireless' communication of sound. Everywhere, it seemed, the technologies of communication – of words, ideas, images and sounds – and of the transportation of the people who produced and consumed them, were becoming transformed. As one century ended and a new one began, there was much talk of a new age dawning, 'art nouveau', of the 'New Woman', of 'novelties'. Almost as if to stamp the transition of the old era to the new, Queen Victoria, the great embodiment of a passing age, died in January 1901, followed a few days later by that other great octogenarian symbol of *his* nation, Giuseppe Verdi, who died in a Milan hotel room just up the road

A growing public soon began to purchase the records of opera stars such as Caruso and the bulky machines on which to play them. Here, Caruso listens to his own recorded voice on a Victor machine. At one stage, the tenor was said to have earned $10,000 a month from his recordings.

from La Scala. The following year, in another room in that same hotel, the young Enrico Caruso was prevailed upon by Fred Gaisberg of the Gramophone and Typewriter Company of London to make his first recordings.

The telephone, photography, film, the piano roll and pianola, the automobile, manned flight, recording and radio all came on stream within a couple of decades or so of each other; cumulatively, they were to transform communications in the twentieth century (rather as the digital revolution has done in our own day). Like everything else, the world of opera found itself transformed by the emergence of these new technologies. In some ways, they fed back directly into the creative process itself. Alfred Roller's innovative lighting effects during the Mahler regime in Vienna would not have been possible without the prior inventions of Edison. Puccini, always intrigued by the latest gadgets, was an early convert to recording; when working on *Madama Butterfly* in 1903, he incorporated authentic Japanese tunes he heard on phonograph records. Thirty years later, Alban Berg composed a carefully palindromic orchestral interlude, to be accompanied by a silent film sequence, as the centrepiece of his opera *Lulu* to mark the turning point in Lulu's life and career. But for all the application of new technologies to the art form itself, their greatest impact on the development of opera was upon its popular dissemination.

*

Edison pioneered not only the light bulb but also the recording cylinder. This, while impressive as a first step, gave only a faintly comprehensible reproduction of the sound it was recording and was expensive to maintain. Soon, the German-born, American-based Emil Berliner developed the far more reliable flat disc and it was this that was to prove the practical foundation of the recording industry. Not only did disc technology enable sound to be recorded and reproduced more accurately; discs could also be multi-copied far less expensively and this, in turn, opened up a large potential market thereby making it feasible to offer major artists big fees.

At first, most recordings tended to offer middle-of-the-road popular artists and repertoire: when an opera singer was on the label, it was usually to perform only the best-known arias plus such lighter, popular numbers as 'Comin' through the Rye', 'The Last Rose of Summer' or 'Home Sweet Home'. As the disc gradually took precedence over the cylinder, the nascent recording industry became more adventurous and more international. Gaisberg, who had learned his craft in his native America, crossed the Atlantic and, with London henceforth as his base, criss-crossed Europe (and later South East Asia) in search of talent, recording as he went. He even went to Russia, hoping to record the voice of the Tsar.

As yet, virtually no recordings were made of the symphonic or 'classical' instrumental repertoire. This was partly because of the assumption that such serious stuff would not appeal to the potential market for recordings, inevitably still very small. It was also a result of the available technology. One side of a ten-inch disc, played at 78rpm, lasted scarcely more than around three minutes, hardly enough to do justice to a Beethoven symphony or sonata; even short songs and arias were often abbreviated and rearranged – and performed fast! – to fit on to disc. Furthermore, sounds produced close to the horn would record well, those more distant poorly, and no symphony orchestra with its wide range of frequencies could be easily accommodated by such a system. The human voice has a more restricted range of frequencies, and a solo singer could be moved closer into the horn when performing quieter sections and pulled away for fortissimo passages. It was not edifying. Gaisberg recalled a complaint from the Wagnerian soprano Frieda Hempel, who doubtless turned up to recording sessions in full prima donna regalia, flowery hat and all, and who disliked the way she was moved bodily forwards or backwards ('all without gentleness') while singing. However, for performers prepared to play by the rules, this early technology favoured the solo singer. The majority of early records of 'classical' music were therefore of opera singers. Contracts included large advances and enticing royalty agreements. These singers may not have recorded complete operas (that would come later). But they were increasingly prepared to submit to disc many of the more important highlights from the operatic repertoire. These were the superstars of their day, the names the recording companies were keen to market.

Thomas Alva Edison, who developed the recording cylinder, was probably America's most versatile inventor. In this photograph, he is shown listening to an early recording.

At first, most of the important 'classical' recordings were made in European cities such as London, Paris and Milan. In the USA, the infant industry still tended to concentrate on 'lighter' artists and repertoire (the 1902–3 Columbia recordings of Met singers did not sell well). However, the success of Gaisberg and his Gramophone Company colleagues was keenly observed from across the Atlantic. Perhaps operatic recordings would sell in America if more aggressively marketed; here, after all, lay the greatest pool of potential customers. The Victor Company took the initiative, set up a factory in Camden, New Jersey, and went on to sign many of the great European operatic stars, among them Caruso, Melba, Plançon, Calvé and Destinn.

In order to hear the voices of these famous figures, a growing public was beginning to purchase not only the records but the machines on which to play them. The bulky 'gramophone' or 'phonograph', complete with revolving turntable and acoustic horn, had somehow to fit elegantly into the middle-class Edwardian-era drawing room, so the Victor Company encased everything in a four-foot mahogany cabinet which it called the 'Victrola'. Records and reproducing equipment did not come cheap. When a dollar bill could buy a multi-course restaurant meal, a star-studded record of the Sextet from Donizetti's *Lucia di Lammermoor* could set you back by $7, while the Victrola was marketed at a cool $200. Yet demand for records and record-playing machines consistently outstripped supply. It was like the rush to television sets in the 1950s, colour TV in the 1970s or the conversion from LPs to CDs a decade later. The Victor Company's investment was well placed; their assets of $2.7m in 1902 had risen to $33.2m by 1917. No wonder they could afford to pay their recording stars astronomical fees.

Gaisberg liked to emphasize what he believed to be the educational value of recording. Nor was he alone. When in 1903 the Columbia Phonograph Company issued its Grand Opera Series ('The First Recordings of Opera in America'), the accompanying brochure concluded:

> These Grand Opera Records will be of special educational value to the student. Those who are striving to work out theories of the production of tone, or are endeavoring to acquire a particular style, know that one of the greatest incentives to success is some concrete examples of what they are striving for, some embodiment of the result which they hope to attain.

It is not the instruction of the teacher which spurs the student to his greatest effort, said the good people at Columbia. Rather:

> it is the voice of the artist who has attained the goal; and that voice must be studied, and studied with care. With these Grand Opera Records the student will have an opportunity to observe minute details of phrasing and enunciation which have hitherto been far beyond his grasp.

Furthermore, recordings would provide an important repository of historic documentation for all future generations to enjoy. You are recording for posterity, Gaisberg would say, as he tried to induce his artists to make a supreme effort in front of the recording horn. Some were inhibited by this, over-anxious perhaps to put down the 'perfect' recording, while others simply let their natural performing instincts take over. Either way, it was perhaps inevitable that many early recordings contained musical errors that at a later period would easily have been rectified by retakes and editing. What we in our hi-tech era might regard as mild imperfections can nevertheless provide a wonderful historical insight into the musical and vocal styles of a generation long since past.

But the greatest impact of recording (contrary to the initial fears of some) was to increase the public appetite for the real thing. And the fact that opera singers were – partly for technical reasons – among the first major recording artists gave their particular art form considerable popular *réclame*. Once people had enjoyed the disembodied voices of Caruso, Melba and the rest in their living rooms, the urge grew to see them in the flesh. Later, the broadcasting of opera was to have a similar effect.

✳

The first full-length, live opera broadcast from the stage of the Metropolitan Opera, New York, was *Hänsel und Gretel* on Christmas Day, 1931. But it was not the first opera to be broadcast; that took place over a decade before. Or even earlier, depending, of course, on what you mean by 'broadcast'. There was, for example, the *théâtrophone* (and its less successful British counterpart the electrophone), a licensed telephone line that could be linked directly to the stage of a theatre. A large box with attached earphones, the *théâtrophone* produced a sound quality that was pretty rudimentary. Proust, who loved music but hated going out unless he had to, admitted that 'on entend très mal' but nevertheless became a subscriber and enthusiastic advocate: the *théâtrophone* enabled you to stay home and revel in your own personal reactions to glorious music played privately, as it were, to you. On 21 February 1911, we find Proust writing to Reynaldo Hahn to say he has listened to the first act of *Maîtres Chanteurs* and, tonight, will hear the whole of *Pelléas*. A newspaper ad at the time announced that, for 60 francs a month, you could have '*Le Théâtre chez soi*' and listed the various theatres in Paris (including the Opéra, Opéra-Comique, Variétés and Comédie-Française) whose offerings you could hear in the comfort of your own home. In 1913, the Théâtrophone company transmitted the Opéra's *Faust* direct to Electrophone subscribers across the Channel while the British company reciprocated with *Tosca* excerpts from Covent Garden.

Telephonic transmissions such as these reached small audiences and were doomed by the advent of wireless broadcasting. The first experiments in opera broadcasting date back to the same period. In America in 1910, the inventor Lee De Forest persuaded Gatti-Casazza to let him place a couple of microphones and a transmitter in New York's Metropolitan Opera, from which, on two successive nights, an erratic signal sent a virtually unrecognizable simulacrum of some of the world's greatest voices to a handful of radio hams in selected spots in Manhattan and nearby New Jersey. Gatti, apparently, tuned in via his office telephone but remained sceptical. After the First World War, the subject was taken up again with rather more seriousness. In England in June 1920, Melba visited the Marconi plant in Chelmsford, Essex, and sang a few items that could be heard not only in London some forty miles away but on the Continent; Tetrazzini did much the same a few months later from her hotel suite in New York, aiming at 'ships within a radius of 400 miles'. In January 1923, the recently founded British Broadcasting Company relayed a performance of *Hänsel und Gretel* by the short-lived British National Opera Company from the stage of the Royal Opera House, Covent Garden, on station 2LO, followed a couple of weeks later by a *Bohème* with Melba.

Before long, broadcasts of complete operas or (more commonly) opera highlight concerts were being relayed across America, some of them introduced by a 25-year-old part-time singer named Milton Cross, later to become

One of the pleasures of hotel life in Edwardian London: listening to direct relays of opera on the Electrophone.

famous as presenter of the Met broadcasts. The number of people with radios was rising rapidly at this time: just over half a million radio sets were sold in America in 1923, a figure that had quadrupled two years later. By 1928, 12 million sets were broadcasting to some 40 million listeners. In spring 1925, at the height of what history likes to dub the 'Jazz Age', the newly created NBC National Grand Opera Company inaugurated a regular weekly broadcast of abridged versions of operas under the conductor and arranger Cesare Sodero. An Italian immigrant (like many in his casts), Sodero had arrived in America around the turn of the century and had been music director at the Edison Phonograph Company before his radio appointment. Sodero was the consummate professional, editing a huge range of operas down to fit a late-night (usually sixty-minute) slot, somehow managing to include all the famous arias and link them seamlessly to music that in the original score might occur ten or twenty minutes later. Everything got the Sodero treatment, from Wagner to Victor Herbert, and the series ran for five years. Artists accustomed to singing uncut versions often found these abridgements difficult. But the challenge was exhilarating. Frances Alda (the former wife of Gatti-Casazza) worried what it would be like performing to an apparently non-existent, silent audience. She soon discovered that listener response came not with applause but by mail. Mountains of it, much of it hugely appreciative from people who had never heard opera before.

The New York Met, therefore, was something of a Johnny-come-lately to the broadcasting of opera. By 1931, when it finally went on the air, America was in the depths of economic depression. Following the stock market crash of 1929, box office revenue had dropped drastically, especially in the more expensive parts of the house. Gatti reports that, over the next three years the Met lost over 30 per cent of its subscribers. He felt like 'the captain of a ship caught in a storm' and knew that emergency steps would have to be taken if the Met was not to founder.

The impetus to broadcast came not from the Met but from the president of NBC, Merlyn H. Aylsworth. Aylsworth approached Gatti a number of times, but Gatti always said no: the opportunity for revenue was attractive, but he did not think that radio would do justice to his singers or his orchestra. Perhaps Gatti had in mind De Forest's experiments back in 1910, or more likely the sound quality relayed to his office during rehearsals. But Aylsworth was persistent. Finally Gatti agreed, his acquiescence doubtless reinforced by a successful demonstration broadcast of *Madama Butterfly* from the Met stage on 23 December 1931 to which he listened in his office. Two days later, the Met's broadcasts went 'live' with *Hänsel und Gretel*.

Nobody knows exactly how many people heard that first Met broadcast on Christmas Day, 1931, but its impact was soon evident. The NBC (opined the *Brooklyn Eagle*) 'is making an excellent effort to bring to American radiolators [*sic!*] the finest there is in music'. Meanwhile, the soprano Lucrezia Bori looked ahead to the day when television, too, would provide 'a new and great stimulus to all things operatic' and broaden the present audience for opera into one 'literally all-inclusive'. The excitement soon spread. A week later, on New Year's Day 1932, Gigli and Bori were singing a matinee performance of *La Bohème*. During the afternoon, a woman rushed up to the Met box office asking if there was a ticket for sale. She was told there was – but didn't she know that the performance was half over? Yes, she said breathlessly: 'I've been listening to the first two acts on the radio, and it's so wonderful I want to see the rest!'

If you had asked American opera lovers in the 1930s 'what first drew you to opera?' chances are most would have talked of listening to their parents' collection of phonograph records. A generation later, and you would likely be regaled with memories of listening to the Met Saturday matinee broadcasts (which continue to this day). Financially, the broadcasts proved a godsend; in the first three months of 1932, they earned the Met a desperately needed $150,000. But the Met's problems were far from over. Gatti had written to everyone on the roster asking them to agree to a 10 per cent reduction in their salaries. This would mean tearing up existing contracts, he acknowledged. But 'when a house is on fire one does not send for lawyers or notaries'. All agreed to the pay cut with the single exception of Gigli, who by then had been with the Met for a dozen years. In April 1932, a further voluntary cut was proposed as it was revealed that the company's capital of $550,000 and most of its reserve had been wiped out; the Met, it seemed, was having to operate at a deficit of from $25,000 to $45,000 a week and was in serious danger of having to close down. Again, Gigli said no. A round robin letter was sent to Gatti complaining of Gigli's behaviour, its signatories including many of the most famous names in opera at the time; shortly afterwards, the great Italian tenor was dismissed.*

The broadcasts were one of a number of ways the Met tried to widen its support base during the difficult years of the Depression. As its fiftieth anniversary approached, a 'Committee for Saving the Metropolitan Opera' was formed with Bori as chairman. There were appeals on the radio, appeals in the press, letters from Bori to the great, the good and the wealthy, and a variety of ingenious events organized, including an opera house ball with all the stars doing their bit (and an on-stage surprise event at which the Wagnerian *Heldentenor* Lauritz Melchior did a circus strong-man act with the diminutive coloratura Lily Pons). In addition, the Metropolitan Opera 'Guild' was set up by Eleanor Belmont (daughter-in-law of August Belmont, who had presided over the New York Academy of Music half a century before, and the first woman to sit on the Met Opera Board). Her mission, said Mrs Belmont, was to enable ordinary New Yorkers to feel that the Met was theirs, 'an integral part of the life of the city': in short, she aimed at the 'democratization of opera'. The Guild, which she chaired, was a 'Friends' organization that brought the Met much-needed cash and popular support. Hitherto, the Met had tended to underwrite its deficits through a handful of large donations from its wealthiest patrons; the Guild enabled it to raise substantial sums through a multiplicity of smaller gifts, at the time a relatively novel approach (not unlike that pioneered by Merola in San Francisco) and widely copied since.

Meanwhile, the Met continued its tradition of taking the opera on an extensive tour each spring, a practice that went back to the earliest days of the Met and was to survive for a century. Back in 1909/10, as Hammerstein's rival company spread its tentacles up and down the eastern seaboard and beyond, the Met had hired a double orchestra and a double chorus and over a hundred soloists and dispatched its variegated troops across the entire eastern half of the country where they gave an aggregate of 163 performances – immediately followed by a high-profile visit under Toscanini to Paris. After the First World War, the company's touring activities were reined in by Gatti for a decade or so, largely limited to regular mid-season engagements in nearby Brooklyn and Philadelphia and, each spring, the ever-faithful Atlanta. But during the Depression the spring tour was expanded again as a valued way of recruiting audiences (not to say Guild members). To this day, many veteran American opera lovers

* Gigli immediately regretted his stance, offering various compromises and issuing a statement saying he would have accepted the same pay cut as everyone else if that had not meant annulling his entire contract. In his *Memoirs*, Gigli acknowledged that he had acted unwisely and tactlessly, 'in a fit of pique', but that at the time he had resented being ordered by 'the almighty Gatti-Casazza' to break his contract 'voluntarily'.

still recall with misty eyes the day back in the 1930s when their parents took them to *Lakmé* or *Lucia* in Philadelphia or Atlanta, or perhaps to an *Aida* in New Orleans with Martinelli or a *Walküre* in Cleveland starring Flagstad and Melchior...

*

For others, the Damascene moment might have been a visit to the cinema. Perhaps it was a movie starring Grace Moore or a Met star like Laurence Tibbett or Risë Stevens – or (most likely of all) Mario Lanza in *The Great Caruso*. The industry dated back to the last years of the nineteenth century when moving pictures were first projected to an incredulous and enchanted public, often in otherwise little-used opera houses. By the 1920s and 1930s, the movies had become the most widespread form of popular entertainment in America; it has been estimated that by 1938 some 80 million Americans (or 60 per cent of the population) were going to the movies each week. A trip to the cinema was certainly a lot cheaper than going to the opera; during the 1925/6 season at the New York Met, the cheapest seat cost $1.50 while a cinema ticket could be obtained for between 10 and 25 cents. Moreover, it is striking to note that the last operas to stake a permanent claim to the popular repertoire were produced shortly before the appearance of the first talking pictures: *Turandot*, one might argue, was thus the end of an era, *The Jazz Singer* the start of a new one. Was film the 'new' opera and the cinema the 'new' opera house? Or, on the contrary, did the rising popularity of film help boost opera by sweeping it along in its generous coat-tails? The relationship between the two art forms and their respective audiences was in fact to prove richly textured.

By 1900, some of the world's leading opera houses were run much like the Hollywood studios of two or three decades later with their big shows, publicity machines and catalogues of contracted artists. Mahler, as we have seen, treated a Vienna Opera singer who wished to appear elsewhere rather as one of the big movie moguls thirty years later would treat a movie star who asked to be released to make a film with another studio.

Some of the big music publishers, too, came to acquire something of the mien of a Hollywood studio. Ricordi bought up the catalogues of a number of its most important rivals and opened up offices abroad. By now, they were no longer simply publishing and selling or renting out copies of musical scores but were also concerned to keep some control over the way their works were staged. There were singers and conductors of whom Casa Ricordi approved and disapproved. They also began issuing 'production books' that spelled out exactly how the sets for a particular opera they published should be designed, how the performers should be dressed, where they should move and how they should be lit.* Gone now were the all-purpose painted flats, the standard 'garden' scene, 'seashore', 'romantic castle' and the rest, nor could the modern prima donna simply open her trunk and pull out her Lucia, Gilda or Violetta outfit. Scenery and costumes had to be specific to their particular operas, and increasingly the publisher itself would commission and provide these. Ricordi also published a magazine which often included high-quality polychrome artwork, produced by its in-house graphics department, proclaiming the latest Ricordi publications. All this helped give the company – like MGM or United Artists – a recognizable style, a brand.

There were artistic parallels, too, between opera and film. Each attempted to create a form of mass entertainment by bringing together a number of different art forms, with the same emphasis on larger-than-life emotions and, perhaps, larger-than-life acting styles. In film, as in opera – and unlike the straight, spoken theatre – it was possible to create large crowd scenes, and ensembles in which several characters expressed conflicting emotions at the same time. You did not get that in Ibsen or Shaw. But you did in a D. W. Griffith movie, just as you did in the quartet from *Rigoletto* or the café scene in *La Bohème*. There were transition scenes in opera, too; many were to find in Wagner's great orchestral set-pieces, such as Siegfried's journey down the Rhine, anticipations of filmic techniques, while those who later resisted Puccini's emotional intensity and derided it as 'film music' often forgot that it was the movie industry that learned from him, not vice versa.

From the earliest years of film, many singers, including famous operatic performers such as Caruso and Farrar, starred in silent movies. Surprising to us, perhaps, but perfectly understandable at a time when film showings were often accompanied not just by a piano but in larger cinemas by a full orchestra. So when Farrar, already a heartthrob in New York (and not just to Toscanini), made a film of *Carmen* in 1915, directed by Cecil B. DeMille, she had a reasonable hope of becoming a nationwide, and possibly an international, celebrity. Her producer, Sam Goldfish (who later changed his name to Goldwyn) felt the same way. 'I believe Miss Farrar will supersede any human being ever seen on the screen,' he was reported as saying, adding that 'she will elevate the moving picture drama to heights never dreamed of.' *Carmen* may not quite have done that. But with its realistic bullfight scene (including supposedly 20,000 extras), its glamorous star and a fifty-piece symphony orchestra playing the music on its much-publicized opening night, the film proved a big hit. It was one of the earliest of (to date) over seventy film, TV or video adaptations of what remains one of the most popular tales in the entire operatic repertoire.

The advent of the talkies should, on the face of it, have been a gift to those who wanted to make films of opera. A few operas were filmed, usually

---

* The idea for these *disposizioni sceniche* seems to have originated with Verdi, based on his experience at the Paris Opéra. Giulio Ricordi himself took a deep personal interest in these and, in collaboration with Verdi, compiled production books in the 1880s for the revised version of *Simon Boccanegra* and for *Otello*.

Opera on (silent) film: Geraldine Farrar on set in *Carmen*, Cecil B. DeMille's 1915 movie.

severely pruned and edited; opera, after all, tends to be a far more static medium than anything a cinema audience would tolerate. Tito Gobbi made a handful of opera films from the late 1940s, as did Plácido Domingo nearly forty years later.

More common, however, and far more popular were feature films such as *Naughty Marietta* or *Rose Marie* that included music and starred attractive actors (Nelson Eddy and Jeanette MacDonald) with operatic-style voices. Sometimes, an aria or two might be introduced into a film to give it a bit of class, or to help 'place' one of the characters. Deanna Durbin sang arias in many of her films, while in *One Night of Love* Grace Moore played the part of a young singer who sets out to achieve her life's ambition, performing a number of arias on the way. Moore herself alternated uneasily between the operatic and film worlds, embellishing both with her beauty but never perhaps completely at home in either. MacDonald sang the 'Liebestod' from *Tristan* in her early movie *Oh for a Man*, and a few years later arias from *Faust* and *Traviata* in a film whose theme song became even more famous: *San Francisco*. The 1943 version of *Phantom of the Opera* opens with Eddy in superb voice singing the drinking song from *Martha*. If Eddy and MacDonald (like Howard Keel later) were actors with good voices, there were also successful films featuring that even rarer breed, top opera singers who looked good and could act: the Met's star baritone, Lawrence Tibbett, received an Academy nomination as Best Actor for his dashing presence in *The Rogue Song*, while Risë Stevens, the Met's captivating Carmen, starred opposite Eddy in *The Chocolate Soldier*. It was not an easy feat to carry off; some great singers (including Caruso and Gigli, like Pavarotti many years later) made feature films that were intended to cash in on their star's fame but most failed dismally. A maladroit screen actor, however celebrated elsewhere, would simply not draw the movie-going public.

The most famous opera movie of the period was one that satirized it. In *A Night at the Opera*, Groucho Marx plays Otis Driftwood, a seedy entrepreneur who tries to inveigle a wealthy widow into handing over a sizeable chunk of her fortune to the cash-strapped New York Opera Company. That way, says Driftwood, she will be welcomed into New York society. In Milan, he introduces her to the solemn, bearded boss of the opera company (a dead ringer for Gatti-Casazza) who is thrilled to know he will now be able to hire a great Italian tenor he has had his eye on. Meanwhile, the singer himself is seen throwing dressing-room tantrums because his girl is friendly with another less starry tenor. Driftwood negotiates a contract with the tenor's representative, Fiorello, paring it down line by line, the entire scene a superb parody of a process familiar to every artist, agent and manager. Later, all the characters cross the Atlantic. Driftwood's tiny stateroom becomes the scene of some of cinema's most famously choreographed chaos while, on deck, great heaving crowds of sunny-tempered (and musical) Italian immigrants consume plateloads of spaghetti. After much mayhem in New York, the denouement features a spectacularly sabotaged performance of *Il trovatore* in which everything that can possibly go wrong at an operatic performance duly does so – all in the interests, of course, of humiliating the arrogant tenor and bringing professional success and true love to his rival. *Trovatore* is an easy target for parody, with its improbable and overblown story, as are the greed and graft of venal agents and the cultural pretentiousness of the wealthy. Some have seen *A Night at the Opera* as a shrewd hatchet job on an expensive, elite, essentially un-American activity. To most, however, it was and remains a brilliant satire of an art form and a profession that are well able to look after themselves, a kind of licensed Carnival in which everything is temporarily permitted to appear topsy-turvy.

*

As new ways of transmitting reproduced images and sounds came on stream in the late nineteenth and early twentieth centuries, opera was undoubtedly a beneficiary. That is to say, more people than ever before could acquire pictures of famous opera singers, hear their voices, see them acting and try playing and singing the music for themselves in their own homes. It may not have been true that 'everyone' in Prague in 1787 was singing and whistling *Figaro*; but by the early 1900s, vast numbers on several continents knew who Caruso and Melba were and what they looked like, while growing numbers were able to hear their voices. Of course, what most people bought, heard and saw were not the real thing but mechanical reproductions. Did the new technologies bring opera to the millions? Or only its simulacrum? Is art still art when mechanically reproduced? 'An imitation of art bears the same relation to art,' thundered a *Times* editorial in 1910, 'as a wax-work to a living man.' Or, in the pithier analogy attributed half a century later to Otto

Klemperer, 'listening to a gramophone record is like going to bed with a picture of Marilyn Monroe!'

Furthermore, the introduction of radio and recording meant that, for most people, the enjoyment of music became essentially passive. The piano, once the sacred centrepiece of the bourgeois home, ceded to the wireless and gramophone while sales of pianos and of sheet music, like the domestic music-making they made possible, went into steep decline. One music publisher ruefully recalled how 'existing transcriptions of classical and romantic music vanished for lack of interest.' Remaining copies were pulped, he said, and existing plates melted down. A 'wide and once highly cultivated and fertile area of musical life has been laid waste', he concluded, noting that most people claiming to enjoy music would henceforth only do so by listening to an interpreter.

Contrary to the direst expectations, however, the invention of mechanical ways of hearing music did not seem to dent people's desire to experience the 'real' thing. A few fastidious souls, in the best Proustian tradition, doubtless preferred listening to reproduced music in the comfort of their own homes rather than hearing it 'live' among all those dirty, coughing people who frequented theatres, opera houses and concert halls. But for the most part, the existence of gramophone recordings, radio relays or opera films seems to have fed but did not sate the curiosity of those who consumed them. The lady who rushed to the Gigli performance at the New York Met having caught the first part on the wireless may have been exceptional. But only in the extent of her zeal.

CHAPTER 16

Repercussions of War

After his return to Italy, Toscanini did what he could for his country, giving concerts for the war effort and in 1917 forming a military band which at one point he conducted in the front line. At the end of each piece, Toscanini is said to have cried out 'Viva l'Italia!' A bass drum was ripped by shrapnel but no-one in the band was hurt and Toscanini was later decorated by the Italian government for bravery under fire. But while he was a passionate Italian nationalist, Toscanini was not particularly expert in the arcanae of international politics. Few artists are. Toscanini's hero, Verdi, might have been aroused by the excitements of the *Risorgimento*; but he was a composer (and farmer), well aware of the vastly superior political sophistication of *his* hero, united Italy's first Prime Minister, Count Cavour. By the twentieth century, as the world became embroiled in a succession of economic downturns, totalitarian ideologies and catastrophic wars, most musicians, like much of the rest of humanity, were swept along paths not of their choosing or understanding.

*

Some of the animosities generated by the Great War can seem peculiarly grotesque when observed through the telescope of history. In Britain, people learned that the Germans raped nuns and cut off the hands of Belgian children, while the royal family thought it prudent to change its name from Saxe-Coburg to Windsor. The Kaiser, cousin of the British king, would be 'squeezed' after the war 'until the pips squeak'. In Germany, a group of prominent intellectuals signed a statement justifying German actions and denouncing the British for allying themselves with the 'barbaric' and 'half-Asiatic' Russians.

In such an atmosphere, the virus of spiralling mutual hatreds was bound to infect the world of opera. Toscanini, while yielding to none in his patriotic support of the Italian war effort, created a furore when including items by Wagner in a concert in Rome. A few days later, a government edict banned all performances of German music in the Italian capital for the duration of the

Toscanini used his skills to maintain troop morale during the First World War, taking a military band to the front line. A proud Italian patriot, he later became a resolute foe of Fascism.

war. Much the same was happening on the other side of the divide, where Bruno Walter, in charge of the court opera in Munich, was constrained to 'curtail' the French and Italian repertoires and was lambasted by the local press for retaining in his orchestra an excellent cellist who happened to be Belgian.

Toscanini's contemporary, friend and sometime sparring partner Puccini, too, became enmeshed in the distorting politics of war. On a visit to Vienna in 1913, Puccini was asked if he might consider writing a waltz-filled operetta. With its German-language text, it would be published in Vienna, where it would receive its premiere, while the composer, who would receive a prodigious fee and royalty agreement, could retain Italian rights. The offer was tempting, but Puccini demurred: operetta with spoken dialogue wasn't quite his line of business, and, in any case, he was committed to the publishing house of Ricordi, by then in the hands of Giulio's son Tito. The following spring, once again in Vienna, Puccini was on the receiving end of what he saw as a series of irritating rebuffs from Tito Ricordi and, perhaps also intoxicated by his celebrity in Vienna, he reconsidered and finally accepted the offer.

Who was really in the driving seat? The easygoing, cigarette puffing Puccini – or the publisher Tito Ricordi?

As Puccini began work, the diplomatic clouds were darkening. When the war that nobody expected broke out in August 1914, the Kingdom of Italy, which was allied to Germany and Austria-Hungary, declared itself neutral (hoping to bargain with the Austrians for border concessions). Many Italians sympathized with the Austro-German cause during the early phases of the war, but Puccini, when asked, simply proclaimed his neutrality, and his friendship for all nations in which his music was performed. In April 1915, Britain and France tempted Italy with offers of greater territorial advantages if it would join the Allied side. Seduced by dreams of reclaiming *Italia irredenta* – territories still 'unredeemed' – Italy duly declared war on Austria-Hungary the following month and, in 1916, on Germany. Vienna had become an enemy capital and Puccini soon found himself widely criticized for trading with the enemy, a hurtful accusation that was particularly acute in the French press, fuelled perhaps by Gallic resentment of his huge popularity among French opera audiences. The eventual result of Puccini's labours was *La rondine*, a through-composed opera (with irresistible waltz tunes), a far more substantial piece than his Viennese backers had expected though in some ways hobbled by its provenance. *La rondine* was published (in Italian) by Ricordi's great rival, Sonzogno, and premiered in Monte Carlo in 1917. It did not reach Vienna until 1920.

*

Everywhere, the insidious effects of war divided former friends and colleagues and skewed artistic judgements. Across the Atlantic, despite growing anti-

German sentiment, America remained neutral until April 1917. At the New York Metropolitan Opera, the general manager, Gatti-Casazza, tried to maintain a sense of artistic integrity and that meant continuing to showcase a number of German works and artists. In his memoirs, Gatti recalls that on 6 April 1917 – Good Friday – the Met scheduled Wagner's Easter opera *Parsifal*, a 'drama of peace and good will among men'. That day, the US Congress voted to enter the war on the side of the Allies. An early casualty was the leading Wagnerian soprano Johanna Gadski. Gadski's husband represented various German munitions firms in the USA; in 1916 he had been accused of conspiracy to blow up the Welland Canal (a charge of which he was acquitted), and their home was said to have been the scene of a celebratory party a year earlier when a U-boat had sunk the *Lusitania*. Once America entered the war, Gadski and her husband returned to Germany.

By autumn 1917, American opinion was turning ever more sharply against everyone and everything German. The Met Board urgently advised Gatti against playing works by German composers, and, at short notice, a revised schedule was put in place, one conspicuously devoid of Wagner. Gatti in consequence had to terminate the contracts of a number of German artists who therefore found themselves stuck in a hostile country with no work. Most were patriotic Germans who, if they had not resented America and its allies before their dismissal, doubtlessly did so thereafter (one sued the Met for breach of contract). Ernestine Schumann-Heink had a son from her first marriage fighting in the German submarine service and two sons and a stepson from her second marriage in the US Navy. Frieda Hempel, an utterly apolitical German prima donna who also excelled in the Met's Italian and French repertoire, found herself accused in some sections of the American press of pro-German sentiments – only to discover, after the war, that the German press had been blackening her name as pro-American.

Similar stories were duplicated elsewhere. Close to a quarter of the musicians in the Boston Symphony Orchestra were German citizens and the orchestra was led by the German conductor Karl Muck. A former music director of the Berlin Opera, Muck was greatly appreciated in Boston by his players and audiences alike. Henry Higginson, the venerable creator and proprietor of the BSO, described him as 'the most industrious, painstaking and the ablest conductor whom we have ever had'. But Muck was also, like many German expatriates, outspokenly proud of his homeland, and wild rumours began to circulate in America about his tangled private life and, absurdly, Muck's supposed espionage on behalf of the Fatherland. Judgements made by Muck on purely artistic grounds – that there should be no ban on German music, or that it was not the job of an orchestral conductor to play the 'Star-Spangled Banner' at serious concerts – came to be regarded as ominously political. Perhaps Muck should have kept his mouth shut and his head beneath the parapet. But that was not his way; Bruno Walter later recalled him as having been 'energetic, firm, and caustically sarcastic'. All this led the BSO to decide that Muck should resign from his post, effective at the end of the 1917/18 season. But before that, in March 1918, at the end of a rehearsal for an Easter performance of Bach's *St Matthew Passion*, US marshals arrested Muck as an enemy alien and he was interned in Fort Oglethorpe in Georgia until the end of the war.* When Bruno Walter met him again in Munich in 1920, he was shocked to discover a 'serious and obviously tired old man of sixty'. Thus did the tensions of war inject their insidious, xenophobic hatreds into what is normally the most international of professions.

Despite such examples of injustice and hardship, it is probably true that, of all the participants in the war, America stood to gain most and lose least, at least musically and operatically. There was not a great deal of opera in Vienna or Berlin in 1918; but in New York it had never stopped. Here, Gatti-Casazza was able to introduce Met audiences to a new generation of young American singers in leading roles, most famously – in the very week following the armistice – the soprano Rosa Ponselle. Ponselle and her sister Carmela, American-born of Italian parents, were young vaudeville singers who had decided to have some operatic training. Their coach knew people at the Met and was friendly with Caruso, who came along one day to hear the girls. As Ponselle recounted the story years later, Caruso reported to Gatti about the sisters, adding that one of them ('he probably said "the fat one" because I was as big as a telephone booth in those days') had just the right voice for Leonora in Verdi's *La forza del destino*, an opera due to receive its first Met production in November. Gatti offered the girls a Met audition at which it was obvious that Rosa, then barely twenty-one, had the makings of an outstanding voice though she was nervous and sang badly. A fortnight later, at a second audition, Gatti recalled that Rosa 'sang perfectly, with a beauty of voice and style that was truly amazing in a young and inexperienced singer'. Ponselle's recollection was that she fainted from nerves. The next thing she knew was that Gatti was offering her *Forza* opposite Caruso. It was an enormous gamble, but one Gatti felt he had to make. The war was coming to an end, many leading singers were stuck in Europe and Gatti needed a Leonora. Caruso was convinced of the girl's talent and it seemed a risk worth running. 'If this American makes good,' Gatti said to Caruso, 'every door will be open to American potentials from that moment on.' And if not, said Gatti, he'd be on the first ship back to Italy.

Ponselle's debut has gone down as the triumphant beginning of one of the great careers in operatic history. It also helped open the profession to US artists, as Gatti had hoped it might. During his tenure, the Met mounted the premieres of some dozen new operas by American composers, among them

---

* Muck wasn't the only one. Altogether, twenty-nine German-born members of the BSO were interned. So were other musicians (such as Ernst Kunwald, conductor of the Cincinatti Symphony).

In November 1918, the American soprano Rosa Ponselle, then aged twenty-one, made her operatic debut at the New York Met in Verdi's *La forza del destino*. Ponselle's triumph helped open the door to a succession of outstanding American singers.

Deems Taylor's *Peter Ibbetson* and Louis Gruenberg's *The Emperor Jones*, both of which starred the magnetic American baritone Lawrence Tibbett. Tibbett was just one of a host of outstanding American singers to enrich the Met's roster from the 1920s on, a tradition that has continued to this day.

*

In much of continental Europe, by contrast, as millions emerged from the ashes of war, opera could hardly have been a priority. Yet even at times of privation and suffering (perhaps then more than ever), people crave art and entertainment. In Russia, for all the horrors of war, revolution and then civil war, the early Soviet period witnessed something of an artistic flowering. If works of music and literature had been the monopoly of a tiny elite in Tsarist days, Bolshevism was determined to bring culture to the masses. Lenin was not primarily interested in matters aesthetic, preferring to leave this to his 'People's Commissar of Public Enlightenment', Anatoly Lunacharsky. Lunacharsky was an intellectual, a music lover and a man of broad cultural interests. In addition to his love of the Russian classics, he was an early convert to the cult of Wagner. To Lunacharsky, as to any educated Bolshevik, it was not hard to see in the *Ring*, as Shaw had done back in the 1880s, a portrayal of the corrosive power of capitalism, the artistic embodiment of Wagner's revolutionary fervour in 1848–9 and his subsequent essay *Art and Revolution*. The Bolsheviks reissued *Art and Revolution* in Russian, Lunacharsky enthusiastically pointing out that 'the revolutionary movement… that gave birth to the great *Communist Manifesto* of our brilliant teachers Marx and Engels was also reflected in the small, lively, deep, and revolutionary brochure of the no less brilliant Richard Wagner.'

The radicalism and speed of the changes Russians were undergoing were accompanied by widespread suffering and distress. To millions, the abdication of the Tsar and the end of the Romanov regime had been a catastrophe, scarcely to be credited, compounded by the humiliation of military failure at the front. The subsequent replacement of Russia's brief bourgeois revolution by one far more extreme in its aims and methods caused further grief, bewilderment and fear. Many artists and intellectuals fled Red Russia, settling in various Western cities: notably Paris, which became home to a substantial community of White Russians, among them Stravinsky, Shalyapin and Diaghilev's Ballets Russes.

Others stayed. The Revolution, they felt, had a unique opportunity to mould a new, better kind of society. According to this view, a human being was like a machine, susceptible to being engineered this way or that according to the forces encountered: what a man or woman sees and hears he or she in part becomes. Social engineering was thus like industrial engineering. In a factory, every nail or rivet has its place in the overall plan; similarly, if the correct scientific forces are brought to bear, the whims of the individual can be rendered subordinate to the needs of the wider society, to the ultimate benefit of all.

This supposed link between art and scientific planning was energetically pursued in newly Sovietized Russia as painters, sculptors and designers debated the merits of 'Futurism', 'Suprematism' and 'Constructivism', poets and novelists dreamed up new forms of society and exponents of the young art of filmmaking argued the didactic benefits of documentary and montage. In the post-Revolutionary quest for social perfectibility, the arts would clearly have a crucial part to play, the new Bolshevik leaders well aware that their hold on power would be strengthened if they could gain the support of the nation's cultural elite. Lunacharsky held a pivotal position here. A sophisticated man of somewhat conservative personal tastes, he argued from the start that the great achievements of the past should be respected, that there should be no wholesale destruction of historic buildings, sale of Tsarist treasures or suppression of the works of Tolstoy or Tchaikovsky, for example. At the same time, Lunacharsky courted major figures in the cultural avant-garde such as the poet Mayakovsky, the artists Malevich and Tatlin and the theatre director Meyerhold. Other artists, too, gave support to the regime: thus, the writer Maxim Gorki seems to have tried to be a positive influence on Lenin while the painter Marc Chagall acted as Commissar for Art in the Vitebsk region.

From the outset, the really revolutionary part of the Bolshevik cultural programme was the attempt to bring artworks to a wider, proletariat audience. Culture, like everything else in the Soviet state, was subject to official planning. To many it was none the worse for that as literacy levels rose and, for the first time, millions of ordinary people were able to read Pushkin and Tolstoy. With their penchant for neologisms and acronyms, the Soviet leadership promoted *Proletkult* (a movement aimed at making culture truly proletarian in origins and appeal) and later RAPP (the Russian Association of Proletarian Writers) and its musical counterpart, RAPM. The regime was quick to appreciate the propaganda value of film, ensuring through Sovkino (later replaced by Soiuzkino) that the latest works of Sergei Eisenstein and others were soon widely available. More traditional art forms were embraced and encouraged, too, as theatres, concert halls and art galleries opened their doors to all who could attend. So, indeed, did those former symbols of the aristocratic elite, the Mariinsky and Bolshoi theatres, enabling factories and trade unions to bring thousands of workers to the opera and ballet for the first time. Such cultural visits, heavily subsidized, were often accompanied by copious educational materials. Furthermore, what happened in Petrograd (as St Petersburg had been renamed in 1914) and the new Soviet capital, Moscow, was paralleled elsewhere as theatres were built, music and dance academies set up, orchestras and theatre companies established and scene painters, carpenters and costume designers given work in provincial towns up and down the land.

The works on display were not for the most part new creations proclaiming the Revolution; as Lunacharsky himself pointed out, no 'revolutionary repertoire' existed. Rather, Russia's virgin opera audiences might find themselves treated to radical new productions of tried and tested classics: not only the great Russian masterpieces such as *Boris* or Tchaikovsky's *Eugene Onegin* but a futuristic *Lohengrin* perhaps, or a *Rienzi* transferred from medieval Rome to the French Revolution, not to mention Meyerbeer's *Le Prophète* set at the time of the Paris Commune and the prospect of *Les Huguenots* reworked as *The Decembrists*. They may have loved the experience or hated it or, more likely, simply been bemused or bewildered by it. Tickets and transport to and from the theatre were free or heavily subsidized. Never mind that the subsidy was in effect taken off the depressed wages of the workers it was designed to benefit; it was presumed they would not notice or, if they did, would not dare complain. So they went, and duly expressed their gratitude to the beloved Soviet state for making such an experience possible.

If one of the ambitions of the Soviet regime was to bring culture out of the closed bastions of the elite and make it available to the masses, they were not unsuccessful. Perhaps the mass exposure to the arts did not produce the new kind of proletarian-led society the Soviet leaders supposedly had in mind. But for many people, creators and consumers alike, the Revolution seemed to have given birth to a sunburst of enthusiastic cultural exuberance, nearly snuffed out by the depredations of civil war and famine but given renewed life by the relative liberalism of the New Economic Policy (NEP) through much of the 1920s and into the 1930s.

*

As the Russian Revolution and civil war unfolded, much of the wider world watched with growing apprehension. Yet its artistic flowering, its apparent capacity to bring imaginative art to a large popular audience, was widely observed and admired. This ambivalence was particularly pronounced in Russia's western neighbour, Germany. Like Russia, Germany had suffered the ignominy of defeat and had lost its empire and emperor, emerging from the Great War in a state of political and social instability and incipient violence. An attempted Communist Revolution in Germany was brutally suppressed from the Right by troops from the Freikorps before a democratic republican constitution was eventually drawn up in Weimar and formally implemented. For a decade, the Weimar Republic lurched from crisis to crisis, eventually snuffed out in 1933 by the advent of Nazism. Yet during its brief, turbulent history, Germany witnessed an explosion of innovative artistic activity, especially perhaps in its musical life.

With military defeat in 1918, a centuries-old system of court patronage of the arts had come tumbling down. There was nothing to replace it with, no surviving Frederick the Great or Mad King Ludwig to finance talented artists, or even a Kaiser Wilhelm to grace the Linden opera with his gruff occasional presence. Post-war, republican Germany had neither the funds nor the political will to subvent expensive arts such as opera. The result, particularly once the currency had been stabilized by the mid-1920s, was an almost uniquely vibrant cultural anarchy. In Berlin, classical concerts and opera rubbed shoulders with the raunchy sounds of cabaret, jazz and the most biting satire. For traditionalists, there was plenty of Beethoven, Schumann and Wagner to be heard. But Berlin, perhaps more than any other city before or since, resonated with the music of contemporary composers. Here, you could have sampled the works of respected neo-romantics such as Strauss, Pfitzner and Zemlinsky or sampled the harsher, modernist sound of Schoenberg and his pupils (Berg's *Wozzeck* was premiered in Berlin in 1925). Some innovative younger composers, such as Hanns Eisler or Kurt Weill (Brecht's collaborator on *The Threepenny Opera*) experimented with musical style, adjusting it according to the politico-social context for which they were writing. Krenek's jazz opera, *Jonny spielt auf*, was a huge box-office success. Schreker, Krenek's teacher and himself one of the most performed of contemporary composers, quit Vienna for Berlin, where he took a prestigious academic post, and Schreker was followed a few years later by Schoenberg, whose Berlin masterclass provided the crucible for many major composers of the next generation. To musicians everywhere, Berlin was the great magnet.

Nor were Berlin's musical tastes exclusively German. One could have heard Debussy and Ravel in Berlin, and Poulenc and Milhaud, Bartók and Janáček. Among Berlin's opera audiences Puccini was a particular favourite, while a Verdi revival began not in Italy but here. Then there were the Russians: Rakhmaninov, Prokofiev, Stravinsky and the latest musical comet to emerge from the Soviet Union, Shostakovich, who first achieved international recognition after a triumphant performance in Berlin under Bruno Walter of his First Symphony. During the later 1920s, when Walter was director of Berlin's Städtische Oper in Charlottenburg, the principal conductor across town at the Staatsoper on Unter den Linden, Frederick the Great's house, was Erich Kleiber; both houses experienced what, in retrospect, came to be regarded as a 'golden age'. There was a third opera house in Berlin, too, the frankly experimental Kroll led by Otto Klemperer. As with Mahler's tenure at the Vienna Hofoper a generation earlier, Klemperer was not at the Kroll for very long. But the impact of his brief tenure – like Mahler's in Vienna – was to be immense.

Klemperer (like Bruno Walter) was a protégé of Mahler, with whom he had worked as assistant conductor. Tall, gaunt and given to moods of depression, Klemperer was, like his late mentor, a Jewish-born convert to Catholicism. His ambition – again, like Mahler's – was to create opera performances that would integrate all the arts, productions that took the staging and designs as seriously as the music. Over the years, Klemperer had worked in a variety of opera houses (Prague, Hamburg, Strasbourg, Cologne) but none had approached his ideal. In 1924, Klemperer visited Russia, returning there to conduct each year until 1929. When not working, he avidly caught up with what was going on in the other arts, especially the theatre, where he attended productions by Stanislavsky and Meyerhold. To an adventurous-minded German artist like Klemperer, Moscow and Leningrad during these years was immensely stimulating as the new Soviet state, in the wake of civil war and cushioned by the relative liberalism of the NEP, underwent its brief but powerful cultural revival. Klemperer's exposure to the Russian avant-garde was to feed into what, in retrospect, can be seen as one of the most influential moments in twentieth-century German operatic history.

In 1926, Klemperer signed a contract to become music director of Berlin's newly renovated Kroll opera, just along from the Reichstag, the German parliament, on what had formerly been called King's Place (Königsplatz) and was in 1923 renamed the Place of the Republic (Platz der Republik). The Kroll was larger than the city's other two opera houses, but it was administratively a satellite of the Linden opera and, as Klemperer rapidly discovered, had even less money than its two rivals. The Kroll was a legatee of the Berlin

Klemperer, seen here in Leningrad in 1925, visited the USSR several times in the 1920s. Some thought his productions at the Kroll influenced by what he had imbibed from the Soviet avant-garde.

Volksbühne, an organization dating from 1890 set up to provide good theatre at affordable prices for a mass audience. In 1920, the Volksbühne had agreed to finance the renovation of the Kroll in return for which the Prussian state theatres – including Berlin's opera houses – would use it as a venue in which to showcase theatrical performances at moderate prices. Soon, however, the German economy collapsed and hyperinflation wiped out the value of the mark, and the Volksbühne had to hand over operations to the state. Thus, when the new theatre opened in 1924, it was constitutionally a branch of the Berlin State Opera (with the Volksbühne having the right to buy up a proportion of the seats to each performance). This meant that Klemperer, who arrived two years later, was an employee of the Prussian Ministry of Culture and, more directly, of the Intendant of the Staatsoper, Heinz Tietjen. Tietjen, an enigmatic character who later became General Intendant of all the Prussian state theatres (and artistic director of Bayreuth), made it clear to Klemperer that the Kroll could not hope to use the very top singers; these would be reserved for the State Opera's Linden house, itself currently undergoing renovation. Indeed, the Linden-based Staatsoper company was actually in temporary residence at the Kroll when Klemperer arrived because the renovation of their theatre had lasted longer than anticipated.

The auguries were not good. Yet when Klemperer finally opened *his* Kroll, in November 1927, he did so in style with a production of Beethoven's opera about freedom: *Fidelio*. Sets and costumes were simple and stylized while musical value was attached less to individual stardom than to ensemble. Some loved it; others, including a number of Berlin's leading critics, hated it. The monumental cubist sets came in for almost universal excoriation. As for the musical side of things, Hanns Eisler thought the evening featured 'provincial singers who had been excellently rehearsed' while Berlin's leading music critic, Alfred Einstein, wrote of the 'fanatical exactitude' of the performance and of an 'exaggerated dependence on the conductor that borders on tyranny'. Klemperer, unmoved, was determined to continue as he had started, putting on a stream of inexpensive, modern-minded productions of every kind of opera, from Mozart and Verdi to works by contemporary composers such as Stravinsky and Hindemith. Some of Berlin's most innovative theatrical designers were drawn to the Kroll as were figures from the modernist school of art and architecture, the Bauhaus. There was nothing sensational about any of this except, perhaps, the central precept: that opera, like all good theatre, had to have resonance in the present. Klemperer, like Mahler before him, was determined to root out anything musical or theatrical that fell back for its effect on comfortable tradition.

Tradition, however, was precisely what many yearned for in a society that, for a decade, had been undergoing a series of rapid, unpredictable transformations. What people wanted, says Klemperer's biographer, was naturalistic productions and a more familiar repertoire. The Volksbühne, in a position to provide the Kroll theatre with half its audience, found that many among its members did not particularly want to attend avant-garde productions of old favourites; nor were they keen on new works they had never heard of. Hindemith's *Cardillac* was no more calculated to appeal to the members of the Volksbühne than a modernistic production of a beloved classic like *Freischütz*. In January 1929, the Kroll tackled Wagner's *Flying Dutchman*. Instead of a great ship, the curtain went up on a series of simple, rectilinear sets whose sharply contrasted light and shade resembled that of the more provocative expressionist films, while the archetypal myth-figures to which audiences were accustomed were replaced by a bunch of ordinary sailors, and girls mending fishing nets. The Dutchman himself was beardless while the putative heroine, Senta, was no blonde, braided Gretchen figure but a redhead peasant girl in a blue pullover. This was to traduce one of the greatest works of German art, blasted some of the critics; blatant communism, thundered others, and all the worse for having been funded by the Prussian state.

Klemperer said later that all he had aimed to produce at the Kroll was 'good' theatre. But his policy of performing new works, and old works in new ways, brought the Kroll a political reputation as a hotbed of radicalism in a city whose political temperature was already dangerously high. The house on the Platz der Republik was, snorted those on the right disdainfully, the 'Republican' opera house. At the same time, the Kroll managed to alienate many among the working classes and *petite bourgeoisie* it had hoped to attract; in Berlin, as in Soviet Russia, there was no necessary concordance between the 'masses' and the avant-garde (the members of the Volksbühne, said Klemperer later, had 'wanted big singers, big arias, big applause'). In short, Klemperer's Kroll drew

The Kroll Opera, home of some of the twentieth century's most innovative and influential operatic productions during the four-year directorship of Otto Klemperer.

fire from both ends of the socio-political spectrum. The end was not long in coming.

In October 1929, two things occurred that gave many a sense of impending doom. The first was the unexpected death aged fifty-one of Gustav Stresemann, Chancellor (and Foreign Minister) of Germany for the past six years. A distinguished statesman with genuinely democratic instincts and intellectual and artistic interests, Stresemann had done much to help lead his nation upon a course of social and political stability, forging good relations with Germany's western neighbours and establishing a sound currency. His death produced a profound shock; 'a day of destiny for all of us', said Klemperer presciently at the time. Three weeks later, the New York stock market collapsed, throwing the financial world into disarray and the Western economies down the road to economic recession. Germany had still not paid off its war debts, imposed in the wake of Versailles, and was particularly hard hit. Unemployment rose and, with it, social discontent. By 1931, theatre subsidies had sunk to barely half their 1928 levels, premieres of new operas from sixty to twenty-eight. The Dresden opera house removed all works from its repertoire that were liable for royalty payments, while in Berlin the Linden reverted increasingly to operetta to attract audiences. Membership of the Berlin Volksbühne dropped drastically and, with it, sales of tickets to the opera. Under these circumstances, Berlin could scarcely continue to sustain three opera houses.

The Kroll was especially vulnerable. One person's doom is another's opportunity and, as a succession of crises piled up upon each other in Germany, the principal beneficiary was the political right: above all, National Socialism. Nazism began to attract a substantial following, initially in a number of cities dotted around the country and then nationwide. Berlin was probably the most liberal-minded city in Germany. Yet even here, anything as apparently subversive as the Kroll was easily targeted and caricatured: the Kroll under Klemperer was modernist, Jewish, Bolshevik, democratic, republican – everything the right detested.

By now, however, the Kroll was also coming to be highly regarded by some of the most influential and discriminating figures in what the theatre critic Alfred Kerr referred to as Berlin's Periclean age. Thomas Mann admired and vociferously supported the Kroll. So did Stravinsky, the philosopher Walter Benjamin and the architect (and director of the Bauhaus) Walter Gropius. A figure as prominent and admired as Klemperer could not easily be sacked. But he could be removed from the Kroll to serve out his contract at the Linden, where the wily Tietjen could keep a close eye on him as he shared conducting duties with Kleiber and others. Klemperer bristled at this proposed loss of artistic independence and brought a legal action which he lost. He was in no doubt, at the time and later, that the closing of the Kroll (and his own demotion) was fundamentally a political decision, not a financial one, but this was hard to prove. He stuck things out at the Linden for a couple of years. In January 1933, the Nazis came to power. Klemperer knew

After the Berlin Reichstag was destroyed by fire, the Nazis transferred their bogus parliamentary proceedings to what had been the Kroll Opera House. Here, Hitler's deputy Rudolf Hess enters the Kroll in 1934.

there was no place for him in a Germany ruled by Hitler. In the wake of the Reichstag fire, he went to see Tietjen and told him that he was going to Zurich. Tietjen made small talk, keeping up a pretence that Klemperer's departure was just for a brief visit. Both men knew Klemperer would never return. After his departure, his beloved Kroll theatre was occupied for a while by – of all things – the Nazi-dominated German parliament pending reconstruction of the Reichstag.

The Kroll Opera had lasted a bare four years and the theatre was destroyed in the Second World War. But Klemperer and the Kroll were to cast an extraordinarily long shadow.

CHAPTER 17

Opera Under the Dictators

Music, proclaimed Goebbels in 1938, was 'the most glorious art of the German heritage'. His Führer would doubtless have agreed. Few heads of state have been such avid and knowledgeable opera lovers as Hitler. Neither Stalin nor Mussolini knew or cared as much about opera as their German counterpart, but all three dictators were quick to grasp its political value. To the Fascist government in Italy, opera was a major part of the nation's cultural legacy, its essentially Italian roots and achievements exploited as such. Stalinist Russia, meanwhile, made great show of bringing high culture to the proletarian masses (while also using it as a way of 'Russifying' the outlying regions of the Soviet empire). Under all three regimes – Fascist Italy, Nazi Germany and the Communist USSR – opera might be said to have enjoyed something of a heyday in the limited but important sense that its institutions and employees were conspicuously encouraged and financed by a state that consciously used the arts as a political tool. State control is at best a mixed blessing and under such brutal regimes as these proved to be a curse for many unfortunates; politically unacceptable artists, as we shall see, were systematically excluded and in some cases imprisoned and murdered. Many fled abroad. And eventually, of course, everyone was engulfed in the horrors of the Second World War. But prior to the outbreak of this catastrophe, the little world of opera offered genuine opportunities under the dictatorships to anyone of talent who was willing and able to toe the harsh political line.

*

Mussolini was the first to come to power, staging his 'March on Rome' (via a railway sleeping car from Milan) in October 1922. Many Italians, including some of the nation's leading artists, welcomed the advent to power of Mussolini and the Fascists. During the sixty-odd years since unification, Italy had lurched through a succession of political and economic crises, periodically augmented by military adventures that had promised more than they delivered. While other European powers were successfully 'scrambling for Africa' in the 1890s, Italy found its chosen adversary, Ethiopia, irritatingly hard to subdue, eventually acquiring an African colony only in 1911 after wresting Libya from Ottoman hands. Italy's belated participation in the Great War on the side of the Allies guaranteed a place at the Versailles peace table. But the outcome disappointed Italian 'irredentists', many applauding the author and aesthete Gabriele D'Annunzio in 1919 when he took it upon himself to invade and occupy the Dalmatian city of Fiume and proclaim it part of Italy.

D'Annunzio was a leading Italian literary figure in the overripe, darkly perfumed, Wagner-intoxicated world of late romanticism. Like Wagner, D'Annunzio drew on the rich mythologies of the past, in his case Virgil and Dante. Part of his appeal lay in the way he tried to live out his life in accordance with his aesthetic; to him, actions were as important as words. Thus, his 1900 novel *The Flame* (*Il fuoco*) is a richly self-indulgent *roman à clef* drawing freely on both his passion for Wagner (whom we see dying in Venice) and his erotic entanglement with the actress Eleanora Duse. Like Wagner, D'Annunzio lived and loved extravagantly, ran up enormous debts and had to flee his creditors by leaving his homeland. In France during the years running up to the Great War, D'Annunzio collaborated for a while with Debussy before returning to Italy to join the war effort, signed up as a fighter pilot and enhanced his heroic status further by losing an eye in the conflict.

D'Annunzio's seductive, highly charged romanticism, in life as in art, intertwined something of the sex-and-violence of the supposedly 'real-life' *verismo* school of Italian opera (which he affected to despise) with *fin-de-siècle* decadence. Today, we would probably find such a figure, not to mention his literary style, intolerably overblown and self-absorbed. But it must be remembered that he was flourishing precisely at the time when the great days of the *Risorgimento* were slipping out of memory, its last heroes and participants passing from the scene. In particular, Giuseppe Verdi, in old age universally regarded as the embodiment of Italy at its finest, died in 1901. By this time, although Verdi was deeply mourned, much of his *oeuvre* had come to be regarded as passé and his final operas *Otello* and *Falstaff* as a little esoteric. People revered him for the *patria* and *libertà* hymned in earlier works. But it was the man almost more than the music that Italians celebrated in the early years of the new century. And the man could be harnessed for political purposes.

In 1913, the year of Verdi's centenary, many cities across Italy held celebratory events, none more extravagant than the great exhibition mounted in Parma from August until October to honour the memory of the duchy's favourite son. There was opera of course. But there was also a bewildering variety of sporting events, industrial and military displays, children's attractions during the day, fireworks at night. Most remarkable was a vast agricultural pavilion filled to overflowing with the products of Italy's evidently prosperous farming community. Not just the fruit and the vegetables, the livestock, meat and dairy products were on display, but the latest products of Italian science: fertilizers, horticultural machinery and forestry equipment. The literature talked of Verdi's 'peasant origins', his love of the land and how, after his various artistic 'battles', he 'loved to restore himself in the serene vision of his countryside'. Verdi (a 'contemplative and Virgilian spirit') had sprung from Italian soil, almost literally it seemed. 'We were nourished by him as by bread,' D'Annunzio had written on Verdi's death, in an ode widely reprinted in 1913. This was not far short of transubstantiation.

The iconic, quasi-religious status imputed to Verdi at the Parma Exhibition was further emphasized by the decision taken by the city authorities to erect a 'National Monument' to the composer. This would take the form of an altar in front of a great semi-circular archway and would portray various allegorical figures with, at their centre, a Rodin-like sculpture of Verdi garbed in the loose vestments of the Ancient world: Socrates, perhaps, or an Old Testament prophet. It was completed after the Great War and inaugurated in 1920.

Nor was Verdi the only musician to be riveted onto the revival of Italian cultural patriotism. Nowadays, it is commonplace to date the origins of opera back to the courts of late-Renaissance northern Italy and to point to Monteverdi as its first 'great' exemplar. In some ways, this oft-repeated narrative is an early twentieth-century construct as Italian musicologists and historians (such as the composer Francesco Malipiero, who spent sixteen years editing all of Monteverdi's known works) strove to present him as the supreme culmination of that greatest of cultural eras, the Italian Renaissance. Monteverdi's supposed status as the founding father of opera, in particular, was confirmed as scholars brought his operas into the foreground of their studies and demoted his madrigals and liturgical compositions as subsidiary. There are hints of this, too, in the early works of D'Annunzio. For all his idolatry of Wagner in *Il fuoco*, for example, D'Annunzio allows his hero to portray the Florentine *Camerata* as having been the first people to edge towards the classically inspired theatrical ideal that Wagner was later to create at Bayreuth, while the uniquely Italian lyrical gift, we read, was embodied in the 'divine' Monterverdi.

The revival of Monterverdi – let alone the broader Early Music revival – can hardly be attributed to D'Annunzio alone,* much though he would doubtless have liked to take the credit. But D'Annunzio did come to have wide appeal in a demoralized nation ill at ease with its recent past and desperate to seek renewed glory. The place to find it, said D'Annunzio, was in Italy's own heroic past. Italy can rise once more and be an inspiration to the world, he proclaimed, just as it had been in ancient times and during the Renaissance. In particular, D'Annunzio called for 'a new kind of art', steeped in the 'heroic blood' of the past: a 'third Rome'. What was needed was the kind of unapologetic brew of cultural nostalgia and military bravura that he

---

* Or indeed to Italians; the first performance of *Orfeo* since the composer's own time took place not in Italy but in Paris under the baton of the French composer and scholar Vincent d'Indy.

Mussolini (left) with one of his supporters, Gabriele D'Annunzio, a flamboyant literary figure and passionate Italian nationalist who tried to forge links between his life and his art.

tried to embody in his own writings and deeds – but writ large. It was but a short step from such a posture to the ideological underpinning of Fascism.

D'Annunzio was a slightly younger contemporary of Puccini, and the two first discussed working together as early as 1894, when Puccini was developing his ideas for *La Bohème*. For nearly twenty years, Italy's most celebrated writer and composer remained periodically in touch. On the face of it, they had much in common: both were steeped in post-Wagnerian romanticism and each was acutely aware of his public reputation and growing marketability. However, the collaboration never materialized, Puccini turning instead to the American playwright David Belasco for inspiration (and later dismissing D'Annunzio, perhaps unfairly, as having 'little feeling for the lyric theatre'). Puccini's single excursion into Dante was a comic one-acter based on a line from the *Inferno*: hardly the high-flown take for which D'Annunzio might have opted. When Mussolini came to power, D'Annunzio was ecstatic. Puccini, a far more down-to-earth character, was flattered when the Duce made him an honorary *Senatore* but liked to joke that he should have named him a *Sonatore* – a noise maker.

The nostalgic romanticism of D'Annunzio was in many respects at odds, too, with the 'Futurism' preached by the poet and patriot Filippo Tommaso Marinetti. Yet both – in marked contrast to the apolitical Puccini – were instrumental in helping pave the way to Fascism. Marinetti and his colleagues produced a stream of manifestos embracing what they regarded as their dynamic, modern-minded, essentially urban aesthetic of power, machinery, speed, force. Like D'Annunzio, Marinetti was a vociferous irredentist, urging Italy to join the Great War in the belief that this would eventually bring together all Italians within their natural boundaries. In the fevered, unstable atmosphere of post-war Italy, backward-looking romantics and speed-inspired Futurists alike yearned for a 'strong man' at the helm. In 1922, he arrived.

*

Operatic life, like much else, stood to gain from an assertive, supportive government, many felt. For some years, the entire opera industry in Italy had been in the doldrums, buffeted by forces with which it was ill-equipped to contend. With the death of Puccini in 1924, an era seemed to pass, no surviving composer having Puccini's talent or appeal. Entrepreneurial impresarios might mount sparkling productions of the latest operas by Mascagni, Montemezzi or Zandonai and the critics and cognoscenti might applaud. But what the wider public wanted was *Lucia*, *Aida* and *Bohème*. Or, indeed, new forms of entertainment altogether. Cinemas began to spring up all over the peninsula, some of them converted opera theatres, and these would offer millions of Italians an inexpensive version of the warm, romantic fare their parents used to seek – rather more expensively – in the opera house. The cinema was to become an even more potent rival to the opera house in Italy in the 1930s after the arrival of the 'talkies'.

If opera was to survive, it clearly needed more professional management. A few houses had adopted a variation of the system pioneered in 1898 when La Scala appointed Gatti-Casazza as a salaried general manager responsible to a board, with the theatre owned and financed by its box-holders and the local municipality. Many smaller theatres, however, continued to stagger on through thick and (more often) thin under variations of the old impresarial system. In 1921, the year before Mussolini's March on Rome, La Scala once again took the lead. Toscanini had returned and, under his leadership and with all his New York experience behind him, a radically new model of operatic management was broached. Toscanini's proposal, backed by some of the most influential figures in Milanese public life, was that La Scala should become a quasi-independent *ente autonomo*, a self-governing 'entity', a non-profit organization responsible for raising its own funds from both public and private sources and able to work cooperatively with both. All other local places of entertainment, including theatres and cinemas, would pay a tax on their earnings, the proceeds of which would be passed to Milan's most prestigious theatre, La Scala. With the adoption of this model, opera in Italy for the first time came to be managed by techniques appropriate to the twentieth century. Before long, a number of Italy's other leading opera theatres followed suit, reinventing themselves as *enti* and setting up a federation by which they might keep in touch and benefit from collective wisdom.

Enter Mussolini. With him came the idea that, if Italy's greatest art form were to make maximum impact, its institutions would need to be coordinated from the top. To Toscanini, of all Italian artists the one most virulently anti-Fascist, it was alarmingly obvious from the outset that government supervision would mean government control. Events soon proved him right. Senior opera appointments, in the theatres themselves and in the ministry consigned to deal with them, were soon going to Fascist sympathizers. There was nothing wrong with that, some felt at the time, if it meant better financing for opera and higher artistic standards. Many musicians had reason to be grateful to Mussolini and his government as, in the words of Toscanini's biographer, the 'sanctification and officialization of opera, and its transformation into High Art, grew year by year'. If the Duce enabled Italy's operatic culture to thrive once more, who among its professionals and its audiences could complain? To this day, Mussolini's name, along with those of the King of Italy and Governor of Rome, is emblazoned above the proscenium arch of the Rome Opera House.

*

Italian Fascism was neither as ruthless nor as elementally cruel as its Soviet and Nazi counterparts proved to be. Nonetheless, the net gradually closed in on all who did not embody and espouse the ruling ideology. The fact that it did so relatively slowly meant that many who might have been able to leave Italy earlier with little difficulty did not consider doing so until it was too late. Like the frog in the pot of water over a low flame, they found it all too easy to bask in the nation's newly acquired pride while remaining blithely oblivious for too long of its potentially lethal nature. No account is more touching than Giorgio Bassani's fictional portrait of the Finzi-Continis, an aristocratic Ferrarese Jewish family living out the twilight of their lives in their fading old estate as the tentacles of Fascism gradually tighten around them. A tennis club withdraws membership, a library refuses entry. Throughout, Bassani's dignified paterfamilias strives to maintain standards of culture and decency. At Passover, a Seder service is held with all the traditional forms properly observed; most around the table, says the narrator, were later devoured in the German crematoria.

Most Italians, including those potentially under threat, were similarly lacking in political foresight and it is hard to criticize the composers, conductors and singers who continued to perform for a government that gave them work and actively encouraged and financed the arts and opera. A few were more percipient. The great Pisa-born operatic baritone Titta Ruffo, brother-in-law of the Socialist leader Giacomo Matteotti, who was murdered by the regime in 1924, was himself an implacable critic of Fascism. Ruffo spent as much time as he could outside Italy, but on a visit to Rome in 1937 had his passport confiscated and had to spend his declining years observing at close quarters the defeat and humiliation of his homeland. Today, his memory is honoured; next time you are in Pisa, seek out the Teatro Verdi, where, if you are lucky, you will be able to enjoy a performance in the Sala Titta Ruffo.

The most ferocious foe of Fascism among Italy's musicians was also its most celebrated. Toscanini was no great political sophisticate; nor were his instincts particularly democratic (as many battered orchestral players who struggled under his demoniac baton over the years would doubtless have testified). He was also a preternatural patriot. After D'Annunzio had occupied Fiume in the name of Italy in 1919, Toscanini took an Italian orchestra to perform there and was decorated for his efforts by the effusive poet. But unlike D'Annunzio, Toscanini was also a relentless opponent of any kind of political *dirigisme* in matters artistic. When governments told artists what to do, Toscanini fearlessly reciprocated.

Signs of what was to come were not long in appearing. As early as the March on Rome, Toscanini privately expressed his disgust with Mussolini. Before the year was out, a group of Mussolini supporters in the Scala audience shouted out for the maestro to play the Fascist anthem, the 'Giovinezza'. Toscanini refused, broke his baton and walked off. The performance was only able to resume after an announcement that the hymn would be played at the end of the evening. After the performance, according to a member of the cast, the singers were told to stay on stage, where they would sing the 'Giovinezza' to piano accompaniment. But Toscanini told them they would do no such thing, ordered them to their dressing rooms and the hymn was apparently played by a solo pianist. The Fascist anthem wormed its way into musical politics again in 1926 at the time of the world premiere of Puccini's final opera, *Turandot*, which Toscanini was to conduct at La Scala. Mussolini let it be known that he would like to attend – in which case, the 'Giovinezza' would of course have to be played. Toscanini's response was that if La Scala wanted *Turandot* and the anthem they had better find another conductor. On the night, Toscanini conducted the opera, and no anthem, and Mussolini decided to stay away (on the spurious grounds that he did not want his presence to distract the public from their devotion to the memory of Puccini).

Toscanini became increasingly uncomfortable in Fascist Italy and was offered the post of principal conductor of the New York Philharmonic (newly amalgamated with Walter Damrosch's New York Symphony in order to create a single super-orchestra). In spring 1929, before leaving La Scala, he took the entire company of over 300 people on what was to prove a triumphant tour to Berlin and Vienna. Critics were uniform in their praise for the quality of the performances, and audiences (which included Furtwängler, Klemperer, Bruno Walter, Max Reinhardt and Siegfried Wagner) were equally impressed. In Vienna, the 21-year-old Herbert von Karajan attended *Falstaff* and was overwhelmed by the complete integration of music and drama, something he thought unimaginable at the Staatsoper. When the company returned to

In 1929, Toscanini took his Scala forces to Berlin and Vienna, receiving a triumphant welcome at each stop and impressing audiences that included Furtwängler, Klemperer, Bruno Walter and the young Karajan. Then, having displayed Italian art at its finest, Toscanini quit Fascist Italy in disgust at its politics.

Milan, they were hailed as conquering heroes. Mussolini sent Toscanini a con-gratulatory telegram packed with pompous Fascistic phraseology, to which Toscanini replied saying merely that in serving his art he knew he was thereby serving his country.

If Toscanini thought that by quitting La Scala for the New York Philhar-monic he was leaving behind his skirmishes with Fascism, time was to deliver a series of further shocks. The worst occurred in 1931, when he was back in Italy to conduct a pair of concerts in Bologna's recently restored Teatro Comunale. Again, the catalyst was a demand, which Toscanini refused, that he perform the 'Giovinezza'. When Toscanini arrived at the theatre for the first concert, his car was surrounded by Fascist thugs who pressed him on whether he would play the anthem, then started jostling and then hitting him. The conductor, suffering minor facial injuries but boiling over with barely controllable fury, was bustled into his car and driven speedily back to his hotel. Before long, a crowd of several hundred Fascist sympathizers gathered in the street below and started yelling obscene taunts up at the 64-year-old maestro. A semblance of calm was eventually restored (thanks in part to the intervention of Toscanini's friend the composer Respighi). But Toscanini and his wife left town in the early hours for Milan. Here, their passports were briefly removed and their home put under government surveillance.

The Bologna incident was reported worldwide. Toscanini, willy nilly, had become one of the most prominent symbols of opposition to totalitarianism. That summer, Toscanini went to Bayreuth, where he had been engaged as the first Italian to conduct in the Wagner holy of holies. Siegfried Wagner had died the previous year and the Festival was now in the hands of his widow, Winifred, who was thrilled at the prospect of having in residence at Bayreuth not one star conductor but two. But Toscanini and Furtwängler had an uneasy relationship, and Toscanini's Bayreuth sojourn was further vitiated by a painful shoulder injury. When pressed to return at the next Festival, scheduled for 1933, he at first demurred. After much wooing by Winifred, Toscanini eventually agreed. Then, in January 1933, Hitler came to power in Germany. Winifred feared she might lose Toscanini and persuaded Hitler to write to the Italian maestro in April saying how delighted he would be to greet him later in the year at Bayreuth. One can only imagine the impact of such a communication on Toscanini. He sent a cagey reply and then, a month later, pulled out. Winifred was devastated, Hitler furious. Toscanini's place was eventually taken by the more compliant Richard Strauss. 'To Strauss the composer,' Toscanini once said memorably, 'I take off my hat. To Strauss the man, I put it on again.'

*

'Did Stalin like music? No. What he liked was the Bolshoi, its splendour and pomposity.' The words are those of the Russian soprano Galina Vishnevskaya, whose early career at the Bolshoi overlapped with the end of the Stalin regime. Stalin 'personally watched over the Bolshoi', recalled Vishnevskaya, and 'went to great lengths for [its] artists', whose relatively high salaries, it seems, were set by Stalin personally. Whenever he visited the opera, Stalin always sat in Box A, over the orchestra, right alongside the stage. Here, he 'felt himself an emperor', enjoying his role as patron of the theatre, rewarding his favourite singers as a nineteenth-century tsar or landowner might have rewarded his favourite serfs. Vishnevskaya surmises that Stalin, a small man with a rather weak voice, probably liked to identify with some of the grandiose tsars he saw on stage, with their sumptuous costumes, their orbs and sceptres, as they bestrode the Bolshoi's elaborate stagings of the great Russian masterpieces. Even – maybe especially – the murderers among them such as Boris Godunov, just as he was intrigued by Eisenstein's screen portrayal of Ivan the Terrible. However, unlike most tsars and emperors (and unlike Napoleon), Stalin had his box at the opera curtained off so that he remained invisible to the audience in the theatre, his presence merely hinted at by what Vishnevskaya called the 'clump of bodyguards' in attendance. The 'little father', to whom all had to make extravagant avowals of love, lived in permanent fear of assassination. Vishnevskaya (who later, with her husband the cellist Mstislav Rostropovich, lived in exile in the West) had no love for the

Soviet system and detested Stalin, that evil genius of her youth. But even she had to admit that, 'on the whole, he was a "good tsar" for the Bolshoi'. The repressions and purges of the 1930s hardly touched any of the leading figures at the Bolshoi. In Soviet Russia, as in Mussolini's Italy or Hitler's Germany, artists whose work found official approval were safe and secure so long as they were able to play the political game.

For those of whom Stalin disapproved, the barbarism was not long in emerging. During the First Five-Year Plan (1928–32), RAPM (the Russian Association of Proletarian Musicians) and its literary counterpart RAPP, cultural appendages of the Plan, monitored the credentials of the nation's composers and authors to ensure they promoted true Soviet values. If you were deemed to have fallen short you were liable to be accused of 'bourgeois tendencies' or condemned as a 'counter-revolutionary', in which case, you might lose your artistic outlets but also perhaps your income, your right to halfway decent accommodation and possibly even your life. In 1932, under the notorious Resolution 'On the Reconstruction of Literary and Artistic Organizations', RAPM and RAPP were replaced by the all-powerful Union of Soviet Composers and Union of Soviet Writers. Before long, 'Socialist Realism' was adopted as the official cultural ideology, in sharp contrast to the sin of 'Formalism', a blanket term used to condemn any art or artefact in which

Outside the Bolshoi Theatre, Moscow, in 1930. Stalin's attendance at the theatre did not yet represent the ominous threat it was soon to become.

formal experimentation (of interest only to elite aesthetes) was deemed to have been given precedence over authentically proletarian content.

The 1932 Resolution and the endorsement of Socialist Realism arose out of a meeting – attended by Stalin – at the home of Maxim Gorki. Ambivalent about the violence the Bolsheviks espoused, and suffering from tuberculosis, Gorki had gone to live in Italy. Sorrento was undoubtedly better for his health than Moscow or Leningrad. But Gorki found Italian Fascism increasingly vacuous and he missed his homeland. The Soviets were keen to have him return and when, after several summer visits to the USSR, Gorki quit Fascist Italy in 1931 to live in Communist Russia, his decision was widely hailed in the Stalinist press. When Gorki endorsed Socialist Realism, he probably considered it a formula designed to harness the incomparable narrative tradition of Russia's great nineteenth-century novelists to the modern excitements and dangers of changing times. In the Soviet lexicon, however, Socialist Realism did not mean gritty tragedies such as *verismo* operas or Zola novels: rather, easily digestible celebrations of the heroic achievements of the Russian people. To Stalin and the Soviet leadership, culture had to be not 'social' but transparently 'socialist' – a blatantly political watchword by which all artistic works and their creators were to be judged, praised or condemned.

In 1934, two unconnected events occurred that were to have huge impact. In January, Shostakovich's opera *Lady Macbeth of the Mtsensk District* was premiered in theatres in both Leningrad and Moscow to enormous acclaim. And at the end of the year, the head of the Communist Party in Leningrad, Sergei Kirov, was assassinated and was succeeded by Andrei Zhdanov (later infamous for straitjacketing Soviet culture after the war). Kirov was an old comrade of Stalin's and had risen to be something of a rival. Just as the Nazis in Germany had deplored the Reichstag fire the previous year and then made ruthless use of the event for their own purposes, Stalin wept crocodile tears for his fallen friend and then embarked upon a policy of massive and cynical brutality that was beyond the imaginings of even his greatest enemies.

Shostakovich's opera is based on a short story by the nineteenth-century author Leskov and tells a brutal story of sex and murder in provincial Russia. Katerina, the small-town 'Lady Macbeth' figure, finds a lover, kills her leering father-in-law and her boring husband and is later transported to a prison camp with her feckless lover, who promptly finds another girlfriend among the inmates. This enticingly gruesome story is told through a richly textured score packed with music that is, as appropriate, ferocious, wistful, grotesque, savage and at times wildly, irresponsibly erotic. In its first year, the opera chalked up over forty performances, most of them sold out, and by the end of 1935 close to 100 in Moscow alone; meanwhile, *Lady Macbeth* was on her triumphant way to opera houses around the world. Then Stalin thought he would like to see this opera everyone was talking about so enthusiastically. Ominously, he did not stay until the end. Two days later, *Pravda* featured a

A striking poster advertising Shostakovich's new opera, *Lady Macbeth of the Mtsensk District*, which had its premiere in Leningrad's Maly Theatre on 22 January 1934.

prominent, unsigned article in which Shostakovich's opera was roundly condemned as 'Chaos [or 'Muddle'] Instead of Music'. From the very beginning, wrote the author, there was a 'deliberately dissonant, confused stream of sound'. The music 'quacks, grunts, and growls'. When there were fragments of melody, they rapidly disappeared again in the subsequent din so that the music was difficult to follow and impossible to remember. As for the subject matter, with its double bed occupying centre stage, it was dismissed as 'coarse, primitive, vulgar'. No wonder the piece was so successful abroad, concluded the writer. For this kind of 'fidgety, screaming, neurotic music… tickles the perverted tastes of the bourgeoisie'. Shostakovich was condemned for having committed the potentially fatal sin of 'Formalism'.

Nobody was in much doubt about the authorship of this piece. If it was not Stalin personally it was certainly written on his authority. Nor, of course, did anybody read it as merely a negative theatre review. With this article, Stalin signalled that henceforth he would demand complete and utter subservience from Soviet artists just as he was doing from politicians and generals. The effects of 'Chaos Instead of Music' on the Russian musical world can be imagined. Some composers, desperate to ingratiate themselves with the murderous regime, produced operatic potboilers that were mounted to great official acclaim, taken off again and rarely or never revived. A handful of musicians managed to produce works of substance, notably Prokofiev, whose *War and Peace* contrived to be a paean of praise to Mother Russia while also celebrating a great Russian novelist, a famous Russian military victory and a quietly victorious general whose strategic genius all recognized as anticipating that of 'the little father' in the Great Patriotic War. Most Soviet composers, however, found it prudent to eschew opera altogether and resort to safer genres. Shostakovich himself, who might surely have had one of the twentieth century's most illustrious operatic careers, never composed another opera, though he contemplated doing so on a number of occasions and in the 1960s returned to *Lady Macbeth*, revising the score and issuing it as *Katerina Ismailova*. He was one of the lucky ones. Many leading Soviet artists and intellectuals, among them Meyerhold, Mandelstam and Isaac Babel, were hounded to cruel and premature deaths. So were millions of their compatriots as forced collectivization, famine, political purges, show trials, mass deportations and the Gulag, followed by the Second World War, took their awful toll.

*

It is common, and rightly so, to talk of the horrors of Nazism, of the ruthless persecution the Hitler regime inflicted upon cultured Germans, Austrians and others, many of whom lost their jobs, their livelihood and perhaps their lives. Many thousands fled abroad, often to the long-term benefit of the nations that gave them refuge. What is harder to appreciate is that, prior to the outbreak of war at least, and even to some extent thereafter, the Nazi regime did much to encourage art and artists of which it approved. Culture became a 'weapon of the state'. This did not necessarily mean that all art had to be slavishly and ideologically 'Aryan'. Of course, there were plenty of toadies ready to produce requisitely muscular sculptures, grandiloquent buildings, upbeat choral arrangements and films and paintings showing happy blond families pulling their weight for the Reich. And the Nazis railed against the 'Jewification' of German culture, its Americanization and 'Negroization' (a cheap shot against the jazz that had become popular during the Weimar years), anathematizing such music as 'degenerate', while anything regarded as 'Bolshevik culture' was similarly labelled. However, the Nazi leadership was too sophisticated to demand total artistic subservience. On the contrary, Goebbels, the minister in charge of culture, was as much concerned with what he regarded as excellence, with the quality of the entertainment available, as with its more narrowly political message. If film and theatre, music, opera and dance could be of demonstrably high quality, that in itself would constitute an ideological triumph for the Reich and spike the guns of those disposed to snipe at the Nazi regime for its supposed philistinism.

Music in particular stood to benefit. The acknowledged pinnacle of Germany's contribution to world civilization, it was regarded by the regime as a weapon (in the striking phrase of one patriotic musicologist) that must not be allowed to rust. One of the many criticisms levelled by the Nazis against their Weimar predecessors was how badly music had, in their view, been neglected. 'Degenerate', non-German music had been allowed to thrive in the uncontrolled, volatile political and economic atmosphere of the 1920s at the same time as state subventions to serious orchestras and opera houses had atrophied. Even the revered Berlin Philharmonic had nearly gone bankrupt in the 1920s and had had to be bailed out by the city council, while its scarcely less impressive sister orchestra, the Berlin Symphony, had been disbanded in 1932.* This was a trend the Nazis (and Hitler personally, a failed artist who fancied himself as something of an aesthete) were determined to reverse. The way to do so, they were convinced, was to coordinate musical activity under a strong, central state authority: in other words, to revive at national level what had worked perfectly well for centuries in many of the traditional princely and ducal courts of Germany. To the Nazis (and to many of the leading modern scholars of the Nazi period), the continuities with the perceived values of the past were at least as striking as the discontinuities.

Shortly after the Nazis' assumption of power, they set up the *Reichskulturkammer*, or Reich Culture Chamber, headed by Goebbels, beneath which were a number of subordinate 'Chambers': one each for music, theatre, visual arts, literature, film, radio, and the press. The man invited to become president of the *Reichsmusikkammer* was Germany's most internationally celebrated opera composer, Richard Strauss. The *RMK* set about trying to boost the musical professions (in something of the spirit of those German courts of earlier times) by establishing proper salary structures, training courses and pension schemes and by giving Germany's leading opera and concert organizations realistic subsidies, thus enabling them to plan ahead. The aim was that, not only in Berlin but all over the country, opera and concert life should thrive once more. When the Nazis came to power, there were 1859 singers and 4889 orchestral players on the books of German theatres; by 1938 those figures had risen to 2145 and 5577.

Musicology, too, was encouraged. Here again, the Reich had no difficulty proclaiming a veneer of continuity with a worthy German past that had been squandered by Weimar. For well over a century, after all, musicologists and music historians, marvelling at the genius of Beethoven and others, had struggled to define what was specifically 'German' about their nation's music. Nor was such a quest confined to students of music – or, indeed, to Germany as scholars throughout much of Europe and North America sought to identify the cultural roots of their nation's 'character'. Music was widely believed to be

* On Hitler's personal insistence, the future financial security of the Berlin Philharmonic was guaranteed by the Reich in October 1933.

particularly revealing of national character, especially that of the ordinary people, the 'folk', and recent musical history was replete with stories of ethnographers (as we would now say) heroically attempting to capture and preserve the surviving remnants of their respective nation's 'folk' music. This was what Bartók and Kodály had been trying to do in Hungary and Vaughan Williams in England during the early years of the twentieth century. Vaughan Williams's essays about 'National Music', including several on folk song, were published in 1934.

So there was nothing particularly revolutionary in the encouragement given by National Socialism to the study of the music of the German *Volk*, on the face of it a perfectly acceptable topic to any 'nationalist' and/or 'socialist'. But here, as in all they did, the Nazis took things to extremes, twisting and bending scholarly inquiry to ensure its conclusions fed directly into the regime's harsh political agenda. Thus, the word *Volk* came to mean not the 'ordinary' people but the German nation itself so that, by intellectual sleight of hand, the music of Germany's great composers was deemed not so much to have been influenced by the music of the German *Volk* or nation as to embody it. And by the German nation, of course, the Nazis did not mean just the nation state, a recent political construction, but the Nordic 'race', that mystical union of northern Germanic peoples that could be traced back to ancient times and whose fortunes they, the Nazi party, were dedicated to revive. German musicologists, hearing the message, researched what they regarded as the specifically 'German' traits in the music of Mozart or Weber, or how the German *Volk* had created the earliest form of polyphony and the major triad through their espousal of the 'lur', an early Nordic instrument. German music it was said (with countless laborious examples from composers from Handel to Bruckner to prove the point) used major more than minor modes, consonance rather than dissonance (while 'Jewish music', needless to say, gravitated in the opposite direction). Any musicologist arguing for conclusions such as these was likely to receive research money and perhaps a salaried academic post.

Of all the musical beneficiaries of the Hitler regime, the greatest was Bayreuth. 'No other head of any great modern state,' says its historian, 'was so fascinated by the arts as this reborn Pericles, as [Hitler] thought of himself.' Hitler was intimately acquainted with Wagner's *oeuvre*, revering it as the epitome of all that was noblest in German culture. Early in his career, he had been welcomed to Wahnfried, the Wagner family home in Bayreuth, where he made a profound impression on Winifred Wagner, the young English-born wife of the composer's son, Siegfried. When Hitler was imprisoned in Landsberg after his 1923 coup attempt, Winifred sent him aid and comfort (and the notepaper on which he was to write *Mein Kampf*), gestures of friendship Hitler never forgot. In 1925, for the first time, he attended the Bayreuth Festival, where Winifred Wagner welcomed him with a bouquet of

Hitler loved Wagner, and was a regular visit to Bayreuth. He is seen here with Winifred Wagner, the composer's (English-born) daughter-in-law, and her sons Wolfgang (back, left) and Wieland.

flowers. The pair called each other 'Winnie' and 'Wolf' and addressed each other as *du*.

The Bayreuth Festival was a private fiefdom of the Wagner family which, like many arts organizations in Weimar Germany, struggled from hand to mouth throughout the 1920s. The Festival was generally held twice in every three years. Between times, Siegfried Wagner, who was in charge, did what he could to appeal for funds, his authority constantly held in check not only by financial constraints but also by the looming presence of his elderly mother Cosima, the arch-conservative guardian of the Wagner flame. In April 1930, Cosima Wagner died aged ninety-two. A few months later, Siegfried followed her to the grave, his duties immediately assumed by his 33-year-old widow (as Cosima herself had once inherited the mantle from 'The Master'). Winifred's burdens were hardly relieved by ill-concealed resentment among some of the female members of the extended Wagner family. But she proved a tough, resilient and imaginative manager, making a number of appointments as she planned the 1931 Festival, notably that of the ubiquitous Heinz Tietjen as her artistic director.

In January 1933, 'Wolf' became Chancellor of Germany. The next month, two weeks after taking office, Hitler attended ceremonies in Leipzig, Wagner's birthplace, to mark the fiftieth anniversary of his death. A fortnight later, the Reichstag building – the very embodiment to many of the failure of Weimar republicanism – went up in flames. In March, on a day replete with symbolic meaning, Hitler convened and addressed the relocated Reichstag in what amounted to a ceremonial inauguration of the Third Reich, later attending a gala performance at the Linden opera of that most celebratory of Wagner's works, *Die Meistersinger*, conducted by Furtwängler. 'Awaken!' sang the gleeful chorus in the final scene, turning joyfully towards their Führer as Hans Sachs invoked the glories of German art.

Hitler's admiration for Wagner remained unabated. So did Winifred's for Hitler. When it became clear that Bayreuth lacked the funds to cover the ambitious programme she had planned for the 1933 Festival, she approached her friend the Chancellor. The upshot was that the Reich agreed to buy tickets in bulk and distribute them to the public at low cost. Hitler, like King Ludwig of Bavaria, saved the Bayreuth Festival. And like Kaiser Wilhelm, he also attended, amidst much cheering, flag-waving and general hullabaloo. Unlike the Kaiser, however, Hitler was clearly absorbed by the performances he attended, and remained in residence for nearly a week. Overt politics were kept outside the holy portals of the Festspielhaus. There was of course no objection to the pictures of Hitler in every shop window, the jovial Storm Troopers lining the streets and drinking in Bayreuth's beer halls, or the swastika banners that hung throughout the little town and on the hillside approaches to the theatre. But for those inside, a discreet note on behalf of the Chancellor requested patrons to refrain from patriotic songs or demonstrations; after all, there was 'no more glorious expression of the German spirit than the immortal works of the Master himself'. For the rest of the decade, this was the pattern as the Bayreuth Festival became more and more a celebration of Nazi power.

This was reflected, too, in the somewhat grandiose productions that characterized Nazi Bayreuth from the outset (in 1933, the final scene of *Meistersinger*, produced by Tietjen, boasted an aggregate of 800 people on stage). Winifred was nevertheless determined that mere spectacle should never impede artistic vision. Rather, her Bayreuth would strive to provide the finest standards available on any stage in Germany. That meant a degree of serious theatrical innovation. Nothing as radical as the kind of productions pioneered at Klemperer's Kroll, of course. But the new approach did mean that (for example) the members of the Bayreuth chorus were directed to act as crowds of interacting individuals rather than being simply arrayed in formal rows: just the kind of thing to anger the conservative old guard who felt Winifred was betraying the true Wagnerian legacy maintained for so long by Cosima. Fortunately for Winifred, she had Hitler on her side (she even persuaded the

Führer to overlook her retention for a while of several outstanding Jewish artists who in her opinion were the finest available). Hitler continued to arrange for German troops to attend Bayreuth, partly no doubt for their cultural elevation but also in an attempt to ensure that Bayreuth could remain solvent. Paradoxically, Winifred Wagner's Bayreuth probably enjoyed a greater degree of artistic independence than any comparable institution – precisely because of the protection provided by her closeness to Hitler and his personal patronage of the Festival.

As time went on, Hitler became increasingly preoccupied with other matters and Winifred found it harder to gain access to him. But Hitler never lost his reverence for Wagner. Of all the gifts he received on his fiftieth birthday in April 1939, the one that moved him most was a set of some of Wagner's original scores and sketches. These priceless manuscripts, once in the possession of King Ludwig II of Bavaria, had been acquired by a group of prominent German industrialists who now presented them proudly to their thrilled and grateful Führer. Winifred, it seems, pleaded with Hitler to deposit them for safekeeping at Wahnfried. But he would not part with them.

*

Richard Strauss was not the only German artist to try and make his peace with the Third Reich. Many welcomed the advent of Hitler. Some were committed Nazis. The painter Emil Nolde, famous for his vivid watercolours, was an early recruit, only to become deeply disturbed when the regime turned against him and even included some of his work in their 1937 exhibition of 'degenerate' art. The sculptor Arno Breker was luckier, providing athletic statues for the 1936 Berlin Olympics which, like the film images of Leni Riefenstahl, were applauded as embodying Aryan perfection. The composer Hans Pfitzner welcomed much that the Nazis seemed to embody, though his precise political views are hard to fathom, mediated as they were through a somewhat spiky and resentful personality.

Others were markedly less enthusiastic, or perhaps thought of themselves as apolitical, and simply kept their heads down and tried to get on with the one thing they knew about: their art. However, adopting a position of what came to be called 'internal exile' was not easy. Every act, even passivity, was a political statement in the Third Reich. No profession was immune to political implications and suspicions: not the surgeon, the school teacher, the judge or the journalist. Artists, too, historically proud of their independent and even oppositional nature, were manoeuvred into political subservience. If they did not comply, their works – and maybe the artists themselves – were liable to be destroyed.

Musicians knew this as well as anyone. The composer Carl Orff continued to work in Germany during the war; his most famous work, *Carmina Burana*, was first performed in Frankfurt in 1937 (and was fiercely criticized by the principal Nazi critics, a fact that did Orff's post-war reputation no harm). Orff and his pupil Werner Egk were commissioned to write music for the Berlin Olympics; that year, Egk was appointed conductor of the Staatsoper, Berlin, a position he held until 1941. The pianist Walter Gieseking worked in Hitler's Reich during the war years, too, as did the young operatic soprano Elisabeth Schwarzkopf. So, for a while, did the choreographer Rudolf Laban, yet another who was commissioned to display his talent at the Berlin Olympics, in his case by devising a spectacular balletic opening ceremony. Goebbels attended the final rehearsal, hated what he saw – and Laban, terrified, later landed up in England.

If it was possible for some to believe initially in the benevolence of the Third Reich, anyone who opposed the regime and its ideology or fell foul of its racial laws rapidly incurred its wrath. Many of Germany's leading musicians were of Jewish background. Bruno Walter was in New York when the Nazis took power in January 1933, but in March he returned to Germany to fulfil conducting engagements in Leipzig and Berlin. As soon as he disembarked, he noticed the newly oppressive atmosphere. Swastika flags were everywhere, and Walter found himself reminded of the anxious, whispered words of the prisoners in *Fidelio*:

> Sprecht leise, haltet euch zurück!
> Wir sind belauscht mit Ohr und Blick
>
> (Speak softly, restrain yourselves
> We are observed by ears and eyes)

Berlin, where Walter had his home, retained something of the free spirit of Weimar days. But when Walter arrived, he was told that there was an urgent message from the people in Leipzig where, it seemed, the local Nazis were planning to prevent his Gewandhaus concert from taking place. Walter hastened to Leipzig to conduct rehearsals and, in the evenings, sat with the courageous head of the Gewandhaus committee as the latter made endless pleading telephone calls. Both men knew that what was at stake was far more than one concert. 'We were two watchmen,' wrote Walter later in an evocative metaphor, 'calling out for help against the creeping fire with which barbarians were threatening culture and its dwelling-place.'

On the day of the concert, Walter arrived at the Gewandhaus for the final rehearsal only to find that the rehearsal and concert had been banned by the Saxon Ministry of the Interior. With heavy heart, he returned to Berlin, where news of the Leipzig debacle had preceded him. On arriving, Walter heard that his upcoming Berlin concert, too, was to be banned. The official reason, as always, was to prevent any 'unpleasant occurrences'. On further inquiry, Walter's agent elicited from a senior official at Goebbels's Propaganda Ministry that, while they did not officially prohibit the concert (which would mean not paying the players), the agent should be aware that 'if you insist on giving the concert you may be sure that everything in the hall will be smashed to pieces'. Under the circumstances, Walter had no option but to pull out. That evening, Bruno Walter left Berlin to live in Austria. The concert went ahead without him. It was conducted by Richard Strauss.

Bruno Walter and Otto Klemperer were of Jewish background, as were thousands of others who fled Nazism while it was still possible to do so, among them many of Germany's leading composers, instrumentalists, singers, musicologists and musical entrepreneurs. Some who left were not Jewish; simply people – such as Carl Ebert and Fritz Busch – who found they could not live and work under so destructive a regime. Ebert, the Intendant of Berlin's Charlottenburg opera, needed a music director and approached his friend Fritz Busch of the Dresden opera. The two men had collaborated occasionally, notably on a landmark production of Verdi's *Un ballo in maschera* in 1932 designed by Caspar Neher. In March 1933, Ebert and Busch met for dinner in Berlin. Busch appeared shaken and told Ebert how he had been booed by Nazi sympathizers in his Dresden theatre a couple of nights before and had had to leave the orchestra pit. Busch, like Ebert, was a high-minded man who had refused to dismiss Jewish colleagues; Ebert, a Social Democrat, gave work to people of various political persuasions, including some on the far left like Neher. Such artistic integrity was clearly not appreciated by the new regime.

During dinner, Ebert was told that his theatre had been occupied earlier that evening by the SA. The next day, he was summoned to see Göring who was Prime Minister of Prussia as well as Hitler's Minister of the Interior. After an inconclusive meeting at which he was subjected to a series of threats and promises all wrapped up in Göring's notoriously oleaginous charm, Ebert was in effect dismissed. Two days later he left for Switzerland.

Busch, too, met Göring, who began by blaming the events in Dresden on 'filthy fellows' and 'nincompoops' in the party who had let things get out of hand. With this, Busch vigorously agreed. But when Göring went on to say how much the Führer wanted Busch to return to Dresden, Busch emphatically refused, knowing that the price he would have to pay would be the loss of artistic independence. Göring resorted to blustering. 'My dear friend,' he said, 'you know we have means at hand to compel you.' Busch was unrepentant. Göring counselled him to think things over for a while; clearly, the Nazis were keen not to lose the services of yet another internationally respected artist. Later, Busch was invited to go to Bayreuth: on the face of it a tempting offer – until it transpired that he would be a late replacement for Toscanini, something he could not possibly countenance.

Early in May, Busch left Germany for ever, initially for a season at the Colón opera house in Buenos Aires. A year later, he was reunited with Ebert as together they pioneered a completely new kind of operatic venture in a most unlikely venue: an English country house in the Sussex downs called Glyndebourne.

*

Klemperer, Walter, Ebert and Busch were among the more prominent figures in the German operatic world to lose their posts as a direct result of Nazi pressure. They were not alone. Within a matter of months after the installation of the Third Reich, Intendants were forced out of over half of Germany's eighty-odd opera houses and replaced by party appointees, while operas by composers or librettists with Jewish or left-wing connections were summarily withdrawn. When Walter left Germany, a workman who had often done odd jobs for the family and a long-time Social Democrat insisted on coming to the station to see him off. 'I suppose you'll have to join the Nazi party,' said the kindly conductor, 'or else you'll find yourself out of work.' The man agreed, mournfully. Then suddenly his face lit up with the hope that maybe lots of other members of Hitler's party 'will be of my kind'. Such naivety was soon impossible as books were burned, people ousted from their jobs because they were politically undesirable and artworks that did not fit the Nazi agenda jeered as degenerate. For some, the true nature of Nazism was first revealed on the 'Night of the Long Knives' in 1934, when (in parallel with the political purges of Stalin) many supposed or potential rivals to Hitler's leadership were murdered. For others, the moment of truth came with the Nuremberg laws the following year which prohibited all sexual relations between Jews and 'Aryans' and stripped Jews of German citizenship. For a while, Jews were permitted to form their own Jewish Culture League in which Jewish artists were permitted to play 'Jewish music' before exclusively Jewish audiences. Some found temporary comfort in this arrangement, citing the high quality of the performances, the opportunity to hear music by otherwise banned composers and the musical sophistication of the audiences these concerts attracted. But the comfort was soon revealed as illusory as the screw continued to tighten.

*

Salzburg was near the German border, an eagle's flight from Hitler's nest at Berchtesgaden. But it had the great virtue of being in Austria. When some of Germany's leading musicians found themselves forced to leave Nazi Germany, they knew they could find a welcome in Vienna or Salzburg. Indeed, the Salzburg Festival, Europe's earliest and finest, became something of a home-away-from-home for artists fleeing Nazism: those who performed at Salzburg were virtually *persona non grata* in Germany and vice versa. After the German contralto Sigrid Onegin backed out of a Salzburg engagement (pleading 'superior orders') and went on to sing instead at Bayreuth, few non-German houses

Teatime in Salzburg. Bruno Walter (left) and his guests Thomas Mann and Arturo Toscanini at the Salzburg Festival around 1935.

were prepared to engage her. On the other hand, when the soprano Lotte Lehmann spurned the offer (from Göring) of a lucrative Berlin contract which would have precluded her from singing outside Germany, she found herself forbidden forthwith to sing in Germany at all. Bruno Walter recalled happy times in Salzburg, relaxing in the home of the author Stefan Zweig in the nearby hills in the company of Toscanini, Lehmann, Thomas Mann and others. The violin virtuoso Fritz Kreisler appeared at Salzburg, and the conductor Erich Kleiber, another émigré from Nazism. When Toscanini conducted opera in Salzburg his principal assistant was Erich Leinsdorf, and for his 1937 *Zauberflöte* the glockenspiel was played by an up-and-coming répétiteur from the Hungarian opera named Georg Solti. Toscanini was pleased with Solti's work. 'See you in Salzburg next year,' said the Maestro, to Solti's delight. Back in Budapest, the opera administration promised to let Solti conduct a performance of his own. The opera would be *Figaro*, and the date of the first performance 11 March 1938. That night, German troops crossed the Austrian border and the following day, welcomed by many and feared by some, marched towards Vienna – the advance party for the *Anschluss* by which Austria was incorporated into Greater Germany.

Overnight, every Austrian became a German citizen. Hitler was ecstatic. So were the vast crowds that greeted him in the streets of Vienna and went to hear his address in the grounds of the Hofburg, Vienna's former imperial palace. Others wondered darkly where he would strike next. In the autumn the Reich annexed the German-speaking Sudeten lands on the Czech borders and the following spring the rest of Bohemia and Moravia. On 1 September 1939, Germany invaded Poland. Hitler's Reich was at war, a conflict that was soon to engulf much of the world and cause incalculable suffering, destruction and death.

CHAPTER 18

Total War

Opera was hardly something to which the desperate citizens of Leningrad could give much thought as they struggled to keep warm and find palatable scraps of food on which to survive. For 900 days, the city was in the iron grip of a siege in which over a quarter of its three million inhabitants would perish. To many, it seemed the entire legacy of Russian civilization was in peril.

Yet at this darkest hour, amidst almost indescribable suffering and destruction, music provided what the historian Boris Schwarz has described as a lifeline for the beleaguered, famished populace. In the depths of winter 1941–2, 'theatres struggled to function,' says Schwarz, 'musicians continued to play, composers managed to write music'. And ragged, starving citizens would somehow stumble their weary way through sub-zero temperatures, past unburied corpses, and assemble in unheated halls to hear a Tchaikovsky concert performed by an orchestra, depleted by sickness and death, whose players would be wearing woollen gloves with just the finger-tips cut out. Shostakovich, evacuated to Kuibyshev, completed his Seventh Symphony and dedicated it to the city of his birth; it was in Kuibyshev in March 1942 that his 'Leningrad' Symphony, played by the evacuated Bolshoi orchestra, received its first performance. In August, this searing composition was performed inside the besieged city itself, the work and the event jointly providing a potent symbol to all who were present of their current struggle and their shared belief in ultimate victory. The 'Leningrad' Symphony has survived the test of time, comparable in its moving evocation of the period in which it was created with Goya's *Disasters of War* or Picasso's *Guernica*. However, the horror and privation of war rarely produce such emblematic masterpieces. No opera was composed or produced during the siege of Leningrad. How could it be? A number of patriotic operas were produced in Moscow once the tide of war had begun to turn. But none (except perhaps Prokofiev's *War and Peace*, left with no definitive version when Prokofiev died in 1953, on the same day as Stalin, and which did not have its premiere until many years later) speaks to audiences today.

*

In the early years of the war, opera became something of a political priority in Nazi Germany, performers receiving exemption from military service and many opera companies continuing to receive official funding and audiences subsidized tickets. To Hitler, it was a matter of pride and importance that, even in time of war, music – *German* music – should be performed throughout the Reich to the highest standards and made available to the widest possible audiences. It is true that many of its outstanding composers and performers fled the Reich, or were imprisoned and even killed by it. Yet, at first, musical standards remained high, especially in Berlin with Furtwängler at the helm of the Berlin Philharmonic and his young rival Karajan at the Staatsoper across town at the Linden. In Vienna, too, operatic standards remained high during the first few years of the war. Marcel Prawy, historian of the Vienna State Opera, was one who escaped the clutches of Nazism, spending much of the war in America. Yet he acknowledges that many of Vienna's top singers were at the zenith of their careers at that time, adding (with the relevant names) that the company had on its books 'two first-class Brünnhildes permanently available, four Hans Sachses and four Siegfrieds', while regular conductors included three of the finest: Furtwängler, Krauss and Knappertsbusch.

In Bayreuth, Winifred Wagner had expected the Festival to be in abeyance for the duration of the war (as it had been during the First World War). But the Führer had other ideas. In April 1940, buoyed by a succession of military victories, he insisted that year's Festival should go ahead. Winifred protested that time and money (not to mention artistic resources) were too short. Nonsense, responded her resourceful friend the Chancellor. He would arrange that the Nazi 'Strength through Joy' movement would guarantee sale of the tickets and bring Germany's worthiest to drink at the inspirational fountain of Wagner. That summer, hordes of bewildered soldiers on leave, workers from Germany's munitions factories and uniformed nurses arrived in Bayreuth on special trains to be greeted as 'Guests of the Führer'. There was little time to enjoy Bayreuth's beer halls or the beauties of the Franconian countryside as the 'guests' were herded into lecture halls, educated on the subtleties of The Master and taken to the Festspielhaus for an uplifting five hours of *Walküre* or *Götterdämmerung*. Brigitte Hamann, Winifred Wagner's biographer, is doubtless correct when she remarks that they 'joined the ranks of those who swore they never wanted to attend a Wagner performance again'. But I doubt whether anyone reported this to Hitler.

Opera was not only a valued political resource at home. As one European nation after another fell before the Nazi onslaught, the shock of defeat was often followed by the prompt visit of a German opera company: presumably an attempt to soften the impact of occupation by impressing the local population with the high cultural standards of its conqueror. In 1940, the Hamburg opera appeared in Oslo and the Frankfurt opera in Belgrade. Paris during the years

Berlin's State Opera House on Unter den Linden, photographed in July 1945. Once Frederick the Great's opera house, the Staatsoper was bombed in April 1941, rebuilt on Hitler's orders, and reduced to a shell by bombing once again in February 1945.

of occupation had visits from a string of top German opera companies, including one in 1941 from the Berlin Staatsoper, led by Karajan, which Winifred Wagner was invited to accompany.

As the tide of war turned against the Axis, even Hitler had to turn his attention away from his beloved opera. Allied bombing expeditions broke through German defences and destroyed or severely damaged many of Germany's leading opera houses. As early as April 1941, Berlin's Linden opera was bombed; Hitler ordered it rebuilt (it was during this rebuilding that the company visited Paris). By 1943, Allied raids on Germany had become more frequent and more formidable. In August, the Hamburg opera house was destroyed, in October firebombs rained down upon Munich's National Theatre and in November it was the turn of Berlin's Deutsches Opernhaus in Charlottenburg, once the home house of Bruno Walter and Carl Ebert. Some opera companies continued to perform in local churches, cinemas, school halls and the like. But by summer 1944, as Hitler survived an assassination attempt and with Germany facing the growing possibility of military defeat, the Reich entered a phase of 'total war'. Henceforth, all activities that did not contribute directly to the war effort were abandoned. Young men such as the future singer Dietrich Fischer-Dieskau and conductor Kurt Masur were drafted into the army while, among Germany's budding operatic sopranos, Gertrud Grob-Prandl checked gas masks and Martha Mödl made hand grenades in a munitions factory.

The final defeat of the 'Thousand Year Reich' was brutal, and total. As Russian troops from the East and Allied forces from the West converged to fraternize on the banks of the Elbe, entire populations in German towns and villages were mown down by vengeful Soviet troops or dispatched to agonizing deaths by Allied bombardment. In early February 1945, Berlin's expensively rebuilt Staatsoper on Unter den Linden, a short walk from some of the Reich's most important governmental buildings, was once again reduced to rubble. A fortnight later, much of Dresden and thousands of its citizens were firebombed, the city's baroque centre and its opera house designed by Gottfried Semper ('the most beautiful theatre ever built', one prima donna called it) destroyed. On 12 March 1945 ('12-3-45'), seven years to the day after the *Anschluss*, the Vienna State opera house, once the proud home of Mahler's Hofoper, took a direct hit. Staff joked that when the final Allied assault on Vienna came at least they could defend themselves with every kind of armament known to man: medieval cannonry, Tudor halberds, the swords of Spanish grandees, Wagnerian spears and helmets and the rest. Useless, said one realist; the only operatic prop that would be of any practical value was probably the Mexican saddle on which the soprano Maria Jeritza used to gallop away in Puccini's *La fanciulla del West*. In April, days before the official end of the war, Bayreuth was bombed, leaving many dead and Villa Wahnfried severely damaged. The Festival Theatre itself was untouched. A few weeks later, an opera-loving American soldier called Joseph Wechsberg, who was part of the occupying force, drove up through bomb-flattened Nuremberg to Bayreuth and went to have a look at Wagner's Festspielhaus:

> The sets for the second Act of *Die Meistersinger* were still on stage, the lovely vision of medieval Nuremberg. The janitor said it was in the middle of the last performance that they had come – and he pointed his forefinger significantly toward the sky.

Wechsberg, fulfilling a lifelong ambition, climbed onto the stage. 'Wahn, Wahn,' he sang: Hans Sachs's great monologue from this very scene. 'Madness, madness…'

And Winifred Wagner's friend 'Wolf'? It is presumed that the conflagration that engulfed his bunker, and with it his body and that of Eva Braun, also destroyed his most valued possessions: his priceless cache of Wagner scores.

*

The death and destruction visited upon wartime Italy were not on the epic scale experienced in Central and Eastern Europe but were none the less traumatic for those involved. Here, as everywhere perhaps, most people were probably less concerned with the ideologies that underlay the war than with how they and their families might find enough to eat and drink and avoid being killed. This became appreciably harder from mid-1943, when Italy itself became a battlefield. The Allies, fresh from victory in North Africa, began forcing their way up the peninsula, a painful process that brought much destruction in its wake. As they advanced, Mussolini was replaced by Badoglio, who secretly began to negotiate armistice terms. In Florence, Titta Ruffo was so elated at the news of Mussolini's fall that he rushed to the window and, with what remained of that giant voice of his, belted out the 'Marseillaise'. A crowd soon gathered outside and joined in. But it was a long time before genuine peace prevailed. The Germans remained a powerful and menacing presence. When they occupied Florence later that summer, Ruffo had to go into hiding. Rome, nominally an 'Open City', continued to be patrolled by German forces while in the north the Germans set up a puppet government and settled in for a protracted fight. An early victim was La Scala, Milan, Italy's premier opera house, bombed in an Allied raid on 16 August. Some time later, a raid on Florence killed the soprano Lina Cavalieri, a dreadful end for a woman who, forty years earlier, had been a star with Caruso at the New York Met and feted for her exceptional beauty.

A man was shot in the square outside Tito Gobbi's home in Rome. Gobbi was one of the lucky ones. A promising young baritone, he was a member of the Rome opera company which had visited Berlin in April 1941 on a cultural exchange programme promoted under the aegis of the Rome–Berlin Axis. Everyone and everything went: singers, chorus, orchestra, scenery, costumes and technical staff. Among Gobbi's loot on his return to Italy was an autographed photograph of Goebbels, whom he had encountered at an official reception. Later, during the dangerous period between the Allied landings and their final arrival in Rome, Gobbi was able to use that photo as a way of putting off the Germans when he was helping to hide a couple of Allied prisoners on the run. If he had been found out he too would have been shot.

Gobbi has left a vivid picture of the dangers and privations in Rome during that anxious transitional period. Water had to be fetched in jars and drums from public fountains. Any minor luxuries, such as milk, tended to be commandeered by the omnipresent Germans. They were everywhere, keeping a grim eye on the cowed population. Gobbi recalls the dread cry 'i tedeschi, i tedeschi'; if you heard this while walking in the streets of Rome, you took to your heels and ran the other way for it signified the proximity of German troops, armed with machine guns, seeking young men to arrest and dispatch to the Reich as forced labour. On one occasion, Gobbi saw Germans approaching and had no chance of escape. So he resolutely turned up the collar of the military-looking overcoat he was wearing and marched boldly past them with a 'Heil Hitler' salute. His acting skills probably saved his life. On another occasion, Gobbi was invited (read 'ordered') to give a performance in Sorrento. He had heard that the theatre there had been destroyed. Never mind. He had to go there anyway. That meant a journey from Rome to Naples followed by a drive around the Sorrento peninsula. Idyllic to you and me, perhaps. But in wartime Italy it proved a near-fatal nightmare journey, dodging bombing raids, across a series of battle zones. In Naples, Gobbi stumbled past collapsing buildings as the air rang with the cries of buried people; in the harbour, he saw a ship take a direct hit and body parts fly past him through the air. After commandeering a series of precarious rides on carts and lorries around the peninsula, Gobbi finally reached Sorrento only to discover, as he had suspected, that there was indeed no theatre and no question of a performance; so he had to retrace his steps and was close to collapse from hunger, thirst and fatigue when he finally reached Rome.

Gobbi's experience was not uncommon. While some Italians continued to cling to Fascist beliefs and collaborate with the occupying Germans, others – like Gobbi – committed minor acts of undoubted heroism. And some (like those featured in Rossellini's 1945 film *Rome: Open City*) risked torture and death by joining the Resistance. Among musicians, it is probably true to say that most, whatever their political opinions, were primarily concerned to utilize their skills to obtain their daily bread. If that meant singing to Goebbels, so be it. You could hardly refuse. Gigli, at that time a far more established and celebrated singer than Gobbi, performed many times for both the Italian and German political hierarchy. He and Gobbi sang together in Rome in 1943–4. One performance of *Tosca* was specially mounted for members of the *Wehrmacht*. Afterwards, the principals were asked to submit to radio interviews. Gigli pleaded sickness and the soprano (Caniglia) slipped away under a thick shawl pretending to be a cleaning woman. That left Gobbi, who describes how he was led, with a machine gun at his back, to a microphone that had been rigged up in a backstage corridor.

It is hard to resist the impression that Gigli was a more enthusiastic collaborator, though perhaps out of naivety rather than political conviction. His memoirs tell of performances before the Nazi leaders and of how he met Hitler on a number of occasions. Hitler 'shook my hand and told me he liked Italian music very much', we read. Another time, Hitler 'applauded tirelessly, and at the final curtain he sent enormous bouquets, tied with the national colours of Germany and Italy'. How charming. Gigli's various encounters with Hitler were brief and formal, he tells us, and the two 'never had occasion to exchange more than a few polite words'. But does he protest too much when he assures us that 'I knew nothing about his political activities'? Some of his compatriots evidently thought so. When Allied troops finally entered Rome in June 1944, Gigli was in for a shock:

Having 'sung for the Germans', I now discovered, to my astonishment, that I was a traitor. The accusation did not come from the
Allies, but from my own countrymen. Threatening crowds besieged
my house in Rome; for months I did not dare to leave it.

Of course he had 'sung for the Germans', Gigli told the officer who came to
investigate him. 'I sang for everyone. I sang for the English and for the
Americans. I sang under the Fascist government, as I would have sung under
the Bolsheviks or anyone else who happened to be ruling Italy.'

Gigli's case did not detain the authorities for long. He was a great singer
with little political sophistication and no malice. Before long, he was back on
the international circuit, memorably giving a series of concert recitals across
Britain and America in the late 1940s and early 1950s, most famously, to
capacity audiences in London's vast Royal Albert Hall where I heard him a
number of times and became utterly enthralled with his incomparably beautiful voice and, through him, with opera.

Most leading Italian musicians, whatever their political views, composed, played or sang at the behest of the Italian political hierarchy if and
when required to do so. Some, including famous opera composers such as
Mascagni, Cilea and Giordano, received awards for their efforts. Many were
sent to appear on behalf of their country in the Third Reich: not only Gobbi
and Gigli, but other top performers such as the conductors Victor De Sabata

Gigli sang for Hitler (pictured) and Mussolini. After the war, however, the tenor soon won
back the hearts of his former enemies, undertaking a succession of exhaustive concert tours
across Europe and the Americas.

(who was part Jewish) and Vittorio Gui. Not all were comfortable with their role. Gobbi clearly was not. The composer Luigi Dallapiccola, whose wife was Jewish, lived in semi-obscurity on the outskirts of Nazi-occupied Florence while working on what was to become his masterpiece, the opera *Il prigioniero* (*The Prisoner*), a powerful plea for freedom. But few made – or dared make – overt protest. Toscanini and Titta Ruffo were in this regard exceptions, as were those (including Bruno Maderna, later a leading figure in the Italian avant-garde) who joined the Partisans.

*

In Italy, cultural collaboration with the Fascist government or German occupiers was often a more or less pragmatic affair, quickly forgiven and even forgotten by most after the war. In the Third Reich, things were different. The Nazi authorities were far more ruthless and thorough in their demands; opponents could hardly dither or hope to keep their heads low, as was possible – with a modicum of luck – in Italy. Dallapiccola or Ruffo may have gone into hiding in German-occupied Florence, but if they had resorted to similar tactics in Stuttgart or Magdeburg they would very likely have been smoked out and dispatched to a labour camp. In the Reich, especially once war had broken out, the pressures to conform to official norms were far stronger than in Italy. As a result, passive or involuntary collaboration was widespread. You marched off to war, or performed in the opera house or concert hall, because you were paid to do so by a regime that would punish you severely if you did not.

Some collaborated more actively. As we have seen, Strauss stepped into the shoes of conductors who had been forced to abandon scheduled performances, and agreed to become president of the *Reichsmusikkammer*. Heinz Tietjen spent the Nazi years, like the rest of his long professional life, adjusting to whichever political wind currently blew strongest, while Winifred Wagner retained her friendship with Hitler, making use of it as best she could in the service of what she saw as her primary task, the maintenance of Bayreuth. Furtwängler was in charge of both the Berlin Philharmonic Orchestra and the Berlin Staatsoper in the first year of the Reich and, as such, an employee of the government, and was also Strauss's vice-president at the *RMK*. When Furtwängler resigned his posts, the directorship of the Staatsoper was handed (on Hitler's express wishes, it was said) to Clemens Krauss, while other prominent conductors in Nazi Berlin included Knappertsbusch and, in due course, the most famous 'K' of them all: Furtwängler's nemesis, Herbert von Karajan. Meanwhile, a number of leading singers made their early reputations under Nazism, notably Elisabeth Schwarzkopf.

Were these and similar figures 'Nazis', to be condemned as such by their post-war contemporaries and by subsequent history? The answer is complex and varies from case to case. Knappertsbusch remained in the Reich but was critical of the Nazis and refused to join the party. Prawy recounts an incident when a broadcast of a Hitler speech interrupted a rehearsal and 'Kna' ostentatiously threw an ashtray at the loudspeaker by way of protest. A more obvious model of the Nazi-era conductor was Clemens Krauss ('it's difficult to compete with features as Aryan as his,' wrote Alban Berg in the late 1920s). When in 1933 Fritz Busch had to pull out of the world premiere in Dresden of Strauss's *Arabella*, of which Busch was a dedicatee, the production went ahead under Krauss, a conductor more amenable to the new regime. Later, after his stint at the Berlin Opera, Krauss moved to the Munich Nationaltheater and then the post-*Anschluss* Vienna Philharmonic. Krauss was banned from appearing in public for a couple of years after the war because of his allegedly pro-Nazi activities. Yet he and his wife, the singer Viorica Ursuleac, were also found to have given covert help to Jews and others escaping from the Reich, in part through the ministrations of a couple of opera-loving English sisters, Ida and Louise Cook. In a moving (if perhaps idealized) account, Ida tells how she and Louise repeatedly visited Germany, initially to 'follow their stars' but increasingly on rescue missions, and how Krauss went so far as to adjust performance dates in order to give the girls a legitimate alibi for their surreptitious activities.

To many, the Hitler regime represented a new start, a government that, unlike its Weimar predecessor, was actively interested in promoting the arts, particularly music, and was headed by a charismatic leader who actually knew and cared about opera. Of course, the Reich represented a ferocious threat to anyone of Jewish origins. But if you were a pretty young blonde 'Aryan' with bags of talent and a capacity for hard work such as Schwarzkopf, the regime offered genuine attractions and opportunities. Schwarzkopf's teacher, Maria Ivogün, was a well-known prima donna of an earlier era and, like many others, an enthusiast for the Nazis. Once launched on her career, during the war, Schwarzkopf sang with the Deutsche (Charlottenburg) Oper, formerly the home house of Bruno Walter and by then under the control of the libidinous Goebbels. And when she fell ill with tuberculosis, Schwarzkopf was (it is said) cared for by a lover who was an SS officer and a doctor. Various dark rumours circulated later about Schwarzkopf's supposed over-compliance with senior Nazi figures. She went on to become one of the leading singers of the post-war world, feted everywhere for the beauty and precision of her artistry. But she always refused to speak publicly about her early years.

Karajan, too, did not much like to talk about the political aspects of his early career. However, because of his youthful prominence his personal history is more easily researched. In 1935, the year he was appointed general music director of the Aachen Opera, the 27-year-old conductor applied to join the Nazi party. Three years later, hailed in the Berlin press as 'Das Wunder Karajan', he was actively wooed by the Staatsoper. After the war, Karajan explained coolly to those investigating his case that joining the party was a logical professional step at the time and of no great political significance;

it was just one of the things you did in the Third Reich if you wanted to get ahead, he said, making it sound rather like the way musicians in the USSR joined the Communist Party. As for the date Karajan was admitted to membership of the party or his card number, these details he claimed to have forgotten. Far from being a party activist or ideologue, said Karajan, he was not in favour with the Nazi regime. Hitler took a personal aversion to him[*] and his professional advance was held back further after 1942, he said, when he married a woman who was one-quarter Jewish.

At the other end of the age range was Richard Strauss, nearly seventy when the Nazis came to power. For all his incomparable gift for rich post-romantic musical composition, Strauss was an urbane professional, primarily concerned with the practicalities of the music business and not at all with politics. What he wanted was to compose music and get it performed, preferably as often and as lucratively as possible, and if that required occasional bowings and scrapings to whomever happened to be in power at the time, so be it. Strauss had a Jewish publisher (Ernst Roth at Universal Edition), a Jewish daughter-in-law and a part-Jewish librettist, Hugo von Hofmannsthal, who died in 1929. When the Nazis came to power, Strauss, Germany's most internationally famous composer, allowed himself to be flattered into the trophy post of the Reich's official top musician. Yet, with a degree of insouciance that verged on the reckless, he continued to work on a new opera with another non-Aryan librettist, his friend Stefan Zweig, a misdemeanour which he got away with but which cost him his presidency of the *Reichsmusik-kammer*. Strauss was not the kind of principled figure who was prepared to stand up to the Nazis. They in their turn were shrewd enough to know the value of his celebrity status and never placed him or his family under serious threat (though his son and daughter-in-law were briefly imprisoned by the Nazis and then kept under house arrest in the last year of the war). So the old man stayed, suffered a bit and carried on writing music as best he could. In the final weeks of the war, Strauss wrote a deeply felt threnody for strings called *Metamorphosen*: an elegy for the destruction of – what? Humanity? Germany? The Reich, that had once promised much but had degenerated into the depths of barbarism? The Munich opera house? Perhaps a little of everything. When American troops arrived at the end of the war, they commandeered villas for their use, giving the residents fifteen minutes to get out. In Garmisch, one US officer was confronted by an elderly gentleman who told him: 'I am Richard Strauss, the composer of *Rosenkavalier* and *Salome*.' Immediately, the officer told his men that this particular villa was off limits.

Of all the top musicians who continued to work within the constraints imposed by the Nazi regime, the one most prominently in the public eye was Furtwängler. Like Strauss, Furtwängler was something of a political innocent.

---

[*] In 1939, Karajan conducted a gala performance of *Meistersinger* without a score in the presence of Hitler, losing his way at one point and incurring the Führer's disapproval.

The conductor Wilhelm Furtwängler in 1939, avoiding the Hitler salute by offering to shake the Führer's hand: a conscientious German musician who struggled (in vain) to put art above politics.

Unlike Strauss, he frequently expressed a deeply romantic belief in the spiritual value of art, particularly music. When the new Nazi government requested him to conduct a gala performance of *Die Meistersinger* to mark the official inauguration of their regime, Furtwängler gave it his all (despite an incipient attack of flu): not for the Nazis, but for Wagner. In the face of Nazi opposition, Furtwängler refused for as long as he could to dispense with the services of Jewish members of his orchestra or of Berta Geissmar, his secretary-cum-assistant, who also happened to be Jewish. The function of art and artists, he wrote in a letter to Goebbels in April 1933, was to unite not to divide; the only meaningful dividing line as far as he was concerned was that which separates good art from bad. Our fight, concluded Furtwängler, should be against the rootless, subversive destructive spirits, not against the real artist. Goebbels sent a carefully worded reply that, on the face of it, looked conciliatory: Furtwängler, like Strauss, was the kind of international celebrity whose good-will the Reich could ill afford to lose. A little later, Furtwängler invited a number of foreign artists, all of them Jewish and/or known to be critics of the Nazis, to perform with the Berlin Philharmonic. One by one, and with deep regret, they turned him down; they admired the stand he was taking, but knew their presence in Berlin would be construed by the Reich as a sign of recognition.

A decisive moment came in 1934 when the Nazis forbade Furtwängler to schedule a new opera by Paul Hindemith, *Mathis der Maler*, a work about the German Renaissance painter Matthias Grünewald. Hindemith was not Jewish. But he was a greatly admired leader of the younger generation of German composers, something of an *avant-gardiste*. For whatever reason, he was anathema to Hitler. To Furtwängler, the director of the Berlin State Opera, a political order such as this undermined his entire authority. It was (wrote Berta Geissmar later) 'as if Mr Churchill suddenly sent a message to Covent Garden telling Sir Thomas Beecham what to do'. In November, Furtwängler boldly published his views about the Hindemith case in a leading newspaper. That day, prolonged, ecstatic applause greeted his appearance at a morning rehearsal for a Berlin concert and, in the evening, at a performance of *Tristan* he conducted at the Staatsoper at which both Göring and Goebbels were present. The man who believed in art had become a principal focus of politics. In December, Furtwängler resigned from his official posts.

In her memoir, Geissmar writes movingly about the mutual respect and affection that existed between Furtwängler and herself. At one point, Furtwängler was announced as Toscanini's successor as director of the New York Philharmonic. However, a (false) press story that he was also to be reinstated to run the Berlin State Opera turned New York opinion against him and the offer was withdrawn. In the end, he remained in the Reich throughout most of the Nazi period. Geissmar, on the other hand, needed to get out, which she managed to do, with Furtwängler's help. She settled in London, working for Beecham, who was the epitome of generosity and kindness. Beecham, she wrote, was like a 'pasha'; to him, 'our Nazi calamities and catastrophes seemed to be a permanent source of amusement'. When Beecham and his recently formed orchestra, the London Philharmonic, were invited to tour Germany in 1936, the conductor insisted she go out ahead to organize details and then join him and the band. With some trepidation, Geissmar set out, had a warm reunion with her former boss, found herself working at one point in her old office at the Berlin Philharmonie, and as an honoured guest at Bayreuth only just managed to avoid meeting Hitler. In the heart of the Reich, the Nazis were forced to proffer their greatest respects to the Jewish Dr Geissmar – or risk losing a highly publicized visit from Britain's most famous (and media-savvy) conductor. The tour went ahead and Hitler himself attended an LPO concert in Berlin which was broadcast. When the Führer was seen to applaud the first item, Beecham said audibly to his players: 'The old bloke seems to like it!' His remark was heard everywhere the concert was relayed and was reported the next day in the British press. But the Nazi press published something even more interesting. During the concert interval, Beecham had received courtesy calls in his dressing room from Furtwängler and others. But a doctored photo appeared in the German papers the next day showing Beecham during the interval visiting Hitler and Goebbels in their VIP box.

Furtwängler, meanwhile, had reached a *modus vivendi* with the Nazi regime and he continued to conduct in Germany and Austria during the war. Never comfortable, Furtwängler accepted no official position from the regime (and never gave the Nazi salute). In January 1945, he fled Germany for exile in Switzerland, possibly saving his life by doing so. At his de-Nazification hearings, Furtwängler told his interrogators that he had felt responsible for maintaining the German musical tradition during the Nazi period. Under a government obsessed with terror and war, he said, he had felt it more important than ever that people should be able to hear Beethoven and his message of freedom and love. After the hearings, Furtwängler was given a clean bill of health and conducted again in Berlin, Bayreuth and Salzburg as well as abroad. But not in the USA, where the 'Furtwängler case' rumbled on in people's minds and in the press and the conductor remained *persona non grata*.

*

A musician who was offered work by the Reich was one of the lucky ones. Many others, regarded as racially or ideologically opposed to Nazism, were herded off to concentration camps. Later, as the camps were liberated, one of the remarkable discoveries was how often inmates had struggled to express their deepest thoughts through art: scratching a portrait or a poem on a wall or a smuggled scrap of paper or twisting pieces of metal into expressive statements of private protest. Or making music. Most often, this simply took the form of singing, often of traditional Yiddish songs, sometimes even protest songs (sung *pianissississimo*, of course, for fear of detection). There was art music in the camps, too: inmates in Dachau performed clandestine classical concerts in a disused latrine, while in Sachsenhausen a chorus was formed and in Buchenwald, remarkably, a string quartet.

Often, music was used by the Nazi authorities for their own entertainment, and also as a cynical tool with which to humiliate their doomed captives. It has been a matter of some wonderment to scholars that camp commanders could spend their days organizing mass murder and their evenings enjoying the supposedly uplifting, civilizing force of great music. Nowhere has humanity stooped lower than in the Nazi camps where enslaved musicians were forced to entertain the very people who planned to kill them.

Theresienstadt (Terezín in Czech) lies thirty miles north of Prague and was primarily used by the Nazis as a transit point in which to collect people for later removal to death camps. But it was also turned into something of a showcase, a 'respectable' prison camp to which they felt they could safely invite outside inspection and show their visitors preselected inmates who, far from planning escape or revolt, were healthy and happy enough to play music and give concerts. Here, the composer Viktor Ullmann wrote songs and piano pieces and drafted a chamber opera, *The Emperor of Atlantis* (a harshly satirical piece about a brutal king who forces humanity into such an orgy of senseless slaughter that Death goes on strike). When the Red Cross visited Terezín in 1944, they were given a performance of the children's opera *Brundibár* by the respected Czech composer (and Terezín inmate) Hans Krása, a work that had been premiered in the camp the year before. Thus, the Nazis used Terezín as a cover for their misdeeds, a cynical insurance policy calculated to soften subsequent accusations should their murderous activities elsewhere ever be revealed. Terezín was in fact a Potemkin village, a thin façade concealing little of substance. Most of its inmates did not have the quasi-privileged existence of its musicians. It has been calculated that of the 140,000 people incarcerated in Terezín, some 33,000 died from starvation, lack of medical care, disease and torture, and of the 87,000 transported to the death camps scarcely 5 per cent survived. Among those sent to Auschwitz and murdered there were Hans Krása and Viktor Ullmann.

Even in Auschwitz there was music. Today, the site is a profoundly moving museum and memorial. Visitors to Auschwitz–Birkenau start their tour by

In Auschwitz, an orchestra of emaciated inmates would serenade fellow prisoners as they were marched out to work each morning and, dropping with exhaustion, back again ten or more hours later.

walking through the notorious entry gates, marked *Arbeit Macht Frei* ('Work Sets You Free'). Here, newly arrived prisoners, herded into the camp in which most would later die, were greeted by orchestral music played by other prisoners. Those among the inmates deemed capable of work would be entertained with further serenades by their emaciated fellows each morning as they were marched out through these gates and, dropping with exhaustion, back again ten or more hours later. Music, for most of those incarcerated in the Nazi concentration camps, could scarcely be more than a memory, a consolation, a tacit point of contact with equally doleful fellow prisoners. For a tiny, lucky handful, it proved a lifeline. One of the players by the Auschwitz gateway each morning and evening was Anita Lasker. When she arrived, it seems the camp's Women's Orchestra lacked a cellist and Anita happened to fit the bill. Anita's cello saved her life.

PART V

The Globalization of Opera
*c.*1945–

CHAPTER 19

Emerging from Apocalypse

As the war approached its end and aftermath, one of the ways in which civilization began to reassert itself was through music. In Leningrad after the siege was finally lifted, many survivors were reduced to living almost like animals, sleeping in dugouts, close to starvation, emotionally desperate. Galina Vishnevskaya, a teenager at the time, remembered seeing a line of German prisoners of war being marched along Nevsky Prospekt; they had to be protected by Russian troops from possible lynching. Yet for all this, people 'literally rose from the dead to reach out for art'. Music theatre poked its head up through the concrete, sniffed the air and, almost miraculously, began to function once more. Vishnevskaya joined a small travelling operetta company, rushed into a marriage (her second) with its director, became pregnant and – squeezing herself into an ever tighter corset – sang and danced throughout that final winter and spring of war 'through the cinders of Russia'. The troupe journeyed as far afield as Murmansk, where the hotel room was overrun by rats. Just after the war was over they toured East Prussia, too, bizarrely sharing their train compartment to Königsberg (later Kaliningrad) with released German prisoners of war being dispatched homewards; when they arrived, they found a dead, flattened city with corpses rotting in the rubble. Here, as everywhere, Galina and her colleagues encountered dreadful performing conditions. There were no washrooms anywhere on these tours, no toilets; just the sub-zero streets. At night, you simply huddled together in whatever shared accommodation was available. When sickness and infection afflicted the troupe, there was no question of cancelling a performance: everyone depended on everyone else. Shoulders bare, Galina and her colleagues shivered their way through some twenty-five performances a month in one bitterly cold hall after another to war-weary soldiers and sailors hunched in their overcoats and caps. It was a penance for performers and audience alike. Yet, somehow, those on both sides of the curtain were determined the show should go on.

*

A broadly similar pattern developed across much of Central and Eastern Europe. Everywhere, people were desperate to put the war behind them, to return to a semblance of peacetime normality. In Vienna, perhaps more than anywhere else, that meant opera, something for which a large Viennese public and many of the city's musicians shared something like the craving of an addict for a hard drug. Conditions in Vienna were not as primitive as in Leningrad, but the city and its population had been deeply scarred by the war. Tens of thousands of Viennese had been killed. For the survivors, housing was hopelessly inadequate, food supplies irregular, electric power spasmodic, communications primitive and public transport almost non-existent. Whole neighbourhoods of Vienna were reduced to rubble and the city was occupied by, and divided between, Austria's recent enemies. This was the city so vividly portrayed in Carol Reed's film *The Third Man*: a once proud imperial capital that, less than thirty years after the fall of the Habsburgs and a mere seven since Austria was joined to Hitler's Reich, was reduced to a sideshow, an impoverished no-man's land lying impotent on the new political frontier. As for opera, the great house on the Ring was a bomb-damaged shell, many of its sets and costumes destroyed, some of its finest performers discredited. Yet Vienna was to witness an operatic resurrection of such vibrancy that misty-eyed opera lovers would reminisce about it for decades to come.

It began at the Volksoper, a middle-sized, unadorned theatre on the city's outer belt or *Gürtel*. The Volksoper had been opened in 1898 to mark the fiftieth anniversary of the accession of Emperor Franz Joseph. It had none of the glamour of the city's State Opera house. What it did have, however, was the all-important virtue of being intact and of having a store of serviceable props and costumes. In normal times, the Volksoper's principal drawing power lay in its stagings of popular operettas by composers such as Johann Strauss, Kálmán and Lehár. But these were not normal times, and from the moment the war ended the Volksoper provided a temporary home for Vienna's premier opera company, the State Opera. Keen to fanfare their return to business as usual, they opened on 1 May with Mozart's *Figaro*, a universally loved piece that had been created in this very city. A superb cast was conducted by Josef Krips, a musician of partly Jewish descent who was warmly welcomed back to Vienna after spending recent years in exile. It seems the Volksoper pulled out all the stops for this production. Or at least all the shiniest props in its store cupboard. Prawy tells how the occupying Russian forces had an eye for gold and, somehow, 'after each interval the scene opened on a few less gilt chairs or golden curtains.' The management seems to have reflected that a student garret would prove more cost-effective on stage than a nobleman's castle, so the next production was *La Bohème*. Sena Jurinac, who had been the Cherubino in *Figaro*, sang Mimì in *Bohème* to the Musetta of Irmgard Seefried; both were in their early to mid-twenties and destined for international celebrity.

On 12 March 1945, the Vienna State Opera took a direct hit in an Allied bombing raid. Staff joked grimly that when the final assault on Vienna came they could defend themselves with medieval cannonry, Tudor halberds, the swords of Spanish grandees and Wagnerian spears and helmets.

Opera was back, it was magnificent, and people poured in to see it, including many music lovers from among the occupying forces. The Volksoper could not accommodate the large potential audience for opera in Vienna and a second theatre was soon called into service. The Theater an der Wien, once Schikaneder's home house, lies just south of the Ring alongside the little river that shares the name of the city. Today, this part of Vienna is dominated by a huge, multicultural open market. But to many opera-starved Viennese in autumn 1945, the principal magnet was the old theatre. It was dilapidated, had not seen a performance since 1939 and was used during the war to store military equipment. When the opera management first visited, the only person to greet them was an old woman caretaker who was growing mushrooms on the stage. Before the theatre could be opened to the public, it clearly needed drastic renovation, some of it carried out by members of the opera chorus who were put to work as emergency carpenters and decorators. When the electricity current failed, the company's director got the authorities to link the theatre directly to the cable that brought heat and light to the occupying forces. Finally, on 6 October 1945, they opened with a work that had had its world premiere in this very theatre: Beethoven's *Fidelio*, that incomparable hymn to freedom.

Over the next few years, the Vienna State Opera company performed at both theatres, developing an ensemble style, initially under the inspiration of Krips, that came to be admired throughout the operatic world. In 1947, the company went on highly successful tours, first to Nice and Paris and then in the autumn to London's Covent Garden. The American opera lover Vincent Sheean was in Vienna towards the end of 1947 and attended a number of performances. At one, a high-octane *Boris* at the Theater an der Wien, the Russians made amends for any earlier kleptomania by flying in – directly from the Kremlin, says Sheean – a quantity of magnificent clothing, gold brocades and heavy museum jewellery in order to add a touch of authentic splendour to the rickety old stage. One evening, Sheean attended a party organized by an American officer concerned with the revival of Austrian culture. Here, he met many of the artists from the opera and found them 'happy as grigs'. There was a great deal of American food and drink at the party, which may have helped. But Sheean sensed they would probably have been just as merry on water. For they knew that 'there was something… heroic being demanded of them just then… and it made them feel rather splendid that they were able to deliver the goods.' Some of the singers Sheean talked to were performing twice a week at each of the two theatres, with rehearsals between performances at one or the other (and sometimes at the Redoutensaal). He expected them to complain about the sheer physical strain of their existence in this cold, damp, severely malfunctioning city. But no. These 'opera lunatics', concluded Sheean, 'seemed to thrive on poor rations.' It was as though 'the severe material limitations of life threw them more utterly than ever into the pursuit of their art – they worked harder, so to speak, because there was literally nothing else to do, and since the ordinary satisfactions were brutally restricted, the satisfaction of making music had to take the place of almost everything else.' It seemed something of old Habsburg Vienna lived on after all.

Indeed, the operatic lights began to twinkle once again throughout much of the old Habsburg empire. In Hungary, there had been no opera to speak of in the latter part of the war as the Horthy regime was replaced by the Nazis and Budapest prepared for the inevitable onslaught by the Russians. When it came, the old castle area high above the Danube was torn apart by ferocious fighting as the Nazis tried in vain to hold out against the Soviets. However, the Pest side of the river remained relatively undamaged and the opera was soon reopened under Soviet auspices. Prague was luckier, at least in the sense that the city was spared serious physical damage. During the Nazi occupation, old German names and forms were reintroduced. Thus, the venerable Estates Theatre was attached to the Neues Deutsches Theater as the Ständetheater. After the war it was renamed once again: not the Estates but the Tyl Theatre after the nineteenth-century playwright, a nominal reassertion of its Czech legacy.

Of all the major opera houses to have been destroyed or seriously damaged by wartime bombing, one of the first to reopen was Milan's La Scala; the emotion of the occasion, a gala concert on 11 May 1946 conducted by the 78-year-old Toscanini, was intensified by the fact that it marked the Maestro's first appearance in Italy since he had fled from Fascism. In Naples, meanwhile, the San Carlo was lovingly brought back from the near dead by an opera-loving officer in the British army of occupation, his work now memorialized by a plaque in the foyer.

In the cities of Germany, as in Vienna, the destruction of the main theatre often led to the temporary commandeering of another. In Munich, they performed opera in that Bayreuth lookalike the Prinzregententheater, in Frankfurt in the Börsensaal, once the hall of the corn exchange. It was a similar story in Dresden, Nuremberg and across much of the former Reich. In Berlin, the old Charlottenburg company moved into the Theater des Westens where – as in Vienna's Theater an der Wien and many another theatre in the German world – they celebrated their return with *Fidelio*. The Staatsoper, meanwhile, performed in the Admiralspalast, later reborn as the Metropole Theatre, while the old Metropole was renovated to become the new Komische Oper, a self-consciously radical re-embodiment of Klemperer's Kroll. By the end of 1947, Berlin, a city almost flattened by heavy bombing a couple of years earlier, boasted three functioning opera companies, one in the western zone and two in the eastern, all of which survive today.

All this was remarkable enough. But it would have required a prophet of exceptional clairvoyance to have foreseen that post-war geopolitics would help turn Britain, for a while at least, into arguably the opera centre of the world.

*

Britain's operatic supremacy had been a long time coming. During the course of this narrative, we have encountered a succession of courageous (or foolhardy) men who have put money and effort into providing opera: partly because they love it, and in some cases (and this has almost always proved foolhardy) because they thought they might make a profit from it. Just occasionally, someone appears with genuine musical and managerial talent and a personal well of cash on which to draw. Such a man was the conductor Thomas Beecham, the son of a wealthy Lancashire industrialist (and manufacturer of Beecham's Pills).

While Beecham was learning his craft in the dying years of the nineteenth century and the early years of the twentieth, a 'Grand Opera Syndicate' would promote short opera seasons at Covent Garden each spring and early summer, while the theatre was also used from time to time by other ad hoc promoters. Some of the world's top singers would appear during GOS seasons, but production and musical standards could be lacklustre. To Max Beerbohm, and he was surely not alone, the chief attraction of the GOS season was the social opportunities it provided, not the music. 'I should not suffer from any sense of loss,' he wrote in 1899, 'if all the scores of all the operas that have ever been written… were to perish in a sudden holocaust tomorrow.' What Beerbohm enjoyed was 'to wander behind the Grand Tier and read the illustrious names printed on the doors of the boxes', or to bump deliberately into 'an hereditary legislator who was once in one of Mr Gladstone's Cabinets' so as to have the honour of apologizing to him. Inside the auditorium, he notes, 'some opera or other' is proceeding. 'The fiddlers are fiddling in a quiet monotone, not loud enough to drown the chatter in the stalls and boxes', while the rows of boxes themselves put him in mind of 'an exquisite panorama of Punch-and-Judy shows'.

Beecham's ambition was to introduce something altogether more disciplined. In early 1910, backed by his father's money, the thirty-year-old conductor took over the Covent Garden theatre himself for what proved to be a sensational month-long season. That summer, he conducted opera at His Majesty's and then booked Covent Garden again for three months in the autumn. The season ended with the London premiere of Strauss's *Salome*, an opera during which the soprano divests herself of her seven veils and at whose culmination she sings ecstatically to the decapitated head of John the Baptist, presented to her on a silver platter, and, in the climactic moment of the opera, kisses its dead lips. Inevitably, Beecham ran into censorship problems but, determined to proceed, he acquiesced in the demands of the Lord Chamberlain and agreed that the opera would (as he wrote later) 'be trimmed so as to make it palatable to the taste of that large army of objectors who would never see it'. Lines were altered to become innocuous, the location shifted from Palestine to Greece and John was renamed, anonymously, 'The Prophet'. As for the final scene, it was agreed the plate could have a blood-stained cover but no head: Beecham squirmed on the first night as he watched his leading lady drooling over what one writer thought looked like a plate of pink blancmange. Scandal and publicity never did the arts much harm, and Beecham's *Salome* performances brought his *annus mirabilis* to a successful conclusion. The Syndicate, clearly outflanked, invited Beecham onto its board.

Beecham struggled to keep opera alive in Britain during the Great War, suffered severe financial problems after the death of his father, bounced back with the help of a generous 'patroness', Lady Cunard, and from 1934 until the outbreak of the Second World War, ever the maverick, was again installed

A supremely gifted musician and a man capable of great wit, elegance and generosity, Sir Thomas Beecham could also be conceited, arrogant and waspish.

at Covent Garden to direct an annual season. Capable of breathtaking generosity verging on bravado (as in his many kindnesses to Berta Geissmar), the elegant, conceited baronet with his silk pyjamas and large cigar also had a waspish side. Many of his contemporaries were badly stung, and Beecham recurrently found himself sidelined by Britain's musical establishment. In 1930, the BBC set up its own symphony orchestra under Adrian Boult; what Boult and the subsidized BBCSO chose to perform, the nation would hear. Beecham's reaction, typically, was to set up his own orchestra, the London Philharmonic, a couple of years later. As for opera, it was true that some of the great international singers and conductors performed in Beecham's annual Covent Garden seasons. But there was a cohort among Britain's wealthy and well-connected who insisted that the best opera in the country was produced not in London but by another rich and eccentric British opera lover in a little theatre he had built alongside his house in Sussex.

After Fritz Busch and Carl Ebert had left Hitler's Germany, the two friends kept in touch; they even found themselves collaborating (as joint directors of a season of German operas at the Teatro Colón in Buenos Aires). In late 1933, Busch, by now in Scandinavia, received a curious message from England. It seemed that his violinist brother Adolf Busch had been performing in Eastbourne on the Sussex coast. He was planning to return to London after the concert but because of impenetrable fog the lady who was driving him suggested they stay over with a cellist friend nearby. That night, talk turned to a Sussex landowner called John Christie who, according to a recent newspaper article, had a small theatre attached to his country house and wanted to perform opera there. A meeting was arranged with Christie, who was evidently serious about his little opera house and talked of starting a regular festival. Christie wanted Adolf Busch to mastermind the whole thing, perhaps with his string quartet providing the nucleus of the orchestra. That wouldn't be possible, he was told. But he might want to contact Busch's conductor brother Fritz.

Fritz Busch was startled by the inquiry, and got in touch with Ebert. The two were hugely sceptical about Christie and his bizarre idea. But early in 1934, Ebert stopped by in England, found his way to Christie's pile in Sussex and met the man himself. He also met Mrs Christie, the singer Audrey Mildmay, whose charm and *savoir faire* helped soften the edges of her ebullient husband. 'If you're going to spend all that money,' she had said to John in words that later became enshrined in Glyndebourne mythology, 'for God's sake do the thing properly!'

Christie knew little about the practicalities of opera or opera houses. He just knew what he liked and that he wanted to please his young soprano wife. How about putting on *Parsifal*, suggested the inveterate and uncritical Teutonophile. Ebert looked at the tiny theatre and replied sardonically that *Parsifal* would be fine if you put your orchestra and singers in the auditorium and the audience on stage. Well, then, replied Christie, what *would* work?

'This intimate theatre simply asks for Mozart's operas.'

Christie was not convinced. 'English audiences don't like Mozart very much.'

'Then we must try to help them to like Mozart,' was Ebert's riposte.

Months later, Ebert and Busch inaugurated the first Glyndebourne Festival. The two opening productions, Mozart's *Le nozze di Figaro* and *Don Giovanni*, were produced with a standard of overall professionalism rarely seen in Britain. The informal contracts manager at Glyndebourne (later general manager) was an Austrian émigré who had previously worked with Ebert in German; his name was Rudolf Bing.

That same year, 1934, Lilian Baylis decided to make London's Sadler's Wells Theatre into an opera house. Decades earlier, Baylis, a poor girl with none of the airs and graces of a Beecham or a Christie, had aided and then succeeded her aunt, Emma Cons, as good fairy to the working people of south London. As the Salvation Army or Toynbee Hall were to the homeless, so Miss Baylis perceived her Old Vic Theatre off the Waterloo Road: a beacon of light, succour to the hungry, an elevation of the spirit. With her droopy face, spinstery bun and unfashionably uneducated accent, Baylis spoke with the conviction of a missionary about the working people who would flock to see good theatre, opera and ballet if only it were made available to them. 'Don't worry, God will provide,' she would promise, as young actors like Sybil Thorndike or Ralph Richardson or singers such as Joan Cross or Heddle Nash anxiously enquired about the costumes they needed for the next night's performance. And miraculously, He usually did.

He also provided Baylis with her audiences. So much so that she bought and refurbished a second theatre: Sadler's Wells in the (then) only marginally more salubrious district of Islington. North Londoners, too, would be given food for the soul. From 1934, Baylis divided the 'Vic–Wells' company into two: the drama troupe would perform exclusively at the Old Vic, while ballet (under Ninette de Valois) and opera were henceforth based at 'the Wells'.

Baylis died in 1937, and once war broke out in 1939 opera in Britain became a matter of little account. Sadler's Wells Theatre was taken over by the Borough of Finsbury as a rest centre for people rendered homeless by the blitz, and the soprano Joan Cross took a tiny Vic–Wells troupe, with no more than a couple of props and a piano, to perform in the factory towns of the north-west, with occasional forays to London's New Theatre (now the Albery). Glyndebourne, strategically sited near the south-east coast, would probably have become a military encampment had it not already been converted to a refuge for children evacuated from London; Rudolf Bing recalled going to Woolworth's in Lewes to place a large order for chamber pots. As for the nation's premier opera house, Covent Garden, this was leased to Mecca Cafés Ltd as a *palais de danse* for the delectation of troops home on leave. How could you put on opera, its former patrons asked one another sadly, when most of the leading artists of recent years were either Germans or Italians, and had therefore become Britain's mortal enemies? Beecham, meanwhile, left for extended visits to Australia and the USA.

The government, concerned to maintain morale, set up the Council for the Encouragement of Music and the Arts and, a little later, the Entertainments National Service Association, both of which dispatched artists and entertainers around the country to keep up the nation's spirits. Despite their titles and putative difference of emphasis, CEMA and ENSA soon proved similar in practice, rivals even. ENSA was run by a popular theatrical producer; but his music supremo was the record producer Walter Legge, lately Beecham's assistant at Covent Garden and after the war one of the UK's most forceful entrepreneurs of classical music. CEMA and ENSA were intended as temporary measures. They were also symptoms of a growing belief in the value of central planning, a concept that received a powerful fillip from the exigencies of war and came to be embodied immediately afterwards in what history calls the Welfare State. Once peacetime returned, the new Labour government not only nationalized the mines and railways and set up a National Health Service; it also transformed CEMA into an Arts Council, a government-financed body specifically empowered to encourage the arts and whose largest single beneficiary, from that day to this, was opera at the Royal Opera House, Covent Garden.

*

The establishment of the Royal Opera House as the permanent home for both a ballet and an opera company came about as a result of determined planning. The Mecca lease on Covent Garden was due to expire in December 1944, with an option to renew unless someone else could be found who would use the theatre for opera and ballet. The chairman of the proprietors asked the impresario Harold Holt whether he might be interested in applying; Holt, who had his hands full, passed on the idea to two of his directors, the music publishers Leslie Boosey and Ralph Hawkes. Mecca were pressing for an early decision. So Boosey and Hawkes took out a five-year lease on the theatre and set up a consultative committee headed by the economist and arts lover Lord Keynes. Their brief, as outlined by Boosey and Hawkes in what would nowadays be called a mission statement, was to establish Covent Garden as a round-the-year international opera house financed – as never before in British history – by a regular government subsidy with no strings attached.

The first thing the committee had to do was to appoint someone to take charge of their theatre. There were several possible contenders, including Beecham, Legge, Bing and Christie. Each, however, was regarded as a wilful, slightly eccentric figure, none of them quite the safe pair of hands the committee sought. Instead, their choice fell upon a relative unknown (in London at least): David Webster. The manager of Liverpool's principal department store, Webster was also chairman of the Liverpool Philharmonic Orchestra and responsible, against considerable opposition, for having retained quality

During the War, the Royal Opera House, Covent Garden, was leased to the Mecca company and used as a *palais de danse*.

music-making on Merseyside throughout the war. With Webster as its general administrator, the Royal Opera House reopened as a theatre in 1946, with ballet, led by de Valois. The creation of a viable opera company took longer. Here, too, the all-important question was whom to entrust with its leadership. Beecham was again a possibility, of course, though his recurrent supercilious sniping ruled him *hors de combat*. Another prominent name was that of John Barbirolli who had returned to England from America during the height of the war to take over Manchester's Hallé Orchestra. Webster, with his Liverpool background, was well acquainted with Barbirolli's gifts. But Barbirolli was profoundly committed to the Hallé and declined. Then there was Joan Cross, the driving force behind the Vic–Wells opera company, a great singer and a powerful personality. But she was a contentious spirit. Her company had none of the glamour or international aspirations that Covent Garden audiences would demand and, in due course, she, Peter Pears and Eric Crozier, buoyed up by the success of Benjamin Britten's latest opera, *Peter Grimes*, seceded from the Sadler's Wells company to set up what was to become the English Opera Group. Webster approached the conductor Eugene Goossens, who had worked with Beecham at Covent Garden in the 1930s, and he also broached the idea with Bruno Walter. Both men lobbed a lot of hard questions in Webster's direction. Webster, dilatory by nature, lost both. Perhaps he was relieved. Such men were potentially over-mighty subjects whom Webster, still struggling with his new job, might have found it difficult to rule.

In the event, the choice fell upon a far less stellar figure. Karl Rankl was an Austrian émigré who had studied with Schoenberg and worked as coach and chorus master in Vienna, Berlin (where he had assisted Klemperer at the Kroll) and a variety of smaller houses in Central Europe before escaping to England in 1939. A refugee thankful for the offer of an important job, Rankl was a practical man of the theatre, a competent composer-conductor who knew the business and would, Webster surmised, get the show on the road. Like a chef with a large kitchen, a series of feasts to prepare and no ingredients, Rankl had to create his operatic fare from nothing: there were no productions to build on, no costumes or sets, no music staff, no chorus, not much of an orchestra. While Rankl toiled, the theatre hosted a visit by the San Carlo Opera of Naples, and the infant opera company opened with a production of Purcell's *Fairy Queen* conducted not by its musical director but by Constant Lambert. The real debut of the company, and Rankl's debut in the pit, came in January 1947 with *Carmen*. It was a decent performance, but no more than that. The heights of Olympus were not to be scaled easily. Perhaps the Covent Garden audiences and critics had been spoiled by hearing singers of the calibre of Gigli and Mario del Monaco with the visiting Naples troupe, while later in the year they were exposed to the Vienna State Opera, whose casts and conductors (Krauss and Krips) Covent Garden could not hope to rival.

Money, at least, was reasonably secure, thanks to the close links that had been created between Covent Garden and the Arts Council, and nobody complained when singers such as Kirsten Flagstad, Hans Hotter and Elisabeth Schwarzkopf agreed to sing in the house. But the critics of the new regime were many and vocal. They wanted to have it both ways. There was much huffing and puffing at the choice of a foreigner as musical director. Yet many also pounced upon the supposed inadequacies of British and Commonwealth artists whom Rankl thought it his job to promote, arguing that by casting Kenneth Neate or Edgar Evans instead of Anton Dermota or Luigi Infantino he was guaranteeing lower standards. Things got worse before they got better. In June 1948, at a highly publicized literary luncheon, Beecham chose to denounce British singers for their 'pleasant but woolly voices', seeming to argue in his acerbic way for a revival of the glamorous international seasons over which he had presided before the war: the best artists from all over the world – but under homegrown management. By appointing Rankl, added Beecham witheringly, Covent Garden had become a laughing stock, proclaiming to the world that Britain could not govern its own musical institutions.

Heading a brief festival of German or Italian opera with imported stars, as Beecham had done in the past, was one thing. What Rankl was trying to do was harder: the formation of a permanent, largely homegrown company capable of high-quality performance of any of the forty-odd works in the standard repertory. For five years, Rankl struggled with this difficult brief. By 1950, the company was well established, with many young British singers holding their own alongside distinguished Continental colleagues. Webster's policy of performing everything in English began to be breached, and top foreign directors and conductors expressed interest in working with the company. Covent Garden was gradually becoming what Webster and Rankl had always wanted it to be: a home of international-quality opera. Ironically, it was Rankl's very success that led to his departure. For the company that he had created had outgrown him, enabling London to become one of the top opera centres in the world.

*

British opera lovers owed much to Rankl. And to Baylis, Beecham, Britten, Christie, Cross, Keynes, Webster and many others. In one sense, these figures had been lucky in that they were tilling in what was, or was soon to become, unusually fertile soil. During the war, many of the top music centres of earlier times (Berlin, Budapest, Munich, Dresden) were far more severely bombed than London, great opera houses from Hamburg to Vienna lying damaged or destroyed. The Cold War that followed helped marginalize many of these cities still further, placing them no longer at the geographical heart of Europe but scattered along the edges of its harsh new political boundary. London, by contrast, found itself centre stage. Britain was the one nation in the whole of Central and Western Europe that had fought Hitler and won and, as such, had tremendous prestige. No other nation held its head so high. Tired and ragged, Britain and its capital emerged from the war to the unaccustomed plaudits of the Western world.

Among its population, furthermore, was a critical mass of Central European émigrés keen to make their contribution. Some were professionally involved with opera while many more were avid music lovers whose regular presence at operas and concerts was greatly disproportionate to their numbers. Perhaps to their surprise, they found post-war Britain keen to overcome its historical reputation as a 'land without music', as Britten's *Peter Grimes*, premiered at Sadler's Wells, proclaimed the world's most talented young opera composer, and the nation's cultural mandarins set up permanent opera and ballet at Covent Garden for the first time and an Arts Council to help fund it. In 1946 the BBC inaugurated its music-and-culture network, the Third Programme, and a year later Rudolf Bing the Edinburgh Festival, which he saw as a kind of British Salzburg. Britten's English Opera Group and Aldeburgh Festival date from this time, while the crowning presence of the 1951 Festival of Britain was its state-of-the-art concert hall, the first permanent public building on such a scale erected in Britain since the war. Beecham bounced back to London and founded another orchestra, the Royal Philharmonic, while his former Covent Garden colleague Walter Legge, now chief producer at HMV, set up what he intended as a super-orchestra, the Philharmonia, with which to make authoritative recordings of the great classics, bringing Karajan to London as its conductor. Legge's timing was immaculate: as the recording business abandoned 78rpm for the LP and embarked upon large-scale recording projects, including many complete operas never before consigned to disc, London with its pool of talented musicians became the industry's city of choice. After twenty years of economic recession, war and austerity, London was once again one of the world's great cultural centres, a city of excitement, innovation and optimism. The Festival of Britain (a 'Tonic to the Nation' the government called it) was a huge success, while the Coronation of Queen Elizabeth II two years later brought immense, cheering crowds onto the streets of London.

The Coronation celebrations included the commission of a new opera, about the first Queen Elizabeth, by Benjamin Britten. The ageing grandees who attended the premiere in their obligatory evening dress, medals and white gloves doubtless expected some simple-minded celebratory pageant, and were nonplussed by *Gloriana*, Britten's deeply reflective work about Elizabeth I's doomed infatuation for the young Essex. Britten was hurt by the cool reception given to a work in which he had included some attractive Tudor pastiche and a ravishing lute serenade, and in the years that followed he turned increasingly to the composition of chamber-scale works which he could control and perform in the safer environment of Aldeburgh. But the

In *Gloriana*, commissioned to celebrate the Coronation of Elizabeth II in 1953, Benjamin Britten wrote a somewhat reflective work about the doomed infatuation of the first Queen Elizabeth (portrayed by Joan Cross) with the young Earl of Essex.

lukewarm reception afforded to *Gloriana* spread a message that radiated far beyond its influence on the opera's composer. By now, a Conservative government was well entrenched and talked of allying culture more closely to commerce. Proposals were progressing for a television channel financed by advertising. Was elite, effete art like *Gloriana* the sort of thing to which huge dollops of taxpayers' money should be devoted? Many thought not. Thus, the principle of state funding of the arts, only recently established in Britain, tottered for a while on its precarious pedestal.

Soon, much else seemed to be tottering. A new generation of 'angry' young novelists and dramatists began to catch the public imagination with their bold criticisms of the values of yesteryear. Royalty was 'the gold filling in a mouthful of decay', scoffed one of John Osborne's characters in *Look Back in Anger*, a play produced in the very year, 1956, in which Britain's dispatch of troops to Suez was widely criticized as the unwarranted intervention of a broken imperial power. In some ways, it was true (as the Prime Minister, Harold Macmillan, told election crowds in 1959) that people in Britain had 'never had it so good' as they enjoyed their first TV sets, cars, washing machines and foreign holidays. Yet, even as Macmillan's premiership ran into the sand and the post-war 'baby boomers' grew into assertive twenty-somethings, other priorities emerged, a string of new, somewhat radical-minded new universities was set up while, outside the walls of academe, Britain's younger generation set international standards in fashion, pop music and trenchant, anti-establishment satire. The 1960s were crucible years for serious arts programmes on television as 'Auntie' BBC, rebounding from the shock of commercial television (introduced in 1955), hitched up her skirts, reached out for newer, younger, audiences, and launched a second channel, BBC2. If millions came to know of Georg Solti, it was not from opera performances at Covent Garden, where he became music director, or from his LPs, but because they had seen Humphrey Burton's television film of the conductor recording Wagner's *Ring*.

By 1971, when Solti left the Royal Opera House, Covent Garden had arguably become what Solti said he wanted to make it: the finest opera house in the world. The company, officially dubbed the 'Royal Opera' in 1968, was by now truly international in scope and ambition, hosting all the world's great singers and producing most works in their original language. Moreover, many of the leading artists on the roster were British, a trend Solti had done much to foster. Audiences on opera nights tended to average around the 2000 mark: more than for ballet even though ticket prices were higher. And the company was by now immensely productive; in the twenty-five years between 1946 and 1971, even though sharing the stage with its sister ballet company, it produced almost as many evenings of opera as the theatre had seen during the fifty years up to 1939.

In much of this, the Royal Opera House management had been greatly helped by the creation in 1964, by the Prime Minister, Harold Wilson, of Britain's first arts minister, Jennie Lee (the widow of Aneurin Bevan, creator of the National Health Service). For all her working-class credentials, Lee proved a generous and able friend of the arts, striking up a good relationship with the opera-loving Chairman of the Arts Council (and Wilson's personal legal adviser) Arnold Goodman. The annual Arts Council grant to the Royal Opera House, half a million pounds in 1960–61, had trebled a decade later. Nor was Covent Garden the only operatic recipient of Arts Council bounty. In 1968, the Sadler's Wells company, buoyed by a series of great successes, moved to one of London's largest West End theatres, the Coliseum, renaming itself half a dozen years later 'English National Opera'. Opera was burgeoning outside the capital, too. Scottish Opera was founded in Glasgow in 1962 while Welsh National, its roots going back to the end of the war, felt secure enough by the early 1970s to professionalize its orchestra and a little later its chorus. And Glyndebourne, long re-established as Britain's premier venue for Festival-quality opera, found itself flattered by imitation as other country house opera ventures began to appear. Meanwhile, a plethora of local, regional and touring companies and opera festivals sought, and mostly found, artists, audiences and finances. Opera in Britain had never before been as popular or as ubiquitous. Or even, perhaps, as good.

CHAPTER 20

Building Opera in America

After the Japanese attack on Pearl Harbor, New York's Metropolitan Opera refrained from scheduling *Madama Butterfly,* sensing its audiences might not feel much sympathy for a Japanese girl wronged by a US sailor. Unlike during the First World War, the Met continued to schedule operas by German composers such as Wagner and Strauss. But for its casts and conductors, the theatre was no longer able to call upon German- or Austrian-based artists or those from occupied Europe, having to rely instead on several distinguished refugees from Nazism as well as a fair sprinkling of Americans. There were plenty of excellent American or American-based artists, too, to keep the Italian repertoire well stocked for the duration. One of the repercussions of both world wars, indeed, was that, by isolating the USA from European talent, the careers of young American artists received a boost.

New audiences to opera, too, were wooed by the wartime Met. Following an announcement that dress codes would be relaxed, a Met Guild publication of 1944 enthused about the presence of newcomers wearing 'the uniform of an army nurse or a private on leave, or just the little black dress or sack suit of the everyday civilian'. The black ties and tiaras, once *de rigueur* at least in the pricier parts of the house, were on their way out.

After the war, a number of famous European artists such as Björling were welcomed back to the Met. Others, regarded by many as tainted by their genuine or imagined cooperation with the Nazi regime, were not. A widespread campaign against Furtwängler prevented him from conducting in the USA, while it was many years before Karajan or Schwarzkopf were invited to the Met.

The most poignant case, perhaps, was that of the Wagnerian soprano Kirsten Flagstad, one of the most outstanding singers in the pre-war Metropolitan. Once war had broken out, Flagstad went back to her native Norway to be with her family. Afterwards, it was widely reported that her husband had collaborated with the occupying Germans and the rumour-mongers whispered that Flagstad had sung for the Nazis and her decision to return been politically motivated. At the very least, the return of so famous a citizen

Kirsten Flagstad spent much of the War in Norway as 'a secluded wife', singing very little, but her husband had collaborated with the Nazis, and after the War some gave the soprano a hostile reception when she sang again in the USA.

to Norway at that time was widely seen as bestowing a level of dignity upon the Nazi occupiers. All who knew Flagstad described her as a simple, unpretentious woman, a proud patriot but no political ideologue. She spent much of the war as 'a secluded wife'(in the words of one historian), singing very little. True, she appeared in Zurich, which involved travelling through Germany, and in Stockholm. Such forays to neutral cities hardly suggested pro-Nazi zeal on her part, though many Norwegians later resented the luxury and security one of their most celebrated citizens had enjoyed during the years of occupation. In spring 1947, Flagstad undertook an American concert tour during which she encountered a number of demonstrations, including stink bombs thrown during a recital in Philadelphia. The influential journalist Walter Winchell sniped away at her in his column ('Please do something about this woman, who before and during the war was not on our team. . . Norway doesn't want her, which is one very good reason for the United States not to take her'). Later in the year, Flagstad sang *Tristan* in Chicago to great acclaim. But no-one approached her from the New York Metropolitan.

Three years later, the Austrian-born Rudolf Bing became general manager of the Met. Initial inquiries revealed little that would have rendered Flagstad *persona non grata* and Bing was keen to invite her back. She had given a recital in Washington after the invasion of Norway at which the German ambassador was present. However, Flagstad had been a guest of the USA at the time, Bing reflected, and America was not then at war. The incident, he decided, was 'long ago and trivial'. Flagstad's husband may have traded with the occupying Nazis, but he had been tried as a quisling after the war and had died shortly afterwards. As for Flagstad herself, wrote Bing, she 'was obviously a non-political person, and the time for punishing her for her husband's misdeeds had ended'. When Bing announced that Flagstad would be returning to the Met, he stated simply that the world's greatest soprano should sing in the world's greatest opera house. To Bing's surprise and consternation, the announcement was greeted with what he described as a 'torrent of vituperation' in the press, much of it ignorant and prejudiced.* Billy Rose, the theatrical impresario and showman who also had a syndicated column, wrote unequivocally that Flagstad had 'entertained the Nazis', adding sarcastically that maybe Bing should engage Hitler's finance minister Hjalmar Schacht as Met budget director and, as wardrobe mistress, the 'Bitch of Buchenwald', Ilse Koch (who was reputed to have made lampshades of human skin). Despite the vehemence of such attacks, Flagstad made a triumphant return to the Met and was warmly applauded by an enormous and enthusiastic audience. Damage had undoubtedly been done, however. When Bing proposed inviting Furtwängler to the Met the following season, he was turned down flat by the Board ('the only time in twenty-two years that I was told whom I could or could not hire').

*

During the years just after the war, the New York Metropolitan was responsible for the only 'live' opera most Americans would have had a chance to encounter. In addition to its season in New York City, the company continued to go on tour each spring, visiting the eastern seaboard and several of the big cities of the South and West. In April 1948, and again a year later, the Met tour included Los Angeles, a city last visited more than forty years before. Typically, a company of some 300 people would set out in April for a month or more, travel on two special trains, with sleeping cars and baggage cars, sojourning for a few days at a time in a succession of hotels. Artists and technical staff found the tours exhausting but enormous fun, offering opportunities to bond with colleagues (doubtless beyond the call of duty in some cases) with whom, in the normal daily run of things back in New York, one might have remained only casually acquainted. Advance publicity helped fill the houses and coffers. Wherever the Met came to rest, the local press gave gleeful reports, often embellished with glamorous photos of posturing celebrity

---

*Bing was no stranger to press headlines during his tenure: in 1955, he invited Marian Anderson to become the first black singer to appear at the Met, and a few years later he was widely reported as having 'Fired Callas'.

The 1948 Met tour arrives in Los Angeles: the last time the Met included LA in the tour was over forty years before.

tenors and basses and be-furred, be-hatted prima donnas posing in front of the train or at the stage door. Meanwhile, during the season proper, a new generation of opera lovers – and potential ticket buyers – was also being nurtured by the broadcasts of the Met's Saturday afternoon matinees.

Yet the Met was far from being the only professional opera company in the USA. The San Francisco Opera, created back in 1923, was very much in business under its indefatigable founder-director Gaetano Merola. There were smaller companies, too: Pittsburgh Opera was established in 1939 and the New York City Opera (initially as City Center Opera) in 1943, while a succession of small, semi-professional companies sprang up during the 1940s, especially in the South, among them Florida (1941), Chattanooga and New Orleans (both 1943), Mississippi (1945), Mobile and Fort Worth (both 1946), Tulsa and Charlotte (both 1948), and Shreveport (1949). Most began by producing short seasons in existing performing arts centres or civic centres, sharing the facility with a local theatre company, orchestra and perhaps a dance troupe. Literally dozens of new opera companies were set up in America (and old ones reconstituted) during the post-war decades, often under the leadership or inspiration of an Italian or German émigré or of an American with European operatic experience. Kentucky Opera was inaugurated in

1952, the year in which Baltimore Opera moved into a proper opera theatre with Rosa Ponselle as its artistic director. New York City Opera gradually built up its reputation under the artistic direction of László Halász and later Julius Rudel, while the mid-1950s saw the launch of companies in Houston (under the inspiration of the Frankfurt-born Walter Herbert), Tulsa, Dallas, Santa Fe and Washington DC. In Chicago, a triumvirate of enthusiasts, including the young Italian-American conductor Nicola Rescigno, announced the launch of a new company, Lyric Opera of Chicago.

With the economic upsurge of the 1960s and 1970s, the existing roster of opera companies was joined by a further string of additions, some of the most successful of which went on to inhabit purpose-built premises. Houston's Wortham Theater Center opened in 1983 while Seattle Opera, starting life in the city's converted Civic Auditorium, moved into its latest sparkling transformation in 2003. John Crosby's Santa Fe company opened in a small, open-to-the-skies theatre in the New Mexican desert in 1957, moving into larger, partially covered facilities in 1968 and, thirty years later, into a state-of-the-art theatre now named after him. In each case, as the company expanded and became more successful, a new building followed, as it had long ago in San Francisco. In two conspicuous cases, however, chicken and egg worked the other way round, as they had done earlier in New York and Chicago. In the nation's capital, Washington DC, and also in Los Angeles, the presence of new theatres helped stimulate the development of what were at the time tiny, struggling companies but which eventually became two of the best of the second-best opera companies in the country.

*

In the early 1960s, Washington was still something of a sleepy, one-industry Southern town. With its transient population of here-today-gone-tomorrow Congressmen, diplomats and politically hued civil servants and lobbyists, 'the District' had few serious pretensions to high culture. As for its longer-term residents, the Dixiecrat senators and their staff, the journalists, jurists and academics, the hoteliers and restaurateurs, they might attend a high-profile visit by a famous orchestra or opera or ballet company once in a while. But for the most part they would have preferred something more – well, more American: a movie, a bourbon on the rocks at the club or a spell on the golf course or out on the Potomac.

There had been opera of a kind in Washington almost since the foundation of the city if you count the musical entertainments, including opera excerpts, that featured in some of the capital's earliest theatres. By the 1850s, Washington had a population of around 50,000 and top singing stars from Europe such as Lind, Patti, Mario and Grisi included it on their circuit. The city was still very much in the making: when Lincoln entered the White House in 1861, the mansion was gaslit but the Washington Monument still lacked its summit and the Capitol building its dome, while not even Pennsylvania Avenue was properly paved. Lincoln, who was later murdered in a theatre, apparently attended the opera several times during the Civil War.

Twenty years later, the city had a population of some 175,000, big enough to warrant a visit from the newly created Metropolitan Opera just four months after the Met's inaugural night in New York. The Met made many subsequent visits – but not in 1910, when Washington's opera buffs revelled in a visit by its great rival, Oscar Hammerstein's Manhattan Opera company, with Mary Garden the star. There was even 'resident' opera in Washington for a while. During the 1920s, a bold opera lover and local singing teacher called Edouard Albion ran a company which, alongside a sequence of hand-to-mouth productions and periodic disasters, also brought Shalyapin to the capital and presented the triumphant reappearance on to the American operatic stage of Johanna Gadski. Gadski's return in 1928 in *Die Walküre* was greeted in Washington with such enthusiasm that after Brünnhilde's entry and battle cry the performance was brought to a brief halt. For a while, Albion's troupe performed in the new multi-purpose Washington Auditorium, struggling on until it finally collapsed in 1936.

'You should have an opera house in Washington.' The speaker was Mary Garden and the year 1949. Her interlocutor was the equally feisty President Harry Truman, known for (among other things) his piano-vamping skills. 'All the great capitals of the world have their opera houses,' Garden went on. 'Every one of them but Washington! I'm going to put that in my next lecture. Do you mind, Mr President?' Truman doubtless nodded politely, shook hands with his visitor and got on with the Cold War. In the event, the person who started what grew into Washington's permanent opera company was not a singer or politician (or a millionaire industrialist or Italian immigrant) but a music critic. Day Thorpe wrote reviews for the *Washington Star*. He approached Paul Callaway, the organist and choirmaster of Washington's National Cathedral, and the pair managed to find enough patrons and sponsors to be able to announce the birth of their infant Opera Society of Washington in 1956. In some ways, Thorpe and Callaway were very purist in their objectives. They were not interested in international stars who would swan in and out (and whom they could never have afforded anyway). Rather, they aimed to present original-language opera, properly rehearsed, with an ensemble of singers booked for the occasion who looked right for their roles and could act. Inevitably, perhaps, these principles were watered down by sober realities. The opening production was of Mozart's *Entführung*, performed in the George Washington University's Lisner auditorium. Although sung in German, it was decided to present the dialogue in English, while scenery and props were assembled from wherever they could be begged or borrowed (including the Turkish embassy) and the orchestra pit was so small that half the players had to sit outside it. Nonetheless, the event proved both an

21 November, 1964: just under a year after the assassination of President Kennedy, the architect Edward D. Stone reveals his plans for Washington's 'Kennedy Center' to Mrs Stephen Smith (sister of JFK) and George R. Marek, vice-president of Washington Opera.

artistic and a social success and Thorpe and Callaway were emboldened to keep going. By 1961, the Opera Society was being invited to perform excerpts from *Zauberflöte* to the Kennedys and Indira Gandhi in the White House.

Audiences and finances remained stubbornly inadequate, however. By the mid-1960s, indeed, funding proved particularly difficult to attract since every local dollar for high culture was being funnelled towards what was by far the largest arts project in Washington's history: the great National Cultural Center taking shape on the bank of the Potomac. The Opera Society survived, later taking its place as one of the permanent occupants of what was by then renamed the Kennedy Center, but only after a number of years in which it had hovered on the edge of extinction. In some ways, it was the building that helped bring the patient back to life.

*

At the opposite end of the country, too, the existence of a building played a major part in the establishment of a permanent opera company. Mrs Dorothy

Buffum Chandler was Chairman of the Hollywood Bowl Association and wife of the publisher of the *Los Angeles Times*. 'Buff' (or 'Buffy') Chandler inspired and energized those responsible for the fluctuating fortunes of the Bowl (which she had helped rescue from imminent closure in 1951) and of the Los Angeles Philharmonic. Her persuasive capacities among the rich and powerful became legendary, as did her forms of fundraising. If symphony concerts 'Under the Stars' did not always fill the Bowl, how about a 'Festival of the Americas' graced by her friend Vice-President 'Dick' Nixon? Then there were the 'Walt Disney Nights' with Disney himself, grinning broadly, 'hereby proclaimed Honorary Governor of the State of California' for the duration, and the Governor himself proclaimed Honorary President of the Bowl! When Disneyland opened in 1955, one of the first letters of congratulation was from Mrs Chandler.

Mrs Chandler wanted her Bowl to be filled to overflowing, partly to fulfil the financial obligations of the board she served, but also because she and her colleagues had an even more ambitious aim in view: the eventual establishment, as the apex of the new Civic Center then being developed up the slope of Los Angeles' Bunker Hill, of a custom-built Los Angeles Music Center, an Acropolis of the performing arts. For over a decade, Mrs Chandler and her troops raised money for this project – eventually over $13 million – from among the great, the good and the wealthy. Finally, in December 1964, the LA Philharmonic, under its young maestro Zubin Mehta, moved into its magnificent new home. The orchestra opened with a brassy fanfare. 'We like the acoustics!' beamed Mehta to an ecstatic audience. Two and a half years later, a brace of new theatres opened across the plaza and the initial building was officially named the Dorothy Chandler Pavilion. Mrs Chandler's dream was complete: new Californian money and Old World culture were firmly united and had erected a superb Parthenon to proclaim their troth. The Music Center complex was built on Temple Street and bounded on its other sides by Grand, First and Hope. Symbolism scarcely comes more potent.

From the outset, the 3250-seat Chandler Pavilion was designed to be the permanent home of the Los Angeles Philharmonic. It was also built with sufficient backstage flexibility to function as a theatre and, before long, found additional tenants. One of the first was the New York City Opera, whose regular autumn visits (in effect replacing those of San Francisco Opera) commenced in 1967. To the wider world, the Dorothy Chandler Pavilion became best known for the next thirty-odd years as the site of the annual Motion Picture Academy Awards: the Oscars.

By the late 1970s, the annual visits to Los Angeles by the New York City Opera were losing support and a somewhat acrimonious break came in 1982. That year, the LA Philharmonic tried its own hand at opera and mounted a costly production of Verdi's *Falstaff* in conjunction with London's Royal Opera, an experiment that was successful enough but could hardly be replicated on

The Hollywood Bowl: home of classical concerts 'Under the Stars'. Dorothy Chandler, Chair of the Bowl Association, dreamed of creating a permanent home for opera in Los Angeles.

a regular basis. However, the link with Covent Garden was to bear fruit a couple of years later when, as the high point of the Arts Festival accompanying the 1984 Los Angeles Olympics, the Royal Opera visited the Chandler Pavilion and brought *Die Zauberflöte*, *Peter Grimes* (with Jon Vickers) and a new production of *Turandot* (with Gwyneth Jones and Plácido Domingo). The visit was a huge success and proved yet again that there was an audience in Los Angeles thirsting for high-quality opera and prepared to pay for it. Domingo, born in Madrid and raised in Mexico, was already on the Board of the LA Music Center Association and deeply conscious of the huge Hispanic population in Southern California to whom he was becoming something of a role model. 'We *have* to do opera here!' he told all who would listen. In October 1984, Peter Hemmings, an Englishman who had run both Scottish and Australian Opera and the London Symphony Orchestra, was appointed by the board to be general manager of a new company, and Domingo agreed to become artistic consultant. Two years later, with Domingo himself starring in *Otello*, the Los Angeles Music Center Opera opened its first season and went on to establish itself as the only permanent company ever to take root in the city. Here, as in Washington, Domingo soon agreed to take on the role of artistic director and later general director. Other singers have managed opera companies in the past; Domingo is the first to have been in charge of two.

✻

Across America, new opera companies and new buildings in which to house them sprang up where none – or nothing comparable – had been before. By all odds the largest, boldest, most costly and most ambitious building project of them all was the one undertaken on New York's West Side. Otto Kahn's soothing words to the incoming general manager, Gatti-Casazza, in 1908, that a new Metropolitan Opera House would soon be built, had rung through the dismal, damp, dingy backstage corridors of the old Met ever since. When Bing arrived, he noted that the theatre had no side stages, rear stage or revolve. This meant that every scene change had to be done on the main stage itself while the audience sat and waited, listening to banging noises behind the curtain. The lighting grid was decades behind European standards. Every production had to be set and struck from scratch and there was nowhere to store scenery or costumes, so that passers-by on New York's Seventh Avenue got used to piles of velvet drapes or crinolines, helmets, swords and scimitars, lying on the sidewalk in boxes or under tarpaulins awaiting collection. Some of the theatre's inadequacies arose from the fact that it filled a tight city block and had nowhere to expand. As its repertoire had grown and productions become more ambitious, the theatre's physical restrictions became ever more onerous.

Over the years, New York's cultural centre of gravity moved gradually uptown and successive Met managements, yearning for a better theatre, considered various sites to the north of Times Square. In the late 1920s, there were plans for a new Metropolitan Opera House to be incorporated into what became the Rockefeller Center; if the drawings by a young architect on the Rockefeller team, Wallace K. Harrison, had been acted upon, what is now the skating rink might have been Metropolitan Plaza. The onset of the Depression put an end to these ideas. Later, there was talk of the Met moving into the Shriners' 'Mecca Temple', the City Center on 55th Street (which in fact became the first home of New York City Opera), or perhaps siting the opera within the confines of Central Park where, like the Metropolitan Museum of Art, it could expand into whatever was its requisite space. After the war came the suggestion that a new Metropolitan Opera be constructed at Columbus Circle where Broadway intersects with 59th Street. This idea, too, was abandoned and the New York Coliseum built instead.

As with any house move, a number of different considerations had to be just right before the upheaval became feasible, among them the location, money, opportunity and the determination to go ahead. Bing was nothing if not determined. The years of Depression and war were over, New York was expanding and the Met needed to move. Around this time, New York's venerable Carnegie Hall (a couple of blocks up from the City Center and the home of the New York Philharmonic) was threatened with sale and possible demolition. Thus, the city's principal symphony orchestra and opera company were both on the lookout for a new home. Wallace Harrison, who had retained his sketches for the aborted Rockefeller Center opera house, wondered whether the opera and orchestra might consider some kind of joint venture. A possible shared location suggested itself. Just south and west of where Broadway crosses Columbus Avenue, broadly between New York's 60th and 70th Streets, were several slum blocks earmarked for redevelopment. Largely occupied by recent immigrants from Puerto Rico, this was the territory of the Jets and Sharks, the gangs in Bernstein's *West Side Story*. A recent Federal Housing Act provided money for urban regeneration; just what was needed for New York's West 60s.

Not everyone, however, thought it was necessarily what the Metropolitan Opera needed: America's leading opera house in the midst of what was at the time a drug-and-crime infested slum. In the fullness of time, New York's Lincoln Center, with the new Met the dominant presence, would become the first multi-institutional centre for the arts in the world – a veritable campus of culture providing a home for two opera houses, two concert halls, a theatre, an arts library and, across the way, a music academy. But the period between its conception and birth was to prove agonizing. Cautiously, the Met and the New York Phil jointly approached John D. Rockefeller III, who agreed his Foundation would help to finance the proposed centre. The sheer complexity of the project boggled the finest minds as 'Lincoln Center Inc' entered into negotiations, and occasional lawsuits, with dozens of existing owners of land and buildings. One of the most intransigent, Joseph P. Kennedy (father of JFK), owned a giant automobile warehouse and he succeeded in delaying proceedings by two years.

The Metropolitan Opera, the largest of all the potential tenants, was present throughout all these complicated manoeuvrings. As plans unfolded, its house-proud general manager found himself fighting a series of battles. Bing had reservations about having a concert hall just along from his opera house, an objection he tactfully expressed in terms of the traffic chaos he thought might ensue. On this, Bing was overruled. Other tussles he won. Thus, the new opera house would have fewer than 4000 seats, not the 5000 favoured by some on his board, a figure that might have brought increased revenue on a popular night but would have made it impossible to produce smaller-scale works such as those of Mozart or – without amplification, which everyone was against – to engage any but the most stentorian voices. Bing was adamant, too, about the quality of the sightlines and acoustics the new auditorium must have, and that the theatre should be equipped with proper side stages and rehearsal rooms and decent space for storage, workshops, washing facilities, administrative offices and the rest, all of which were woefully inadequate in the old house. Good European that he was, Bing also demanded windows that actually opened, preferably throughout the building but at least for his own office. He also prevailed upon his friend Marc Chagall to design a pair of canvases on operatic subjects with which to embellish the giant picture windows on either side of the façade of the new building.

As often happens on such mammoth projects, much was trimmed as work progressed and budgets soared. Much to Bing's distress (and Harrison's), the new Met was already too small on the day it opened. Toilet facilities were (and remain) inadequate, while the corridors on either side of the auditorium at orchestra level are too narrow to accommodate comfortably the crowds leaving at the end of a performance. Nor was the building properly equipped to house the expanding seasons, the greater number of productions and the ambitious sets it was soon required to accommodate. There was another battle, too, that Bing fought and lost. If he was initially disturbed at the prospect of his opera house lying cheek by jowl with a concert hall, he was aghast when it was proposed to bring on site not only the ballet company from New York's City Center but, in the same multi-purpose theatre, the City Center Opera Company. 'I was under the impression that Lincoln Center aimed at the highest cultural achievements,' he sniffed, arguing that, with two opera companies in adjacent buildings, the wider public might confuse the two to the inevitable detriment of the Met. Worse, the State Theater erected to house the New York City Ballet and Opera companies, designed by one of America's most distinguished architects, Philip Johnson, was completed first. So Bing suffered the indignity of seeing NYCO inaugurate its new premises on Lincoln Center while his own house remained a building site. Worse, where NYCO scored a bullseye with the 25-year-old Domingo starring in Ginastera's brand new *Don Rodrigo*, the opening night at the new Met some months later featured a jinx-beset premiere of a soon-to-be-forgotten opera by Samuel Barber.

Time plays strange tricks. Once the Met had bedded down successfully in its new location, the building became a top attraction and the opera company retained its reputation as America's finest. People visiting Lincoln Center would congregate around the fountain in the central plaza and look up at the Met's five arches, redolent of those at Venice's St Mark's, the outer ones embellished by the great Chagall canvases, while a glimpse through the theatre's front doors revealed a red-carpeted curved central staircase to the treasures beyond. To those who attended performances, the somewhat four-square auditorium may have lacked the glamour of its predecessor or its sense of proximity to the stage, but sightlines and acoustics were excellent considering the size of the place. Audiences gasped with pleasure as the sunburst chandeliers, which seemed likely to impede many people's view of the stage, dimmed just before curtain-up and rose towards the ceiling like so many spiders climbing up their webs. Meanwhile, in the State Theater, the New York City Opera under Julius Rudel's artistic leadership presented a more adventurous repertoire than the Met and nurtured a stable of outstanding singers, several of whom went on to have major international careers,

The elaborately curved central staircase: one of the most striking (and frequently photographed) features of Wallace K. Harrison's 'new' Metropolitan Opera House, inaugurated in 1966.

among them not only Domingo but also José Carreras, Cornell MacNeil, Sherrill Milnes, Samuel Ramey, Beverly Sills* and Shirley Verrett. In the longer run, however, the NYCO suffered more than the Met from the proximity between the two, a disadvantage not helped by the fact that it had to share its theatre with a sequence of dance companies. By the early new century, the Met was producing one richly grandiloquent production after another (and, in common with many theatres, losing audiences in the wake of 9/11) while the NYCO was casting about for a new home, a quest that was to prove unsuccessful and in 2007 was finally abandoned. For the foreseeable future, it seemed, New York's two opera companies, the Metropolitan and the City Opera, would remain uneasy neighbours beneath the shared umbrella provided by Lincoln Center.

*

By the final decades of the twentieth century, there were opera companies and houses all over North America. In San Francisco, the company that Merola had founded and nurtured grew and thrived under his successor (and former chorus master), Kurt Herbert Adler, while Carol Fox and then Ardis Krainik presided over many seasons of high-quality opera in Chicago. Some of the finest productions of Wagner were staged in Seattle while St Louis became

*Sills went on to become general manager of the NYCO, chairman of Lincoln Center and, finally, chairman of the Metropolitan Opera – the company from which Bing excluded her as a singer for many years.

noted for excellently produced opera in English and the Glimmerglass Festival for its adventurous repertoire and imaginative stagings. Many companies took pride, too, in producing the operas of recent and contemporary American composers while American singers, directors and conductors became prominent not just across North America but throughout the operatic world. By 2000, there were well over one hundred professional opera companies in the USA and Canada, 70 per cent of them formed since 1960 and well over half since 1970. The number of professional performances of opera across North America rose from just over 1300 in 1980 to 2100 twenty years later.

Opera was not universally welcomed. Some regarded it dismissively as a pastime appealing to a mere handful of cognoscenti and patronized by far fewer people than went to good, accessible, egalitarian, easily comprehensible all-American entertainments such as film, jazz or the Broadway musical. Many felt there was something almost sissyish about an interest in opera, a form of entertainment 'real men' would not want to attend unless – and then only reluctantly – at the behest of their wives. A 2002 poll cited non-opera goers as listing, among other reasons they would be unlikely to attend, that they did not understand the art form, would feel 'intimidated' and 'uncomfortable' at the opera, had no-one they could go with and felt they would not understand the story. Almost two-thirds of respondents said that foreign language was a major barrier to attendance. Others cited the high price of tickets, a preference for other forms of performance art and, in many cases, a simple lack of time or interest. What would induce them to go to the opera? They might be enticed by a famous performer such as Pavarotti, they said, or if invited by a friend or family member. But many noted that their spouses or friends did not enjoy opera, others adding that it was 'upper-crusty' or 'elitist'.

Yet for all the resistance, millions of Americans across the country clearly took to opera both as art and as event. In some places, a particularly dynamic personality at the helm could be an important factor: a musician such as Merola or Domingo, perhaps, or a wealthy patron like Samuel Insull or 'Buffy' Chandler. Or of course an inspiring general manager: without John Crosby there would probably have been no Santa Fe Opera; without David Gockley, Houston Grand Opera might never have become a major presence; and without Glynn Ross and Speight Jenkins it is hard to believe Seattle would have become America's Bayreuth. Local political and economic conditions, too, could have an impact: the fact that the San Francisco city fathers decided to finance a war memorial complex and include an opera house in the designs gave opera in their city a massive boost, while the onset of Depression helped reduce the labour costs involved in building the War Memorial Opera House. In Chicago, by contrast, where a new opera house had just been completed, the Depression almost brought high-quality opera to a standstill. Each location, too, had its own social conditions. Minnesota Opera produced

Dvořák's *Rusalka*, confident this would help draw in members of the state's large Czech community. In Washington DC, Martin Feinstein and later Domingo could appeal to donors with the argument that high-quality opera would be a worthy embellishment to the nation's capital. In Los Angeles, by contrast, Domingo's Latino background could be used to help boost the local profile of his opera company.

There was also a wider picture. Not only were the great majority of America's opera companies founded since the Second World War; a remarkably high proportion were in the South and Southwest and dated from the 1970s or later, while several in traditionally cultured northern cities struggled to stay in business. This was paralleled by broad demographic trends. During the decades following the war, many of the traditional heavy industries of the north began to experience increased competition from abroad and chronic labour disputes at home. Many factories and even entire industries faced closure. Meanwhile, large inner-city ghettoes became the focus of social unrest and rebellion. Gradually, many entrepreneurial northerners began to desert the 'Rustbelt' states of the old industrial north for the 'Sunbelt' states of the south and west. What began as a stream had developed into a flood by the end of the century. Between 1990 and 2000, the population of the greater Houston area grew by over 25 per cent, making it by 2005 the seventh-largest metropolitan area in the United States. Greater Atlanta during the same period grew by a colossal 38.4 per cent, becoming by 2005 the nation's ninth-largest metropolitan area. Dallas–Fort Worth, the nation's fifth-largest metropolitan area by 2005, had experienced a 29.4 per cent growth in population during the final decade of the twentieth century, and broadly similar trends were experienced in Miami–Fort Lauderdale, greater Los Angeles and countless other, smaller but rapidly expanding towns and cities throughout the South and West.

In many of these thrusting new conurbations, opera came to be something of a civic badge of honour, alongside museums, art galleries and other cultural and educational amenities. The much-vaunted American sense of local and regional pride was partly a function of sheer distance; if you lived in Miami, Houston or Los Angeles, you were more likely to support your local theatre, orchestra, dance company or art museum than another hundreds or thousands of miles away in New York or Chicago. There is a loose parallel here with eighteenth-century Italy or Germany, where every self-respecting town had its palace and its opera house. The great cities of the United States were not self-governing states, of course, much less monarchies or duchies. But like Parma and Palermo, Mannheim and Munich, the muscular new Sunbelt centres drew part of their identity from the well-endowed cultural institutions they were able to display. Opera thus came to be widely regarded as a defining characteristic of a healthy city that also wanted to attract corporate headquarters and an educated workforce, an essential element in the civic infrastructure. Like glassy skyscrapers and 'shi-shi' restaurants, opera was a conspicuous indication of the presence of wealth and culture, a proclamation of civic success.

Opera in the USA never received more than a minute proportion of its budget from government sources, whether federal, state or local. In 2005, barely one quarter of 1 per cent of the New York Met's annual budget of $220m came from public funds. Where protesters in Milan might demonstrate against government subsidies to La Scala or the British press resent Lottery funds going to Covent Garden, similar animosity has scarcely been apparent in the United States. It was not quite true that government in the USA did not help subsidize opera. It did, by enabling those who supported opera to claim tax exemption on their donations; this was, in effect, a 'foregone subsidy', one that took the form of the government foregoing the tax revenue it would otherwise have collected. There was, however, an essential difference between this form of subsidy and the direct grants more common in Europe where citizens knew that a proportion of their taxes would be used to support cultural institutions such as opera companies. In the USA, the decision was left to the individual donor. The federal government, in other words, offered citizens the opportunity to make tax-exempt donations to the social or cultural amenities of their choice, and it was up to the opera company to persuade potential donors that this was where they should direct their largesse.

As they did so, Joe Citizen was bombarded from all sides. Why go (or donate) to the opera when downtown was packed with so many other forms of evening entertainment, not to mention such modern domestic pleasures as were offered by television, DVDs or the Internet? And why support the opera or symphony, widely seen as representative of a traditional European culture, over (say) the requirements of a disability group struggling to finance a sports facility, a local hospice or an Afro-American theatre or improvisatory dance group? These were hard arguments for opera companies to address. Yet the very multiplicity of claims on the American donor was one of opera's strengths. Precisely because opera in America co-existed alongside so many other forms of cultural activity, it could reasonably claim that it survived and thrived not because it was placed there by kings or princes or governments but because people had called it into being and wanted it. This helped give it a legitimacy increasingly emulated elsewhere as opera went global – and traditional ways of defending and financing it came to be widely undermined.

CHAPTER 21

Opera Goes Global

Back around 1900, few countries other than Italy or Germany could boast more than one or two major opera houses or permanent, professional companies. A century later, there were a hundred or more in the USA, three or four of them among the most highly reputed in the world. There was opera, too, in Cape Town, Istanbul, Reykjavik, Rio, Seoul and Singapore, new houses emerging in Tokyo, Toronto, Tel Aviv, Tenerife, Oslo, Cardiff and Copenhagen, and old ones rebuilt or rebuilding in London, San Francisco, Barcelona, Buenos Aires, Tallinn, Milan and Venice. *Aida* was produced alongside the Nile and *Turandot* in the Forbidden City. Across the world the 'Three Tenors' became as celebrated as pop stars, while a typical evening at any reputable European opera house might feature, say, a Czech opera with local-language surtitles performed by singers drawn from North or South America, Eastern or Western Europe, Australasia, South Africa or Asia. Bangkok was planning its first *Ring* cycle. And in the entire southern hemisphere, the most famous building was an opera house.

*

There had been opera in Australia since the earliest days of European settlement, as we have seen, most of it produced by touring companies, and it usually found an audience. When Melba toured Australia with the J. C. Williamson theatre company in 1911, 1924 and 1928, large numbers poured out to see and hear her. In the 1930s and 1940s, attempts were made to establish resident companies, first in Melbourne and later Sydney, but it was only in the mid-1950s that the idea of permanent opera began to take firm root. To some, the idea of having a national opera had come to be regarded almost as a badge of national pride: analogous, perhaps, to the national airline, Qantas, that brought the young Queen Elizabeth II to Australia in 1954. Australians revelled in what was the first visit to their country by a reigning monarch. Later that year, a trust was set up with the aim of establishing national ballet, drama and opera companies. In honour of the Queen, it was named the Australian Elizabethan Theatre Trust (the AETT).

The 1965 'Sutherland–Williamson' tour visited the main cities in Australia with seven operas. Joan Sutherland herself appeared in five, including several (such as Bellini's *La sonnambula*) with the young and little known Luciano Pavarotti.

Two years later, the Olympic Games came to Australia for the first time. One by-product of the excitement and pride generated by the Melbourne Olympics (as in Los Angeles twenty-eight years later) was a determination to help boost the arts. That year, 1956, was also the bicentenary of the birth of Mozart, and the AETT agreed to fund what was in effect Australia's first national opera company. With four Mozart operas as its core repertoire and using the orchestras of the Australian Broadcasting Commission, it performed in Melbourne and a number of other cities. The company came to be dubbed the Elizabethan Trust Opera Company and acquired as music director the man who had got Covent Garden opera started after the war, Karl Rankl. If Rankl had expected an easier workload and more recognition than he had experienced in London, he would have been disappointed. Performances took place in theatres not built for opera and the events themselves were more often reported in the society pages, alongside the fashions seen at the races, than in the arts pages. Money was hard to raise and early seasons had to be curtailed or even cancelled. Rankl resigned but the company limped on.

There the story of permanent opera in Australia might have remained were it not for the efforts of another great Australian diva. That and the indomitable Williamson company under its veteran director Sir Frank Tait. In 1965, the 'Sutherland–Williamson' tour (which included the young Italian tenor Luciano Pavarotti) took seven operas to all the main cities in Australia.

Joan Sutherland herself appeared in five of the operas, and everywhere she sang, the theatre was sold out. When the opera was the little-known *L'elisir d'amore*, starring the equally unknown Pavarotti and no Sutherland, tickets cost less but there were empty seats. Many people had evidently paid to see a 'name' or a 'star', or to enjoy sharing the applause for a globally famous compatriot, more than to hear high-quality opera as such. However, audiences were enthusiastic and the tour garnered considerable publicity. After one matinee starring Sutherland, the demand for repeated curtain calls ate into the time the backstage staff needed to strike the sets and prepare for the evening performance of another opera, so that the curtain went up half an hour late. At the end of the final performance of the tour, Sutherland came on stage one final time to sing 'Home, Sweet Home' to an ecstatic audience, as Melba had done before her, the Melbourne *Age* reporting that 'women in evening gowns stood on seats and applause continued for forty minutes'. What the whole enterprise confirmed was that there was undoubtedly a public for opera in Australia, though it had to be shrewdly marketed and potential audiences carefully coaxed. Whatever the inadequacies of the supply side, in other words, the potential demand for opera in Australia was substantial.

One other thing made it happen. Fort Macquarie was a tram depot on the tip of Bennelong Point, a spit of land overlooking Sydney harbour. After the war, trams began to be phased out and the decision was made, under the leadership of the New South Wales Premier, Joseph Cahill, to redevelop the land as the site of an opera house. Cahill was not known to be an opera lover. But he was keen to leave monuments to his premiership, and he seems to have been impressed by the arguments of Eugene Goossens, director of the NSW State Conservatorium of Music at the time, that the city deserved decent music venues. Cahill saw to it that the Sydney Opera House was pushed through as a prestige project, to be funded in large part by a lottery with contributions from the state and federal exchequers. A widely publicized international architectural competition was won by the Danish architect Jørn Utzon. From Utzon's early designs, it rapidly became clear that his stupendously curvilinear building, topped by towering white sails (or shells, or sharks' fins), would be almost impossible to construct given the current state of architectural technology. Costs rose, compromises were introduced and Utzon resigned. In the event, the building, originally budgeted at A$7m, came in at well over A$100m and took nearly fifteen years to construct. Once it finally opened in 1973, the great, gleaming edifice provided a magnet for opera lovers from all over the world. Moffatt Oxenbould, for many years the artistic director of what became Opera Australia, worked as a stage manager on the Sutherland–Williamson tour and was also among the first generation to work in the new building. He long remembered how, as the complex gradually took shape, the excitement and optimism he felt put him in mind of the end of *Rheingold* when the gods cross the rainbow bridge into Valhalla.

By the time the house opened, Australia was led by one of the few governments in its history to place culture high up the political agenda. Gough Whitlam was not Prime Minister for long (he was ousted in a constitutional *cause célèbre* late in 1975). But while he reigned in Canberra, the arts received unaccustomed federal funding and political goodwill.* For the first time there was in Sydney the prospect of regular if not full-time employment for a company of operatic soloists, choristers, orchestra, wigmakers, scene painters, carpenters and stage managers. People visited from all over the continent to see the famous edifice by the harbour, while opera lovers from Europe and America, seeking to escape the privations of the northern winter, found Sydney within their sights as long-haul jet flights became cheaper and more frequent.

The Sydney Opera House was exciting as a piece of sculpture (and one of the first public buildings in Australia to instal effective air-conditioning). But there were also disappointments. The complex was in fact a multi-purpose centre containing several auditoria of varying sizes. The largest was originally intended for opera, the second for concerts and a third to accommodate drama. When it was nearing completion, the Sydney Symphony Orchestra had a full season and a regular audience base while the young opera company struggled to put on a six-to-seven-week season. Not surprisingly, the orchestra demanded the largest of the performance spaces and this duly became the concert hall. The opera was consigned to a smaller auditorium containing only 1500 seats (which meant low ticket revenue), a small pit (which meant no large-scale Wagner or Strauss), variable acoustics and no decent wings or backstage space. In due course, the opera company grew in size and ambition, performing for something like eight months each year in what was a frankly inadequate space, and Sydney's opera people began to talk about the serious renovations their theatre required.

Renovation would create its own problems. For a start, what would you renovate? Given the fact that the famous sails atop the complex were also the side walls of its performance spaces, it was hard to think how the opera theatre could be provided with decent wing space without altering the external structure of the building itself. Nor, for the same reason, could the orchestra pit or the seating capacity of the house be appreciably expanded. If it were decided to go ahead with limited, practical renovations, these, unless minuscule, would necessitate a period of closure. The impact of this on the audience for opera in Sydney could easily be imagined. Of all the world's

---

* In some of the states, too, the early/mid-1970s were good years for the arts. Conspicuously so in South Australia, where the cultured and liberal-minded Governor, Don Dunstan, sought to raise the profile of his capital city. The Adelaide Festival Theatre opened in the same year as the Sydney Opera House, 1973, but on time and within its A$20m budget. Twenty-five years later, this was the city and this the theatre that staged Australia's first complete production of Wagner's *Ring* cycle.

The most famous building in the southern hemisphere: a new opera house takes shape.

opera houses, that in Sydney probably had the highest proportion of non-locals among its audiences. It was the building that most visitors wanted to see more than the opera itself. Bennelong Point was always packed with crowds from all over Australia and abroad, taking photographs, milling around, climbing the steps to the box office. The great tour liners that docked in Sydney harbour were bursting with passengers anxious to go to the opera, if only for an act before going on to dinner. When the main opera houses in Barcelona, London, Milan and San Francisco underwent rebuilding, the companies had to work hard to retain their audiences, appearing in a variety of other theatres around town. In Sydney, ticket sales could well plummet if the opera company were to perform once again in 'ordinary' theatres.

One possible solution, at least in theory, would be to move the centre of gravity of what was supposedly a national company from Sydney to Melbourne for the duration. On paper, this might have appeared a sensible idea. Melbournians would tell you about the valiant efforts by Gertrude Johnson back in the 1930s to create a permanent company in their city, while the theatre in the Melbourne Arts Centre inaugurated in the 1980s was far better equipped than the Sydney Opera House. Furthermore, the city had a cultural and intellectual (and operatic) history every bit the equal of anything its brasher counterpart could boast. Here, however, we enter murky waters. The rivalry between Sydney and Melbourne dates back to the nineteenth century and remains as vigorous and sometimes as acrimonious today as ever.

When the Sydney-based Australian Opera merged with the Victoria State Opera in 1996 to produce what became known as Opera Australia,* Sydney-siders saw it as a rational amalgamation making for a truly national company while in Melbourne it was widely denounced as yet another crude grab for dominance by its rival. For all these reasons, it was hard to imagine the Sydney Opera House being put out of commission for a sustained period or the fabric of the building being subjected to substantial reconstruction. Nor could the headquarters of Opera Australia be easily moved to Melbourne without a political fight. So, at least for the time being, it seemed likely that things would remain much as they were.

Further dilemmas, too, confronted what was now Opera Australia. As an avowedly national rather than international company, it was both a show-case and a nursery of domestic talent, a stance reinforced by union and visa restrictions on the number of non-Australian singers the company could engage. While it helped nurture the skills of many Australian singers who went on to make big careers elsewhere, its development was profoundly influenced, and not always for the better, by the harsh facts of geography. Anyone attending performances by Opera Australia, whether in Sydney or on tour elsewhere, was likely to catch a well-rehearsed show by a team of talented artists who could sing, act, move and, in general, create a satisfying, fully rounded performance. This sense of ensemble, of all the artists moving in the same direction, could communicate a sense of artistic integrity some-times lacking in old-fashioned European houses where poorly rehearsed guest stars would step into unfamiliar productions to deliver their showpiece arias. But what could you do in Sydney or Melbourne if your Tamino or your Scarpia called in sick? Opera Australia, unlike the flagship European and American companies, could not afford to train and pay principal covers for every role and often had to rely in a crisis upon other less experienced members of the company. Nor did OA have anything like the range of talent available a mere plane-hop away that could normally be relied upon by American or European companies. Sydney and Melbourne were some twenty-five or more flying hours and eight or ten time zones away from most of the world's main opera centres.

The 'tyranny of distance' cast further shadows. Few of the world's top singers would normally agree to appear in Australia in opera at the height of their careers. Some would schedule a succession of concerts across Australia, perhaps under the auspices of the ABC, as part of a wider promotional tour, and a number of Australian singers with big international careers (notably Sutherland) would make a point of performing back home when they could. But, for most, the idea of staying 'Down Under' for the lengthy period required for the rehearsal of opera and subsequent run of performances

*It was nearly dubbed Australian National Opera until it was pointed out that the acronym, ANO, was Italian for anus.

was out of the question. Australian audiences were therefore unlikely to encounter the kind of supreme singing that, in the words of the experienced critic Roger Covell, 'makes you delirious with excitement and sends you spinning homewards in a dream'. For that, Australians generally had to travel elsewhere.

*

Yet for all this, it remains true that Australia has produced many singers of high quality, some of them going on to make important international careers -- far more of them, it would seem, than are warranted by its population size. The common explanation points to the wonderful sunshine and the open-air lifestyle Australians are able to enjoy. But sunshine in itself does not make for great voices; if it did, operatic history would celebrate more Greek or Portuguese singers and fewer from Russia or Scandinavia. The explanations go deeper.

The professional opera singer, like the athlete, works in a highly competitive world. Those who reach the top reap abundant rewards while there, but are liable to encounter as many snakes as ladders. As it happens, Australia has produced not only a disproportionate number of gifted opera singers but also far more than its fair share of successful athletes and sports champions. Great numbers of Olympic medals often go to Australian athletes, while any list of the most celebrated Australians in the nation's history would surely include the singers Melba and Sutherland and the cricketer Don Bradman.

A number of parallels suggest themselves between the two kinds of profession. Some are obvious. Sporting prowess and good singing both depend upon the practitioners' robust good health and the capacity to perform at maximum physical and mental capacity precisely when required, and both kinds of performer stand to benefit from a healthy natural environment. The memoirs of top opera singers are packed with instances of the sheer physical wear and tear involved in what, for lesser mortals, might seem one of the most exhausting of professions. Most of us, when tired from the strain of recent illness or lack of sleep, can manage to undertake the normal toil of our workaday lives. But for an opera singer, a day at the office often means having to stand through six hours of rehearsal, or to sing a strenuous role before a demanding audience that has paid good money to hear you at your best. Nobody wants to see a Bradman or a Melba off form. The typical Australian, wrote the historian Geoffrey Blainey, has prized 'determination, stamina, courage and the will to succeed'. Blainey was writing about Australia's attitudes towards its sportsmen. But his words could have been applied just as much to its singers.

In addition, opera like athletics provided talented Australians with an avenue of social mobility, a pathway towards greater status and money in a society largely devoid of traditional forms of social hierarchy. Australians might have freed themselves from many of the older, stuffier British institutions, priding themselves on cutting down tall poppies and treating everyone equally. But no society can be totally egalitarian and most crave indications of social hierarchy, whether imported or homegrown. In Australia, the two merged as British influence was ousted with one hand and retained with the other. Thus, many Australians, while contemptuous of the pretensions of the 'Poms', long continued to relish the residues of British pomp and circumstance, sharing a 'cultural cringe' towards the perceived superiority of what was still widely regarded as the 'mother country' (it is a moot point whether Don Bradman brought greater glory to Australia by humiliating England's cricketers or by crowning his career by receiving a knighthood from the King). Opera and athletics, furthermore, both offered the prospect of international travel, for prowess in each was portable. And if you managed to make a name for yourself abroad, you were more likely to be given star treatment back in Australia. Bradman had to score centuries in England before he became truly celebrated back home and Sutherland to star at Covent Garden. When Sutherland returned to Australia for her triumphant tour in 1965, she was welcomed everywhere by a sobriquet, 'La Stupenda', she had earned in Italy.

Nor is the analogy between sport and opera limited to the career patterns of performers for there are similarities, too, in the nature of their respective audiences. Australia may be famous for its great open spaces, piercing sunshine, leaping marsupials, red deserts and sandy seashores. It is the size of the continental United States and contains less than one-tenth the population. What is less often remembered is that the great majority of those twenty million Australians live clustered in or near half a dozen major cities, all of them on or near the coastline. The characters portrayed in such TV soaps as *Neighbours* or *Home and Away* are far more representative than the mythologized 'Outback' images projected by Crocodile Dundee or the canvases of Sidney Nolan. Since soon after colonization, Australia developed into an essentially urban and suburban society containing a large middle class with abundant leisure time in which to enjoy its disposable income. Blainey writes that Melbourne and Sydney were probably 'the first large cities in the world where a majority of the wage-earners ceased their working week by two o'clock on the Saturday afternoon and were thus free to play or watch games'. Add to this a mania for the erection of exciting new buildings, and what do you get? A spectator culture on a massive scale, every town having its theatre, its sports stadium and a plenitude of pubs, inns and park space for people to gather in their numbers before and after the event. They still do: the main cricket grounds in Sydney and Melbourne and the adjacent facilities accommodate crowds that dwarf anything the so-called 'mother country' can match, while huge audiences turn out for the amplified, open-air opera performances or celebrity concerts now promoted around the country during Australia's long, balmy summer evenings. There are enthusiastic audiences, too, for the professional-level, domestically produced opera that is now on show every year in all the capital cities of Australia, while singers from Australia are regularly cast nowadays throughout much of the operatic world. Perhaps it is not so surprising after all that the only country whose most universally recognized building is an opera house is not one of the sedate nations of old Europe but the land of the thrusting egalitarian and the self-confessed larrikin.

*

By the beginning of the twenty-first century, opera had become the latest chic in several of the wealthier capitals of Asia. In both Japan and South Korea, there was a widespread and enthusiastic (some would say fanatical) audience for opera, performances at the New National Theatre in Tokyo starting early so that Japan's salarymen could attend the show and still do the long commute home afterwards. In China, new houses were erected in a number of cities, among them Shanghai and Hangzhou, while the appearance of a space-age, bubble-topped Grand National Theatre (the 'Egg', they nicknamed it) in the heart of Beijing became a controversial talking point. None of the shiny new culture centres emerging in Asia was intended to produce year-round opera; there was as yet neither the money nor the audience for anything so ambitious. Rather, they would aim to showcase a handful of operatic productions each year, or perhaps a mini-festival, alongside a diet of more popular and/or traditionally Asian fare. In the event, operatic standards varied, audiences were not particularly discriminating (tending to cheer any visiting star from the West) and money for opera here, as everywhere, proved scarce.

Much of the opera produced in Asia relied in small or large part on the presence of European or American talent. Sometimes, the spark came from a homegrown dynamo, usually someone part-educated in the West. Thus, Hong Kong's Lo Kingman was responsible for many operatic productions not only in Hong Kong itself but also in a number of cities in China. Educated at Hong Kong's Diocesan Boys' School, Lo later had the chance to study stage design and direction in the opera theatres of Rome, Naples and Perugia. In 1993, he became director of the Academy for Performing Arts, and he was a pivotal figure in the establishment of the Hong Kong Philharmonic and Sinfonietta orchestras, the Hong Kong Arts Festival and the Hong Kong Cultural Centre and Arts Centre.

In Bangkok, similarly, opera was the passion of an entrepreneurial Thai musician, Somtow Sucharitkul, who – like Lo Kingman – was the very embodiment of East–West cultural fusion. Educated at Eton and Cambridge, Somtow went on to spend twenty years in Los Angeles before returning to his native Thailand. A skilled composer and conductor, he also became known as a prolific author of gothic and horror novels. A man of huge ambition and

The 'Egg' is gradually hatched: Beijing's National Theatre for the Performing Arts designed by the French architect Paul Andreu.

a natural romantic, Somtow launched Bangkok Opera in 2000, carefully navigating his infant company through what were initially choppy waters. In due course, things began to stabilize. Wolfgang Wagner was persuaded to come out and inaugurate the Thailand Branch of the International Wagner Society, while mutually beneficial links were forged with opera companies in Singapore and Malaysia. A sequence of productions in Bangkok, including Western repertoire pieces and new works (among them Somtow's own compositions), helped the company attract audiences and press attention, to the point that Somtow felt confident enough to announce plans for a *Ring* cycle.

Critics argued that Somtow was merely transplanting into modern Asia an art form produced by and for a different time and place. Not at all, he would riposte, arguing that Asia was in a good position to reinvigorate and augment a Western culture that had in some respects lost its way. That might mean writing new operas calling upon both oriental and occidental musical and dramatic traditions, or else producing the great works of Mozart, Verdi, Wagner or Puccini at a high musical level in modern-minded stagings designed to appeal to educated Asian audiences: on the one hand, Somtow's own opera about the ancient Thai royal family and, on the other, a *Zauberflöte* with the three boys entering on a *tuk-tuk*, *Aida* placed in ancient Siam or a Buddhist-inspired *Ring*. In his own compositions, Somtow incorporated an often richly textured fusion of both Eastern and Western harmonic and instrumental traditions. Some found the attempt to draw on the two traditions a little facile, a form of musical political correctness; others admired Somtow's capacity to cross cultural boundaries in a world of rapidly disintegrating certainties.

Without a determined figure like Somtow, there would probably have been no Bangkok Opera, certainly no company prepared to take on the *Ring*. By 'company', I refer to what Somtow himself calls self-deprecatingly a 'cottage industry' run from his private home. Here, he would compose, maintain a copious correspondence, sit on the phone, negotiate and sign contracts, hold auditions and rehearsals, and purvey and consume generous quantities of coffee. The British singer Michael Chance, who worked with Somtow, recalled how the sheer busyness of this home-cum-office reminded him of what must have been the atmosphere in Handel's house in London's Brook Street back in the 1730s. Like Handel, Somtow was composer, impresario, artistic director, fund-raiser and principal performer all rolled into one. Like Handel, too, he was assiduous in his cultivation of the high and mighty on whose goodwill his entire enterprise depended. Somtow, who could trace his own ancestry back to a branch of the Thai royal family, dedicated some of his compositions to the current King or Queen and portrayed the historical monarchy and social elite in his operas. This was shrewd politics (again, the model of Handel springs to mind). Modern Thailand, after all, retained a traditional, hierarchical social structure while the country's politics tended towards tight central control with a strong military presence; anyone wishing to do something as audacious as to found and develop an opera company would only have been able to do so if guaranteed goodwill from the top. And this, Somtow somehow managed to obtain.

The importance or popularity of opera in Asia should not be exaggerated. It was never likely to be more than a niche interest appealing to a small number. Like Dr Johnson's dog standing on its hind legs, the more surprising thing was that Western opera took root in Asia at all. The compliment was hardly returned: in no Western cities, even in an age much taken by the appeal of 'World Music', was traditional Peking Opera or Japanese Noh theatre likely to reach an enthusiastic or sizeable public. It may have been easy to caricature those attending the Tokyo New Theatre or the Thailand Cultural Centre in Bangkok as affluent, well-educated, well-travelled locals and visiting foreigners all keen to display their cultural sophistication. But there were plenty of such people among the opera-going public in Europe and America, too. The fact remains that opera – an extravagant, expensive and quintessentially Western art form – clearly found an audience of sorts in the East. And, to the benefit of opera goers everywhere, a succession of fine singers emerged from Asia's music academies, many going on to successful careers in the West.

*

Opera had gone global. It was also popular. In North America, which experienced perhaps the most spectacular burgeoning of operatic activity, most permanent or semi-permanent opera companies managed to attract a healthy audience. Main season attendance in the USA rose between 1983 and 2000 from 2.5 million to 4.3 million and overall opera attendance, 1980–2000, from 5.5 million to 6.7 million. By 2000, something like 3.3 per cent of the adult population of the United States attended opera each year, a figure rising at a faster rate than the adult population as a whole and faster, too, than the equivalent statistic for dance, symphony concerts or theatre, each of which was experiencing slight audience shrinkage. Opera audiences, not surprisingly perhaps, tended to be better educated and more affluent (and older) than the population as a whole. Yet there was evidence that opera was the only 'classical' art form that was seeing the median age of its audience being slightly lowered. These figures must be understood as starting from a low base. In 2002 (in the wake of 9/11, which for a while depressed audiences at most forms of entertainment), 11 million people attended Broadway shows, 17 million attended musicals and 26.5 million visited art museums, while symphony concerts had an aggregate audience of 30 million – figures opera could never hope to match. But the rapid rise in the quantity and quality of opera performed in America in the later decades of the twentieth century, and the size of the audience it attracted, is remarkable and, in its scale and timescale, perhaps unparalleled.

Opera was widely popular, too, in its original European heartland. In Copenhagen, the new opera house was intended not to supplant but to supplement the existing theatre, while in reunited Germany, for all its economic woes, something like ninety different theatres continued to present some 7000 opera performances in a typical year (6946 opera performances, according to 2002 statistics). In France, there was an audience for high-quality opera not only in Paris but in Aix, Bordeaux, Lyon, Nice, Strasbourg and elsewhere.

*

As opera reached out to ever wider audiences, this inevitably fed back into the nature of what was being produced. One symptom, or by-product, of operatic globalization was the growing trend for particular operatic productions, often with similar casts, to be shown in a number of different centres. This was not entirely new. Certain works on the margins of the popular repertoire had often had a vogue for a while, usually because of the popularity (and marketability) of particular singers. Mary Garden hugely boosted the fortunes of Gustave Charpentier's opera *Louise* in the first twenty years of the last century, while a deciding factor when several top houses mounted Verdi's *Luisa Miller* in the mid-1970s was the readiness of Domingo, Pavarotti and Carreras to take on this opera at that stage of their careers. More recently, the early careers of Gheorghiu and Alagna helped fuel revivals of Gounod's *Roméo et Juliette* while the stratospheric facility and comedic gifts of Juan Diego Flórez and the French soprano Natalie Dessay persuaded Vienna, London and New York to bring back Donizetti's *La Fille du régiment*.

La Fille was a co-production. By the turn of the millennium, it was becoming increasingly common for opera companies to share productions. Perhaps the chosen work or composer had a centenary coming up, or a celebrity singer was about to record the work and keen to help promote it. Much of the detail, artistic and administrative, could be discussed via email, fax and the occasional conference-call. Assuming everything was sorted out satisfactorily, the outcome would normally be an initial run of performances by the lead company and then, later in that season or the next, the same production – often with the same principals – would turn up in the schedules elsewhere. Audiences in several countries would be able to enjoy decently financed, well-rehearsed performances that their home company alone could scarcely have afforded. Meanwhile, the production team, and perhaps a starry soloist or two, would be paid for a total of maybe twenty performances rather than just the half-dozen or so that any one house would normally think it prudent to mount in a season. And the management of several companies could be reasonably certain of recouping their initial expenditure.

Co-productions represent the heavy division of a movement that also recruited the foot soldiers of the profession into its ranks. Today, any number of operatic mercenaries are able to deploy their artillery across the operatic battlefield. Maybe the military analogy is inappropriate; there are probably fewer battles at today's efficiently run opera houses than in the past, except perhaps on stage. But most solo singers are mercenaries, at least by comparison

Lauren Pelly's witty staging of Donizetti's *La Fille du Régiment*, featuring the formidable vocal and comedic talents of Natalie Dessay (right, with Alessandro Corbelli), was a co-production shared by the Vienna State Opera, London's Covent Garden and the New York Metropolitan.

with their more sedentary predecessors (or with today's salaried orchestral players and chorus members). Once established, few operatic soloists remain contracted to long service in a specific house, preferring to remain free to sell their talents, normally through an agent, to the highest bidder, often amortizing the cost of learning a difficult part or an unfamiliar opera by reprising the role elsewhere. If Covent Garden's Germont, Gurnemanz or Golaud has a resourceful and well-connected agent, he may well be booked to do the same role a season later – doubtless for a higher fee – in Houston, Lyon, Hamburg or Naples.

Arguably, the spread of opera – like that of T-shirts, fast food and hotel chains – had the effect of homogenizing the product. Some sensed a loss of what used to be called a 'house style'. At (say) Mahler's Hofoper, Ebert and Busch's Glyndebourne or Klemperer's Kroll, productions tended to be stamped with the overall authority and philosophy of those at the top, a kind of aesthetic family feeling that differentiated what you saw there from what was available elsewhere. For a decade from the mid-1980s, when Peter Jonas, Mark Elder and David Pountney ran English National Opera at the London Coliseum, a succession of exciting productions by what came to be dubbed the 'Powerhouse' regime had an unmistakably muscular edge to them.

People began to talk, too, of the erosion of national styles of musical production and performance. Toscanini was often praised for the instinctive *italianità* he brought to the works of Verdi while Furtwängler was said to have an innately German feeling for Wagner. Among singers, the most lauded exponents of Italian opera long tended to be from Italy or at least Mediterranean Europe, few of whom were thought wise to assay the works of Wagner. The simplistic identification of composers and performers with the music of their homeland was always misleading; the Verdi revival in the first half of the twentieth century was spearheaded not in Italy but in Germany, Toscanini was one of the finest Wagner conductors of his time, while the most idiomatic exponent of such archetypally French operas as *Thaïs*, *Louise* and *Pelléas* was the Scottish-born Mary Garden. But by the twenty-first century, such exceptions had become the rule as hordes of successful performers traversed the operatic world, found their way in several languages, consumed a global cuisine and became inured to a sequence of indistinguishable hotels and airport lounges. It was no longer a matter of comment if a talented French or Japanese singer starred in a Verdi opera, an Italian conductor excelled in *Boris* or *Werther* or a new production of *Carmen* in America was directed or designed by a Russian or an Israeli. In such a world, 'national' styles were at a premium and 'house' styles ever rarer.

A further contribution to the apparent homogenization of opera across the world came from recordings. Between around 1970 and the 1990s, particularly as CDs replaced LPs, new recordings of all the best-known operas and many more obscure ones poured off the presses and made big money

Few Londoners got to visit the Dresden opera in the days of Wagner or Strauss. But by the twenty-first century, new opportunities had opened up for opera audiences around the world.

LONDON HAS A NEW HIGHLIGHT:
THE OPERA IN DRESDEN.

Daily nonstop from Gatwick to Dresden. Book at ba.com

SAXONY. STATE OF THE ARTS.   ba.com

for their companies and artists. Sensing a rising tide of consumer interest, companies such as EMI (Angel in America), Decca (London), Polygram and Deutsche Grammophon – and later the giant corporations who bought them – also transferred to CD much in the back catalogue. The cornucopia reached a peak in the early 1990s in the wake of the initial triumph of 'The Three Tenors'. Far from deterring the audience for live opera, recordings helped feed the appetite: people craved to see and hear the stars in the roles they had committed to disc. One result was that the leading recording artists were everywhere in demand. Another was that millions among the record-buying public thought they knew what their favourite operas should sound like: anyone who sang the role of Tosca was likely to be compared with Callas, every Rodolfo with Pavarotti, Otello with Domingo, Lucia with Sutherland. Performers, too, if familiar with the recordings of their great exemplars, could find it hard not to model aspects of their interpretations on what they heard. In due course, the development of video recording meant that a production from Salzburg or Paris might be seen as well as heard a year later in private homes from Tucson to Tokyo, Rome to Rio, Perth to Perth.

For many reasons, then, the latter part of the twentieth century probably saw a diminution, if not the end, of distinctive operatic styles as between one centre and another. The operatic caravan, containing a troupe of peripatetic singers and productions, seemed to be increasingly on the move across the operatic map, setting down briefly in one country after another and bringing much the same kind of smooth, all-purpose international product to each. Maybe. But the news was by no means all bad, especially if one result was that opera audiences in many countries now had a chance to sample some of the best the world had to offer. What they heard, furthermore, was in some respects more 'authentic' than anything available to their immediate predecessors.

*

Imagine you are attending a concert in London's Royal Festival Hall, the Berlin Philharmonie or perhaps the concert hall at the Sydney Opera House or Disney Hall in Los Angeles. You find your seat and settle down to read the programme. A celebrated 'period' orchestra will perform works by Bach and Haydn on original instruments under a conductor who is an acknowledged expert on authentic, 'historically informed' performance style. You are evidently about to be transported back to just the kind of music-making the composers themselves might have experienced in eighteenth-century Leipzig or Esterházy. Or perhaps you are at a prestigious opera house such as the Opéra Bastille in Paris or Berlin's Deutsche Oper about to enjoy Mozart or Wagner. Here, too, you can be confident that the latest scholarship has been brought to bear to ensure that what you are about to hear is as close as possible to what the composers intended.

During the second half of the twentieth century, a generation of scholar-musicians emerged who devoted themselves to the quest for authentic perform-ance practice. Handel came increasingly to be played on baroque violins with strings of gut not of metal and the keyboard continuo in *Figaro* or *Così* on a harpsichord not a piano. A fiddle made in 1770 was self-evidently more appropriate for Gluck than one made in 1970, the brazen buzziness of a valveless trumpet more fitting than a sleek modern instrument. Unfortunately, most eighteenth-century harpsichords, violins or trumpets were owned by private connoisseurs or locked away in museums, too rare or perhaps insuffi-ciently robust to be taken on the performing circuit. So a revival of traditional instrument-making occurred as new equivalents of old instruments were manufactured, careful fabrications of the originals. Nor was the quest for authentic instrumentation confined to 'Early Music'; no longer was a tuba considered adequate, for example, where Berlioz or Verdi had specified the ophicleide or the cimbasso.

The quest for historical authenticity went far beyond the instruments on which players performed. An instrument, after all, is mute. When Heifetz was complimented by an admirer on the wonderful sound his violin made, he is said to have looked quizzically at his Strad, put it to his ear, and replied sourly that so far as he could tell it made no sound whatever. The point, of course, is the nature of the music-making. Here, there was a veritable revolution in the latter half of the twentieth century as musicians and musicologists struggled to revive not only the instrumentation for which compositions had been written but also the pitch at which they would have been played (in the eighteenth century often a good semitone lower than in the late twentieth) and, in general, their composers' detailed intentions about how they wanted their works to be performed. Printed scores were compared with original manuscripts and mistakes corrected while cuts were opened up in operas that had traditionally been given in edited versions. Operas which their composers had subsequently altered and adapted were subjected to scholarly debate about precisely which version the composer had favoured and whether the 'final' version was always necessarily superior to the 'original'.

One by-product of this new musical historicism was that it helped widen the standard operatic repertoire as neglected works by early composers were taken out of the cupboard, dusted down and performed. By the turn of the millennium, it was no longer unusual for a major opera house to schedule operas by Monteverdi or Cavalli, while previously little-performed operas by well-known composers (such as Mozart's *Idomeneo* or *La clemenza di Tito*) now began to enter the operatic mainstream.

Further insights followed. In the Vienna of Mozart's or Beethoven's time, most halls and orchestras were smaller than today's, and instruments less penetrating. The implication for our own times? That the overtures to *The Magic Flute* or *Fidelio*, for example, were probably intended to be given with less gravitas and more of a spring than our grandparents were used to. Modern singers, for their part, tended to perform rather differently from their predecessors two or three generations earlier. Recordings reveal some celebrated artists from the past taking what we have come to regard as a great deal of liberty, sliding from note to note, holding on to the high ones an unconscionable time and interpolating grace notes where none was indicated. Today's purists baulk at unmarked use of appoggiatura or portamento or the sundry sighs and grunts of singers simulating the throes of high passion. Better to be more precise, more accurate, more obeisant to the wishes of the composer: this was the new orthodoxy. Today's Cavaradossi or Canio would be asked to sing, not gulp, the last lines of his big tragic aria and no longer would the Duke, however fine his voice, be permitted to overpower his colleagues in the *Rigoletto* Quartet.

As scholars published new critical editions of the *oeuvre* of one composer after another, removing generations of accumulated excrescences in the process, audiences were increasingly likely to be offered what the composer had wanted them to hear. No longer would any major house offer a truncated *Walküre*, while few productions of *Don Carlos* would now omit the opening Fontainebleau act that helps explain all that follows. Tasteful ornamentation in baroque or bel canto arias replaced the extravaganzas favoured by an earlier generation of singers, and conductors learned to observe the correct slides and slurs, trills and tempi, rests, rhythms and rubato.

Yet we must be careful here. For a start, as musical performance became more 'authentic' around the world, operatic production (as we will see in the next chapter) became interestingly more innovative and diverse. There is much else, too, that differentiates the experience of opera in our own times from anything available in the past. Modern theatres are less likely to burn down, better equipped with facilities for comfort and safety, and often air-conditioned. Nor do today's audiences turn up in horse-drawn carriages and wear wigs or top hats, camisoles or crinolines. For all the admirable authenticity of the musical scores and the style in which they are performed, the overall experience of opera for twenty-first-century audiences is very different from that of earlier times. Moreover, the historical filter through which we experience artworks of the past is overlaid with the jagged sights and sounds of modernity. We cannot listen to *Figaro* or *Traviata* through the ears of those to whom these works were first performed. Today's opera goers have heard Bartók and Stravinsky, know about Auschwitz and Hiroshima and are at home in a world of film, jet planes, computers and global terrorism. We smile when we think of the emperor who told Mozart his opera contained 'too many notes' or of Beethoven's contemporaries finding his music discordant. Their operas, and those of Verdi or Strauss, reach modern ears through a sensibility markedly different from that of the times in which they were composed, a fact that no amount of authentic performance practice can alter. If your view of operatic history is limited to a list of musical texts, be comforted that you are often able to hear performances that sound much as originally intended. But in the broader sense, the replication of the operatic experience of earlier times is impossible.

Nor, I suspect, would most of us want it if it were available. Even musically. We may not be absolutely certain how composers such as Cavalli or Handel performed their own works. But we do have first-hand evidence of how Richard Strauss or Edward Elgar conducted their own scores or how some of Puccini's favourite singers performed his arias; there are recordings to tell us. One of the most striking things about those recordings is what would nowadays be regarded as the 'old-fashioned' style of the orchestral playing: the greater variations of tempo and a wealth of vibrato and glissandi – analogous in a way to the vocal idiosyncrasies – that most nowadays regard as vulgar and unacceptable. Thus, modern performances of works by such composers tend to 'improve' upon the originals, playing with a streamlined precision that is not always evident in the recordings of the original creators. Strictly speaking, this might be regarded as an abnegation of historical authenticity. Most modern performers would probably say, rather, that today's musical standards are higher than those of a century ago and that we are able, therefore, to give the work of these composers a greater degree of

'Old music in modern surroundings' became the template in opera theatres around the world, such as the Opéra Bastille, Paris, which opened in July 1989 on the bicentenary of the French Revolution.

accuracy than they themselves would normally have expected to hear. In short, that the present is able to improve upon the past.

Which brings us back to the Deutsche Oper, Opéra Bastille and Sydney Opera House. You may or may not like to see Mozart or Verdi operas in modern buildings of concrete, steel and glass; perhaps you prefer a great temple of the arts from an earlier era such as Covent Garden, La Scala or the Barcelona Liceu – all of them recently rebuilt. Either way, what most opera houses around the world were offering by the early new century was a succession of more or less 'authentic' musical revivals from an earlier era, performed in a modern or heavily restored building containing good sightlines from most seats, an audience that arrives on time, and facilities such as electric lighting, air-conditioning, elevators, flush toilets and adjacent parking facilities and/or good public transport, all of which would have been unimaginable a century or two ago. This basic formula – old music in modern surroundings – became the template in opera theatres around the world, and few who attended were disposed to complain. Where controversy lay was in the way the canon of 'old' works came to be produced.

CHAPTER 22

New Ways of Presenting Old Works

As opera went global, it reached out to wider audiences than ever before: not only in the multiplicity of opera houses that sprang up around the globe but also on television and radio, CD and videodisc, and at a plethora of arena, open-air, big-screen, country house and educational event. The musical performance might be scrupulously 'authentic' or sung to the accompaniment of anything from a solo piano to an amplified 100-piece orchestra, while the overall experience became more user-friendly, whether in the theatre, piazza, cinema, classroom, park or stadium. 'Opera for All' was the new buzzword among managements as old and young, black and white, gay and straight, rich and poor were all invited to climb onto the operatic omnibus. Not everybody chose to do so, while some who did doubtless found the experience uncongenial, hopping off at the next stop. But many came and stayed.

Yet for all the squeaky-clean physical modernity on offer to twenty-first-century audiences, the music generally performed remained resolutely rooted in the past, the standard repertoire coalescing around a small number of works by composers long dead. Try as they might, managements found it difficult obtaining audiences for 'unknown' works, old or new. Of course, people turned out to see a highly hyped production tied, perhaps, to an anniversary, a controversial production or the presence of a famous star. But for audiences, performers and managers everywhere, the staple operatic diet settled down to a repertoire of perhaps forty or fifty acknowledged favourites written during the 'long' nineteenth century, from Mozart's *Entführung* (1782) to Puccini's *Turandot* (1926). The origins of this 'canonization' of the repertoire have roots deep in operatic history.

*

In Mozart's day, or that of Weber or Bellini, most opera house bosses, like their audiences, looked forward to the production of freshly minted works each season. As with today's movie business, 'new' generally sold a lot better than 'old'. That began to change from around the middle of the nineteenth

In the 1840s, new works by Halévy or Meyerbeer could attract a full house. A century later, these composers were little performed while few new operas proved popular, audiences preferring a recurrent diet of old favourites by Mozart, Verdi, Wagner and Puccini.

century as a recognized canon of existing works gradually began to emerge that (like the plays of Shakespeare) came to be regarded as great hallmarks worthy of repeated public presentation. Until as late as the 1920s, new and old continued to co-exist in reasonable harmony, audiences flocking to what they regarded as the best of both: *Louise* as well as *Lucia*, *Tosca* and *Tannhäuser*, *Rosenkavalier* and *Rigoletto*. However, it was increasingly clear by then that fewer and fewer new works were establishing themselves as part of the standard repertoire, the world's opera houses and audiences relying more and more on a handful of works created in a rapidly receding past. This remains largely the case to this day.

Even more remarkably, perhaps, the components of the 'standard repertoire' itself have changed remarkably little over the past hundred years. True, Victorian audiences rarely encountered Mozart's *Così* (now a great favourite) but flocked to works by Meyerbeer rarely performed today. Gounod's *Faust* and *Roméo et Juliette* or Ponchielli's *La Gioconda* slipped down the league table of popularity while a few works by earlier composers (Monteverdi, Handel, Gluck) and more recent ones (Berg, Britten) gradually edged their way up. Nonetheless, it is instructive to compare the dozen or so titles most frequently performed at the world's leading opera houses a century ago and now. What is most striking is the consistency of the core repertoire over time and across the map. Around 1900, few major opera houses felt they could do without *La traviata*, *Aida*, *Lohengrin*, *Die Walküre*, *Carmen* and (by the early twentieth century) *La Bohème*, *Tosca* and *Madama Butterfly*. As one might expect, Italian operas had an edge over German ones in Italy while Wagner was more often produced in the German and Nordic countries. Similarly, works such as *Boris Godunov* and *Eugene Onegin* were at or near the top of the list (with Mozart and Wagner a long way down until recent times) in Russia. Despite such differences, however, most of the key works have remained consistently among the more frequently produced throughout the operatic world.

This historic shift, from 'new' works to 'old', took both practical and aesthetic form. We have caught hints of the practicalities here and there as our narrative has criss-crossed the highways of operatic history. In Italy in the first half of the nineteenth century, we encountered many a beleaguered impresario anxious lest he fail to secure a promised new opera in time: Lanari enlisting the police against Bellini's librettist Felice Romani to get him to deliver a text by the agreed date, Merelli soft-talking the young Verdi into writing an opera in order to help fill a gaping hole in the Scala schedule. Few singers could rely on the reprise of familiar roles, even the most celebrated having to learn several new ones each season. The tenor Adolphe Nourrit, working for Barbaja in Naples in the 1830s, reported that he was obliged:

> to rehearse every day, to get a new role in my head every month, never to know one day what I am to sing the next. Hardly to be certain in the morning what one will be called upon to do in the evening, and not to be excused for anything short of fever!

As for the composer, Verdi found himself launched by his success with *Nabucco* on a *métier* requiring him to produce a regular stream of operas against a relentless succession of tight deadlines. It was a career pattern that Rossini had opted out of in his thirties and which later played a part in the breakdown of Donizetti's physical and mental health. The fact was that the opera-going public expected novelty. If an impresario or his artists failed to deliver, they would jeopardize their chances of employment the following season.

By the latter part of the century, things were changing. The emergence of a handful of powerful publishing firms, allied to the development of internationally enforceable copyright laws, began to offer successful composers the chance of greater financial security. This enabled them to spend more time polishing a smaller number of compositions. Increasingly lengthy gaps tended to elapse between the composition of Verdi's mature works, a luxury he could never have afforded earlier; his first fifteen operas were produced in ten years (1839–49) while his last five appeared in 1862 (*La forza del destino*), 1867 (*Don Carlos*), 1871 (*Aida*), 1887 (*Otello*) and 1893 (*Falstaff*).

Verdi provided a gold mine to his publishers, Ricordi. But composers do not live for ever, and publishers became increasingly shrewd in how they marketed existing stock. Casa Ricordi was something of a brand leader, actively encouraging new productions of older works. They also continued to produce a stream of new works by relatively unknown composers: every opera lover was on the lookout for the next Verdi or Wagner. So were the music publishers, some of whom would agree to retain a promising youngster for a few years as he struggled to find his compositional voice and marketability. Thus, Puccini received payment from Ricordi as he edged his way towards *Manon Lescaut* while Sonzogno retained Giordano, who went on to compose *Andrea Chénier*. But the signs increasingly suggested that all but the most talented among the new generation were in danger of being eclipsed by the growing popularity of the old.

The shift can be expressed in aesthetic terms, too, especially in the German world. In 1820–25, fewer than a quarter of the works programmed by the Leipzig Gewandhaus Orchestra were by dead composers; a generation later (by which time Mendelssohn had revived works by important predecessors such as Bach), that figure had more than doubled. 'Serious' music, as we have seen, came to be given moral status and its greatest progenitors almost deified, Beethoven being joined in the pantheon of 'genius' by Bach, Mozart and others. The noblest form of music (and therefore arguably the highest form of art) was 'absolute' music: chamber works, symphonies and the like. Opera, while frequently performed and much loved, was regarded by some as entertainment of a lower, commercial kind with words, characters and plots and its association with the theatre. An article published in Vienna in 1829 recounts sadly how the members of a choral society, 'spoiled by easy-to-perform, agreeable, and flashy opera music', were not able to adjust to the 'strict, serious tone' of their new director, a church organist keen to teach them masses and oratorios. In due course, however, opera followed suit. Wagner, adopting a highly romantic view of art and the artist, made it his life's mission to bring salvation to society through the medium of his multifaceted music dramas. In time, his works came be regarded as embodying quasi-sacred significance and his Bayreuth theatre the qualities of a temple.

We may smile at the romantic conception of art and the artist as spiritual forces in a pedestrian world bringing enlightenment to the philistines. But many, and not only in Germany, shared this perspective. During the mid- and later nineteenth century, opera houses resembling Greek temples were erected in half the capitals of Europe and attended by a public that was quiet and respectful once the performance had started. The operas these audiences attended were increasingly drawn from an agreed repertoire of 'great' works, often performed by the same artists who, having learned a role for London or Paris, could by now travel in some speed and comfort to display it that same year to an adoring public in New York or Buenos Aires. At first, the emerging canon was far from watertight. Like a swimming pool, it was periodically refreshed by fresh draughts as older fare drained away, the 'grand operas' of Auber and Halévy, for example, coming to be replaced in popular esteem by more recent French works such as *Faust* and *Carmen*. But these soon became embedded, alongside the creations of Wagner and Verdi, with a handful of acknowledged masterworks by earlier composers. During the decades on either side of 1900, new operas continued to be produced in considerable numbers, but few except a handful by Puccini or Strauss proved durable. Meanwhile, many opera singers, accustomed to the soaring phrases of earlier styles, often found the thick orchestration of late romanticism difficult to surmount and the jagged musical line of modernism hard on the voice. A singer such as Mary Garden or Caruso still expected to appear in a stream of premieres; Plácido Domingo sang a tiny handful, mostly written expressly for him, none of which entered the mainstream. By his time, most opera singers, like the audiences to whom they performed, preferred to revisit a collection of acknowledged classics than to venture into unfamiliar and (in all senses) unrewarding territory.

The situation familiar to Barbaja, Nourrit or Donizetti was thus reversed as operatic taste converged around what came to be regarded as the standard repertoire: the agreed works that opera goers knew, loved and would pay to see and revisit. These works constituted more than a repertoire; they were a 'canon', a collection of art works carrying a patina of moral and ideological value. Everybody's favourite operas were not just good box office. They were also widely regarded as examples of an uplifting form of high art, created by a handful of figures most of whom were long dead and touched by genius.

Throughout the twentieth century and into the twenty-first, new operas continued to be composed and produced, some of them of outstanding quality. Meanwhile, the Early Music revival retrieved from the archives works scarcely known since their composers' own day. Nothing on the opera stages of the world exceeds the impact of a powerful production of the Orpheus operas by Monteverdi or Gluck, or of Berg's *Wozzeck* or *Lulu* or Britten's *Peter Grimes*, *Billy Budd* or *Midsummer Night's Dream*. But not one of these has entered the standard repertoire around the world. All are special occasions, usually performed with visiting stars in the principal roles. When *Grimes* is regularly performed all over the world in English by the same locally recruited casts who routinely sing *Carmen* in French and *Tosca* in

Italian it may be said to have entered the operatic 'canon'. But that day is sadly not yet.

*

As popular taste crystallized around a small number of constantly repeated works, various subsidiary professions received a boost. Musicology and the study of musical history, scarcely important academic fields in the early nineteenth century when the repertoire was constantly refreshed by novelty, grew exponentially in the twentieth, the intellectual microscope focused with ever-greater intensity onto the music of the past. Systematic music criticism, too, developed into a recognized profession during the nineteenth century and the considered views of such diverse figures such as François-Joseph Fétis, Eduard Hanslick, Robert Schumann and George Bernard Shaw, expressed at length in their respective journals, came to be widely consulted. The critic may not be able to 'control the stars' (wrote the exasperated Shaw, contemplating the 'bouquet-throwing' encouraged by one diva from the USA); but at least he could 'administer the stripes'.

Not only the music itself but the way it was performed came to be minutely analysed and of paramount interest. And, in the case of opera, how it was staged. If the canon of operatic works regularly performed came to be stubbornly fixed in the past, the same cannot be said of the productions they received. Latter-day music directors may have striven to perform their scores 'as the composer intended'. Stage directors, by contrast, often seemed to reject historical authenticity. This is hardly surprising. The sets, stage machinery, lighting and acting styles of Monteverdi's or Mozart's day would have struck later generations as risible. By modern times, theatres were equipped with a range of facilities that earlier practitioners could scarcely have dreamed about: revolves, side stages, TV monitors, digitized lighting systems and the ability to deploy and strike the most complex three-dimensional sets in the twinkling of a brief intermission. Into this theatre marched a new-style professional who simply did not exist during the earlier history of opera: the producer, or director.

In the past, a creative and energetic composer such as Wagner or Verdi might concern himself with the sets, props and costumes to be used in a production of his work, and the moves and visible emotions of the characters. More commonly, such details would be left to the house management and the performers themselves. Leading singers often provided their own costumes; after all, Patti or Melba, who travelled with wardrobes packed with sumptuous gowns and priceless jewellery, surely knew what suited them better than some little sempstress employed by Covent Garden or the Paris Opéra. Nor did the Pattis or Melbas consider it incumbent upon them to turn up to all the rehearsals of a production in which they were billed as the star. An emissary could come and tell them all they needed to know. After all, it was *their* Violetta, Lucia, Juliette or Mimì people had paid to hear and see and, assuming they sang like angels, who would dare criticize their acting?

In due course, figures such as Mahler or Klemperer, picking up the Wagnerian concept of the *Gesamtkunstwerk*, attempted to integrate all the arts in their productions, bringing in directors and designers from the theatrical world and casting singers who could act and looked right for their parts. Progress was slow. When Rudolf Bing took over the New York Met in 1950, he was appalled at the many routine, unimaginative productions on the roster, a shortcoming he made it his first task to correct. Bing had some difficulty at first persuading singers such as Melchior, Björling or Di Stefano to attend rehearsals. But in this, as in most other respects, Bing usually prevailed. Across the Atlantic, Covent Garden's David Webster sacked Tito Gobbi for non-appearance at rehearsals. Soon, every self-respecting operatic management was insisting that production values were as important as musical ones. Gobbi, as it happened, was a superb actor. But Melchior and Björling and many of their contemporaries and immediate successors were not. Crowds flocked to see them, and later Sutherland, Caballé, Jessye Norman and Pavarotti, not because of their dramatic abilities but because of their voices.

By the final years of the century, things were changing. For one thing, the core operatic repertoire appeared to have become stuck, as we have seen, after the appearance of *Rosenkavalier* and *Turandot*. One way opera might be helped to remain a living art form was by producing old works in new ways. The profession of producer, scarcely known in 1900, was paramount by 2000. Increasingly, it often seemed, performances came to be reviewed more as drama than as music, the production getting greater coverage than the singing. Audiences, too, in an age of DVD and the TV close-up, came to expect opera singers to inhabit all aspects of whatever character they were portraying, while artists, in their turn, were generally more prepared to take direction. Richard Jones, one of the more radical among the new generation of opera directors, recalled working as a junior assistant on an *Aida* production in the early 1980s starring Pavarotti and Ricciarelli: 'it was absurd,' Jones recalled later (2007), 'how many conditions they imposed', adding that singers and audiences were now more receptive to what imaginative direction could add. Increasingly, artists came to be cast not only for their ability to sing their roles but also to look and act the part. The press made much unkind fuss when the magnificent but (at that time) portly American soprano Deborah Voigt was dropped from a Covent Garden production of Strauss's *Ariadne auf Naxos* in 2004 and her place taken by the more pulchritudinous Anne Schwanewilms. Three years later, Covent Garden had a triumph on its hands with the waif-like Natalie Dessay, a flat-chested tomboy in overalls, starring as Donizetti's 'Daughter of the Regiment' – a role last portrayed at the ROH forty years earlier by the big-boned Joan Sutherland. By now, few opera houses, audiences or producers tolerated mere 'stand-and-deliver' performances; the reign of the fat or immobile Manrico, Mimì or Brünnhilde was coming to an end. You could no longer simply 'park and bark'.

The increasing prominence of the 'singer-actor' was one symptom of the ever-growing significance attached to operatic production. Opera, it was said, must (like any other kind of drama) speak to the audiences to whom it was directed if it were to make an impact, to touch on reference points they would recognize. Sometimes, this was done with blazing directness: setting *Fidelio* in a Nazi concentration camp, for example, or in Guantánamo, or representing Wotan as a capitalist factory owner and the Nibelungen as his wage slaves. More often, the message was presented emblematically: disguised, satirical or deliberately designed to overthrow the comfortable nostrums of past productions. During the final decades of the twentieth century, a number of stage directors, several of them working in East Germany and then internationally, brought a radical, neo-Brechtian approach to operatic production, angering and exciting audiences in equal measure. As a new young generation of directors picked up the message, it seemed to some opera goers that the production 'concept' was too often taking precedence over the music. The European opera house, at one time plagued by the imperious prima donna or dictatorial maestro, was now said to be suffering from a new disease: *Regietheater* or 'produceritis'. Some spectators were excited, others outraged, as they encountered Mozart's Despina as a waitress in a roadside greasy spoon, Don Giovanni shooting heroin or feasting on the carcass of a dead horse, Otello suppressing a gay obsession with Iago, naked buggery in the first scene of *Rigoletto* (the Duke's court *is* supposed to be decadent) or a group of Verdi conspirators sitting on a row of toilet seats. Every now and then, an imaginative director would find a way of producing a much-loved classic that would find truly widespread appeal. Jonathan Miller's *Rigoletto*, revived again and again by English National Opera, placed the action in New York's Little Italy in the 1950s. Another ENO production, Anthony Minghella's 2005 *Madame Butterfly*, made abundant use of traditional Japanese theatrical imagery and was chosen by Peter Gelb to open his first season as general manager of the New York Metropolitan a year later.

In general, the leading American houses tended to favour more conventional productions. Joseph Volpe, Gelb's predecessor at the New York Met, said he hated productions by 'pedants' who essentially rewrote works according to their own 'vision' rather than presenting them in terms the audience could understand. His *Ring* and *Rigoletto* were big and beautiful and the public loved them. And there is little doubt that some among the new breed of opera directors relished the sheer perversity or shock value of what they brought to their stagings. The best among them, however, came to their task intimately familiar with the music drama they were setting and keen to illuminate it as best they could, and were able to work just as creatively with their musician colleagues as did more traditionally minded directors. The one

In Anthony Minghella's imaginative production of *Madame Butterfly*, the heroine's little son is played not by a child actor but through traditional Japanese-style puppetry.

thing on which all were agreed was the constant need to re-produce the works of the past so that they had meaning for the present. Audiences and critics might be angered by gratuitously offensive post-modernism; but this was usually more interesting than a bland production of a revered classic that merely tried to re-create the stage pictures popular in a bygone age.

*

There was another thing, too, seemingly small in itself but immensely resonant, that marked out the operatic experience in the global age. By the late twentieth century, performances of the standard repertoire in most of the leading opera houses of the world were being performed in their original language. What could be more 'authentic' than playing *Lohengrin* in German, *Carmen* in French and *Aida* in Italian? This is how these works were written and how their composers and early audiences first heard them. Yet the return to original-language production – for that is what it was – represented something of a revolution.

A century ago, most singers spent the greater part of their careers as members of an ensemble in their home (or adopted) country. Opera houses usually performed in the language of their audience, or else perhaps in Italian since that was conventionally deemed the language of opera; *Faust*, composed to a French text, was sung in Italian the night the New York Metropolitan opened. A generation later, that opera was performed in Berlin with the young American soprano Geraldine Farrar as Marguerite. Farrar sang in Italian and the chorus in German, while Farrar's greatest hit while in Berlin was Massenet's *Manon* which she performed, as would have been expected, in German. In the 1930s, Björling learned his craft singing operas in Swedish, Flagstad in Norwegian. By that time, the multinational casts that performed at the New York Met or at Covent Garden's pre-war Italian or German seasons sang the great canonic works in their language of composition. But the tradition of vernacular language continued to be widely accepted, by artists and audiences alike, until well into the second half of the twentieth century. Thus, we find Schwarzkopf learning *Traviata* in English for a post-war production at Covent Garden, while Gigli routinely included Italian-language versions of the Farewell aria from Wagner's *Lohengrin* or the tenor romance from Bizet's *Les pêcheurs de perles* in his London recitals. The young Callas sang *Tristano* and *La Walkiria* in Italy, while in Paris the Opéra continued to advertise Wagner's *Vaisseau fantôme*, Verdi's *Le Trouvère* or *Le Chevalier à la Rose* by Richard Strauss.

By the end of the century this had changed, all but a handful of major opera companies performing the standard repertoire in the original language. There were good artistic reasons for this: the composer had the sounds and stresses of the original text in mind while composing the music. It made professional sense, too: a better passport was provided by acquiring the role of Carmen in French or Tosca in Italian than knowing them only in Dutch, Danish or English. Caruso or Gigli, for all their travels, lived in a bubble of *italianità*; their latter-day successors were citizens of the world jetting from country to country, continent to continent, offering a luxury commodity that had to be as universally recognizable as a BMW or a Rolex.

One might have expected some audience resistance. As we have seen, people who do not like opera have often singled out the fact that it is performed in a 'foreign' language. Whether in the columns of the London *Spectator* in 1711 or in response to sophisticated modern opinion polls, it was the 'foreignness' of opera and the fear that they 'wouldn't understand it' that many cited as a deterrent to attendance. If people can understand what's going on, Lilian Baylis used to say in her forthright way (and she spoke for many), they'll come to performances. If so, the turn to original-language performance in more recent times might seem to have been counter-productive. Why would potential audiences in the twenty-first century be any more receptive than those of earlier times to opera performed in a language they did not understand? An important part of the answer lies in the invention and widespread adoption of surtitles (or 'supertitles') – vernacular versions of the operatic text projected above the proscenium or on individual seat-backs: the operatic equivalent of movie subtitles.

Surtitles were first introduced in Toronto in 1983 by Lotfi Mansouri, the general director of the Canadian Opera Company (and later of San Francisco

Opera), and they were rapidly adopted elsewhere. From the outset, critical opinion was radically divided. Some, especially among the cognoscenti, argued that titles were intrusive, distracting audiences from what was happening on stage; instead of watching the opera they were watching the projected text. It was like going to the tennis at Wimbledon and watching the scoreboard instead of the match. 'You go to opera to listen and to watch, not to read,' fulminated Rodney Milnes, at the time editor of the British journal *Opera*, in November 1986. 'You read beforehand.' As for singers, they 'loathed' them, it seemed. Surtitles, Milnes concluded, were 'a denial of everything that theatre stands for', something he would fight 'tooth and claw'. The letters column in subsequent editions bristled with opinionated point and counterpoint. A singer's agent wrote in to say that in his experience titles had 'vitalized audiences and made them much more aware of the music drama at hand. Does the Editor read so slowly,' he added archly, 'that he is unable to absorb the information without being distracted by it?'

Similar debate occurred elsewhere as one company after another began to experiment with the new idea. At the New York Metropolitan Opera, its music director, James Levine, let it be known that titles would be introduced at the Met 'over my dead body'. Did singers really loathe titles? Yes, if they heard an audience laughing before they had sung the witticism translated

So that's what they're singing! Surtitles show Rodolfo (in Act I of *La Bohème*) inviting a hesitant Mimì into his studio.

above them. Did it make them lazy with their enunciation now that most in the audience were not listening to the words anyway? Probably not, but who could be sure? The debate went back and forth, among audiences and performers, in the musical press and in the operatic corridors of power. Like all new technologies, surtitles had their blips in the early years and were an easy object of fun: I remember a *Figaro* in the 1980s where Barbarina had the audience in hysterics when her little song proclaimed 'I have lost it! I have lost it!', and a *Don Giovanni* in which 'Viva la libertà!' was translated as 'Hurry for Freedom!' (and did one opera house really have Cavaradossi proclaim that his beloved Tosca had 'a black eye'?). Sometimes the system broke down completely, only to restart later out of sync with what was happening on stage. In time, however, things settled down as those responsible learned the tricks of their new trade. From 2002, New York's Metropolitan placed titles on seat-backs, a procedure later adopted elsewhere, some companies offering various language options – and the opportunity to switch the whole thing off – at the touch of a button. And James Levine remained at the Met.

More controversial was the use of surtitling for vernacular-language performances. A storm burst over the head of English National Opera, a company committed to opera in English, when it announced in 2005 that, in response to public demand, it was introducing surtitles. To David Pountney, the company's former head of production, a surtitle was analogous to a 'celluloid condom inserted between the audience and the immediate gratification of understanding.' In a variation on the sexual theme, the conductor Paul Daniel opined that surtitles had the effect of making audiences 'passive and castrated'; if you are just having the information fed to you, said Daniel, you cannot feel an opera 'in the bollocks'. And, in a shift from sex to violence, former ENO boss Peter Jonas said sourly that if that was what people wanted why not hold public executions on the stage of the Coliseum? Many feared that the introduction of English-language surtitles for English-language performances spelled the end of ENO's entire *raison d'être*. Others pointed out that, however carefully a singer might enunciate, few could render their words clearly audible in all parts of so large a house. The very nature of opera, indeed, with its stratospheric passages, rapid runs, multi-voice sections and often thick orchestral accompaniment tended to militate against the clear audibility of the text. Debate was fierce, but the ENO stuck to its decision and went ahead with its new policy.

As opera went global, so did surtitles. By 2000, John Rockwell of the *New York Times* thought the value of titles was obvious to all; they were so widely and immediately appreciated by the vast majority of opera goers, he wrote, that they hardly seemed controversial any more. 'And think of the advantages! Long, complex operas are rendered instantly comprehensible and engaging to a wide audience.' Rockwell also sensed that the introduction of titles, by bringing the drama of opera to the foreground, may have helped widen the repertoire by giving managements the courage to stage new compositions or unfamiliar early operas. And, of course, by enabling audiences to understand the details of what was being said, they helped facilitate more imaginative production. In 2005, Henrietta Bredin wrote of surtitles: 'They're here to stay. There is no longer any point in discussing whether or not opera performances in languages other than English should have surtitles. Everyone's doing it now.'

'Everyone's doing it now.' Surtitles were the new operatic democracy. With what can only be regarded as a nice symmetry, Bredin's article appeared in the *Spectator*.

*

By the turn of the century, a profound conceptual rift had opened up at the heart of what the operatic world expected to hear and see. On the one hand, performances came to be sung more often than not in their original language (backed up by vernacular titles) while the musical presentation, similarly, tended to defer increasingly to the carefully researched intentions of the composer. In these respects, the operatic experience, if not 'authentic' (nothing could be totally so), became increasingly 'historically informed'. Yet at precisely the same time, the dramatic side of operatic presentation was often deliberately plucked from its historical roots, familiar works being produced in styles their creators would not have recognized. Musical values, in other words, were fastidiously conservative, dramatic ones sometimes provocatively avant-garde. On occasion, this discrepancy could make for conflict as this or that singer or conductor, evidently unhappy with a production in which they were booked to appear, was reported as having quit as a result of 'irreconcilable artistic differences'. In February 1994, the Russian conductor Gennadi Rozhdestvensky walked out of a Covent Garden production of Massenet's *Chérubin* in which the director was said to have asked him to adopt slower musical tempi to fit the production. A few years later, Christopher Hogwood withdrew from an Opera Australia production of *Der Freischütz* he was due to conduct in which, among other things, the director planned to place an interval in the middle of Act II of Weber's carefully constructed three-act drama. 'Smart cookie,' commented the *Sydney Sunday Telegraph* critic of Hogwood (15 September 2002) after slamming the production.

More often, thoughtful stage directors and open-minded musicians worked in reasonable harmony together in the hope that their combined efforts would produce work whose impact exceeded the sum of its constituent parts. Thus, as opera went global, it was revivified, if not with a steady stream of major new additions to its core repertoire, by a marriage of musical integrity and dramatic modernity. Like all marriages, this one had its darker moments. But the net outcome was to help pump new blood into an essentially old-fashioned art form as it reached out to ever wider audiences.

CHAPTER 23

The Show Must Go On...

In September 2006, Berlin's Deutsche Oper scheduled a production of Mozart's *Idomeneo* featuring the severed head of (among others) the prophet Muhammad. After police warnings that security at the opera house might be put at risk, the performances were cancelled.

All art is in part political. By which I do not mean merely that it reflects or criticizes the values of the power structures of its day, though opera has done this often enough throughout its history. Early *opera seria* frequently depicted the kind of kings and princes who commissioned it, albeit in historical or allegorical form, while at times of political repression the operatic stage has been used to represent the (suitably disguised) aspirations of the angry and the dispossessed. Political passions have been acted out, too, not only on stage but in or around the opera house itself. Napoleon was acclaimed at the opera after surviving a failed assassination attempt; the Duc de Berry was not so lucky, his murder sparking the closure of the opera house where he fell. In 1858, bombs were thrown by a frustrated Italian nationalist at Napoleon III when he and the Empress were approaching the opera in Paris (hence the separate, safer imperial entrance to the new house designed by Garnier), while in 1893 an anarchist hurled a bomb into the stalls of Barcelona's premier showcase of class and wealth, the Liceu opera house, killing a score of spectators. In more recent times, when President de Gaulle of France made a state visit to London in 1960, Queen Elizabeth II accompanied him to the Royal Opera House, echoing a similar visit by their predecessors, Queen Victoria and the Emperor Napoleon III. President Kennedy, hosting a dinner for the daughter (and later successor) of the Indian Prime Minister, invited the Opera Society of Washington to the White House to provide the entertainment, while one of President Mitterrand's proudest achievements was the creation of a new opera house in Paris. At the height of the Cold War, singers from Warsaw Pact countries were sometimes denied visas to sing in the West. To this day in Israel the music of Wagner is widely regarded as unacceptable. As for those Berlin performances of *Idomeneo*, they were reinstated after a political outcry. 'If concern about possible protests leads

LA DYNAMITE EN ESPAGNE

'Dynamite in Spain' (1893). Political passions have often overflowed in the opera house – and not only onstage.

to self-censorship then the democratic culture of free speech is in danger,' declared the Culture Minister, Bernd Neumann.

Opera has always needed powerful figures prepared to embrace (and finance) it. For centuries, it could count on the sponsorship of political leaders, from princely patrons to variegated twentieth-century dictatorships and democracies. By the turn of the twenty-first, however, despite its unprecedented global popularity, opera was becoming politically marginalized: a specialist, 'niche' interest that received progressively less public attention and which governments were increasingly disinclined to encourage. When Blair, Berlusconi, Bush, Chirac or Putin visited each other, they might dress up for a formal dinner at a castle or palace, or helicopter over to their host's countryside pile to be seen buddying together in tie-less mufti. But the last place that generation of foreign dignitaries or their successors normally wanted to be seen taking their counterparts was to the opera. When France's President Sarkozy and his new wife Carla Bruni made a state visit to London in 2008, an evening at the opera with the Queen and Prince Philip would have been unthinkable.

The change had come about partly for reasons of finance. In the decades immediately following the Second World War, most of the democracies of Western Europe put public money into high culture, including opera. The principal opera companies in France, Italy and West Germany received some two-thirds of their budgets from the public exchequer, the Dutch even more, recouping most of the rest from ticket sales. Britain – in this as in much else, straddling European and American models – received appreciably less from government, though the Royal Opera, English National Opera and the new regional companies were all principal beneficiaries of Arts Council largesse without which they could not have functioned. People opposed to funding the arts through tax revenues had no difficulty pointing to examples of wastage and feather-bedding: several Italian companies, for example, employed a large staff but in a typical season had more dark nights than performances. Hungry recipients, on the other hand, complained no doubt justifiably that the money was never sufficient to guarantee the highest operatic standards. How else, they would ask when challenged, could this most expensive of art forms survive? As any opera boss would tell you, ticket sales in a house containing 2000 seats or less can never provide more than a fraction of the costs: if you increase ticket prices too sharply, you will alienate a proportion of your potential audience base; lower them and your revenue will drop. And if you try to fill the house by producing nothing other than sure-fire hits, you will betray the artistic standards you are there to uphold. In America, the biggest houses contained three or even four thousand seats; on a good night, that represented a lot of revenue, but still not enough to keep a company in business.

Unlike most other businesses, furthermore, the world of opera could not easily increase its 'productivity'. Of course, a house or company might be able to tighten up on its administrative procedures, mount more perform-ances, keep salaries on the low side and rely on a smaller chorus and cheaper sets and costumes. However, any substantial reduction in rehearsal time, for example, would tend to eat into artistic standards and there was no way the proverbial triangle player could be given more notes to play than the score demanded; a performance of *Aida* in the twenty-first century required the same-sized orchestra as in the nineteenth, but the players would expect considerably enhanced pay and conditions. Thus, the performance of opera – as opposed to the production of wheat, cars or toothbrushes – had built-in costs, inflationary by their very nature, that no amount of efficiency measures could offset. Herein lay one of the fundamental challenges to those running the world's opera companies.

In the USA, as we have seen, opera was heavily dependent on tax-deductible private donations, which tended to fluctuate with the vicissitudes of the stock market. Did this mean having to accommodate the conserva-tive artistic tastes of the wealthiest benefactors (an accusation frequently hurled from across the Atlantic)? Sometimes perhaps. The opera-loving Sybil Harrington, widow of a Texas oil millionaire, who bankrolled sixteen Met productions during the 1980s and 1990s, liked her opera big and glossy. Some

Sybil Harrington, widow of a Texas oil millionaire, bankrolled many productions at the New York Met, among them Franco Zeffirelli's *Turandot*.

found Zeffirelli's Met *Bohème* or *Turandot* (both financed by Harrington) gaudy and over-peopled, in the manner of a 1930s Hollywood movie. Audiences loved them; where once they had applauded the entry of the 'star' singer, they now applauded the *mise en scène*, an experience unknown to most European directors or designers. Some Europeans were inclined to be snooty about this. We are able to be experimental, they would say, and put on new works and thought-provoking productions of familiar ones, while in America they have to play safe and please their diamond donors with one glitzy old favourite after another. Cultural and intellectual integrity, it was maintained, were less likely to be compromised by funding from public than from private sources, especially if filtered through a committee of 'the great and the good'.

Such arguments were comforting so long as they continued to be accepted by both parties: donor governments and those who received their bounty. But during the 1980s and 1990s, opera lost a great deal of the political clout it had once been able to take for granted as political opinion in many European capitals found a renewed enthusiasm for privatization. The arts, like everything else, should learn to rely increasingly on their market, it was said. Governments did not donate large amounts of public money to football clubs, rock venues or gourmet restaurants; why should they do so to symphony orchestras or dance or opera companies? If people wanted opera so much, surely they could find a way of paying for it. People with no particular interest in opera labelled it 'elitist'.

As the chill new wind started to blow, many a straw began to bend. In Britain, Kent Opera, an entrepreneurial company which had attracted such talents as Jonathan Miller and Roger Norrington, collapsed under pressure of reduced public funding. A few years later, Scottish Opera was starved of public funds almost to the point of disbandment. Nor was Covent Garden immune. Arts Council grants to the Royal Opera House rose from £1.4 million to £20 million between 1970 and 1997 but inflation meant the purchasing value of the grant had virtually halved. When in 1995 the ROH received a rebuilding grant from Britain's National Lottery, the popular newspaper the *Sun* furiously denounced the award, proclaiming that 'the people' did not want their money 'squandered on the minority pastimes of the well-heeled when genuine causes like medical research charities are losing out'. One senior Covent Garden executive was asked on live TV how he could justify an award to the opera house when people were dying for lack of dialysis machines.

The Royal Opera House weathered a succession of ferocious storms, losing several chief executives in the process, and in 1997 the house closed for a long-overdue rebuild. By the early twenty-first century, once it had settled into its renovated premises, the company's revenue was coming in roughly equal amounts from three types of source: public money (the Arts Council), private money from 'development' (commercial sponsorship, merchandising, Friends' organizations etc.) and box office revenue. Where once government had provided 60 per cent of the ROH's costs, it was now providing little over 30 per cent. When in 2007 the Minister for Culture, Media and Sport removed money from the arts budget to help top up funds for the 2012 Olympics, there was a howl of outrage from the arts community but to little avail. A year later, the national economy, apparently so buoyant, found itself stumbling into a steep downturn.

Britain was not alone. In Italy, the formerly state-financed opera houses were run from the mid-1990s by foundations funded in part by sponsorship deals and private investment, though they also received money from national and regional government. A decade later, the Berlusconi government cut Italy's national arts budget by nearly a fifth (19.2 per cent), and opera houses felt the pinch most acutely. Several, including companies in Florence, Genoa and Naples, attempted to stave off bankruptcy by selling assets such as warehouse space, sacking chorus members, reducing rehearsal times and cancelling productions. In Germany, where reunification incurred severe economic restraints, many of the states and municipalities, in the old West as well as the poorer East, had to rein in their arts budgets. Sponsorship was hard to raise except in the largest, wealthiest cities and *Länder*; 'we have already given you our money,' said local bankers and industrialists in places like Erfurt or Bremen, pointing to the taxes they and their companies had to pay, which were among the highest in Europe. In the newly reunited capital, Berlin, plans by the municipal government to 'rationalize' the city's three opera companies by amalgamating them (and perhaps phasing out the smallest, the Komische Oper) were only quashed after a series of high-profile threats of resignation in the music world, notably that of Barenboim at the Staatsoper, whom the city could ill afford to lose, and a highly unusual intervention by the federal minister for culture.

Further East, the winds were often icier still. After the collapse of Communism, many institutions in the former USSR were privatized. One consequence was that thousands of musicians, hitherto accustomed to a secure career pattern, found themselves on reduced wages or out of work. Some sought employment elsewhere. Before long, opera companies all over Western Europe were besieged by applications from often talented Russians, Ukrainians and others, only too happy to take work for what locals would have regarded as a pittance. Entire companies from the old Warsaw Pact tried to replenish their depleted coffers through exhaustive tours of the West; Valery Gergiev's Mariinsky company,* buttressed by the support of Vladimir Putin, became the brand leader, but others dragged their tawdry *Aida* or *Turandot* from town to town, seemingly condemned, like the Flying Dutchman, to a life permanently on the move. Perhaps it was not surprising that many of post-Soviet Russia's leading performers, in common with the lemming-like flow of less celebrated singers and instrumentalists, chose to live and work mainly abroad. The inequities and abuses of capitalism, it seemed, were no more capable than Communism of persuading Russia's musicians to stay home.

*

As political leaders attended fewer operas and found less public funding for it than their predecessors, they were merely reacting to new realities. Modern governments had more calls on the public purse than earlier ones, while the onset of worldwide recession a few years into the new century rendered arts funding ever more precarious – whether from public or private sources. In the USA, no less than the subsidized sector in continental Europe, economic downturn caused seasons to be curtailed, productions to be cancelled, staffing levels and salaries trimmed and, in some cases (Connecticut Opera, Baltimore Opera, Opera Pacific in southern California), total close-down. The New York Met, finding its $300m endowment fund reduced in value by a third and facing a substantial deficit, raised much-needed cash in early 2009 by putting up its Chagall canvases as collateral against an earlier loan from JP Morgan Chase.

Opera was being marginalized in other ways, too. In earlier times, initially in Italy then in much of Europe, the opera house had often been the principal place of entertainment available in the evenings to the well-to-do about town: the covered piazza where they might meet their social peers and enjoy the show. There were alternatives. A troupe of actors or puppeteers might be passing through town, or a travelling circus. Or you might choose to host, or to attend, a glittering *soirée*, complete with a charming hour or so of good music. Or else stay home in front of the fire – in which case it was probably a game of cards, a hot toddy and early to bed. For the young and the louche, there may have been an officers' club (or worse) for late-night drinking and womanizing and the odd fight, while their more sober counterparts might have headed off

*Formerly the Kirov. The company reverted to its original name, just as its city itself became St Petersburg once again in place of Leningrad.

towards an improving lecture or religious meeting. But there was no cinema or bowling club to attend, no floodlit sports arena, no telephone with which to chat to friends, no radio, television or Internet to distract eye and ear. If you wanted to have a good evening's entertainment, the opera was the location of choice. In many provincial towns, there was to all intents and purposes no other.

In the twentieth century, this was no longer true as huge numbers flocked to the movies or into giant stadiums to revel in the excitements and frustrations of sports events or to enjoy amplified performances by pop groups and rock stars. In many ways, the cinema and stadium became the latter-day counterparts to the opera house of an earlier age, twentieth-century temples offering the exhilaration of being present at a communally shared, somewhat ritualized socio-artistic experience. Further alternative forms of entertainment took hold, and the salience of opera was correspondingly punctured. By the first few years of the new millennium, the urban middle classes, their numbers swollen by increasing affluence, were pouring out onto the streets at night and at weekends into a variety of new, glossy emporia. In Sydney, an efflorescence of boutique stores and restaurants around Circular Quay provided powerful counter-attractions to the Opera House while even London, once regarded as something of a gastronomic pit, was dotted with *haute cuisine* restaurants, open-air cafés and newly gentrified pubs. London's vaunted theatrical life continued to flourish, many of its shows crossing the Atlantic thereby helping New York's Great White Way to sparkle ever more brightly. In most of the great cities of the developed world, indeed, large numbers of educated people found themselves bombarded by a bewildering variety of cultural attractions competing for their money and attention: not just such traditional fare as museums, art galleries, theatres, concerts and opera, but also late-night shopping, gourmet restaurants, multiplex cinemas, 'alternative theatre', rock clubs, gay and lesbian bars, comedy venues, gyms and sports centres. Did you spot opera in the midst of that list? It was easy to miss. Opera was no longer the prince of urban entertainments, as it had once been, but merely one small player having to jostle for recognition in a cultural world increasingly crowded with alternatives, a minority interest *comme les autres*.

*

If the political and socioeconomic status of opera had changed, so had that of the intrepid men (and a handful of women) running and financing the opera 'business'. Most opera houses and companies had once been owned and financed by powerful ruling families: directly, in the case of court opera, or else by leasing a theatre or the land on which to build one to a manager or impresario or to a company that would hire one. Such models were largely swept away by the French Revolution and Napoleonic wars. Vestiges remained, for example in Bavaria where Wagner's fortunes were revived, both economically and artistically, by the beneficence of an opera-loving king. More commonly, aristocratic patronage moved into the shadows, the wealthy and high-born often doing what they could to encourage opera but no longer owning it. By the twentieth century, a noble name or title might have made you a valued member of an operatic board and perhaps a prominent donor. But the only hereditary aristocrats normally seen backstage were those who chose to work in opera in a professional capacity. During the First World War, when Bruno Walter was conducting opera in Munich, one of his violinists was a prince of the blood, Prince Ludwig Ferdinand, a popular figure who accepted his place when, occasionally, Walter had to demote him down the orchestral pecking order if they were playing a particularly difficult score. Half a century later, the transition of London's Sadler's Wells to become English National Opera was overseen by a hard-working operatic polymath, the Earl of Harewood, who was the company's managing director and also, but entirely incidentally, a cousin of the Queen.

There was nothing particularly romantic about the world of the opera manager in the twentieth century as, day after day, and most evenings, meetings were held, finances sought, contracts negotiated, artists hired and fired, shows attended, late-night dinners consumed. In his autobiography, the Met's Rudolf Bing reproduces a cross-section of the memos that issued from his office. One concerns the purchase of too many typewriters, another the best way of dealing with latecomers, while a third asks the chorus to be careful not to 'crowd out' soloists in the backstage elevator. The man who operates the elevator should be provided with a little stool to sit on, says Bing in another memo, while elsewhere he has to issue a stern warning against backstage smoking. Decorum during curtain calls is of concern at one point, as is the alarm expressed by the Met's Carmen, Risë Stevens, at the realistic way one or two tenors have 'killed' her in the final act (Bing asks that they be issued with rubber-bladed knives).

Periodically, the crises were a great deal more serious. Entire companies have sunk without trace, their captain and crew lost beneath the unforgiving waves of operatic bankruptcy, while again and again we read of opera houses succumbing to fire, often with considerable loss of life and of the financial investments of those in charge. Countless performances have been lost, too, by strike action. With the emergence of labour unions, strikes became more formalized. In January 1906, shortly before a Met performance of *Faust* starring Caruso, the chorus, long aggrieved at their paltry wage level, announced they would not be going on that night; the show went ahead, but with parts of the opera omitted or reorchestrated – and, of course, no 'Soldiers' Chorus'. Half a century later, Bing found himself having to negotiate with fourteen different unions at the New York Met. A bitter dispute with one of them, the American Guild of Musical Artists (AGMA), led to the formal cancellation of the 1961/2 season (some of it later reinstated after arbitration by President

Kennedy's Secretary of Labor), but the Met was closed again by strike action in autumn 1969 and again in 1980.

What place was there in all this for art? Over the centuries, managements have commissioned any number of new works which have been duly composed, cast, learned, rehearsed and performed, only to be consigned to the waste bin of operatic history. Among the few that have survived, some of the most famous (for example, *Il barbiere di Siviglia*, *La traviata*, *Carmen*, *Madama Butterfly*) received deeply discouraging opening nights before achieving later success. Many others, from *Rinaldo* to the *Ring*, began life as artistic triumphs but financial flops.

Occasionally, an 'angel' has appeared, someone whose love of opera is matched by deep and generous pockets: a Harold McCormick, for example, or a Sybil Harrington. But even angels can have faulty wings. In the late twentieth century, the American-based, Cuban-raised millionaire Alberto Vilar pledged vast sums to selected opera companies in America and elsewhere. For a while, every opera magazine showed photos of Vilar with Domingo, with Gergiev or with the Met management, while his name was nailed prominently into place all over the operatic world onto auditorium walls, seat backs and at the top of donor lists. Among the companies Vilar helped finance was London's Royal Opera. Covent Garden, no longer able to rely on the receipt of adequate public funds, was actively seeking private sponsorship. When the rebuilt theatre reopened in late 1999, its most spectacular new feature was the redeployed Floral Hall, now a glistening social space: the 'Vilar Floral

Rudolf Bing, the Met's general manager, found himself pulling the strings in more ways than one.

Hall', it was soon dubbed, while the Royal Opera's nursery programme for outstanding young singers became the 'Vilar Young Artists Programme'. Then, in 2005, as various unfortunate business practices came to the attention of the law-enforcement authorities, Vilar's generosity turned from a shower into a trickle, then dried up completely as opera houses around the world reverberated to the clunk of his name being dropped.

*

Opera by the end of the twentieth century had become something of a niche interest, struggling for funds, attention and audiences in an environment full of fiercely competitive counter-attractions, and there was no reason to presume it would ever recover the kind of priority it had once enjoyed. Early in the twenty-first century its problems were exacerbated further by the onset of economic recession. Yet for all its setbacks, whether artistic, political or financial, operatic life somehow managed to survive. It might even be said to have thrived, the art form and its derivatives proving popular not only in its traditional heartlands but around the world and its aggregate audiences growing almost on a par in some places with attendance at sports events. Part of the reason had to do with the jet plane, the growth of travel, the internationalization of the media and the introduction of the Internet and digital technology: the same technological forces, in other words, that contributed towards the 'globalization' of other interests, activities and commodities. For the world of opera, these innovations provided both opportunities and hazards.

In many ways, the advent of digital technology proved a boon for the opera world as it forced people throughout the business to re-address the ways in which they reached out to their audiences. To some extent, this was merely a matter of office procedure as company staff learned to transfer their lists of subscribers and 'friends' from paper to computer files, communicate via email and introduce websites and online booking. Moreover, opera companies were now able to share information, resources and productions far more easily than before thanks to new electronic forms of communication, groups of them coming together under mutually beneficial umbrella organizations such as Opera America and Opera Europa (each with a hundred or more members).

In other ways, digitization was to prove more of a challenge. The recording industry had always thrived on innovation. In its early years, as we have seen, the available technology had favoured small forces, notably the individual singer with piano accompaniment. The arrival of the electric microphone in 1925 enhanced the quality of sound obtainable in the studio and the introduction of the long-playing record after the Second World War and later the CD boosted the recording of longer works, including operas. All this brought incomparable boons as a vast bank of recorded sound was gradually built up enabling the opera lover, at the touch of a button, to compare modern singers with predecessors going back, through Callas and Di Stefano to Gigli, Galli-Curci, Melba and Caruso. By the early 1990s, in the wake of the 'Three Tenors' phenomenon and with the CD industry at its height, the 'classical' market accounted for something close to 10 per cent of records sold worldwide. This kind of level could not however be sustained. Soon, a succession of small independent labels, by keeping their overheads low, contracting less-expensive artists and concentrating on a particular gap in the market, took a collective bite out of the profits of the industry giants (who tended to respond by trying to buy them up). More worrying for large and small alike was the overall decline in the percentage of record sales going to the classical market, a figure that sank towards the floor and was only stabilized around the 3–4 per cent mark by the aggressive marketing of a number of essentially pop talents as 'classical'. In part, this reflected the more general marginalization of classical music, including opera. But the arrival of the Internet, downloads, the DVD, MP3, iPod, Blu-ray and High Definition television showed signs of throwing the entire industry into disarray as record sales dropped, studio recordings came close to standstill and the CD looked threatened with eventual extinction.

One person's crisis is another's opportunity. As the once-powerful recording companies saw their fortunes slump, some entrepreneurial opera companies, building on a tradition of large-scale, open-air concerts, went on to produce and promote their own DVDs and in some cases to broadcast selected performances over new digital radio channels or project them direct from the stage onto giant screens. In 2006/7, the New York Metropolitan Opera initiated the live, HD transmission of Met performances directly on to the screens of movie theatres in North America and Europe (and via tape delay in Japan). The response was impressive, new cinemas being added throughout the four-month, six-opera experiment to accommodate audience demand. Overall, an aggregate audience of some 325,000 people worldwide watched the relays. The Met immediately announced an expansion of the scheme for the following season; in December 2007, its *Roméo et Juliette* relay starring Anna Netrebko reached a worldwide cinema audience of nearly 100,000 on some 600 screens. The experiment proved exspensive: a risky one perhaps, as economic recession set in. But the Met's lead was nevertheless followed by other opera companies, among them the San Francisco Opera, Milan's La Scala and Britain's Royal Opera. Meanwhile, Covent Garden bought Opus Arte, a DVD production company with an impressive backlist of opera recordings made at (inter alia) Glyndebourne, Netherlands Opera and Madrid's Teatro Real. The intention was to expand the list to include not only Covent Garden itself but further partners, thus building up and marketing worldwide a library of high-quality DVDs of live opera performances and, in due course, ploughing a proportion of the resulting profits back into the participating houses. Perhaps it was only a question of time before the world's opera theatres would routinely beam their shows – live or 'on demand' – in HD imagery and surround sound directly onto the world's TV screens or onto various portable platforms, much like sporting events. This could be done on a pay-to-view basis, with – who knows? – perhaps a higher premium for people wishing to choose their own camera angles and watch their chosen stars up close. As I write, experiments are being done with 3-D high-definition discs and even what is being dubbed the HVD, or holographic versatile disc.

As opera reached out to audiences via a plethora of new platforms, those on the artistic side, too, had to learn to adjust to new realities as rehearsal processes and production techniques were revolutionized by closed-circuit television, radio communications, computerized scenic effects and digitized lighting plots. For them, too, the digital age brought its downsides. Leading figures on the modern operatic stage were no longer being asked to go into the studio to record their entire repertoire as their predecessors had done; posterity would already be flooded with recorded material from a hundred years of back catalogue, liberally augmented by copyright-light material from all those 'live' DVDs, so that the opportunities for even the most celebrated singers of the new century to earn subsidiary rights correspondingly diminished. On the other hand, the innovations of the digital age provided singers with a host of new opportunities for popularity and publicity as fan websites and download opportunities proliferated and a rapidly expanding range of employment opportunities beckoned, all backed by management companies and sophisticated music agencies at ease with a complex system of international fee structures and currency convertibility. By the early twenty-first century any top-quality singer with good looks was liable to be marketed rather like a pop idol or soccer star. On the front cover of its winter 2007 brochure, Britain's Royal Opera featured a fine young Russian soprano with the words: 'TURBOCHARGED: Marina [Poplavskaya] can do 0–60 in one second. Decibels that is. One voice. Complete Control. Total Power. Va Va Voom.' They did not publicize the young Ponselle or Callas like that!

Here, too, there were hazards. Celebrities, after all, can fall as rapidly and as publicly as they rise. For a while, in the later 1990s, Angela Gheorghiu and Roberto Alagna were marketed by their recording company as opera's 'golden couple'. By the early 2000s, as reports abounded about how 'difficult' they could be, the profession's publicists moved on, alighting for a while on Anna Netrebko and Rolando Villazón. Within a matter of barely three or four years, Villazón, suffering from a series of well-publicized ailments, cancelled several months of performances while (in the words of Canadian soprano Adrianne Pieczonka in a widely reported 2007 interview) everyone was already 'looking for a new Anna Netrebko' even though Netrebko was only in her mid-thirties. The world of opera, sniffed Pieczonka, was becoming

They did not publicize the young Ponselle or Callas like this!

'like a pop-star culture', a sentiment mirrored by the British mezzo-soprano Alice Coote, who said that everyone in the opera world was 'galvanised by a fear of whether they'll be around tomorrow'. When the German tenor Endrik Wottrich was criticized for having pulled out of a Bayreuth performance because of a cold, he gave an unusually frank interview about the pressures of his profession to the *Frankfurter Allgemeine Zeitung*. 'We are faced with the choice of performing and being attacked because we sing one false note,' said Wottrich angrily, 'or being attacked because we are taking care of ourselves.' Let us hope that 'Marina' manages to outlast the temporary super-celebrity thrust upon her by the publicists of Team Covent Garden and enjoys the successful, long-lasting international career the modern world is able to offer.

Perhaps the greatest beneficiaries of operatic globalization and digitization were its audiences. Anyone, anywhere, could potentially find out what was being performed across the operatic world. What was advertised in Singapore or Sydney also sprang out at you from your laptop in Moscow, Cape Town or Buenos Aires. You were planning a visit to Berlin or Barcelona and wanted to spend an evening at the opera? You could book your theatre seats online as easily as your flight or hotel room. There was more opera outside the opera house than ever before, too. A proliferation of small-scale touring companies, often with no more than a rudimentary chorus or orchestra, took their shows to school halls and civic centres, while shrewd entrepreneurs found new audiences for opera, or opera excerpts, by promoting summertime performances in elegant open-air or country house environments. If all its forms are taken into account, our earlier proposition – that opera was more popular than ever before – is easy to sustain. 'Classical' radio stations sprouted up everywhere and operatic music was commonly used to back TV ads while the aria or voice of your choice was increasingly just a download away. And if you wanted to know what to think about a particular opera, artist or production, you did not have to seek out the column by an accredited music critic, but could check a variety of views online including those of bloggers keen to add their views to the mix. In many ways, the increasing global appeal of opera was a reflection of increasingly homogenized consumption patterns among the world's wealthy, rather like the spread of exotic holidays, expensive fashion accessories and gourmet restaurants. With economic *embourgeoisement* came a taste for pricey pastimes.

Did all this indicate a genuinely widespread appreciation of opera, or just its heartless commercialization? Opera on the iPod, DVD or cinema or TV screen is hardly the 'real thing'. Even in the opera house itself, quality was perhaps being sacrificed on the altar of quantity, some said, variously bemoaning the introduction of surtitles, the application of 'acoustical enhancement' into opera houses or the vogue for laser-lit, amplified arena opera or for sub-Glyndebourne country house opera. Familiar operas were being co-produced in often bland or gratuitously offensive productions, cried the cognoscenti, little new was being added to the repertoire, and the classical recording industry only survived by repackaging its back catalogue and by aggressively marketing a handful of 'crossover artists'. Some of the latter were sold as 'classical' artists, even as 'opera singers', and may have had their voices operatically trained. But none was really an 'opera singer' if what was meant by that term – one might have thought by definition – was someone who sang in performances of opera. Gone were the days, it was said (accurately enough), when an educated public would eagerly anticipate the latest opera by a celebrated composer and perhaps buy the libretto. By the early 2000s, millions looked forward to the latest Brad Pitt movie or mass-market musical; but a new opera scarcely registered on the Richter scale of popular interest.

Perhaps opera was becoming essentially a museum art, subsidized by increasingly tight-fisted governments and self-serving corporations, attracting an ageing and wealthy public prepared to visit and revisit a small number of highly wrought works whose provenance dated from an ever-receding past. Like obsessive stamp collectors or train-spotters, opera lovers would 'collect' their favourite works and singers with almost religious devotion while often lacking a broader critical sense or intellectual curiosity.

This characterization of the opera house as a museum for obsessives is harsh and misleading. Yet, like many caricatures, it contains perhaps a grain of truth. For the global spread of opera highlighted a cruel paradox. On the one hand, a greater number of people than ever before had the time, money and inclination to buy into opera in its various manifestations. That is, 'opera' was becoming more popular than ever before. Yet, at the same time, we have seen how this supposedly popular art form came to be increasingly marginalized by press and politicians as no more than a minority niche interest which slipped further and further down their list of priorities. As we regard the trajectory of the past 400 years, it might seem that we have been chronicling the rise, ascendancy, decline and fall of an old-fashioned, expensive, elite art form whose time has come and (nearly) gone.

*

There are, however, grounds for optimism about the future of opera as a live art form. In the first place, it is not true that the operatic repertoire was not being extended. Anyone seriously devoted to opera would know and love many works created in recent decades. The repertoire was also extended backwards. By the early twenty-first century, it was common practice around the operatic circuit to produce works by Monteverdi, Handel and Gluck with perhaps the occasional outing of an opera by Cavalli, Haydn or Salieri. Opera lovers notoriously complained (they always had) that the latest crop of singers was not as good as in the old days; and it may have been true that big-voiced Verdi and Wagner tenors and sopranos were even fewer than in the middle of the twentieth century. But alongside the baroque revival came a startlingly talented crop of singers capable, as most of their immediate predecessors were not, of doing superb justice to the subtleties of pre-classical opera. There may have been no Flagstad or Melchior in 2000, no Leontyne Price or Franco Corelli; but few singers in the mid-twentieth century had had the quieter virtuosity of Lorraine Hunt Lieberson, Cecilia Bartoli or David Daniels.

In addition to the extension of the operatic repertoire, both forwards and backwards, the old favourites continued to be produced all over the world. Unlike the pots and paintings in museums, operas are nothing if not newly produced. You may (or may not) like *Wozzeck* or *Billy Budd* or 'modern' productions of older works. But audiences would probably enjoy attending the opera a lot less if all they saw were slavish reproductions of the original *Figaro*, *Lucia* or *Rheingold*. The theatre has long since moved beyond candle lighting, swimming machines and semaphore acting styles, as great works of the past are made to speak to the audiences of the present.

Opera, always the most multimedia of art forms has survived into what is now a multimedia age. Today, we have learned to expect and accept a multiplicity of messages concurrently directed towards us, a ceaseless patchwork of sounds, lights and images. Whether we are walking down a busy city street, travelling in a bus or train resonating to an orchestra of mobile phones, wandering through an echoey, music-filled shopping mall or attending a big-league sports match, you and I are everywhere bombarded by a raft of rapidly shifting sights and sounds, while few cafés, restaurants, hotel lobbies or supermarkets remain music-free. If you choose to relax at home surfing the TV to see what is on offer, chances are you will soon encounter a split screen containing talking heads and action shots at one and the same time, with text ribbons at top and bottom and perhaps an interactive button in the top right-hand corner. As for the Internet, do not complain about the recurrent bubbles, buttons and flashing offers, for they are its economic lifeblood. As people became increasingly inured to multimedia platforms, they were in a sense catching up with a composite form of communication that opera helped pioneer centuries before.

This will surely continue in future years as imaginative people harness the latest technologies and create new artworks that integrate music, song, drama, dance, poetry, props, costumes, scenery and lighting. Will the results necessarily be operas? Perhaps the very concept of 'opera' will become less restricted than it is now. Many already argue that the definition of opera should be widened as new audiences are wooed. If *Die Fledermaus* and *The Merry Widow* can be mounted by opera companies, and some of the works of Gilbert and Sullivan, perhaps *Carousel* and *West Side Story* are operas too, and Spanish *zarzuela* and Sondheim musicals. And if they, why not *Evita*? This is not a question of the quality of the works concerned, but rather their genre: there are plenty of works we might all agree are 'operas' but which make for a tedious evening's theatre, while some of the best (*Zauberflöte*, *Fidelio*, *Carmen*) link musical numbers with spoken dialogue, like Gilbert and Sullivan or a Broadway musical. In 2004, Britain's National Theatre had a big hit on its hands with a brilliantly produced, hugely obscene and somewhat sacrilegious show called *Jerry Springer – The Opera*. Not something Covent Garden or the New York Metropolitan were in a hurry to showcase.

Changing circumstances lead to changing styles of artwork. In decades to come, the world will surely see a massive increase in migration, primarily from the poorer parts of the world to the wealthier. All migrations bring culture in their wake. As our world becomes increasingly multi-ethnic and large Asian subcultures find their place in Sydney and Melbourne, Los Angeles becomes more Latino and London and Paris absorb ever-growing Muslim populations, this will surely have an impact upon what is produced, how and to whom in the world's music theatres. Already, Western tastes are learning to absorb 'World Music' and 'Fusion', while dance groups featuring African or Asian styles are reaching enthusiastic Western audiences. If Verdi and Wagner can be successfully staged in Beijing and Bangkok, maybe Western theatres will reciprocate and dip their toes deeper into the swirling, nourishing waters of non-European styles of music drama.

Another future trend may involve greater integration between what we currently define as classical and popular music. No such division was obvious in Mozart's day (though people certainly differentiated between music

Jerry Springer – The Opera was a huge (and controversial) theatrical success. Next stop Covent Garden?

composed for the church and that composed for the stage or as a diversion for those who had commissioned it). Later, with the moral elevation of the idea of 'art', distinctions developed not only of function but also of hierarchy: serious music was for the educated, popular music for the masses. By the second half of the twentieth century, there was scarcely any meeting point between, on the one hand, the music of Schoenberg, Boulez or Stockhausen and that of Duke Ellington, Sinatra or the Beatles.

Latterly, however, signs appeared of a new meeting of minds, styles and audiences. Some 'classical' conductors would schedule jazz or movie music at orchestral concerts, and established opera stars recorded pieces by Richard Rodgers, Lennon and McCartney, Yves Montand or Andrew Lloyd Webber. A number of serious composers, meanwhile, began to explore new ways of reaching out to a wider public, initially through a quasi-religious idiom, or via the kind of hypnotic repetitions that came to be dubbed 'minimalism' (in 1996, the composer John Adams said his current plan was 'not to write for operatic voices but for singers who can work in a variety of pop styles'). Then, as powerful new computer systems came to attract the compositional talents of classical and pop musicians alike, the supposed distinction between the two genres became further blurred. If these convergent trends continue, future operas may no longer be definable as 'classical' but, rather, embody a fusion of styles and genres aimed to appeal to the widest possible audience. In which case, one might imagine Mozart and Schikaneder allowing themselves a gentle smile of satisfaction before they turn over and go back to sleep.

As for the subject-matter of music theatre half a century from now, this will surely reflect the preoccupations of the time, rather as many nineteenth-century operas portrayed powerful rulers and admiring or angry crowds, and those of a century later (such as Berg's *Wozzeck*, Schoenberg's *Moses and Aaron*, Britten's *Peter Grimes*, Stravinsky's *Rake's Progress*) the frustrations and anxieties of anomic individuals at odds with those around them. One can imagine the music dramas of the 2050s and 2060s featuring situations arising from the migration from one culture to another, or from the trials imposed by desertification, floods and fires (or portraying love and death – or immortality – in outer space*). Maybe they will even be populated by symbolic flute-playing princes, amorous birdmen and Zoroastrian high priests...

If the art of opera has a future, what of the public it will need to attract? Here, the prognosis is somewhat ambivalent. Demographically, there are grounds for cautious optimism. Today's opera audiences typically include a dispropor-tionate number of people in their fifties and above. In the developed parts of the world, people tend to live longer than in the past and, in older age, to have more disposable time and income than their juniors. This pattern seems likely to continue, with the over-sixties in some countries set to approach 40 per cent of the population. Yet there are clouds on the horizon. Managements, concerned to groom and nurture audiences of the future, strive to bring younger people into the opera house with educational projects, cheap ticket schemes, schools' matinees and the like, and some of these youngsters undoubtedly catch the operatic bug. But economic projections suggest that few were likely to enjoy the financial security (let alone the final salary pensions) that their parents' and grandparents' generation learned to take for granted.

Opera managements will thus have to work hard if they are to have any chance of refreshing their audience base. In this, as in much else, opera will be no different from other branches of entertainment. Maybe the operatic expe-rience of the future will become increasingly like that of a sports event, with audiences becoming more vociferous, opera companies developing fan clubs and opera houses putting burgers and beer (or their health-food equivalents) on their menus. Already by the early twenty-first century, as we have seen, star singers were being marketed like sports celebrities. Some were finding the pressures of the profession oppressive. It was widely reported that some singers, like their sporting counterparts, were resorting to performance-enhancing drugs: not only beta-blockers to calm nerves before going on stage but, in some cases, cocaine, serious alcohol abuse or steroids in the form of cortisone to control inflamed vocal cords or ease the achievement of high notes. It is hard to see how the abuse of drugs will be eliminated in future years, though devel-opments in biochemistry may be able to reduce their deleterious effects.

In addition to sport, other forms of public entertainment might point to future trends in the opera world. Many of the newest opera houses were built,

* The first opera placed in space that I know of (and saw) was Blomdahl's *Aniara* (1959).

like multi-screen cinemas, to incorporate two or three variably sized auditoria. Everywhere, pains were taken to ensure that a night at the opera, like a visit to a superstore or shopping centre, was a multifaceted 'experience' offering not just a theatre trip but food, drink and attractive 'retail outlets'. The Austrian town of Bregenz on the edge of the Bodensee offered a complex including both a conventional indoor theatre and a huge open-air stadium from which thousands of spectators could watch a massively amplified, spectacularly designed performance produced on a stage floating on the lake like a giant liner. Opera was becoming an adjunct of cultural tourism as upmarket companies identified a wealthy clientele eager to visit the world's opera centres, an alliance further cemented as performances came to be tied to historic and 'heritage' sites, building on such successful precedents as Finland's Olavinlinna Castle, the Roman arena in Verona or the courtyard of the Archbishops' Palace in Aix-en-Provence. In less grandiose venues (such as those used by Graham Vick's innovative Birmingham Opera Company), imaginative producers began to experiment with ways of drawing audiences into the drama as active participants as a means of reducing the traditional division between spectators and performers.

Fifty years hence, the nature and experience of opera will doubtless have altered still further. Climate change, for example, will surely have had an effect on all aspects of life, including the world of opera. Methods of travelling to and from theatres, of heating and cooling public buildings and of illuminating and powering theatrical productions (indoor and outdoor) may be very different from what we commonly expect today, while we could be the first and last generation to assume that cheap air flights can routinely transport opera's producers and consumers to and from the cities of their choice. Maybe the Internet will bring about the demise of the 'official' music critic as anybody's view is rendered equally accessible online to everyone else who might be interested.

There are further directions, too, in which science may take us. At present, most opera houses claim to eschew amplification unless for a specific musical or dramatic effect. But the art and science of sound projection are becoming ever more sophisticated, some houses introducing 'electronic acoustic enhancement' systems in which microprocessors control multiple loudspeakers and microphones placed around a performance space. The results can be subtle but persuasive. In Berlin, for example, the Staatsoper (under Barenboim) agreed to instal the 'Lares' system, raising the auditorium's reverberation time for certain Wagner performances from 1.2 seconds to 1.7. If full-scale amplification in the theatre ever becomes the norm, however, the implications for opera would be considerable. Why, for example, would aspiring singers need or want to produce an 'operatic' voice – a particular kind of focused, diaphragm-supported sound that was developed in order to be able to fill theatres? To anyone inclined to define opera as music theatre sung with an 'operatic voice', amplification could herald the eventual demise of the genre, so that anyone with a trained soprano or baritone as we recognize it would come to be valued, like today's thatchers or wigmakers, primarily for having retained a near-obsolete skill. Or perhaps the operatic voice will simply be consigned, like that of the castrato, to history.

Advances in acoustical science might go further still: for example, to enable any imperfection – a mispronounced word or a note sung or played slightly flat – to be automatically 'corrected'. Perhaps there will in any case be fewer imperfections to correct if performers come to make increasing use of drugs. It is a daunting thought. Part of the excitement of live opera has always resided in what one might call the risk factor: the fact that real human beings are attempting to achieve something very difficult in our presence, and the corresponding sense of excitement when they succeed. As future developments in biotechnology continue to enhance the effects of drugs, maybe our grandchildren will come to be entertained by a race of genetically engineered super-singers, a contingent of 'Stepford Sopranos' whose incomparably beautiful faces, voices and bodies genuinely warrant the soubriquet 'diva'.

*

Opera – the art form and the event – will undoubtedly continue to evolve as it continues to respond, like everything else in our culture, to the pressures and opportunities of globalization, democratization and the latest technologies. Economic vicissitudes, too, will play a major role; nobody can predict with confidence how opera, that most expensive of art forms to produce, will survive an extended period of worldwide recession. But if there is one thing of which we can be reasonably certain, it is that the 'Artworks of the Future' will include forms of multimedia entertainment it is impossible for us to envisage. Will the enjoyment of 'opera' become a solitary and passive experience, a kind of musical computer game for aesthetic zombies? For some, perhaps. Others will seek out something more interactive, perhaps harnessing their imagination to the latest technologies to create their own multimedia pastimes. Or revelling in the pleasures of stadium opera on a scale currently unimaginable: maybe something global, on the model of today's 'rolling' pop concerts beginning in Auckland or Sydney and ending eighteen hours later in Los Angeles or San Francisco. By then, who knows, supersonic (or 'virtual') transport might be such as to enable those who wish to be present throughout. Or perhaps they will simply monitor the events, as and when they choose, at the time or thereafter, on the single, portable all-purpose digital device that will doubtless by then combine all today's computerized functions.

And perhaps there will still be millions around the world who will want to go out and experience great opera performed 'live' in the theatre by real, talented and vulnerable human beings. Let us hope that the thrill of the genuine article is never expunged, that it is enhanced and not obliterated by

An imposing venue for opera tourists: Olavinlinna Castle in Savonlinna, Finland.

whatever the production styles and technological developments employed. A live, theatre-based, digitally derived, 'virtual' *Ring* could become as much a standard-bearer over the next half-century as Wieland Wagner's Bayreuth productions were in the last. If so, the size and social base of opera audiences might come to parallel those for such post-Wagnerian movie sagas as *Star Wars* or *The Lord of the Rings*. In which case, be prepared for mass-market writers, composers, producers and directors to widen radically the limits of what you and I think of as opera. Or perhaps to get rid of the word 'opera' altogether. Would that matter? Perhaps not. As I said at the outset, the 'O' word was never very helpful in the first place.

Notes

Introduction

Among 'the efforts of a number of notable and courageous pioneers' who have tried to link the history of music to its wider social, political and economic context, I have in mind e.g. John Rosselli's writings on the operatic professions in nineteenth-century Italy; William Weber's analysis of the emerging middle-class audience for concerts of classical music; the volume on *Opera Production and its Resources* in the series on the history of Italian opera edited by Lorenzo Bianconi and Giorgio Pestelli; the work on opera in seventeenth-century Venice by Ellen Rosand and more recently Beth and Jonathan Glixon; that of Robert D. Hume and Judith Milhous on the finances of eighteenth-century opera in London; and the researches of William L. Crosten, Anselm Gerhard, Steven Huebner and James H. Johnson on opera audiences in nineteenth-century Paris and of Jennifer Hall-Witt on those in London. Meanwhile, a number of economists and economic historians with an interest in the arts – such as William Baumol, Cyril Ehrlich, Bruno Frey and F. M. Scherer – have come to the topic from the other side, as it were, and enriched further our understanding of the historical relationship between music and money.

PART I: Down the Road from *Arianna* to *Zauberflöte* (*c.* 1600–1800)

1. The Birth of Italian Opera

Ellen Rosand discusses Anna Renzi's career, and quotes from Giulio Strozzi's view of Renzi, in *Opera in Seventeenth-Century Venice*, pp. 228–35. Quotations from John Evelyn are from his *Diaries*, June 1645 and January 1646. For more on the origins of opera in seventeenth-century Venice, see Notes to Chapter 2.

John D. Drummond in *Opera in Perspective* traces the history of opera back through the insights of cultural anthropology to prehistoric times; he also has chapters on music drama in ancient Greece and Rome as well as medieval Europe before arriving, a third of the way through his book, in the cultural world of the Italian Renaissance. For more on the *Camerata*, see the collection of documents edited by Claude V. Palisca; Palisca has also made an English-language translation of Vincenzo Galilei's *Dialogue on Ancient and Modern Music*. My references to Galilei are also drawn from Oliver Strunk, *Source Readings in Music History: The Renaissance*, pp. 112–32; James Reston Jr, *Galileo: A Life* (Beard Books, 2005), p. 10; and Jamie James, *The Music of the Spheres: Music, Science, and the Natural Order of the Universe* (Springer, 1995), pp. 98–9. The idea that opera arose *ab initio* from the intellectual discussions of the *Camerata* and the lyrico-dramatic genius of Monteverdi is to some extent a twentieth-century construct and was given especial currency in Fascist Italy (see Chapter 17).

On the Florentine *intermedi*, see James M. Saslow, *The Medici Wedding of 1589*. Also, chapter 10 of Iain Fenlon's *Music and Culture in Late Renaissance Italy*. The quotation ('Through the depredations of time') is from a pamphlet by Bastiano de' Rossi and is reproduced in Piero Weiss (ed.), *Opera*, p. 6. Grazzini's mock lament is quoted in the chapter by Franco Piperno on p. 47 of Lorenzo Bianconi and Giorgio Pestelli (eds.), *Opera Production and Its Resources*. For an art historian's approach to the iconography of the *intermedi*, see Roy Strong, *Art and Power* (Boydell, 1984), chapter IV, pp. 126–52.

On Monteverdi and *Orfeo*, see John Whenham (ed.), *Claudio Monteverdi*. Iain Fenlon has investigated the birth of opera and, in particular, the circumstances surrounding the creation of *Orfeo*; his pioneering work in this area is *Music and Patronage in Sixteenth-Century Mantua*. See also his essay 'The Mantuan Stage Works', in Denis Arnold and Nigel Fortune, *The New Monteverdi Companion* (in which he quotes Carlo Magno as writing to his brother in Rome); also, Fenlon's essay 'Monteverdi, Opera and History', which is included in *The Operas of Monteverdi* (one of English National Opera's Opera Guide series edited by Nicholas John), and Fenlon's chapter ('Early Opera: The Initial Stage') in James Haar (ed.), *European Music, 1520–1640* (Boydell and Brewer, 2006). For a detailed consideration of the correspondence between Francisco and Ferdinando Gonzaga, see Fenlon's essay in Whenham, *Claudio Monteverdi*. For some of the detective work and speculation regarding the room in which *Orfeo* was first performed, see Fenlon's article 'Monteverdi's Mantuan *Orfeo*: Some New Documentation' (*Early Music*, XII (1984), pp. 163–72), and Paola Besutti, 'The "Sala degli Specchi" Uncovered: Monteverdi, the Gonzagas and the Palazzo Ducale, Mantua' (*Early Music*, XXVII:3 (August 1999), pp. 451–65). Monteverdi's letters are edited by Denis Stevens; the lengthy epistle of 2 December 1608 spelling out what 'fortune' has given and taken away is on pp. 51–4. For more on the creation and first performance of *Orfeo*, see Thomas Forrest Kelly, *First Nights: Five Musical Premieres*, chapter 1, to which Kelly appends English-language translations of surviving documents. Some parallels are drawn between the lives and subsequent reputations of Monteverdi and his near contemporaries Caravaggio and John Donne in the first chapter of Herbert Lindenberger's *Opera in History*. For a fictionalized account of life in the Gonzaga court in Monteverdi's time, see Clare Colvin's novel *Masque of the Gonzagas* (Arcadia Books, 1999). Tourists visiting the ducal palace in Mantua today will find little mention (even in the gift shop) of Monteverdi, let alone of *Orfeo*: a sharp reminder of the indifference of most people, even cultural tourists, to the subject-matter of this book!

On the development of seventeenth-century opera in general, see the chapter by Tim Carter in Roger Parker (ed.), *The Oxford Illustrated History of Opera*. Carter writes about the origins of opera in Rome on pp. 17–20; the description of *Sant'Alessio* is by a Frenchman, Jean-Jacques Bouchard, and is reproduced in Weiss (ed.), *Opera*, p. 33. Much of Carter's scholarly work concerns the Renaissance origins of opera; see, for example, his *Monteverdi and His Contemporaries* (Ashgate, 2000).

2. The Opera Business, Italian Style

For Anna Renzi's contract, see Beth and Jonathan Glixon, *Inventing the Business of Opera*, pp. 199–200; theirs is the best recent study of the practicalities of early operatic life in Venice. Much of my material is drawn from their researches, and from Ellen Rosand's seminal work on the subject, *Opera in Seventeenth-Century Venice*; Rosand discusses Renzi's career on pp. 228–35. For more on Renzi, see Beth L. Glixon, 'Private Lives of Public Women: Prima Donnas in Mid-Seventeenth-Century Venice' (*Music & Letters*, vol. 76, no. 4, November 1995, pp. 509–31). The Glixons and Rosand are among a number of scholars to tackle the question of why commercial opera began when and where it did, in Venice, in 1637 (see Rosand's chapter in the Roberta Montemorra Marvin and Downing A. Thomas anthology *Operatic Migrations*). Another is Edward Muir in his article 'Why Venice? Venetian Society and the Success of Early Opera' (*Journal of Interdisciplinary History*, XXXVI:3, Winter 2006). For an important early investigation of the origins of the 'business' origins of opera, including in Venice, see Lorenzo Bianconi and Thomas Walker, 'Production, Consumption and Political Function of Seventeenth-Century Opera' (*Early Music History*, vol. 4, 1984, pp. 209–96). In addition, much can be learned from Simon Towneley Worsthorne's *Venetian Opera in the Seventeenth Century*, especially his opening chapters on the historical background and the theatrical context of early seventeenth-century Venetian opera. See also the early studies by Henry Prunières, notably his article 'Opera in Venice in the XVIIth Century' (*The Music Quarterly*, XVII: 1, January 1931, pp. 1–13). The biographical section in Jane Glover's study of Cavalli (pp. 11–39) remains valuable. All studies of early opera in Venice are indebted to the writings of Cristoforo Ivanovich, who in 1681 chronicled operas seen in Venice since 1637 and the various opera theatres at which they had been produced; edited excerpts of Ivanovich's appendix (about the running of the theatres themselves) can be found in Piero Weiss, *Opera* (pp. 34ff.).

The acrimonious correspondence with Anna Felicita Chiusi is taken from Beth L. Glixon, 'Private Lives of Public Women', pp. 520–21. The quotations from librettists are from Rosand, *Opera in Seventeenth-Century Venice*, pp. 167–8. The letter from Cesti to Faustini is quoted by the Glixons in *Inventing the Business of Opera*, p. 167, and that from John Dodington addressed to the Doge in ibid., p. 302. The French commentator who wrote of people attending the opera for their *divertissement particulier* is quoted in Bianconi and Walker, 'Production, Consumption and Political Function', p. 227.

On castrati, see John Rosselli, 'The Castrati as a Professional Group and a Social Phenomenon, 1550–1850' (*Acta Musicologica*, vol. 60, fasc 2, May–August 1988, pp. 143–79); for a more convenient source for much of Rosselli's material, see chapter 2 of his book *Singers of Italian Opera*. See also Patrick Barbier, *The World of the Castrati*, and Richard Somerset-Ward, *Angels and Monsters*, chapter 4. See also Nicholas Clapton's biography of Moreschi. Burney's description of the young castrati lying 'by themselves in a warmer apartment upstairs' is in Burney, *Music, Men, and Manners in France and Italy 1770*, p. 185, and his comment about church choirs being made up of the 'refuse of the opera houses' is on p. 164. For Burney's encounters with Farinelli and Caffarelli, see pp. 90–93 and 193.

On *opera seria* and the ways it would tend to mirror the power structure of its patrons and audiences, see, for example, Reinhard Strohm, *Dramma per musica* and, more recently, Martha Feldman, *Opera and Sovereignty*. Feldman's work is remarkable for its fusion of musicological analysis with insights drawn from cultural anthropology.

Burney's comments about the size of Italian theatres, the 'noise and indecorum' of audiences and the need of the performers to 'bawl' in order to be heard (in contrast to the 'silence which reigns at London and Paris') are on p. 90 of *Music, Men, and Manners*. The quotation from Samuel Sharp about the opera being 'a place of rendezvous and visiting' is from Samuel Sharp, *Letters* (R. Cave, 1767), p. 78. That from de Brosses about Hasse's dislike of French music is from pp. 346–7 of M. R. Colomb (ed.), *Le Président de Brosses en Italie: lettres familières écrites d'Italie en 1739 et 1740* (Paris, 1861); other quotations from de Brosses are taken from the excerpts in Weiss, *Opera*, and from Enrico Fubini (ed.), *Music and Culture in Eighteenth-Century Europe*, chapter 4 (which also includes excerpts from the writings of Burney and Sharp). Leopold Mozart's letter about the cold weather in Naples and Wolfgang's desire for a tan is dated 29 May 1770, while Wolfgang's about the King standing on a stool is dated 5 June. Chapter 4 of Barbier's *The World of the Castrati*, on 'The Theatre in Italy', includes quotations from the *Travel-Diaries of William Beckford*, from which I have borrowed. Jeremy Black has written two books on the eighteenth-century Grand Tour, each containing a chapter about the arts: *The British Abroad* (chapter 12), and *Italy and the Grand Tour* (chapter 14, which deals with the reactions of British visitors to Italian opera); I am indebted to Black's researches for quotations, direct and indirect, from Lord Stanhope, Edward Thomas, Thomas Brand, Lord Charles Somerset, Garrick and Charles Abbot. The story of Casanova, Henriette and the opera box in Parma is from Giacomo Casanova, *History of My Life*, translated by Willard R. Trask (Johns Hopkins University Press, 1997, chapter 4), pp. 54–5.

3. Opera Crosses the Alps – and the Channel

On the place of music in the court of Louis XIV, see Robert M. Isherwood, *Music in the Service of the King*. Peter Burke's *The Fabrication of Louis XIV* is a pioneering study of the creation and diffusion of what we would call political 'image'. The proclamation issued by Louis XIV in 1672 establishing the French Académie Royale de Musique is reproduced in Piero Weiss (ed.), *Opera*, pp. 40–43. Richard Taruskin's description ('the courtiest of court operas') is from *The Oxford History of Western Music*, vol. 2, p. 86. Taruskin's comment that early opera was the product and expression of 'a tyrannical class' and was 'only made possible by the despotic exploitation of other classes' is from ibid., p. 14. It was the seventeenth-century Duke of Brunswick who sold his subjects as soldiers (ibid., p. 15, quoting Manfred Bukofzer, *Music in the Baroque Era* (Norton, 1947)).

A useful summary of the place of musical performance, including opera, in eighteenth-century Paris can be found in the article by Jean Mongrédien entitled 'Paris: The End of the Ancien Régime', in Neal Zaslaw (ed.), *Man & Music* (see especially pp. 85–96 on opera). For documents illustrating the management (and mismanagement) of opera in Paris from 1672 to 1770 and the practical experience of opera-going, see Caroline Wood and Graham Sadler, *French Baroque Opera*, pp. 1–40. For the development of *opéra comique*, see David Charlton, *Grétry and the Growth of Opéra-Comique*; also Michael Robinson's article, '*Opera buffa* into *opéra comique*', in Malcolm Boyd (ed.), *Music and the French Revolution*. James H. Johnson, in *Listening in Paris*, addresses the question: why were audiences at the Opéra so noisy in 1750 and so reverential by 1850? My account of opera at the Palais Royal owes much to Johnson's researches. For a detailed description of the theatre in the Palais Royal, see the article by Barbara Coeyman in John Hajdu Heyer (ed.), *Lully Studies*. See also R. H. F. Scott, *Jean-Baptiste Lully*.

Burney's comments about how 'the lights at the opera house… affect my eyes in a very painful manner' are from *Music, Men, and Manners*, p. 53. The reference to Marie Antoinette complaining about the smoke in the theatre is from Johnson, *Listening in Paris*, p. 13. Selected documents from the *Querelle des Bouffons* can be found in Oliver Strunk (ed.), *Source Readings in Music History: The Classic Era* (pp. 45–80); Enrico Fubini (ed.), *Music and Culture* (chapter 2); and Weiss (ed.): *Opera*, pp. 106–11.

Many historians have written of the intersection between commerce and culture in early eighteenth-century London, among them John H. Plumb and Roy Porter. For a vivid description of Handel's London, see Peter Earle, *A City Full of People: Men and Women of London 1650–1750* (Methuen, 1994). Handel is the subject of many biographies, from Mainwaring (first published in 1760, a year after Handel's death and said to be the first biography of a major musician) to the volumes published in the 1980s and 1990s by Christopher Hogwood, Jonathan Keates, H.C. Robbins Landon and Donald Burrows. Winton Dean's two-volume work concentrates primarily on the operas but contains much biographical material. The story about Handel threatening to fling Cuzzoni out of the window is from Mainwaring (in a footnote), pp. 110–11. See also the article by James Wierbicki, 'Dethroning the Divas: Satire Directed at Cuzzoni and Faustina' (*The Opera Quarterly*, vol. 17, no. 2, Spring 2001, pp. 175–96). For detailed documentation about Handel and his life, see Otto Erich Deutsch (ed.), *Handel: A Documentary Biography*.

For the early history of the Haymarket theatre, see Daniel Nalbach, *The King's Theatre*. See also Judith Milhous and Robert D. Hume, 'The Haymarket Opera in 1711' (*Early Music*, XVIII, November 1989). Also Judith Milhous and Robert D. Hume, 'Heidegger and the Management of the Haymarket Opera, 1713–17' (*Early Music*, XXVIII:1, February 1999). A detailed description of the King's Theatre in Handel's time can be found in Mark A. Radice (ed.), *Opera in Context*, pp. 95–109. The French visitor who described his visits to Handel operas in 1728 was Pierre-Jacques Fougeroux; his letter (which includes two references to how much audiences liked drinking and smoking) is in Donald Burrows, *Handel*, pp. 460–62.

The relationship between Handel's early operas and the political context of their times is analysed by Paul Monod in 'The Politics of Handel's Early London Operas, 1711–1718' (*Journal of Interdisciplinary History*, XXXVI:3, Winter 2006). See also David Hunter, 'Handel among the Jacobites' (*Music and Letters*, LXXXII, 2001). Hunter writes of the nature of Handel's audiences in 'Patronising Handel, Inventing Audiences: The Intersection of Class, Money, Music and History' (*Early Music*, XXVIII, February 2000). Here, Hunter shows it is anachronistic to suggest that Handel was writing for, or even attracting, a 'middle-class' audience. On the contrary, the 'middling sort' in Handel's day constituted a tiny proportion of the English population, few of whom could have afforded tickets, much less a subscription, to the opera. Rather, Handel's appeal was primarily directed towards a small but wealthy aristocracy and the patronage its top echelons could supply; it was only after his death, according to Hunter, that he became the composer of the 'middle classes'.

On the Royal Academy of Music, see C. Steven LaRue, *Handel and His Singers: The Creation of the Royal Academy Operas, 1720–1728* (Clarendon, 1995). Also, the essay by Elizabeth Gibson in Stanley Sadie and Anthony Hicks (eds.), *Handel Tercentenary Collection* and, in the same book, Carole Taylor's essay analysing why Handel gradually distanced himself from Italian opera. The rivalry between Handel's Royal Academy of Music and the Opera of the Nobility is one of the sub-plots of the feature film *Farinelli*, directed by Gérard Corbiau and starring Stefano Dionisi (1994). In addition, see two articles by Judith Milhous and Robert D. Hume, 'New Light on Handel and the Royal Academy of Music in 1720' (*Theatre Journal*, vol. 35, no. 2, 1983); and 'The Charter for the Royal Academy of Music' (*Music & Letters*, vol. 67, no. 1, January 1986). For estimates of Cuzzoni's income, and a detailed consideration of the finances of opera in Handel's London, see Milhous and Hume, 'Opera Salaries in Eighteenth-Century London' (*Journal of the American Musicological Society*, XLVI, no. 1, 1993), and Robert D. Hume, 'The Economics of Culture in London, 1660–1740' (*Huntington Library Quarterly*, May 2006).

Hogarth's attitude towards Italian opera is discussed in Jeremy Barlow, *The Enraged Musician*; see especially chapter 7 (pp. 161–98).

On Farinelli, see Milhous and Hume, 'Construing and Misconstruing Farinelli in London' (*British Journal for Eighteenth-Century Studies*, no. 28, 2005). The satirical poem 'And there the *English* Actor goes…' is from a song of 1735 and is reproduced in Milhous and Hume, 'Construing and Misconstruing Farinelli in London'. 'But why this Rout about a lousy Shilling?' is from 'A Trip to Vaux-Hall: Or a General Satyr on the Times' by 'Hercules Mac-Sturdy, of the County of Tiperary, Esq' (1737), reproduced by David Coke in the booklet to accompany a 1978 exhibition at Gainsborough's House, Sudbury, Suffolk, entitled *The Muse's Bower: Vauxhall Gardens 1728–1786*. Farinelli left England in 1737 for Spain where, at the invitation of the Queen, and for an enormous salary, he became personal servant to her husband, Philip V, his duties being to sing each evening to the King in the hope of soothing the monarch's depression and melancholia. Farinelli never returned to England. His defection to the Spanish court caused great resentment in London, not least to the beleaguered Opera of the Nobility to whom he was still contracted, and press stories abounded about his insatiable avarice. The story acquired a political spin. This was a time of growing commercial tension between England and Spain and opposition commentators in London noted sourly that more fuss was made among the British ruling classes (that is, the Prime Minister, Walpole) by the loss of Farinelli to Spain than by that of impounded British shipping. Both, it was suggested, were examples of unprincipled Spanish 'depredations'. Two years later, war broke out between the two countries (the 'War of Jenkins' Ear'). The political dimensions of Farinelli's departure for Spain are well described by Thomas McGeary in 'Farinelli in Madrid: Opera, Politics, and the War of Jenkins' Ear' (*The Musical Quarterly*, vol. 82, no. 2, Summer 1998, pp. 383–421). After Philip V's death in 1746, Farinelli stayed on in Spain for another dozen years, producing a series of operas and other magnificent theatrical extravaganzas, many of them in collaboration with the famed librettist Metastasio, before finally retiring to Bologna.

For the broader cultural context in early Hanoverian England, see John Brewer, *The Pleasures of the Imagination*. Brewer is excellent on the popularity of *The Beggar's Opera* and on Tyers and Vauxhall Gardens. David H. Solkin outlines the history of Vauxhall, and of Jonathan Tyers' attempts to gentrify the gardens and his installation of the Roubiliac statue, in chapter 4 of *Painting for Money*. For detailed treatment of the Roubiliac statue and its messages see Suzanne Aspden's essay '"Fam'd Handel Breathing, tho' Transformed to Stone": The Composer as Monument' (*Journal of the American Musicological Society*, vol. 55, no. 1, Spring 2002); also, her extensive list of 'Works Cited'.

In addition to articles by Hume and/or Milhous cited above (and their contributions to Grove), see:

Robert D. Hume, 'The Politics of Opera in Late Seventeenth-Century London' (*Cambridge Opera Journal*, vol. 10, no. 1, 1998, pp. 15–43)
Robert D. Hume, 'The Sponsorship of Opera in London, 1704–1720' (*Modern Philology*, vol. 85, no. 4, May 1988, pp. 420–32)
Donald Burrows and Robert D. Hume, 'George I, the Haymarket Opera Company and Handel's "Water Music"' (*Early Music*, XIX:3, August 1991)
Judith Milhous and Robert D. Hume, 'Box Office Reports for Five Operas Mounted by Handel in London, 1732–1734' (*Harvard Library Bulletin*, XXVI, no. 3, July 1978)
Robert D. Hume: 'Handel and Opera Management in London in the 1730s' (*Music & Letters*, vol. 67, no. 4, October 1986)

Linda Colley writes about the adoption of Handel as an icon of British national pride, especially once he concentrated on oratorio, in *Britons: Forging the Nation 1707–1837* (Yale University Press, 1992), pp. 31–3.

4. Cultural Confluence in Mozart's Vienna

For the relationship between culture and politics in eighteenth-century Europe, see T. C. W. Blanning, *The Culture of Power and the Power of Culture*, a work that argues for the emergence of a 'public sphere'. In *The Triumph of Music* (Allen Lane, 2008), Blanning plots the ascendancy of music over other arts in Europe since the eighteenth century. See also Thomas Bauman, *Opera and the Enlightenment*. Several of the essays in Neal Zaslaw (ed.), *The Classical Era,* are of value here, especially those by Zaslaw himself ('Music and Society in the Classical Era'), Bruce Alan Brown ('Maria Theresa's Vienna'), John A. Rice ('Vienna under Joseph II and Leopold II'), Cliff Eisen ('Salzburg under Church Rule'), Christopher Hogwood and Jan Smaczny ('The Bohemian Lands'), and Thomas Bauman ('Courts and Municipalities in North Germany' – especially the section on Frederick the Great, pp. 242–6).

There have been many biographies of Frederick the Great, from Carlyle's monumental Victorian-era work via Nancy Mitford a century later to the volume by David Fraser (Allen Lane, 2000). My favourite among recent studies of that monstrous but musical monarch is James R. Gaines's evocative description of the visit of Bach to the flute-playing king in *Evening in the Palace of Reason*. See also E. H. Helm, *Music at the Court of Frederick the Great*. Blanning writes of Frederick the Great and music in both the books cited above; see also his article 'Frederick the Great and German Culture', in *Royal and Republican Sovereignty in Early Modern Europe: Essays in Honour of Ragnhild Hatton's Eightieth Birthday*, eds. G. C. Gibbs, Robert Oresko and Hamish Scott (Cambridge, 1996).

For Casanova's memories of his life as a violinist, see Giacomo Casanova, *The Story of My Life* (single-volume, edited version, Penguin, 2000), pp. 143ff. Bach's complaint that the Leipzig authorities were 'odd and little interested in music' is from his letter to Georg Erdmann, quoted in Hans T. David and Arthur Mendel, *The Bach Reader: A Life of J. S. Bach in Letters and Documents* (W. W. Norton, 1945), pp. 125–6. The statement about being 'constantly exposed to undeserved affronts' is quoted in Charles Sanford Terry, *Bach, a Biography* (OUP, 1928), p. 216.

Maria Theresa's warning to her son that he had no need of 'a composer or of useless people' such as young Mozart is in Deutsch, *Mozart: A Documentary Biography,* p. 138. Niemetschek describes the visit of the Mozarts to the court of Maria Theresa in his *Life of Mozart,* pp. 15–17. For more on the court of Maria Theresa (including Mozart's visit as a child), see the early chapters of Antonia Fraser's biography of Marie Antoinette. Mozart's resentment at the dining arrangements ('at least I have the honour of being placed above the cooks') is expressed in his letter of 17 March 1781. On his painful dismissal from the employment of Archbishop Colloredo by Count Arco later that year and his comment 'Salzburg is no longer the place for me', see his letters of 9 and 13 June. For Haydn's complaint about being a '*Kapell-*Servant', see the essay by László Somfai ('Haydn at the Esterházy Court') in Zaslaw (ed.), *Classical Era,* p. 289.

Blanning has written about the status of the musician in *The Culture of Power,* pp. 81–3, and *The Triumph of Music,* chapter 1. A statistical analysis of the social and economic position of musicians in the eighteenth and nineteenth centuries is provided by F. M. Scherer in *Quarter Notes and Bank Notes.* For the cultural context of Joseph II's Vienna, see Derek Beales, *Joseph II,* and *Enlightenment and Reform in Eighteenth-Century Europe* (see especially chapter 4, entitled 'Mozart and the Habsburgs'), and his chapter on 'Religion and Culture' in Blanning (ed.), *The Eighteenth Century.* Mozart's Vienna years are the subject of Volkmar Braunbehrens, *Mozart in Vienna.*

Much of the material on Mozart's adult life in Vienna draws upon Mozart's letters, edited by Emily Anderson; the collection of documents edited by Otto Erich Deustch; and contemporary memoirs, especially those of Da Ponte and Michael Kelly. Kelly writes of Mozart's love of punch and billiards, and of his Sunday concerts, on p. 113 of his *Reminiscences,* while the description of the three-way contest between Mozart, Salieri and Righini (whom Kelly calls Rigini), of Mozart being 'touchy as dynamite' and of the Emperor deciding to put Mozart's opera 'instantly' into rehearsal is on pp. 130–31. Da Ponte's entertaining if somewhat self-serving description of the background to *Figaro* can be found in his *Memoirs,* pp. 149–51 and 159–61. For more on Beaumarchais, see the biography by Frédéric Grendel and, of course, the three 'Figaro' plays. Da Ponte's racy description of the way he wrote the libretto for *Don Giovanni* is on pp. 174–5 of his *Memoirs.* Recent biographies of Da Ponte are by Anthony Holden and Rodney Bolt.

For the hazards of freelance life in Joseph II's Vienna and how Mozart dealt with them see the essay by Dorothea Link in Simon P. Keefe (ed.), *The Cambridge Companion to Mozart.* Many often-repeated stories about Mozart have their origins in the biography initiated by Constanze Mozart's second husband, Georg Nikolaus Nissen, completed after Nissen's death and originally published in 1828. For purposes of the present study, I have found much of value in the work of, among others, David Cairns, Alfred Einstein, Peter Gay, Jane Glover, Daniel Heartz, Wolfgang Hildesheimer, H. C. Robbins Landon, Julian Rushton, Maynard Solomon and Nicholas Till (not to forget Mörike's delicious – but avowedly fictional – *Mozart's Journey to Prague*). Also, Harald Salfellner's *Mozart and Prague* which provides a link between works such as these and the broader historical context. Niemetschek writes of the popularity of *Figaro,* and of its appearance in a piano version and arranged for wind quintet etc. in his *Life of Mozart,* p. 35. The colourful description of the crowd at the *Don Giovanni* premiere, with the mud, beer and almond milk, as well as Mozart's exclamation 'My Praguers understand me', are from the doctor and writer Alfred Meissner (who is quoted by Salfellner, *Mozart and Prague,* as is the *Prager Oberpostamtszeitung*).

Detailed descriptions of the Burgtheater and the Freyhaus theatre can be found in the essay by Malcolm S. Cole in Mark A. Radice (ed.), *Opera in Context,* pp. 111–45. For more on Schikaneder, the Theater auf der Wieden and the origins of *Die Zauberflöte,* see Honolka's biography of Schikaneder, especially chapters 4 and 5, and chapter X in Robbins Landon's volume about Mozart's final year. Recent research suggests that Mozart may have contributed informally to previous works put on by Schikaneder at the Wiednertheater; see David J. Buch, 'Mozart and the Theater auf der Wieden' (*Cambridge Opera Journal,* vol. 9, no. 3, 1997, pp. 195–232). The site of the Freyhaus is on the right bank of the Wien river, south of the Karlskirche, between the Wiedner Hauptstrasse and Margaretenstrasse.

Mozart describes the piano competition with Clementi (and Joseph's '*Allons,* fire away') in a letter to his father of 16 January 1782. The statement 'It was formerly a strong custom that our great princely houses maintained their own house orchestras…' is from the 1796 *Jahrbuch* of Johann Ferdinand von Schönfeld and is quoted in Tia DeNora, *Beethoven and the Construction of Genius,* p. 40. The analysis of subscribers to Mozart's 1784 concert is quoted in John A. Rice's essay in Neal Zaslaw's *The Classical Era,* p. 127. The theory that Mozart was a secret and excessive gambler, and the statistics of his earnings and of the Puchberg loans, are quoted in the official guidebook (and audioguide) at the 'Mozarthaus' on the Domgasse, the largest of the dozen or so apartments the constantly peripatetic Mozarts occupied in Vienna.

Mozart's letter ('There is no monarch… I should be more glad to serve') is dated 17 August 1782. Robbins Landon's quote about musicians having had 'a bad name which they earned for themselves with their crude manners [and] lack of education' and being 'treated as inferiors in the great houses' is from *Mozart's Last Year*, p. 25, as is the newspaper ad for a musician who has to double as a *valet-de-chambre*.

PART II: Revolution and Romanticism (c. 1800–1860)

5. Napoleon and Beethoven

Beethoven's inscription ('Love liberty above all things…') is from Michael Hamburger (ed.), *Beethoven*, p. 23. The outburst 'I do not write for the masses' was reported by the singer Josef August Röckel. Röckel's memories of working with Beethoven on *Fidelio* were written down long after the event, but ring true and are included in O. G. Sonneck, *Beethoven*, pp. 60–68, and Piero Weiss (ed.), *Opera*, pp. 156–62.

In *Quarter Notes and Bank Notes*, F. M. Scherer shows that the transition from a world of musical patronage to that of the freelance musician working in a market economy occurred gradually over time. Mozart's career can thus be read as emblematic of what was a radical if long-term historical process.

On opera and opera-going in Napoleon's Paris, see James H. Johnson, *Listening in Paris*, chapter 9. For a more general survey, see Patrick Barbier, *Opera in Paris*, and Jean Mongrédien, *French Music from the Enlightenment to Romanticism*, chapter 3 *passim*. Also of interest are some of the contributions to Malcolm Boyd (ed.), *Music and the French Revolution*; see, for example, Elizabeth Bartlett on the repertoire at the Opéra during the Reign of Terror, and Cynthia M. Gessele on the French Conservatoire de Musique. For Napoleon's insistence that 'no opera… be staged without my authorization', see Barbier, *Opera in Paris*, p. 15, and for his ignorance of *Don Giovanni*, p. 7. The basic decree whereby Napoleon attempted to reduce and rationalize the theatres in Paris was issued on 8 June 1806, supplemented by order of the Ministry of the Interior in April 1807 and ratified in July. For a summary, see Barbier, *Opera in Paris*, p. 9; for more detail, and a quotation from the original decree, see Hervé Lacombe, *The Keys to French Opera in the Nineteenth Century*, p. 245 (and note 53 on p. 383). James H. Johnson tells of Napoleon rushing to the opera after an assassination attempt in *Listening in Paris*, p. 167; the references to it being impolite to talk or blow one's nose during music, and to audience members calling out to others to be quiet, are from Johnson, ibid., p. 172. Napoleon's admiration for Crescentini is recounted by Barbier, *Opera in Paris*, pp. 22–3.

In addition to Röckel, the principal contemporary and near-contemporary sources of information about Beethoven (including his relationships with Schikaneder, Sonnleithner, Cherubini, the Viennese nobility and with his nephew and various women) are the 'Biographical Notes' by Franz Wegeler and Ferdinand Ries (*Remembering Beethoven*) and the biography by Schindler, both produced by people who knew Beethoven well and whose work originally appeared within a few years of his death. The authoritative multi-volume biography by Thayer appeared in the 1860s and 1870s; I used the 1970 edition by Elliot Forbes. Sebastian Mayer's comment ('my brother-in-law would never have written such damned nonsense') is from Thayer, p. 384. For a good modern biography of Beethoven, see that by Maynard Solomon. Beethoven's wish that he could be 'above having to wrangle and bargain with publishers' and be paid an annual salary is quoted in Hamburger (ed.), *Beethoven*, p. 32.

Much has been written about the romantic 'image' associated with Beethoven and how he came to acquire it. Particularly illuminating are Alessandra Comini, *The Changing Image of Beethoven*; Tia DeNora, *Beethoven and the Construction of Genius*; and Esteban Buch, *Beethoven's Ninth*. On the writing, rehearsing and rewriting of *Leonore/Fidelio*, see Paul Robinson (ed.), *Fidelio*. Also, the essay by David Galliver in Malcolm Boyd (ed.), *Music and the French Revolution*.

6. After Napoleon: Opera as Politics, Art and Business

Stendhal's reaction to Naples's rebuilt San Carlo opera house is in *Rome, Naples and Florence*, pp. 354–5, and his description of Pasta's singing from his *Life of Rossini*, p. 379.

The contributors to Alexander Ringer (ed.), *Music & Society: The Early Romantic Era* write about developments in musical life in Paris, Vienna, Berlin, Dresden and Leipzig, Italy, London, Moscow and St Petersburg, the USA and Latin America. For more on the development of romantic opera (especially in France), including the significance of their historical settings and the growing prominence of the chorus and of stage design, see David Charlton (ed.), *The Cambridge Companion to Grand Opera*, especially the contributions by Hervé Lacombe, Simon Williams and James Parakilas (who quotes the figures for chorus members in the Paris Opéra on p. 77); also Sarah

Hibberd's essay about *La Muette de Portici*. For more on the significance of opera in Paris, c. 1820–50, see Chapter 8. For culture (and cultural nationalism) in nineteenth-century Russia, see Notes to Chapter 10.

On the emerging, almost religious reverence for 'art' and the idea of the artist as 'genius', see Tia DeNora, *Beethoven and the Construction of Genius*. Beethoven's funeral is discussed by Esteban Buch in *Beethoven's Ninth*, chapter 6; for Beethoven's funeral and the oration written by Grillparzer, see p. 111–14. Tim Blanning considers the romantic concept of 'genius' (and quotes the Grillparzer text) in *The Triumph of Music*, pp. 95–101, and the 'sacralization' of European culture, including music, in Tim Blanning, (ed.), *The Oxford History of Modern Europe* (OUP, 1996), pp. 135–8. George Eliot refers to Liszt in *Daniel Deronda* (Penguin, 1967), p. 280, and her description of Klesmer is on p. 282. Friedrich Wieck is quoted in Harvey Sachs, *Virtuoso* (Thames & Hudson, 1982), p. 54, and Henry Reeves on p. 52.

The most detailed modern biography of Verdi is by Mary Jane Phillips-Matz. She includes Verdi's 1848 letter to Piave (pp. 230–31) and his reminiscence of the origins of *Nabucco* (pp. 106–7). For greater integration of Verdi's life and work, see the writings of Julian Budden, George Martin, Charles Osborne, Roger Parker, John Rosselli, Frank Walker and William Weaver. Several authors (Walker, Rosselli, Parker) have investigated the reception of Verdi's *Nabucco* between its first performance in 1842 and the revolutions of 1848–9 and in particular the oft-repeated story that 'Va, pensiero' became rapidly adopted as a quasi-nationalistic hymn. To Parker (*Leonora's Last Act*, chapter 2), what is striking is how little this particular chorus was picked out in contemporary reviews, except to admire it within its general musico-dramatic context. The elevation of 'Va, pensiero' to special status appears to date from much later (not least to Verdi's own mythologizing of its importance in his later autobiographical sketch). While Parker is in demythologizing mode, he also adduces evidence that, far from having given up composition at this time, Verdi had been actively seeking further commissions. For Verdi's early encounters with censorship, see John A. Davis, 'Opera and Absolutism in Restoration Italy, 1815–1860' (*Journal of Interdisciplinary History*, XXXVI:4, Spring 2006, pp. 569–94); and Andreas Giger, 'Social Control and the Censorship of Giuseppe Verdi's Operas in Rome 1844–1859' (*Cambridge Opera Journal*, vol. 11, no. 3, pp. 233–65).

For the origins of the name of the 'Nabucco pipeline' I am indebted to Christian Dolezal of OMV Gas & Power GmbH, official spokesperson for the Nabucco Project.

Donizetti's early years under the tutelage of Simon Mayr are described in the biographies by William Ashbrook (pp. 10–13) and Herbert Weinstock (pp. 5–12). The quotation about Barbaja 'sniffing the odour of true merit' is from the novelist Giuseppe Rovani (author of *Cento anni*) and is quoted in William Weaver, *The Golden Century*, p. 28. Barbaja's attempts to keep Nourrit in Naples are from Henry Pleasants, *The Great Tenor Tragedy*, pp. 55–6 and 61. For Rossini's recollection of his meeting with Beethoven, see Edmond Michotte, *Richard Wagner's Visit to Rossini*, pp. 38–46.

Much work on the opera 'business' in nineteenth-century Italy is contained in three pioneering books by John Rosselli: *The Opera Industry in Italy from Cimarosa to Verdi*; *Music and Musicians in Nineteenth-Century Italy*; and *Singers of Italian Opera*. See also the chapter by Roger Parker ('The Opera Industry') in Jim Samson (ed.), *The Cambridge History of Nineteenth-Century Music*. Donald Sassoon writes of the many opera houses built or renovated in post-Napoleonic Italy in *The Culture of the Europeans*, pp. 262–3. Rosselli's *Opera Industry* is a detailed study of the role of the operatic impresario and contains much excellent material about Barbaja, Lanari, Merelli and others. On the changing status (and recompense) of the librettist, see chapter 4, by Fabrizio della Seta, in Lorenzo Bianconi and Giorgio Pestelli (eds.), *Opera Production and Its Resources*. The story of Bellini's problems with Felice Romani and of Lanari involving the police is recounted in the biographies by Stelios Galatopoulos (pp. 258–61), Leslie Orrey (pp. 48–9) and John Rosselli (pp. 106–8, 112–16). For more-detailed treatment of Romani and the nature of his profession (including the librettist's relationship with the impresario and the composer), see Alessandro Roccatagliati, 'Felice Romani, Librettist by Trade' (*Cambridge Opera Journal*, vol. 8, no. 2, 1996, pp. 113–45). On the fame and fortune of Eugène Scribe, see Sassoon, *Culture of the Europeans*, p. 289. For more on the relationship between Italian opera composers and their audiences, see C. Sorba, 'To Please the Public: Composers and Audiences in XIXth Century Italy' (*Journal of Interdisciplinary History*, XXXVI:4, Spring 2006, pp. 595–614).

I am grateful to Gabriele Dotto, Director of the Ricordi Archives, for material about the history of Casa Ricordi. For a brief summary, see Richard Macnutt, 'The House of Ricordi' (*The Musical Times*, vol. 120, no. 1632, February 1979, pp. 123–5). According to John Rosselli (*Music and Musicians in Nineteenth-Century Italy*, p. 114), no fewer than 245 arrangements of all or parts of Verdi's 1843 opera *I Lombardi* were issued during the ten years following its first performance.

Patrick Barbier in *Opera in Paris*, p. 211, quotes a French newspaper in 1829 complaining sarcastically about the 'unfortunate' Malibran earning just over 94,000 francs that year and wondering whether a fund might be set up to help 'this poor woman'. A cheap meal in a Paris restaurant around this time could have been obtained for less than a franc according to Sassoon (*Culture of the Europeans*, p. 250). On the fees earned by top singers, Rosselli reports (*Music and Musicians*, p. 83) that Pasta and Malibran earned 1000 francs per performance in the 1830s – a level not surpassed until the 1870s. In Paris, according to Barbier (*Opera in Paris*, p. 155), Pasta would have earned between 30,000 and 35,000 francs a year. See also Susan Rutherford, *The Prima Donna and Opera* (especially chapter 5), and Rupert Christiansen, *Prima Donna* (especially chapter 2). Rosselli tells of Strepponi singing the role of Norma six times in a week, and of the soprano who had to learn twenty-six roles in a season, in *Music and Musicians*, pp. 77–8. For a re-examination of the prima donna's so-called *aria di baule* or interpolated 'suitcase aria', see Hilary Poriss, 'Making Their Way through the World: Italian One-Hit Wonders' (*19th-Century Music*, vol. 24, no. 3, Spring, 2001, pp. 197–224). For more on the lives and careers of celebrated women singers, see Chapter 12.

For Rossini's contract for *Il barbiere di Siviglia* and Verdi's correspondence about his contract (for *Ernani*) with Venice, see Bruno Cagli, 'Verdi and the Business of Writing Operas' (especially pp. 112–14), in William Weaver and Martin Chusid (eds.), *The Verdi Companion*. Pasta's 1826 contract with the King's Theatre, London, is discussed, and quoted, in Susan Rutherford, *The Prima Donna and Opera*, pp. 167–8.

The story of the three French composers at the café refusing to pay their bill is told in Sassoon, *Culture of the Europeans*, p. 508. The anecdote also appears (featuring a single composer) in Ernest Roth, *The Business of Music*, p. 33.

7. Opera Reaches New York – and the Wider Frontier

The quotation from Increase Mather is taken from Susan Castillo, *Colonial Encounters in New World Writing, 1500–1786: Performing America* (Routledge, 2005), pp. 56–7. For more on attitudes to theatre in Colonial America (including the quotations from William Penn and Michael Wigglesworth), see Paul Kuritz, *The Making of Theatre History* (Paul Kuritz, 1988), pp. 238–40. A description and analysis of opera in pre- and post-Revolutionary Boston (including Puritan hostility to the theatre) can be found in David Mackay, 'Opera in Colonial Boston' (*American Music*, vol. 3, no. 2, Summer 1985). For the early history of opera in New Orleans, see John Dizikes, *Opera in America*, chapter 3.

Da Ponte's reminiscences about the García visit are in his *Memoirs*, pp. 446–9. See also the biographies of Da Ponte by Anthony Holden and Rodney Bolt. For a detailed description of the visit (including the quotations from the diary of Robert Dale Owen), see James Radomski, *Manuel García*, chapter 9. April Fitzlyon tells of the Garcías in New York, and of Malibran's suffering at the hands of her father, in *Maria Malibran*, pp. 35–55. Clara Fisher Maeder's observation that audiences would applaud whenever Dominck Lynch did so is from her memoirs, p. 31. See also Karen Ahlquist, *Democracy at the Opera*. For this section, newspaper reports proved particularly fruitful. So did Vera Brodsky Lawrence, *Strong on Music*, a lengthy study based on (and greatly expanded from) the diaries of the New York music lover George Templeton Strong; for the García visit, see pp. xliv–lvi.

For an insight into operatic life in nineteenth-century Latin America, see John Rosselli, 'The Opera Business and the Italian Immigrant Community in Latin America 1820–1930: The Example of Buenos Aires' (*Past and Present*, no. 127, May 1990, pp. 155–82).

The most comprehensive study of the establishment of opera in Australia is the three-volume work by Alison Gyger; the first, *Civilising the Colonies*, covers the years to 1880 (the 1834 quotation about 'Bonnets and Hats' is on p. 13). William Lyster and his touring companies are treated in Harold Love's *The Golden Age of Australian Opera*. For the early history of Melbourne, see chapter 7 of Asa Briggs, *Victorian Cities* (Penguin, 1968). Anna Bishop is the subject of a biography by Richard Davis, while Catherine Hayes's life is by Basil Walsh. I am grateful to Elizabeth Silsbury and Jula Szuster (Adelaide), Therese Radic (Melbourne), Roger Covell, Alison and David Gyger, Moffatt Oxenbould and Graham Pont (Sydney) for much help and encouragement as I learned about the establishment and history of opera in Australia. In addition to their books listed in the Bibliography, see the essays by Szuster and by Robyn Holmes in Andrew D. McCredie (ed.), *From Colonel Light into the Footlights: The Performing Arts in South Australia from 1836 to the Present* (Pagel, 1988).

For the development of opera in California, see George Martin, *Verdi at the Golden Gate*, especially the earlier chapters which describe the development of theatrical and musical life in San Francisco during and just after the gold rush. In addition, see chapter 10 in John Dizikes' *Opera in America*; also, Joan Chatfield-Taylor's illustrated history of opera in San Francisco (in which the singer who camped in his bedsheets, Alfred Roncovieri, is quoted). The quotation about gentlemen ejecting 'tobacco juice' is from Quaintance Eaton, *Opera Caravan*, p. 86. For the sheer volume and popularity of opera in antebellum America see Katherine Preston, *Opera on the Road*.

For the importance of the piano as an iconic fixture in every bourgeois home in the later nineteenth century, see Cyril Ehrlich, *The Piano*. The same title was given by Jane Campion to her 1992 movie, starring Holly Hunter as a mute nineteenth-century Scottish migrant to remote, coastal New Zealand whose obsession with her piano provides the central focus and springboard of the plot. For more on the importance of the piano in nineteenth-century homes, see Notes to Chapter 11.

Mapleson's quotation about the frantic train journey to Chicago is from his *Memoirs*, p. 257; his comments about 'Frisco' as 'the toe of the stocking' and the near revolt by his Italian chorus are on pp. 260 and 262. For Melba in Australia, see her own *Melodies and Memories* (especially chapters 17 and 22, from which my quotations are drawn) and the biography by John Hetherington. Also, a touching memoir of Melba by her granddaughter, Lady Pamela Vestey. Mark Twain's observations about audience behaviour in America and Europe are from *A Tramp Abroad* (OUP, 1996), pp. 87 and 95. For more on the behaviour of American audiences at opera (and other 'highbrow') entertainments, see, for example, Lawrence Levine, *Highbrow Lowbrow*, Part III.

8. L'Opéra

For an overview of the principal opera companies in Paris, *c.*1815–50, and of the corresponding operatic genres (*grand, comique, italien*), see Patrick Barbier, *Opera in Paris* (especially chapters 2 and 7); the essays in Part I of David Charlton (ed.), *The Cambridge Companion to Grand Opera* (especially chapter 2 by Hervé Lacombe); William L. Crosten, *French Grand Opera*; Jane F. Fulcher, *The Nation's Image*; the opening chapter in Anselm Gerhard, *The Urbanization of Opera*; Hervé Lacombe, *The Keys to French Opera in the Nineteenth Century*; Alexander Ringer (ed.), *Music & Society: The Early Romantic Era* (especially chapter 2 by Ralph P. Locke). Also, chapter 7 in William Atwood's *The Parisian Worlds of Frédéric Chopin*, and James H. Johnson, *Listening in Paris* (especially chapters 10 and 14). All discuss, *passim*, the career of Louis Véron as manager of the Opéra, the subject of a study by John Drysdale. I am grateful to James Johnson for educating me *in situ* about the nineteenth-century history of opera in Paris during a congenial day in 2005.

For an evocative picture of the Parisian 'salon', see, for example, S. Kracauer, *Offenbach and the Paris of His Time*, chapter 5; the quotation from Flotow is from pp. 45–6. See, too, Barbier, *Opera in Paris*, pp. 201–3 (where he quotes Marie d'Agoult on Henriette Sontag) and Atwood, *Parisian Worlds*, chapter 4. Giulio Ricordi's reactions to a Rossini *soirée* are quoted in Gaia Servadio, *Rossini*, p. 209.

A detailed description of the Salle Peletier – the home of *grand opéra* for much of this period – can be found in the essay by Karin Pendle and Stephen Wilkins in Mark A. Radice (ed.), *Opera in Context*, pp. 171–207. Johnson describes the decline of the Opéra in the 1820s, *Listening in Paris*, pp. 185–6. For Rossini's years at the Théâtre-Italien, see ibid., pp. 184–5; also Richard Osborne, *Rossini*, chapter 10, and Servadio, *Rossini*, pp. 124ff. The statistics about the number of performances of Rossini works at the Italiens are from Barbier, p. 185.

The three main operatic institutions in Paris were not the only ones. See, for instance, Mark Everist, *Music Drama at the Paris Odéon 1824–28*; Everist's opening chapter contains an excellent summary of conditions in Paris as the city tried to cope with the onset of industrialization and a massive increase in population. In the 1850s and 1860s, Paris saw the rise and demise of another opera company, the Théâtre-Lyrique, whose history has been chronicled by T. J. Walsh; it was at the Lyrique that Gounod's *Faust* had its premiere (in 1859). See also Katharine Ellis, 'Systems Failure in Operatic Paris: The Acid Test of the Théâtre-Lyrique', in Annegret Fauser and Mark Everist (eds.), *Music, Theater, and Cultural Transfer: Paris, 1830–1914* (University of Chicago Press, 2009).

For an investigation into the nature of the Paris opera audience (and considered scepticism over the extent to which it became more 'bourgeois'), see Steven Huebner's article 'Opera Audiences in Paris 1830–1870' (*Music and Letters*, vol. 70, no. 2, May 1989, pp. 206–25); it is from Huebner that I have taken the statistics of subscribers, ticket prices, working-class incomes etc. as well as the quotations about the 'inferior classes' and 'good company'. See also Gerhard, *Urbanization of Opera*, pp. 25–33. For the numbers in the Opéra chorus and *corps de ballet*, see Hervé Lacombe in Charlton (ed.), *Cambridge Companion to Grand Opera*, pp. 29 and 31. The reasons why opera audiences became quieter and more attentive are explored in Johnson, *Listening in Paris*. Berlioz's description of his early visits to the Opéra is from chapter 15 of his *Memoirs* (his determination to silence talkative neighbours is on p. 82). On the correspondence between the urbanization of Paris and the development of opera in the city, see Gerhard, *Urbanization of Opera*. For a detailed analysis of the nature of audiences attending performances of classical music in London, Paris and Vienna during the first half of the nineteenth century, see William Weber, *Music and the Middle Class*.

For opera in the French provinces, especially Lyon, see Jean Mongrédien, *French Music from the Enlightenment to Romanticism*, pp. 138–58. The Bovary visit to the opera in Rouen is in Gustave Flaubert, *Madame Bovary*, pp. 231–41.

The quotations from Balzac's *Old Goriot* are from p. 93 (Rastignac's 'first day on the battlefield of Parisian civilization'); p. 165 ('People with a box at the Italiens have heaven's own luck!'); p. 92 ('owns a side-box at the Opéra and goes to the Bouffons too'). We learn of Mme Beauséant's visits to the opera with both husband and lover on p. 81, while Rastignac adjusts his cravat on p. 37. The novel is full of references to the opera and the social value of attending; on pp. 149ff., for example, Rastignac finds himself whisked off by Mme Beauséant to the Italiens, where he 'passed from enchantment to enchantment' – none of it to do with the work being performed, which is not even mentioned. The character of Foedora in Balzac's *The Wild Ass's Skin* was widely thought to have been modelled on Rossini's second wife, Olympe Pélissier. The quotation from *Eugénie Grandet* is from p. 110.

Stendhal describes the 'pedants' and 'dilettanti' in his *Life of Rossini*, pp. 315–16. Johnson discusses the *dilettanti* and the claque in *Listening in Paris*, pp. 191–6 and 246–8, and Barbier in *Opera in Paris*, pp. 199–201 and 126–8. On the claque, see also Lacombe in Charlton (ed.), *Cambridge Companion to Grand Opera*, pp. 38–9. For a frank and amusing inside account of a twentieth-century claque (at the Vienna Staatsoper), see Joseph Wechsberg, 'My Life in the Claque', *The New Yorker*, 19 February 1944, p. 22; later adapted as chapter 8 of Wechsberg's *Looking for a Bluebird*.

The description of Louis Philippe's abdication comes from the memoirs of Charles George Barrington, secretary to Lord Palmerston. Barrington heard the story from a 'foreign gentleman who, if not present, heard the story from one who was'. The relevant extract from Barrington's *Recollections* is reprinted in Daniel Snowman (ed.), *PastMasters* (Sutton, 2001), p. 197. For Offenbach's triumphs at the 'Bouffes' at the 1855 World Exhibition in Paris, see Kracauer, *Offenbach*, pp. 129ff., and Peter Gammond, *Offenbach: His Life and Times*, pp. 37ff. A detailed description of Napoleon III's 1855 visit to Covent Garden can be found in Ivor Guest, *Napoleon III in England*, pp. 126–8. Immediately after the return of the French Emperor and Empress, Queen Victoria reflected at some length about the character of Napoleon III, his apparent moral ambiguity and his belief in his 'Star' (see Christopher Hibbert (ed.), *Lives and Letters: Queen Victoria in her Letters and Journals* (Penguin, 1985), pp. 131–2).

For Debussy's comments about the Opéra Garnier, see Paul Holmes, *Debussy* (Omnibus Press, 1989), p. 61, and Roger Nichols, *The Life of Debussy* (CUP, 1998), p. 165.

9. Fires of London

For the history of the Royal Opera House, Covent Garden, see Harold Rosenthal, *Two Centuries of Opera at Covent Garden*; also Henry Saxe Wyndham, *The Annals of Covent Garden Theatre*. Wyndham writes of the 1856 fire in volume ii, pp. 201 *et seq*. The early years of the Gye regime and the fire of 1856 are dealt with on pp. 72–114. See pp. 110–11 for quotations from the *London Journal* (the women were 'disgustingly attired…' and the men 'consisted of thieves…'). The description of Bunn's actors and dancers ('half attired, with enamelled faces…') 'pattering' from one theatre to another can be found in Rosenthal, *Two Centuries of Opera*, pp. 48–9. The social history of opera in nineteenth-century London provides a central focus in Jennifer Hall-Witt, *Fashionable Acts: Opera and Elite Culture in London, 1780–1880*. The statistics on nineteenth-century theatre fires are quoted in Patrick Carnegy, *Wagner and the Art of the Theatre*, p. 67. Theatre fires were less common by the late twentieth century, but among opera houses damaged or destroyed were those in Cairo (where *Aida* was premiered), Barcelona, Frankfurt, Bari and Venice (the last three resulting from arson).

On the 1808 fire, rebuild and 'O.P. Riots', see Rosenthal, *Two Centuries of Opera*, pp. 21–6. My account of the 'O.P. Riots' also draws on contemporary documentation supplied by the ROH Collections.

Lumley's account of his stewardship of Her Majesty's Theatre (*Reminiscences of the Opera*) is now thought to have been authored in large part by Harriet Grote, to whom the book is dedicated (see Hall-Witt, *Fashionable Acts*, pp. 160 and 302). Lumley (or Grote) is nevertheless revealing about the infuriatingly unpredictable behaviour of Jenny Lind, the one star on whom he relied in his otherwise doomed rivalry with Gye. Lumley's problem was that Lind had previously signed a contract with Bunn of Drury Lane, a contract she later regretted and from which she asked Bunn in vain to release her. Bunn, knowing of the more lucrative offer from Lumley of Her Majesty's, went on to take Lind to court, won his case and was awarded damages of £2500 (see report in *The Times*, 23 February 1848, p. 7). Lind's solicitor was also Lumley's, and Lumley may well have paid Lind's court expenses (as well as the resulting damages). For a detailed consideration of the court case, see George Biddlecombe, 'The Construction of a Cultural Icon: The Case of Jenny Lind', in Peter Horton and Bennett Zon (eds.), *Nineteenth-Century British Music Studies*, vol. 3 (Ashgate, 2003), especially pp. 56–9.

One of the two Italians who went bankrupt after restructuring Covent Garden as an opera house in 1846–7 was Giuseppe Persiani, a minor composer and the husband of the (very major) opera singer Fanny Persiani. Delafield's bankruptcy resulted from excessive private overspending as well as on theatrical productions (see the court report in *The Times*, 5 November 1849, p. 7).

The quotation from Chorley (the 'old house' beaten 'out of the field') is from Henry F. Chorley, *Thirty Years' Musical Recollections*, p. 325.

Frederick Gye's diaries belong to Gye's descendants but are lodged in the Royal Opera House Collections, Covent Garden, where Francesca Franchi (Head of Collections) and Julia Creed (Archivist) kindly gave me access to them. For more on the Gye diaries as a whole, see Gabriella Dideriksen and Matthew Ringel, 'Frederick Gye and "The Dreadful Business of Opera Management"' (*19th-Century Music*, vol. 19, no. 1, Summer 1995, pp. 3–30).

For Weber in London, see John Warrack, *Carl Maria von Weber*, chapter XVIII. Rupert Christiansen writes of Wagner in London in *The Victorian Visitors*, pp. 42–81. Verdi first visited London in June 1847 for the premiere of *I masnadieri* starring Lind. In a letter to Giuseppina Appiani dated 27 June, he wrote how 'I've been suffering this fog and smoke which suffocates and depresses me.' The theatres in London were packed out, he reports, adding that 'if I could just stay here for a couple of years, I would carry off a bagful of these *holy, holy* pounds' (see Charles Osborne (ed.), *Letters of Giuseppe Verdi*, p. 45; and Mary Jane Phillips-Matz, *Verdi*, p. 216). For a flavour of operatic life in mid-Victorian London, see, for example, Chorley, *Thirty Years' Musical Recollections*, and, for a slightly later period, George Bernard Shaw, *London Music in 1888–89* and *Music in London 1890–94*.

PART III: *Opera Resurgens (c. 1860–1900)*

10. Culture and Politics in Central and Eastern Europe

The struggle for 'national identity' in music is the subject of a chapter by Jim Samson in Jim Samson (ed.), *Man and Music: The Late Romantic Era*. John Tyrrell, in *Czech Opera*, places its subject in historical context; see especially the opening two chapters, the first on Czech nationalism and the second on theatres. Richard Taruskin writes of Smetana and the development of Czech opera in *The Oxford History of Western Music*, vol. 3, pp. 443–63. Ivan T. Berend writes on romanticism and nationalism in *History Derailed: Central and Eastern Europe in the Long Nineteenth Century* (University of California, 2003); see especially chapter 2. Excellent essays on Smetana and the Prague of his time are included in Olga Mojzisová (ed.), *Bedřich Smetana: Time, Life, Work*, published by the Smetana Museum in Prague. My understanding of Czech operatic history has been further enhanced by conversations in Prague with Ivan Ruml, Jiří Nekvasil and Jan Spacek, to each of whom my thanks. I attended (and reviewed) a performance of *Libuše* at the Prague National Theatre on 1 November 2000.

Tolstoy describes Natasha's visit to the opera in *War and Peace*, Book 2, Part 5, sections 8–11. Verdi's *La forza del destino* was produced in St Petersburg's Bolshoi Kamenny theatre (not the newly built Mariinsky) on 10 November 1862; his fee was 33,000 roubles (George Loomis, 'Verdi in St Petersburg' (*Opera*, July 2001, pp. 789–96)). For reactions to the premiere of *Forza*, see Mary Jane Phillips-Matz, *Verdi*, pp. 454–6.

Julie A. Buckler writes of the opera houses and audiences in Imperial Russia in the opening chapters of *The Literary Lorgnette*, a study of the mid-century Russian love of Italian opera and of its presentation in literature (including *War and Peace*). For an introduction to music and culture in nineteenth-century Russia, see Rosamund Bartlett's chapter ('Russian Culture, 1801–1917') in Dominic Lieven (ed.), *The Cambridge History of Russia*, vol. 2 (CUP, 2006). Richard Taruskin's *Defining Russia Musically* is illuminating on the relationship between Russia's music and its elusive and shifting sense of 'national character'; on p. 225 he makes the point that it was only at the opera that radicals had the right of assembly. See also Taruskin's and David Brown's studies of Mussorgsky. For Taruskin on Stasov, the 'mighty little band' (as he translates Stasov's term) and the search for authentic Russian cultural traditions, see *The Oxford History of Western Music*, vol. 3, pp. 463–78. Orlando Figes writes about Stasov and the Balakirev circle in *Natasha's Dance*, pp. 175–90 and 390–99, and about Mamontov and his Private Opera on pp. 198–204. For more on high culture and Russian national identity, see Geoffrey Hosking, *Russia and the Russians: A History* (Harvard University Press, 2001), pp. 344–50.

A vivid example of how little known were the works of Mussorgsky and his colleagues outside their immediate circle is provided by an anecdote reported in Harvey Sachs, *Toscanini*, pp. 61–2. In 1898, Aloys Mooser, a Swiss musicologist and keen mountaineer, took shelter from an alpine storm halfway up Mont Blanc in a cabin, where he encountered a group of Italian climbers. One was the 31-year-old Arturo Toscanini. The two quickly discovered their shared musical interest. Warming themselves with soup and stretched out on camp beds, Mooser mentioned that he was currently living in St Petersburg and attached to the Imperial Theatres. Toscanini asked ('point-blank'): 'So you have seen *Boris Godunov*?' Mooser was astonished, reflecting later that 'there weren't twenty people in the west' who knew *Boris* at that time (twenty-four years after its pre-miere). Even in St Petersburg, 'the official milieu, the court, the public, many professional musicians and the majority of the press considered Mussorgsky a sort of failure bereft of talent', none of his works appearing on the imperial stages. Toscanini, it seems, had somehow obtained a copy of the score of *Boris* and studied it, and he swore to Mooser in their ice-covered hut perched at 3350 metres that one day he would conduct the work (he did, at the New York Metropolitan in March 1913).

It has been said (see Bryan Magee, *Aspects of Wagner*, p. 35) that by the time of Wagner's death the number of books and articles about him had exceeded 10,000 and had overtaken those about any other human being except Jesus Christ and Napoleon. I will mention rather fewer here. Useful Eng-lish-language biographies of Wagner include those by Ernest Newman, Robert W. Gutman and Barry Millington. See also the essays in Barry Millington (ed.), *The Wagner Compendium*, especially those on the historical and intellectual background. One of Millington's own essays nicely punctures a number of myths about Wagner (including the alleged size of the Wagner bibliography). Some of the complex links between Wagner's work and his personal history and circumstances are examined in John Deathridge, *Wagner beyond Good and Evil*. Cosima Wagner's *Diaries* provide close-up doc-umentation of Wagner from 1869, shortly after she joined Wagner at Triebschen on Lake Lucerne, to his death in 1883. For descriptions of Wagner by many who knew him, see Stewart Spencer, *Wagner Remembered*.

Most deal at length with Wagner's relationship with King Ludwig. Ludwig's comments about Wagner ('I am nothing... Unique and Incomparable') are taken from Spencer, *Wagner Remembered*, pp. 174, 183. See also Manfred Eger's essay 'The Patronage of King Ludwig II' in Ulrich Müller and Peter Wapnewski (eds.), *Wagner Handbook*, in which Eger assesses the aggregate amount of Ludwig's subventions. On the idea of a festival of Wagner's operas in Munich (and an illustration of the proposed theatre by Semper), see Patrick Carnegy, *Wagner and the Art of the Theatre*, pp. 52–4. The first Munich Opera Festival took place in 1875 (a year before Wagner's own festival in Bayreuth); it became an annual event in 1901 when the Prinzregententheater – modelled on the Bayreuth Festspielhaus – was inaugurated, and continues to this day.

Wagner's meeting with Ludwig's representatives in February 1874 and his subsequent 'ill humour' are documented in Cosima Wagner's *Diaries*, pp. 203–4. For Wagner's deception towards the monarch, see Gutman, pp. 442–4. Frederic Spotts (*Bayreuth*, p. 37) refers to Wagner's 'brazen fleec-ing of the King's treasury'. Spotts is excellent on the origins of Bayreuth, the building of the theatre and the first Festival. Tchaikovsky's comments on the first Bayreuth Festival are taken from Robert Hartford (ed.), *Bayreuth*, pp. 52–6; Hartford also includes selections by Lilli Lehmann, Grieg, Saint-Saëns and others. Wagner is quoted as referring to Emile Ollivier as 'a good and intelligent person [who] shares his country's insolence' in the *Diaries* on p. 87 and to the Kaiser as possessing 'certain qualities...' on p. 89; he reprimands his doctor over Alsace and Lorraine on p. 72. Cosima's exhila-ration at Bavaria, Saxony and Württemberg fighting as a German army is on p. 69.

Wagner's disillusionment with the new German Reich was evident within a couple of years of its establishment; Cosima notes his comments that he is 'not to be counted among the ranks of... patriots' and is 'nailed on the cross of the German ideal' on 4 September 1873 (*Diaries*, pp. 185–6). 'We might... have a German Reich, but... no German nation' is from April 1874 (p. 206). The *Diaries* record many occasions when Wagner talked of leaving Germany for the USA. 'When R. now talks about emigrating to America,' she wrote in July 1877, 'I no longer have the courage to speak against it' (p. 285). Wagner's pleasure in gazing on the map of America is on p. 378, his desire to leave the Reich and his comments on 'cruel and indifferent people' on p. 385. 'I have made up my mind to go to America' is on p. 396. Thomas Mann later wrote that the 'German spirit' meant everything to Wagner, the 'German state' nothing (Thomas Mann, *Pro and Contra Wagner*, p. 193).

Cosima wrote of the Wagners' 1877 visit to London (they stayed in Orme Square) in her *Diaries* pp. 280–84. While her husband went to rehearsals, Cosima was a busy cultural tourist visiting the National Gallery, Zoo and British Museum. Much of the Wagners' social time was spent with their friends the Leweses (George Eliot and her partner) with whom Cosima attended the first concert, only to be horrified by the 'double echo' of the Royal Albert Hall. Rupert Christiansen speculates on the audiences that would have attended Wagner's London concerts (*The Victorian Visitors*, chapter 2); even if the Royal Albert Hall was half empty, Christiansen points out (p. 67), some 20,000 people would have bought tickets, a number that speaks highly of the musical sophistication of London.

Wagner's encounter with the man in the Naples tram is from Cosima Wagner's *Diaries*, p. 376.

For a detailed description of the way Wagner was perceived by admirers (and others), during and after his lifetime, in various different countries, see the essays in David C. Large and William Weber (eds.), *Wagnerism in European Culture and Politics*. On Wagner's anti-Semitism, see, for example, Barry Millington's essay 'Wagner and the Jews' (from Millington's *Wagner Compendium*, pp. 161–4), the essay by Dieter Borchmeyer in Müller and Wapnewski (eds.), *Wagner Handbook*, and Jonathan Carr, *The Wagner Clan*, chapter 5.

11. New York's Gilded Age

Giacosa's *Impressions of America* was based on a visit made in 1898 and published in 1908. An English-language translation is included in Oscar Handlin (ed.), *This was America: As Recorded by European Travelers in the Eighteenth, Nineteenth and Twentieth Centuries* (Harper Torchbook, 1964); Giacosa's description of New York's Little Italy is on pp. 402–3. In later years, many Italian opera singers enjoyed the home-away-from-home provided by New York's Little Italy; Gigli (a self-confessed 'nationalist about food') describes – a little improbably – how he would go to Mulberry Street and 'buy Chianti and smoked raw Parma ham and parmesan cheese, herbs such as basil and rosemary and marjoram, pasta and olive oil, fresh-roasted coffee and grassini' (*Memoirs*, p. 123).

Professor Wunsch is first mentioned on p. 16 of Willa Cather's *The Song of the Lark*. Thea expresses her desire 'to go to Germany to study' on p. 75. The description of Fred going to 'ball games, prize-fights, and horse-races' when in Chicago, but when in Germany to opera (and 'scarcely knowing when the soup ended and the symphony began') is on p. 242. The 'opera house' in Moonstone, as Cather describes it (p. 56), is scarcely more than a small village hall.

On the impact of German music and musicians in late nineteenth-century America, see Joseph Horowitz, *Classical Music in America*, Book 1, and John Dizikes, *Opera in America*, chapter 22. For a detailed analysis, see Jessica C. E. Gienow-Hecht, 'Trumpeting Down the Walls of Jericho: The Politics of Art, Music and Emotion in German–American Relations, 1870–1920' (*Journal of Social History*, Spring 2003). Also, James H. Stone, 'Mid-Nineteenth-Century American Beliefs in the Social Value of Music' (*The Musical Quarterly*, vol. 43, no. 1, January 1957, pp. 38–49). The stories of Carl Bergmann (an early conductor of the New York Philharmonic) playing Wagner and of Theodore Thomas his violin are from the article by Gienow-Hecht. Bergmann was responsible for several American 'firsts': the first known Wagner performance (1852), the first all-Wagner concert (1853) and the first performance of an entire Wagner work (*Tannhäuser* in 1859).

Wagner is quoted as having said that 'the masterpieces of music are kept alive, not at the theatres and concert-halls, but at the pianofortes of lovers of music' (Bernard Shaw, *Music in London 1890–94*, vol. II, p. 139). The number of pianos in the homes of middle-class families rose dramatically in Europe and America during the second half of the nineteenth century, peaking around the early years of the twentieth. In 1850, Britain produced around 23,000 pianos and the USA 10,000; by 1910 the British number had more than trebled and the American figure risen to an astonishing 370,000 (Cyril Ehrlich, *The Piano*, Appendix II, p. 222).

For Lind's tour of America, see Joan Bulman, *Jenny Lind*, chapter X; also, Dizikes, *Opera in America*, chapter 12. For more on the plethora of small-town American opera houses of the period, see Dizikes, ibid., chapter 25. The New York Academy of Music is described in ibid., pp. 166–7. Mrs Vanderbilt's thwarted desire for a box and the subsequent emergence of the Metropolitan Opera is on pp. 216–19. The Vanderbilt story also appears on p. 4 of Irving Kolodin's *The Story of the Metropolitan Opera* and on p. 13 of Martin Mayer's *The Met*. My description of the origins of 'the Met' relies heavily on Kolodin, Mayer and Dizikes and on that flamboyant nemesis of the Met, 'Colonel' Mapleson.

Mapleson's first American tour (1878–9) is the subject of chapter 21 of his *Memoirs*. Patti is a dominant figure throughout the *Memoirs*. Mapleson describes Patti's extravagant railroad carriage on p. 208 and prints her contract on pp. 235–7. The rivalry between Patti and Gerster is the specific focus of chapter 30; Gerster's comment that there is 'nothing wrong in a man kissing a woman old enough to be his mother' is on p. 205. Mapleson's description of the first Cincinnati Opera Festival as 'undoubtedly the most daring musical enterprise ever attempted' is from his *Memoirs*, p. 142.

For the early years of the Metropolitan Opera, New York, see Kolodin and Mayer; also, Dizikes (pp. 219–22). Details of performances and casts can be found in William H. Seltsam, *Metropolitan Opera Annals*. Mapleson's (understandably) muted version of events is in his *Memoirs*, chapters 27 and 28 *passim*. Press quotations about the opening of the Met are taken from the *New York World* and the *New York Times*.

For the role of Leopold Damrosch and his son Walter, see Dizikes, chapter 22 (pp. 231–46). Also, the autobiography of Walter Damrosch himself, *My Musial Life*, especially pages 51–63. An evocative picture of the social cachet associated with the Metropolitan Opera is presented in Eric Homberger, *Mrs Astor's New York*, pp. 224–37.

12. *Prima la donna*

Information about the lives of famous women opera singers is derived from a wide range of individual biographies, memoirs and autobiographies, most of them cited in the Bibliography. Also, books about collections of opera singers, including Rupert Christiansen, *Prima Donna*; Henry Pleasants, *The Great Singers*; Peter G. Davis, *The American Opera Singer*; Charles Neilson Gattey, *Queens of Song*; Lanranco Rasponi, *The Last Prima Donnas*; and Richard Somerset-Ward, *Angels and Monsters*. See also John Rosselli, *Singers of Italian Opera*, chapter 3, and *Music and Musicians in Nineteenth-Century Italy*, chapter 5 *passim*. Susan Rutherford, in *The Prima Donna and Opera*, considers in detail the private and public lives of the female opera singer during the nineteenth and early twentieth centuries; the quotations from Kellogg and Nordica are from chapter 4.

For Lilli Lehmann's comments to 'Lena Geyer', see Marcia Davenport, *Of Lena Geyer*, p. 72. Geraldine Farrar writes of Lehmann ('a hard taskmaster...') in *Such Sweet Compulsion*, p. 62. Blanche Marchesi reports on Emma Eames's coldness in *Singer's Pilgrimage*, p. 51. Melba writes of studying with Mathilde Marchesi in *Melodies and Memories*, pp. 16ff. Mary Garden's impressions of Marchesi are in *Mary Garden's Story* (with Louis Biancolli), pp. 15–17. Renée Fleming describes her encounters with Schwarzkopf in *The Inner Voice*, pp. 50–52; Horne's with Lotte Lehmann are in *My Life*, pp. 59–67. Mathilde Marchesi's comments ('What pupil is allowed to study for three years...?') are quoted in John Hetherington, *Melba*, p. 60. Chapter 3 of Susan Rutherford, *The Prima Donna and Opera*, is devoted to the subject of tutors and tuition. The 1833 letter to Spontini about Schröder-Devrient is by the Dresden-based composer Rastrelli and is quoted in ibid., pp. 182–3. Rosselli tells of Renzi as having being labelled a 'courtesan' in *Music and Musicians*, p. 62, while Christiansen refers to Mayhew as identifying the prima donna as a 'sort of courtesan' in *Prima Donna*, p. 9. For a witty summary of the popular image of the modern 'prima donna', see Fleming, *Inner Voice*, pp. 68–9.

With the recent growth of gender studies, much has been written about the place of women in opera: female composers of opera, the major operatic roles written for women, and the singers who have undertaken them. See, for example, Carolyn Abbate, *Unsung Voices*, which analyses the physical impact composers intended to impart through the music they gave their fictional heroines; also, the essays in Mary Ann Smart (ed.), *Siren Songs*. Catherine Clément, in a richly embroidered but deeply contentious book *Opera, or the Undoing of Women*, concentrates on the plots, pointing out how frequently operas written by men feature the suffering and death of women; the English-language edition is introduced by a leading American feminist writer about music, Susan McClary. Linda and Michael Hutcheon take up some of these themes in their pioneering books *Opera: Desire, Disease, Death* and *Opera: The Art of Dying* (pointing out *en passant* that the core operatic repertoire probably features just as many suffering and dying men as women). Opera, since its early beginnings, has frequently addressed the topic of death; it was the central topic of Monteverdi's *Orfeo*. In the nineteenth century, the subject of death became something of an *idée fixe* in the arts where it was recurrently aestheticized, anaesthetized and romanticized.

On male homosexuality and opera, see Wayne Koestenbaum, *The Queen's Throat*, a highly imaginative and engaging attempt to explain the preoccupations of the 'opera queen' (from the 'inside', as Koestenbaum might have said). The Lind and Melba stories are on p. 24. Paul Robinson (author of *Opera and Ideas*), in a review of Koestenbaum, reflects on some of the reasons opera has attracted so strong a response from gay men; see 'The Opera Queen: A Voice from the Closet' (*Cambridge Opera Journal*, vol. 6, no. 3, November 1994, pp. 283–91). The quotations about fops and dandies, and how they dressed, are from George Charles Grantley Fitzhardinge Berkeley, *My Life and Recollections*, vol. 3 (Elibron Classics, 2003), pp. 37–8, originally published in 1866. The description of 'Fops' Alley', and the comment about the 'Fop', 'Dandy' and 'Swell', are from Benjamin Lumley, *Reminiscences of the Opera*, pp. 62–3 (on the authorship of Lumley's *Reminiscences*, see Notes to Chapter 9).

13. The Lion Tamers: The Ascendancy of the Conductor

For the cultural life of Vienna at the time of Mahler, see William M. Johnston, *The Austrian Mind*, Carl Schorske, *Fin-de-Siècle Vienna*, and Hilde Spiel, *Vienna's Golden Autumn*. Music and society are discussed in two chapters on Vienna by Paul Banks (on 'absolutism and nostalgia' and 'fin-de-siècle

Vienna') in Jim Samson (ed.), *Man and Music: The Late Romantic Era*. The pivotal place of Jews in Viennese cultural life is examined in Steven Beller, *Vienna and the Jews*. Many of Vienna's leading musical figures were of Jewish or part-Jewish descent, among them Mahler, Goldmark, Schoenberg, Zemlinsky, Kálmán, the violinist Arnold Rosé, the musicologist Guido Adler and the conductors Klemperer and Bruno Walter. For more on the art and culture of early twentieth-century Vienna and the wider German-speaking world, see Daniel Snowman, *The Hitler Emigrés*, pp. 3–43.

A number of accounts of the history of the Vienna opera house appeared soon after its reopening in 1955, among them Spike Hughes, *Great Opera Houses*, pp. 30–66, and Heinrich Kralik's *The Vienna Opera* (Methuen, 1963), an illustrated revision of a book first published in 1955. See also the illustrated labour of love by the Vienna State Opera's long-term dramaturg, Marcel Prawy, entitled *The Vienna Opera*.

The second and third volumes of Henry-Louis de La Grange's four-volume biography of Mahler cover Mahler's Vienna years; see also Kurt Blaukopf, *Mahler*, chapter 7. The quotations from artists who worked with Mahler, including Schumann-Heink and Slezak, are taken from Norman Lebrecht, *Mahler Remembered*; the person who said Mahler 'treated his musicians like a lion tamer his animals' was the Budapest-born, American-Jewish musicologist Alfred Sendrey. Alma Mahler's comment that Mahler's musicians 'feared' him is from a BBC interview with Jeremy Noble in the early 1960s shortly before her death. Her comment is endorsed by a series of interviews, recorded in 1964 for station KPFK, Los Angeles, between William Malloch and musicians who played in the New York Philharmonic under Mahler's baton in 1909–11.

Mahler was not the only operatic celebrity to be followed in the streets. Gatti-Casazza recalled (*Memories of the Opera*, pp. 32–5) how as a young man he had spotted Verdi leaving his apartment in the Palazzo Doria in Genoa and walked discreetly behind him as the 75-year-old maestro strolled through the streets, bought a paper and boarded a horse-car. Years later, when Gatti recounted this to Verdi, the old man smiled and said: 'What a waste! At that age, with a good vigorous pair of legs under you, you should have been following a pretty girl!'

For a history of conducting, see José Antonio Bowen (ed.), *The Cambridge Companion to Conducting* (CUP, 2003), especially Part II. Bowen himself writes on 'the rise of conducting', gently demolishing Spohr's claim to have been the first to use a baton (but what did Spohr mean by a baton?). Raymond Holden, one of Bowen's contributors, has examined the work of famous conductors from the German-speaking world, including Mahler, in *The Virtuoso Conductors*. See also Elliott W. Galkin, *A History of Orchestral Conducting in Theory and Practice*. Norman Lebrecht traces the rise of the celebrity conductor in *The Maestro Myth*, a book that features feet of clay as much as magic batons. Berlioz recalls his irritation when a conductor tapped his bow on the desk, in his *Memoirs*, p. 196.

Otto Klemperer, towards the end of his life, told the BBC's John Freeman: 'I have composed my whole life, and I do it today as I did it 60 years before. And I've very few works published... but I hope it will become more. (JF: Would you like to be remembered as a composer?) YES! (Have you found deeper satisfaction as a composer?) YES!' (from *Face to Face*, BBC Archives, 1961).

John Rosselli deals with the musical and operatic scene in post-*Risorgimento* Italy in *Music and Musicians in Nineteenth-Century Italy*, chapters 7 and 8 *passim*. See also his *Singers of Italian Opera*, especially pp. 202–7 where he discusses the life (and plight) of the chorus singer, and Rosselli's chapter ('The Decline of a Tradition') in Jim Samson (ed.), *Man and Music*. On the role of the impresario, see Rosselli's *The Opera Industry in Italy from Cimarosa to Verdi*. Julian Budden writes illuminatingly about 'The Musical World of the Young Puccini' in William Weaver and Simonetta Puccini (eds.), *The Puccini Companion*. For more on the *Scapigliatura*, see, for example, Mary Jane Phillips-Matz, *Verdi*, pp. 466ff., and Michele Girardi, *Puccini*, chapter 2.

The most comprehensive modern biography of Toscanini is by Harvey Sachs (see also his *Reflections on Toscanini* and *Music in Fascist Italy*). The biography by Howard Taubman was written towards the end of Toscanini's life and is at times somewhat circumspect; nor did Taubman have access to the detailed documentation available to Sachs. Toscanini's postcard from Bayreuth is quoted in Sachs, *Toscanini*, p. 72. Sachs writes of Toscanini's first periods at La Scala and the New York Metropolitan in chapters 3 and 4 of *Toscanini*. See also Gatti-Casazza's *Memories of the Opera*, chapters 3, 4–5 *passim*. For a description of the Gatti–Toscanini years at the Met, see Martin Mayer, *The Met*, pp. 81–134, *passim*. Bruno Walter tells how he first heard about Toscanini from Mahler; when he himself finally met the Italian maestro, the first thing that flashed through his mind, he recalls, was 'Lucifer!' (Bruno Walter, *Theme and Variations*, p. 307).

Both Mahler and a thinly disguised Toscanini ('Guido Vestri') appear in Marcia Davenport's novel *Of Lena Geyer*, originally published in 1936. When 'Vestri' comes to the Met from Italy, he is 'like a fire sweeping through the singers and the orchestra and making them blaze as they [have] never done before'. Vestri is described as 'a small man, thin and nervous, and rather jerky in his

movements, with a sharp, penetrating voice and black eyes that snapped and glittered as he talked...
He was quite capable of remaining in repose but one always felt that at any moment he might
spring, like the tiger Lena compared him to, and do something fierce and wild.' Lena reports that,
in rehearsal, 'she almost expected him to resort to gunpowder to blow some of (her fellow cast
members) out of their faults.' Vestri 'is probably cruel and selfish and jealous', she acknowledges,
and 'has the most awful temper. But I tell you I think he is the most fascinating man I ever saw' (*Of
Lena Geyer*, pp. 304–7).

On Hammerstein, see John Frederick Cone, *Oscar Hammerstein's Manhattan Opera Company*.
Also, Irving Kolodin, *The Story of the Metropolitan Opera*, pp. 203–23, and John Dizikes, *Opera in
America*, pp. 321–36. Melba's highly coloured account of how she was wooed by Hammerstein can
be found in *Melodies and Memories*, pp. 167–9; for Hammerstein's more down-to-earth account, see
Cone, pp. 35–9.

Details of performances and casts at the Met during the Toscanini era can be found in William
H. Seltsam, *Metropolitan Opera Annals*. Harvey Sachs discusses Toscanini's 1915 departure from
the Met in *Toscanini*, pp. 127–32.

PART IV: Opera in War and Peace (*c.* 1900–1950)

14. Opera Goes West

For the history of opera in Chicago, see Robert C. Marsh (completed and edited by Norman
Pellegrini), *150 Years of Opera in Chicago*, and Edward C. Moore, *Forty Years of Opera in
Chicago* (Horace Liveright, 1930). See also John Dizikes, *Opera in America*, chapters 23 and 34.
Mapleson's report on the 1885 Chicago Opera Festival is in his *Memoirs*, pp. 230–34. A thoroughly
documented history of the Chicago Auditorium can be found in Joseph M. Siry, 'Chicago's
Auditorium Building: Opera or Anarchism' (*Journal of the Society of Architectural Historians*,
vol. 57, no. 2, June 1998, pp. 128–59). Siry quotes Peck on pp. 137 and 138. He also quotes
Dankmar Adler (p. 133) as attributing the Auditorium to the 'wish of Chicago to possess an Opera
House larger and finer than the Metropolitan'. The Chicago Auditorium is now part of Roosevelt
University on Michigan Avenue. For Mary Garden, see her entertaining autobiography (with Louis
Biancolli), *Mary Garden's Story*; also, the biography by Michael Turnbull. For statistics of per-
formances and productions in Chicago and New York in the 1930s, see Marsh, *150 Years*, pp. 109
and 111.

On Gaetano Merola and the San Francisco opera, see Arthur Bloomfield, *50 Years of the San
Francisco Opera*; also Joan Chatfield-Taylor, *San Francisco Opera*, chapter 2, and Dizikes, *Opera in
America*, pp. 467–8.

Much of the material about opera in Los Angeles in this chapter and in Chapter 20 was first
researched, in the archives of the Los Angeles Opera, in connection with my book *Plácido Domingo's
Tales from the Opera* which was written to accompany the 1994 BBC television series of the same
name. In addition, I am grateful to Bernard Greenberg and Gary Murphy for further information
and source material.

15. Spreading the Message

On the early history of recording, see Roland Gelatt, *The Fabulous Phonograph*, and Timothy Day,
A Century of Recorded Music; much of my detail is drawn from their accounts. See also Colin
Symes, *Setting the Record Straight*, which includes chapters on, for example, the 'domestication of
the concert hall', the iconography of record covers, gramophone magazines, record collections etc.
A crucial text is Fred Gaisberg's *Music on Record*; the story of recording Caruso is on pp. 51–2 (and
in Gelatt, pp. 114–15). Caruso's comment that he earned $10,000 per month is from Enrico Caruso
Jnr and Andrew Farkas, *Enrico Caruso*, p. 360.

For the *théâtrophone* and electrophone, see Peter Young, *Person to Person: The International
Impact of the Telephone* (Granta, 1991), especially chapters 4 and 6. Also, P. J. Povey, *The Telephone
and the Exchange* (Pitman, 1979), and R. A. J. Earl, *Vintage Telephones of the World* (Institution of
Electrical Engineers, 1988), chapter 4.

For the early history of broadcast opera, especially in the USA, see two articles by Jim
McPherson in *Opera Quarterly* (vol. 16, no. 1, Winter 2000, pp. 5–23, and vol. 16, no. 2, Spring 2000,
pp. 204–23). The figures for radio sets in America in the 1920s are cited by Tim Blanning, *The
Triumph of Music*, p. 205. Interestingly, the NBC National Grand Opera Company was created
before the establishment of what became its parent organization, the National Broadcasting
Company. Frances Alda's comment about the postal appreciations of her operatic broadcasts is

quoted by McPherson in the first of his articles and is from her book *Men, Women and Tenors*. Harold Rosenthal mentions the early broadcasts of opera from the stage of London's Royal Opera House in *Two Centuries of Opera*, p. 415. On the Met broadcasts, see Paul Jackson's three volumes, all published by Amadeus Press: *Saturday Afternoons at the Old Met: The Metropolitan Opera Broadcasts, 1931–1950* (2003); *Sign-Off for the Old Met: Metropolitan Opera Broadcasts, 1950–1966* (1997); and *Start-Up at the New Met: The Metropolitan Opera Broadcasts 1966–1976* (2006). I am grateful to Robert Tuggle, Director of Archives at the Metropolitan Opera, for additional material about the origins of the Met broadcasts.

The story of the lady who asked for a Met ticket in mid-matinee is from Gigli, *Memoirs*, p. 173. Gatti writes of the Met's financial crisis and the dismissal of Gigli in *Memories of the Opera*, pp. 313–15. See also, Irving Kolodin, *The Story of the Metropolitan Opera*, especially pp. 25–9, and Martin Mayer, *The Met*, pp. 175–9. According to Gigli (*Memoirs*, pp. 174–5), the second 'voluntary' salary cut was to be 25 per cent. The round robin to Gatti was dated 12 April 1932 and complained that Gigli had 'profited from the sacrifice which we have made to keep the Metropolitan going'. His behaviour, it said, 'disturbs the harmony and endangers the safety of our institution'. The thirty-two signatories included the conductors Bellezza, Bodanzky and Serafin and a veritable Who's Who of world-class singers, including Bori, De Luca, Martinelli, Melchior, Pinza, Pons, Ponselle, Rethberg and Swarthout. Gigli's statement that he would have accepted the same pay cut as everyone else was quoted in the *New York Tribune*, 7 May 1932. Gatti, Gigli felt, had a grudge against him while the artists who had signed the round robin had 'acted in a tricky way, protesting their friendship to me and at the same time signing an offensive and untruthful letter'. For a reassessment of the whole sorry story, see the article by Graeme Kay in *Opera*, May 2004, pp. 522ff.

For more on the Met tours, and a list of every tour engagement, performance and cast from 1883 to 1956, see Quaintance Eaton, *Opera Caravan*.

The 'production books' for *Simon Boccanegra* and *Otello*, edited and translated by Hans Busch and accompanied by much documentary material, were published by the Clarendon Press, Oxford (2 vols.) in 1988.

For detailed studies of the history of opera on film, see Marcia Citron, *Opera on Screen*; Richard Fawkes, *Opera on Film*; and the *Encyclopedia of Opera on Screen* by Ken Wlaschin. David Schroeder, in *Cinema's Illusions, Opera's Allure*, writes of the parallels between opera and film, emphasizing film's debt to Wagner. Jeremy Tambling, in *Opera, Ideology and Film*, considers the political dimension of art before going on to consider a number of specific examples of operas on film. See also Michael Grover-Friedlander, *Vocal Apparitions: The Attraction of Cinema to Opera* (Princeton University Press, 2005). The estimate that 80 million Americans were visiting the cinema weekly in 1938 is quoted in Blanning, *Triumph of Music*, p. 168.

On the decline in piano sales and the rise in those of the gramophone, see Cyril Ehrlich, *The Piano*, pp. 184ff.; Ehrlich's statistics show a clear relationship between the two. The publisher who commented on the demise of amateur music-making and the 'passivity' of music lovers in the age of the radio and gramophone was Ernst Roth in *The Business of Music*, chapter 5. On the wider implications of the reproducibility of art, see Walter Benjamin's much-quoted essay 'The Work of Art in the Age of Mechanical Reproduction' written in 1936. This has been frequently reproduced by means which Benjamin could scarcely have imagined: today, his text is easily available on the Internet.

16. Repercussions of War

For Toscanini's activities during the First World War (including the brass band he created and conducted at the front, and the concert in Rome that included Wagner), see Harvey Sachs, *Toscanini*, pp. 132ff. Bruno Walter writes of having to 'curtail' the French and Italian repertoire, and of his Belgian cellist, in *Theme and Variations*, p. 244. Puccini's chief French accuser was Léon Daudet (son of the writer Alphonse Daudet), while composers such as Dukas and d'Indy led the French opposition to Puccini and his works. For the wartime storm over *La rondine*, see Mosco Carner, *Puccini*, pp. 202–11.

Joseph Horowitz describes American cultural Germanophobia during the First World War in *Classical Music in America*, pp. 265–9. Gatti-Casazza writes of his wartime problems at the New York Metropolitan in *Memories of the Opera*, pp. 178–84. See also Irving Kolodin, *The Story of the Metropolitan Opera*, pp. 313–15, and Martin Mayer, *The Met*, pp. 135–6. Frieda Hempel described her frustrated attempts to keep the politics of war at a distance in *My Golden Age of Singing*, pp. 186–9. For Karl Muck at the BSO and his subsequent arrest and internment, see Horowitz, *Classical Music in America*, pp. 83–6. Walter's descriptions of Muck before and after internment are from *Theme and Variations*, p. 261.

For Ponselle's reminiscences of her rise to fame, see James A. Drake, *Rosa Ponselle*, pp. 16–23.

Also Gatti-Casazza, *Memories of the Opera*, pp. 201–3. There had been a number of important US opera singers before Ponselle, women especially (such as Eames, Nordica, Fremstad, Homer, Farrar). Those whose careers took off in the 1920s and 1930s include Paul Althouse, Grace Moore, Charles Kullman, Gladys Swarthout, John Charles Thomas, Lawrence Tibbett and the Canadian Edward Johnson who, before becoming general manager of the Met, had a successful career as an operatic tenor under the name Edoardo di Giovanni; by the time America entered the Second World War, Met audiences had also begun to hear the names and voices of Jan Peerce, Eleanor Steber, Risë Stevens, Helen Traubel and Leonard Warren. Details of Met performances and casts can be found in William H. Seltsam, *Metropolitan Opera Annals*.

On music in the early USSR, see Boris Schwarz, *Music and Musical Life in Soviet Russia*, Parts I and II. A detailed exploration of Russian attitudes towards Wagner and his works during the Soviet period is contained in Rosamund Bartlett, *Wagner and Russia*, chapter 7. For a description of some of the more memorable stagings of Wagner in early Soviet Russia, see ibid. and Patrick Carnegy, *Wagner and the Art of the Theatre*, pp. 208–26. See also the essay by Bernice Glatzer Rosenthal on 'Wagner and Wagnerian Ideas in Russia' in David C. Large and William Weber (eds.), *Wagnerism in European Culture and Politics*, especially pp. 227ff.; the quotation from Lunacharsky about Wagner's *Art and Revolution* is on p. 234. For a broader view of the arts in post-1917 Russia and, in particular, the arts as a form of social engineering, see Orlando Figes, *A People's Tragedy: The Russian Revolution, 1891–1924* (Pimlico, 1996), pp. 732–40, and *Natasha's Dance*, chapter 7.

For an overview of art, culture and the wider political context of Weimar-era Germany, see Walter Laqueur, *Weimar*; Laqueur writes about music on pp. 155–62 and (on operetta and jazz) pp. 249–53. Peter Gay, in *Weimar Culture*, covers similar ground but through a more psychoanalytical perspective. For Klemperer's visits to the Soviet Union, see Peter Heyworth, *Otto Klemperer*, vol. 1, pp. 212–24. 'Soviet avant-garde theatre,' writes Heyworth (p. 218), 'undoubtedly opened new perspectives that influenced Klemperer's own approach to the stage when he became director of the Kroll Opera in 1927.' Heyworth deals with Klemperer's years at the Kroll in chapters 11–16 *passim*; the quotations from Hanns Eisler and Alfred Einstein are from p. 260. See also Heyworth's *Conversations with Klemperer*, pp. 55–70. For the Kroll's controversial Wagner stagings (especially the *Fliegende Holländer*), see Carnegy, *Wagner and the Art of the Theatre*, chapter 8.

Heinz Tietjen was for a while the most powerful man in German theatre. Born in Tangier, son of a German diplomat and a mother of English descent, Tietjen was an imaginative stage director and a not inconsiderable operatic conductor. He was also a great survivor, managing to adapt to whatever regime was in power and working successfully under Weimar, the Third Reich and postwar West Germany (when he became Intendant of the Hamburg opera). Klemperer (in Heyworth, *Conversations*, p. 70) recalled with some bitterness Tietjen's apparent cold indifference to his fate at their final interview. To Bruno Walter (*Theme and Variations*, pp. 297–300), Tietjen was one of the strangest, most impenetrable of men. He might give you a friendly smile, Walter recalled, then suddenly the shutters would come down. 'Never a spirited or spontaneous – to say nothing of interesting – word came from his lips.'

17. Opera Under the Dictators

Goebbels spoke of music as 'the most glorious art of the German heritage' at the 'Reich Music Days', a national music festival mounted in May 1938 in Düsseldorf.

Italy under Mussolini

The authoritative book on the Mussolini period is Harvey Sachs, *Music in Fascist Italy*. On pp. 55ff., Sachs discusses opera and its institutions, including the development of the idea of the opera house as *ente autonomo*. He devotes his final chapter to 'The Toscanini Case'. For a comprehensive treatment of Toscanini's brushes with Fascism and Nazism, see Sachs, *Toscanini*, chapter 6.

On the Verdi centenary exhibition see Laura Basini, 'Cults of Sacred Memory: Parma and the Verdi Centennial Celebrations of 1913' (*Cambridge Opera Journal*, vol. 13, no. 3, pp. 141–61, 2001). For the Fascist espousal of the idea of opera as essentially the creation of the *Camerata* and Monteverdi (and Malipiero's leading role in the Monteverdi revival), see Andrew Dell'Antonio, '*Il divino Claudio*: Monteverdi and Lyric Nostalgia in Fascist Italy' (*Cambridge Opera Journal*, vol. 8, no. 3, November 1996, pp. 271–84). D'Annunzio discusses the relative claims of Wagner and the Italian *Camerata* to the revival of Greek-style theatre on pp. 88ff. of *The Flame*. Wagner is revered. But he is not an Italian. 'Nothing could be further from the *Oresteia* than the *Ring* cycle,' asserts D'Annunzio's *alter ago* (p. 89). 'The Florentines of the house of Bardi have penetrated far more deeply into the essence of Greek tragedy,' he says. The pioneers in this attempt to 'develop the harmonious in all human energy, to show the complete human being with all the means of art' were geniuses of the Italian Renaissance such as Caccini, Peri and Emilio de'Cavalieri – above all, 'the greatest innovator of all…, the divine Monteverdi' (p. 90). The call for 'a new kind of art' steeped in 'heroic blood', and for a 'third Rome', are on p. 100. For Puccini's attitude towards possible collaboration with D'Annunzio, see Mosco Carner, *Puccini*, pp. 119–21, and Michele Girardi, *Puccini*, pp. 200–201. Puccini's one-act comedy based on a line in Dante is *Gianni Schicchi*.

Marinetti set out his stall in his first Futurist Manifesto, published in 1909. 'We shall sing the love of danger, the habit of energy and boldness,' he announced, adding that 'the essential elements of our poetry shall be courage, daring and rebellion.' Futurists, he proclaimed, 'wish to glorify war, the only giver of health'. And he ended with what amounted to a catalogue of what Futurists embraced, a list including 'great crowds', 'revolutions', 'arsenals', 'factories', 'broad-chested locomotives prancing on the rails like huge steel horses' and 'aeroplanes, the sound of whose screw is like the flapping of flags'.

Giorgio Bassani's *The Garden of the Finzi-Continis* is published by Quartet (1992).

The USSR under Stalin

Galina Vishnevskaya's memories of 'Stalin nights' at the Bolshoi are contained in her autobiography, pp. 93–8. According to Volkov (*Shostakovich and Stalin*, p. 129), Stalin genuinely enjoyed classical music. His favourites were the great Russian operas and ballets, but it seems he also enjoyed Bizet and Verdi.

For sources on the place of music and opera in immediately post-revolutionary Russia, see Notes to Chapter 16. Boris Schwarz describes operatic and musical life in early Stalinist Russia in some detail in chapters 3–7 of *Music and Musical Life in Soviet Russia*; the story of Shostakovich's *Lady Macbeth of Mtsensk*, its initial success and the damning *Pravda* article, is on pp. 119ff.

One of the more graphic accounts of the *Lady Macbeth* incident is that in Shostakovich's own *Testimony*, pp. 80ff. This 1979 volume of Shostakovich's memoirs 'as related to and edited by Solomon Volkov' should be treated with caution. The basic facts about the composer's life are not in dispute. What is questionable is how close Volkov really was to Shostakovich, how much time the composer gave him and, in general, how far these supposed 'memoirs' are genuinely Shostakovich's and how far they are Volkov's reconstruction and elaboration based on limited access (and on interview material published elsewhere). A number of experts, having dissected the detail and asked (in vain) to see the original manuscript or other forms of evidence, have concluded that Volkov cashed in on meetings he had with the composer that were neither as close nor as frequent as he suggested. The first, and to my mind devastating, condemnation of Volkov's credentials can be found in Laurel E. Fay, 'Shostakovich versus Volkov: Whose Testimony?' (*Russian Review*, vol. 39, no. 4, October 1980, pp. 484–93).

Testimony raises other issues in addition to the question of its authenticity. At many places in these memoirs, Shostakovich speaks with bitterness about those he encountered and worked with. Much of his life – and much of his music – was undertaken in a spirit of defiance, it seems, an unspoken revolt by an unwilling victim of an intolerable and intolerant regime whom he had to placate in order to remain alive. Thus, Shostakovich says that the prison scene at the end of *Lady Macbeth* was 'to remind the audience that prisoners are wretched people and that you shouldn't hit a man when he's down'. Even after the *Lady Macbeth* debacle, Shostakovich believed he could continue to criticize the Stalin regime, if not directly then in code, in music. Overall, *Testimony* reads like something of an apologia, a self-justification, an attempt by the composer to exonerate himself from any blame for cooperating with the political system under which he lived.

This was a message many in the West were anxious to hear. When *Testimony* appeared, the Cold War was still at its height and the book fed straight into a welcome anti-Soviet narrative. Music lovers in particular were understandably keen to believe that all that noisy anger and grotesquerie in much of Shostakovich's *oeuvre* was his way of signalling his fury with the regime while managing to stay – just – this side of prosecution, persecution and perhaps the *Gulag*. However, to many Shostakovich scholars, even some of his greatest admirers, such a gloss was simply impossible to square with the facts which, inevitably perhaps, were more complex. Thus, Richard Taruskin, picking up from Laurel Fay, argued in *The New Republic* (20 March 1989) that *Lady Macbeth*, far from amounting to a critique of the Soviet system, portrays virtually every character except Katerina as a 'class enemy' to be eliminated. The opera, said Taruskin, 'remains a profoundly inhumane work of art. Its chilling treatment of the victims amounts to a justification of genocide.' In *Lady Macbeth*, in other words, Shostakovich was not trying to criticize the Stalinist system but to endorse it. The *Pravda* article was therefore all the more significant: for in it, Stalin was showing that under his rule no-one in the USSR was safe – not even its favourite and most loyal musical son. Taruskin has written widely on Shostakovich. See his book *Defining Russia Musically* (Princeton University Press, 1997). Also, his essay 'Who was Shostakovich?' (*The Atlantic Monthly*, CCLXXV:2, 1995, pp. 62–72). For more on Shostakovich, see Rosamund Bartlett (ed.), *Shostakovich in Context*; also, the biographies by Laurel Fay and Elizabeth Wilson. Volkov returned to answer his critics in *Shostakovich and Stalin*; see pp. 111–42 for his take on the *Lady Macbeth* saga.

Germany under Hitler

For the place of music and musicians in Nazi Germany, see Michael Meyer, *The Politics of Music in the Third Reich*; Michael Kater, *Twisted Muse*; and Erik Levi, *Music in the Third Reich* (especially chapter 7, which concentrates on opera). The statistics of singers and orchestral players employed by German theatres are taken from Levi, p. 181. See also Levi's contributions to John London (ed.), *Theatre under the Nazis* (Manchester University Press, 2000), in which Levi writes on 'Opera in the Nazi Period'; and to Michael Balfour (ed.), *Theatre and War 1933–45: Performance in Extremis* (Berghahn Books, 2001), in which Levi contributes a chapter entitled 'Towards an Aesthetic of Fascist Opera'. Levi points out that direct political censorship of opera during the Nazi period was not as systematic or stringent as might have been expected, and that the somewhat conservative operatic culture of the time was not confined to the Third Reich. For a well-informed summary of music and musicians in Nazi Germany, see the opening chapter of Pamela Potter, *Most German of the Arts*. Potter is primarily concerned with the state of musicology under Nazism. For Nazi-era musicology and race, see Potter, pp. 78–9, 178–9; on the idea of the *Volk*, p. 49; on the 'lur', polyphony and major musical modes, pp. 134, 216, 208. Potter writes on the 'Germanification' of Handel on pp. 221–8. As an indication that the historical search for the roots of 'national character' was not confined to Germany, see, for example, chapters 2–5 of Peter Mandler, *The English National Character: The History of an Idea from Edmund Burke to Tony Blair* (Yale University Press, 2007).

Despite the official emphasis on German music under the Third Reich, the three most performed operas as late as the 1938/9 season were *I Pagliacci*, *Cavalleria Rusticana* and *Madama Butterfly*. Wagner, at the top of the league table of the most performed operatic composers in 1932–3, had slipped in popularity well behind Verdi by 1939/40. For detailed figures, see Levi, *Music in the Third Reich*, pp. 192–3. On the Verdi revival in Nazi Germany, see Gundula Kreuzer, 'Verdi in the Third Reich' (*Opera*, December 2001).

Berta Geissmar, Furtwängler's assistant, who was Jewish, has left a vivid description of the deteriorating situation in *The Baton and the Jackboot*.

On Hitler and Bayreuth see Frederic Spotts, *Bayreuth*, especially chapter 5. Also, Brigitte Hamann's biography of Winifred Wagner, chapters 7–13. Hamann writes of Siegfried Wagner's death, Winifred's early management of Bayreuth and the political and musical events of 1933 on pp. 142–212. Jewish artists whom Winifred Wagner was at first able to retain included the conductor Leo Blech and the singers Emanuel List and Alexander Kipnis. For a highly critical 'inside' view of Winifred Wagner's Bayreuth, see *The Royal Family of Bayreuth* by Friedelind Wagner, the rebel among the Wagner children; Friedelind was befriended by Toscanini and went to live in the USA. An interestingly reflective view is provided by a Wagner of the next generation, Friedelind's niece Nike Wagner (born in 1945), in *The Wagners*, chapter 12. A. N. Wilson has written a fictionalized account of the relationship between Winifred Wagner and Hitler in *Winnie and Wolf* (Hutchinson, 2007).

Hitler's adulation of Wagner went back to his youth when, attending the opera with his friend August Kubizek, a Wagner performance 'could affect him almost like a religious experience, plunging him into deep and mystical fantasies' (Ian Kershaw, *Hitler: 1889–1936*, p. 21). The two men next met nearly thirty years later, in 1939, when Hitler invited Kubizek to Bayreuth, showed him over Wahnfried and took him to visit Wagner's grave in the gardens of the villa. Hitler, deeply moved by the memories jogged by the presence of his old friend, told Winifred of a performance the two men had attended in Linz of *Rienzi*, Wagner's romantic early opera about a populist leader in medieval Rome. 'It was at that moment that it all began!' said the Führer, with deep meaning, as he quoted some inspirational lines from the text (Hamann, *Winifred Wagner*, pp. 307–9; Kershaw, *Hitler: 1889–1936*, p. 610, note 128).

For a description of some of the Tietjen–Preetorius productions at Bayreuth during the 1930s, see Spotts, pp. 176ff. Also, Patrick Carnegy, *Wagner and the Art of the Theatre*, pp. 272–5.

Bruno Walter writes of his early encounter with the Third Reich, his cancelled concerts in Leipzig and Berlin and his departure from Germany in *Theme and Variations*, pp. 325–30. Strauss was not comfortable replacing Walter in Leipzig, and donated his fee to the orchestra (Michael Kennedy, *Richard Strauss*, p. 274). For the Nazi demonstrations in the Dresden and Berlin Charlottenburg opera houses, the encounters with Göring by Carl Ebert and Fritz Busch and the subsequent departure of each from Germany, see Fritz Busch, *Pages from a Musician's Life*, pp.

201–13, and Peter Ebert's biography of his father, *In This Theatre of Man's Life*, pp. 77–9. The cultural impact of refugees from Nazism is the subject of Daniel Snowman, *The Hitler Emigrés*.

On the Salzburg Festival, Brigitte Hamann writes (*Winifred Wagner*, p. 191) that under its director, (the 'non-Aryan') Max Reinhardt, the Festival became 'a sanctuary for artists displaced from Germany, and soon came to be seen as the "Jewish" counterpart of "German" Bayreuth'. In due course, adds Hamann, it became politically impossible for artists to perform at both festivals. For Lotte Lehmann's account of how she refused to accept a Berlin contract offered by Göring, see Stephen Brook (ed.), *Opera: A Penguin Anthology*, pp. 163–6. According to the singer Viorica Ursuleac, the real reason Lehmann refused Göring's contract was that he would not agree to let her sing certain coveted roles that were Ursuleac's preserve. There was no love lost between the two women, and Ursuleac remained especially embittered that, as she saw it, Lehmann 'did nothing but spread stories that I was a dedicated Nazi. Nothing could have been further from the truth' (Lanfranco Rasponi, *The Last Prima Donnas*, p. 136). Bruno Walter writes about Salzburg in *Theme and Variations*, pp. 336–44. For Solti's early encounter with Toscanini, see Sir Georg Solti, *Solti on Solti*, pp. 33–6. After the *Anschluss* of March 1938 and the incorporation of Austria into the Greater German Reich, the Salzburg Festival was strictly off limits to any Jewish or anti-Nazi musician.

18. Total War

Boris Schwarz writes of the USSR during the Second World War and of the siege of Leningrad in *Music and Musical Life in Soviet Russia*, pp. 175ff. After the fall of Communism, the city of Kuibyshev was renamed Samara just as Leningrad reassumed its original name of St Petersburg. Galina Vishnevskaya provides a vivid first-hand picture of life in Leningrad during the siege of 1941–3 in *Galina*, pp. 26–39.

Marcel Prawy writes of 'two first-class Brünnhildes' etc. in *The Vienna Opera*, p. 164. On the 1940 Bayreuth Festival and the 'Guests of the Führer' in its audiences, see Brigitte Hamann, *Winifred Wagner*, pp. 322–7.

During the occupation of France, the Paris Opéra hosted visits from the Berlin Staatsoper and the Mannheim and Cologne companies among others, gave the first performance in France of Pfitzner's *Palestrina* and featured Wagner performances with leading artists from top German and Austrian houses.

The singer who recalled Dresden's Semperoper as the most beautiful ever built was Elisabeth Höngen (Lanfranco Rasponi, *The Last Prima Donnas*, p. 312). Höngen left Dresden for Vienna in 1943, a move which, as she said to Rasponi, probably saved her life. The jokes about the historic armaments at the Vienna State Opera are reported in Prawy, *Vienna Opera*, p. 165. Joseph Wechsberg was later a distinguished journalist best known for his regular contributions to *The New Yorker*; for his memory of the Bayreuth Festspielhaus, see *The First Time Around*, pp. 187–8.

Harvey Sachs writes about musicians in wartime Italy in chapter 9 of *Music in Fascist Italy*. He mentions Titta Ruffo's premature excitement at the fall of Mussolini (and the death of Cavalieri) on p. 203. Tito Gobbi recounts his wartime memories in the early chapters of *My Life*; see especially pp. 44–63. Rossellini's film *Roma: Città Aperta* contains scenes highly reminiscent of parts of *Tosca*, including a Scarpia-like German officer-in-charge who orders the offstage (but audible) torture of an heroic Roman libertarian and patriot, while the film ends with the execution of another by firing squad.

Gigli writes of his activities in Fascist Italy (and his brief meetings with Hitler) in his *Memoirs*, pp. 177–215. 'I knew nothing about his political activities,' says Gigli on p. 192, while the passage about being regarded as a traitor for having 'sung for the Germans' is on p. 213. Sachs writes about Mascagni's frequent and somewhat fawning contacts with the Mussolini government; it seems Giordano and Cilea kept more of a distance but accepted official recognition when it was offered (*Music in Fascist Italy*, pp. 106–21). In addition to Maderna, another who joined the Partisans was Riccardo Malipiero, nephew of the composer Gian Francesco Malipiero, who, since the early years of Fascism, had been a supporter of Mussolini.

Much has been written about German and Austrian musicians who remained and worked in the Third Reich and the degree of culpability that should attach to them in consequence. For an overview, see Michael Kater, *Twisted Muse*; Kater devotes much of chapter 2 to Knappertsbusch, Krauss, Karajan and Schwarzkopf, while Furtwängler, Strauss and Pfitzner are covered later in the book on pp. 195–221. Kater's subsequent book, *Composers of the Nazi Era*, includes chapters on Egk, Hindemith, Weill, Hartman, Orff, Pfitzner, Schoenberg and Strauss. On Winifred Wagner, see chapter 14 of Brigitte Hamann's biography which deals with Winifred's de-Nazification hearings (which resulted in her being excluded from any future influence over the Bayreuth Festival); also, Nike Wagner, *The Wagners*, chapter 12.

The story of Knappertsbusch throwing an ashtray at a loudspeaker broadcasting a Hitler speech is in Prawy, *Vienna Opera*, pp. 154–5. A kindly side of Clemens Krauss is revealed by Ida Cook in *We Followed Our Stars*, in which she describes how Krauss and his wife Viorica Ursuleac gave surreptitious help as Ida and her sister Louise smuggled refugees out of the Third Reich. Schwarzkopf's wartime history has remained peculiarly elusive, despite the determined efforts to uncover the details by armies of researchers – not least Michael Kater, by whom Schwarzkopf resolutely refused to be interviewed. Prawy reports (*Vienna Opera*, p. 170) that in occupied Vienna after the war, Schwarzkopf 'was once banned by the British but cleared by the French, and later banned by the Russians and cleared by the Americans'.

Karajan was more forthcoming, replying matter-of-factly when required to do so and (according to some) conveniently smoothing over or even falsifying awkward facts. Thus, Robert C. Bachmann (*Notes on a Career: Karajan*, Quartet, 1990) writes of 'fact-blurring' and even of what he calls 'facticide'; in response to a question from Bachmann, Karajan said that, to him, joining the Nazi party was like someone keen to climb the Eiger having first to become a member of the Swiss Mountaineering Club (p. 85). Richard Osborne has probably got it about right. In the Preface to his *Conversations with Karajan* and in Appendix B of his biography of Karajan, Osborne examines in detail Karajan's decision to join the NSDAP (and the confusion arising from earlier writing, such as Roger Vaughan's biography, as to whether this was in 1933, 1935 or both). Osborne also publishes in his biography the minutes of Karajan's March 1946 interrogation by the Austrian de-Nazification examining board (chapter 21) and the main body of the deposition he presented to them (Appendix C).

On Richard Strauss, see the biography by Michael Kennedy; the Nazi background (and occasionally foreground) of Strauss's last years pervades much of the text from p. 269 to the end. Kennedy describes Strauss's replacement of Bruno Walter in Leipzig in chapter 20, and examines his presidency of the *Reichsmusikkammer* in chapter 21. For a poignant portrait of Strauss at the end of the war, his composition of *Metamorphosen* and the story of Strauss encountering the occupying American forces, see pp. 361–3. See also Alex Ross, *The Rest is Noise*, pp. 323–44, *passim*. The story of Strauss and his relationship with Stefan Zweig is the subject of Ronald Harwood's 2008 play, *Collaboration*.

On Furtwängler, Berta Geissmar's *The Baton and the Jackboot* is revealing, as are Furtwängler's *Notebooks* and the essays and addresses collected in *Furtwängler on Music*. The complexities and ambiguities of Furtwängler's position in the Third Reich are the subject of detailed and sympathetically inclined research in Fred K. Prieberg, *Trial of Strength*, and lie at the core of Ronald Harwood's 1995 play (later made into a film), *Taking Sides*. Prieberg reproduces an English-language translation of Furtwängler's April 1933 letter to Goebbels in chapter 3, note 27 (pp. 339–40). For more on Furtwängler, see Sam H. Shirakawa, *The Devil's Music Master*; also, the final chapter in Michael Meyer, *The Politics of Music in the Third Reich*. For the continuing 'Furtwängler case' in the USA, see Daniel Gillis, *Furtwängler and America*.

The story of Beecham's visit to Germany with the LPO is told in Geissmar, *Baton and the Jackboot*, chapters 21–8 *passim*. Friedelind Wagner (*The Royal Family of Bayreuth*, p. 133) tells how Hitler pursued Beecham and finally got to meet him. Hitler, accustomed to people who 'heiled' briskly then waited in deferential silence, was apparently overwhelmed by the dynamic English conductor, who completely monopolized the conversation. After the meeting, the irrepressible Beecham summed it up by saying: 'Now I know what is wrong with Germany.'

George Steiner (in *Language and Silence: Essays on Language, Literature, and the Inhuman*, Penguin, 1969) addresses the apparent paradox that 'a man can read Goethe or Rilke in the evening, that he can play Bach and Schubert, and go to his day's work at Auschwitz in the morning'. Steiner considers the implications for our traditional assumption that 'culture is a humanizing force, that the energies of spirit are transferable to those of conduct'.

Shirli Gilbert has written about music in the concentration camps in *Music in the Holocaust*. There were six orchestras in Auschwitz. For Anita Lasker-Wallfisch's experiences in Auschwitz, see *Inherit the Truth*, pp. 68–86. The leader of the Auschwitz Women's Orchestra was Alma Rosé, daughter of Arnold Rosé, the leader of the Rosé Quartet and for many years of the Vienna Philharmonic Orchestra. Arnold Rosé's wife (and Alma's mother) was a sister of Mahler. For more on Alma Rosé, who died in Auschwitz in 1944, see Richard Newman, *Alma Rosé*.

PART V: The Globalization of Opera (*c.* 1945–)

19. Emerging from Apocalypse

Galina Vishnevskaya writes that 'people… rose from the dead' in *Galina*, p. 39, and describes her early experiences with a touring company on pp. 42–7.

For a summary of the histories of opera at Covent Garden, La Scala, Vienna and the New York Metropolitan since 1945, see Susie Gilbert and Jay Shir, *A Tale of Four Houses*.

Marcel Prawy writes of opera in post-war Vienna in *The Vienna Opera*, pp. 166–78 and Vincent Sheean of his memories of Vienna in late 1947 in *First and Last Love*, pp. 210–13. The occupying powers evidently had different attitudes towards de-Nazification. To the Western governments, it was primarily a process of re-education while to the Soviets its chief purpose was to purge former Nazis (see Pamela M. Potter, *Most German of the Arts*, chapter 8, especially pp. 248–9). Prawy (*Vienna Opera*, p. 170) reports that Schwarzkopf 'was once banned by the British but cleared by the French, and later banned by the Russians and cleared by the Americans'.

For Toscanini and the emotional reopening of La Scala, Milan, see Harvey Sachs, *Toscanini*, pp. 288–91.

Max Beerbohm writes of Covent Garden in *More* (Bodley Head, 1899; quoted in Hugh and Pauline Massingham, *The London Anthology* (Phoenix House, 1950)), pp. 261–2.

For Beecham, see the biography by John Lucas; Lucas writes of the 1910 season in chapter 5. Beecham's own recollections of his 1910 Covent Garden season (ending with the *Salome* saga) are in *A Mingled Chime*, pp. 87–105. Harold Rosenthal, in *Two Centuries of Opera at Covent Garden*, writes of Beecham's 1910 season on pp. 344–58 and the Beecham seasons of the late 1930s on pp. 476–550. On the origins of Glyndebourne, and Ebert's first encounter with John Christie, see Peter Ebert, *In This Theatre of Man's Life*, chapter 8. See also the histories of Glyndebourne by Spike Hughes (especially chapter 4) and John Jolliffe (chapter 2). Bing's memories of working at Glyndebourne are in *5000 Nights at the Opera*, chapters 7–10. See also Wilfrid Blunt, *John Christie of Glyndebourne* (Geoffrey Bles, 1968). On Lilian Baylis, see the biography by Elizabeth Schafer. Baylis is recalled by many who knew and worked for her and the Vic–Wells companies. See, for instance, Tyrone Guthrie, *A Life in the Theatre* (Hamish Hamilton, 1960). Also, the biography by Richard Findlater; and Harcourt Williams, *Old Vic Saga* (Winchester Publications, 1949).

The origins of CEMA and of its successor the Arts Council are described in Andrew Sinclair, *Arts and Cultures: The History of the 50 Years of the Arts Council of Great Britain* (Sinclair-Stevenson, 1995) and, with engaging cynicism, in Richard Witts, *Artist Unknown: An Alternative History of the Arts Council* (Little Brown, 1998).

For the emergence after the war of what became 'the Royal Opera', see Rosenthal, *Two Centuries of Opera*, and Frances Donaldson, *The Royal Opera House in the Twentieth Century*, both of which tend to see the ROH through a somewhat privileged, roseate glow. For a harder critical edge, see Norman Lebrecht, *Covent Garden*. On Webster, see Montague Haltrecht, *The Quiet Showman*; Boosey and Hawkes's manifesto is quoted in ibid., pp. 51–2. For Beecham's broadsides against Rankl, see ibid., pp. 107–9, and Lebrecht, *Covent Garden*, pp. 107–10. John Tooley writes about Webster and the Rankl years in *In House*, pp. 1–21, and about Solti on pp. 25–35. Rankl's appointment was officially as 'Musical Director', a title that, by Solti's time, was commonly abbreviated to 'Music Director', the term generally in use since. For Rudolf Bing and the Edinburgh Festival, see George Bruce, *Festival in the North: The Story of the Edinburgh Festival* (Robert Hale, 1975), and chapters 12 and 13 of Bing, *5000 Nights*. Bing recalls his first impressions of Edinburgh on pp. 93 and 110. For more on Britten and *Gloriana*, see Humphrey Carpenter's biography of the composer, especially chapter 6. Also, Lord Harewood, *The Tongs and the Bones*, pp. 134–8. On the Solti years at Covent Garden, see *Solti on Solti*, chapter 5. Also Donaldson, *Royal Opera House*, chapter 11; Gilbert and Shir, *Tale of Four Houses*, chapters 9 and 10; and Montague Haltrecht, *Quiet Showman*, pp. 264–301 *passim*. The most colourful narrative about the Solti years, and the importance of Arts Council funding under Jennie Lee and Lord Goodman, can be found in Lebrecht, *Covent Garden*, chapter 7. For a more patrician view of Lee and Goodman, see Lord Drogheda, *Double Harness*, pp. 280–328 *passim*. Also, Lord Goodman's own memoirs, *Tell Them I'm on My Way*, *passim*, and Patricia Hollis's biography of Jennie Lee, chapter 9.

20. Building Opera in America

For the history of the Met during and just after the war, see Irving Kolodin, *The Story of the Metropolitan Opera*, pp. 497–586 and, more briefly, Martin Mayer, *The Met*, pp. 218–20. Details of performances and casts can be found in William H. Seltsam, *Metropolitan Opera Annals*. The comment about audience members wearing a nurse's or private's uniform is from Mary Ellis Peltz, *Your Metropolitan Opera* (Met Opera Guild, 1944), p. 4.

On Flagstad's problems in post-war America, see Mayer, *The Met*, pp. 227–8 and 241–3; Rudolf Bing, *5000 Nights at the Opera*, pp. 154–5; John Culshaw, *Ring Resounding*, pp. 54–5; and Kolodin, *Story of the Metropolitan Opera*, pp. 570–71. Billy Rose's column about Flagstad appeared in syndicated form across the USA, but it was killed by the *New York Herald Tribune*, which sensed possible libel. Rose immediately severed his connection with the *Tribune* and signed up with the more populist *New York Daily News*. Bing writes that bringing Marian Anderson to the Met was 'among my proudest moments at the house' (*5000 Nights*, p. 228); he devotes chapter 21 (pp. 231–48) to the Callas saga.

For a thoroughly documented history of the Met tours, see Quaintance Eaton, *Opera Caravan*. Met tours became increasingly expensive, especially as air travel took the place of rail; Bing referred to the long spring touring as 'the albatross hung around the neck of the manager of the Metropolitan' (*5000 Nights*, p. 249). The Met's tours were brought to an end in 1985.

On opera in Washington DC, see the text by Mary Jane Phillips-Matz in a coffee table book, *Washington National Opera: 1956–2006*, published by the company. Edouard Albion's real name was Harold Meek. For the rise and fall of his Washington National Opera Company, see Jim McPherson, 'Mr Meek Goes to Washington: The Story of the Small-Potatoes Canadian Baritone Who Founded America's "National" Opera' (*The Opera Quarterly*, 20:2, 2004, pp. 197–267). McPherson recounts how Shalyapin's appearance in *Faust* at Washington's new Auditorium in January 1925 caused ructions between the great Russian bass and the Chicago Opera, with whom he subsequently parted company. From the late 1940s, Washington became home to the National Negro Opera Company which also had chapters in other American cities. Mary Garden tells of her encounter with Truman in *Mary Garden's Story* (with Louis Biancolli), pp. 282–3.

Dorothy Chandler's shrewd courting of Disney in the 1950s was to pay handsome dividends half a century later when a new concert hall funded by the Disney family across the road from the Chandler Pavilion became home of the Los Angeles Philharmonic, enabling LA Opera to become sole resident of the Chandler. On the earlier history of opera in Los Angeles, see Chapter 14 and Notes.

The history of New York City Opera, from its foundation until the 1970s, has been written by Martin L. Sokol; for the move to the Lincoln Center, see chapter 20. For more on the move of the Met and NYCO to the Lincoln Center, see Bing, *5000 Nights*, chapter 25; John Dizikes, *Opera in America*, pp. 528–31; Mayer, *The Met*, chapter 8; Beverly Sills and Lawrence Linderman, *Beverly*, pp. 159–60 and 297–8; and Joseph Volpe, *The Toughest Show on Earth*, chapter 5. See also Alan Rich, *The Lincoln Center Story*.

The statistics about opera companies, performances and audiences are taken from material provided by Opera America. The figures quoted should be regarded as indicating no more than broad general trends; some include data from Canada while others are strictly limited to continental United States. Opera America defines a 'professional' opera company in the USA or Canada as one that regularly produces at least two performances of at least two operatic works per annum and pays its performers and its administrative staff.

21. Opera Goes Global

Alison Gyger has documented the history of opera in Australia between 1950 and the opening of the Sydney Opera House in *Australia's Operatic Phoenix*. For an authoritatively informed insider's view which takes the story up to the end of the century, see Moffatt Oxenbould, *Timing is Everything*. For the history of opera since the 1950s in South Australia, especially Adelaide, see Elizabeth Silsbury's *State of Opera*. Norma Major describes the 1965 Sutherland–Williamson tour in her biography of Sutherland on pp. 105–14; Sutherland herself covers the tour in her autobiography, pp. 185–98. Geoffrey Blainey writes of the importance of sport in Australian social history in *A Shorter History of Australia* (Vintage, 2000), chapter 9. In addition to Melba and Sutherland, a partial list of Australian singers who went on to develop successful international careers would include Florence Austral, Jeffrey Black, June Bronhill, John Brownlee, Geoffrey Chard, Marie Collier, Peter Coleman-Wright, Ronald Dowd, Lauris Elms, Sylvia Fisher, Elizabeth Fretwell, Lisa Gasteen, Joan Hammond, Yvonne Kenny, Marjorie Lawrence, Elsie Morison, Deborah Riedel, John Shaw and Jonathan Summers.

My understanding of the growing popularity of opera in Asia was enhanced when lecturing at the Hong Kong Academy for Performing Arts in 2002 at the invitation of its director, and opera enthusiast, Lo Kingman. I am also grateful to Somtow Sucharitkul, and to Michael Chance, for helping check the accuracy of my account of opera in Bangkok. For more on the growing popularity of opera in Asia, see the July/August 2006 edition of *Opera Now*, which contains a number of feature articles (including one by Robert Turnbull about Bangkok Opera).

Figures on opera attendance in the USA were supplied by Opera America; those on visitor numbers to Broadway shows, museums and symphony concerts were taken from US Government Census data.

The movement to revive the 'authenticity' of musical performance was primarily concerned with Early Music. See Harry Haskell, *The Early Music Revival*, especially chapter 7 on the revival of baroque opera and chapter 10 on historicist productions of Mozart and Rossini operas. Also, Nicholas Kenyon (ed.), *Authenticity and Early Music*. One of those at the forefront of recent operatic scholarship is Philip Gossett, whose insights and reflections can be read in *Divas and Scholars*. Musical pitch varied widely in earlier times. During the nineteenth century, as international travel became more common (and lines of longitude and Greenwich Mean Time were established), a series of meetings sought to standardize musical pitch, a quest not officially finalized until the twentieth century at the International Standardizing Organization meeting in London in May 1939, confirmed in 1953. Today, however, there are indications that pitch continues to rise, singers often performing Mozart a semitone higher than in his day.

22. New Ways of Presenting Old Works

For a consideration of *Turandot* as arguably the last opera to enter the popular repertoire, see, for example, William Ashbrook and Harold Powers, *Puccini's Turandot: The End of the Great Tradition* (Princeton University Press, 1991). For detailed statistics illustrating the consistency of the standard operatic repertoire over the past century or so (as well as its interesting variations), see George Martin, *The Opera Companion*, pp. 669–701. Martin (writing in 1962) pointed out that Verdi was the only composer to prove consistently popular throughout the operatic world. The most-performed operas at Covent Garden between 1882 and 1982 (according to the ROH publication 'About the House', Summer 1982) were: *Carmen* (448 performances), *Aida* (439), *La Bohème* (423), *Rigoletto* (411), *Faust* (409), *Don Giovanni* (347), *La traviata* (323), *Madama Butterfly* (311), *Cavalleria rusticana* (309) and *Tosca* (298). In Nazi Germany, operas by Verdi were performed more than those of Wagner (see Notes to Chapter 17).

Adolphe Nourrit's comments about working in Naples are from Henry Pleasants, *The Great Tenor Tragedy*, p. 99.

The development of a musical (and operatic) 'canon' has been researched by William Weber, much of whose work focuses on the relationship between the audiences for music and the repertoire performed. See his pioneering work, *Music and the Middle Class*. Also Weber's article 'Redefining the Status of Opera: London and Leipzig, 1800–1848' (*Journal of Interdisciplinary History*, XXXVI:3, Winter 2006), and chapter 1 in David C. Large and William Weber (eds.), *Wagnerism in European Culture and Politics* (in which Weber gives figures for works by dead composers performed at the Leipzig Gewandhaus). The story of the choral society 'spoiled… by opera music' is recounted in David Gramit, *Cultivating Music*, p. 129. Shaw's comment about stars and stripes is from *London Music in 1888–89*, p. 160; the offending American prima donna was Nordica.

On the emergence of the opera producer, or director, Patrick Carnegy (*Wagner and the Art of the Theatre*, p. 3) argues that Wagner's revolutionary insistence on the coordination of singing, acting, design and movement 'shaped the subsequent course of opera' and, indeed, resonated throughout the subsequent history of Western theatre. Rudolf Bing writes of the poor quality of Met productions in *5000 Nights at the Opera*, pp. 139ff.; for Webster's sacking of Gobbi, see Montague Haltrecht, *The Quiet Showman*, pp. 192–7. The correspondence columns of *Opera* often raised the penchant of opera critics to concentrate more on production than vocal or musical performance (see, for example, the letters page in the edition of November 2000, or the sustained attack by Brian Kellow in that of October 2008). The comments by Richard Jones are from an interview in the *Guardian*, 17 May 2007. For Joseph Volpe's dislike of certain kinds of 'modern' operatic production, see *The Toughest Show on Earth*, p. 123. Many writers on opera in recent decades expressed their distaste for 'modern' productions. See, for example, Henry Pleasants, *Opera in Crisis*, chapter 3, which is entitled 'The Plague: Produceritis'. For a sympathetic study, see Tom Sutcliffe's *Believing in Opera*, which includes chapters on the work of many seminal figures, among them Patrice Chéreau, Ruth Berghaus, David Alden, Peter Sellars, Richard Jones and Graham Vick. Sutcliffe is opposed to surtitles, arguing (p. 7) that they 'encourage audiences to refer back to and draw on their generalized memory of the work they are hearing… rather than respond to the specific performance of the moment'.

The introduction of English-language surtitles at ENO was announced in June 2005. The reactions of Pountney, Daniel, Jonas and others were widely reported, and not only in the musical press (see, for example, the article by Charlotte Higgins in the *Guardian* on 8 June 2005 in which all three were quoted). The trio first used the 'condoms' analogy in Nicholas John (ed.), *Power House*, p. 44. John Rockwell's advocacy of surtitles appeared in an article in the February 2000 edition of *Opera*. The article by Henrietta Bredin appeared in *The Spectator*, 4 June 2005.

23. The Show Must Go On…

The Berlin *Idomeneo* was a revival of an earlier production. Its cancellation led to heated debate, widely reported in the world's press, about the conflicting demands of security and artistic freedom. Chancellor Angela Merkel was quoted as condemning the cancellation as 'self-censorship out of fear', while a culture spokesman for her conservative bloc in Parliament accused the opera house of 'falling on its knees before terrorists', adding that the cancellation was 'a signal to other stages… to put on no works that criticize Islam' (*New York Times*, 26 September 2006). See also the article by Anne Applebaum in the *Washington Post*, 3 October 2006, and, for the reinstatement, the *Washington Post*, 18 December 2006.

The (utterly non-political) Bulgarian bass Boris Christoff was denied a US visa at the height of the Cold War; see Rudolf Bing, *5000 Nights at the Opera*, p. 166.

For more on the built-in inflation involved in musical (including operatic) performance, see W. J. Baumol and W. G. Bowen, 'On the Performing Arts: The Anatomy of their Economic Problems' (*The American Economic Review*, vol. 55, 1 March 1965, pp. 495–502). Also, F. M. Scherer, *Quarter Notes and Bank Notes*, pp. 199–200. Joseph Volpe writes about Mrs Harrington and the opera productions she financed at the New York Met in *The Toughest Show on Earth*, chapter 9.

For the fate of Kent Opera, see *Opera*, January 1990 (p. 23), and the editor's article 'Anatomy of a Murder' the following month (pp. 160–61). The figures for Arts Council grants to the Royal Opera House, 1970–97, are quoted in Norman Lebrecht, *Covent Garden*, p. 487; Lebrecht quotes the reaction of the *Sun* to the ROH Lottery grant on p. 393. The reduction in the Italian cultural budget under Berlusconi and its impact on opera houses was widely reported (see, for example, Richard Owen in *The Times*, 3 February 2006, and John Allison's editorial in *Opera*, April 2006). For a well-documented description of musical life in post-Communist Russia, see Rosamund Bartlett, 'The Post-Soviet Musical Landscape' (*Slavonica*, vol. 13, no. 1, April 2007, pp. 7–25). In an article about Valery Gergiev 'The Loyalist', (*New York Times Magazine*, 12 March 2009), Arthur Lobow wrote about the Mariinsky director's close links to Vladimir Putin – and quoted Richard Morrison of the London *Times* as comparing the relationship with that of Wagner and Ludwig II of Bavaria.

The decision by the New York Metropolitan Opera to collateralize its Chagall canvases was first reported in *New York* magazine; for details, see the article by Daniel J. Wakin in the *New York Times*, 3 March 2009.

The political and economic marginalization of opera was not confined to Europe. In Argentina, the country's leading opera company, based at the Teatro Colón in Buenos Aires, came close to collapse in 2002, singers and staff remaining unpaid and new contracts unsigned, while the house was rocked by a succession of high-profile resignations (fifty miles down the road, meanwhile, the rebuilt opera house at La Plata had to abort much of its first season for lack of funds). A spokesperson for the Colón put it ruefully: 'How can you feed your cat or dog if you can't feed your children?' (see report by Karyl Lynn Zietz in *Opera Now*, March/April 2002, pp. 6–8). The Colón was closed for refurbishment in November 2006 and was due to reopen in time for the theatre's centenary in May 2008. Severe funding problems made this impossible and the event was rescheduled for the year of Argentina's bicentenary, 2010.

Bruno Walter writes affectionately about Prince Ludwig Ferdinand in *Theme and Variations*, pp. 245–6. For the life and career of Lord Harewood, see his engaging memoir *The Tongs and the Bones*. Bing reproduces some of his Met memos in *5000 Nights*, pp. 214–23.

John Rosselli writes of the plight of nineteenth-century Italian choruses and their resort to strike action in *Singers of Italian Opera*, pp. 202–8. On the Met chorus strike of January 1906, see Irving Kolodin, *The Story of the Metropolitan Opera*, pp. 196–9. For the Met strikes of 1961 and 1969, see Bing, *5000 Nights*, pp. 264–74; Mayer, *The Met*, pp. 297–303, 320–23; Volpe, *Toughest Show*, pp. 61–5; and Fiedler, *Molto Agitato*, pp. 49–57 and 84–5.

Alberto Vilar was arrested at Newark International Airport on 26 May 2005, indicted in New York for fraud and money laundering in early June, and found guilty in 2008.

For a trenchant and highly entertaining description of the decline of the classical recording industry, see the first half of Norman Lebrecht's *Maestros, Masterpieces and Madness*; Lebrecht concentrates primarily on the doings and misdoings of the big companies and the people who ran them. The intersecting histories of the major classical recording companies in the late twentieth century are complex. Polygram (part of the Dutch group Philips) was sold to Seagram, the owners of Universal Studios. Meanwhile, Columbia Records and what was once RCA-Victor had become part of the Bertelsmann Group, rebranded as BMG. BMG later merged with the Japanese giant, Sony, who had long since swallowed up CBS Records. By the early new century, the four giants in a rapidly declining classical market were Universal (a subsidiary of Seagram), Sony-BMG, EMI and Warner. Merger mania continued. In 2000, the French communications giant Vivendi merged with Seagram and the French media company Canal Plus to form Vivendi Universal (who later sold Universal Pictures to NBC while retaining Universal Music). Meanwhile, Warner and EMI, each anxious to revive its ailing recording arm, danced attendance on each other with a succession of merger and buyout proposals which to some looked more like a dance of death. While the big players suffered, a handful of small, independent companies (such as Naxos, Hyperion, Chandos) managed to survive by discovering niche markets, while, increasingly, artists made their own recordings and marketed them on the Internet.

It is almost *de rigueur* for every seasoned opera goer to bemoan the lack of great singers compared with an earlier age. In the 1890s, Melba's teacher, Madame Marchesi (quoted in John Hetherington, *Melba*, p. 61) rued the decline of the vocal art: 'Oh, holy art of singing,' she wrote, 'how sad a fate hath befallen thee!' Forty years later, however, Giulio Gatti-Casazza looked back to that very period, sensing 'an enormous chasm' dividing the great figures of his youth from those of the present (*Memories of the Opera*, p. 38). An American opera expert, whose experience included the heyday of Caruso and Farrar at the Met, felt that he and his contemporaries could but envy those who were around back in the 1850s to hear Lind and the young Patti (George Odell, quoted in Mayer, *The Met*, p. 10).

Figures for cinema attendance at Met relays were provided by the Metropolitan Opera; see also the *New York Times*, 19 December 2007. Nick Kimberley writes about some of the potential 'platforms' for opera dissemination (including mention of the HVD) in the November 2008 edition of *Opera*.

The interview with Alice Coote was published in *The Times* (London) on 21 March 2008. For a useful pull-together of the views of Adrianne Pieczonka, Endrik Wottrich and others, including discussion of the use of drugs by opera singers, see the article by Associated Press writer George Jahn dated 22 August 2007; also, 'Divas Battle Booze, Drugs, Depression' in the *Sydney Morning Herald*, 24 August 2007. The pressures under which opera singers live and work was the theme of the editorial in the May 2008 edition of *Opera*.

The popular inaccessibility of much 'classical' music in the twentieth century (and its possible re-contact with a wider audience) provides a major theme in books by Julian Johnson (*Who Needs Classical Music?*) and Ivan Hewett (*Healing the Rift*). The quotation from John Adams is from an interview in *Opera Quarterly*, vol. 13, 1996.

For the implications of introducing amplification into the opera house, see the lecture by John Tomlinson to the Royal Philharmonic Society, 21 March 2000 (edited version: *Opera*, July 2000, pp. 768–75). On opera and technology more generally, see the July/August 2007 edition of *Opera Now*.

Select Bibliography

The following bibliography contains some of the principal (mostly modern-era) books consulted and/or quoted which may be of interest – and should prove reasonably accessible – to the non-specialist English-language reader. They are listed in the editions I used. I have not listed what was probably my most consistently consulted source: *The New Grove Dictionary of Music and Musicians* (second edition), edited by Stanley Sadie and John Tyrrell and published (by OUP) in January 2001, which I consulted online almost daily. Nor have I listed the huge body of social and cultural histories to which I had recourse during my researches, the almost equally large army of specifically musicological books, or the many journals, articles or reviews or selections from specialist archive collections consulted. Where any of these are quoted or referred to directly in the text, see the relevant section in the Notes, above.

Abbate, Carolyn, *Unsung Voices: Opera and Musical Narrative in the Nineteenth Century* (Princeton University Press, 1991)

Adorno, Theodore, *Introduction to the Sociology of Music* (Seabury Press, New York, 1976)

Ahlquist, Karen, *Democracy at the Opera: Music, Theater, and Culture in New York City, 1815–1860* (University of Illinois Press, 1997)

Alda, Frances, *Men, Women and Tenors* (Houghton Mifflin, 1937)

Anderson, Emily (ed.), *The Letters of Mozart and His Family*, rev. edn (Macmillan, 1997)

Anderson, Emily (trans.) and Alan Tyson (ed.), *Selected Letters of Beethoven* (Macmillan/ St Martin's Press, 1967)

Arblaster, Anthony, *Viva la Libertà! Politics in Opera* (Verso, 1992)

Arnold, Denis and Nigel Fortune (eds.), *The New Monteverdi Companion* (Faber and Faber, 1985)

Ashbrook, William, *Donizetti* (Cassell, 1965)

—, *Donizetti and His Operas* (CUP, 1982)

Atwood, William, *The Parisian Worlds of Frédéric Chopin* (Yale University Press, 1999)

Balzac, Honoré de, *Eugénie Grandet* (Penguin, 1985)

—, *Old Goriot* (Penguin 2006)

—, *The Wild Ass's Skin* (Penguin, 1977)

Barbier, Patrick, *Opera in Paris, 1800–1850: A Lively History* (Amadeus Press, 1995)

—, *The World of the Castrati: The History of an Extraordinary Operatic Phenomenon* (Souvenir Press, 1998)

Barlow, Jeremy, *The Enraged Musician: Hogarth's Musical Imagery* (Ashgate, 2005)

Bartlett, Rosamund, *Wagner and Russia* (CUP, 1995)

— (ed.), *Shostakovich in Context* (OUP, 2000)

Bauman, Thomas, *Opera and the Enlightenment* (CUP, 2006)

Beales, Derek, *Enlightenment and Reform in Eighteenth-Century Europe* (I. B. Tauris, 2005)

—, *Joseph II: In the Shadow of Maria Theresa 1741–80* (CUP, 1987)

Beaumarchais, Pierre-Augustin Caron de, *The Figaro Trilogy* (OUP, 2003)

Beauvert, Thierry, *Opera Houses of the World* (Thames and Hudson, 1996)

Beecham, Sir Thomas, *A Mingled Chime: Leaves from an Autobiography* (Hutchinson, 1944)

Beller, Steven, *Vienna and the Jews 1867–1938: A Cultural History* (CUP, 1990)

Bennett, Joseph, *Forty Years of Music: 1865–1905* (Methuen, 1908)

Bereson, Ruth, *The Operatic State: Cultural Policy and the Opera House* (Routledge, 2002)

Berlioz, Hector (ed. David Cairns), *The Memoirs of Hector Berlioz* (Gollancz, 1969)

Bianconi, Lorenzo and Giorgio Pestelli (eds.), *Opera on Stage* (University of Chicago Press, 2002)

—, *Opera Production and Its Resources* (University of Chicago Press, 1998)

Bing, Rudolf, *5000 Nights at the Opera* (Doubleday, 1972)

Björling, Anna-Lisa and Andrew Farkas, *Jussi* (Amadeus Press, 1996)

Black, Jeremy, *The British Abroad: The Grand Tour in the Eighteenth Century* (Sutton, 2003)

—, *Italy and the Grand Tour* (Yale University Press, 2003)

Blanning, T. C. W., *The Culture of Power and the Power of Culture: Old Regime Europe 1660–1789* (OUP, 2002)

—, *Joseph II* (Longman, 1994)

— (ed.), *The Eighteenth Century: Europe 1688–1815* (OUP, 2000)

— (ed.), *The Nineteenth Century: Europe 1789–1914* (OUP, 2000)

Blanning, Tim, *The Pursuit of Glory: Europe 1648–1815* (Allen Lane, 2007)

—, *The Triumph of Music: The Rise of Composers, Musicians and Their Art* (Allen Lane, 2008)

Blaukopf, Kurt, *Mahler* (Allen Lane, 1973)

Blom, Eric, *Mozart* ('Master Musicians' series, J. M. Dent, 1974)

Bloomfield, Arthur, *50 Years of the San Francisco Opera* (San Francisco Book Co., 1972)

Bokina, John, *Opera and Politics: From Monteverdi to Henze* (Yale University Press, 1997)

Bolt, Rodney, *Lorenzo Da Ponte: The Adventures of Mozart's Librettist in the Old and New Worlds* (Bloomsbury, 2006)

Boyd, Malcolm (ed.), *Music and the French Revolution* (CUP, 1992)

Braunbehrens, Volkmar, *Mozart in Vienna 1781–1791* (Grove/Weidenfeld, 1989)

Brener, Milton, *Opera Offstage: Passion and Politics behind the Great Operas* (Robson, 2003)

Breslin, Herbert, *The King and I: The Uncensored Tale of Luciano Pavarotti's Rise to Fame by His Manager, Friend, and Sometime Adversary* (Broadway Books, 2004)

Brewer, John, *The Pleasures of the Imagination* (Farrar, Straus and Giroux, 1997)

Brook, Stephen (ed.), *Opera: A Penguin Anthology* (Penguin, 1996)

Brown, David, *Mussorgsky: His Life and Works* (OUP, 2002)

—, *Tchaikovsky*, 4 vols. (Norton, 1986–1992)

—, *Tchaikovsky: The Man and His Music* (Faber and Faber, 2006)

Buch, Esteban, *Beethoven's Ninth: A Political History* (University of Chicago Press, 2003)

Buckler, Julie A., *The Literary Lorgnette: Attending Opera in Imperial Russia* (Stanford University Press, 2000)

Budden, Julian, *The Operas of Verdi*, 3 vols. (OUP, 1973–81)

—, *Puccini, His Life and Works* (OUP, 2002)

—, *Verdi* (Dent, 1985)

Bulman, Joan, *Jenny Lind: A Biography* (James Barrie, 1956)

Burke, Peter, *The Fabrication of Louis XIV* (Yale University Press, 1994)

Burney, Charles, *Music, Men, and Manners in France and Italy 1770* (Eulenberg Books, 1974)

Burrows, Donald, *Handel* (OUP, 1994)

Busch, Fritz, *Pages from a Musician's Life* (The Hogarth Press, 1953)

Cairns, David, *Berlioz*, 2 vols. (Penguin, 2000)

—, *Mozart and His Operas* (Allen Lane, 2006)

Carnegy, Patrick, *Wagner and the Art of the Theatre* (Yale University Press, 2006)

Carner, Mosco, *Puccini: A Critical Biography* (Duckworth, 1974)

Carpenter, Humphrey, *Benjamin Britten: A Biography* (Faber and Faber, 1992)

Carr, Jonathan, *The Wagner Clan* (Faber and Faber, 2007)

Caruso, Enrico, *Caruso's Caricatures* (Dover Publications, 1977)

Caruso Jr, Enrico and Andrew Farkas, *Enrico Caruso: My Father and My Family* (Amadeus Press, 1997)

Cather, Willa, *The Song of the Lark* (OUP, 2000)

Charlton, David, *French Opera 1730–1830: Meaning and Media* (Ashgate, 2000)

—, *Grétry and the Growth of Opéra-Comique* (CUP, 1986)

— (ed.), *The Cambridge Companion to Grand Opera* (CUP, 2003)

Chatfield-Taylor, Joan, *San Francisco Opera: The First Seventy-Five Years* (Chronicle Books, 1997)

Chorley, Henry F., *Thirty Years' Musical Recollections* (Knopf, 1926)

Christiansen, Rupert, *Prima Donna: A History* (The Bodley Head, 1984)

—, *The Victorian Visitors: Culture Shock in Nineteenth-Century Britain* (Grove Press, 2000)

Citron, Marcia J., *Opera on Screen* (Yale University Press, 2000)

Clapton, Nicholas, *Alessandro Moreschi: The Last Castrato* (Haus, 2004)

Clément, Catherine, *Opera, Or the Undoing of Women* (Virago, 1989)

Comini, Alessandra, *The Changing Image of Beethoven: A Study in Mythmaking* (Rizzoli, 1987)

Conati, Marcello (ed.), *Interviews and Encounters with Verdi* (Gollancz, 1984)

Cone, John Frederick, *Oscar Hammerstein's Manhattan Opera Company* (University of Oklahoma Press, 1966)

Conrad, Peter, *A Song of Love and Death: The Meaning of Opera* (Chatto & Windus, 1987)

Cook, Ida, *We Followed Our Stars* (Hamish Hamilton, 1950)

Cooke, Mervyn (ed.), *The Cambridge Companion to Twentieth-Century Opera* (CUP, 2005)

Crosten, William L., *French Grand Opera: An Art and a Business* (Da Capo, 1972)

Culshaw, John, *Ring Resounding* (Secker and Warburg, 1967)

Curtiss, Mina, *Bizet and His World* (Secker and Warburg, 1959)

Da Ponte, Lorenzo, *Memoirs of Lorenzo Da Ponte* (ed. Elizabeth Abbott, Dover Publications, 1967)

Dahlhaus, Carl, *Nineteenth-Century Music* (University of California Press, 1989)

Damrosch, Walter, *My Musical Life* (George Allen and Unwin, 1924)

D'Annunzio, Gabriele, *The Flame* (Quartet Books, 1991)

Davenport, Marcia, *Of Lena Geyer* (Avon, 1982)

Davis, Peter G., *The American Opera Singer: The Lives and Adventures of America's Great Singers in Opera and Concert, from 1825 to the Present* (Anchor Books, 1997)

Davis, Richard, *Anna Bishop: The Adventures of an Intrepid Prima Donna* (Currency Press, 1997)

Day, Timothy, *A Century of Recorded Music: Listening to Musical History* (Yale University Press, 2002)

Dean, Winton, *Handel's Operas* (vol. 1: OUP, 1987; vol. 2: Boydell & Brewer, 2006)

Deathridge, John, *Wagner beyond Good and Evil* (Bloomsbury, 2008)

Del Fiorentino, Dante, *Immortal Bohemian: An Intimate Memoir of Giacomo Puccini* (Crown, 1962)

DeNora, Tia, *Beethoven and the Construction of Genius: Musical Politics in Vienna, 1792–1803* (University of California Press, 1997)

Deutsch, Otto Erich (ed.), *Handel: A Documentary Biography* (Da Capo, 1974)

— (ed.; trans. Eric Blom et al.), *Mozart: A Documentary Biography* (Stanford University Press, 1965)

Dizikes, John, *Opera in America: A Cultural History* (Yale University Press, 1993)

Domingo, Plácido, *My First Forty Years* (Weidenfeld and Nicolson, 1983)

Donaldson, Frances, *The Royal Opera House in the Twentieth Century* (Weidenfeld and Nicolson, 1988)

Donington, Robert, *Opera and Its Symbols: The Unity of Words, Music and Staging* (Yale University Press, 1990)

Drake, James A., *Rosa Ponselle: A Centenary Biography* (Amadeus Press, 1997)

Drogheda, Lord, *Double Harness* (Weidenfeld and Nicolson, 1978)

Drummond, John D., *Opera in Perspective* (University of Minnesota, 1980)

Drysdale, John, *Louis Véron and the Finances of the Académie Royale de Musique* (Peter Lang, 2003)

Dumas *fils*, Alexandre, *La Dame aux Camélias* (OUP, 2000)

Eaton, Quaintance, *Opera Caravan: Adventures of the Metropolitan on Tour 1883–1956* (Da Capo, 1978)

Ebert, Peter, *In This Theatre of Man's Life: The Biography of Carl Ebert* (The Book Guild Limited, 1999)

Ehrlich, Cyril, *The Piano: A History* (OUP, 1990)

Einstein, Alfred, *Mozart: His Characters, His Work* (Panther, 1971)

Evans, Sir Geraint, *A Knight at the Opera* (Michael Joseph, 1984)

Everist, Mark, *Music Drama at the Paris Odéon 1824–1828* (University of California Press, 2002)

Farrar, Geraldine, *Such Sweet Compulsion: The Autobiography of Geraldine Farrar* (The Greystone Press, 1938)

Fauser, Annegret, and Mark Everist (eds.), *Music, Theater, and Cultural transfer: Paris 1830–1914* (University of Chicago Press, 2009)

Fawkes, Richard, *Opera on Film* (Duckworth, 2000)

Fay, Laurel E., *Shostakovich: A Life* (OUP, 1999)

Feldman, Martha, *Opera and Sovereignty: Transforming Myths in Eighteenth-Century Italy* (University of Chicago Press, 2007)

Fenlon, Iain *Music and Culture in Late Renaissance Italy* (OUP, 2002)

—, *Music and Patronage in Sixteenth-century Mantua* (CUP, 1981)

Fiedler, Johanna, *Molto Agitato: The Mayhem behind the Music at the Metropolitan Opera* (Nan A. Talese/Doubleday, 2001)

Figes, Orlando, *Natasha's Dance: A Cultural History of Russia* (Allen Lane, 2002)

Findlater, Richard, *Lilian Baylis: The Lady of the Old Vic* (Allen Lane, 1975)

Fitzlyon, April, *Maria Malibran: Diva of the Romantic Age* (Souvenir Press, 1987)

—, *The Price of Genius: A Life of Pauline Viardot* (John Calder, 1964)

Flaubert, Gustave, *Madame Bovary* (Penguin, 1952)

Fleming, Renée, *The Inner Voice: The Making of a Singer* (Penguin, 2005)

Forbes, Elliot (ed.), *Thayer's Life of Beethoven* (Princeton University Press, 1970)

Forsyth, Michael, *Buildings for Music: The Architect, the Musician, and the Listener from the Seventeenth Century to the Present Day* (MIT Press, 1985)

Fraser, Antonia, *Marie Antoinette: The Journey* (Phoenix, 2002)

Frolova-Walker, Marina, *Russia: Music and Nation: From Glinka to Stalin* (Yale University Press, 2007)

Fryer, Paul and Olga Usova, *Lina Cavalieri: The Life of Opera's Greatest Beauty, 1874–1944* (McFarland, 2003)

Fubini, Enrico *Music and Culture in Eighteenth-Century Europe: A Source Book* (University of Chicago Press, 1994)

Fulcher, Jane F., *The Nation's Image: French Grand Opera as Politics and Politicized Art* (CUP, 1987)

Furtwängler, Wilhelm, *Furtwängler on Music: Essays and Addresses* (Scolar Press, 1991)

—, *Notebooks 1924–54* (Quartet, 1991)

Gaines, James, *Evening in the Palace of Reason: Bach Meets Frederick the Great in the Age of Enlightenment* (Harper, 2005)

Gaisberg, F. W., *Music on Record* (Robert Hale, 1947)

Galatopoulos, Stelios, *Bellini: Life, Times, Music* (Sanctuary, 2002)

Galilei, Vincenzo (trans. Claude V. Palisca), *Dialogue on Ancient and Modern Music* (Yale University Press, 2003)

Galkin, Elliott W., *A History of Orchestral Conducting in Theory and Practice* (Pendragon, 1989)

Gammond, Peter, *Offenbach: His Life and Times* (Midas Books, 1980)

Garden, Mary and Louis Biancolli, *Mary Garden's Story* (Simon & Schuster, 1951)

Garlington, Aubrey S., *Society, Culture and Opera in Florence, 1814–1830: Dilettantes in an 'Earthly Paradise'* (Ashgate, 2005)]

Gartenberg, Egon, *Vienna: Its Musical Heritage* (Penn State University Press, 1968)

Gattey, Charles Neilson, *Queens of Song* (Barrie & Jenkins, 1979)

Gatti-Casazza, Giulio, *Memories of the Opera* (John Calder, 1977)

Gay, Peter, *Mozart* (Phoenix, 2000)

—, *Weimar Culture: The Outsider as Insider* (Penguin, 1974)

Gedda, Nicolai, *My Life and Art* (Amadeus Press, 1999)

Geissmar, Berta, *The Baton and the Jackboot: Recollections of Musical Life* (Hamish Hamilton, 1944)

Gelatt, Roland, *The Fabulous Phonograph 1877–1977* (Collier Macmillan, 1977)

Gerhard, Anselm, *The Urbanization of Opera: Music Theater in Paris in the Nineteenth Century* (University of Chicago Press, 1998)

Gigli, Beniamino, *The Memoirs of Beniamino Gigli* (Cassell, 1957)

Gilbert, Shirli, *Music in the Holocaust: Confronting Life in the Nazi Ghettos and Camps* (Clarendon Press, 2005).

Gilbert, Susie and Jay Shir, *A Tale of Four Houses: Opera at Covent Garden, La Scala, Vienna and the Met since 1945* (HarperCollins, 2003)

Gillis, Daniel, *Furtwängler and America* (Manylands Books, 1970)

Girardi, Michele, *Puccini: His International Art* (University of Chicago Press, 2000)

Glixon, Beth L. and Jonathan E. Glixon, *Inventing the Business of Opera – The Impresario and His World in Seventeenth-Century Venice* (OUP, 2006)

Glover, Jane, *Cavalli* (Batsford, 1978)

—, *Mozart's Women: His Family, His Friends, His Music* (Pan, 2006)

Goodman, Arnold, *Tell Them I'm on My Way* (Chapmans, 1993)

Gossett, Philip, *Divas and Scholars: Performing Italian Opera* (Chicago University Press, 2006)

Gramit, David, *Cultivating Music: The Aspirations, Interests, and Limits of German Musical Culture, 1770–1848* (University of California Press, 2002)

Grendel, Frédéric, *Beaumarchais: The Man Who was Figaro* (Macdonald and Jane's, 1977)

Grey, Thomas S., ed, *Richard Wagner and His World* (Princeton University Press, 2009)

Guest, Ivor, *The Ballet of the Second Empire* (Pitman, 1974)

—, *Napoleon III in England* (British Technical and General Press, 1952)

Gutman, Robert W., *Richard Wagner: The Man, His Mind and His Music* (Pelican, 1971)
Gyger, Alison *Australia's Operatic Phoenix: From World War II to 'War and Peace'* (Pellinor, 2005)
—, *Civilising the Colonies: Pioneering Opera in Australia* (Pellinor, 1999)
—, *Opera for the Antipodes: Opera in Australia, 1881–1939* (Currency Press, 1990)
Hall-Witt, Jennifer, *Fashionable Acts: Opera and Elite Culture in London, 1780–1880* (University of
     New Hampshire Press, 2007)
Haltrecht, Montague, *The Quiet Showman: Sir David Webster and the Royal Opera House*
     (Collins, 1975)
Hamann, Brigitte, *Winifred Wagner: A Life at the Heart of Hitler's Bayreuth* (Granta, 2005)
Hamburger, Michael (ed.), *Beethoven: Letters, Journals and Conversations* (Jonathan Cape, 1966)
Harewood, Lord, *The Tongs and the Bones: The Memoirs of Lord Harewood* (Weidenfeld and
     Nicolson, 1981)
Hartford, Robert (ed.), *Bayreuth: The Early Years* (Gollancz, 1980)
Haskell, Harry, *The Early Music Revival: A History* (Thames and Hudson, 1988)
Headington, Christopher, Roy Westbrook and Terry Barfoot, *Opera: A History* (Arrow, 1991)
Heartz, Daniel, (ed. Thomas Bauman), *Mozart's Operas* (University of California Press, 1990)
Helm, E. H., *Music at the Court of Frederick the Great* (University of Oklahoma Press, 1960)
Hempel, Frieda, *My Golden Age of Singing* (Amadeus Press, 1998)
Henstock, M. E., *Fernando De Lucia: Son of Naples, 1860–1925* (Amadeus Press, 1990)
Hetherington, John, *Melba: A Biography* (Faber and Faber, 1967)
Hewett, Ivan, *Healing the Rift* (Continuum, 2003)
Heyer, John Hajdu (ed.), *Lully Studies* (CUP, 2000)
Heyworth, Peter, *Conversations with Klemperer* (Gollancz, 1973)
—, *Otto Klemperer: His Life and Times* (CUP, 2 vols., 1983, 1996)
Hildesheimer, Wolfgang, *Mozart* (Dent, 1990)
Hobsbawm, Eric, *The Age of Empire: 1875–1914* (Abacus, 1997)
Hogwood, Christopher, *Handel* (Thames and Hudson, rev. edn, 2009)
Holden, Anthony, *The Man Who Wrote Mozart* (Weidenfeld and Nicolson, 2006)
Holden, Raymond, *The Virtuoso Conductors: The Central European Tradition from Wagner to
     Karajan* (Yale University Press, 2005)
Hollis, Patricia, *Jennie Lee: A Life* (OUP, 1997)
Homberger, Eric, *Mrs. Astor's New York: Money and Social Power in a Gilded Age* (Yale University
     Press, 2002)
Honolka, Kurt, *Papageno: Emanuel Schikaneder: Man of the Theater in Mozart's Time* (Amadeus
     Press, 1990)
Hope-Wallace, Philip, *Words and Music* (Collins, 1981)
Horne, Marilyn, *My Life* (Atheneum, 1983)
Horowitz, Joseph, *Classical Music in America: A History of Its Rise and Fall* (W. W. Norton, 2005)
—, *Wagner Nights: An American History* (University of California Press, 1994)
Hughes, Spike, *Glyndebourne: A History of the Festival Opera* (Methuen, 1965)
—, *Great Opera Houses: A Traveller's Guide to Their History and Traditions* (Weidenfeld and
     Nicolson, 1957)
Hutcheon, Linda and Michael, *The Art of Dying* (Harvard University Press, 2004)
—, *Opera: Desire, Disease, Death* (University of Nebraska Press, 1996)
Isaacs, Jeremy, *Never Mind the Moon: My Time at the Royal Opera House* (Bantam, 1999)
Isherwood, Robert M., *Music in the Service of the King: France in the Seventeenth Century*
     (Cornell University Press, 1973)
Jablonski, Edward (ed.), *Gershwin Remembered* (Faber and Faber, 1992)
Jackson, Stanley, *Caruso* (W. H. Allen, 1972)
Jefferson, Alan, *Lotte Lehmann 1888–1976* (Julia MacRae, 1988)
Jenkins, John, *Mozart and the English Connection* (Cygnus Arts, 1998)
John, Nicholas (ed.), *Power House: The English National Opera Experience* (Lime Tree, 1992)
—, (series ed.), *The Operas of Monteverdi* (Calder Publications/English National Opera, 1992)
Johnson, James H., *Listening in Paris: A Cultural History* (University of California Press, 1995)
Johnson, Julian, *Who Needs Classical Music? Cultural Choice and Musical Value* (OUP, 2002)
Johnson, Victoria, Jane F. Fulcher and Thomas Ertman (eds.), *Opera and Society in Italy and France
     from Monteverdi to Bourdieu* (CUP, 2007)
Johnston, William M., *The Austrian Mind: An Intellectual and Social History 1848–1938*
     (University of California Press, 1976)
Jolliffe, John, *Glyndebourne: An Operatic Miracle* (John Murray, 1999)

Jordan, Ruth, *Fromental Halévy: His Life and Music 1799–1862* (Kahn and Averill, 1994)

Kater, Michael, *Composers of the Nazi Era* (OUP, 2000)

—, *Twisted Muse: Musicians and Their Music in the Third Reich* (OUP, 1996)

Keates, Jonathan, *Handel: The Man and His Music* (The Bodley Head, 2008)

Keefe, Simon P. (ed.), *The Cambridge Companion to Mozart* (CUP, 2003)

Kelly, Michael, *Reminiscences* (OUP, 1975)

Kelly, Thomas Forrest, *First Nights: Five Musical Premieres* (Yale University Press, 2000)

—, *First Nights at the Opera* (Yale University Press, 2004)

Kendall, Alan, *Gioacchino Rossini: The Reluctant Hero* (Gollancz, 1992)

Kennedy, Michael, *Richard Strauss: Man, Musician, Enigma* (CUP, 1999)

Kenyon, Nicholas (ed.), *Authenticity and Early Music: A Symposium* (OUP, 1988)

Kershaw, Ian, *Hitler 1889–1936: Hubris* (Penguin, 1999), *Hitler 1936–1945: Nemesis* (Penguin, 2001)

Kimbell, David, *Italian Opera* (CUP, 1991)

—, *Verdi in the Age of Italian Romanticism* (CUP, 1981)

Klein, Herman, *The Golden Age of Opera* (Routledge, 1933)

Koestenbaum, Wayne, *The Queen's Throat: Opera, Homosexuality and the Mystery of Desire* (Da Capo Press, 2001)

Kolodin, Irving, *The Story of the Metropolitan Opera 1883–1950: A Candid History* (Alfred A. Knopf, 1953)

Kracauer, S., *Offenbach and the Paris of His Time* (Constable, 1937)

La Grange, Henry-Louis de, *Gustav Mahler*, 4 vols. (Victor Gollancz, 1974; OUP, 1995–2008)

La Grange, Henry-Louis de and Günther Weiss (eds.), *Gustav Mahler: Letters to His Wife* (Faber and Faber, 2005)

Lacombe, Hervé, *The Keys to French Opera in the Nineteenth Century* (University of California Press, 2001)

Laqueur, Walter, *Weimar: A Cultural History 1918–1933* (Weidenfeld and Nicolson, 1974)

Large, David C. and William Weber (eds.), *Wagnerism in European Culture and Politics* (Cornell University Press, 1984)

Lasker-Wallfisch, Anita, *Inherit the Truth 1939–1945* (de la Mare, 1996)

Lawford-Hinrichsen, Irene, *Music Publishing and Patronage: C F Peters: 1800 to the Holocaust* (Edition Press, 2000)

Lawrence, Vera Brodsky, *Strong on Music: The New York Music Scene in the Days of George Templeton Strong, 1836–1875. Vol I: Resonances: 1836–1850* (OUP, 1988)

Lebrecht, Norman, *Covent Garden: The Untold Story: Dispatches from the English Culture War, 1945–2000* (Simon & Schuster, 2000)

—, *The Maestro Myth: Great Conductors in Pursuit of Power* (Simon & Schuster, 1991)

—, *Maestros, Masterpieces and Madness: The Secret Life and Shameful Death of the Classical Record Industry* (Allen Lane, 2007)

—, *Mahler Remembered* (Faber and Faber, 1987)

Lehmann, Lotte, *Wings of Song* (Kegan Paul, 1938)

Leppert, Richard, and McLary, Susan (eds), *Music and Society: The Politics of Composition, Performance and Reception* (CUP, 1987)

Levi, Erik, *Music in the Third Reich* (Macmillan, 1994)

Levine, Lawrence, *Highbrow Lowbrow: The Emergence of Cultural Hierarchy in America* (Harvard University Press, 1990)

Lindenberger, Herbert, *Opera: The Extravagant Art* (Cornell University Press, 1984)

—, *Opera in History from Monteverdi to Cage* (Stanford University Press, 1998)

Londré, Felicia Hardison, *The History of World Theater from the English Reformation to the Present* (Continuum, 1991)

Love, Harold, *The Golden Age of Australian Opera: W. S. Lyster and His Companies, 1861–1880* (Currency Press, 1981)

Lowerson, John, *Amateur Operatics: A Social and Cultural History* (University of Manchester Press, 2005)

Lucas, John, *Thomas Beecham: An Obsession with Music* (Boydell and Brewer, 2008)

Lumley, Benjamin, *Reminiscences of the Opera* (Da Capo, 1976)

Maeder, Clara Fisher (ed. Douglas Taylor), *Autobiography of Clara Fisher Maeder* (The Dunlap Society, 1897)

Magee, Bryan, *Aspects of Wagner* (OUP, 1988)

—, *Wagner and Philosophy* (Penguin, 2000)

Mainwaring, John, *Memoirs of the Life of the Late George Frederic Handel* (Da Capo, 1980)

Major, Norma, *Joan Sutherland* (Queen Anne Press, 1987)

Mallach, Alan, *The Autumn of Italian Opera: From Verismo to Modernism, 1890–1915* (Northeastern University Press, 2007)

Mann, Thomas, *Pro and Contra Wagner* (Faber and Faber, 1985)

Mapleson, James Henry (ed. Harold Rosenthal), *The Mapleson Memoirs* (Putnam, 1966)

Marchesi, Blanche, *Singer's Pilgrimage* (Grant Harris, 1923)

Marek, George R., *A Front Seat at the Opera* (George G. Harrap, 1951)

— (ed.), *The World Treasury of Grand Opera: Its Triumphs, Trials and Great Personalities* (Harper and Brothers, 1957)

Marsh, Robert C. (completed and edited by Norman Pellegrini), *150 Years of Opera in Chicago* (Northern Illinois University Press, 2006)

Martin, George, *Aspects of Verdi* (Robson Books, 1988)

—, *The Opera Companion: A Guide for the Casual Opera-Goer* (Macmillan, 1962)

—, *Verdi, His Music, Life and Times* (Macmillan, 1963)

—, *Verdi at the Golden Gate: Opera and San Francisco in the Gold Rush Years* (University of California Press, 1993)

Martorella, Rosanne, *The Sociology of Opera* (Praeger, 1982)

Marvin, Roberta Montemorra and Downing A. Thomas (eds.), *Operatic Migrations: Transforming Works and Crossing Boundaries* (Ashgate, 2006)

Mayer, Martin, *The Met: One Hundred Years of Grand Opera* (Thames and Hudson, 1983)

Melba, Nellie, *Melodies and Memories: The Autobiography of Nellie Melba* (Thomas Nelson Australia, 1980)

Mérimée, Prosper, *Carmen* (Hesperus Press, 2004)

Metropolitan Opera, *The Metropolitan Opera: The Radio and Television Legacy* (Museum of Broadcasting, New York, 1986)

Meyer, Michael, *The Politics of Music in the Third Reich* (Peter Lang, 1991)

Michotte, Edmond (trans. and ed. Herbert Weinstock), *Richard Wagner's Visit to Rossini* (University of Chicago Press, 1968)

Millington, Barry, *Wagner* (Princeton University Press, 1992)

— (ed.), *The Wagner Compendium: A Guide to Wagner's Life and Music* (Thames and Hudson, 1992)

Mintzer, Charles, *Rosa Raisa: A Biography of a Diva with Selections from Her Memoirs* (Northeastern University Press, 2001)

Mongrédien, Jean, *French Music from the Enlightenment to Romanticism 1789–1830* (Amadeus Press, 1996)

Moore, Gerald, *Am I Too Loud? Memoirs of an Accompanist* (Hamish Hamilton, 1962)

Moran, William R. (ed.), *Nellie Melba: A Contemporary Review* (Greenwood Press, 1985)

Mörike, Eduard, *Mozart's Journey to Prague* (John Calder, 1957)

Müller, Ulrich and Peter Wapnewski (eds.; trans. and ed. John Deathridge), *Wagner Handbook: The Full Story of the Man, His Music, and His Legacy* (Harvard University Press, 1992)

Myers, Rollo (ed.), *Richard Strauss & Romain Rolland: Correspondence* (Calder and Boyars, 1968)

Nalbach, Daniel, *The King's Theatre, 1704–1867: London's First Italian Opera House* (The Society for Theatre Research, 1972)

Newman, Ernest, *The Life of Richard Wagner* (CUP, 1976)

Newman, Richard, *Alma Rosé: Vienna to Auschwitz* (Amadeus Press, 2003)

Niemetschek, Franz (trans. Helen Mautner), *Life of Mozart* (Leonard Hyman, 1956)

O'Connor, Garry, *The Pursuit of Perfection: A Life of Maggie Teyte* (Gollancz, 1979)

Orrey, Leslie, *Bellini* (J. M. Dent, 1973)

Osborne, Charles (ed.), *Letters of Giuseppe Verdi* (Gollancz, 1971)

Osborne, Richard, *Conversations with Karajan* (OUP, 1991)

—, *Herbert von Karajan: A Life in Music* (Pimlico, 1999)

—, *Rossini* (Dent, 1987)

Oxenbould, Moffatt, *Timing is Everything: A Life Backstage at the Opera* (ABC Books, 2005)

Palisca, Claude V., *The Florentine Camerata: Documentary Studies and Translations* (Yale University Press, 1989)

Parker, Roger, *Leonora's Last Act: Essays in Verdian Discourse* (Princeton University Press, 1997)

— (ed.), *The Oxford Illustrated History of Opera* (OUP, 1994)

Peltz, Mary Ellis, *Behind the Gold Curtain: The Story of the Metropolitan Opera: 1883–1950* (Farrar Straus, 1950)

Phillips-Matz, Mary Jane, *Leonard Warren: American Baritone* (Amadeus Press, 2000)

—, *Verdi: A Biography* (OUP, 1993)

Pleasants, Henry, *The Great Singers: From the Dawn of Time to Our Own Time* (Simon & Schuster, 1970)

—, *The Great Tenor Tragedy: The Last Days of Adolphe Nourrit As Told (Mostly) by Himself* (Amadeus Press, 1995)

—, *Opera in Crisis: Tradition, Present, Future* (Thames and Hudson, 1989)

Plumb, John H., *England in the Eighteenth Century* (Penguin, 1951)

Porter, Roy, *English Society in the Eighteenth Century* (Penguin, 1981)

—, *London: A Social History* (Hamish Hamilton, 1994)

Potter, John, *Tenor: History of a Voice* (Yale University Press, 2009)

Potter, Pamela M., *Most German of the Arts: Musicology and Society from the Weimar Republic to the End of Hitler's Reich* (Yale University Press, 1998)

Prawy, Marcel, *The Vienna Opera* (Weidenfeld and Nicolson, 1970)

Preston, Katherine K., *Opera on the Road: Traveling Opera Troupes in the United States, 1825–60* (University of Illinois Press, 2001)

Price, Curtis, Judith Milhous and Robert D. Hume, *Italian Opera in Late Eighteenth-Century London: The King's Theatre, Haymarket, 1778–1791* (OUP, 1995)

Prieberg, Fred K., *Trial of Strength: Wilhelm Furtwängler and the Third Reich* (Quartet, 1991)

Puritz, Gerd, *Elisabeth Schumann: A Biography* (Deutsch, 1993)

Radice, Mark A. (ed.), *Opera in Context: Essays on Historical Staging from the Late Renaissance to the Time of Puccini* (Amadeus Press, 1998)

Radomski, James, *Manuel García (1775–1832): Chronicle of the Life of a 'Bel Canto' Tenor at the Dawn of Romanticism* (OUP, 2000)

Raeburn, Michael, *The Chronicle of Opera* (Thames and Hudson, 1998)

Randall, Annie J. and Rosalind Gray Davis, *Puccini and the Girl: History and Reception of 'The Girl of the Golden West'* (University Chicago, 2005)

Rasponi, Lanfranco, *The Last Prima Donnas* (Gollancz, 1984)

Raynor, Henry, *Music and Society since 1815* (Barrie & Jenkins, 1976)

Rich, Alan, *The Lincoln Center Story* (American Heritage, 1984)

Ringer, Alexander (ed.), *Music & Society: The Early Romantic Era: Between Revolutions: 1789 and 1848* (Prentice Hall, 1991)

Robbins Landon, H. C., *Handel and His World* (Weidenfeld and Nicolson, 1984)

—, *Mozart and Vienna* (Thames and Hudson, 1991)

—, *The Mozart Compendium: A Guide to Mozart's Life and Music* (Schirmer, 1990)

—, *1791: Mozart's Last Year* (Thames and Hudson, 1988)

Robbins Landon, H. C. and John Julius Norwich, *Five Centuries of Music in Venice* (Thames and Hudson, 1991)

Robinson, Paul, *Opera and Ideas: From Mozart to Strauss* (Harper & Row, 1985)

— (ed.), *Fidelio* (CUP, 1996)

Rosand, Ellen, *Opera in Seventeenth-Century Venice: The Creation of a Genre* (University of California Press, 1991)

Rosenthal, Harold, *Two Centuries of Opera at Covent Garden* (Putnam, 1958)

Ross, Alex, *The Rest is Noise: Listening to the Twentieth Century* (Fourth Estate, 2008)

Rosselli, John, *The Life of Bellini* (CUP, 1996)

—, *The Life of Verdi* (CUP, 2000)

—, *Music and Musicians in Nineteenth-Century Italy* (Amadeus Press, 1991)

—, *The Opera Industry in Italy from Cimarosa to Verdi: The Role of the Impresario* (CUP, 1984)

—, *Singers of Italian Opera: The History of a Profession* (CUP, 1992)

Roth, Ernst, *The Business of Music: Reflections of a Music Publisher* (Cassell, 1969)

Rushton, Julian, *Mozart: An Extraordinary Life* (ABRSM, 2005)

Russell, Dave, *Popular Music in England, 1840–1914: A Social History* (Manchester University Press, 1997)

Russell, John, *Erich Kleiber: A Memoir* (Deutsch, 1957)

Rutherford, Susan, *The Prima Donna and Opera, 1815–1930* (CUP, 2007)

Sabor, Rudolph, *The Real Wagner* (André Deutsch, 1987)

Sachs, Harvey, *Music in Fascist Italy* (Norton, 1987)

—, *Reflections on Toscanini* (Robson, 1991)

—, *Toscanini* (J. B. Lippincott Co., 1978)

Sadie, Stanley and Anthony Hicks (eds.), *Handel Tercentenary Collection* (Macmillan, 1987)

Salfellner, Harald, *Mozart and Prague* (Vitalis, 2003)

Samson, Jim (ed.), *Man and Music, Vol. 7: The Late Romantic Era: From the Mid-19th Century to World War I* (Macmillan, 1991)
— (ed.), *The Cambridge History of Nineteenth-Century Music* (CUP, 2001)
Saslow, James M., *The Medici Wedding of 1589* (Yale University Press, 2006)
Sassoon, Donald, *The Culture of the Europeans: From 1800 to the Present* (HarperCollins, 2006)
Saunders, Frances Stonor, *Who Paid the Piper? The CIA and the Cultural Cold War* (Granta, 2000)
Schafer, Elizabeth, *Lilian Baylis: A Biography* (University of Hertfordshire Press, 2007)
Scherer, F. M., *Quarter Notes and Bank Notes: The Economics of Music Composition in the Eighteenth and Nineteenth Centuries* (Princeton University Press, 2004)
Schindler, Anton Felix, *Beethoven As I Knew Him* (Faber and Faber, 1966)
Schmidgall, Gary, *Literature as Opera* (OUP, 1977)
Schorske, Carl E., *Fin-de-Siècle Vienna: Politics and Culture* (Random House, 1980)
Schroeder, David, *Cinema's Illusions, Opera's Allure* (Continuum, 2002)
Schwarz, Boris, *Music and Musical Life in Soviet Russia, 1917–70* (Barrie & Jenkins, 1972)
Schwarzkopf, Elisabeth, *On and Off the Record: A Memoir of Walter Legge* (Faber and Faber, 1982)
Scott, Michael, *The Record of Singing*, 2 vols. (Duckworth, 1977, 1979)
Scott, R. H. F., *Jean-Baptiste Lully: The Founder of French Opera* (Peter Owen, 1973)
Secrest, Meryle, *Somewhere for Me: A Biography of Richard Rodgers* (Bloomsbury, 2002)
Seligman, Vincent, *Puccini among Friends* (Macmillan, 1938)
Seltsam, William H., *Metropolitan Opera Annals: A Chronicle of Artists and Performances* (H. W. Wilson Co./Metropolitan Opera Guild, 1947)
Senici, Emanuele (ed.), *The Cambridge Companion to Rossini* (CUP, 2004)
Servadio, Gaia, *Rossini* (Constable, 2003)
Shaw, Bernard, *London Music in 1888–89 As Heard by Corno di Bassetto* (Constable, 1937)
—, *Music in London 1890–94*, 3 vols. (Constable, 1932)
Sheean, Vincent, *First and Last Love* (Random House, 1956)
—, *Orpheus at Eighty: A Study of Giuseppe Verdi* (Cassell, 1959)
Shirakawa, Sam H., *The Devil's Music Master: The Controversial Life and Career of Wilhelm Furtwängler* (OUP, 1992)
Shostakovich, Dmitri (ed. Solomon Volkov), *Testimony: The Memoirs of Dmitri Shostakovich* (Faber and Faber, 1981)
Sills, Beverly and Lawrence Linderman, *Beverly: An Autobiography* (Bantam, 1987)
Silsbury, Elizabeth, *State of Opera: An Intimate New History of the State Opera of South Australia 1957–2000* (Wakefield Press, 2001)
Skelton, Geoffrey, *Wagner at Bayreuth: Experiment and Tradition* (Barrie & Rockliff, 1976)
Slezak, Walter, *What Time's the Next Swan?* (Doubleday, 1962)
Slonimsky, Nicholas, *Perfect Pitch: A Life Story* (OUP, 1988)
Smart, Mary Ann, *Siren Songs: Representation of Gender and Sexuality in Opera* (Princeton University Press, 2000)
Snowman, Daniel, *The Hitler Emigrés: The Cultural Impact on Britain of Refugees from Nazism* (Pimlico, 2003)
—, *Plácido Domingo's Tales from the Opera* (BBC Books, 1994)
—, *The World of Plácido Domingo* (The Bodley Head, 1985)
Sokol, Martin L., *The New York City Opera: An American Adventure* (Macmillan, 1981)
Solkin, David H., *Painting for Money: The Visual Arts and the Public Sphere in Eighteenth-Century England* (Yale University Press, 1992)
Solomon, Maynard, *Beethoven* (Schirmer, 1979)
—, *Mozart: A Life* (HarperCollins, 1996)
Solti, Sir Georg, *Solti on Solti* (Chatto and Windus, 1997)
Somerset-Ward, Richard, *Angels and Monsters: The Story of Male and Female Sopranos in Opera* (Yale University Press, 2004)
Sonneck, O. G. (ed.), *Beethoven: Impressions by His Contemporaries* (Dover, 1967)
Spencer, Stewart, *Wagner Remembered* (Faber and Faber, 2000)
Spiel, Hilde, *Vienna's Golden Autumn 1866–1938* (Weidenfeld and Nicolson, 1987)
Spotts, Frederic, *Bayreuth: A History of the Wagner Festival* (Yale University Press, 1994)
Steen, Michael, *Enchantress of Nations: Pauline Viardot: Soprano, Muse and Lover* (Icon Books, 2007)
Stendhal, *Life of Rossini* (Calder and Boyars, 1970)
—, *Rome, Naples and Florence* (John Calder, 1959)
Stevens, Denis (ed.), *The Letters of Monteverdi*, rev. edn (Clarendon Press, Oxford, 1995)

Strohm, Reinhard, *Dramma per musica: Italian Opera Seria of the Eighteenth Century* (Yale University Press, 1997)

Strunk, Oliver (ed.), *Source Readings in Music History: The Renaissance/The Baroque Era/The Classic Era/The Romantic Era* (Norton, 1965)

Summers, Judith, *The Empress of Pleasure: The Life and Adventures of Teresa Cornelys – Queen of Masquerades and Casanova's Lover* (Viking, 2003)

Sutcliffe, Tom, *Believing in Opera* (Faber and Faber, 1996)

Sutherland, Joan, *A Prima Donna's Progress: The Autobiography of Joan Sutherland* (Weidenfeld and Nicolson, 1997)

Symes, Colin, *Setting the Record Straight: A Material History of Classical Recording* (Wesleyan University Press, 2004)

Tallis, Michael and Joan, *The Silent Showman: Sir George Tallis, the Man behind the World's Largest Entertainment Organisation of the 1920s* (Wakefield Press, 1999)

Tambling, Jeremy, *Opera, Ideology and Film* (St Martin's Press, 1987)

— (ed.), *A Night in at the Opera: Media Representations of Opera* (University of Luton Press, 2003)

Taruskin, Richard, *Defining Russia Musically: Historical and Hermeneutical Essays* (Princeton University Press, 1997)

—, *Mussorgsky: Eight Essays and an Epilogue* (Princeton University Press, 1993)

—, *The Oxford History of Western Music*, 6 vols. (OUP, 2005)

Taubman, Howard, *Toscanini* (Odhams, 1951)

Thacker, Toby, *Music after Hitler 1945–1955* (Ashgate, 2007)

Till, Nicholas, *Mozart and the Enlightenment: Truth, Virtue, and Beauty in Mozart's Operas* (Faber and Faber, 1994)

—, *Rossini: His Life and Times* (Midas Books, 1983)

Timms, Susie, *Titiens: Her Majesty's Prima Donna* (Bezazzy, 2005)

Toller, Owen, *Pfitzner's 'Palestrina': The Musical Legend and Its Background* (Toccata Press, 1997)

Tooley, John, *In House: The Story of Covent Garden* (Faber and Faber, 1999)

Traubel, Helen, *St. Louis Woman* (Duell, Sloan and Pearce, 1959)

Turnbull, Michael T. R. B., *Mary Garden* (Amadeus Press, 1997)

Tyrrell, John, *Czech Opera* (CUP, 1988)

Vaughan, Roger, *Herbert von Karajan: A Biographical Portrait* (W. W. Norton, 1986)

Vestey, Pamela, *Melba: A Family Memoir* (Pamela Vestey, 2000)

Vishnevskaya, Galina, *Galina: A Russian Story* (Harcourt Brace Jovanovich, 1984)

Volkov, Solomon, *Shostakovich and Stalin: The Extraordinary Relationship between the Great Composer and the Brutal Dictator* (Little, Brown, 2004)

Volpe, Joseph, *The Toughest Show on Earth: My Rise and Reign at the Metropolitan Opera* (Knopf, 2006)

Wagner, Cosima (ed. Geoffrey Skelton), *Cosima Wagner's Diaries*, one-volume abridgement (Yale University Press, 1997)

Wagner, Friedelind, *The Royal Family of Bayreuth* (Eyre and Spottiswoode, 1948)

Wagner, Gottfried, *Twilight of the Wagners: The Unveiling of a Family's Legacy* (Picador, 1997)

Wagner, Nike, *The Wagners: The Dramas of a Musical Dynasty* (Phoenix, 2001)

Walker, Frank, *The Man Verdi* (Dent, 1962)

Walsh, Basil, *Catherine Hayes: The Hibernian Prima Donna* (Irish Academic Press, 2000)

Walsh, T. J., *Second Empire Opera: The Théâtre Lyrique Paris 1851–1870* (John Calder, 1981)

Walter, Bruno, *Theme and Variations: An Autobiography* (Hamish Hamilton, 1947)

Walton, Benjamin, *Rossini in Restoration Paris: The Sound of Modern Life* (CUP, 2007)

Warrack, John, *Carl Maria von Weber* (Hamish Hamilton, 1968)

Weaver, William, *The Golden Century of Italian Opera from Rossini to Puccini* (Thames and Hudson, 1980)

Weaver, William and Martin Chusid (eds.), *The Verdi Companion* (W. W. Norton, 1979)

Weaver, William and Simonetta Puccini (eds.), *The Puccini Companion* (W.W. Norton, 1994)

Weber, William, *Music and the Middle Class: The Social Structure of Concert Life in London, Paris and Vienna* (Croom Helm, 1975)

— (ed.), *The Musician as Entrepreneur, 1700–1914: Managers, Charlatans and Idealists* (Indiana University Press, 2004)

Wechsberg, Joseph, *The First Time Around: Some Irreverent Recollections* (Little, Brown and Company, 1970)

—, *Looking for a Bluebird* (Houghton Mifflin, 1945)

—, *The Opera* (Weidenfeld and Nicolson, 1972)

Wegeler, Franz and Ferdinand Ries, *Remembering Beethoven: The Biographical Notes of Franz Wegeler and Ferdinand Ries* (Deutsch, 1988)

Weinstat, Hertzel and Bert Wechsler, *Dear Rogue: A Biography of the American Baritone Lawrence Tibbett* (Amadeus Press, 1966)

Weinstock, Herbert, *Donizetti and the World of Opera in Italy, Paris and Vienna in the First Half of the Nineteenth Century* (Methuen, 1964)

—, *Rossini: A Biography* (OUP, 1968)

—, *Vincenzo Bellini* (Knopf, 1971)

Weiss, Piero, *Opera: A History in Documents* (OUP, 2002)

Whenham, John (ed.), *Claudio Monteverdi: Orfeo* (CUP, 1986)

Wilson, Alexandra, *The Puccini Problem: Opera, Nationalism and Modernity* (CUP, 2007)

Wilson, Elizabeth, *Shostakovich: A Life Remembered* (Faber and Faber, 1994)

Wlaschin, Ken, *The Encyclopedia of Opera on Screen* (Yale University Press, 2004)

Wood, Caroline and Graham Sadler, *French Baroque Opera: A Reader* (Ashgate, 2000)

Worsthorne, Simon Towneley, *Venetian Opera in the Seventeenth Century* (Clarendon Press, 1954)

Wyndham, Henry Saxe, *The Annals of Covent Garden Theatre from 1732 to 1897*, 2 vols. (Chatto & Windus, 1906)

Zaslaw, Neal (ed.), *Man & Music: The Classical Era: From the 1740s to the End of the 18th Century* (Prentice Hall, 1989)

Index

Figures in **bold** refer to illustrations.
Titles of operas are listed under their composers; theatres and opera companies
are listed under their respective cities.